Praise for *The Black Banners*

"One of the most valuable and detailed accounts of its subject to appear in the past decade."

—*Economist*

"The F.B.I. is so shrouded in secrecy; Soufan's book provides some transparency."

—Concepción de León, *New York Times*

"Most Americans first heard of FBI agent Ali H. Soufan in the spring of 2009. That's when he testified from behind a black curtain in the Senate Judiciary Committee's hearing room. . . . Now Soufan has fired another salvo, . . . detailed descriptions of what unfolded behind the closed doors of the world's interrogation rooms. . . . Soufan's story provides a new and important window on America's battle with al-Qaeda."

—*Washington Post*

"Any American would benefit from reading this book, and it is a must-read for U.S. warfighters, foreign policy makers, historians, and intelligence and law enforcement personnel."

—LTC Douglas A. Pryer, U.S. Army, Afghanistan, *Military Review*

"An earnest and raw memoir from someone whose knowledge of al Qaeda and early U.S. investigations of them rivals anyone's. . . . Soufan has written a richly detailed account of the most important recent years for the counterterrorism community."

—*Lawfareblog*

"It is packed with facts that rarely, if ever, have appeared in the media; and it is written in an anecdotal style reminiscent of a Tom Clancy espionage thriller that is easy and enjoyable to read."

—Middle East Policy Council

"To those inside the U.S. government Soufan has long been something of a legend. He conducted the most effective and fruitful interrogations of Al Qaeda suspects during the war on terrorism, and save for some inexplicable failures by the CIA, he and his team might well have prevented 9/11. Soufan has since left the FBI and written a gripping account of his experiences, brimming with details about Al Qaeda and its historical development."

—*Harper's Magazine*

"Almost nobody is better placed to write a book about Al-Qaeda's war against America, and Washington's counter-offensive, than Ali Soufan. . . . [*The Black Banners*] is an absorbing account of America's fightback after 9/11, full of revealing or amusing details. . . . [T]his book is cheering as well as fascinating, because it reveals the dedication of those who defend us, as well as the weird frailties of those who try to kill us."

—*Sunday Times*

"By putting a human face on the al-Qaeda operatives, he helps us to understand their motives and various and sometimes clashing personalities. . . . There is much to get through in the detailed background story of bin Laden and al-Qaeda, but the revelations uncovered are worth it; this is a story that had to be told."

—*Booklist*

THE
BLACK BANNERS

■ DECLASSIFIED ■

THE
BLACK BANNERS

▪ DECLASSIFIED ▪

How Torture Derailed the
War on Terror after 9/11

ALI SOUFAN

with Daniel Freedman

W. W. NORTON & COMPANY
Independent Publishers Since 1923

For information about permission to reproduce selections from this book, write to
Permissions, W. W. Norton & Company, Inc., 500 Fifth Avenue, New York, NY 10110

For information about special discounts for bulk purchases, please contact
W. W. Norton Special Sales at specialsales@wwnorton.com or 800-233-4830

Manufacturing by LSC Communications, Harrisonburg
Book design by Ellen Cipriano
Production manager: Anna Oler

ISBN 978-0-393-54072-7
ISBN 978-0-393-34349-6 (pbk.)

W. W. Norton & Company, Inc., 500 Fifth Avenue, New York, N.Y. 10110
www.wwnorton.com

W. W. Norton & Company Ltd., 15 Carlisle Street, London W1D 3BS

1 2 3 4 5 6 7 8 9 0

For Heather, Connor, Dean, and Dylan
   —my peace of mind

CONTENTS

MAP   x

FOREWORD   xiii

PROLOGUE   xix

NOTE TO READERS   xxix

PART 1 · THE EARLY YEARS

1. The Fatwa and the Bet   3

2. Osama Air   33

3. The Northern Group   56

PART 2 · DECLARATION OF WAR

4. The al-Qaeda Switchboard   75

5. Operation Challenge and the
    Manchester Manual   97

6. "You'll Be Singing Like a Canary"   1 2 1

7. Millennium Plot   1 3 1

PART 3 ▪ USS *COLE*

8. A Naval Destroyer in Yemen?   1 4 9

9. The Hall of Death   1 6 8

10. "We're Stubborn, but We're Not Crazy"   1 8 5

11. The Human Polygraph Machine   2 0 9

12. "What Is al-Qaeda Doing in Malaysia?"   2 2 8

13. Bin Laden's Errand Boy   2 5 4

PART 4 ▪ THE ATTACK THAT CHANGED THE WORLD

14. The Binalshibh Riddle   2 7 1

15. "What Dots?"   2 8 4

16. The Father of Death   3 0 6

PART 5 ▪ A NEW WORLD ORDER

17. Bin Laden's Escape   3 4 3

18. DocEx   3 5 0

19. Black Magic   3 5 6

PART 6 ▪ THE FIRST HIGH-VALUE DETAINEE

20. Abu Zubaydah   373

21. The Contractors Take Over   393

22. "We Don't Do That"   411

PART 7 ▪ SUCCESSES AND FAILURES

23. Guantánamo Bay   439

24. 45 Minutes   484

25. The Crystal Ball Memo   502

PART 8 ▪ FINAL MISSIONS

26. Leaving the FBI   511

27. Undercover   518

POSTSCRIPT   525

CONCLUSION   531

ACKNOWLEDGMENTS   539

PRINCIPAL CHARACTERS   545

KEY DOCUMENTS AND ARTICLES CITED   569

PHOTOGRAPH CREDITS   573

INDEX   575

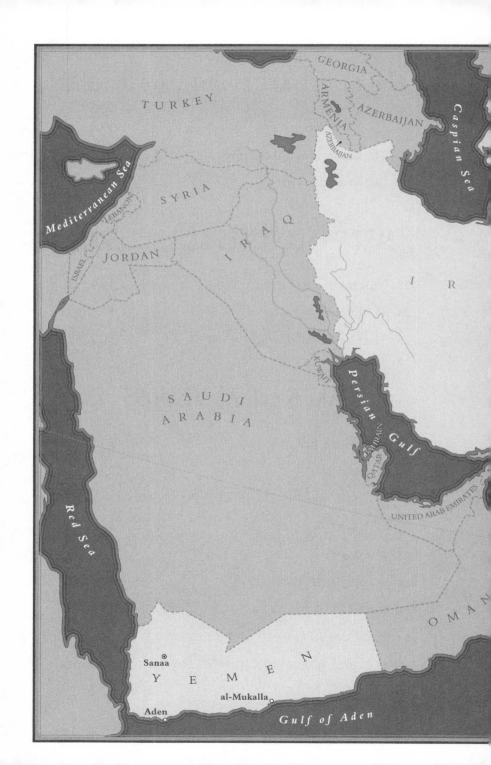

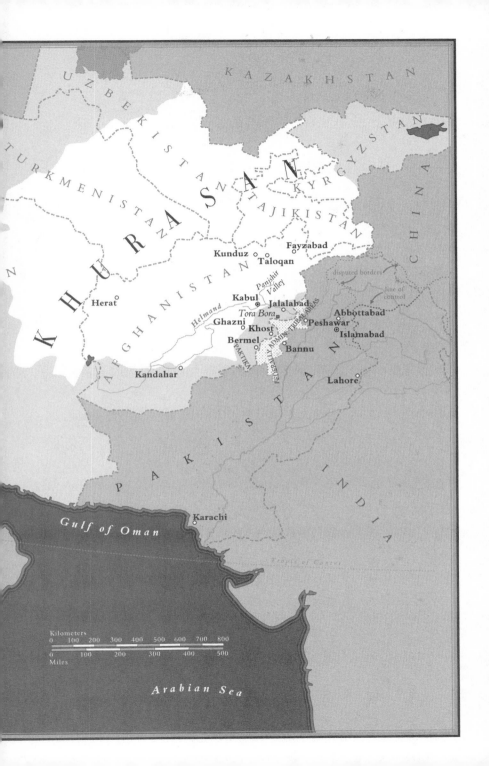

FOREWORD

The publication of this new edition of *The Black Banners* is an event of historic significance. When the book was first published, the Central Intelligence Agency insisted that large portions of it be cut—"redacted," in intelligence-speak—for what it claimed were reasons of national security. On many pages the redactions were so severe that there were more black lines than complete sentences, and the narrative was unintelligible. These were often the most important passages in the book. Now, the CIA has recognized that its own redactions were unwarranted, and it has reversed its decision. That in itself is a victory for freedom of information.

Moreover, the book corrects the record on a crucial matter of national security. Following 9/11, the CIA adopted so-called enhanced interrogation techniques (EITs)—in plain language, torture—as a means of extracting information from terrorist suspects. These techniques produced no actionable intelligence, as we know from the findings of the agency's own inspector general. But certain politicians and officials muzzled this truth for the sake of their own reputations. They censored critics of the techniques, while allowing proponents to speak freely. Thus emboldened, the torturers could paint a straightforward yet misleading picture: simply waterboard a suspect and the intelligence would flow. In response, those of us who knew the truth could offer little besides bare denials. When challenged to explain how the information was really obtained, we could say only, "I'm sorry, that's classified."

In its new, unredacted form, *The Black Banners* presents the full facts. At long last, readers can see the torture for what it is, and how it failed, through the eyes of someone other than a proponent of those techniques. No less importantly, they will see for themselves how vital intelligence was really obtained, without force or violence.

The prohibition on torture has since been reaffirmed; but it would be foolish to assume that the matter has been confined to the history books. Periodically, political efforts are made to revive the techniques. On the campaign trail in 2016, candidate Trump promised a return to waterboarding—a technique whereby the detainee is taken to the very brink of drowning—together with "a hell of a lot worse than waterboarding." At rallies around the country, this line drew cheers. My hope is that this book, by presenting the dismal reality of enhanced interrogation, will help stave off any temptation to return to techniques that produce nothing of value, help terrorists recruit more followers, and make all Americans less safe.

An Abuse of Office

Beginning in 2002, I witnessed the U.S. government's implementation of interrogation techniques better suited to authoritarian dictatorships— sleep deprivation, forced nudity, freezing temperatures, confinement in what amounted to coffins, and of course waterboarding. I harbored little sympathy for those subjected to these torture methods—they were, for the most part, hardened terrorists responsible for the deaths of dozens or hundreds or even thousands of innocent people. Two things did trouble me, however. On a moral level, we just don't do this kind of thing in America; we are meant to be better than our enemies. And on a practical level, the techniques plainly did not work. Again and again, I saw otherwise cooperative subjects clam up under torture. Concerned that the failure to produce intelligence from these people was compromising America's national security, I protested up the chain of command. The torture continued. It was still going on when I left the FBI in 2005.

After the Bush administration left office, the Department of Justice declassified internal memos on the enhanced interrogation techniques. The Senate held hearings about the torture program. I testified. No official who authorized the EITs would appear, and for good reason—testimony under oath would have forced them either to admit that the techniques didn't work or to commit perjury.

I wrote *The Black Banners* because I felt that my firsthand account of the war on terror—before, during, and after 9/11—would add something of value to an important conversation, of which torture was just one aspect. I submitted the manuscript to the FBI for review, as required by both my contract and considerations of national security. There followed a considerable amount of back-and-forth, but the process was a constructive one. I responded to all the bureau's concerns, and we agreed on a final version. Then, out of courtesy, the FBI forwarded the manuscript to the CIA.

The agency responded with 181 pages of "concerns" about the book. Nearly every one of these was baseless. Many were downright frivolous. For example, I was faulted for using terms defined on the CIA's own website; for reporting facts stated in the *9/11 Commission Report*; and for quoting from the *Congressional Record*. Like Yossarian in *Catch-22* "censoring" adjectives and adverbs, the agency even declared war on pronouns, forbidding me to use words like "I" and "me" and "my."

In truth, the CIA officials handling the matter never believed anything I wrote was classified; indeed, they faxed the entire manuscript to me over an unsecured line, only later to claim—in response to my challenges—that material sent to me in this manner was classified. These are hardly the actions of an organization with any genuine concern for national security. Its real motivation was less honorable: to preserve the agency's reputation in the face of overwhelming evidence that one of its most controversial programs had failed. Redacting my book was a straightforward abuse of office, in violation of executive orders, federal law, and the right of the American people to know what their government does in their name. But with a publication deadline looming,

I had no choice but to release the book with long passages—in some cases, entire pages—blacked out.

Suspicions about the CIA's motives can be confirmed by looking at some books the agency *did* approve for publication. As early as 2007, former CIA director George Tenet published a memoir that discussed torture in detail—albeit with a much more positive spin on the matter. Later, around the same time it was redacting *The Black Banners*, the CIA approved a book by Jose Rodriguez—the CIA official who ordered tapes of the enhanced interrogation techniques destroyed because, as he stated in a subsequently declassified e-mail, it would make him and his team "look terrible." Rodriguez's book covered many of the same events as mine; he even quoted alleged conversations between me and the terrorist suspect Abu Zubaydah. The CIA did not find this objectionable. It was the same story in 2016 with a book by one of the architects of the EITs, the CIA contractor James Mitchell.

A Story That Can Now Be Told

Things began to change in 2018, when I was approached by the Oscar-winning filmmaker Alex Gibney and the Pulitzer Prize–winning journalist Raymond Bonner. They were working together on a documentary about torture and wanted to interview me for the film. I've never made any secret of my opposition to the CIA's purported classification of the material in my book; but I take my obligations seriously. With regret, I told Alex and Raymond that I wouldn't talk about anything still hidden, no matter how unjustly, behind those redactions.

Alex and Raymond literally made a federal case out of it. With the help of the Media Freedom and Information Access Clinic at Yale Law School, they sued the CIA, challenging its prepublication review on First Amendment grounds. Chief Judge Colleen McMahon of the Southern District of New York gave the agency time to reconsider, and, in an act of institutional humility for which the CIA deserves eternal credit, this time it gave the book a fair review. At the end of that process, it reversed its original redactions. While it requested minor changes to terminology and names, arguably justified by the need to preserve the secrecy of methods and sources, none of those impact the narrative.

This unredacted version of the book includes updates, photographs, and an index not available in the original edition. We also updated the Principal Characters section of the book.

Eighteen years on from the first sanctioned EITs, the public can finally read the complete story. *The Black Banners* shows in vivid, first-person detail how actionable intelligence—including information cited by proponents of torture as an example of its success—was actually obtained using nonviolent methods. It demonstrates how the Bush administration's dogmatic commitment to torture caused it to ignore genuine intelligence produced using other means, thus allowing deadly attacks to proceed that otherwise might have been prevented. It reveals the battles between intelligence operatives in the field—including many courageous CIA colleagues—and the political leadership in Washington. At the same time, and no less importantly, my account also outlines the interrogation techniques that *did* work—the time-honored psychological methods enshrined in U.S. law enforcement, intelligence, and military traditions.

Ironically, in trying to silence me, the officials who redacted the original edition of this book did a great if unintentional service to the truth: if my account was not true, they would not have tried to censor it. Readers will find the reality documented in *The Black Banners* far more intriguing than the vainglorious fiction of the pro-torture narrative— and far more troubling. As I write in chapter 25, "There is no way to describe the feeling of knowing you could have stopped a terrorist attack if only your government had supported you." Readers of this unredacted edition will be left with similar feelings again and again. They will ask why any of this was allowed to happen, why it was covered up for so many years, what might be done to prevent such events in the future, and how those responsible might at long last be made to face up to the consequences of their actions.

Bringing the whole story to light has been the work of many hands. In particular, I want to thank my attorney and longtime friend David Kelley for the many hours he has poured into this fight. My thanks likewise go to Marlon Martinez of the FBI's Office of General Counsel and to U.S. Attorneys Sarah Normand and Chris Connolly of the Southern District of New York. I also want to thank the CIA review board for giving the manuscript another look—and being willing to correct the errors of the past.

My supporters from the worlds of intelligence, law enforcement, the military, and politics are too numerous to name here, but they have my gratitude for encouraging me to keep up this fight when it seemed hopeless. In particular, let me acknowledge the late Senator John McCain, himself a victim of torture at the hands of the North Vietnamese regime, who graciously expressed the hope that, through my experiences, all Americans would come to know the truth about these techniques.

Special thanks to my partner and coauthor on this book, Dan Freedman, for his wise counsel, thoughtful guidance, and steadfast friendship. Without Dan, I never would have finished the first draft, let alone gotten through the months and years of wrangling over the text.

Most of all, I want to thank Alex Gibney and Raymond Bonner, together with the team at the Yale Law School Media Freedom and Information Access Clinic, led by David Schulz, Charles Crain, Simone Seiver, Jacob van Leer, and Katrin Marquez. Their efforts show that, in America, provided you fight long and hard enough, the truth will out.

Ali Soufan,
September 8, 2020

PROLOGUE

So it is said that if you know your enemies and know yourself,
you will win a hundred times in a hundred battles.

—Sun Tzu, *The Art of War*

"You can't stop the mujahideen," Abu Jandal told me on September 17,
2001. "We will be victorious." We sat across a rectangular table from
each other in a nondescript interrogation room with unadorned white
walls in a high-level national security prison in Sanaa, the capital of
Yemen. The prison was operated by the country's central intelligence
agency, the Political Security Organization (PSO), the complex also
serving as its headquarters. PSO officials in traditional Yemeni dress
were ranged on plastic chairs along one wall, observing the conversation. Abu Jandal—the name means "father of death"—was the most
senior al-Qaeda operative in custody; he had served as Osama bin Lad-
en's personal bodyguard and trusted confidant. We got to him through
Fahd al-Quso, a Yemeni al-Qaeda operative involved in the October
12, 2000, bombing of the USS *Cole*. Quso had identified, in a photograph shown to him the previous evening, a man whom we knew to be
Marwan al-Shehhi, who was on board United Airlines Flight 175 when
it crashed into the south tower of the World Trade Center. Shehhi had
once stayed at a safe house in Afghanistan operated by Abu Jandal.

I gave my partner, Naval Criminal Investigative Service (NCIS)
special agent Robert McFadden, a bemused look. He raised his eye-

brows and smiled at Abu Jandal. Only training and experience enabled Bob and me to smile and appear relaxed, because below the surface we were seething. "You'll find that you have underestimated America," I replied, speaking in Arabic, "but tell me, why do you think you'll be victorious?"

Abu Jandal had been in prison in Yemen for eleven months in the aftermath of the *Cole* bombing because of his connections to al-Qaeda. Top American security officials were anxiously waiting to see what intelligence we could get from him to help us understand who had destroyed the World Trade Center and part of the Pentagon. We suspected that it was al-Qaeda, but there was as yet no definite proof, and Bob and I had been ordered to identify those responsible for the attacks "by any means necessary"—a command that neither of us had ever received before. Quso's leading us to Abu Jandal was our first indication that al-Qaeda may have been responsible for the attack, but the connection between the two men could have been a coincidence.

Among the thousands of people listed as dead or missing in the World Trade Center were several whom Bob and I knew, including my former boss and mentor at the Federal Bureau of Investigation (FBI), John O'Neill, and a friend and colleague, FBI special agent Lenny Hatton. In Abu Jandal we had someone who took satisfaction in America's pain. Yet a display of anger or the slightest betrayal of the sense of urgency we felt would jeopardize our efforts to get information from him. An interrogation is a mind game in which you have to use your wits and knowledge of the detainee to convince or steer him to cooperate, and essential to this is to show that you are in control. If a suspect thinks that you lack knowledge of what he's talking about or sees that you are flustered, enraged, or pressed for time—these would be signs that he was winning and shouldn't cooperate. We kept the fake smiles plastered on our faces and let Abu Jandal speak.

"You want to know why?" Abu Jandal asked rhetorically, with his usual gusto, as his face broke into one of his trademark broad grins. We had learned that he loved to lecture us—and that was when we could get him to slip up.

"Sure," I said.

"I'll tell you why," he continued. "The hadith says," and he began quoting: "'If you see the black banners coming from Khurasan, join that army, even if you have to crawl over ice; no power will be able to stop them—'"

Abu Jandal paused for a second to catch his breath, but before he could finish the hadith, I continued it for him: "' —and they will finally reach Baitul Maqdis [Jerusalem], where they will erect their flags.'" His grin momentarily left his face, and with surprise in his voice he asked me: "You know the hadith? Do you really work for the FBI?"

"Of course I know that hadith. It's narrated by Abu Hurairah, although it's questionable whether that actually was said by the Prophet," I said, "and I know lots of hadith. As I told you before, the image you have of America and of her people, like me, is all wrong."

Hadith are reported sayings and doings of the Prophet Muhammad, and I was to hear that reputed hadith from many al-Qaeda members I interrogated. It was one of al-Qaeda's favorites.

Khurasan is a term for a historical region spanning northeastern and eastern Iran and parts of Turkmenistan, Uzbekistan, Tajikistan, Afghanistan, and northwestern Pakistan. Because of the hadith, jihadists believe that this is the region from which they will inflict a major defeat against their enemies—in the Islamic version of Armageddon. Bin Laden's 1996 declaration of war against the United States—a main text for al-Qaeda members—ends with the dateline "Friday, August 23, 1996, in the Hindu Kush, Khurasan, Afghanistan." It's not a coincidence that bin Laden made al-Qaeda's flag black; he also regularly cited the hadith and referenced Khurasan when recruiting, motivating, and fund-raising. Al-Qaeda operatives I interrogated were often convinced that, by joining al-Qaeda, they were fulfilling the words of the Prophet.

It is an indication of how imperfectly we know our enemy that to most people in the West, and even among supposed al-Qaeda experts, the image of the black banners means little. Westerners instead focus on al-Qaeda's use, in its propaganda, of its strikes on the United States— the August 1998 East African embassy bombings, the October 2000 attack on the USS *Cole*, and, of course, 9/11. Such references are obviously important to the organization, but al-Qaeda's use of the black banners is in many ways even more important, because it adds the crucial religious element. If you go into Internet chats rooms where al-Qaeda sympathizers and supporters converse (in Arabic), the black banners are regularly cited.

The hadith has been quoted before in Islamic history: for instance, during the revolution that overthrew the Umayyad Caliphate, the second of the major caliphates set up after the death of the Prophet. The Umayyads were overthrown by the Abbasids in a rebellion that was initiated in Iran, which was then called Khurasan—and the rebels' banners were black. The hadith was also quoted during the fall of Constantinople and the Muslim conquest of Spain.

Many Muslim scholars question the authenticity of the hadith, including the influential cleric Sheikh Salman al-Oadah, jailed for opposing the Saudi government's decision to allow U.S. troops into the country to counter Saddam Hussein's invasion of Kuwait. In his 1996 declaration of jihad, bin Laden quoted Oadah approvingly as being a fellow opponent of troops in the kingdom. Subsequently, however, the sheikh went firmly on record as opposing al-Qaeda, having seen the destruction and death the organization has caused; and he has become a major voice critical of al-Qaeda in the Muslim world. The sheikh, asked about the authenticity of the hadith, said: "The hadith about the army with black banners coming out of Khurasan has two chains of transmission, but both are weak and cannot be authenticated. If a Muslim believes in this hadith, he believes in something false. Anyone who cares about his religion and belief should avoid heading towards falsehood."

There are other hadith that refer to the black banners, including another al-Qaeda favorite: "The black banners will come from the East, led by mighty men, with long hair and long beards; their surnames are taken from the names of their hometowns and their first names are from a Kunya [an alias]."

Abu Jandal quoted it to Bob and me, and I asked him if this was the reason al-Qaeda members let their hair and beards grow long, and change their names so their first reflects an alias and their second, their hometown. He smiled and told me I was right, and told me how it applied to him: while his real name was Nasser Ahmad Nasser al-Bahri, he called himself Abu Jandal al-Jadawi; al-Jadawi means "from Jeddah," which is where he grew up.

Ali al-Bahlul, al-Qaeda's media relations secretary and bin Laden's personal propagandist, whom I interrogated in Guantánamo Bay, Cuba, in 2002, was certain that the coming of al-Qaeda's black banners heralded the apocalypse, which would be followed by the triumph of Islam. "The current war is between the three religions, Christianity, Judaism, and Islam," he told me, "and is the battle of Armageddon predicted in the Old Testament, the New Testament, and the hadith of the Prophet." In Bahlul's mind, because all of this is ordained by God and the holy books, any atrocities and murders of innocent people committed by al-Qaeda are completely justified, and are part of a "heavenly plan." He added, with complete sincerity, "It is a difficult and painful road we are taking, but jihad eases all sorrows."

Asymmetrical organizations like al-Qaeda often develop their own countercultures, with special texts, lore, and codes of conduct, which are usually outside the boundaries of their society's, or religion's, accepted norms. With al-Qaeda this is seen in the leadership's seizing upon questionable hadith and promoting them to the status of most cited and respected of texts. In addition, there is the canonization of events that have become part of the collective consciousness, which in a sense allows believers to create their own religion within Islam. These events include bin Laden's 1996 declaration of war against the United States, his 1998 fatwa, and his 1999 Eid sermon, along with "successful" attacks such as the 1998 East African embassy bombings, the 2000 bombing of the USS *Cole*, and 9/11.

This lore that they have created for themselves leads al-Qaeda members to believe that they are part of something bigger than they are. Al-Qaeda's aims are well known—to defeat the "crusaders," drive them out of the Arabian Peninsula, and create a worldwide Islamic state—but what binds the operatives together is this narrative that convinces them that they're part of a divine plan.

The counterculture extends not only to scripts and events but to justifications for actions taken that Muslims would normally frown upon. The use of suicide bombing and the killing of innocent people are obvious examples, but extremists through the ages have justified the death of innocents in "war" for a higher cause, and that is not new to al-Qaeda. Indeed, al-Qaeda relies on the interpretations of a thirteenth-century Syrian cleric named Taqi ad-Din ibn Taymiyyah, who justified the killing of bystanders.

What's even more telling is how morally corrupt (in Islamic terms) some al-Qaeda members are. I was shocked when I first discovered that many top operatives did not live according to Islamic principles. Both 9/11 mastermind Khalid Sheikh Mohammed (KSM) and his nephew Ramzi Yousef, the mastermind of the 1993 World Trade Center bombing, were well known in the brothels of the Philippines; Ziad Jarrah, one of the 9/11 hijackers, loved nightclubs and was living with a girlfriend; and Abdul Rahim Hussein Muhammad Abda al-Nashiri, the mastermind of the USS *Cole* bombing and later head of all al-Qaeda operations in the Arabian Peninsula, was living with a Russian prostitute. Islam also strictly bans the consumption of alcohol, and yet Mohammed Atta, the head of the 9/11 hijackers, was an alcoholic and pounded shots in a bar prior to 9/11, while other hijackers visited strip joints.

It's a tragic irony that these terrorists—who claim to be joining al-Qaeda for the defense of their religion and because they believe in the hadith that say that the war of Armageddon is upon us—disregard the most basic tenets of their religion in the process. They're in violation of the very Islamic law they're fighting to impose.

When I first began interrogating al-Qaeda members, I found that while they could quote bin Laden's sayings by heart, I knew far more of the Quran than they did—and in fact some barely knew classical Arabic, the language of both the hadith and the Quran. An understanding of their thought process and the limits of their knowledge enabled me and my colleagues to use their claimed piousness against them. I would even engage them in religious debate and convince them to cooperate and confess.

▪ ▪ ▪

"Now that you've tested me on a hadith," I said to Abu Jandal, "let me test you on one."

"Sure," he replied eagerly.

"Let me first ask you whether Christians and Jews are allowed in Mecca and Medina."

"Of course not," he replied, shaking his head and giving a condescending smile, "that's a silly question. Everyone knows they're forbidden. Even the Saudi Arabian monarchy, which welcomed infidels into the Arabian Peninsula, wouldn't dare allow them in Mecca and Medina."

"And why aren't they allowed into Mecca and Medina?"

"Because they're holy places."

"Are you familiar with the hadith where the Prophet has dealings with his Jewish neighbor?" I asked.

"Of course."

"Where did those conversations happen?"

"In Medina."

"Did the Prophet commit a sin by allowing a Jew to live next door to him in Medina?"

"Umm," Abu Jandal stuttered, and, after a pause, he replied, "No, the Prophet didn't sin, the Prophet of course never sinned."

"So tell me," I pressed, "if the Prophet said it was okay for a Jew to live next door to him in Medina, how can you say you know more than the Prophet and that Jews and Christians can't live in Medina today?"

Abu Jandal didn't have an immediate response. Thinking for a few moments, he said: "But it is different after the Prophet's death, because on his deathbed, according to the hadith, he said to expel all infidels from the Arabian Peninsula."

"Hold on," I said, "we both know that the Prophet forbade the writing of any hadith during his lifetime, as he wanted the focus to be on the Quran. Hadith were only written about one hundred years later. So you're choosing what the Prophet allegedly said over what he actually did?"

Abu Jandal was at first silent, and then, looking flustered, he said, "Well, there are scholars who determine this."

. . .

When the radio was first introduced in Saudi Arabia, conservative Wahhabi clerics denounced it as "the devil hiding in a box." Wahhabism traditionally is suspicious of new technology, viewing modernity as an evil that takes people further away from the ideal way of life as practiced by the Prophet. The clerics demanded that King Abdul Aziz, Saudi Arabia's founder and ruler, ban the radio and behead the Westerners who had brought it into the country.

The king relied on the clerics for domestic support and could not just dismiss their demands. "If what you say is true," he told them, "then we must ban the devil's work, and we will behead those behind it."

"You are a great and wise king," the clerics responded, excited that he was siding with them.

"And so," the king said, "we will hold a public trial tomorrow about this devil box, and it will be brought before me." The king then secretly told the engineers working on the radio to make sure that the Quran was playing at the time of the trial.

The next day, with the clerics present, the king ordered the radio to be brought before him. "Turn this box on," he ordered, and as it was switched on, passages from the Quran were heard. The king, pretending to be confused, turned to the clerics and asked: "Can it be that the devil is saying the Quran? Or is it perhaps true that this is not an evil box?" The clerics conceded that they had been mistaken, and there was no more labeling of the radio as the devil's box.

People ask what is the most important weapon we have against al-Qaeda, and I reply, "Knowledge." What King Abdul Aziz understood is that often the most effective way to beat extremists is to outwit them. As Sun Tzu wrote in *The Art of War*, when we know our enemy's strengths and weaknesses, and when at the same time we know our capabilities—that's when we are best placed to achieve victory.

This is true in anything from deciding how to interrogate a suspect—whether to torture him or to outwit him to get information—to dealing with rogue states: do we simply resort to force, or do we first try to understand their thought processes and internal divisions and try to manipulate them? It's the difference between acting out of fear and acting out of knowledge.

Our greatest successes against al-Qaeda have come when we understood how they recruited, brainwashed, and operated, and used our knowledge to outwit and defeat them. Our failures have come when we instead let ourselves be guided by ignorance, fear, and brutality. These failures explain why the approximately four hundred terrorists who were members of al-Qaeda on 9/11 have been able to last in a war against the greatest power on earth longer than the combined duration of the First and Second World Wars.

This book tells the story of America's successes and failures in the war against al-Qaeda—from the origins of the organization right through to the death of Osama bin Laden on May 2, 2011 (May 1 in the United States)—with the aim of teaching people the nature of our enemy and how it can be defeated. I was fortunate to work alongside many heroes from the FBI, the Central Intelligence Agency (CIA), the NCIS, and other military agencies, and to work under great FBI leaders, such as Directors Robert Mueller and Louis Freeh, who understood the threat and what needed to be done. The successes in this book are theirs.

Note to Readers

The story is told firsthand through what I saw and learned, and wherever possible I have used dialogue to allow readers to experience situations as they happened. These exchanges are as I remember them, or as colleagues and terrorists recounted them to me. Other conversations are drawn directly from official transcripts, wires, and unedited court documents. I am grateful to my former colleagues who took the time to look through the manuscript and verify what they read. Naturally, with the passage of time it's difficult to remember conversations precisely word for word, and I trust that the reader will appreciate this when reading the conversations, and will understand that any errors are, of course, my own.

The reader should also be aware that this book was subjected to self-censorship to protect sources, methods, and classified material. It also went through the official government prepublication approval process. I have assigned certain CIA officers and government figures names other than their own; the practice will be obvious to the reader because anyone whose identity is thus obscured is referred to by a single first name only.

The aim of the book is to teach people how to understand al-Qaeda and how we can defeat them in the future, and any offense to specific individuals is unintended.

• • •

In on-site signage and much official government documentation, "Guantánamo" is unaccented when the word appears as part of the name of the American naval base and detention facility, but since the name of the bay itself is accented, and because that is the spelling recognized by readers and preferred by most mainstream publications, I have used it throughout.

PART 1

———————

THE EARLY YEARS

1

The Fatwa and the Bet

Winter 1998. "So, Ali, now let me ask you a personal question." I was having dinner with John O'Neill, my boss and the FBI special agent in charge of the National Security Division in the FBI's New York office. We were at Kennedy's, on West Fifty-seventh Street in midtown Manhattan, sitting at a table by the fireplace. It was John's favorite spot in the restaurant, especially when the weather was cold, as it was that evening.

John and I had spent the previous few hours discussing a memo I had written on a figure then little-known outside government circles, Osama bin Laden, who had just issued a fatwa declaring war against America. It was this memo that had brought me—a rookie in the bureau—to the attention of John, one of the most senior members in the office. Someone of my standing would usually have had to go through several chains of command to reach John O'Neill.

We had just finished dessert, and John was cradling his preferred drink, Chivas Regal with seltzer. His question signaled that he was done talking terrorism and now wanted to get to know me as a person. This was something he liked to do with all new agents he took under his wing, a colleague had told me. The question appeared to be a good sign.

The thought that he was considering taking me under his wing made me smile inwardly. John was an FBI legend and was known to be one of the few senior U.S. government officials who understood the necessity of making counterterrorism a national priority. To others, the war on drugs, foreign governments spying on us, and other nonterrorism-related matters were of greater concern. For anyone who believed, as I did, that a response to acts of terrorism carried out by violent Islamist groups needed to be prioritized, working alongside John was where you wanted to be.

"Sure, boss," I answered. "What's your question?"

"What I want to know, Ali," he said, leaning forward and looking at me and swirling his drink in the palm of his left hand, "is why did you join the bureau? What led you, a boy born in Beirut, from a family of intellectuals, to our ranks? You're not a typical recruit." Ending with a statement rather than a direct question was customary for John, and on that note he gave a quick smile, leaned back in his chair, and took a sip of his drink.

I studied John as he asked the question. He was, as usual, immaculately dressed, wearing one of his trademark double-breasted suits and expensive brogues, with a Rolex watch on his wrist. John didn't dress like a typical government employee. He valued looking good over saving for the proverbial rainy day (government salaries don't allow both).

I noticed the bulge near his left ankle as he leaned back and stretched out his legs. While John was too senior to be a street agent knocking on doors asking questions anymore, like any good agent he always kept his weapon by his side. In John's case it was a 9 mm gun. He didn't mind if people saw it, either: in truth, it could have been pushed a bit more discreetly toward his inner leg, but along with being a classy dresser John also cultivated a tough-guy persona—perhaps to show he wasn't a typical senior manager and was still "one of the boys," or even to intimidate people, if necessary.

While John did have an element of showmanship to him, he was one of the hardest-working and most effective senior agents in the bureau.

"When you're that good, you can be a tough guy and wear expensive suits. Apparently it works," I once told a colleague who criticized John's appearance and affect.

John's question made me slightly nervous. I laughed, struggling to appear at ease. I was trying hard to make a good impression, and my answer wasn't the typical "I-always-wanted-to-join-the-bureau-from-when-I-was-a-little-kid-because-I-want-to-protect-our-country-and-the-FBI-is-the-best" that most supervisors would have wanted to hear—and what most people in my shoes would have given.

John wasn't a typical supervisor. His conversation with me was laced with no-nonsense blunt talk and honesty about successes and failures, and he didn't shy away from profanities. My instinct was that John probably wouldn't like a soppy answer anyway. But I was still with someone far higher than me, and part of me felt the temptation to play it safe.

That part of me lost the debate going on inside my mind. "You're not going to believe me," I said, trying to find a way in.

"Try me," John responded.

I took a sip of my drink. "Well," I said, "it was a bet . . ."

"A bet?" John repeated, raising his left eyebrow.

"Yes," I replied with a guilty grin. "My fraternity brothers made a bet with me, and with each other, on how far I could get through the bureau's selection process. I never expected to make it all the way, but I passed every level, even the polygraph . . ." I paused. "And when the offer came from the bureau it was too tempting to pass up, and here I am today."

"You're kidding me," John said, and then started laughing. "Well, I see you're honest—I like that, ha!" He shook his head, still smiling. "Cheers," he continued, raising his glass, and we both downed the remainder of our drinks. He added, with his signature smile, "And they say gambling doesn't pay off."

My path to the FBI did start as a bet. I got my undergraduate degree at Mansfield University, in rural Pennsylvania, and there the vice president of student affairs, Joe Maresco—with whom I had a close relationship, as I was president of the student body—suggested, during a conversation about my prospects, that the perfect job for me might be working for the FBI.

I thought he was crazy. I didn't think I met the profile of an agent. I was an Arab American born in Lebanon. I was also a fraternity boy, and I enjoyed all the revelry that entailed. I certainly didn't fit in with the straitlaced white bureau types I envisioned—an image shaped by television shows. Nor had I ever considered a career in law enforcement or intelligence. It was as if Joe had suggested I join the circus or become a Formula One race car driver—it had never crossed my mind.

As I walked through the door of my fraternity house after my conversation with Joe, a few of my housemates were sitting on the couches, watching television, and I repeated, half-laughing, his career recommendation. They started laughing, too. "If you send in an application you'll probably get it back in the mail a few weeks later marked 'Return to Sender,'" one guy said. Another chimed in: "You won't even pass the physical." A third added: "They'll probably think it's a joke application . . ."

"I think he could do it," another countered. "If he could convince everyone in the university to raise funds for a new student center, he could convince some drug dealers to come clean." He was referring to a campaign I had led persuading everyone, from the students to the school administration, to donate to the building cause.

And the debate began, with no one, including myself, taking Joe's advice seriously.

Still, for the next few days I reflected on what Joe had said and began to find myself intrigued: now that I thought about it, a career in the FBI could be exciting. More than that, my nature has always been to not accept that there is something I can't do, and my fraternity brothers' insisting that I had no chance was such a challenge. I was always the child who, given a dare, accepted it. I got that partly from my father, who loved adventures, and it was partly due to the circumstances of my childhood: the Lebanon of my youth was a war zone, and, after that, things like the dark or being locked in a closet just didn't frighten me.

One of my earliest war memories is of hugging the bottom of the stairs in my house as bombs exploded in our neighborhood. (The center of a house, where the stairs were, was said to be the safest part.) We would huddle silently, listening as windows shattered and rubble fell. Sometimes, after what seemed like an eternity of silence, screams would shatter the quiet as people discovered dead bodies and severely injured loved ones.

My father used to tell me what Lebanon was like before the civil war, when Beirut was the Paris of the Middle East, as people liked to say, and when the country was renowned for its culture, intellectuals, and natural beauty; but I never knew that country. I grew up in a land that was a country only in name. Part was occupied by regional powers, and the rest was divided among different Lebanese ethnic and religious groups who ran their areas like feudal fiefdoms. Turf wars broke out regularly, and the losers were always ordinary civilians. I remember once crouching on the floor of our house as two militias battled each other from the two ends of our street, and we didn't know when it would end, or if we would survive. Everyone in Lebanon knew someone who was killed in the violence. I lost two classmates in a single semester in fifth grade.

To this day I vividly remember, down to minute details, Palestinian militants pulling up in jeeps outside homes in our neighborhood, swinging their machine guns toward the occupants, and ordering them to hand over their car keys. People had no choice but to obey, as there was no effective police force to appeal to for help.

A few months after my conversation with Joe, there was a career fair, and the bureau had a booth, reminding me of the bet. A few days later I decided to send in an application—more out of curiosity than anything else. I still didn't know much about what the bureau did, beyond the conventional knowledge and what I'd "learned" from some social science classes, movies, and, of course, the television shows. But after I submitted the application, I spent some time researching the FBI.

The information was mostly new to me. I discovered that the bureau was created in 1908—given its prominence today, I had thought it would

have been around longer. I also learned that only under J. Edgar Hoover
had it been built into the powerful law enforcement tool it is today,
which makes the bureau's successes and reputation even more impressive. The application process includes tests of all sorts, from physical to
aptitude, along with lots of interviews, often spaced out over months.
As I jumped through the hoops, my friends started a pool betting on
how long I'd last.

During the polygraph tests—while I was hooked up to the
machine—the polygrapher asked: "Have you ever done anything that
would embarrass you if your mother knew about it?"

"Yes," I replied, which puzzled him: it was not the answer he was
expecting. I jokingly explained to him that the machine probably wasn't
programmed to take in how strict the ethics of a Muslim mother can be.

After completing the long series of interviews and tests, for almost
a year I didn't hear anything from the bureau, and I began to think
that my application had failed somewhere and that they had forgotten to notify me. It didn't bother me too much, as applying to the
bureau had been more a source of amusement than anything else, and
I certainly hadn't been basing my future on the FBI. I was planning
on a career in academia, and as I was finishing up at Mansfield, I had
applied to do a master's degree in international studies at Villanova
University. By the time I was at Villanova, I had almost completely
forgotten about the bureau, and so it was a surprise to receive a letter
of acceptance as I was finishing and preparing to move to England to
pursue a PhD. I went back and forth in my mind as to what to do, with
friends and family divided in their recommendations. Ultimately the
bureau's offer was too tempting to pass up. The idea of being an agent
appealed to my sense of adventure, as did the chance to help protect
America, a country I had come to love dearly. I loved it because of the
welcome it had given me and my family and because, having grown
up in a country pulled apart by sectarian discord, I had come to appreciate the greatness of the United States and admire the ideals that had
created the nation.

I was fascinated by the protections the U.S. Constitution provides citizens. While the Constitution and the Pledge of Allegiance may perhaps seem largely symbolic to many Americans, to those of us who have lived with alternatives, they are filled with meaning. I know that the protections offered therein are very necessary.

The idea of being part of something bigger than me prevailed. I accepted the offer, and, in November 1997, after sixteen weeks of training at the FBI Academy, in Quantico, Virginia, I joined the bureau as a special agent, assigned to the New York office.

The FBI's New York field office, located in downtown Manhattan, in many ways resembles the city in which it is housed: it's full of colorful characters who are not afraid to voice their opinions and for whom politeness is often an unnecessary convention that gets in the way of making a point. The bluntness, the jokes, and the camaraderie of the NYO were, to me, far more appealing than the cold and formal atmosphere of many offices.

I did have an advantage over other out-of-towners in my ability to adjust, however. While New York City was entirely different from the rural Pennsylvania that had been my home in previous years (and which I loved), the lively characters did remind me in different ways of some of the interesting figures of my childhood in Beirut, and this helped me feel at home. Before new recruits are assigned to specific squads, they rotate through different sections of the office, starting with the applicants' squad (conducting background checks), then moving on to special operations (doing surveillance), and finishing at the command center—ensuring that newcomers gain an understanding of all the work the office does. This boosts camaraderie between squads and efficiency for the bureau as a whole, with everyone coming to know the roles and capabilities of other teams. It is also meant to help the recruits see which squads appeal to them, and it gives senior management a chance to see rookies at work before deciding where to place them.

Through the rotation period we met senior agents from different divisions who gave us advice and explained what their groups did. What most interested me was counterterrorism, and the senior people in this area whom I met were Pat D'Amuro, assistant special agent in charge (ASAC) of counterterrorism, and John O'Neill, who was Pat's superior, running the entire National Security Division.

In college I was always interested in the effects of nonstate actors on global stability. My experience in war-torn Lebanon shaped my view that groups like the Irish Republican Army, Hezbollah, the Palestine Liberation Organization, and Hamas can be more influential than the states themselves in setting political and security agendas. My graduate research focused on the cultural approach in international relations. Most of my professors were students of the realism school, which maintains that a country's national interest is central to how it acts, but I always believed that realism in many ways is shaped by the cultural lenses of different peoples. My research developed into a hobby, and gradually led me to follow the activities of a Saudi Arabian millionaire named Osama bin Laden.

What piqued my interest was reading newspapers from the Middle East. I kept up with them in order to stay up to speed on my Arabic and because I obviously retained an interest in the region. Bin Laden's name often appeared; there was a fascination with him among many in the Middle East, as he had given up a life of privilege to go fight with the mujahideen against the Soviet Union in Afghanistan and had then maintained the life of a fighter.

Over time I noticed bin Laden's declarations toward the United States growing increasingly aggressive, and it became clear to me that someone with his pedigree and resources was going to be very dangerous someday. I began following him more seriously, turning him from an academic interest into part of my job: actively searching the Arab media for his name and keeping a folder of interesting articles about him.

Bin Laden was the seventeenth child (out of an estimated fifty-four) of Mohammed bin Awad bin Laden, a household name in much of the Middle East. Born to a poor family in the south of Yemen, Mohammed had moved to Saudi Arabia, working as a porter before starting his own construction business. He built a reputation as a good builder and attracted the attention of the Saudi royal family, which began using him for their projects. Commissions started with roads, then moved on to palaces, until he was given the highest honor: renovating the Grand Mosque—al-Masjid al-Haram—in Mecca.

While Mohammed had a reputation for integrity in business, in his personal life he was more lax. He married a total of twenty-two women, often "marrying" and divorcing in a single day, as Islam forbids more than four wives at a time. Osama was the product of Mohammed's tenth marriage, to a Syrian woman named Hamida al-Attas; he was born on March 10, 1957.

True to form, Mohammed divorced Osama's mother soon after his birth to marry someone else. Mohammed was killed on September 3, 1967, when his private plane crashed while landing in southwest Saudi Arabia. Osama was ten; his image of his father was based less on personal interaction than on the legend of his father's building a company from scratch. The company continued to flourish after Mohammed's death, and the young Osama grew up with a desire to emulate his father in building something great.

After a religious upbringing, a young and devout Osama bin Laden traveled to Afghanistan in 1980 to join the fight against the Soviet invaders. While bin Laden did reportedly participate in some battles, due to his Saudi contacts he developed a reputation as a financier and worked with the charismatic cleric Abdullah Azzam in operating Makhtab al-Khidmat—the innocuously named Bureau of Services, which channeled money and recruits into Afghanistan. MAK was founded by Azzam in the early 1980s in Peshawar, Pakistan, and boasted global outposts, including in the United States, where its center of activity was al-Farouq Mosque, on Altantic Avenue in the Boerum Hill section of Brooklyn.

Osama bin Laden was in many ways a product of the mixture of two extremes of 1970s Saudi Arabia: a militant version of Wahhabism and Saudi wealth. Oil had transformed the Saudi government budget from $9.2 billion (1969–1974) to $142 billion (1975–1979). Many lucrative contracts went to the Saudi Binladin Group, as the family business was called, ensuring Osama and his many siblings a steady stream of money.

The Saudi state also used its newfound wealth to spread its Wahhabi sect of Islam across the world, building mosques and madrassas (religious schools) wherever it could while at the same time allowing strict Wahhabism to dictate most domestic law. This created some problems for the luxury-loving royals, whose indulgences were often at odds with their own laws. They solved this dilemma by buying homes and yachts on the French Riviera and in other showy places and playing out their fantasies there, all the while acting like pious Muslims at home. By satisfying their desires abroad, they simply put enough distance between the exercise of these two warring impulses so that Saudi citizens and, more importantly, clerics couldn't see them acting against their religion.

Wahhabism by itself is a peaceful version of Islam, as attested to by the millions of Muslims in Saudi Arabia and the Gulf states who are practicing Wahhabis and have nothing to do with violence or extremism. The extremism and terrorism arise when Wahhabism, a puritanical form of Islam with a distrust of modernity and an emphasis on the past, is mixed with a violent form of Salafism (a strand of Islam that focuses heavily on what pious ancestors did). An even more potent combination occurs with the introduction of the idea of *takfir*, wherein Muslims who don't practice Islam the same way are labeled apostates and are considered to be deserving of death. The result is like mixing oil and fire. It was in Afghanistan, during the first jihad, when Muslims from all across the world came to fight the Soviets, that these concepts combusted. Wahhabis came from Saudi Arabia and the Gulf, Salafis primarily from Jordan, and *takfiris* mainly from North Africa (Algeria, Morocco, Libya, and Egypt). *Takfir* was popular among the North African jihadists, as they had been fighting their own (nominally Muslim) regimes and therefore had to justify their terrorism and the killing of fellow Muslims in the process.

The Saudi government encouraged and helped young men travel abroad to fight in the Afghani jihad. This served a dual purpose of ensuring that Wahhabism influenced the mujahideen and enabling the country to get rid of would-be religious troublemakers by sending them abroad. It also helped shape the future of Afghanistan by helping to facilitate the rise of the Taliban.

And so Osama and hundreds of others headed to Afghanistan, their mission endorsed by the government both financially and operationally.

While I was doing my initial rotation, in February 1998—I was on the applicants' squad, performing background checks—I read in an Arabic newspaper, published in London, about the fatwa signed by bin Laden and other radical clerics, sanctioning the murder of American citizens anywhere in the world. The statement had been issued in the name of the World Islamic Front. It claimed that because America had declared war on God, it was the duty of every Muslim to kill Americans: "The ruling to kill the Americans and their allies—civilians and military—is an individual duty for every Muslim who can do it in any country in which it is possible to do it, in order to liberate al-Aqsa Mosque [Jerusalem] and the holy mosque [the Grand Mosque, in Mecca] from their grip, and in order for their armies to move out of all the lands of Islam, defeated and unable to threaten any Muslim."

Unaware of any existing bureau focus on bin Laden, and seeing that his rhetoric had morphed from vague utterances to direct threats, I wrote a memo explaining who he was and recommending that the FBI focus on the threat he posed to the United States. I gave the memo to my applicants' squad supervisor, who said that she would pass it to Kevin Cruise; she explained that Kevin was on the I-49 squad, under whose purview bin Laden fell. After receiving the memo, Kevin asked to see me. He introduced himself and explained what I-49 did—it focused on Sunni terrorist groups, including Jemaah Islamiah (JI) and Egyptian Islamic Jihad (EIJ). It covered the first World Trade Center bombing and after that had kept a focus on bin Laden, given the link between the plot and people in bin Laden's orbit.

I showed Kevin portions of bin Laden's August 1996 declaration of war against America, issued in response to the U.S. presence in the Arabian Peninsula: "Terrorizing you, while you are carrying arms on our land, is a legitimate, reasonable and morally demanded duty. It is also a rightful act well known to all humans and all creatures. Your example and our example are like a snake that entered into a house of a man and got killed by him. The coward is the one who lets you roam freely and safely while carrying arms in his country." Kevin was fully aware of the background information and said that the FBI was already pursuing a criminal case against bin Laden. Daniel Coleman was the bureau's bin Laden expert, and Kevin later introduced me to him. At the time, Dan was assigned to the CIA's Alec Station, set up by the agency's Counterterrorism Center (CTC) in 1996 to monitor bin Laden's activities. (Initially the CTC was called the Counterterrorist Center.) Kevin also introduced me to the other members of the I-49 squad, and we discussed the fatwa, agreeing that it was a serious warning and that an increased focus on bin Laden was needed. Kevin told us that the other branches of government were in agreement.

In May 1998, at the surveillance phase of the new agent rotation—I was working a mob case—I was paged by the office. I called in and was patched through to Kevin.

"Ali," he said, "bin Laden has just done an interview with ABC. He's talking openly about attacking the United States." Later that afternoon, I stopped in to watch it. The interview, which occurred as an offshoot of a press conference called by bin Laden, was conducted by John Miller (who later went to work for the FBI), and bin Laden was direct: "Today, however, our battle against the Americans is far greater than our battle was against the Russians. Americans have committed unprecedented stupidity. They have attacked Islam and its most significant sacrosanct symbols. . . . We anticipate a black future for America. Instead of remaining United States, it shall end up separated states and shall have to carry the bodies of its sons back to America."

"What do you think?" Kevin asked. I shook my head.

"That's it," I told him, "that's the third warning. First there was the 1996 declaration of jihad, then the February fatwa, and now he's going public straight to the American people. I think it's a warning that al-Qaeda is about to attack. We need to be prepared."

We didn't realize how right we were. Two months later, the U.S. embassies in Nairobi, Kenya, and Dar es Salaam, Tanzania, were bombed.

My initial rotation was up, and it was time to decide on a squad. I had become friends with a few agents in I-40, which dealt with Palestinian terrorist groups like Hamas, as well as terrorist-sponsoring countries, like Iraq under Saddam Hussein. The squad supervisor, Tom Donlon, who had been the case agent on several important cases, including the 1993 World Trade Center bombing, took me to see Pat D'Amuro.

On Pat's desk was a box filled with packets of Advil, Tylenol, and other painkillers—"for all the headaches related to the task force," he liked to joke. I spent a fair amount of time with him that day. He spoke about his experience in running a task force made up (at the time) of more than thirty-five federal, state, and local agencies handling virtually every terrorist group and state sponsor of terrorism around the world, and of the importance of agents remembering that they are bound by the Constitution. He said that we should never forget about the end-game—disrupting terrorist plots while keeping all options on the table, including prosecutions in a court of law.

Tom Donlon told Pat that he thought I was a suitable candidate for counterterrorism, based on my educational background in international affairs and my personal background—as someone born in Lebanon and fluent in Arabic. Pat asked if I was interested in joining the Joint Ter-rorism Task Force (JTTF). He explained that the JTTF was the first such effort in the nation, and that it was made up of various squads that covered virtually every terrorist group in the world, as well as the states that sponsored them. Agents, investigators, analysts, linguists, and other specialists comprised the team, drawn not only from the bureau but from other law enforcement and intelligence agencies. I gratefully accepted the invitation.

Pat then took me to meet John O'Neill, whose office was on the twenty-fifth floor of the FBI building. I stared for a few seconds out the window; John had the corner office, with huge windows and a view of lots of Manhattan: you could see the Empire State Building. We sat down on couches next to a coffee table piled with books on French art and Ireland, and we spoke about terrorism.

I was familiar with Tom Donlon's track record from some of the people on his squad, and as a new hire it was exciting for me to work under such an experienced agent. Tom had also agreed that I would continue to help the I-49 squad, and so I did operational work for I-40—tracking suspects and questioning people—and spent the rest of my time analyzing intelligence and working with agents on I-49 matters.

I was briefed on the investigations I-40 was running, and I spent my early weeks monitoring suspicious activities carried out by what we thought might be front organizations for terrorist groups. I also worked on foreign counterintelligence matters targeting state sponsors of terrorism, but as those cases are still classified, the stories can't be told here.

I continued to research different terrorist organizations, with a special focus on religious radical groups. Tom Donlon encouraged me to write a memo on the subject—"to spread the knowledge around," as he told me. I was more than happy to draft it. Among the people to whom Tom passed the memo was John O'Neill, who, I later learned, in turn distributed it across the entire terrorism branch management.

"Ali, what you working on?" I heard a voice say behind me. It was late in the evening, and I thought I was the only one left in the office. The voice was John O'Neill's. I didn't expect him to be around this late, let alone approach me at my desk. John laughed, realizing that he had startled me.

"Well?"

"Sorry, boss, you scared me." I worried that I had looked foolish.

"Don't worry," he said, as if reading my mind. "And great paper, by the way. I like that you took the initiative to write it, and the analysis was sharp. Good work."

"Thank you, sir."

"Next time you write something, send it directly to me as well."

"Yes, sir, I will."

"It's late and you're probably hungry. Let's go out to dinner and chat. I also had some questions I wanted to ask you."

The bartender at Kennedy's, Maurice, whom many in the law

enforcement community and the FBI viewed as the best bartender in New York, welcomed us with his warm Irish smile. A waitress led us to John's usual table, and we started discussing my memo. John, I quickly saw, was the kind of leader who saw no shame in admitting when he didn't know something, and he was appreciative when gaps in his knowledge were filled.

"What do you think makes this guy tick?" he asked, about twenty minutes into the conversation. He was referring to Osama bin Laden, whose activities we had been discussing.

"To understand that, we probably need to start with the global, regional, and local context—what surrounded him as he entered the scene," I replied.

"Where would you start?"

"The key moment is 1979."

"Why 1979?"

"Osama bin Laden was twenty-three in 1980, when he went to Afghanistan to join the mujahideen fighting the Soviet Union. The events of the previous year, 1979, had a big impact on the way that he and countless other young Muslims across the region saw their countries, their religion, and their role in the world—and it shaped their worldview and subsequent actions."

"And those events were?"

"The Iranian revolution, the signing of the peace agreement between Israel and Egypt, the Iranian hostage crisis, the seizure of the Grand Mosque in Mecca, and the Soviet Union's invasion of Afghanistan. They all happened in 1979."

With the Iranian revolution and the overthrow of the shah, an Islamic state was established under Ayatollah Ruhollah Khomeini. It was the first success of a political Islamic movement in modern history, and its effect was felt across the Muslim world: Shiite communities elsewhere now had a protector as well as a similar goal to aim toward, and Sunnis—especially the more radical groups in Egypt and Saudi Arabia—dreamed of repeating the revolution within their own framework. Other Sunnis saw a Shiite theocracy as a threat to Sunni Islam's dominance in the region and were motivated to try to counter it and strengthen their own influence.

Khomeini's seizure of power was itself a revolution in Shiite political thought. The traditional view is that an Islamic regime can't be established until the return of the twelfth, "missing" imam. Until then the ideas of Islam can be used to bring about a just society, but not an Islamic state. Khomeini broke with this traditional view, and he justified his actions—over the objections of dissenting clerics—by advocating the doctrine of *Velayat-e faqih*, or rule of jurisprudence. He argued that religious leaders can be ambassadors of the twelfth imam and therefore can establish an Islamic regime prior to his return.

Of course, modern political Islam wasn't created by Khomeini alone. He drew many of his ideas and religious justifications from Sunni Islamic thinkers, chief among them the Egyptian author and intellectual Sayyid Qutb (1906–1966).

Qutb was a member of the Muslim Brotherhood, an organization founded by Hassan al-Banna in 1928, when Banna was a twenty-two-year-old teacher of Arabic. The Muslim Brotherhood sought ultimately to create a state based on Sharia, or Islamic law. Its aim was to build its own social network by providing social services to the lower classes. The movement arose, in part, to challenge the rule of King Farouk, who was seen as corrupt and without sympathy for the poor. The Brotherhood was organized into small cells of five-member units, making it difficult for the king's security services to penetrate it—if one cell was cracked, the rest of the group would remain untouched. When the government officially tried to disband the Muslim Brotherhood two decades after its founding, the organization's membership rolls numbered more than a million.

Qutb joined the group shortly after Banna's death and through it met Colonel Gamal Abdel Nasser and other military leaders plotting to overthrow King Farouk. They were looking for allies, and the Brotherhood, with its strong support among the lower classes, seemed ideal. Together the military officers and Brotherhood leaders carried out the successful 1952 coup.

While both groups wanted to replace the king, their ideas for what should come next differed, with Nasser planning a secular government (and championing the idea of Arab nationalism) and the Brotherhood seeking an Islamic government (and pushing political Islam). Although it was Nasser who took power after the king's fall, he offered Qutb a position in the cabinet, as minister of education. Qutb declined, saying that the position wasn't senior enough for him, and began publicly challenging the regime, calling for an Islamic state.

In 1954 a member of the Brotherhood, Mohammed Abdel Latif, attempted to assassinate Nasser, firing eight shots at him from twenty-five feet away. All of them missed. While panic broke out in the assembled crowd, Nasser remained calm and simply declared: "If Abdel Nasser dies . . . each of you is Gamal Abdel Nasser . . . Gamal Abdel Nasser is of you and from you and he is willing to sacrifice his life for the nation." The crowd cheered him and the event was widely reported across the country, causing Nasser's popularity to soar. He used the opportunity to crack down on the Brotherhood, throwing many members, including Qutb, in jail.

Qutb was reportedly severely tortured, and the experience drove him to write his most influential work, *Milestones—Ma'alim fi al-Tariq*—which he had friends and family smuggle out of prison and circulate. In the book, he argues that according to Islam only God has sovereignty, and that for an ordinary person such as Nasser to serve as sovereign is the equivalent of idolatry. Such a system, Qutb writes, results in *jahiliyya*—the state of ignorance that preceded the life of the Prophet Muhammad. To Qutb, the modern state and Islam were incompatible, and those behind the modern state were pulling Muslims in the wrong direction.

Qutb's doctrine held that those who tortured him and his fellow prisoners, and indeed any citizens of the state (who by implication authorized the torture), could not be real Muslims—no real Muslim would inflict torture on another. Therefore, he argued, the torturers were *kafirs,* or nonbelievers, deserving of a sentence of apostasy, or *takfir*.

The background to sentencing someone as a *kafir* lies in the mid-seventh century, when Imam Ali, the Prophet's son-in-law, decided, as caliph, to compromise with a political opponent rather than engage in a war. His action prompted a rebellion by the Kharijites, who assassinated Ali and declared that only they were the true Muslims—all others were apostates and must be put to death. The Kharijites called themselves al-Shurat ("the buyers"), a reference to their buying a place for themselves in the next world. Kharijites ("those who went out") was the name given to the group by other Muslims because of their extreme views. Charges of apostasy and other measures imposed by the Kharijites had no scriptural basis: according to the Quran, only those who worship idols and who persecuted the Prophet and the early Muslims can be considered apostates. Hence the Kharijites took to manipulating Quranic passages and Islamic doctrine to justify their deeds.

Qutb also drew on radical thinkers such as the Pakistani Sayed Abul A'ala Maududi, his contemporary, and much earlier figures, such as Ibn Taymiyyah. One target of Ibn Taymiyyah's theological wrath was the Arab Muslims' Mongol conquerors, converts to Sunni Islam. He charged them with apostasy and declared, furthermore, that anyone who dealt with them or even so much as stood near them when they were being attacked could be killed—even if they were pious Muslims. His rationale was that if the bystanders were sinful Muslims, then it was fitting that they were killed, and if they were devout Muslims and unworthy of death, they'd simply go straight to heaven—thus no harm would be done by killing them. Either way, according to his logic, the killers were committing no sin by killing bystanders.

One doesn't have to look far in Islamic theology to see how wrong this view is: the Quran states that anyone who kills an innocent person shall be treated "as if he had murdered all of mankind." That refers to any human being, regardless of religion. It also states: "As for anyone who kills a Muslim deliberately, his repayment is Hell, remaining in it timelessly, forever. God is angry with him and has cursed him, and has prepared for him a terrible punishment." To this day Ibn Taymiyya's arguments are used by *takfiri* terrorists—those who accuse other Muslims of being apostates—to justify the killing of innocent people. Some who subscribe to it don't have enough knowledge of Islam to know how wrong it is, and others knowingly misuse it to justify violence.

Qutb was hanged in 1966. Beforehand, the regime offered him

mercy on the condition that he recant his views, but he refused, allegedly telling his sister, "My words will be stronger if they kill me." He surely was right in that sense, as his ideas have been used by everyone from Khomeini to bin Laden. Khomeini was fond of employing Qutb's imagery and conceptual arguments: just as Qutb, for example, compared Nasser (whom he viewed as a tyrant) to Pharaoh, Khomeini likened the shah to the biblical Pharaoh, and by his logic whoever challenged the Pharaoh took on the role of Moses. Given Khomeini's international prominence as the leader of Iran, his use of Qutb's ideas and arguments gave them wide circulation in the Muslim world.

In March 1979, one month after the Iranian revolution, Egypt and Israel signed the peace treaty that formally completed the Camp David Accords of the previous year. In the Middle East, the agreement was seen as a betrayal of the Palestinians and undermined the Arab world's solidarity against Israel. As a consequence, Egypt faced isolation throughout the Muslim and Arab world and was suspended from the Arab League. Islamist radicals in Egypt were enraged: Sadat, in the years before his assassination by extremists in 1981, had tried to sell himself as a religious president, in contrast to Nasser, who battled the Islamists and imprisoned Qutb.

On November 4, 1979, Iranian students attacked the U.S. Embassy in Tehran, taking fifty-two Americans hostage in retaliation for the United States' having allowed the shah into the country for cancer treatment. The failed U.S. rescue attempt in April resulted in the hostages being scattered around Iran; they were not released until January 1981—444 days after they had been seized. While the student leaders who overran the embassy hadn't sought Khomeini's approval before they acted, he supported them once it became clear that they were loyal Islamists who had pledged fealty to him. For the duration of the 444 days, the United States under Jimmy Carter seemed powerless to respond, and the forces of political Islam appeared to be on the rise.

Sixteen days after the attack on the embassy, on November 20, the destruction of a holy place shook the Islamic world when extremists seized al-Masjid al-Haram and took pilgrims hostage. The mosque surrounds the Kaaba, which is said to have been built by Abraham and is the place that Muslims turn to face when they pray five times a day. It is considered the first house of worship and the holiest site in Islam. The extremists declared that the Mahdi, the redeemer of Islam, had arrived—it was one of their leaders—and called on Muslims to obey him. Using the Grand Mosque's loudspeaker system, which could be heard throughout Mecca, they announced that the Saudi leadership had been corrupted by the West and demanded that the monarchy be replaced, that all ties with the West be cut, and that a stricter version of Islamic law be introduced into the country.

It took two weeks for the mosque to be fully retaken, and hundreds of pilgrims and Saudi troops were killed in the process. Afterward, the Saudi monarchy made concessions to radical clerics, imposing stricter Islamic laws on the population. In a sense, the extremists won.

Khomeini and other leaders, paradoxically, blamed the United States for what had happened, and anti-American riots broke out in several countries, including Pakistan, the Philippines, Libya, and the United Arab Emirates. The U.S. Embassy in Islamabad, Pakistan, was seized by a mob and burned to the ground, and the same happened in Tripoli, Libya.

The Soviet Union's invasion of Afghanistan was the final momentous event of 1979. The Soviets had been active in the country since the establishment of a Marxist-leaning Democratic Republic of Afghanistan in the spring of 1978. When the Marxist government could no longer contain the Afghan mujahideen, who wanted a religious state, Soviet troops entered Kabul to prop up their allies.

Muslims across the world rallied to protect the country from the Soviet "infidel" invaders. The invasion, and the creation of a new enemy for radical Muslims, served Egypt and Saudi Arabia well; both countries saw a chance to offload their domestic extremists by supporting their traveling to Afghanistan to join the jihad. Together the two countries poured billions of dollars into Afghanistan to support the mujahideen. The United States, eager to fight communism, also provided covert funding and training for the fighters.

One of the most influential figures in the Afghan jihad was Abdullah Azzam, a Palestinian cleric. A student of Qutb, Azzam had been a lecturer at King Abdul Aziz University, in Jeddah, before moving to Pakistan in 1979 to teach at the International Islamic University in Islamabad and to be closer to Afghanistan. When the Soviets invaded Afghanistan, Azzam issued a fatwa, entitled "Defense of the Muslim Lands, the First Obligation after Faith," in which he declared that it was a *fard ayn*, or personal obligation, for Muslims to defend Afghanistan against "the occupiers." Other important clerics participated in the fatwa, including Saudi Arabia's grand mufti, Abd al-Aziz bin Baz, giving it even more weight.

Azzam's slogan, "Jihad and rifle alone. No negotiations. No conferences and no dialogue," gives an indication of his worldview. His speeches influenced bin Laden—who had been a student at King Abdul Aziz University when Azzam was there—to join the mujahideen. Other top terrorists, including Ramzi Yousef, were also swayed by Azzam's arguments and appeals. Azzam had established Makhtab al-Khidmat to facilitate the movement of mujahideen to Afghanistan. He arranged guesthouses and training camps to prepare recruits for battle, opened fund-raising and recruitment branches around the world—including the one in Brooklyn—and himself recruited thousands of individuals to fight.

"Thousands of young Arabs traveled to Afghanistan," I told John, as we finished discussing what had happened in 1979. "Many were inspired by the ideology outlined by Azzam and other similar-minded clerics. Others were disenchanted with the oppressive regimes and lack of opportunity back home and sought an adventure. Most Muslims who came just provided muscle. Bin Laden's advantage, of course, was that he brought his own funding, which drew others to him and bought their loyalty."

The dessert dishes had long been cleared by the waitress, but John was keen to continue chatting and getting to know me on a personal level. When that conversation finished, we looked at our watches and saw that it was past 1:00 AM.

It turned out that it wasn't uncommon for John to be in the office late at night, and it often seemed that he never slept. He was usually in the office before anyone else, and he was the last one at his desk at night. And when he did leave in the evenings, it was to entertain foreign law enforcement and intelligence officials who were visiting or to take colleagues out to discuss work.

If John didn't have a dinner to go to, he would walk around the office to see who was there. He often stopped at my desk and invited me out. After a few weeks of finding me always there, he just started calling me at my desk; he'd tell me to meet him outside for dinner, and we would continue our discussions wherever we'd left off the last time.

John had a few favorite restaurants, and his choice was determined by what kind of food he was in the mood for and what time of night it was. For steak, he loved Cité, on West Fifty-first Street. If it was very late, we would head to 1st, on First Avenue. (He would tell me that it was "the place where all the good chefs in the city go after-hours.") If he was looking for a more social evening, he'd choose Elaine's.

A place John especially liked taking officials from other countries was Bruno's, owned, "ironically," as John liked to say, by an Albanian. "The best Italian food in the city, and the guy's Albanian." There was a table on the second floor that the manager would reserve for John if he knew he was coming. An exceptional Israeli piano player usually played Frank Sinatra songs, but when John had guests he would take requests from our group.

During the investigation into the 1998 East African embassy bombings, we were entertaining Tanzanian officials, and John asked the piano player for "an African song." Without pause the pianist started playing the 1920s Solomon Linda tune "Mbube" ("The Lion Sleeps Tonight"), more or less as rendered in the Disney film *The Lion King*, with its chorus of "In the jungle, the mighty jungle." When we took Saudi officials there and John requested a Middle Eastern song, the piano player opened with "Desert Rose."

John always tried to make foreign officials feel at home, so if there was a good restaurant in New York that served food from their countries, we went. In 1999, we were working with Saad al-Khair and his fellow Jordanian intelligence officers on the Millennium Operation, the investigation that thwarted a terrorist plot to attack American and

Israeli targets in Jordan on and around January 1, 2000. We took the Jordanians to a place called Cedars of Lebanon. The restaurant's live band often played traditional Arabic songs, which our visitors loved.

John understood the importance of personal relationships. Foreign law enforcement and intelligence officers could make life either difficult or easy for us, depending upon how cooperative they were. John endeared himself to them. When a British official's wife had cancer, John spent time researching the best hospitals in New York and helped the couple plan their trip. In turn, officials treated him and his team well when we traveled to England.

Most of our counterparts came to adore John. A phone call from him achieved much more than official cables. I saw this firsthand when I was in England taking part in Operation Challenge, the investigation that disrupted al-Qaeda and EIJ activity there. The relationship was one of honesty and friendship, not diplomatic niceties. One evening when our colleagues from Scotland Yard were visiting, John raised his glass during dinner and told them, "Unless you get your side to help more, the queen's going to end up living in Northern Ireland." No offense was taken—they knew John spoke from the heart, out of genuine concern for us all—and we got the help we wanted.

The bureaucracy didn't always understand the importance of John's dinners and entertaining and sometimes refused to give funding approval. In those cases John would just put the dinner on his own credit card. I learned to do the same, telling others, as John had told me, "We're not in the bureau to save money, we're here to save lives."

As the bureau began investigating bin Laden and al-Qaeda, agents began uncovering an American contingent with ties to the group. It wasn't only bin Laden who saw Azzam as his mentor; several Americans fell under Azzam's spell when he toured the United States in the 1980s to raise funds for the mujahideen and recruit believers to go to Afghanistan. Among the Americans lured were Wadih el-Hage, Essam al-Ridi, and Ihab Ali.

El-Hage was born in Lebanon to a Christian family but raised in Kuwait, where his father worked. There he began hanging out with

Muslim friends, who introduced him to the Quran and to the faith, and eventually he converted to Islam. His family was outraged by the conversion and shunned him. The Kuwaitis who sponsored his conversion sent him to the United States to be educated.

When the Soviets invaded Afghanistan, el-Hage, inspired by Azzam's sermons, left the United States and went to Pakistan to aid his Muslim brothers. Taking the alias Abed al-Sabour al-Lubnani (the Lebanese) and serving as an aide to Azzam, he translated military books for fighters to use and performed administrative work. While working for Azzam, he met the young Osama bin Laden, and the two formed a relationship.

In 1985 el-Hage returned to the United States, and a year later he graduated from the University of Southwestern Louisiana. He married an eighteen-year-old American Muslim named April, moved to Arizona, and, in 1989, became a naturalized U.S. citizen. El-Hage traveled regularly back to Peshawar to work for bin Laden.

Essam al-Ridi was born in Egypt in 1958 and spent his childhood in Kuwait. He studied engineering in Karachi, Pakistan, but civil unrest prevented him from finishing his degree, so he moved to Texas, where he enrolled in the now-defunct Ed Boardman Aviation School, in Fort Worth. Returning to Kuwait, he was unable to find a job, so he moved back to the United States and worked as an instructor at the flight school.

Ridi met Abdullah Azzam first in Pakistan and then again at a Muslim American Youth Association convention in the United States. Ridi had helped organize the convention, and Azzam was one of the guest speakers. They stayed in touch, discussing how Ridi could help in Pakistan, and eventually they both traveled there. Ridi spent his first night at Azzam's house and at some point met the Afghani mujahideen leader Abdul Rasul Sayyaf.

Ridi's time in Pakistan was marked by perpetual dissatisfaction and the desire to return to the United States, about which he spoke repeatedly to Azzam. He wasn't sure that his services were actually required in Pakistan, so eventually he asked Sayyaf, "Will my help be needed here, or can I help from the United States?" When Sayyaf asked him to describe his skills, he replied, "I know how to fly and travel around the world."

"There is no need for flying," Sayyaf told him, "but we need someone to travel and ship things."

For eighteen months Ridi procured items for the mujahideen— such as night vision goggles from the United States and range finders from England. He was traveling every fifteen to twenty days, visiting countries from Japan to Kuwait. He complained to Azzam several times, telling him that he couldn't do it alone much longer, and Azzam always said there was no one to spare to help him.

In 1985, having adopted the alias Abu Tareq in Afghanistan, Ridi weighed his options. His Egyptian passport was about to expire, and as this was what allowed him to travel, he needed to get it renewed; but he had never stopped looking for an excuse to leave Pakistan. He resented people like bin Laden—rich outsiders who controlled decision making—but when he raised such objections, he was ignored. In the end he returned to the United States and resumed work as a flight instructor in Texas.

When he left, he told Azzam: "I'm not needed here, and I'm not in line with the ideology. It will be best if I move back home, but I'll still provide the help you need." Resettled in the United States, he continued to purchase items for the mujahideen, packing them in Wadih el-Hage's luggage for el-Hage—who had partially assumed the role Ridi had abandoned—to take back to Pakistan. On occasion, Ridi semi-reluctantly traveled back to Afghanistan, as in 1989, when the mujahideen had difficulty adjusting the scope on long-range .50-caliber sniper rifles he had purchased in the United States and shipped to them. The fighters' unfamiliarity with the weapons forced a trip whose sole purpose was for Ridi to show them, in person, how to fix the sights.

Initially Ridi's reservations about bin Laden made him wary of working with him; he viewed himself as a purist and continued to be suspicious of the wealthy Saudi who had no military experience, only very deep pockets, and who nonetheless saw himself as a military leader. Ridi stayed true to his promise to Azzam to remain on call, however, and whenever bin Laden or other mujahideen wanted him to procure what they needed—and usually it was Wadih el-Hage who phoned with instructions—he would do so, traveling around the world for equipment, some of which is reportedly still being used by al-Qaeda.

Ihab Ali, known for his operational alias, Nawawi, was another Egyptian who moved to the United States with his family, attending high school in Orlando, Florida. Inspired by Azzam, he traveled to Afghanistan to fight the Soviets. He trained at the Airman Flight School, in Norman, Oklahoma, before traveling to Sudan to join up with bin Laden, to whom he, like Ridi, had been introduced by Azzam, in Afghanistan.

At the time, the U.S. government knew that individuals like these three men were traveling to Afghanistan, but because of American support for the mujahideen, they were not stopped, as they were committing no crime. While the men didn't know each other well in the United States, they met abroad and built relationships with each other and with other Arab mujahideen, such as bin Laden.

The United States government played a major role in supporting the Afghan jihad against the Soviets. American involvement was in no small part driven by Democratic congressman Charlie Wilson, of Texas, who pushed for the Pentagon to send surplus cash to Afghanistan. Many American intelligence officials and political leaders believed that striking a blow to the Soviets in Afghanistan would deliver the United States a big cold war victory. CIA director William Casey believed that the fight needed to be waged in the third world. Under his guidance the CIA did everything it could to support the mujahideen, even printing translations of the Quran in the hope of encouraging people in Uzbekistan and other countries to rise up against the Soviets.

The United States used Pakistan as a conduit to the mujahideen, distributing weapons and money. Pakistan was a willing helper, as President Muhammad Zia-ul-Haq, who had seized power in a 1977 military coup, didn't want the Soviets on his border. It was in Pakistan's interest to have a friendly Afghanistan instead.

Ironically, while the United States was supporting one group of Islamic fighters in Afghanistan, the mid-1980s saw a rise in religiously motivated terrorist attacks against American citizens and interests. In

1983, Hezbollah suicide attacks on marine barracks in Lebanon killed more than 250 Americans. Hijackings by terrorists elsewhere in the Middle East also claimed American lives.

To address the growing threat, in 1984 Ronald Reagan signed National Security Decision Directive (NSDD) 138, "Combating Terrorism." The director of Central Intelligence (DCI) established the Counterterrorism Center the following year. At first it focused largely on Hezbollah and secular leftist terrorist groups, rather than emphasizing Muslim Brotherhood–inspired groups. A new, interagency committee on terrorism was also formed by the National Security Council.

While these changes were being made, however, U.S. aid to the mujahideen continued to increase. The CIA also committed support to guerrilla attacks in Tajikistan and Uzbekistan and to a Pakistani intelligence initiative to recruit Muslims worldwide to fight with the mujahideen.

The biggest problem was that Washington did not have a strategy in place for what would happen after the Soviet withdrawal in 1988. Instead, Washington's focus was on the Iraqi invasion of Kuwait and the first Gulf War, along with the fall of the Soviet Union. Al-Qaeda, meanwhile, was busy setting up a Nairobi cell to arm and train Somali warlords to fight the U.S. troops deployed to the country.

I often met with John to discuss terrorism matters, and his focus never shifted; he was married to his work and to the FBI. Pat D'Amuro used to get annoyed when John would call him every hour during investigations to ask questions and micromanage. Pat wanted him to ease up and give him a break. John's reply didn't vary: "You have to let it consume you; there is no break." Years later, during the USS *Cole* investigation, when I was the case agent and John was out of the country, I understood how Pat felt. John called me every hour; and he told me, as he had told Pat, that I needed to let it consume me.

To John the reality was simple: "The bad guys work nonstop, so do we." To be in John's trusted inner circle you needed to give your all, as he did, or you were out. People who were pushed out resented John for it. I understood their anger—it's natural to want to spend time with your family—but I saw John's perspective, too: we were in a race against the clock.

What upset other people about John was that he liked to be the center of attention. During a dinner at Cité with Pat D'Amuro and another agent, Kenny Maxwell, who much later succeeded Pat as head of the JTTF, John repeatedly referred to New York as "my city." Kenny—Irish, like John—had lived in New York his entire life. John, born in Atlantic City, had worked mainly in Chicago and Washington, DC.

Kenny told John, "This is my city. You're from Chicago." John didn't like the insinuation, and soon the two Irish guys were yelling at each other and Pat had to calm them down. Anybody who didn't acknowledge John's need to be center stage or who tried to outshine him might be told off for it.

John was killed on 9/11 in the World Trade Center, and stories came out afterward about his messy personal life. He was a complicated human being, but as a boss, I never saw anything but the best from him—and I worked with him on many high-profile cases. I never saw his personal life affect his work or judgment.

In April 1988 the Soviets announced that within nine months they would withdraw from Afghanistan. The question for the mujahideen, after celebrating their victory, was what should come next. Some decided to stay in Afghanistan and use it as a base of operations for jihad elsewhere. Others returned home, seeing their religious duty as having been fulfilled and wishing to resume normal lives. Many went off in search of new conflicts—in places like Bosnia, Chechnya, the Philippines, and Algeria.

Those who decided to stay gathered in Peshawar to decide upon their next steps. They were in agreement that the network they had built to fight the Soviets shouldn't be allowed to collapse, and that the momentum should be maintained, so they set up a new group, called The Base—al-Qaeda in Arabic—to coordinate their actions. Bin Laden was chosen as the leader of the new group, which had a defined structure, with a *shura*, or advisory, council, along with military, political, financial, security, religious, and media committees. His rise to prominence was in large part due to his wealth and fund-raising ability, which brought him friends, influence, and power among the mujahideen.

Among the mujahideen leaders there was disagreement over direction and priorities. MAK head Abdullah Azzam, who had been bin Laden's mentor, wanted to focus on rebuilding Afghanistan, and then to support the Palestinians against Israel. Bin Laden, however, wanted to focus on "the head of the snake," namely the United States—a position he was supported in, and encouraged to take, by Ayman al-Zawahiri, who had considerable influence among Egyptian Islamists. Zawahiri was one of the leaders of Egyptian Islamic Jihad, the underground group aimed at creating an Islamic state in Egypt and then using Egypt as a launching pad for jihad against the West. In 1980 he had traveled to Pakistan to join the Afghan jihad, believing that his group could obtain in Afghanistan the training they needed for success in Egypt.

Bin Laden and Zawahiri bonded and had great use for each other: Zawahiri and his group found bin Laden's financial support and network indispensable, and bin Laden, in turn, was attracted to Zawahiri's sense of direction and his experience. After warning bin Laden of his need for enhanced security, Zawahiri offered his own men as protection; hence the al-Qaeda leader came to be surrounded by Egyptians, who helped shape his and his organization's focus.

Among the Egyptians was Amin Ali al-Rashidi, known as Abu Ubaidah al-Banshiri—he acquired the name al-Banshiri in Afghanistan, where he had fought in an area called the Panjshir Valley. Banshiri was a former Egyptian police officer who became al-Qaeda's military commander. His deputy, Tayseer Abu Sitah, better known as Mohammed Atef or by his al-Qaeda alias Abu Hafs al-Masri (al-Masri meaning "the Egyptian"), had also served as a police officer. The fact that someone like Abu Sitah operated under multiple names shows the complexity of trying to unravel the identities of everyone in the group.

The head of al-Qaeda's religious committee was Mamdouh Mahmoud Salim, who took the name Abu Hajer al-Iraqi. He was a Kurd who had fought in Saddam's army and alongside bin Laden in Afghanistan, where the two became close friends. While Abu Hajer wasn't a cleric—he was an engineer by training, and had memorized the Quran—bin

Laden believed that he was a pious figure, and he loved to hear him recite passages from the Quran. The Islamic thinkers whom Abu Hajer liked to quote included Qutb and Ibn Tamiyyah.

The disagreement between Azzam and bin Laden ended on November 24, 1989, when an improvised explosive device (IED) that had been placed under Azzam's car killed him and his two sons. Responsibility was never assigned, but it was suspected that Zawahiri was connected. While before Azzam's death Zawahiri had denounced him in public, after his death he pretended that they had been the best of friends.

Bin Laden, as head of al-Qaeda, wasn't supreme over all mujahideen; al-Qaeda was only one among many Sunni groups vying for dominance. Another leader offering a vision was Omar Abdul Rahman, the "Blind Sheikh," so called because childhood diabetes had left him sightless. Rahman led al-Gamma'a al-Islamiyya (the Islamic Group), a rival of Zawahiri's group. Others influential in Afghanistan were Ramzi Yousef and his uncle Khalid Sheikh Mohammed, who operated independently and had no desire to be under bin Laden's command.

When bin Laden returned to Saudi Arabia in 1990, he was welcomed as a hero among ordinary people, but the Saudi regime was wary, having grown concerned about his actions. He was seen as a troublemaker, having worked in 1989, for instance, on a plot to overthrow the Marxist government in South Yemen.

The ultimate break between bin Laden and the royal family came when Saddam invaded Kuwait. Bin Laden told the royals that he and his army of mujahideen could defend the kingdom, but his offer was rebuffed, as the Saudis knew that bin Laden and his band of fighters would be no match for Saddam's army. Instead they welcomed U.S. troops to fight Saddam.

Bin Laden was furious at being spurned, and at the royals for allowing "infidel" troops into Saudi Arabia. He publicly denounced the royal family. They took away his passport as a form of punishment, but in the spring of 1991, with the help of sympathizers in Saudi Arabia, he made it to Peshawar. He was later securely transported, by an Egyptian named Ali Mohamed, to Sudan.

2

Osama Air

Bin Laden's move to Sudan was not a hasty decision or one made strictly under duress. Years before 1991, he had begun to realize that the Saudi regime was growing increasingly frustrated with him, and he had started considering other locations. When the tipping point came and the Saudis tried to silence him by confiscating his passport, he already had a new base lined up.

One option had always been to return to Afghanistan, where he had flourished in the past; another was to set up a new base in Sudan. In 1989, when the National Islamic Front (NIF) took control of Sudan in a coup, declaring a desire to turn Khartoum into the center of an international Islamic network, the NIF sent an invitation to bin Laden to move his organization to the country. It was then that he began to consider Sudan seriously.

He sent operatives, led by Abu Hajer, to meet with the new Sudanese leaders and evaluate the country's suitability as a base of operations. Abu Hajer came back with a positive report, telling bin Laden and other al-Qaeda members that the NIF leaders were devout Muslims and that al-Qaeda would have the necessary freedom to operate effectively from the country. Abu Hajer also brought back books written by NIF religious leader Dr. Hassan al-Turabi, whom al-Qaeda members tended to mistrust because he had studied at the Sorbonne. Abu Hajer said: "Studying in Europe doesn't make someone a bad person. Turabi is a noted scholar. He has memorized the Quran, he knows a lot about Islamic law, and in fact for forty years he served *da'wa*"—the act of inviting others to study Islam, sometimes with the aim of converting them.

Bin Laden made a deal with Turabi and the Sudanese authorities whereby they would give al-Qaeda the freedom to operate, and in exchange he would invest in the country and help the regime fight Christian separatists in the south. Once the deal was finalized, bin Laden sent Jamal al-Fadl (then his secretary) and others to prepare for his arrival. It was in 1991 that the preparations were completed and the move accomplished.

Every Thursday after the sunset prayer, all al-Qaeda members in Khartoum gathered at one of the farms the organization owned to hear a lecture given by bin Laden or someone else on jihad and on the organization's mission. At the first such meeting, bin Laden told his followers that their mission in Sudan would be to build al-Qaeda, eventually turning it into an international network that would not only support others waging jihad but which would be capable of launching its own operations. From 1992 to 1995, as events such as the first Gulf War and the conflict in Somalia shaped the narrative of the terror network, operatives undertook the large-scale procurement of equipment and supplies that began to mark al-Qaeda's institutional and operational evolution.

Essam al-Ridi was at his home in Texas when the phone rang on a fall day in 1993.

"As-Salāmu `Alaykum, my brother." He recognized the voice as belonging to Wadih el-Hage. El-Hage had offered the traditional greeting: Peace be upon you.

"Wa `Alaykum as-Salām, Abu Abdallah Lubnani," Ridi replied, returning the greeting. "How are you?"

"Alhamdu lelah," el-Hage replied: Praise be to God. "And yourself?"

"Alhamdu lelah."

"So why are you calling, my friend? What can I do for you?"

"I've got a message from the sheikh."

"I guessed as much," Ridi replied with a hearty laugh. It was usually with some request from bin Laden that his old friend el-Hage called him these days.

"So what can I do for Abu Abdullah?" Ridi continued, referring to bin Laden by one of his aliases: the father of Abdullah. Abdullah is the name of bin Laden's eldest son, and referring to him thus was an expression of respect, as it's considered a great honor in the Muslim world to have a son.

"He wants you to buy an airplane for him," el-Hage replied. He explained that bin Laden had asked that the plane be delivered to Khartoum International Airport.

"An airplane?" As a trained pilot and flight instructor, Ridi knew how to go about purchasing a plane. "What type of plane does Abu Abdullah want, and how much is he willing to spend?"

"Something that has a range of more than two thousand miles," el-Hage replied, "for no more than three hundred fifty thousand dollars." He explained that bin Laden wanted to transport Stinger missiles from Peshawar to Khartoum.

"You have to be careful transporting weapons, you know," Ridi said. "You need to make sure you get permission from the countries on both ends, or you'll find yourself in trouble."

"Don't worry, we've got permission from the authorities in Peshawar and Khartoum. But that's why we need the two thousand miles. We can't risk running out of fuel and being forced to land elsewhere—it will be chaos."

Ridi found a suitable plane; the seller even agreed to give him a 9 percent commission for arranging the purchase, a fact Ridi chose not to divulge to el-Hage. In any case, his profit was never realized; inexplicably, el-Hage dropped the allowance for the plane to $250,000. "This is the price that the sheik has decided on, so see what you can do," he told Ridi.

Ridi argued that the terms were impossible. He knew what was out there; they would never be able to get what they wanted for $250,000. At last, however, he found a decommissioned military aircraft for $210,000 that had a range of 1,500 miles. "It's in storage in Tucson, Arizona, and hasn't been used in a while," he told el-Hage, "so I need to get it checked and fixed." When el-Hage asked him how he would get it to the airport, Ridi replied, "I'll fly it there myself."

El-Hage said that he had one final request to convey: bin Laden wanted Ridi to work for him as a pilot. Ridi demurred, suggesting that they discuss the offer in Khartoum. He had the plane refurbished and repainted, updated its equipment, and took off from Dallas–Fort Worth. Minus-65-degree weather while flying caused the plane to malfunction, and a window cracked on the way. It took him a week to get there.

El-Hage met him at the airport and inspected the plane. He was full of praise for Ridi. "It looks good. Well done."

"For what it cost, it's good," Ridi shrugged. The journey had exhausted him.

El-Hage took him to his own home and later they dined with bin Laden, to whom Ridi presented the keys to the aircraft. They agreed to meet at the airport the following morning so that bin Laden could inspect the plane. Ridi rose early to clean it—the exterior was dirty from the flight—but bin Laden failed to show at the appointed time, and Ridi spent several idle hours before getting in touch with el-Hage, who apologized and summoned him to the office for a meeting.

Ridi arrived at a residential building in the Riyadh neighborhood of Khartoum. El-Hage, manning the front desk, greeted Ridi warmly. Besides performing the duties he had inherited from Ridi, he had taken over as bin Laden's secretary following the departure of Jamal al-Fadl, one of the first members of al-Qaeda. Fadl, who was Sudanese, had spent several weeks training el-Hage in the management of the office. Beyond el-Hage's desk was an office that belonged to Abu Jaffar (Abu Khadija al-Iraqi), bin Laden's business manager; the interior office was bin Laden's. Ridi was ushered into bin Laden's office by el-Hage.

Bin Laden was wearing a white thawb (a traditional Arab garment) and had a black beard. "I'm sorry for not coming this morning," he said to Ridi. He spoke quietly, with a Saudi accent, his voice seeming to betray a hint of shyness. "But I've got a new request for you now. I'd like you to stay here in Sudan and work for me. I'll pay you twelve hundred dollars a month."

"Before we discuss any job offer," Ridi replied, "there's something that I need to say to you on a personal level. You may know that when we were both in Afghanistan, I resented the fact that you were a rich man with no military background or experience trying to be a military leader. That was one of the reasons I left Afghanistan. Now that you have the experience, it's a different situation, so my view has changed."

Bin Laden thanked Ridi and explained the particulars of the job. "You will fly the plane for me personally. You will also use it for crop dusting." Bin Laden owned farms that grew crops from which vegetable oil was produced. "And you'll fly the crops to other countries to be sold."

"That's three jobs," Ridi replied. "Which one is for twelve hundred dollars?"

"That's for all three. This, you should know, is the highest I'm paying my officers."

"It might be the highest, but I've heard that there's high inflation here in Khartoum," Ridi replied. "I've also heard that schools are expensive for expatriates. So is furniture. It's not a healthy environment. Living here is going to cost me more than twelve hundred dollars a month. Even if you're paying this salary to your top officers, it doesn't mean I should be paid the same. I'm doing a different job, and have different expenses."

"That's the highest, so consider it," bin Laden said. "And just so you know, in case you do still have any of your concerns, this is not jihad, this is strictly business."

Ridi later confirmed, with el-Hage, that the proposed salary was one of the highest bin Laden paid. Nonetheless, he turned it down. But he assured bin Laden that he was still prepared to "help you as usual whenever you need it." After getting reimbursed for his expenses, Ridi flew to Peshawar, where he spent time catching up with old friends from his days in Afghanistan, and then returned to the United States.

True to his word, Ridi continued to run missions for bin Laden when asked. Sometimes it involved flying the plane; at one point, he traveled to Khartoum to take five Arabs to Nairobi. Their job was to join cells being set up in Somalia. Other times, Ridi helped purchase weapons and matériel.

About a year and a half went by with no calls to fly the plane. Ridi took a job in Egypt with an airline but soon was summoned, once again, by el-Hage. "Brother, can you come to Sudan to fix up the plane and make it workable so it can be used for business?" When Ridi asked what had happened, el-Hage explained that the plane simply hadn't been used for a while and was languishing at the airport. "We haven't been able to get it to work since last time you used it."

Ridi pointed out that flying directly from Egypt to Sudan to meet with bin Laden was likely to raise government suspicion. Bin Laden was involved in weapons smuggling through Egypt; he had been sending caravans with weapons to meet Egyptian terrorists in the desert. Intelligence operatives were closely monitoring anyone with ties to bin Laden, and Ridi didn't want to come to their attention. "That's fine, meet me in Nairobi," el-Hage suggested. "That's where I'm now based."

"Why are you here now?" Ridi asked el-Hage in Nairobi.

"I'm working for a charity called Help Africa People." The improbable name gave Ridi an indication of what was going on.

"A charity?"

"It's really a cover for our efforts in Somalia and here," el-Hage replied with a smile.

Ridi laughed. "I guessed as much."

Their discussion turned to the plane. Ridi said that in order to get it ready to be used for business, he would need a copilot.

"Okay, Ali Nawawi will help you. He'll meet you in Khartoum."

Ridi flew to Khartoum, checked into the Hilton hotel near the airport, and then met Nawawi at the airport. The two men examined the plane and found that it had a flat tire, and that some of the other tires had melted from the heat. The engine was full of sand, and the batteries were dead. Parts of the plane were rusty from disuse, and the craft was filthy. They also couldn't find the keys. A few al-Qaeda operatives had met them at the airport; they, too, didn't know where the keys were.

Nawawi went off to hunt for the keys, and Ridi stayed to work on the plane. The keys were eventually located, and after the two men had finished making the necessary repairs and had checked the hydraulics and run a series of tests, they decided that they were ready to see how the plane handled. It took off without incident. After touching down on the runway a few times and going back up into the air without slowing down, Ridi decided that the plane was operational and that it was time to land properly. They touched down successfully, but when Ridi tried applying the brakes, nothing happened.

"We've lost the main hydraulic or the main brake system," he told Nawawi. "I'm going to try the alternate brake system." As the more experienced pilot, he was in control. The alternate brakes failed to work, and he tried the hand brakes. When this, too, failed, he shut down the engine. The plane continued to speed along the runway.

Ridi was sweating, but his voice was calm and his hands steady; his professional training had kicked in. They were still traveling fast—about sixty knots—and he found himself quickly explaining the obvious to Nawawi: that they would soon run out of runway space. He aimed the plane at a sand dune. "When we crash into the dune, take off your seat belt and get out of the plane—because it might explode," he told Nawawi.

About five seconds later the plane veered off the runway and crashed into the dune, which brought them to an abrupt halt. The impact jerked their heads forward, but their seat belts prevented their bodies from following. Ridi unbuckled his belt and jumped out of his seat. He switched off the hydraulic system and the plane's electric system to try to avoid an explosion, and opened the door. As he was about to jump out, he saw that Nawawi, in a state of shock, had remained in his seat, belt still buckled. He rushed to release Nawawi's seat belt and dragged him out of the plane.

Everyone in the airport was staring at them. "I've got to get out of here quick," Ridi told Nawawi, who had started to come to his senses.

"It's not our fault. Bin Laden won't blame you," Nawawi said.

"That's not what I'm worried about. Khartoum is full of Egyptian intelligence tracking bin Laden and people working with him. Everyone knows this is bin Laden's plane. It's the only private plane in the airport. I don't want Egyptian intelligence associating me with him. That will cause me a lot of problems."

They reached a security guard on the runway. "Are you okay?" the guard asked the two men.

"I'm fine, but I need you to drop me at the terminal," Ridi told him. The guard agreed to do so, and, leaving Nawawi to fend for himself, Ridi went straight from the terminal to the Hilton, packed his bags, and returned to the airport. He booked himself on the first flight out of Khartoum—it happened to be going to Addis Ababa—and from there caught a flight to Cairo.

That was the end of what was later nicknamed, by a few of us in the bureau, "Osama Air."

On the surface it looked as if bin Laden was in fact engaged in legitimate business in Sudan. He established companies such as Ladin International, an investment company; Wadi al-Aqiq, a holding company; al-Hijra, a construction business; al-Themar al-Mubaraka, an agricultural company; Taba Investments, an investment company; Khartoum Tannery, a leather company; and Qudarat Transport Company, a transportation company, which all seemed to perform legitimate work. The construction company, for example, built a highway from Khartoum to Port Sudan. At the same time, operatives used the businesses as a means of traveling around the world to purchase weapons, explosives, and equipment and to aid foreign fighters. The businesses were the perfect cover to avoid attracting attention from intelligence services.

Bin Laden began to create a worldwide network for helping fellow jihadist groups, establishing an Islamic Army *shura* to coordinate efforts. On the council were representatives from, among other groups, the Libyan Islamic Fighting Group (LIFG) and EIJ, the latter represented by Zawahiri. Bin Laden sent funds, weapons, trainers, and fighters to the Moro Islamic Liberation Front (MILF) and the Abu Sayyaf Group, both in the Philippines, and Jemaah Islamiah, which was based in Indonesia but was spread across Southeast Asia. Trainers were sent to Kashmir and Tajikistan, and a guesthouse was opened in Yemen—a central point for the entire region. Simultaneously, al-Qaeda members were sent to these groups to learn from their experiences and to pick up skills. Al-Qaeda members even went to the Bekaa Valley, in Lebanon, where they received training from the Shiite group Hezbollah. While al-Qaeda is a radical Sunni group that views Shiites as heretics, for the purpose of learning terrorist tactics they were prepared to put their religious differences aside.

In late 1992, once the basic network was set up, bin Laden and other al-Qaeda leaders plotted where they might begin striking U.S. targets. They settled on the Horn of Africa. American troops were in Somalia as part of Operation Restore Hope—an international United Nations–sanctioned humanitarian and famine relief mission in the south of the country, which the United States had begun leading in December of 1992. Abu Hafs al-Masri was sent to Somalia to evaluate precisely what the United States was doing in Somalia; in the resulting report, he termed the U.S. presence an invasion of Muslim lands but conceded that, because of the different tribal groups in the country, it would be tough for al-Qaeda to operate there. Based upon Abu Hafs al-Masri's report, al-Qaeda's leaders issued a fatwa demanding that the United States leave Somalia.

Al-Qaeda trainers were on the ground during the Battle of Mogadishu (also known as Black Hawk Down), on October 3–4, 1993, when two U.S. Black Hawk helicopters were shot down during an operation. After a chaotic rescue mission, 18 Americans and more than 1,000 Somali fighters were killed. The world saw the lifeless bodies of American soldiers being dragged through the streets, and President Clinton soon afterward ordered U.S. troops to withdraw from Somalia. Bin Laden celebrated the withdrawal as a major victory and often told his followers that this episode showed how America was weak, and how al-Qaeda could beat the superpower by inflicting pain.

After al-Qaeda was set up in Sudan, the leadership decided that the group needed a presence in Somalia. Nairobi was deemed the perfect entry point. Operatives, claiming to be aid workers, would fly to Nairobi and then take a small plane to the border; from there they would drive. Bin Laden sent his trusted lieutenant Khalid al-Fawwaz to lead the Nairobi cell. Fawwaz opened several businesses, the first in precious gems, and formed NGOs that purportedly helped Africans but which were actually a cover for al-Qaeda operatives who passed through on their way to Mogadishu. Once the cell was operational, bin Laden sent Fawwaz to London to run al-Qaeda operations focusing on logistics and public relations. Fawwaz worked under cover of the Advice and Reformation Committee, an NGO established on July 11, 1994, that advocated reforms in Saudi Arabia. Wadih el-Hage was sent by bin Laden to replace Fawwaz in Kenya.

El-Hage's secretary in Nairobi was Fazul Abdullah Mohammed, one of whose aliases was Harun Fazul. Born in the Comoros Islands, Harun Fazul attended a radical Wahhabi school and then went to Afghanistan, where he got involved with al-Qaeda. (He was eventually killed, on June 10, 2011.) The Nairobi cell helped operations in Somalia and also began planning al-Qaeda's first solo mission and announcement of their presence on the world stage: they intended to simultaneously bomb the U.S. embassies in Nairobi and Dar es Salaam.

In late 1993 or early 1994, al-Qaeda's financial chief, Madani al-Tayyib, who was also known in al-Qaeda circles as Abu Fadhl al-Makkee, summoned Jamal al-Fadl. "We've heard that someone in Khartoum has got uranium, and we need you to find out if it is true. If it is, we want to buy it." Al-Qaeda was constantly looking for weapons and chemicals to use in their operations against the United States.

"How should I find out?" Fadl asked.

"Go to Abu Dijana. He knows more about it." Abu Dijana was a senior al-Qaeda operative from Yemen.

Fadl met with him and was told that there was a Sudanese official named Moqadem Salah Abdel al-Mobruk who knew about buying and selling uranium.

"Do you know how I can reach him?" he asked Abu Dijana.

"No, but you're Sudanese—use your contacts to find out."

Fadl asked around and eventually found someone who said that he knew the official. "Why do you want to meet him?" the man asked.

"I'm told he knows how we can get uranium, and if he does, we'd like to buy it."

Within a week the man had arranged the introduction, and Fadl found himself face-to-face with Salah Abdel al-Mobruk. Fadl was soon to become involved in the kind of negotiation that characterized many of al-Qaeda's early dealings: the banal graft, mind-numbingly tedious phone calls, and cordial middlemen—which both obscured and amplified the nature of the transactions and the magnitude of what was being accomplished.

"I do know about the uranium," Mobruk told Fadl. "There's a guy called Basheer who will help you."

Mobruk arranged a meeting between Fadl and Basheer, whose reaction to the request for uranium was one of surprise and almost stupefaction, though whether his response was genuine or a pose was impossible to tell. "Are you serious? You want to buy uranium?" he asked Fadl.

"Yes, I am. I know people who are serious and want it."

"Do they have money?"

"They do, but they first want more information about the uranium, such as the quality of it and what country it's made in. After that they'll talk about the price."

Basheer quickly warmed to the task. "I will give you the information," he said. "The price will be a million and a half dollars, and we need the money given to us outside Sudan. I'll also need a commission, as will Salah Abdel al-Mobruk. And tell me this: how will you check the uranium?"

"I don't know, but I have to go to my people and tell them what you told me, and I'll get you an answer."

Fadl met with Abu Rida al-Suri, an al-Qaeda financier. Like Jamal al-Fadl, Abu Rida was one of al-Qaeda's original members. Born Mohammed Loay Baizid in Syria, he had spent a considerable amount of time in the United States, including several years studying engineering in Kansas City. "It sounds good," Abu Rida told Fadl. He added, "We'll just have to check the uranium."

"How will you check it?"

"We have access to a machine, an electric machine, that can check it. But first we need to take a look at the cylinder containing the uranium, which will tell us about the quality of it and which country it is made in." Abu Rida wrote down for Fadl a list of questions al-Qaeda had and the information they wanted, and told him to get the answers.

Fadl returned to the middleman and told him that he needed to meet Basheer again to discuss the uranium, on the basis of Abu Rida's questions. The middleman provided a rendezvous point and asked Fadl to meet him there in several days' time at ten in the morning. "You can bring Abu Rida al-Suri with you, if you want," he added.

On the appointed day, Fadl and Abu Rida drove to the location given to Fadl by Basheer, who suddenly materialized alongside them in a jeep. "Leave your car here," he told them. "Come with me and we'll go to the uranium." They got into his jeep and sped north out of Khartoum, eventually leaving the main road and pulling up outside a house. "Let's go," Basheer instructed them. Ushering them inside the house, he got them settled, then disappeared and returned with a big bag. Out of the bag he pulled a cylinder. It was a few feet long and had words engraved on it. Basheer handed it to Abu Rida.

Abu Rida examined the writing and spent about five minutes inspecting the whole cylinder, all the while jotting down information in a notebook. He conferred briefly with Basheer before they all left. Basheer dropped them off at their car in Khartoum.

Once they were alone, Abu Rida tore the sheet of information from his notepad and handed it to Fadl. "Take this to Abu Hajer, and whatever he says we should do is okay with me."

Fadl did as he was told. It was a brief meeting, with little time wasted on anything other than the task at hand. Abu Hajer studied the page and said, "Tell them we'll buy it."

At his third meeting with Basheer, again brokered by the middleman, Fadl told Basheer, "My people want to buy the uranium." Basheer once again asked how they planned to check the uranium, and Fadl explained, "We're waiting for a machine to come from outside Sudan to check it."

"How long will that take?"

"I don't know. But Abu Rida will handle everything. He's the financier."

Fadl reported back to Abu Rida, telling him how to get in contact with Basheer.

It became apparent to Fadl that his part in the negotiation had come to an end. "Great job," Abu Rida said, and gave him ten thousand dollars.

"What's this for?" Fadl asked. He could not have been more surprised than if Abu Rida had instructed him to return to Basheer a fourth time with more questions.

"For your hard work."

After purchasing the uranium—for the full $1.5 million asking price, plus the payment of commissions to the various fixers along the way—al-Qaeda discovered that they had been duped: it wasn't uranium that they had purchased but red mercury, which was useless to them.

Years later, when I was in London, investigating the al-Qaeda cell there as part of Operation Challenge, we were going through files belonging to Fawwaz and other cell members in London, and I read a lab report from Austria identifying the substance as osmium.

Born in Egypt in 1935 and married to an American, Dr. Rashad Khalifa was a liberal imam in Tucson, Arizona. He had moved to the United States in the late 1950s; his son Sam Khalifa went on to play shortstop for the Pittsburgh Pirates in the early to mid-1980s. A biochemist, Khalifa imputed properties to numbers, believing that they determined events in life, and even alleged that the miracles of the Quran were revealed through mathematical equations. He allowed male and female congregants to pray together in his mosque, Masjid Tucson, and didn't demand that they wear traditional Muslim dress, even for prayers. Khalifa also publicly opposed radical *takfiri* ideas that others in the local

Muslim community—especially radical Egyptians—espoused, such as labeling fellow adherents of Islam who didn't accept their views as *kafirs*, or nonbelievers.

A rival Tucson mosque, the Islamic Center, situated about ten miles from Masjid Tucson, served the more radical members of the local Muslim community, including Wadih el-Hage. The Islamic Center's congregants often discussed Khalifa and their displeasure with what he was preaching. By the late 1980s, their complaints about the imam had reached other radical communities across the United States.

On a Friday in January 1990, el-Hage received a call from a man who said that he was a visitor from New York and that he was waiting at the Islamic Center to see him. They met at the mosque; el-Hage later described the man vaguely and unhelpfully as a tall Egyptian who wore glasses and had a long beard. The man told el-Hage that he was visiting Tucson to investigate Rashad Khalifa. "I've heard that his teachings contradict what all Muslims agree on," the man told el-Hage. He spoke of Khalifa's willingness to allow men and women to pray together, and of his theories about numbers in the Quran. *Scientific American* had called Khalifa's well-received annotated translation of the Quran, published under the title *Quran: The Final Testament*, "an ingenious study," which did nothing to address his critics' objections. El-Hage invited the visitor back to his house for lunch.

During the meal, the visitor raged against Khalifa. He told el-Hage that he had tried to go to Masjid Tucson to pray but hadn't been allowed in because of his long beard. Peering through a window of the mosque, he had seen men and women worshipping together and had grown even angrier. According to el-Hage, the visitor simply left after this catalogue of grievances.

Later that month, Dr. Khalifa was found murdered in the kitchen of his mosque. Wadih el-Hage later said he felt that Khalifa's killing was justified. The murder remains unsolved.

On November 5, 1990, Meir Kahane, a right-wing American Israeli rabbi and onetime member of the Israeli parliament, was giving a speech at a Marriott hotel in New York City. When he finished, members of the audience gathered around him to congratulate him. A gun was fired, and the bullet hit Kahane in the neck, killing him. While trying to escape, El Sayyid Nosair, an Egyptian who had immigrated to the United States in 1981, was wounded in a shootout and apprehended.

A subsequent investigation found that an Egyptian named Mahmud Abouhalima had provided Nosair's gun and additional weapons for the attack. The weapons allegedly had been bought for Abouhalima by el-Hage, whom he had met at an Islamic conference in the United States in 1989. Nosair was a member of the group of radical Islamists in New York led by the Blind Sheik, Sheikh Omar Abdul Rahman.

Abdul Rahman, having mastered the Quran in Braille, had gone on to study at Cairo's prestigious al-Azhar University. He had been arrested by the Egyptian regime in connection with the assassination of Sadat—accused, among other acts, of having written a fatwa that prompted the murder—and reportedly he had been tortured in prison. In the end he was acquitted but expelled from Egypt. He traveled to Afghanistan, where he met up with Abdullah Azzam, under whom he had once studied.

Abdul Rahman then moved to the United States to take control of Azzam's organization's U.S. assets, despite being on the U.S. State Department terrorist watchlist. The visa was given to him in Sudan by a CIA official. On arriving in the United States, the Blind Sheikh began recruiting more followers, raising funds, and denouncing the United States, using many of the same arguments as Qutb, whom he greatly admired.

In early 1991 el-Hage received a phone call from Mustafa Shalabi, a young Egyptian immigrant who ran the al-Kifah Center, located in Brooklyn's al-Farouq Mosque. Shalabi asked el-Hage to come to New York for two weeks to take care of the center while he went to Pakistan. The center was part of Makhtab al-Khidmat, and Shalabi was effective at recruiting followers and raising funds.

After the Soviet Union pulled out of Afghanistan, there was a dispute in the center about how to handle approximately $100,000 in leftover funds. Shalabi, whose loyalty was solely to Azzam, wanted to send the money to Afghanistan to help the people there rebuild. The other faction, led by the Blind Sheikh, wanted to use the funds for jihad in other countries, especially in Abdul Rahman's Egypt. Shalabi had decided to travel to Pakistan to see Azzam and try to resolve the dispute. El-Hage would run the center in his absence.

When el-Hage arrived in Brooklyn, he went to meet Shalabi at a prearranged location, but Shalabi never showed up. He didn't show up on the appointed day, and he didn't show up the next day, either. A week later Shalabi's body was found in an apartment he had shared with Mahmud Abouhalima. An investigation found that Shalabi had been murdered on March 1, 1991—the day el-Hage got to New York. While el-Hage was in New York, he also went to Rikers Island prison to visit El Sayyid Nosair.

After Shalabi was killed, the Blind Sheikh's followers took control of the center, and it became a training ground for radicals. One the most popular trainers was Ali Mohamed, who had helped move bin Laden to Sudan. Ali Mohamed joined the United States Army in the 1980s; at the same time, he was also a member of Zawahiri's EIJ, thus functioning as a double agent. He was in the habit of bringing U.S. Army manuals to the center to train fighters, among them El Sayyid Nosair.

On February 26, 1993, a vehicle parked in the underground garage of the World Trade Center exploded, ripping a hole through seven stories, killing six people and injuring more than a thousand. The aim had been to blow up one tower, causing it to topple into the next one—bringing them both crashing down—but the explosives weren't powerful enough.

The FBI's New York field office took control of the investigation. Forensic investigators on the scene identified part of the vehicle as being from a rental van that had been reported stolen in New Jersey by Mohammed Salameh, a Palestinian who was illegally in the United States. He had been calling the rental office to get his $400 deposit back.

FBI agents arrested Salameh on March 4 and soon arrested others connected to the plot, including Nidal Ayyad, the engineer who had procured the chemicals for the bomb. The investigation found that

Ramzi Yousef, a Kuwaiti of Pakistani origin, had parked the van. Educated in England, he had entered the United States in 1992 with fraudulent documents but then claimed political asylum—which was granted.

Yousef had fled to Pakistan after the attack, and the evidence showed that the plot was planned either at or in the vicinity of a training camp in eastern Afghanistan, near Khost, called the Khaldan camp; Yousef and the other plotters had met there. The investigation also led the bureau to al-Farouq Mosque in Brooklyn, the al-Kifah Center, and the Blind Sheikh. Salameh, Abouhalima, Nosair, and the Blind Sheikh all became subjects of investigation following the bombing. The investigation uncovered the fact that the men were hatching a second plot—to attack New York City landmarks, including the United Nations, the FBI office, the Lincoln and Holland tunnels, and the George Washington Bridge.

FBI special agent John Anticev was the case agent for the Kahane murder, and intelligence from that operation led to the bureau's identifying members of the World Trade Center cell. Anticev and his partner, New York Police Department (NYPD) detective Louis Napoli, had a source who had penetrated the second terrorist cell, which was preparing to attack the New York City landmarks.

Through the investigation into the World Trade Center bombing and the investigation into the thwarted landmarks plot, an operation that the FBI called Terrorstop, the name of one American citizen kept appearing: Wadih el-Hage. The FBI began to search for him, with Dan Coleman leading the investigation, and it was discovered that el-Hage was living in Nairobi, where he worked with Abu Ubaidah al-Banshiri, al-Qaeda's military leader and second in command, and Harun Fazul, Banshiri's secretary.

El-Hage's Nairobi house was eventually raided, on August 21, 1997. Dan Coleman wanted to shake the tree and see what happened, as the FBI didn't have any direct case against el-Hage. They found his address book, which included the names of Nawawi—Ridi's copilot when they crashed bin Laden's plane—and Ali Mohamed, the al-Qaeda double agent in the U.S. military. On el-Hage's personal computer was also a letter from Harun Fazul, in which Harun warned that he believed the cell in Nairobi was being monitored: "There are many reasons that lead me to believe that the cell members in East Africa are in great danger, which leaves us no choice but to think and work hard to foil the plans of the enemy who is working day and night to catch one of us or gather more information about any of us." Harun also recounted that it had been reported, in a British newspaper, that someone close to bin Laden had been cooperating with the Saudi intelligence services. He believed it to be Madani al-Tayyib, al-Qaeda's financial chief, who had worked with Fadl to purchase the uranium. Harun said that he was trying to verify his hunch and that Tayyib's betrayal, if verified, would be "terrible news." He urged greater security precautions.

Tayyib was close to bin Laden, having married his niece. He had lost a leg in the Soviet jihad. Weakened and in constant pain since the amputation, he had traveled to Europe to get treatment—enlisting the help of Fawwaz, bin Laden's man in London. In London he surrendered to the Saudis, hoping that they would help him attend to his medical needs. He told them all he knew about bin Laden's and al-Qaeda's finances, but the Saudis never shared this or gave the FBI access to Tayyib, claiming later that they did give the information to the CIA. The news of Tayyib's defection from al-Qaeda became public in 1997.

Years later, in early 2002, when I was interrogating suspects at Guantánamo Bay, Cuba, I received a call from Major General Michael Dunlavey, the commanding officer of Joint Task Force 170, set up by the Pentagon to coordinate interrogations. Dunlavey asked me to come see him. "I've got Madani al-Tayyib in our custody," he said excitedly. "He's a top al-Qaeda guy. He knows all about their money."

I walked across the camp to Dunlavey's office. "Are you sure you've got him?" I asked.

"Yes, I am, we've questioned him."

"But I heard the Saudis have him locked up."

"Well, it's him. He is not cooperating yet. He"—Dunlavey gestured to an officer standing nearby—"is interrogating him."

"Did you see Madani al-Tayyib in person?" I asked the officer.

"Yes, I did."

"How many legs does he have?"

"What do you mean?"

"His legs. Does he have one or two legs?" I asked.

"He's got two."

"Two real legs."

"Yes."

"Then it's not Madani al-Tayyib," I said, "because he's an amputee."

Pleased that the matter had been put to rest, Dunlavey turned to the officer and said jocularly, "You see, you can't regrow limbs."

By the mid-1990s there was growing international pressure on Sudan over its hosting of bin Laden. Beginning in 1992, bin Laden and members of al-Qaeda's religious rulings committee had published fatwas instructing people to attack U.S. troops based in the Saudi Arabian Peninsula. Between 1992 and 1995, al-Qaeda members, using vehicles associated with bin Laden's businesses, transported weapons and explosives from Khartoum to the Port of Sudan for shipment to Saudi Arabia. In November 1995, a car bomb exploded in Saudi Arabia outside a training facility run jointly by the United States and the Saudis; the perpetrators were led by Khalid al-Saeed, a close associate of bin Laden's. In June 1996, a truck bomb exploded in the Khobar Towers complex in Dhahran, Saudi Arabia, which housed U.S. servicemen. Nineteen Americans were killed and 372 wounded. The FBI investigators concluded that the attack had been carried out by Saudi Hezbollah. However, this did not stop al-Qaeda from taking credit. In his 1996 declaration of war, bin Laden boasted, in a poem invoking Qiblah, or the direction Muslims face for prayers, that he had not betrayed the Saudi king but that the king had betrayed the Grand Mosque by allowing infidels into the kingdom:

> The crusader army became dust when we detonated al-Khobar
> With courageous youth of Islam fearing no danger,
> If they are threatened: "The tyrants will kill you,"
> They reply, "My death is a victory."

I did not betray the king, but he did betray our Qiblah,
And he permitted, in the holy country, the most filthy of humans
I have made an oath by God, the Great, to fight whoever rejected the
   faith.

Pressure on Sudan also came from Libya, as the Libyan Islamic Fighting Group, allied with al-Qaeda, was dedicated to overthrowing longtime dictator Colonel Muammar al-Gaddafi's rule and setting up an Islamic state. Their opposition to Gaddafi was rooted in the concept of *takfir*: even though Gaddafi was a practicing Muslim, he was not allowing them to establish Sharia law and was instead establishing his own version of a socialist regime. Sudan eventually bowed to Libyan pressure and told bin Laden that all Libyan members of al-Qaeda and affiliated groups needed to leave the country. Some took positions in al-Qaeda cells elsewhere—for example, Anas al-Liby, a computer expert, traveled to London. Others left al-Qaeda, feeling that bin Laden had betrayed them by not standing up for them.

In June 1995, when Hosni Mubarak was visiting Ethiopia, an assassination attempt was carried out on the Egyptian president by the al-Qaeda affiliate EIJ. Years later, when I interrogated Ibrahim Ahmed Mahmoud al-Qosi, a Sudanese al-Qaeda member, he told me that Abu Hafs al-Masri gave him $5,000 to deliver to the would-be plotters and that, after the attack failed, the perpetrators hid in Sudan. The international community sanctioned Sudan after it refused to hand them over.

None of these incidents was capable of bringing an end to bin Laden's tenure in Sudan: as long as he was spreading his wealth among the Sudanese leadership, the country was happy to have him. But when the Saudis decided to squeeze bin Laden financially—forcing the Saudi Binladin Group to stop sending him money—he faced real problems. Internally, he found it increasingly difficult to pay al-Qaeda members' salaries; more importantly, his largesse in Sudan came to an end. The Sudanese decided that it was no longer worth bearing the burden of bin Laden and told him it was time to leave. On May 19, 1996, on a rented plane, he flew to Afghanistan accompanied by his trusted followers.

· · ·

Two days later, on May 21, Abu Ubaidah al-Banshiri was aboard a ferry, the MV *Bukoba*, on Lake Victoria, traveling between two ports in Tanzania, from Bukoba to Mwanza, on his way home from visiting family members. The main purpose of the al-Qaeda military commander's trip had been to oversee military operations in Kenya. Banshiri's brother-in-law, Ashif Mohamed Juma, was traveling with him. The ferry's capacity was 480 passengers, but it was carrying at least 1,200.

Abu Ubaidah and Juma had purchased tickets in a second-class cabin. Their room was about 7 by 10 feet, and it had four sets of bunk beds. They shared the cabin—Juma on one of the top bunk beds and Abu Ubaidah beneath him—with five other people. At a point in the crossing, where the water was 110 feet deep, the ferry started swaying wildly from side to side—its stabilizer wasn't working.

Juma had been napping but was awakened by the rocking. "Abu Ubaidah," he shouted, "something is wrong."

"Don't worry," Abu Ubaidah replied. "We're fine, go back to sleep. Allah is with us." About five seconds later the boat tilted to one side and capsized. Screams were heard as people were thrown out of their beds. The cabin door was now located above Abu Ubaidah and Juma's heads. Juma used some of the furniture to climb up and pull himself out. The others followed suit as water began seeping in. As Abu Ubaidah was climbing out—using the cabin door to propel himself—the door came off its hinges and he fell back into the cabin. Juma screamed his name and tried grabbing him, but a wall of water came crashing through the corridor, dragging Juma away. He tried to keep his head above water and found himself repeatedly knocking into bodies—whether the people were alive or dead he could not tell. He managed to swim out of the ship and then tried to swim toward what he thought was land.

He quickly realized that he would never reach land, and swam back toward the ferry, hoping to find something to grab onto. Other passengers were on floats, and he grabbed one, praying that Abu Ubaidah had somehow miraculously made it out alive. Two hours later a rescue ship arrived, and the survivors were taken to the port of Mwanza. Juma searched in vain for Abu Ubaidah. Back home, he passed the message to Abu Ubaidah's al-Qaeda colleagues that he had drowned. The news reached bin Laden two days later, on May 23. He was devastated; not only was Abu Ubaidah his trusted deputy and the most effective and popular military leader al-Qaeda had, but bin Laden was counting on his guidance as he prepared to rebuild al-Qaeda in Afghanistan.

Bin Laden at first hadn't believed that Abu Ubaidah had drowned. He suspected that he had been murdered, and he ordered Wadih el-Hage and Harun Fazul (both then in Nairobi) to investigate. Harun got to Mwanza first and began searching for Abu Ubaidah's body, taking boats out on the lake to look for clues. Two weeks later el-Hage joined him. They stayed for two more weeks, before returning to Nairobi. From there they sent a report to bin Laden, stating their belief that Abu Ubaidah in fact had drowned. The FBI later found news television footage from the port capturing Harun frantically looking for Abu Ubaidah.

Faced with replacing Abu Ubaidah as al-Qaeda's military commander, bin Laden appointed Abu Hafs to the position. A second vacancy—head of the East African cells—was filled by Abdullah Ahmed Abdullah, better known in al-Qaeda circles as Abu Mohammed al-Masri. In East Africa he operated under the alias Saleh.

In December 1994, Ramzi Yousef, then living in Manila, drew up plans both to assassinate Pope John Paul II when the pontiff visited the Philippines and to place bombs inside toys on U.S. airlines flying out of Bangkok. The attacks were referred to as the Bojinka plot. Yousef's partner in the latter plan was his uncle Khalid Sheikh Mohammed. A Kuwaiti born to Pakistani parents, KSM had been yearning to get more actively involved in jihad ever since his nephew had earned notoriety for the World Trade Center bombing almost two years earlier. KSM had an identical twin brother who had allegedly been killed in Afghanistan during the first jihad.

Yousef had successfully conducted a trial run of the Bojinka plot, leaving a bomb under a passenger seat on a flight from Manila to Tokyo on December 11, 1994, that ripped apart the body of a Japanese businessman. The bomb also tore apart the cabin floor, exposing the cargo hold below, but the pilot was able to make an emergency landing on Okinawa.

Yousef had successfully shown he could get a bomb on a plane—all that was needed to bring down the plane were more explosives.

With the test a success, Yousef hunkered down in Manila with KSM and began preparing to build bombs that would do far more damage. During a preparatory session, however, a fire started in Yousef's apartment, and the police raided it and found evidence of the plot. Yousef somehow evaded arrest and went to Pakistan to continue to carry out his plan. On February 7, 1995, Pakistani intelligence officers captured him in Islamabad. Khalid Sheikh Mohammed—who had sent his nephew $600 just prior to the World Trade Center bombing, a transaction he perhaps now feared could be traced, implicating him—was in Qatar at the time. When he learned that Yousef had been arrested, he went into hiding.

Yousef was flown from Pakistan to Stewart Air National Guard Base, in Newburgh, New York, which is under the jurisdiction of the Southern District despite its distance from downtown Manhattan. At the base, he was transferred to an FBI helicopter to be flown to Manhattan. As the helicopter passed over the World Trade Center, one of Yousef's guards nudged Yousef and pointed to the towers. "You see, it's still standing," he said.

"It wouldn't be if we'd had more money," Yousef replied.

3

The Northern Group

Bin Laden had reason to resent having to leave Sudan: not only had his assets in the country been seized, but the Saudi monarchy had forced his family to cut him off, leaving him struggling financially. Still, he was returning to Afghanistan, a country that had played a significant role in his development, transforming him from a directionless Saudi millionaire into a respected mujahideen leader. A theme that bin Laden liked to promote to his followers was that their travels were like the Hijra—a reference to the year 622, when the Prophet was forced to leave Mecca and go to Medina. What at first had seemed to be a defeat for the Prophet had turned into a great advantage, as from the safety of Medina he gained followers and developed the religion, then spread it across the globe. Bin Laden often invoked comparisons between himself and the Prophet, whose work he wished to further. He was in the habit of quoting the Prophet, and he tried modeling his life on his—fasting, worshipping, even dressing accordingly—and making sure people noticed. In bin Laden's mind, as I deduced from investigating al-Qaeda and its leadership, the appropriate prostration, when combined with rigorous, painstaking attention to public image, served to rally his spirits and those of his followers: his belief in himself grew, and the reverence with which his followers viewed him deepened. Through this combination of inner drive and public adulation he could continue the work that the Prophet had begun.

Al-Qaeda wasn't starting from scratch in Afghanistan. In Sudan, bin Laden had built al-Qaeda into a global network, and this included setting up training camps and guesthouses across Afghanistan and Pakistan. His operatives had also formed relationships with Pakistani intelligence officials, and they had paved the way for bin Laden to be welcomed by the Taliban.

Bin Laden was curious to meet Mullah Omar, his new host and the leader of the Taliban. He didn't know what Omar looked like; he was something of a recluse, and, as the Taliban had banned photography, no photographs had ever been taken of him, or at least none that were publicly available. He did know that Omar was blind in one eye—he had lost his sight while fighting with the mujahideen against the Soviets and their supporters.

Bin Laden was also eager to obtain a greater understanding of the Taliban itself. They had sprung seemingly out of nowhere in 1994 and had quickly imposed, on the parts of the country under their control, an interpretation of Islam based more on Pashtun tribal rituals than on religious tradition. All forms of entertainment were banned: television, sports—even, famously, kite flying. Girls' schools were closed down, and women were not allowed out of their homes. Men without beards were arrested. The strictures amounted to a form of religious extremism unprecedented in Afghanistan, where religious tolerance had prevailed historically. The majority of the Muslim population in Afghanistan belong to the Sunni Hanafi sect, which is considered the most liberal of the four schools of law in Sunni Islam; most of the rest are Shiites.

Named after its founder, Imam Abu Hanifa, Hanafi jurisprudence is known for its use of reason in legal opinions, and for its decentralized decision making. These two traits helped make Hanafis into the most tolerant of Sunnis, and explain the historical coexistence and mutual prosperity of Sunnis and other Muslims, as well as Hindus, Sikhs, and Jews.

The shift in Afghanistan came with the Soviet jihad (1979–1989), when Saudi money came pouring into the country and, with these funds, clerics who espoused the far more unyielding Wahhabi version of Sunni Islam. Wahhabism, the dominant form of Sunni Islam in Saudi Arabia, is seen either as indistinguishable from Salafi Islam (the name means "forefather," and practice is ideally based on unadulterated, centuries-old principles) or as a more strictly fundamentalist branch of Salafiya. As more and more Wahhabi clerics gained influence, Wahhabism began to spread among Pashtuns. Particularly vulnerable and susceptible to its precepts were the illiterate and the poor, many of whom simply followed what the clerics told them. When Wahhabism mixed with the *takfiri* ideology popularized by Qutb, intolerance and extremism resulted, and the jihadi Salafi movement was born.

The appeal of an alliance between the Taliban and al-Qaeda was also based on a shared connection to (or, perhaps more accurately, a manipulation of) traditional Wahhabism. The Taliban had imposed their Pashtun tribal code, Pashtunwali, on the areas they controlled, and then labeled those laws Sharia law. In reality their pre-Islamic tribal laws, while having become infused with elements of Islam over the ages, did not accurately represent Islamic Sharia. The Taliban also lacked the Islamic scholars and jurisprudence to support what they were doing. Wahhabism, with its reverence for old traditions and ancient moral conduct, was the closest form of Islam to the Taliban's religious interpretations, and so they relied on Wahhabi scholars for religious justification.

Al-Qaeda claims to be a Wahhabi group, and it mixes traditional Wahhabism with Salafi and *takfiri* ideas—popular among jihadists— to create its own brand of terror. With both al-Qaeda and the Taliban claiming similar interpretations of Islam, an alliance between them in many ways was a natural theological marriage. Of course, al-Qaeda and the Taliban practice versions of radical Islam that are very different from each other. Al-Qaeda, for example, doesn't subjugate women to the same extent as the Taliban. And both al-Qaeda's and the Taliban's forms of Islam are very different from traditional Wahhabism as practiced in Saudi Arabia and the Gulf states.

After the Soviet Union withdrew from Afghanistan in 1989, it took the victorious mujahideen another three years to topple the Soviet-backed dictator President Muhammad Najibullah. Various mujahideen commanders now in charge subsequently took control of different parts of the country, and most ordinary fighters returned home; others went to madrassas to study Islam. The fighters who returned home eventually saw that the mujahideen commanders were as corrupt as the regime they had replaced, and that true Islam, as they understood it from the standpoint of their Saudi-funded madrassas, was not being practiced or enforced. Groups of fighters, led by Mullah Omar, the leader of one small madrassa, began to come together with the idea of taking control of the country.

They called themselves the Taliban, from *talib*, meaning "student," particularly a student of Islam. Supported by Pakistan and endorsed by the governments of Saudi Arabia and the United Arab Emirates, Taliban groups began growing in size and imposing their ultrastrict version of Islam. It was not a coincidence that the leaders of the Taliban came from the most uneducated and backward of Pashtun tribes. In Mullah Omar's town, for example, girls had never had any schools in the first place.

As the Taliban gained control of more and more parts of the country, it began hosting radical Islamist groups from across the world, inviting them to use Afghanistan as a base. One such group was al-Qaeda. Worldwide reaction to the gradual takeover of Afghanistan by the Taliban was decidedly mixed. The United States initially supported the Taliban, which was seen as a barrier to the Shiite Iranian expansion in Afghanistan, and U.S. officials also welcomed the Taliban's opposition to the drug trade. The fact that the Taliban was religiously intolerant—infamously destroying (together with al-Qaeda) two sixth-century Buddhas carved into a cliff in central Afghanistan—and were oppressive to women was not enough to change U.S. policy.

When the Taliban captured Kandahar in April 1996, Mullah Omar removed the rarely seen eighteenth-century Cloak of the Prophet Muhammad from the mosque in which it resides, showing it to the assembled crowd as part of an effort to demonstrate that he had been ordained by God to lead Afghanistan. His followers named him Amir al-Mu'minin, "commander of the faithful"—the emir of the country.

The Taliban took Kabul on September 26, 1996, and their first action was to capture Muhammad Najibullah, who had been driven from power and was living in a United Nations compound. They castrated the former president, dragged his body around the city tied to a jeep, shot him, and hanged him and his brother from a pole. The action brought forth a stream of recruits from madrassas, including those in Pakistan.

The largest grouping of opponents of the Taliban was the Northern Alliance, led by the charismatic mujahideen general Ahmed Shah Massoud. Called the Lion of Panjshir after the valley in which he was born (Panjshir means "valley of five lions"), Massoud, a Tajik and a devout Muslim, was one of the most successful commanders fighting the Russians, with numerous victories to his credit. He had also fought the communists in Afghanistan. The Soviets had come to see him as an unbeatable master of guerrilla warfare. However, Massoud's weakness was that he was a poor diplomat, and the fact that he was a Tajik in a tribal society with a Pashtun majority prevented his rise to power before the Taliban came to dominate the country—and prevented would-be allies from joining the Northern Alliance. Nonetheless, many in the West eventually came to see him as the best hope in stopping the Taliban.

"Brothers, listen to me, I have something important to say." Muhannad bin Attash stood up and raised his hands in the air to silence the young men who had been chatting among themselves. They fell silent and turned to face him. It was mid-1996, and they were gathered at an al-Qaeda–funded guesthouse on October Street in Sanaa, where young men in the neighborhood sympathetic to the radical jihad movement frequently gathered. Muhannad first reminded his audience of the heroics of the previous generation of mujahideen who had expelled the

Russians from Afghanistan, and then, having sufficiently riled them up, told them that their opportunity had now come. He had, he continued, an important message from Osama bin Laden for them.

By this point the young men were listening intently. Muhannad was a persuasive speaker, and bin Laden was well known and admired for his role in the first Soviet jihad. Most of the young fighters were not newcomers to jihad, having served in Afghanistan, Chechnya, and Bosnia. Once again the enemy was the Russians, Muhannad said. And this time Russia had sent fighters into Tajikistan—to take control of that country and from there expand further into Muslim lands. The young men asked Muhannad how they could help Sheikh Osama counter the Russians. Muhannad replied that he was traveling the next day to Afghanistan to see bin Laden and would send back instructions.

Muhannad returned to Afghanistan, accompanied by another al-Qaeda member, Sa'ad al-Madani, later a bin Laden bodyguard. The two men went to see the al-Qaeda leader at the Jalalabad training camp. Muhannad had known bin Laden for most of his life. Their fathers had been friends growing up in Yemen, and Muhannad's father had sent Muhannad to fight with bin Laden; he had soon become one of his most trusted aides.

Muhannad reported to bin Laden that he had the recruits that the al-Qaeda leader had asked him to find.

When bin Laden returned to Afghanistan from Sudan, his terrorist organization was in bad shape. Not only had the forced move from Sudan damaged morale, but funds were severely depleted, and, even more importantly, new recruits were not lining up. The death of Abu Ubaidah on Lake Victoria, too, had left a hole.

There was no shortage of young Muslims willing to engage in jihad. Many had been inspired by the Afghan jihad against the Soviets and by the theological arguments put forward by leaders like Abdullah Azzam to fight "oppressors" in Bosnia and Chechnya. They traveled to those places through the same infrastructure that supported the Afghan jihad—the recruitment channels, funding, NGOs, and travel facilitators were all still in place. The problem was that al-Qaeda's jihad was nontraditional, and most young Muslim fighters didn't relate to it. Their definition of the obligation of jihad centered on physically righting wrongs and expelling aggressors who were actually occupying Muslim lands or oppressing Muslims. According to this thinking, the first Afghan war was justified because the Soviet Union had invaded Muslim lands. They fought in Bosnia and Chechnya because they were told that Muslim women and children were being raped and slaughtered.

The idea of a secret war of terrorism was unfamiliar to them. (Egyptians, through Zawahiri and others, were the only ones truly familiar with this type of war and its theological justifications.) The broad goal of fighting America didn't make sense to the young fighters. What Muslim lands was America occupying? What crimes was America perpetrating against Muslims? These were the questions young men asked al-Qaeda recruiters. Their past experience with America had been positive—the United States had been on the side of Muslims in Afghanistan, Bosnia, and Chechnya.

Bin Laden realized that to rope these young men in, he needed to create a traditional enemy for them to fight. The Tajik militants fighting the Russians at the time announced that they would welcome new fighters. Providing conventional battles and an enemy would surely bring some of the former mujahideen and veterans of the Bosnian and Chechnyan wars back to Afghanistan: the land of jihad, as bin Laden loved to call it.

After discussing details with bin Laden, Muhannad sent a fax to the guesthouse in Sanaa about two weeks following his and Sa'ad al-Madani's return to Afghanistan, instructing the emir in Sanaa to inform those who had been present when he had spoken that the Tajik front "was open for jihad." He provided directions for those wishing to join him at the front. Among the young men who would heed the call to arms was Abu Jandal.

Later in 1996, forty fighters showed up in Taloqan, Afghanistan, which served as the base camp for the Tajik jihad. Most of the forty were from the Arabian Peninsula (Yemen and Saudi Arabia); two were from Pakistan. The Tajik contingent called themselves Katibat al-Shimal, literally "the Northern Battalion" but known as the Northern Group (not to be confused with the Northern Alliance) because of the location of their operations: in the north of Afghanistan, near the Tajik border. Muhannad introduced the new fighters to the leader of the group, Hamza al-Ghamdi, standing unnoticed in their midst. When he came forward, a hush fell over the group: Hamza was a legend in Afghanistan from the first Soviet war. He had fought many storied battles against the Soviets; in the 1987 Battle of Jaji, in Jalalabad, he, bin Laden, and fifty mujahideen were said to have held off two hundred Soviet Spetsnaz. Hamza was muscular and strong and loved to wrestle.

He trained the new recruits hard, and they gained deep respect for his skill and commitment. Once he deemed them ready, the group moved to Badakhshan, which served as a staging area before the entry into Tajikistan. They settled outside the city of Fayzabad; Hamza knew its Afghan military commander, Khirad Mand, from the first Afghan jihad, and Mand agreed to give the Northern Group his protection. A week later they marched toward Tajikistan. It was snowing when they arrived at the border, making it impossible for them to travel any further, so they set up camp there for the night.

The next morning they were visited by Abdullah Noori, the leader of the Tajik mujahideen and of Hizb Wahdat Islami, a Tajik Islamic party. Abdullah Noori addressed the fighters. "Thank you for coming. We are honored that you are helping us. We need you to remain here for now while my Tajiks scout the area for Russians. My men are more familiar with the terrain and are less likely to be spotted and captured."

Hamza agreed to the plan. Eight hours later Noori returned to announce that his scouts had found Russians stationed at the border and that entering Tajikistan would be prohibitively dangerous. They would have to wait until the Russians moved on. Asked how long that would take, Noori replied, "Days, or even weeks, we don't know." The Northern Group settled in uncertainly.

One evening Hamza summoned Salim Hamdan, a promising recruit. "We can't stay here much longer," he told the young man. "Our group members are having problems with the local Afghanis. They keep demanding more money, weapons, and supplies from us. We keep giving them things, and they keep asking for more. We worry that if we don't give them what they want, they'll try to hand us over to the Russians."

Hamdan was considered trustworthy and honest. Hamza told him, "I need you to travel to Fayzabad and tell Khirad Mand what is going on." The Afghan military commander who had given the new mujahideen his protection had not accompanied them.

Hamdan did as he was told, returning two days later. "Mand says we should leave this area," he told Hamza, "and if we go to Fayzabad, he'll give us his protection." Hamza agreed that they had to leave. They traveled back to Taloqan and then went to Kunduz, a city in northern Afghanistan, where they stayed at a Tajik refugee camp, one of several set up for those fleeing the civil war. Their aim was to get to Jalalabad or Kabul. The main routes, however, were cut off, as the Taliban and the Northern Alliance were engaged in heavy fighting.

Hamza contacted a Northern Alliance commander he knew from the Soviet jihad; the commander helped the new fighters leave, and they eventually made it to Kabul. Hamza, Hamdan, and another operative, known as Qutaybah, stayed behind at the border to tie up loose ends. They then boarded a Northern Alliance helicopter in Taloqan and flew to the Panjshir Valley.

In Kabul, the young Northern Group fighters fell into a period of disgruntlement and began assailing Muhannad with questions about the purpose of their being in Afghanistan. They had several legitimate gripes: that they had come to fight but were instead running; that they had come to engage the Tajiks in battle but that that conflict appeared to have ended; and that they did not wish to get caught in an Afghani civil war.

"Brothers, I understand your frustration," Muhannad told the young men, "but before you go home, I want you to meet Sheikh Osama. He has specifically asked to see 'the brothers of the Northern Group.' You've come all this way—at least hear what this great jihadist has to say."

The al-Qaeda leader hosted them at his Jihad Wal training camp, where he and his top associates, Abu Hafs al-Masri, Saif al-Adel, and Saleh (by now using the alias Abu Mohammed al-Masri), greeted them and explained al-Qaeda's goals. Bin Laden spoke of what was going on in Saudi Arabia: "the plundering of oil by the Americans and their imperialist plans to occupy the Arabian Peninsula and the Holy Lands."

Of the forty fighters, twenty-three members of the group left the training camp to return home. Abu Jandal, who remained, explained to me years later: "The brothers from the Northern Group are fighters who fight the enemy face-to-face. They don't understand bin Laden's war and the new jihad, so they went home."

For three days the remaining members of the group listened as bin Laden presented them with news clippings and BBC documentaries designed to convince them that the presence of U.S. troops in Saudi Arabia and the Arabian Peninsula was an "occupation." "You therefore have a duty to expel the infidels from the peninsula, as the Prophet has ordered," bin Laden told them. He said that if they had any additional questions, they should address Muhannad. The problem was that a degree of unease had begun to infiltrate the group, with certain members having grown suspicious of Muhannad. They had come to realize that Muhannad was much closer to bin Laden than they had previously understood. Muhannad told those who consulted him that bin Laden's jihad was just, and that they—Arabs from the Gulf—needed to ensure that Egyptians who had surrounded bin Laden didn't run al-Qaeda.

Jihad meant different things to different fighters. The Egyptians had what they viewed as jihad back home: assassinations and bombs to try to topple their government. Others, who had fought in Bosnia, Somalia, and Chechnya, saw the Egyptian version of "jihad" as terrorism; to them, jihad meant fighting face-to-face.

Eventually all of the remaining fighters agreed to pledge *bayat*, or allegiance, to bin Laden. A few offered only a conditional *bayat*, agreeing to join al-Qaeda and fight America with the proviso that if a jihad effort with a clearer justification existed on another front, they would be free to join that instead.

In addition to Abu Jandal, among the members of the Northern

Group who joined al-Qaeda at this time were Walid bin Attash (a younger brother of Muhannad's), whose nom de guerre was Khallad; Abdul Rahim Hussein Muhammad Abda al-Nashiri; Salim Hamdan; Mohamed Rashed Daoud al-Owhali; and Jaffar al-Hada. Not only Abu Jandal but all of the rest of this group were fighters bin Laden had privately marked as future key operatives. Their names became central to the subsequent al-Qaeda attacks on the embassies in Africa, the USS *Cole* bombing, and 9/11.

In mid-1996, a few weeks before bin Laden had departed for Afghanistan, Madani al-Tayyib had called Jamal al-Fadl into his office in Khartoum. Since the uranium job, Fadl had continued to handle missions for al-Qaeda. He walked into Tayyib's office with his usual big smile. "As-Salāmu `Alaykum. Brother, how are you?"

"Wa `Alaykum as-Salām," Tayyib replied without a smile.

"What's wrong?" Fadl asked.

"I want to speak to you about a serious matter. Somebody told me that you're taking a commission on our goods that you are selling." One of Fadl's jobs at the time was to sell goods al-Qaeda produced to local businesses.

"That's not true."

"Somebody very reliable told us that you are."

"I'm not," Fadl replied. "Have them bring evidence. It's a lie!"

Fadl was taken to a meeting with more al-Qaeda officials. Again Tayyib confronted him, and again Fadl denied it.

"Look, Jamal, a guy named Fazhil who you do business with—you know him, right?" Fadl nodded. "He told someone, who told us, that you take a commission."

Confronted with more evidence, Fadl relented. "Okay," he said, shaking his head, "I'm sorry, I did take a commission." He had been charging local businesses a commission in exchange for selling them al-Qaeda's goods, netting himself around $110,000.

"I must say that we cannot believe you did this. You were one of the first people to join al-Qaeda. How could you steal from us?"

Fadl's face went red and he stared at the floor to avoid the look of condemnation in Tayyib's eyes. "Please forgive me," he said. "I will try my best to get the money back."

"What should we tell bin Laden? He knows you swore *bayat* to him. We know that you're basically a good person, and that you fought hard in Afghanistan. Why do you need the money?"

"The truth is that we are working hard, but the Egyptians are earning more money than the rest of us," Fadl replied. His reply was a reflection of the constant tension in al-Qaeda between Egyptians, who dominated leadership positions and who were therefore paid more than other operatives, and members from elsewhere. Many of the Egyptians came with more experience, which is why they were higher up in the group. There was general resentment over the perceived inequity.

"That's no excuse to steal."

Fadl returned to Tayyib with about a quarter of the money he owed. The rest he had already spent, buying land for his sister and for himself. He had also bought a car. When he confessed to Tayyib that he could not come up with the remainder of the money, Tayyib told him that he needed to speak to bin Laden.

The al-Qaeda leader had been briefed on the matter. "I don't care about the money," bin Laden told him. "I care about you. You were with us from the start in Afghanistan. We give you a salary, we give you everything. When you travel we give you extra money. We pay your medical bills. So why do you need to steal?"

"For the reasons we have spoken about before, Abu Abdallah— because the Egyptians get more money than the rest of us, and they joined al-Qaeda later. It's not fair."

"That's still no reason to steal," bin Laden replied. "If you need the money you can always come to us. You can say, 'I want a house' or 'I want a car'—and we'd give it to you. But you didn't do that. You just stole the money."

"I'm sorry, and I've given back what I have left, but I don't have any more. I ask for your forgiveness and hope that you can grant it, and that you can accept my apology. I did my best, and I wish to remain a member of al-Qaeda."

"There's no forgiveness until you bring all of the money back," bin

Laden replied. The two men had arrived at a stalemate: Fadl continued to maintain that the salary scale was biased, and bin Laden argued that if he forgave Fadl, other members of the organization would think that it was all right to steal as long as they sought forgiveness.

Finding himself in a bind, Fadl walked into an American embassy in one of the countries in the Horn of Africa. He waited in a line for visa applications, and when he got to the front of the line, he was was greeted by a female clerk. "I don't want a visa," Fadl said, "but I have some information for you about people who want to do something against your government."

The woman hesitated, unsure what to do. A brief conversation ensued, and she explained to Fadl that she would bring the issue to a colleague. She disappeared to another part of the embassy. Twenty minutes later she returned and asked Fadl to come into an inner office to resume the conversation.

"I was in Afghanistan," Fadl began, "and I work with a group that is trying to make war against your country. They are trying very hard to do this. Maybe war inside the United States or maybe against the U.S. Army outside. They also are planning to bomb an embassy."

The clerk asked Fadl how he had come by this information. "I worked with them for more than nine years," Fadl said, "and now I've left the group. If you help me, I'll tell you everything you need." She asked Fadl where he was living, and he explained that he was living in a hotel and gave her the address.

"Don't leave the hotel," the clerk instructed him. "Stay out of sight." She left the room to obtain cash for Fadl. "Here's some money to keep you going," she told him.

Fadl returned to the embassy a few days later and met with the same clerk. She had more questions and was trying, he sensed, to verify that he was a credible source. He answered all of her questions, and she asked him to return later that week, which he did, meeting more officials. Eventually Fadl met with Dan Coleman and two assistant U.S. attorneys from the Southern District of New York, Patrick Fitzgerald and Kenneth Karas.

Originally he didn't tell them why he had left al-Qaeda, but he gave them enough information for them to determine that he could be believed. He returned to the embassy repeatedly for further questioning. About two weeks into the process, his interlocutors told him that they knew he had committed some offense in Sudan, and that if Fadl could not tell them what it was, they couldn't trust him. Assuming that they must have somehow found out about the money he had been skimming off the top of his deals with local businesses, he sheepishly confessed, and with that he opened up: telling his questioners, in great detail, about an organization called al-Qaeda, its structure, its leaders, its members, and its operations.

Being back in Afghanistan reconnected bin Laden to the "golden chain" of money from Saudi Arabia, the United Arab Emirates, and elsewhere that had once funded the mujahideen and that now was funding the Taliban in the same way. Funding rippled out to al-Qaeda through Taliban channels, but bin Laden reactivated his own connection to the network. In this way he was able, beginning in 1996, to begin adding to his Afghani bases, buying construction equipment to help him build caves and facilities; he also continued to build his operations around the world. The cash that poured in from sympathetic Saudis, in particular, enabled him to make deeper inroads into countries such as Albania and Yemen, as well as into London.

Bin Laden's oath of loyalty to Mullah Omar, which by 1997 had become public knowledge, gave al-Qaeda freedom of movement, allowing the group to use the Afghani national airline to transport money, weapons, and operatives, and relieving them of any worries about crossing controlled borders. Bin Laden in turn provided money to the Taliban, and among the gifts he lavished on Mullah Omar was a house for him and his family.

Bin Laden promised the Taliban that he would keep a low profile, but soon he was attracting attention, notably following his March 1997 interview with Peter Arnett on CNN. Shortly after, Mullah Omar had bin Laden moved to Kandahar, where he himself was headquartered, so that he could keep a closer watch on him.

The CNN interview was bin Laden's first television appearance, and questions were submitted in advance. When asked about criticisms he had made of the Saudi royal family, he accused them of being "but a branch or an agent of the U.S.," and he spoke about his jihad against America. The Saudis were furious—especially so because they were funding the Taliban—and Prince Turki bin Faisal al-Saud, director general of al-Mukhabarat al-Aamah, the Saudi Arabian intelligence agency, received a promise from Mullah Omar on behalf of the Taliban that bin Laden would be expelled.

On February 23, 1998, al-Qaeda issued its second fatwa declaring war against the United States:

> The Arabian Peninsula has never—since God made it flat, created its desert, and encircled it with seas—been stormed by any forces like the crusader armies spreading in it like locusts, eating its riches and wiping out its plantations. . . . For over seven years the United States has been occupying the lands of Islam in the holiest of places, the Arabian Peninsula, plundering its riches, dictating to its rulers, humiliating its people, terrorizing its neighbors, and turning its bases in the Peninsula into a spearhead through which to fight the neighboring Muslim peoples. . . . The ruling to kill the Americans and their allies—civilians and military—is an individual duty for every Muslim who can do it in any country in which it is possible to do it, in order to liberate the al-Aqsa Mosque and the holy mosque [the Grand Mosque] from their grip, and in order for their armies to move out of all the lands of Islam, defeated and unable to threaten any Muslim. This is in accordance with the words of Almighty God: "and fight the pagans all together as they fight you all together," and "fight them until there is no more tumult or oppression, and there prevail justice and faith in God."

. . .

"Enough about al-Qaeda," Jamal al-Fadl said to me one day after we had spent the morning talking about bin Laden at an FBI safe house, "let's play soccer." He had a big grin and the look of a little kid. Soon after he had agreed to cooperate, Fadl had been moved to the United States and put into the Witness Protection Program. He became known to the U.S. intelligence community as "Junior" and was a source of extensive information for us.

Before he arrived, we had little understanding of what exactly al-Qaeda was and how it operated. Even in 1997, the CIA's Counterterrorism Center described bin Laden as an "extremist financier." It was information that Fadl told us that enabled the United States to credibly indict bin Laden in 1998. He explained the organization's structure, cover businesses, and the entire network from its inception until 1996, the day he walked into the U.S. Embassy in the Horn of Africa.

Junior, to my initial surprise, didn't seem to be religious. Non-work conversations focused on money, women, and soccer. Fadl was born in 1963 in Ruffa, Sudan, and had lived in the United States. He had worked at al-Farouq Mosque, helping Mustafa Shalabi raise funds for Afghanistan. On Shalabi's recommendation he had traveled to Afghanistan to fight, picked up the alias Abu Bakr Sudani, and joined al-Qaeda—becoming only the third member of the organization, he claimed.

I met Junior only a few times; he was primarily handled by my fellow FBI agents Mike Anticev (John Anticev's brother) and Mike Driscoll, who had the tough job of managing him: Junior's taste for the good life made it difficult, at times, to keep him under control. At one point he tried to coach a local girls' soccer team, and another time, while he was meant to be hiding his identity, he told a state trooper who'd pulled him over for speeding that he knew Osama bin Laden. Dan Coleman also had to weigh in as a father figure to push Junior to do the right thing.

All the trouble was worth it. The information Junior gave the FBI on al-Qaeda included details of its setup, payroll, and banking networks, even its travel warnings: don't dress like a Muslim (wear Western clothes and shave your head); carry cologne and cigarettes. It was also Junior who outlined the story of al-Qaeda's efforts to purchase the bogus uranium.

Eight months before September 11, 2001, Junior appeared as a key prosecution witness in federal court in Manhattan in the trial of various al-Qaeda members, including Wadih el-Hage, accused of involvement in the 1998 East African embassy bombings. He explained to the judge and jury what he had told Dan Coleman and the prosecutors years earlier—how al-Qaeda operated, what he did for them, what the front companies were, and the individuals he knew.

The U.S. government's indictment of bin Laden, informed largely by intelligence gained from Junior, had been secured almost three years earlier: on June 10, 1998, bin Laden was charged with being the leader of a terrorist organization and with planning, and taking part in, terrorist activities. On November 4, 1998, the indictment was unsealed and updated to include the East African embassy bombings.

While the United States was thus pursuing bin Laden, he continued to be a cause of concern to Saudi Arabia. He had persisted in publicly criticizing the Saudi government, and he supported terrorist acts against the kingdom. In the spring of 1998, Prince Turki, on behalf of Saudi Arabia, had asked the Taliban to expel bin Laden. According to Turki, Mullah Omar agreed. The promise, however, wasn't kept.

PART 2

DECLARATION OF WAR

4

The al-Qaeda Switchboard

By early 1994, the al-Qaeda cell in Nairobi tasked with planning attacks against U.S. targets in Africa was operational. Led by bin Laden's trusted lieutenant Khalid al-Fawwaz, the cell established front businesses and charities as a cover for its presence in the city—and for bringing personnel, equipment, and money into Africa. Among the charities was el-Hage's Help Africa People.

In charge of the casing of targets was the double agent Ali Mohamed, one of Ayman al-Zawahiri's, and Egyptian Islamic Jihad's, most daring and successful operatives. Fluent in several languages, charismatic, and fit, Mohamed had had a seventeen-year career in the Egyptian military. Officers from his unit in the Egyptian army had killed President Sadat. Like Mohamed, they were EIJ members. At the time of the assassination, Ali Mohamed was attending a program in the United States.

After leaving the Egyptian army, Mohamed had worked as a security adviser to both EgyptAir and the CIA. He had moved to the United States, married an American woman, Linda Sanchez (whom he met on his first flight over), and acquired U.S. citizenship. In 1986 he joined the U.S. Army and was sent to Fort Bragg, where he lectured on Islamic culture and politics.

He took a leave from the army to train "brothers in Afghanistan," a hiatus for which the army granted approval, and he also regularly took leave to help EIJ and al-Qaeda, on missions ranging from training bin Laden's bodyguards to helping plan operations. The guides and maps that he had initially taken and photocopied from the U.S. Army proved so useful in training al-Qaeda and EIJ members that Mohamed eventually refashioned much of the material into his own pamphlet. He was known in al-Qaeda circles under the alias Abu Mohamed al-Amriki ("the American")—a tribute to his successfully duping the CIA and the U.S. military.

In May 1993 Mohamed attempted to join the FBI as a translator, admitting to the agent in San Jose who interviewed him that he had connections to a terrorist group in Sudan. The name al-Qaeda meant little to the agent, but he referred the matter to the Department of Defense. Years later, when the bureau requested a transcript of the DoD's subsequent conversation with Mohamed, the DoD said that it had been lost.

Among the operatives working with Mohamed in 1994 in Nairobi was Anas al-Liby. Born in Tripoli and identifiable by a scar on the left side of his face, Liby joined al-Qaeda in Afghanistan after standout performances at various training camps. Apart from his considerable computer skills, he rose to become one of the terrorist group's most efficient operatives and often trained other members. With Mohamed and Liby in Nairobi, but for a different purpose, was L'Houssaine Kherchtou. A Moroccan who was one of al-Qaeda's earliest recruits, Kherchtou was training in a flight school in Nairobi to become bin Laden's personal pilot.

The three men knew each other well, as both Kherchtou and Liby had been among a group of select new al-Qaeda trainees to whom Mohamed had taught surveillance in Afghanistan a few years earlier. Liby, in turn, had trained the group in the use of computers for operational purposes.

Posing as tourists, in December 1993 Mohamed and his team conducted surveillance of different sites in Nairobi, including the U.S. Embassy and the United States Agency for International Development (USAID). The men also surveyed possible British, French, and Israeli targets. Khalid al-Fawwaz paid for the team's expenses and equipment as they took pictures, monitored traffic and crowds, and learned where security cameras and guards were positioned. Kherchtou's apartment in Nairobi often served as a makeshift darkroom, and when the team completed their surveillance they wrote up a report, which included their recommendations for where to strike. In their view, the best option was to attack the U.S. Embassy in Nairobi.

They traveled to al-Qaeda headquarters in Khartoum and briefed bin Laden on their findings. He agreed with their assessment, and after studying the map they had drawn of the U.S. Embassy, he pointed to a spot along the perimeter of the building and told everyone gathered, "Here's where a truck can be driven in for a suicide attack."

Al-Qaeda was organized so that different cells were responsible for different parts of an operation. Often one cell would set up cover businesses in a country, another would conduct surveillance of targets, a third would carry out the attack, and a fourth would clean up afterward. This separation helped ensure that if one cell were compromised, other operatives would be safe.

Having succeeded in their part of the operation, Ali Mohamed and his cell were dismissed, and the cell that would carry out the operations traveled to Nairobi. A separate cell traveled to Dar es Salaam, where a similar attack on the U.S. Embassy there was being planned. Al-Qaeda had decided to launch simultaneous attacks in order to garner as much attention as possible. Bin Laden calculated that while one attack could be downplayed, the ability of a terrorist organization to inflict simultaneous attacks showed not only the strength of the group but also American weakness, both of which would help with future al-Qaeda recruitment and with the organization's aim of inflicting harm on the United States.

The chief of the twin operations was the Egyptian operative known both as Abu Mohammed al-Masri and as Saleh, though he also used a fraudulent Yemeni passport under the name Abdullah Ahmed Abdullah. The explosives expert was another Egyptian operative, Abu Abdul Rahman al-Muhajir (Muhsin Musa Matwakku Atwah), who would later become al-Qaeda's chief bomb maker.

The suicide bombers were handpicked by bin Laden: two Saudis, Mohamed al-Owhali and "Jihad Ali," for Nairobi; and an Egyptian, Hamdan Khalif Alal—known as "Ahmed the German" because of his blond hair—for Dar es Salaam. Owhali was known in al-Qaeda as Moath al-Balucci. Jihad Ali's birth name was Jihad Mohammed Ali al-Harazi, and his al-Qaeda alias was Abu Obeydah al-Maki; during the Nairobi operation, he also went by the single name Azzam. The three men were informed of their mission, which they eagerly accepted, and they filmed martyrdom videos.

The leadership decided that the attacks would occur on Friday, August 7, 1998, at 10:30 AM, the time of day when Muslims are meant to be in the mosque at prayer. Therefore, al-Qaeda's theologians argued, anyone killed in the bombing could not be a real Muslim, as he wasn't at prayer, and so his death would be an acceptable consequence.

In Afghanistan, a few days before the bombings, Saif al-Adel, by now al-Qaeda's security chief, approached Salim Hamdan, who had acquired the alias Saqr al-Jadawi and had been elevated to the position of personal driver for bin Laden. "Saqr, I need you to fix that car from the sheikh's convoy," Saif al-Adel said, pointing to one of the cars.

"I'm sure it's fine," Hamdan replied.

"Make sure it's tuned up. We'll probably be on the move soon."

The vehicles bin Laden used had tinted windows, and the bodyguards who rode with him carried Kalashnikov machine guns and rocket-propelled grenade (RPG) launchers. Hamdan himself always carried a Russian-manufactured Makarov handgun, although in the event of attack, his main role was to drive bin Laden to safety. They regularly rotated the cars—this was Hamdan's responsibility—so that the convoy would not be easily identifiable, and they chose not to use Land Cruisers with mounted weapons, as the Taliban leaders did, since those vehicles attracted too much attention.

Bin Laden usually sat in the rear and listened to tape recordings of the Quran, religious lectures, or lectures on other Islamic topics. Other times, he just closed his eyes and relaxed. His repose was only disturbed if Zawahiri, Abu Hafs, Saif al-Adel, or another senior al-Qaeda leader was riding with him, in which case a range of topics might need to be discussed, even operations.

On the evening before the bombing, Abu Hafs called a meeting at the mosque in bin Laden's Kandahar compound. He read a list of the names of people who would have to leave the compound immediately and head to Kabul and said that they would be transported by plane. In the meantime, bin Laden, Zawahiri, Saif al-Adel, and Sheikh Sa'eed al-Masri, an al-Qaeda *shura* council member who replaced Madani al-Tayyib on the financial committee, would go to another facility in Kandahar.

Bin Laden wanted to travel with as small an entourage as possible to avoid being noticed, so he didn't take his ever-present security detail with him. Abu Jandal later remarked to me, "It was strange to see those guys leaving the compound driving their own trucks, with their families in the back." Later, Saif al-Adel returned and told Abu Jandal to dig trenches around the compound, especially next to the guard posts, as "the Americans are going to bomb us soon."

Abu Jandal knew the suicide bombers well: he had once chastised Owhali for playing with a grenade with the safety pin out. Owhali and Abdul Aziz al-Janoubi—an alias for Ahmed Mohammed Haza al-Darbi, the brother-in-law of 9/11 hijacker Khalid al-Mihdhar (alias Sinan al-Maki)—had been fooling with the grenade, took out the pin, and didn't know how to put it back in. Abu Jandal put the pin back in and made the two of them crawl around the base they were training at as punishment.

Owhali had also been stationed as a bodyguard outside the press conference bin Laden gave following his May 1998 meeting with ABC journalist John Miller. The press conference was conducted in the Jihadwol training camp in Khost, Afghanistan; also present were Saif al-Adel, Zawahiri, and Abu Ata'a al-Tunisi, head of military training before he was killed fighting with the Taliban against the Northern Alliance.

Abu Ata'a al-Tunisi was the son-in-law of Adbullah Tabarak, who over-saw the team of bodyguards charged with protecting bin Laden.

Jihad Ali served as a bin Laden bodyguard and was the cousin of Abdul Rahim Hussein Muhammad Abda al-Nashiri; both were mem-bers of the Northern Group. Nashiri's al-Qaeda alias was Mullah Bilal, and Jihad Ali—known for his jokes—nicknamed him "Bulbul," Arabic for a kind of bird. When Jihad Ali was selected as the bomber, Nashiri and Khallad prepared him, and Nashiri phoned Jihad Ali's mother—his aunt—to tell her that her son had been martyred.

The designated suicide bomber for Tanzania, Ahmed the German, was an explosives trainer whom other operatives had accused of liking "little boys." This greatly upset him and he complained to Abu Jandal, who assured him that the accusations must be false.

The Nairobi bombing occurred at 10:35. A Toyota Dyna truck carry-ing the bomb exploded near the rear of the U.S. Embassy, killing 12 Americans and 201 others. It was morning rush hour, and cars, buses, and other vehicles were lined up in traffic outside the embassy, includ-ing a bus carrying schoolchildren. A multistory secretarial college was demolished, and the U.S. Embassy and a Cooperative Bank building were severely damaged.

Four minutes later, at 10:39, a white Suzuki Samurai truck blew up next to the U.S. Embassy in Dar es Salaam, killing eleven people. Hun-dreds were injured in the two attacks.

When the news of the bombing reached them in Afghanistan, Abu Jandal, Hamdan, and the rest of bin Laden's entourage went to Kabul to be with him. They all kept a low profile: as Hamdan later said, "This was the first time that bin Laden was essentially going face-to-face with the Americans, and he was unsure of what the response would be."

It was around 5:30 AM on August 7 when my beeper went off, snap-ping me out of sleep. I rolled over, grabbed the pager from my bedside table, and took a look at the message: it was from my supervisor, Tom Donlon, telling me to contact him at the office.

I jumped out of bed, picked up my house phone, and dialed the office. I heard Tom's voice come on the line.

"Tommy, it's Ali. I got your page. What's going on?"

"The American embassies in Nairobi and Dar es Salaam were bombed this morning. It looks like suicide bombers drove trucks into the embassies and blew themselves up. There are a lot of casualties. Details are still coming in." Tom spoke rapidly, barely pausing between sentences.

I silently gathered my thoughts. "Do we know who is responsible?"

"It's unclear. I think it may be your guy," Tom replied. "Hurry up and come straight to the office."

I put on some clothes and ran out of my apartment. At the office, the mood was somber. I nodded to my colleagues but didn't stop for hellos or small talk. Everyone else was similarly focused: eyes on the television set, watching incoming reporting, or reading reports about the attacks or standing in small knots of intense conversation.

I printed out all reports of the bombing that had reached our system, along with the two claims of responsibility for the attack that had been sent to media outlets, and started analyzing them. Every few minutes, new details kept coming in.

About twenty minutes after I had arrived, Tom came to my desk. "So, Ali, what's your guess on who is behind the attacks?" he asked.

"Based on my reading of these reports and open sources," I said, "my guess is al-Qaeda and Osama bin Laden."

"Why do you think that?"

"For a start, that's where his recent fatwas have been pointing. He issued a fatwa on February 23, 1998, declaring jihad against the West, and in my opinion it was a warning that an al-Qaeda attack would be launched soon." Tom nodded and said he remembered the fatwa and the memo on it that I had distributed to colleagues.

Bin Laden's fatwa had stated: "We—with God's help—call on every Muslim who believes in God and wishes to be rewarded to comply with God's order to kill the Americans and plunder their money wherever and whenever they find it. We also call on Muslim *ulema* [legal scholars], leaders, youths, and soldiers to launch the raid on Satan's U.S. troops and the devil's supporters allying with them, and to displace those who are behind them so that they may learn a lesson." In addition to bin Laden, the fatwa had been signed by Zawahiri, then head of EIJ—his group had not yet merged with al-Qaeda and he had not yet become bin Laden's deputy—and other prominent Islamic terrorists.

"Besides the fatwa, is there anything else indicating that it's likely bin Laden is behind the attacks?" Tom asked.

"There is. Take a look at the claims of responsibility for the attacks," I said, showing Tom what I had printed. "The language mirrors past statements by bin Laden."

I had underscored some of the lines in the two statements and showed them to Tom, along with the similar lines that appeared in past bin Laden declarations, which I had kept from earlier research. "That's a good catch," Tom said. "Let's go to the command center, and you can tell John O'Neill your theory. Headquarters is deciding whether this should be an NYO case or a WFO case."

The FBI's Washington, DC, field office, or WFO, had responsibility for almost all overseas attacks. Al-Qaeda attacks were the exception, and they were normally handled by the New York field office. This was because the office of origin (OO) for al-Qaeda was New York. Under the bureau's OO system, whoever first opens an official case on a particular subject or group—there are fifty-six FBI offices across the country—subsequently handles all related matters. This ensures that work is not duplicated and that institutional expertise from past investigations is retained and built on rather than having to be relearned by a new office every time another incident occurs.

However, because the WFO was the first port of call for overseas attacks, and because al-Qaeda had not officially claimed responsibility for the embassy bombings (thus the case had not automatically been given to NYO), a WFO team was already en route to Nairobi to begin investigating. Before NYO could start investigating, we had to convince headquarters that al-Qaeda was involved.

Tom and I walked across the street from our office to the Joint Terrorism Task Force command center. It was packed with representatives of every U.S. intelligence and law enforcement outfit with offices in New York City, including the CIA, the U.S. National Security Agency (NSA), and the police department. In the center of the room, at the podium, manning the secure phones and conversing with headquarters in Washington, were John O'Neill, Pat D'Amuro, and other senior FBI agents.

"Ali believes that al-Qaeda is responsible for the attacks," Tom told John and Pat, "and he's got a convincing explanation."

I repeated what I had told Tom a few minutes earlier.

"Good thinking," John said when I had finished. "I want you to help draft a memo to headquarters in Washington explaining why we think the attack has bin Laden's signature. Come with me."

I followed John from the podium to a side room. Sitting at a round table reviewing files were Kevin Cruise, from the I-49 squad, and an NYPD detective, Tom Corrigan, who was also attached to I-49. Both Kevin and Tom were al-Qaeda experts. John instructed the three of us to prepare a memo for headquarters outlining why we thought al-Qaeda was responsible.

I wrote down the analysis I had given John and the others, and Kevin and Tom added historical and other classified information that bolstered the claim. They had been privy to intelligence reports on al-Qaeda cells in the region, specifically in Nairobi, and added those details to the memo. When we completed it we showed it to John, who gave it his approval and sent it off to headquarters.

A reply came back about thirty minutes later that headquarters had accepted the arguments in our memo. An NYO team was to be assembled: half would go to Nairobi and the other half to Dar es Salaam. Senior officials decided that Pat D'Amuro would lead both groups. Arrangements were made for everyone to leave in a few hours.

While the decision was being made as to who would make up the team, John came up to me. "Good work on the memo," he said, putting his arm around me.

"Thanks, boss," I said.

"Listen," John continued, "I don't want you to go to Nairobi. I need you here with me. We'll have enough agents on the ground there, but I could use your insights here."

In Nairobi the FBI team worked with local law enforcement and intelligence services to begin piecing together the attacks, gathering evidence, performing forensic analysis, questioning witnesses, and following leads. REWARD FOR JUSTICE posters were issued by the State Department and distributed worldwide.

At the same time, Department of Justice prosecutors from the Southern District of New York flew in and worked with local officials to establish protocol for conducting the investigation. This was essential, as our interest was not just in finding those responsible but also in ensuring that we would be able to convict them in a U.S. court—and use evidence gained for other potential al-Qaeda–related prosecutions.

We needed to make certain that all parts of the investigation— from the handling of evidence to the conducting of interviews and interrogations—met federal standards, so that evidence, testimony, and confessions would be admissible in U.S. courts. Counterterrorism is a continuous process. The result of any operation might end up in court, so it is prudent to have the legal process in mind in order to keep all options open.

While my colleagues were doing the hard work on the ground in Nairobi, I worked with John and others in New York both in providing assistance to the Nairobi team and in tracking the broader al-Qaeda network. One city we started focusing on was London. The British capital had been the location from which al-Qaeda had distributed bin Laden's declaration of jihad and other statements. It was also where media outlets such as CNN and ABC had arranged their meetings with bin Laden.

John contacted senior British officials to urge them to take the al-Qaeda threat seriously and to help us investigate alleged al-Qaeda members in London and throughout the United Kingdom. They were at first reluctant to do anything about the presence of EIJ and al-Qaeda operatives in London, who didn't seem to be harming British interests.

I did further analysis on the claims of responsibility. The two were almost identical, the only difference being the location and the names of the shadowy "platoons," or cells, that had carried out the bombings. The Nairobi claim announced that the bombing had been planned by the platoon of Martyr Khalid al-Saeed and carried out by operatives from the Arabian Peninsula (referring to Saudi Arabia); the Dar es Salaam claim said that the bombing had been planned by the platoon of Abdullah Azzam and carried out by an Egyptian. The names of the platoons honored Islamist terrorist heroes: Khalid al-Saeed was one of the terrorists behind the November 1995 attack on U.S. servicemen in Riyadh, Saudi Arabia (an act for which he had been praised by bin Laden), and Abdullah Azzam was an original mentor to many of al-Qaeda's members, widely considered to be the father of the Arab mujahideen in Afghanistan. Azzam's base had been in Afghanistan, so this pointed to a connection between Afghanistan and the attack. Moreover, the parties in both claims, employing language similar to that used by bin Laden in previous fatwas, referred to themselves as being part of the Islamic Army for the Liberation of the Holy Places.

On August 10, three days after the bombing, Debbie Doran, an I-49 agent manning the phones in the FBI's command post in Nairobi, took a call from someone who reported seeing a "suspicious Arab man with bandages on his hands and stitches on his forehead." The caller then appeared to have second thoughts and signaled that he was going to hang up.

The FBI runs in Debbie's blood: her father was a special agent in charge in New York. When she signed up for the bureau, she knew exactly the long hours it would entail, and she is willing to be consumed by important work. Debbie coaxed the caller to stay on the line by assuring him that anything he told her was confidential. It was clear to her from his voice—almost a whisper, with a distinct element of fear—that he worried that saying too much might put him in danger. Debbie spoke of the bombing and reminded him of his moral duty to find the killers of so many innocent people.

The caller told her where he had spotted the man and provided a description. An undercover team was dispatched. Among the agents were Stephen Gaudin and an NYPD detective named Wayne Parola. Stephen, newly assigned to the SWAT team in the New York office, had been with the U.S. Army Special Operations Forces. Though at the time he lacked in-depth knowledge of al-Qaeda, he had a remarkable talent for communicating with suspects, a function of his natural empathy and people skills. He would later put this gift to use in key interrogations. The assignment to Nairobi changed Stephen's career path: he was to become a central member of the FBI's al-Qaeda team. Wayne Parola was a member of the JTTF and brought a lot of experience. Italian, stocky, with a black beard, he walked the walk, talked the talk, and fit the role of an NYPD detective.

Wayne, Stephen, and the rest of the team staked out the location, and a man who matched the description given to Debbie soon appeared. The agents monitored him, waiting for an opportune moment to grab him. When the moment presented itself, they apprehended and subdued him. A search produced eight hundred-dollar bills. The man had no identification or documents.Unsure how serious his injuries were, the team took him to a hospital to be evaluated by a doctor.

John Anticev led the questioning at the hospital, conducted at the detainee's bedside. John had been the case agent for Terrorstop, the 1993 New York City landmarks operation, and he was both an experienced interrogator and schooled in radical terrorism, a fact he soon impressed upon the patient-detainee.

"What's your name?" John asked.

"My name is Khaled Saleem bin Rasheed," the man replied. Asked where he was from and what he was doing in Nairobi, the man replied that he was from Yemen and that he was looking for business opportunities.

John didn't challenge his story. Instead he asked him how he had been injured. Rasheed replied that he had been in the Cooperative Bank at the time of the bombing, and that he had been knocked down by the explosion. He had checked himself into the hospital, where he had gotten stitches and where his injuries had been bandaged.

John nodded and jotted down everything he said, in the meantime analyzing his words and studying his moves. He asked Rasheed if he was comfortable and whether he had had a chance to pray. Rasheed said that he had, and John went on to ask him a series of seemingly routine questions about his religious beliefs and his views on the United States, the Taliban, and related matters.

Rasheed settled into his bed and engaged John. He seemed to enjoy the discussion, welcoming the chance to "educate" John on these subjects. John steered the conversation to Abdullah Azzam and noticed that Rasheed gave a slight, seemingly involuntary smile upon hearing the name. It was clear that he was knowledgeable about the theology used as a basis for Islamist radicalism, and he, in turn, was impressed with John's knowledge.

Rasheed had reached a point at which he was completely at ease. John was relaxed, calm, smiling, and polite. He gave Rasheed the impression that he respected him, and Rasheed clearly appreciated it— he smiled back and happily chatted.

As Rasheed was midway through a sentence, John interrupted him and in a swift movement placed a piece of paper and a pen in front of him, telling him sternly, "Write down the number you called after the bombing."

Rasheed froze, bewildered by the change in John's manner and tone. John repeated, "Write down the number!" The certainty with which he gave the command stunned Rasheed, who almost robotically wrote down a phone number. He then put down the pen and stared blankly at John. He was shaking. He had no idea how John knew he had called a number.

In fact, John didn't know; but his hunch had paid off, and now the FBI team had in custody someone who not only had effectively admitted a role in the bombing but had supplied an important lead.

John asked a follow-up question about the number, but Rasheed wouldn't say anything else.

As the interrogation was taking place, another team of agents was investigating Rasheed's cover story. They went to the hospital where he claimed to have been treated following the bombing and to the airport to see if they could find his landing card or any other information. At the hospital, after questioning staff and doctors, they discovered that a janitor had found Rasheed's belongings stashed on a windowsill above a toilet seat. Among the belongings were truck keys and bullets. They were sent to the FBI forensic team that was analyzing the remains of the truck used for the bombing. The keys were found to match the suicide truck's locks.

The agents who had gone to the airport found a landing card under the name Khaled Saleem bin Rasheed. Following up on the landing card information took them to a villa in Nairobi that appeared to have been used by the bombers—residue from explosives was found throughout.

At the same time, we traced the telephone number Rasheed had written down to a man in Yemen named Ahmed al-Hada. By monitoring the number, we found that it appeared to be used as the main contact number for al-Qaeda in Yemen, and that calls placed from it went regularly to a satellite phone that U.S. authorities had already been monitoring because it belonged to Osama bin Laden. There were several calls from bin Laden's satellite phone to the Hada switchboard and from Hada to Nairobi. The al-Qaeda link to the bombing was clear.

On the day of the embassy bombings, a Palestinian al-Qaeda operative named Mohamed Sadeek Odeh was arrested at the airport in Karachi. He had flown in from Kenya, and Pakistani authorities had noticed that the picture on his passport was fraudulent. He was questioned for several days before being rendered, on August 14, to Kenyan authorities and then transported —on the Pakistani prime minister's plane—to Nairobi. Pat D'Amuro and a team assigned to meet Odeh and his handlers at the Nairobi airport found themselves faced with an unexpected dilemma: the prime minister's plane didn't have enough fuel to fly back to Pakistan.

Eventually the fuel tank was filled. A Kenyan official asked pointedly, "But who will pay?"

Pat spotted a CIA plane on the runway. "Bill it to them," he deadpanned.

The next day, August 15, John Anticev and his team were given access to Odeh. They started off by advising him of his rights, as guided by the bureau and the Department of Justice, and Odeh signed the form, acknowledging that he understood its contents. He went on to admit his involvement in the plot, and he outlined his path to al-Qaeda. He had gone to high school in the Philippines and had become interested in jihad after watching videos and listening to tape recordings of lectures by Abdullah Azzam. In his final year of high school, Odeh needed a thousand dollars, which his father agreed to send him. Upon receiving the money, he asked a cleric whether he should use it to finish his studies or to travel to Afghanistan to join the mujahideen. The cleric told him to head to Afghanistan. There he attended the al-Farouq camp, near Khost, later joining al-Qaeda. He was trained in assassinations and learned how much explosive power was needed to bring down different types of buildings.

Once his training with al-Qaeda was complete, Odeh was sent to Somalia and then Kenya. His first assignment in Kenya was to set up a fishing business, whose proceeds were used to help finance the Nairobi cell. His second assignment was to work with explosives. Odeh explained to the interrogators that in late July 1998, Khalfan Khamis Mohamed, Mustafa Mohamed Fadhil, and other al-Qaeda members had gathered in Dar es Salaam to grind TNT to be used in the bombing. The two of them had met Fahid Mohammed Ally Msalam and Ahmed the German in House 213 in the Ilala district of the city to make final preparations. With the help of operative Ahmed Khalfan Ghailani, they had loaded boxes of TNT, cylinder tanks, batteries, detonators, fertilizer, and sandbags into the back of the truck to be used.

Odeh explained that on August 1, 1998, Saleh had told him that all members of al-Qaeda had to leave Kenya within five days. That same day, Ghailani checked into the Hilltop Hotel in Nairobi, and the following day, Odeh and Harun Fazul met with other al-Qaeda members there. At about the time this meeting was taking place, al-Qaeda members Sheikh Ahmed Salem Swedan and Mustafa Mohamed Fadhil, following instructions, left Nairobi on Pakistan International Airlines Flight 744, bound for Karachi via Dubai; and on August 3, Fahid Mohammed

Ally Msalam purchased tickets for himself and Odeh on Pakistan International Airlines Flight 746, scheduled to depart on August 6.

Odeh joined other al-Qaeda members at the Hilltop Hotel, where they remained in touch with the team in Dar es Salaam. On August 5, in preparation for meeting bin Laden in Afghanistan following the next day's flight to Karachi, Odeh shaved his beard and got new clothing. While accomplishing his shopping errands, he took a walk along Moi Avenue, near the U.S. Embassy. On August 6, Saleh and Ghailani left Nairobi for Karachi on Kenya Airways Flight 310, and Odeh (using a false name) and Msalam departed on Flight 746.

Among other details Odeh shared with the interrogators was the role Harun Fazul played in al-Qaeda, specifically his role in writing reports for the leadership. He wrote in code; if anything fell into the wrong hands, al-Qaeda's plans would still be safeguarded. Odeh gave the questioners examples: "working" meant "jihad," "potatoes" meant "hand grenades," "papers" meant "bad documents," and "goods" meant "fake documents."

"Can you give an example of how these words would be used?" Anticev asked.

"If we say, 'How were the goods from Yemen,'" Odeh replied, "it would mean 'we need fake documents from Yemen.'" Odeh said that Harun's reports were faxed to Pakistan and from there taken by courier to al-Qaeda's leaders.

On August 27 John Anticev flew with Odeh from Kenya to Stewart Air Base, where an FBI team was waiting to collect him and continue questioning him. I was one of the members of that team. I stepped onto the plane and gave John a hug. "Welcome home," I said. "Great work." This was an understatement. John and the team in Kenya had done a tremendous job. Odeh, wearing a dark jumpsuit, was taken by a SWAT team onto a helicopter and flown to a jail in New York.

On August 20, thirteen days after the bombings, I was in the middle of a conversation with John O'Neill about al-Qaeda operations in London when we heard a run of expletives and shouts from people gathered in front of a television screen nearby.

We ran over and watched a reporter announce that President Clinton had ordered the firing of missiles from navy vessels in the Arabian Sea to bomb sites in Sudan and Afghanistan believed to be run by, or connected to, bin Laden. The sites included a pharmaceutical plant in Khartoum and al-Qaeda training camps near Khost. David Cohen and Charlie Seidel from the CIA had called John only minutes before to warn him that the bombing was about to take place.

This, the reporter said, was the U.S. retaliation for the embassy bombings. Crowds in Sudan and elsewhere in the Arab and Muslim world were protesting the strikes; the United States was seen as having attacked without cause or warning, killing innocent people.

"What are they doing?" shouted one colleague in disbelief, voicing what we were all feeling at that moment. "Don't they realize we've got agents on the ground in hostile territories?"

"Why the hell didn't they at least tell us first that they were going to do this?" I asked John. He shrugged as I followed him to a side office off the command post and called Pat D'Amuro to check on the security of the agents on the ground in Nairobi and Dar es Salaam, all now easy targets for anyone wishing to avenge the U.S. strikes. If the FBI had known about the bombings in advance, our agents would have been pulled out or taken off the streets until the issue died down.

Headquarters instructed all personnel on the ground in East Africa to keep a low profile until the furor over the attacks had subsided. Being in Nairobi and Dar es Salaam was already dangerous enough: al-Qaeda had just attacked there and likely still had the means to attack again.

There were many phone calls home that day from the two African cities—FBI agents assuring their loved ones back home that they were safe. There was some talk that President Clinton had ordered the strikes to distract attention from his ongoing Monica Lewinsky scandal, but I didn't believe, nor did I want to believe, that national security would be used in such a manner. Still, whoever had decided to keep the FBI out of the loop took a great risk with American lives.

The emir of one of the camps bombed was Hassan al-Khamiri. The bombing had a devastating effect on him, deepening his hatred of the

United States and prompting him to ask bin Laden if he could martyr himself in an upcoming al-Qaeda operation.

Rasheed was brought back in for further interrogation, this time by Stephen Gaudin and Wayne Parola. Neither of them spoke Arabic, so a translator was furnished by the WFO. He was an older man and Rasheed saw him as a father figure; the two bonded.

Stephen and Wayne began by asking Rasheed the questions John Anticev had asked at the start of the original interrogation: What was he doing in Nairobi? What was his connection to the bombing? Rasheed initially gave the same answers he had supplied previously. Stephen and Wayne confronted him with the evidence; in addition, Stephen gave him Meals Ready to Eat (MREs), instant rations for U.S. soldiers abroad. Rasheed was fascinated with the idea of an instant meal, found the MREs to be tasty, and especially loved the cookies that came with them. Gradually his stonewalling gave way to a kind of resignation. Seemingly overwhelmed by the weight of the evidence, he simply declared: "Here's what I want. I want to be tried in America, not Kenya, because America is my enemy. If you promise me this, I'll tell you everything."

The FBI discussed his request with the Department of Justice, and it was agreed that there was no reason not to accede to it: we would have wanted to try him in the United States anyway, as he had attacked U.S. embassies and murdered U.S. civilians. Assistant U.S. attorney Pat Fitzgerald drew up a document stating that the United States would endeavor to get him extradited to the United States for a trial.

Rasheed was presented with the document and an Arabic translation. He seemed happy with it. After it was signed, he said: "Thank you, and now I have something to tell you." He paused, and then continued, "My name is not Khaled Saleem bin Rasheed. I am Mohamed al-Owhali, and I'm from Saudi Arabia." Having fulfilled his role as a suicide bomber without in fact dying—a feat he would eventually explain—Owhali had fled the scene of the attack and was alive to tell the FBI his story.

He said that his path to al-Qaeda had been through the Khaldan training camp. While the camp was not controlled by al-Qaeda, it was in the habit of letting the leadership know about promising recruits. Owhali had been one such recruit. He told the interrogators with pride that his skills had distinguished him from fellow recruits and that he had been recommended to al-Qaeda. In due course, he had met bin Laden. Owhali told the interrogators that he had found himself agreeing with everything that bin Laden said.

He pledged *bayat* to bin Laden and joined al-Qaeda. Soon after, he asked bin Laden for a mission. Bin Laden told him that something would come his way. Eventually bin Laden summoned Owhali and told him that he would be part of an effort to inflict a mighty blow against the United States—he would help bomb the U.S. Embassy in Nairobi. On July 31, he had flown from Pakistan to Afghanistan to Dubai, where he had missed his intended flight to Nairobi, not arriving till August 2.

Owhali took the interrogation team through everything he knew about the bombing, from the bomb maker—whom he identified as the Egyptian known as Saleh—through to his actions on the day of the attack. He was not a proficient liar, and when he tried to withhold information or protect the identity of his friends, the interrogation team caught him out.

Around May 1998, Harun Fazul, who was to serve as a guide for Owhali and his fellow designated bomber Jihad Ali during their time in Nairobi, rented a villa, at 43 New Runda Estates. On August 4, Owhali, Harun, and other al-Qaeda members reconnoitered at the U.S. Embassy. On the fifth, sixth, and seventh, Owhali called Hada's switchboard in Yemen from a phone at the villa. On the morning of the bombing, at around 9:30, Harun accompanied the bombers from the villa to the embassy. They traveled in a convoy, led by Harun in his own truck, with Owhali and Jihad Ali following in the bomb-laden truck. Owhali was equipped with four stun grenades, a 9 mm Beretta handgun, bullets, and keys to the padlocks on the bomb truck.

At around 10:30 AM, Harun threw a stun grenade at embassy guards to engage and distract them while Owhali and Jihad Ali continued on toward the building. Harun drove off, his part in the mission finished. As Owhali and Jihad Ali got closer to the embassy, they reached a point where gates and another set of guards prevented them from going any further. Owhali jumped out—it had been agreed that his role would be to detonate himself at these very gates in order to enable Jihad Ali to explode himself and the car close enough to the embassy to do damage. Brandishing the stun grenades, Owhali shouted at a guard to open the gates. The guard refused, and Owhali threw a grenade at him. Seeing the commotion and the explosion, Jihad Ali began firing a pistol at the embassy, causing people to scatter.

Owhali was unsure what to do: his mission had been to help Jihad Ali get as close to the embassy as possible. Although the gates were still closed, the guards had dispersed, and Jihad Ali was in fact now close enough to fulfill his mission. For Owhali to blow himself up would be considered suicide rather than martyrdom—forbidden under Islam. It was a fine distinction, but one of importance to Owhali. After making a quick calculation, Owhali began to run away—and was knocked over and injured by the explosion when Jihad Ali blew himself up.

Owhali entered a nearby hospital, disposing of his remaining bullets from his gun in the bathroom in which they were later found and placing a few other belongings on the window ledge. He told the nurses and doctors who treated him that he had been a victim of the blast. After being stitched up and bandaged, he left the hospital and contacted al-Qaeda through the Hada switchboard, reporting what had happened. He asked that someone send him a passport and money. A thousand dollars was transferred, which Owhali used to buy new clothes. He was planning his escape from Nairobi when he was picked up.

Owhali was flown to the United States and, once jailed, was asked who his next of kin was. He pointed to Stephen Gaudin. Owhali was tried in 2001 and sentenced in federal court to life without parole, along with Wadih el-Hage and two other operatives involved in the bombings, Mohamed Odeh and Khalfan Khamis Mohamed.

Ali Mohamed was arrested in September 1998 when he tried to flee to Egypt after being subpoenaed for his connection to the bombings. He pled guilty in May 1999 but was never sentenced. To date he is awaiting sentencing and is being held in a secure location. Pat Fitzgerald had long been pressing for Mohamed to be tried and convicted, and when I went with Pat to debrief him in jail, the former double agent seemed shaken.

The investigators followed up on Owhali's leads, all of which proved accurate. We later learned that in the days after the Nairobi bombing, Harun Fazul hired people to clean the villa at 43 New Runda Estates, and around August 14 he left Nairobi for the Comoros Islands. In Dar es Salaam, Khalfan Khamis Mohamed cleaned the premises at House 213 in Ilala and made arrangements for the cleaning and discarding of the grinder used to prepare the TNT. On August 8, he left Dar es Salaam for Cape Town. A full picture emerged of how the attacks had been planned and carried out, and the prosecution teams began planning the indictments and trials of bin Laden and other al-Qaeda leaders for their roles.

The searches of the different facilities, safe houses, and offices used by al-Qaeda generated valuable documents, phone numbers, and photographs of many al-Qaeda members. At the Help Africa offices, agents recovered passport-size photos used to issue bogus identification cards. The photos were of the entire al-Qaeda leadership, in addition to most of the main operatives from the period bin Laden was based in Sudan. The pictures became the basis for one of our first al-Qaeda "photobooks," a term the agency uses for mug shots and other pictures of suspects relevant to an investigation.

At the same time, our investigative interest now had taken new directions. First there was Yemen: it was clear that al-Qaeda members were based there and were using the country for operations. The fake passports used by Owhali (in the name of Rasheed) and other terrorists involved in the attacks were issued in Yemen, with Hada's phone number the main means of communication. Then there were leads pointing to al-Qaeda in London. We had started investigating London in 1996 because bin Laden's media office was based there. After the East African embassy bombings, British authorities had finally arrested Khalid al-Fawwaz and two of Zawahiri's operatives. Working with Scotland Yard, we had found that the claims of responsibility for the attacks had been faxed by Zawahiri's two Egyptians, Adel Abdel Bary and Ibrahim Eidarous, from The Grapevine, a copy shop across the street from a residence on Beethoven Street used by the group's media operatives. We dubbed it the Beethoven Office.

Two of the agents involved in the Dar es Salaam investigation were Abby Perkins and Aaron Zebley. Both were instrumental in apprehending and gaining a confession from Khalfan Khamis Mohamed—a confession that helped convict him and get him a life sentence in the eventual embassy bombings trial.

In the second half of 1999, bin Laden met with some thirty graduates of a special "close combat" training session at Loghar training camp. Assembled by Khallad, the members of the group were viewed as special operatives. Khallad brought in a Pakistani trainer to teach the operatives hand-to-hand combat, and Tae Kwan Do and other martial arts.

After the session was finished, the students were sent to Kandahar to see bin Laden. He congratulated them on graduating and lectured them about the East African embassy bombings, divulging operational details, including the vehicles and explosives used, and explaining, in particular, the reasons for the Nairobi attack: one, Operation Restore Hope, in Somalia, which he claimed had resulted in the death of thirty thousand Muslims, had been directed from the Nairobi embassy; two, the embassy was the base of support for Sudanese rebel leader and politician John Garang de Mabior; and, three, it was the biggest center of American intelligence in East Africa.

Among the group to whom bin Laden offered this justification were Khalid al-Mihdhar and Nawaf al-Hazmi, two of the 9/11 hijackers.

5

Operation Challenge and the Manchester Manual

July 1999. "We've got one more important order of business," said Tom Donlon, the I-40 squad leader. We had finished reviewing some operations we were running. Everything from the agenda had been covered, so I turned to Tom, curious about what he might have to say.

"It's Ali's birthday today," he continued, looking at me with a smile, and on cue the squad broke into a rendition of "Happy Birthday," and cupcakes were pulled out from where they had been hidden under the table.

As we were about to start eating, there was a knock at the door, and Tom Lang, the supervisor of the I-49 squad, stuck his head into the room. "I need to speak to you, Ali," he said quietly. I was still splitting my time between the two squads, and Tom Lang was my I-49 boss.

"Happy birthday, Ali," Tom Donlon said with a grin. "It looks like we'll have to have the party without you."

I followed Tom Lang into the hallway. "What's going on?"

"We've got a big problem. The British are about to release Khalid al-Fawwaz, Adel Abdel Bary, and Ibrahim Eidarous, the al-Qaeda and EIJ leaders in London."

"What? Why?"

Well-known Islamists and members of EIJ's *shura* council, Bary and Eidarous had moved to London in 1996–97, signaling the growing importance of the city as a base for the terrorist movement. Al-Qaeda and EIJ were working toward a merger, and the two groups shared personnel, office space, and equipment. But they still had separate command structures; the EIJ *shura* council had not yet approved the merger, something Zawahiri was pushing hard for. Bary, appointed by Zawahiri in May 1996 to lead EIJ's London cell, had subsequently been demoted to deputy with the arrival, in September 1997, of Eidarous. Former head of EIJ in Europe, Eidarous had been stationed in Baku, Azerbaijan, before the move to London.

Fawwaz was living in London as a Saudi dissident, having claimed political asylum in the UK. London was the ideal place for Fawwaz to operate, bin Laden had decided: almost every news outlet in the world had representation there, and the British authorities tended to turn a blind eye to the activity of Islamist radicals as long as they didn't pose an obvious threat. This unofficial policy had earned London the name "Londonistan" from frustrated French intelligence officials and had brought scorn from law enforcement and intelligence services around the world. The policy wasn't even popular among many in the UK security services, especially within Scotland Yard. The Anti-Terrorism Branch of the police, SO13, had been monitoring al-Qaeda and EIJ operatives and understood the threat they posed. However, Scotland Yard was overruled.

Although we had urged the British to arrest Fawwaz, Bary, and Eidarous in 1996, they had refused. As the men had done nothing but communicate with people the United States found "problematic," and as they were not directly connected to terrorist attacks, there had been no evidence to support arresting them at that point. They had finally been arrested following the East African embassy bombings, based upon evidence of their connection to the attacks provided by the FBI.

"The British just told us that a judge said they don't have enough evidence to keep them locked up anymore," Tom said to me.

"What do you mean? There are piles of evidence—enough to keep them locked up for life. I've spent the last couple of months decoding documents and sending files to London with evidence for them to use."

"I know, I know," Tom said, shaking his head, "the fault isn't on our end, but somehow the ball has been dropped, and now the British are saying that we've got twenty-four hours to make the case for continuing to hold them or they'll have to release them." Tom explained that assistant U.S. attorneys Ken Karas and Pat Fitzgerald were expecting Dan Coleman, senior FBI agent Jack Cloonan, and me to meet them at the Southern District offices to put together a complaint to be filed in the UK requesting the extradition of the three men.

"I see. So we have to have them arrested again based on new evidence, and use that for the extradition case?"

"As long as they remain in jail, I don't care how you manage it. But those guys are dangerous and can't be released."

It was an open secret that anyone who wanted to reach bin Laden could do so by going through Fawwaz. When Peter Bergen and Peter Arnett interviewed bin Laden for CNN in 1997—his first interview with a Western media outlet—they went through Fawwaz. Documents that we later found in Fawwaz's office described the process of bringing the two journalists to meet bin Laden. They were taken to Afghanistan by an associate of Fawwaz's, Abu Musab al-Suri, a Syrian known among jihadists as a prolific writer and strategist; his real name is Mustafa Setmariam. In Afghanistan, Abu Musab handed them over to Saif al-Adel, a member of al-Qaeda's military committee, who ran a series of "security checks," including scanning them with a handheld metal detector to check if they were carrying weapons or had any tracking devices. Abu Musab's notes report that the scanner didn't work but that Saif al-Adel thought it was important to make the CNN crew think it did. Saif al-Adel, bin Laden, and other al-Qaeda members later joked with each other about having fooled Bergen and Arnett.

The notes record that on this trip Abu Musab asked bin Laden for details about certain operations and that bin Laden was not forthcoming. "I can't share this with you," he said, "as you are in the enemy's belly." Later Abu Musab left Europe and returned to Afghanistan.

When John Miller interviewed bin Laden in 1998—almost two months before the East African embassy bombings—he, too, first traveled to London to meet Fawwaz, who, with an associate, assisted the ABC team in traveling to Islamabad and from there to Afghanistan, where bin Laden awaited them. It was also from Fawwaz's London office that bin Laden had sent missives denouncing the Saudi royal family for having allowed U.S. troops into the Arabian Peninsula. Bin Laden's vitriolic statements targeted Sheikh bin Baz (Abd al-Aziz bin Baz), the official head of all Saudi clerics. Bin Laden denounced bin Baz's 1990 fatwa, which specified that foreign troops should be permitted in the kingdom.

On August 6, 1998, the Saudi-owned pan-Arab daily *al-Hayat*, which is distributed around the world, published a message from EIJ and Zawahiri: "We wish to inform the Americans that their message has been received, and we are preparing our answer, with the help of God, in the only language they will understand." The following day, the East African embassies were blown up.

Zawahiri was referring to a raid a month earlier, in Albania, during which Albanian authorities, aided by the United States, had arrested members of an EIJ cell. The raid was conducted following intelligence reports that the cell was planning an attack on U.S. interests in Albania. The operatives were handed over to the Egyptian authorities, as they were wanted in Egypt for their involvement in a series of terrorist attacks, and tried along with others captured elsewhere. (Still others—such as Eidarous and Abdel Bary—were tried in absentia.) The case was named Returnees from Albania, given the country of origin of a large number of the detainees.

Albania had become a favorable location for EIJ and other Egyptian Islamist terrorists, as the chaos following the fall of the communist regime—and, subsequently, the Balkan war that had begun in 1991—created perfect conditions for their operations. Because of the disorder in the country, many legitimate Islamic organizations and NGOs opened offices to help the local population, and EIJ operatives could pretend to be part of that.

• • •

Our investigation into the East African embassy bombings uncovered a lot of evidence connecting Fawwaz, Abdel Bary, and Eidarous to the attack. The satellite phone that bin Laden had used to communicate with the cell responsible for the attack, and with other al-Qaeda members around the world, had been purchased through Fawwaz for bin Laden, for example; and Fawwaz, of course, had been the original head of the Kenya cell before his transfer to London.

FBI agents were sent to London on thirty-day rotations to work with the British on the case, which Scotland Yard called Operation Challenge. John O'Neill also asked for all evidence to be sent to New York for me and the other agents in I-49 to analyze. Pat D'Amuro and John asked me to take the lead on evaluating the evidence and sending reports to London, as my knowledge of al-Qaeda, coupled with my fluency in Arabic, meant that the usual laborious process of waiting weeks for documents to be translated and then analyzed could be avoided.

On the computer in Fawwaz's residence, we found a file entitled "The Message," which had been created on July 31, 1996. It was an early version of bin Laden's 1996 declaration of jihad, which Fawwaz had sent to media outlets on August 23, 1996. He had also sent a note to the media outlets vouching for the authenticity of the fatwa's authorship.

His phone records revealed that on February 22, 1998, he had received calls from bin Laden's satellite phone and had contacted the offices of the London-based paper *al-Quds al-Arabi*. The next day, a fatwa entitled "International Islamic Front for Jihad on the Jews and Crusaders," calling for Muslims to kill Americans and signed by bin Laden and Zawahiri, had been published in *al-Quds*.

In a letter dated May 7, 1998, Abu Hafs, al-Qaeda's number-two military leader, told Fawwaz about bin Laden's support of a fatwa by the Ulema Union of Afghanistan, declaring jihad against the United States. In his letter Abu Hafs made recommendations to Fawwaz as to where the fatwa should be published. One week later, on May 14, Fawwaz had it published in *al-Quds*.

We also uncovered evidence highlighting the roles Abdel Bary and

Eidarous played in the terrorist network, such as a copy of the August 6, 1998, threat from Zawahiri to retaliate for the arrests in Albania, which had been received by Abdel Bary before publication. There was correspondence between Eidarous and Zawahiri linking both of them to al-Qaeda. On October 29, 1997, for example, Eidarous had asked Zawahiri to call Abdel Bary's cell phone. The next day, several calls to the same number had been made from bin Laden's satellite phone.

There was a letter from June 1998, in which Zawahiri stated that Eidarous was the leader of EIJ in London, and a letter from July 1998, in which Abdel Bary affirmed his commitment to EIJ and accepted that he would follow orders. We understood that he had originally voiced unhappiness that Ediarous was coming to London and replacing him as head of the London cell.

In New York we focused on sorting the evidence and following up on leads that directed us elsewhere: to Albania, Sudan, Azerbaijan, and other places. We were never told about any deadlines on the British side, and we were under the impression that the British would continue to hold the men—as the evidence was so compelling—until we were ready to begin building a criminal case.

It was therefore a shock when Tom Lang told me that the members of the London cell were about to be released. The situation in London wasn't being helped by the thirty-day rotation schedule. Agents spent much of their time getting up to speed on the investigation rather than moving the case forward.

But when the message came through that they were about to be released, we knew that we couldn't allow that to happen: if they were released, they'd be on the first plane to Pakistan, and from there to Afghanistan, and it would be a long time before we'd see them again. Perhaps never.

The five of us in New York—Pat, Ken, Dan, Jack, and I—spent that night, the night of my birthday, in Pat's office going through evidence. The operatives' use of multiple aliases complicated the process of building the case, as we had to establish their identity each time. In the trunk of Eidarous's car, which he seemed to have used as a sort of filing cabinet for EIJ material, we had found incriminating documents under the names Abbas and Daoud, which were clearly Abdel Bary and Eidarous, respectively. To prove this, we went through the group's phone books and cross-referenced names, aliases, and numbers. One of Pat's greatest skills is his memory, which is almost photographic. At one point we were missing a certain piece of linking evidence, and Pat remembered that the issue had come up in the trial of the Blind Sheikh. So he went to the evidence storage area of the Southern District and located a tape with the testimony we needed, thereby establishing the connection.

By the end of the night, we had finished putting together a complaint and sent it to London. It was filed, and the British agreed to hold Fawwaz, Abdel Bary, and Eidarous. Pat D'Amuro appointed me case agent for Operation Challenge and told me to head to London, with Ken Karas, to ensure that there were no more mistakes, and that we would win the upcoming legal battle to extradite the three men to the United States for trial.

Our time in London turned out to be an extended version of that all-nighter in the Southern District: Ken and I, working with Scotland Yard detectives, combed through thousands of documents, linking names, aliases, and terrorist activities in order to make the case against the three men. At first Ken struggled to find a barrister to represent us in court in England. Someone had been recommended, and she was the first candidate Ken approached. She told him: "I'm not going to embarrass myself by taking what clearly is a losing case." That was a prevalent attitude, and he got told no a few more times until he secured someone.

The barrister we ended up with was a talented court performer, but he had no experience dealing with terrorist cases or al-Qaeda. We had to teach him about al-Qaeda and terrorism from scratch, and even had to coach him in how to pronounce operatives' names. On our first day in court, after successfully pronouncing "Zawahiri," he turned to Ken and me and gave us a big smile.

Up against us was a lawyer who had made a career of representing IRA terrorists and who was known for her hostility to the British authorities, earning herself the nickname "the wicked witch." With the arrest of al-Qaeda and EIJ members, she had decided to take up their cause. One day during the trial, Ken and I walked through the court doors with a Scotland Yard detective at the same time as the defense lawyer, and Ken, being a gentleman, stepped aside and held open the door for her. "Haven't you done enough damage?" she asked, glaring at him, before storming through. Ken and I looked at each other in shock, and the Scotland Yard detective said, shrugging, "See what we have to deal with."

We won the case at the magistrate level. The defense then appealed the case to the Royal Court of Justice, where we won again. The defense then appealed to the House of Lords—the highest court in Britain—and we defeated them there, too. To many in the British government, the press, and academic circles, our victory came as a great surprise. They all apparently underestimated the evidence we had amassed.

To celebrate our victory in the House of Lords, Ken, Joe Hummel, and I went out to dinner with a bunch of guys from SO13: the head of the branch, Alan Fry; his deputy, John Bunn; and a few of their colleagues. Joe Hummel, a friend from I-40, is called Joey Hamas within the bureau because of the work he did cracking down on the Palestinian terrorist group.

Alan and John had invested time, resources, and personal capital in supporting us in our investigation and in the trial—and in convincing elements of the British government supportive of the Londonistan policy to back us. The Scotland Yard officials had been criticized in many quarters for wasting their time on a "failed" case—so it was a great vindication for them, and a testament to their skills, that we all won. We simply could not have done it without our British partners' expertise, efforts, and support.

The night began at Shepherd's, a restaurant frequented by Members of Parliament and owned by Michael Caine, who had just won a best supporting actor Oscar. We continued our celebration in John Bunn's office. After months of hard work and virtually no sleep we felt we deserved it, and stayed till the early hours of the morning.

. . .

"Welcome back, Ali. Well done," John O'Neill said to me a few days later. We had just sat down to dinner at Cité.

"Thanks, boss. It was tough, but it was worthwhile—obviously in terms of us winning the case, but also because of what I learned about al-Qaeda and its global network."

"That's very good," John said. "Al-Qaeda is one of the greatest threats that we'll face in the future—despite the fact that most in the U.S. government don't, or won't, recognize it yet. So I'm glad that you're at least building up the skills that will be needed in the long fight ahead."

The thousands of documents, letters, and pieces of communications that we had analyzed to build the case against the London cell had given me a deep understanding of how al-Qaeda and EIJ operated and of their internal dynamics. This would later prove to be an invaluable aid both in our investigations into the group and when conducting interviews and interrogations of its members.

We had learned that within EIJ there was opposition from members of the *shura* council to Zawahiri's quest for EIJ to merge formally with al-Qaeda. Those members wanted EIJ to stick to its original aim of toppling the Egyptian regime, and not to take up bin Laden's cause of global jihad. One member of the council, Hani al-Sibai, for example, wrote a letter to Zawahiri warning that if EIJ joined al-Qaeda and took bin Laden's funding he would eventually control them. "He who owns my food owns my decisions," Sibai wrote.

Our investigation had also uncovered leads pointing to EIJ and al-Qaeda operations in other countries. We had learned that the head of EIJ's *shura* council was based in Yemen, and that there were cells in Italy, Albania, and Azerbaijan. (One letter we uncovered detailed an attempt by Eidarous to buy a farm in Azerbaijan, which was known to have a good weapons laboratory.) I had traveled to London thinking that there was one case to solve, but returned to New York with a host of new leads to follow up on.

During dinner John and I also discussed what it was like working with Scotland Yard. John knew the famous British law enforcement outfit well from the time he had spent in London. Like John, I returned from England with a favorable impression. I had bonded with the SO13 guys and had enjoyed working alongside them.

Often when we worked in foreign countries a challenge we faced was dealing with local officials whose methods of collecting evidence and conducting interrogations didn't match our standards—which risked rendering evidence and confessions inadmissible in U.S. courts. Evidence needs to be logged as soon as it is recovered and a chain of custody maintained—that is, it must be established that the evidence has been in the custody of a trustworthy, identifiable person from the time of recovery, with a member of a law enforcement agency present. These individuals have to be prepared to testify in court—as such, they cannot be undercover agents—and it must be shown that there was no chance of the evidence's having been tainted. The requirements are the same in the UK, so we faced no problems.

While we were in London I saw that Scotland Yard, with its focus on tracking, apprehending, and convicting terrorists, had problems with MI5, the British internal intelligence service. One day, after we had successfully wrapped up Operation Challenge, Joe Hummel arranged for Ken and me to brief MI5. Joe told us that they were especially interested in the al-Qaeda–EIJ network in the UK and how it connected with other cells around the world. SO13 officers accompanied us to MI5 headquarters, and we gave a thorough briefing. During the question-and-answer session that followed, an MI5 official told me: "What you've said about what's going on the UK is very detailed. Much of it is new to us. How do you know about all of this?" His question and tone implied that he thought we were running our own operations in their backyard without coordinating with British authorities.

"Most of this information," I said, "is from the great work that SO13 has been doing."

The SO13 officers in the room couldn't hide their smiles, and after we left they told us that all the intelligence from Operation Challenge had been given to MI5 but that they hadn't even looked at it. They had assumed that, because it came from law enforcement, it wasn't worth analyzing.

"That's a problem between law enforcement and intelligence agencies across the world, to varying degrees," John said after I'd described the exchange, "and I fear that it's a growing problem here in the United States. I've been warning about it, but I'm not sure people are paying attention."

"It's a dangerous attitude," I said. "Don't they realize we're all on the same side?"

John shook his head and said, "Some people don't get it."

A few months later I had a similar experience with the CIA after receiving a complaint from them that we hadn't shared the intelligence on "al-Qaeda's WMD [weapons of mass destruction] program." We replied that all such information was contained in the Jamal al-Fadl and Operation Challenge files on the uranium fiasco, and that those files were in their possession. There was no real WMD program.

In 1999, a few weeks after I had returned from London, I was having lunch at my desk and Tom Lang, the I-49 supervisor, came and sat beside me. "Ali," Tom said, "I need you to go to Albania. The CIA is running some operations there and they need your help, given your experience with al-Qaeda and EIJ's European network."

"When do I need to leave?"

"In a few hours."

"Thank God I'm single. I'll go pack my things."

The East African embassy bombings had sharpened the U.S. government's focus on Albania. Given the warning message from Zawahiri's group that had appeared in *al-Hayat* the day before the bombing, we had thought, at first, that the bombings might have some links to Albania. Separate intelligence reports came in on possible plots against U.S. interests in Albania, so the renewed focus was maintained. Suspected EIJ members in Albania were put under surveillance. One day the head of the EIJ cell in Albania, Ashraf, was spotted carrying a letter. Guessing that it contained intelligence, the Albanian security services made a move to try to arrest him. He attempted to flee, throwing his letter into the bushes. He was stopped and the letter was retrieved. It was addressed to Eidarous, in his position as head of EIJ in London, and congratulated him on the group's "weddings." The term was used by al-Qaeda and EIJ to describe suicide bombers—believed to be in heaven, marrying virgins. The letter went on to state that preparations were under way for "our own weddings here." Security at all U.S. institutions in Albania was stepped up, and the CIA and FBI intensified our monitoring and investigating.

There was no direct flight from New York to Albania, so I took what was then the best option: flying Austrian Airlines from New York to Vienna and from there to Tirana, the Albanian capital. The airport in Tirana was primitive: just a house and a basic runway that was really only suitable for landing in good weather. The captain warned, as we took off from Vienna, "If the weather is bad we won't be able to land in Tirana, but the good news is that the weather is clear . . . for now."

"When you land in Tirana, stay next to the plane," Tom Lang had told me in a briefing before I'd left New York. "Whatever you do, don't go anywhere and don't give your passport to anyone. Just wait by the plane. The CIA guys will pick you up."

While everyone else from the flight filed into the house next to the runaway that served as the baggage and customs hall, I stayed next to the plane. "Excuse me, sir, you need to head into the customs hall," a stewardess told me. "It's okay," I said, "I'm waiting for someone here." Shrugging, she walked off. A few Albanians security officials approached me. They wore civilians clothes but carried weapons and walkie-talkies.

"Please go into the customs area," one of the officials said to me. "You can't stand here."

"I'm sorry, but I've been told to wait here."

"Who are you?"

"I'm waiting for someone to pick me up." (I didn't mention from where.) They conferred with each other in Albanian, took another look at me, and walked off. For the next ten minutes I stood there, waiting, my only companion a stray dog that had wandered over to stare at me.

Then, seemingly from nowhere, I spotted two 4x4 vehicles speeding down the runway, heading toward me. The vehicles came to an abrupt stop right next to me, and a door was flung open. Several men were inside each 4x4. From the vehicle closest to me, an American voice shouted, "Jump in."

I wasn't just going to jump into any car in Albania, so I looked in and asked, "Who are you?"

I noticed that the 4x4s were American-made, typically the kind the U.S. government uses; and the men inside looked like Americans. "We're the people you're waiting for," one of the men replied, "and if you're Ali Soufan, we're here to pick you up."

"That works for me," I said, and climbed in.

"Do I need to do anything about Customs?" I asked as the car started moving.

"Not here," the man replied with a grin. "Welcome to Albania."

"The entire area is pretty much a ghost town," a CIA colleague told me, as he drove me through the part of Tirana where diplomatic missions used to be based. "Entire compounds have been evacuated. No one wants to be here now," he continued. "But then again, it's not like people would want to be here anyway."

"So, how bad is it?" I asked.

"Not as bad as it was then, of course," he said, referring to the early 1990s and the Balkan war, "but you still have remnants of groups up to no good, and the Iranians are doing their part to keep this area unstable. For ten dollars you can easily buy a used AK-47."

"From what I've heard, there's also a problem with Russian and criminal gangs?"

"The Russian mafia is especially influential, and other criminal gangs are trying to take advantage of the lawlessness here."

The U.S. Embassy in Albania was closed following the uncovering of a plot by EIJ to bomb the building, and all nonessential personnel had been sent back to the United States. The embassy was deserted except for the U.S. ambassador, security personnel, and a few other officials. The CIA personnel had moved to a remote covert location. We checked in with them, and the CIA chief briefed me on the operations the organization was running and the missions they needed my support on.

"Who else is here besides you working on this?" I asked.

"There's only a few of us here, so we're spread pretty thin. We get others in to help, but they're in for short stints, so we lack the continuity I would ideally want."

At a local hotel, all of us had rooms on the same floor, and I went upstairs around midnight, exhausted from traveling. I fell asleep as soon as my head hit the pillow. At around 3:00 AM I was awakened by gunfire. I recognized the sound of AK-47s being fired and rolled off the bed, grabbing my gun from my bedside table. I crouched on the floor, trying to get a sense of where the gunfire was coming from.

I opened my door and went into the corridor. Other U.S. personnel had already gathered. "What's going on?" I asked no one in particular.

"Don't worry," an officer told me. From his tone I guessed that he had been in the country for a while. "The presidential palace is not far from here, and often at night stray dogs run in packs on the grounds there. The guards fire rounds from their machine guns to scare the dogs off. Go get some sleep."

I spent the next few weeks working with the CIA officers on identifying terrorists, gathering intelligence, and disrupting threats. The chief and his men treated me like one of their team, and we developed a good relationship. It helped that we were a small group, which encourages closeness. Operating under a threat also brings people together. We knew Iranian agents were monitoring us, as were al-Qaeda and EIJ members—all of whom had reason not to want us in the country. We always had to be vigilant and rely on each other for backup.

Sometimes the best of precautions were frustrated by the fact that we were in Albania, which was very backward in those years. One evening I went out to eat with two CIA officers, both temporarily assigned to the country. When we returned to our car, it wouldn't start. The battery had died.

It was late, the electricity had been cut off, and the neighborhood was deserted—we had been the only patrons in the restaurant. We had no choice but to push the car to try to restart it. One guy sat behind the wheel, and the other guy and I pushed the car.

"Ahh," the guy with me yelled, and then I didn't see him anymore.

I shouted his name and heard a muffled response: "I'm down here." He had fallen into an uncovered manhole in the road. Realizing it was nothing serious, we started laughing, and helped him out of the hole. We could not stop laughing. Finally we were able to restart the car, and hours later we got back to the hotel, exhausted and covered in dirt but happy to have arrived safely.

During our fast-paced operation, other intelligence services were made party to our investigation. Following long-standing protocol, we appreciated the secrecy of the foreign services' cooperation and the sensitive nature of their involvement. It was essential to keep their participation confidential at all costs. Brash disclosures could have a profound impact on other ongoing operations, not to mention the fact that they might damage relationships with our partners and unnecessarily jeopardize sensitive sources and methods. Because those partners had different rules and standards relating to collection of evidence and chain of custody procedures, some of the incriminating evidence that had been collected became legally tainted and could not be used in a U.S. court.

As a result, the prosecutors declined to bring cases against a few of the EIJ operatives, including Hani al-Sibai. As of this writing, Sibai is still living freely as a political refugee in London, where he runs an Islamic organization. The Egyptians, however, using the evidence we collected, convicted him in absentia of being a member of EIJ's *shura* council and of involvement in terrorist acts.

There were also several EIJ members who were able to escape from the country and thereby from the investigation into the East African embassy bombings. For instance, we discovered that an operative who used the alias Abdul Rahman al-Masri and who had connections to Yemen had found his way to Italy, where he was staying with Sibai's brother-in-law in Turin. Because of the alias, we thought at first that he might be the bomb maker Abu Abdul Rahman al-Muhajir, and that he had helped build the bombs detonated in 1998. We knew that Muhajir used a fake Yemeni passport and was Egyptian.

I traveled to Italy, along with other FBI agents and assistant U.S. attorney Pat Fitzgerald, to determine if Muhajir and Abdul Rahman al-Masri were indeed the same person. We were assisted in Turin by members of the Italian Division of General Investigations and Special Operations, or Divisione Investigazioni Generali e Operazioni Speciali (DIGOS). The team was headed by Giuseppe Petronzi, from the counterterrorism department. The Turin police arrested the individual; however, upon questioning we found that he wasn't Muhajir but another EIJ operative from Albania (with the same alias). We found weapons and wigs where he was staying, along with correspondence between him and Hani al-Sibai in which Sibai, working from London, had tried to arrange fake passports. While we hadn't found Muhajir, we had broken up an EIJ plot in Italy.

The challenge in working with the Italians was one of language. Although much later in the process we worked with Massimo De Benedittis, a DIGOS officer who was fluent in English (and whose nickname was "Kaiser"—all Italian officers in the division had what they called "war names"), when we first arrived not a single officer spoke English fluently, and none of us spoke Italian. The FBI representative who spoke Italian, and who would normally have handled the assignment, was out of the country on personal matters. We communicated through an interpreter who spoke Italian and Arabic. She translated from Italian to Arabic, and I then translated from Arabic to English for my colleagues.

During one conversation, in broken English, Petronzi kept referring to "Louis."

"What do you mean?" I asked.

"Louis, Louis," he said, pointing at the suspect. The suspect wasn't named Louis, so I thought perhaps there was someone else involved whom we didn't know about. If not that, I jokingly speculated, he might be talking about Louis Freeh, the director the FBI.

Eventually, through the translator, I discovered that he wasn't saying the name Louis but *lui*, the word for "him." This became a running joke between Petronzi and us—happily, he always saw the funny side of things. We became good friends with him and Kaiser and other members of their team, and their assistance and hospitality created a lasting bond between us.

While we were tracing leads and striving to disrupt possible threats by al-Qaeda, other agents and analysts from I-49 were also tracking terrorists connected to the East African embassy bombings. Their efforts uncovered Nazih Abdul Hamed al-Ruqai'i—the real name of Anas al-Liby, the Libyan al-Qaeda member who had cased the Nairobi embassy with Ali Mohamed. He was found to be residing in Manchester, England.

John O'Neill assembled a team to accompany him to the UK. We were met in London by SO13 detectives, and together we boarded a train to Manchester. There we were met by local police detectives assigned to assist us, and John asked me to brief the team on Liby. "Anas al-Liby is a senior al-Qaeda operative," I told them. "He's a computer expert and was part of the team that did surveillance on the embassy in Nairobi. This is potentially a big win for us."

"What are we looking for?" a detective asked.

"We're looking for any notes, pictures, or documents, anything related to al-Qaeda, the embassy bombings, or the Libyan Islamic Fighting Group, which he's also a member of, as well as being a member of al-Qaeda. We need to find in his possession evidence linking him to the bombings, or we won't be able to hold him."

Liby's location was raided, and he was caught before he could escape. He was brought down to the police station for preliminary questioning, and in the meantime his property was searched and all potential evidence was brought into the office. In his interview with the British police he didn't cooperate and denied involvement in terrorism.

As the detectives searched through Liby's computer files and possessions, it soon became apparent that in this case, unlike raids on other operatives, there was no "smoking gun" evidence that would tie Liby to the attacks and allow us to hold him. He was one of the more intelligent al-Qaeda operatives and had closely observed how we'd arrested other operatives: beyond going into hiding, he had destroyed as much evidence as he could. His computer hard drive had been cleared, and no incriminating files were found.

"Sorry, we're going to have to release him," a Manchester police detective told us. "Under British law we can't continue holding him just on suspicion. We need concrete evidence. And in his interview he denied everything."

"But if you release him, you can be certain he'll skip town before we have time to sort through all the evidence and find something—which I'm sure is there," John said.

"Sorry, it's British law."

Liby was released and evaded the team that was sent to follow him. We didn't know where he had disappeared to, but we were pretty certain he was on his way to Afghanistan. While he fled, our British partners gave us access to all evidence recovered from his residence. We searched through his computer files and other property, consoling ourselves with the thought that, though we had lost the man, we would find something of use against al-Qaeda.

Searching through one pile of files, documents, and books in Arabic, I saw what looked like a log or journal. I pulled it out from the pile and flicked through; it was full of photocopied handwritten pages. I turned to the first page, and on it was a note saying: "It is forbidden to take this out of the guesthouse." I started reading and saw that it was full of "lessons" (as the book termed it) for terrorist operatives, covering everything from "necessary qualifications" to espionage techniques, to "torture methods." It was written by an EIJ instructor based on his experiences in Egypt fighting the Mubarak regime.

Once I had skimmed a substantial portion of it, I told the team that it looked to be something of considerable interest.

"What is it?" asked Jack Cloonan, the senior agent on the team.

"It's the training manual that operatives, I'm guessing al-Qaeda operatives, use. It lists everything from how they should conceal themselves to the importance of conducting special operations."

"But does that actually lead us to any terrorists?" an officer asked.

"Not directly, but it will. This teaches us exactly how the terrorists are taught to think and prepare themselves for operations and interrogations. It offers insight into their mind-set, and behavior patterns we need to watch for. So it should help us catch them and, when we catch them, understand how to interrogate them successfully."

"Can you give an example of what the book says?" John asked.

"Sure. For example, this chapter contains instructions on how covert operatives should act. They're told not to reveal their real names, even to other members. They are told to remove anything that indicates they are Islamists. For example, beards, long shirts, copies of the Quran, or greetings such as 'May God reward you' are to be avoided.

"They're also told to avoid visiting public spaces such as libraries and mosques. They should avoid attracting any attention to themselves. It even says here that they need to be careful where they park. And they're warned not to speak to their wives about what they're doing.

"Another chapter here," I said, reading as I spoke, "is on the cell model they use, which is the cluster model—where cell members don't know members of other cells."

"Why is that?" John asked.

"It says so that if one part of the cell is caught, everyone else won't be compromised. They don't even know the communication methods that members of other cells use. And cell members are told not to recognize one another in public."

"That's amazing," declared an FBI colleague.

"It is. Look at this section here on safe houses. The manual says that ground-floor facilities are preferred, as they offer more escape options. All safe houses must have contingency plans for speedy evacuation, as well as secure areas to hide documents. And anyone going into a safe house needs to have sufficient cover—so as to avoid attention. No two safe houses should be rented from the same office, or in the same area—they're very careful."

"What does the section on interrogations tell them to do if caught?" John asked.

"Hold on," I said, and I went to that section and sped through its pages. "What's interesting is that it warns operatives that they'll be subjected to torture when caught. It tells them to hold off as much as they can, especially for the first forty-eight hours."

"Why forty-eight hours?" another colleague asked.

"It says because that will give fellow cell members enough time to reorganize, rendering information less valuable."

"And it tells them to expect to be tortured?"

"Yes, this manual is actually written warning them what would happen if the Egyptian or another Middle Eastern government arrests them. It says their sisters and mothers will be raped in front of them and they themselves will be sodomized by dogs."

"And they have to bear it?"

"They're told that their reward will come in heaven, but that they can pretend to cooperate in order to trick the interrogator."

"Meaning what?" John asked.

"It says they should give information to the interrogator, so the interrogator thinks the terrorist is cooperating, but really the information he gives up isn't valuable."

Later translated into English, the Manchester Manual, as it came to be known, was used by CIA contractors to justify the use of so-called enhanced interrogation techniques (EITs) authorized by the administration of President George W. Bush. To anyone who understood the point of the manual, this is ironic, as the manual teaches terrorists to expect and endure far worse. It is no surprise that these harsh techniques failed to work.

"Ali, I want you to head to Pakistan. We've got a potentially very important source who has come in, and I want you to evaluate him," John O'Neill told me a few weeks later. It was early in 2000.

"Sure, boss, what's the backstory?"

"It's an Afghani man who approached an agent from the Drug Enforcement Administration [DEA] in Peshawar saying that he had been working with Arabs and al-Qaeda in Pakistan and Afghanistan and didn't like them, so he wanted to work with the U.S. against them."

"That's pretty convenient for us," I said.

"You'd think, but the DEA agent passed him on to the CIA—the source didn't have anything on drug trafficking, so he was out of their area of interest. But when the source met with the agency, he was told that they weren't interested and they sent him away."

"Why?"

"Apparently they think he is full of it and lying, but our FBI guy there, Chris Reimann, called me to say he thinks this guy is the real deal. Go to Pakistan," John continued, "and meet him and evaluate him. And if he's credible, get information and arrange a permanent way of contacting him."

"Yes, sir."

"One more thing. Make sure you thank him and let him know we're appreciative."

Mike Dorris, who was assigned to the FBI office in Islamabad and was crucial in recruiting the source, later explained the situation to me in more detail. "The CIA asked the source a series of questions about bin Laden. He didn't know much about the main target [bin Laden], as he dealt with midlevel al-Qaeda guys, not the leadership. The CIA official therefore deemed him to be a useless source."

"That's pretty bad," I said, shaking my head.

"It gets worse. The source then came back to the DEA twice, again saying he wanted to share information. The first time, the DEA again passed him to the CIA official, who again turned him away. But the second time, thankfully, the DEA agent included me. I realized this source could be of use, so I sent you guys a message through Chris Reimann."

In Pakistan the DEA agent arranged for us and another FBI agent, Jennifer Keenan, from I-49, to meet the man. When the CIA got wind of the meeting, a different officer from the agency came. As we had flown all the way from New York to meet the source, the officer guessed that he was probably more valuable than his colleague had thought.

Unlike Junior, the man didn't know much about the top-level al-Qaeda operatives, but he was able to tell us about midlevel operatives—and other radical terrorists whom we had never heard about. And for the ones we knew a little about, he filled in gaps. It was clear he disliked al-Qaeda, both from a personal and an ideological point of view, and he gave us whatever information he thought was valuable. We tilted the questions toward what we thought would be of use, and he answered anything we asked.

"I don't know bin Laden, but I know Khallad, and if you know Khallad, you know a lot about bin Laden," he told me during one conversation.

"Who is Khallad?"

"Khallad is a one-legged operative known as bin Laden's 'errand boy.' His family is very close to bin Laden's family, as their fathers were friends. Khallad's whole family is involved in al-Qaeda. His older brother, Muhannad, was killed in Afghanistan fighting with the Taliban—in the same battle where Khallad lost his leg. There's also a younger brother called al-Bara"—Abdul Aziz bin Attash—"who actually looks very much like Khallad and is currently jailed in Yemen."

I didn't tell him that I had heard the name Khallad before. It had come up during the questioning of Owhali, the failed suicide bomber from the East African embassy bombing. Owhali had said that when he and Jihad Ali made their martyrdom videos, the people holding the cameras were Khallad and Nashiri. At the time, we thought that he probably meant Khalid, a common name; but Stephen Gaudin, Owhali's interrogator, insisted it was Khallad. Now we knew who Khallad was—and that he was someone important we should be on the lookout for.

"Who else is very valuable to bin Laden?" I later asked the source.

"I know two individuals bin Laden trusts with his life."

"Who are they?"

"Abu Jandal and Saqr al-Jadawi," he said, using Salim Hamdan's alias. "They may be Saudis. Abu Jandal is bin Laden's personal bodyguard and Saqr, his driver. Bin Laden trusts them so much that he has them live on either side of his house, and he had them marry two sisters so they would become blood relatives." Our conversation continued, through the interactions he had had with these al-Qaeda operatives to some of the fugitives from the East African embassy bombings, including the main facilitator, Abu Mohammed al-Masri (Saleh). At one point he told us about Abu Zubaydah, another major operative. "He is the emir of a training camp and is one of the major smugglers and terrorist facilitators in Afghanistan." Abu Zubaydah, we would learn, served as Khaldan's external emir; its internal emir was Ibn al-Shaykh al-Liby.

"Is Abu Zubaydah a member of al-Qaeda?"

"No, he isn't, and he spends his time in Pakistan."

We wrote up all the information the source had given us, and it was deemed both credible and significant by FBI analysts back in the United States. We thanked the man and arranged a method to maintain contact. We also briefed the CIA chief on our evaluation of the information that had been supplied.

When I returned to the United States I found that the CIA was now interested in our man. I traveled with my supervisor at the time, John Liguori, and my partner, Steve Bongardt, to Langley (CIA headquarters) to brief the agency. There we found that there was an internal CIA disagreement—between the CTC and the Near East Division—about who from their side would handle him. Apparently neither had a similar source in the country, so this would be a major asset.

As far as shared access with the CIA was concerned, we didn't mind it at all; the source could be useful to us both. The agency had expertise in safely handling sources. Nevertheless, in the past—in the East African embassy bombings investigation, in Albania, and in other cases—evidence had been tainted and made unusable for prosecutions because CIA officers had, in fact, mishandled the chain of custody; or there were discrepancies between information that went through CIA channels and what was reported in FBI channels. This can cause considerable problems during the prosecution phase; one doesn't know which to trust. To make matters clear this time, John Liguori spelled out the terms. "One thing needs to be clear," he told the CIA, "the source is our source. He's a criminal source who is providing information on the fugitives from the East African embassy bombings. The intelligence we gain might be used for investigations and prosecutions. You are welcome to use him as well, but all meetings need to be done jointly and we have to be included in the reporting. All information needs to be coordinated because it will one day be used in a court of law."

"Absolutely," a senior CIA officer told us. "We respect that."

"Good," John said. "Remember, any intelligence gained has to be exactly the same in your reports as in our 302 reports, so that when it comes to court, there are no contradictions." The 302 is a form used for reporting information that is likely to become testimony. It contains a digest of the interview conducted.

They readily agreed to our terms.

I traveled a few times with Steve Bongardt to Pakistan to meet the source. We made efforts to protect him; we didn't want Pakistani or other intelligence agents knowing about our meetings with him. Whenever we were in the country, Pakistani agents tried to tail us. They weren't very efficient, which made it easy to lose them. Sometimes, however, we enjoyed playing games with them to show them how ridiculous the situation was. One time, after we had finished our mission and were ready to go home the next morning, Steve and I walked out of our rooms, went to the elevator, and spotted a man who had been following us for a few days. While he claimed to be a receptionist on our floor, he repeatedly popped up wherever we were, and he didn't wear a hotel uniform or seem to do any administrative work. As the elevator doors opened, we stepped in, and he followed us in.

"Oh, excuse me," I said out loud. "I forgot something." Steve and I stepped out of the elevator, and the "receptionist" jumped out.

"Actually, I have it," Steve said, playing along, and we both stepped back in—as did the man.

We jumped out, and he jumped out. "You're burned," I told him with a big smile. "Tell them they need to send someone else to follow us." His face went red, and he walked off.

6

"You'll Be Singing Like a Canary"

L'Houssaine Kherchtou, chosen by al-Qaeda's leaders to serve as bin Laden's personal pilot, returned to Sudan from flight school in Nairobi in 1995 to find his pregnant wife begging on the streets of Khartoum for money for a Cesarean section. Al-Qaeda's security rules had prevented him from contacting her, and he was unaware that she had been reduced to begging. He told her tearfully that he would take care of the money, and checked her into the main hospital in Khartoum.

Kherchtou then went to see Sheikh Sa'eed al-Masri, al-Qaeda's financial chief, in the office the latter shared with bin Laden and other al-Qaeda leaders. "I need money to pay the hospital bill for my wife's Cesarean section," he told Sa'eed al-Masri. "It's five hundred dollars."

"I'm sorry, there is no money. We can't give you anything," Sa'eed al-Masri said apologetically. After a pause he added: "Why don't you take your wife to the Muslim hospital?"

The Muslim hospital offered free care to the poor; conditions were known to be terrible. Kherchtou would never take his wife there. He knew that al-Qaeda had been having financial difficulties since bin Laden's loss of family funds following his expulsion from Saudi Arabia;

Kherchtou had been told not to renew his pilot license, which also cost five hundred dollars. He also knew, however, that al-Qaeda still had money. He had seen fellow operatives purchasing fake passports and other items needed for missions. The health of his wife and future child should be a priority, too, he believed, and he didn't understand why they wouldn't spare the money, especially for someone who had been so loyal and long-serving. One of al-Qaeda's first operatives, Kherchtou felt the sting of the rejection when he recalled his service to the organization in Afghanistan, Nairobi, and elsewhere.

"If it were your wife or your daughter who needed a Cesarean, would you take her there?" Kherchtou asked Sa'eed al-Masri.

"Well . . . ," Sa'eed al-Masri replied. He found himself caught off-guard by Kherchtou's challenge, and he knew, in his heart, that Kherchtou was right.

Kherchtou seized on Sa'eed al-Masri's silence to press forward: "Why don't you borrow money for me so I can pay for the procedure, and I will pay you back later?"

Sa'eed al-Masri shook his head. "I'm sorry. I can't do anything until bin Laden comes back."

Bin Laden was out of the office, but Kherchtou knew that this was Sa'eed al-Masri's decision. "I've been with al-Qaeda since 1991. Is this how you repay loyalty? Consider the health of my wife." He stormed out of the office, fuming. Beyond the refusal to give him money, he also resented how Egyptians like Sa'eed al-Masri were running al-Qaeda. "I would have shot him if I had had a gun," Kherchtou told friends when recounting the conversation. "All the money goes to Egyptians, and the rest of us they treat like second-class citizens."

While Kherchtou remained on al-Qaeda's payroll after that incident, continuing to run errands between Khartoum and Nairobi for bin Laden, he began to drift away from the organization. And when bin Laden announced, in 1996, that al-Qaeda was relocating to Afghanistan, Kherchtou didn't follow him. Instead he sent his family back home to Morocco, telling al-Qaeda's leaders that he wanted his children to get a decent education, and that there were no suitable schools in Afghanistan. He continued to work in Nairobi, but no longer saw the al-Qaeda leadership regularly and emotionally distanced himself from them.

"Ali, we've got a potentially important lead in understanding al-Qaeda," Debbie Doran told me. It was a few weeks after the East African embassy bombings, and all our efforts were focused on tracking those responsible and deepening our understanding of the organization.

"What's the lead?" I asked.

Debbie told me that her team had found a letter dated a few days before the bombing, signed by Mzungu, an alias Kherchtou used. They had also found that Kherchtou, like other al-Qaeda members, had been arrested by Kenyan authorities but then released from jail at the request of a Western intelligence agency—and that that intelligence agency had taken him out of the country.

"Was he involved in the bombing?" I asked Debbie.

"We don't exactly know. He was in Nairobi at the time of the bombing, which makes it interesting. He interacted with the cell members." After the Kenyans arrested him, the Western intelligence agency intervened—they had been working on using him as a source, and convinced the Kenyans to release him. The FBI nicknamed him Joe the Moroccan, a translation of one of his aliases, Yousef al-Maghrebi.

"They made a deal with Joe," Debbie continued, "agreeing that they'd have him released so he could travel back to Khartoum. In exchange, he would meet with their intelligence operatives there and report on al-Qaeda's activities. He agreed to the deal and returned to Khartoum, telling al-Qaeda members that he was released because he had convinced the Kenyans that he was a businessman with no connection to the terrorist plot. Once in Khartoum, he failed to make any contact with the Western intelligence agency.

"That's where we come in," Debbie concluded. "We need to go and find out about him, and then see if we can do a better job recruiting him. If he did live with the Nairobi cell members and was with al-Qaeda from the start, he could be an important source."

• • •

I traveled with Debbie to the country whose intelligence agency had been working with Kherchtou, and at first the agency denied knowing anything about him. However, when we presented the evidence we had on their dealings with him, and explained that he could be an important source for us in tracking and prosecuting those responsible for the East African embassy bombings, they admitted that they had been trying to work with him. They agreed to turn over their files to us.

From the files we learned that they had been in contact with him directly after the embassy bombings and had learned about his connections to the al-Qaeda cell in Nairobi. The files contained a good deal of information on Kherchtou—on his background and some of his work for al-Qaeda. In addition, there was valuable personal information that I mentally noted would be useful when interviewing him, such as al-Qaeda's refusal to give him money for his wife's Cesarean.

Our next challenge was to work out how we could get hold of him, as Sudan was highly unlikely to agree to an extradition request, and any request we made was likely to tip Kherchtou off that we were looking for him. We discussed trying to apprehend him but ruled it out because it posed too many security risks, and, more importantly, because it reduced the likelihood that he would cooperate with us—which was our primary hope. Instead we contacted Direction de la Surveillance du Territoire (DST), the Moroccan intelligence service, which agreed to help. Moroccan immigration officials sent a message to Kherchtou in Khartoum that there was an issue with the immigration status of his children and that he should return home to resolve it. Thinking that he just had to deal with a routine bureaucratic problem, he flew to Morocco. Upon landing, he was picked up by the intelligence agency, which took him to a safe house in Rabat, the Moroccan capital, where we were waiting.

"Hi, L'Houssaine. How are you?" I asked in Arabic. "Are you comfortable?"

"Yes," he replied, staring at me with a puzzled expression. I guessed that he was trying to work out who I was, where we were, and what was going on.

"You speak English, right?" I asked.

"A little," he replied in English.

"Well," I said, switching to English, "let's speak in English, but when it's easier we can speak in Arabic."

"Okay."

"Let me introduce myself," I continued. "My name is Ali Soufan and I'm with the FBI. With me are my colleagues from the U.S. government, led by our boss, John O'Neill. The others here are Jack Cloonan and Pat Fitzgerald."

He looked at me in surprise. He didn't think that here in Morocco he'd be in the hands of the United States. The safe house was in a rural area about thirty minutes' drive from Rabat. The scenery was beautiful, as was the house itself. The food was fresh and of the highest quality, and there was plenty to drink, creating a relaxed atmosphere. None of it made sense to him.

At first we just chatted with Kherchtou about himself, his family, and other harmless topics that he was comfortable talking about. He answered politely but was clearly nervous about being with Americans and suspicious of us. After a half-hour of small talk, I turned to him and said: "Now, look, L'Houssaine. We know all about you and your history with al-Qaeda. It is in your interest to cooperate fully with us. If you do, we in turn will treat you well." He didn't say anything. I continued: "Now we know al-Qaeda didn't treat you like you deserved to be treated." Kherchtou straightened up and looked directly at me. "You know what I'm referring to, don't you?" I asked. He shook his head slowly.

"Remember when your wife needed a Cesarean section, and she was forced to beg on the streets of Khartoum for the money? Remember how angry you were when al-Qaeda refused to give you the five hundred dollars needed for that operation? That's how al-Qaeda treats one of its most loyal members?" He again shook his head, and there was a pained expression on his face.

"That's not the way you treat anyone who is in need of charity," I continued. "We both know it's not the way a good Muslim would treat a neighbor, let alone a devoted colleague. What's clear to me is that al-Qaeda has no respect for you. It doesn't care about you or the health of your wife, and you don't owe them anything."

A few tears rolled down Kherchtou's face. "You're right," he said, wiping away the tears. There was some anger in his eyes, too. "There was no excuse for that," he told me, and he began to talk about the outrage he felt at the time. "They couldn't spare five hundred dollars for my wife after everything I'd done!"

"They broke their covenant to you," I said, "and they showed you their true nature."

I stopped speaking, letting what I'd said sink in. We were all silent for about a minute. I then asked, "Would you like some tea?" He nodded. I poured some into a cup for him. He took a sip and placed his cup back on the table.

"Now, L'Houssaine, here's your choice," I said. "You can cooperate with us, work with us, and we will treat you well. You see how respectfully we've treated you so far; that's what we're like. Or you can refuse to cooperate, in which case you'll spend your life in jail. I know what you're going to choose. I believe by the time you've finished with us you'll be singing like a canary."

The conversation was in Arabic, and the Moroccan intelligence agents in the room, who followed every word, couldn't believe what I had said. They told me afterward that they were shocked that I had spoken to him so directly and had made such a bold prediction. Years after this encounter, a fellow FBI agent, Andre Khoury, was serving in the FBI Legat (the legal attaché office within the U.S. Embassy) in Rabat. Local intelligence agents asked him, "Do you know Ali Soufan? Did you hear about the time he told L'Houssaine Kherchtou that he'd end up 'singing like a canary'?"

Andre laughed when he told me the story a few years later.

John spent time bonding with Moroccan officials to ensure we got their continued cooperation. One evening we went out to dinner with the heads of DST, and John raised his glass and declared: "A long time ago the king of Morocco asked my country for help against pirates. The United States agreed, and Morocco was one of the first countries to ever make a treaty with the United States, and we've had a proud friendship since. Today the United States is asking Morocco for help, and it's been nice to see how warmly you've returned the favor."

The toast was cheered by the Moroccans, who seemed touched by the reminder of the friendship. I was sitting next to Debbie and said, "No one knows how to make toasts and win friends like John."

After that first conversation Kherchtou began opening up more. To continue to make him feel comfortable, we stayed away from asking for sensitive information about al-Qaeda and instead focused on his life, his family, his travels, and his aspirations, building a relationship with him. He was naturally talkative, and on safe topics he engaged well. Pat Fitzgerald, for his part, expertly established rapport with him and reeled him in.

After a few hours of conversation, we took Kherchtou out to a pizza place in Rabat for a change of scenery. He was interested in the United States and we told him what it was like living there. We gently broached the subject of his going into the Witness Protection Program if he cooperated with us, and we explained the benefits to him. He was especially interested in hearing about the satellite television options in America after I told him about the availability of channels in Arabic.

As we were leaving the pizza place, he seemed to be deep in thought and had a confused look on his face. "Is everything okay?" I asked. He shook his head. I could tell from his eyes that he was nervous. "Look," I told him, "I can tell you're nervous being with us. But let me tell you something: I'm nervous, too."

His eyes opened wide. "Why?" he asked.

"Well, I can't believe that I was just sitting and eating pizza with an al-Qaeda guy."

He laughed. "Not anymore. I'm not an al-Qaeda guy anymore."

"That makes me feel better," I told him with a smile, "and that means you'll be happy to work with us." I put my arm around him and we both laughed.

· · ·

Back at the safe house, Kherchtou began discussing terms for cooperating. "Will I go to jail?" he asked.

"We can't make any promises," Pat told him, "but here's what you need to do. You will fly to the United States and plead guilty to being a member of an organization dedicated to killing Americans, but you will become a cooperating witness, and a judge may decide to not sentence you. I will ask the judge to show you leniency because you're helping us."

Pat did some questioning to ascertain whether Kherchtou would be a good cooperating witness. I paid close attention and learned many techniques, such as how to play your cards close to your chest and lull someone into a false sense of security and then trap him on small details. While interrogation techniques are taught at the FBI Academy, being in a classroom is very different from being in an interrogation room and seeing an expert questioner at work. With Pat I saw, firsthand, how to use what you know to your advantage. We told Kherchtou that under the Witness Protection Program he would be given a new identity to ensure that no al-Qaeda agents or sympathizers could find him. And in the program he could lead a new life, enjoying all the good things America had to offer.

"Okay," he replied simply. And with that he began telling us all about al-Qaeda, how it operated, how they recruited, training camps they used, what bin Laden did daily, and so on. We started debriefing him by asking him to tell us about his path to al-Qaeda, which would teach us about their recruitment as well as their training process. He told us that after high school he had gone to a catering school and had worked in France and Italy. In Milan he had attended an Islamic center, where he was encouraged to travel to Afghanistan. He trained for combat, met bin Laden, and joined the organization.

"What happens in al-Qaeda guesthouses?" I asked.

"On entering the guesthouse you give in all your valuables—your money, passport, and all forms of ID—and they give you a nickname, usually linked to where you're from. They tell you that you're giving in all your valuables and ID so that if you're killed or caught, your captors won't know who you are." He said that his nickname was Abu Zaid Maghrebi and that he had also picked up the alias Abu Talal.

"What camp did you train in?"

"Al-Farouq." The camp turned out many of al-Qaeda's premier fighters.

"What did you learn there?"

"How to use regular firearms, antiaircraft weapons, and other basic guerrilla warfare skills."

"Who were your trainers?" I asked, and thus the debriefing went. After al-Farouq, Kherchtou had attended the Abu Bakr Sadeek camp, also located near Khost. It was run by Khalid al-Fawwaz—we were very familiar with him from Operation Challenge. With Kherchtou at Abu Bakr Sadeek was Odeh, operating under the alias Marwan.

Kherchtou went on to tell us about how he was trained, at one point, by Ali Mohamed, Zawahiri's man in the U.S. Army. Abu Hafs had told him in advance that "Abu Mohamed al-Amriki is very strict, and you have to be patient with him. He often uses bad words and is not an observent Muslim, but he's very skilled."

Kherchtou was later sent to Kenya to learn how to fly, so that one day he could become bin Laden's personal pilot. While in Nairobi attending flight school, he helped operatives who were passing through Kenya on their way to Somalia and other locations. Sometimes on trips between Nairobi and Khartoum he was given money to take to operatives in Kenya; the largest sum was ten thousand dollars.

Kherchtou filled in for us where Junior had left off. This was 1999, and Junior had left in 1996. Those were important years for al-Qaeda, so the information Kherchtou gave us was priceless.

On September 21, 1999, we flew with Kherchtou to the United States, and other agents were waiting for us at the airport. We took Kherchtou to an undisclosed location, and I went home, exhausted. As soon as I got there, the phone rang. An FBI agent was calling from the site. "Ali, Joe wants to speak to you—he's insisting."

"Okay, put him through."

"Hi. Ali?" I heard Kherchtou's voice.

"Hi, how are you?"

"I'm good, but where are you?"

"I'm at my home, resting."

"But these people are asking me questions and talking about plans for me, and I want you to be here to advise me."

"My friend, I need to get some rest and see my family tonight. I've been away from them for a while. But tomorrow I will come and see you."

The next day I drove to the safe house. As I walked through the door Kherchtou jumped up and greeted me with a big hug. He was clearly nervous about being in the United States and was unsure how things would work out. I was a friendly face he had come to trust.

We chatted and discussed the trials for the East African embassy bombings, for which he would serve as a witness. I also gave him a copy of the writings of the Lebanese American poet and writer Kahlil Gibran, whom we had discussed a few days earlier. His face lit up. "Thank you, Ali, so much."

Kherchtou went on to serve, alongside Junior, as a star witness in the East African embassy trials, ensuring the conviction of four al-Qaeda terrorists—men he had previously worked with. Because of his cooperation, he was not sentenced; as we had promised, he was indeed put in the Witness Protection Program.

The last time I saw him was immediately after the USS *Cole* was bombed, on October 12, 2000. We had debriefed him before we headed to Yemen to see if he knew anyone who might be involved. "I wish I could come with you to help investigate," he told me as we parted.

"I know, but you can help from here," I told him. "Keep telling us anything you think of."

7

Millennium Plot

After 1996, when he was back in Afghanistan, Osama bin Laden focused on remodeling al-Qaeda. In Sudan, the group had primarily acted as a sponsor of terrorism through bin Laden's business enterprises. Now bin Laden worked specifically and in detail on building al-Qaeda into an international terrorist organization that launched attacks under its own name. He built a network of safe houses and training camps across Pakistan and Afghanistan, and the group acquired a more intricate structure and became better organized.

At the same time, bin Laden still tried to use non–al-Qaeda groups to further his aims. He recognized that al-Qaeda's stated goal of expelling infidels from the Arabian Peninsula had limited appeal to many of the would-be terrorists who were flocking to Afghanistan for training. Many of the Islamic groups that sent their fighters to the country— such as those from Libya, Morocco, and Algeria—didn't care about America. Their focus was on the immediate enemy: their governments back home, which they accused of being insufficiently Islamic. These groups utilized non–al-Qaeda training camps like Khaldan and focused their efforts on overthrowing their home governments.

Mostly *takfiris* in their outlook, they knew bin Laden's record of using non–al-Qaeda operatives and resented his use of their operatives to further his aims.

Khaldan predated al-Qaeda, having been established during the Afghan jihad against the Soviets. Neither its external emir, Abu Zubaydah, nor its internal emir, Ibn al-Shaykh al-Liby, was a member of al-Qaeda, and these emirs prized their independence. Khaldan was known to be an independent camp. Ibn al-Shaykh al-Liby's responsibility was running it, while Abu Zubaydah—who had built a reputation as a top terrorist facilitator in Afghanistan—helped recruits and camp graduates with travel documents, funds, and safe houses.

While bin Laden understood why other groups, wary of al-Qaeda poaching their members, distanced themselves from him, he still wanted to have a connection with them. He thought that in the future they could perhaps work together and, more importantly, that their aims of hitting their domestic governments could mesh with his aims—especially if those countries had American or Western targets in them. Therefore, while he avoided getting directly involved with the members of other groups, he decided to support these operatives and the camps they attended indirectly. He funneled funds to non–al-Qaeda camps—including Khaldan—and delegated people who were associated with him to build relationships with Khaldan-trained operatives. One such operative was Khalil Said al-Deek.

An American Palestinian of Jordanian descent, born in Jenin, on the West Bank, Deek got a diploma in computer science in the United States and operated under the alias Abu Ayed al-Phalastini ("the Palestinian"). He had close connections to the Blind Sheikh, Omar Abdul Rahman, and was involved in a group that in 1992 planned to strike at targets in Los Angeles; the plot fell apart because Deek left the group to fight in Bosnia. He later fought in Afghanistan, where he fell in with bin Laden and senior al-Qaeda members.

Because of his U.S. citizenship, Deek was able to travel freely in the West and most of the world. He formed links with al-Qaeda cells and Islamic groups in Gaza, Turkey, Pakistan, the UK, and elsewhere.

In Britain he liaised with the al-Qaeda cell led by Khalid al-Fawwaz and worked with the British Pakistani operative Mozzam Begg to collect funds for Afghanistan.

Using his computer skills, Deek put together an electronic version of the *Encyclopedia of Jihad*—a multivolume manual created by Afghani-based mujahideen in the 1980s—and gave copies of the CD to operatives who were planning attacks. In Afghanistan he maneuvered among other groups and independent camps to see who could be of use to al-Qaeda. He formed a close relationship with Abu Zubaydah. It was a natural friendship: the two had similar backgrounds (they were both Jordanian Palestinians) and similar ideas about Islamic extremism. Through this relationship, al-Qaeda money and ideas flowed easily into the Khaldan camp.

Among other close connections was one that Deek formed with veteran fighter Khadr Abu Hoshar. Abu Hoshar had joined the mujahideen in Afghanistan in the late 1980s and fought against the Soviet Union. When he returned to Jordan he got involved in a terrorist group, the Army of Mohammad, that planned to launch operations to overthrow the Jordanian government—which the group viewed as being insufficiently Islamic.

After a stint in prison for plotting against the government, Abu Hoshar traveled between Yemen and Syria and established a cell with like-minded *takfiris*. They espoused the teachings of Abu Mohammed al-Maqdisi, a radical cleric based in Jordan who advocated, among other *takfiri* principles, that Sharia law was the only valid law, and that any who failed to uphold it were infidels. Abu Hoshar's main partner in this cell was a fellow Palestinian Jordanian named Raed Hijazi, whom he had met in May 1996 in the Yarmouk Palestinian refugee camp in Syria.

Hijazi, born in California to Palestinian Jordanian parents but raised in Saudi Arabia and Jordan, immersed himself in Islam and became radicalized with help from a local mosque in California. The mosque helped him travel to Afghanistan and gain admission to Khaldan, where he took classes in weapons and explosives. He learned quickly and became a skilled operative, acquiring the aliases Abu Ahmed al-Amriki (for the country of his birth) and Abu Ahmed al-Howitzer—because of his proficiency in operating the artillery device. Hijazi also developed relationships with Deek and Abu Zubaydah, and together the four men began plotting attacks within Jordan.

The idea was to bomb Christian, Israeli, and American targets in Jordan in the year 2000. They settled on attacking the Christian holy sites of Mount Nebo and the site along the Jordan River where Jesus was baptized; the border crossing with Israel; and the Radisson SAS Hotel in Amman—all of which they calculated would be packed with visiting tourists for the millennium. If successful, they would then launch a second wave of attacks.

Most of the coordination for the plot took place in Pakistan and was led by Deek and Abu Zubaydah. The planners met in the al-Iman Media Center in Peshawar, which was run by Deek. He was assisted by a convert to Islam from California, Adam Yahiye Gadahn, who operated under the alias Azzam the American and later became a spokesman for al-Qaeda.

Abu Hoshar and Hijazi recruited members for their cell in Jordan, Turkey, and Syria; more operatives came via Deek's center. Some were al-Qaeda members; others were not. Most were Jordanians or Palestinian Jordanians, and what united them was a desire to carry out an operation in Jordan. As Western targets were going to be attacked, al-Qaeda sent operatives to help, and Deek indirectly funneled money from bin Laden to the group. The non–al-Qaeda members didn't know that al-Qaeda money was supporting the operation; they believed, instead, that Deek's funding came from independent donors.

Abu Hoshar and Hijazi's planning got delayed when Abu Hoshar was arrested upon his return to Jordan from Syria and put in jail for eighteen months for plotting against the regime. During his imprisonment, Hijazi returned to the United States and started driving a cab in Boston, apparently to raise additional money for the plot.

After Abu Hoshar was freed in 1998, the two began gathering supplies and training operatives. The group also raised money through robberies and the sale of fraudulent documents in Jordan. Hijazi traveled back and forth between Jordan, London, and Boston to help gather supplies and bring in money. In London he was supported by another Palestinian radical, Abu Qutadah, a self-described cleric whose *takfiri* fatwas had already resulted in the slaughter and murder of many Muslims around the world, especially during the 1990s Algerian civil war.

Using his U.S. passport, Hijazi traveled to the UK, where he met al-Qaeda operatives and purchased walkie-talkies that would be used as remote-control detonators for the bombs, along with other materials for the plot. While in London, Hijazi also stopped in at the American Embassy to renew his U.S. passport.

After getting everything he needed from London, he left England and went to Israel, and from there he traveled by bus to Jordan. He entered at the northern border crossing that the group was planning to attack, in order to case the route, and took notes on a map of the area.

To gather explosives without attracting attention, Hijazi got a license to work as a jeweler—so that he could legally purchase nitric acid and other chemicals needed for bomb making. (The bombs were to be similar in structure to the one built by Ramzi Yousef in 1993.) Deek gave them a CD copy of the *Encyclopedia of Jihad*, which offered instruction in building bombs.

They rented a house in Marka, Amman, a poor neighborhood, and dug a hole to hide the chemicals they were accumulating. It took them two months to get it deep enough—they told neighbors they were building an extra bathroom. They collected weapons and detonators, along with fraudulent documents to use in the attacks. Hijazi also owned a farm that they used as a location to test explosives without people hearing and getting suspicious. A year of acquisition and hoarding—they bought only small quantities at a time in order to avoid attracting attention—finally produced the necessary cache of matériel.

The operatives who were to be used in the attack were sent to Abu Zubaydah's Khaldan camp for training. Operatives who couldn't travel to Afghanistan were taken to Syria and then to Lebanon; from there they were transported to training grounds by a member of the Palestinian Islamic Jihad (PIJ), using IDs belonging to Iranian Revolutionary Guards.

In June 1999, Abu Hoshar sent Hijazi and three others to Abu

Zubaydah for advanced explosives training. After the training was completed, Hijazi traveled to Syria. He planned to wait there until December 6, at which point he'd enter Jordan. The operation would take place during Ramadan: Muslims who are martyred during that time, according to radical Islamist lore, are promised a special place in heaven.

October 1999. The waiter had just put my steak down in front of me when my pager went off. The page was from FBI special agent and veteran al-Qaeda expert Dan Coleman, at the JTTF. I told Heather, my girlfriend (later, my wife), that I'd be right back—we were in the middle of a Saturday night dinner in Union Square, in downtown Manhattan—and I went into a phone booth at the back of the restaurant to call Dan.

"Ali, there's something going on in Jordan. You have to fly there tomorrow," he said quickly, in his usual direct-with-no-small-talk manner, and wished me good luck. He couldn't give me any details about the operation; the line at the restaurant was not secure. I returned to Heather and told her we'd need to finish up dinner, as I had to go abroad in less than twelve hours.

At JFK Airport the next morning I met Pat D'Amuro, who would be leading the mission for the first few days. We flew to Amman and were met at the airport by Scott Jessee, the FBI representative in Tel Aviv. (The FBI back then did not have a representative in Jordan, so all matters were covered operationally by the Tel Aviv office.) I knew Scott well from my time in Pakistan, where we'd crossed paths, and I was glad to have him as part of the team; he is a very effective operative.

After checking in with the embassy and getting briefed by the CIA, we all went to the headquarters of the Jordanian intelligence agency, Dairat al-Mukhabarat al-Ammah—the General Intelligence Directorate (GID). The GID headquarters is marked by a black flag and an inscription, in Arabic, of their motto: "Justice has come." It was not our first time meeting Saad al-Khair, the famed GID chief (then deputy chief), and his team. We had worked with them before and had been much impressed by their knowledge and operational skills. We had confidence that our investigation would be a success.

Saad was known to be a savvy and straightforward operative, as well as someone you didn't want to be on the wrong side of. Just mentioning his name put fear into the hearts of would-be offenders and others who had made the mistake of crossing him. Tall, handsome, always immaculately dressed, courteous and a real gentleman—and with a cigar almost always in his hand—Saad reminded me of the good foreign intelligence official you'd see helping James Bond in a movie. He was sharp and could read people well, and he had no time for people who played games with him or lied to him. His distinctive smile seemed to say: you can't fool me.

Saad understood the human mind and human nature, and he used his intelligence to outwit his enemies. He told me how he personally went undercover to disrupt threats, apprehend killers, and serve justice to those who threatened his beloved Jordan. Saad passed away in December 2009 after suffering a heart attack, and his stories still resonate. He will always be dear to my heart. One story—made famous by the journalist and novelist David Ignatius and in the movie *Body of Lies*—has Saad handing a phone to a jihadist whom he is trying to persuade to cooperate. On the line is the jihadist's mother. When she hears her son's voice, she starts thanking him and praising him, which confuses him. Finally, she says: "Thank you so much for the television and money you sent me. You're such a good boy." In a moment he understands that Saad has sent his mother these gifts, telling her that they are from her son, and he begins to cry. He realizes that he can cooperate with Saad and reveal the identity of his accomplices and have his mother continue to think he's been helping her, or he can refuse to cooperate and break her heart—as she'll find out he hasn't really sent her money and a television. He decides to cooperate.

Saad and the Jordanians briefed us on the plot, which they were in the early throes of uncovering: a Jordanian cell was planning to attack Western targets in Amman at the stroke of the new millennium. One of the key suspects was Khadr Abu Hoshar. The FBI was being brought in because the targets were also U.S. interests and because U.S. citizens were involved: Khalil Deek and Raed Hijazi.

. . .

Working nonstop with the Jordanians on uncovering the plot, we were quickly impressed with the caliber of their agents. They were expert at monitoring suspects in Jordan and had developed leads tracking the operatives involved from Afghanistan and across the Middle East. We told them what we had learned about al-Qaeda from operations in the UK, Albania, and elsewhere, and they, in turn, taught us a lot about al-Qaeda's worldwide operations. The Jordanians left no stone unturned in protecting their country from potentially devastating attacks.

I was the only FBI agent continuously working in Amman on the millennium threat, as the other agents rotated in and out of the country—usually for two weeks at a time. We worked from the U.S. Embassy and shared space with others in the embassy. Before I arrived I had been warned about the CIA liaison, whom I will call Fred. He had been a translator at the FBI New York office and had applied to be an agent but had been rejected, after which he had joined the CIA. He was said to have held a grudge against all FBI agents after that.

My problems with him started within the first couple of days, after Pat D'Amuro received a phone call from FBI headquarters saying that my reporting of intelligence and Fred's reporting of the same events didn't match up. This meant that Washington didn't know whose information to trust. The further problem was that American citizens were involved, and if intelligence didn't match, we would have difficulty prosecuting the case.

An investigation was done and the Jordanians were consulted, and all concerned were advised that my reporting was correct and Fred's was faulty. Fred's basic failure was that he had a tendency to jump to conclusions without facts. For example, in one memo he reported that the group that had been identified within Jordan was training with the Lebanese terrorist group Hezbollah, which he also took to mean that the Jordanian group was linked to Iran as well, as Iran is Hezbollah's main sponsor. In my reporting I made no mention of Hezbollah and said only that the Jordanians were linked to Palestinian terrorist groups. Fred drew this faulty conclusion because the Jordanian group had trained in the Bekaa Valley: he knew that Hezbollah operated in the Bekaa Valley, so that was his "proof" of Hezbollah's involvement.

Because of his flawed analysis, a total of twelve CIA cables—intelligence reports—had to be withdrawn. If portions of a cable are shown to be inaccurate, the entire cable is viewed as unreliable and suspect. The presumption is that one can't trust the accuracy of the person writing it; therefore, it's rendered useless. Happily, the problems with the CIA did not impair our working relationship with the GID, which carried over into the personal. Our partners regularly took us to dinner and even family events. We enjoyed each other's company and appreciated being able to share skills and impart different insights.

Months after we had left Jordan, Saad and his team came to visit us in New York. John O'Neill and Pat D'Amuro rolled out the red carpet. The operatives who had worked with us in the field honored me by having dinner at my place, a small one-bedroom apartment. It was the evening of the NFL Super Bowl, and it was snowing. My partner Steve Bongardt; Mark Rossini, the FBI agent detailed to the CIA's Counterterrorism Center; Fred; and assistant U.S. attorney Pat Fitzgerald all attended. We ate and joked for hours, and it was a night to remember.

During the Jordanian investigation, the GID gave the chief of operations, Alvin—later the CTC's Sunni extremists chief—a box of evidence to go through. Alvin took it into his office, dumped it in the corner, and never looked through it. Nor did he tell me or my FBI colleagues about it. The division of labor in this instance was that Saad had delegated the task to Alvin, trusting him to go through the box carefully.

A few days later I was chatting with Alvin in his office and noticed the box in the corner. "What's in there?" I asked.

"Oh, it's nothing," he said. "The Jordanians gave us junk to look through." His view was that if it was important, the Jordanians wouldn't have just passed it along to us.

"Let me take a look," I said, and started going through it. It was far from being junk. "Alvin, this is important stuff here," I told him, pulling out one piece as an example. It was a map, with a few locations marked on a route from Israel to Jordan.

Alvin and I returned the evidence to Saad so that his officers could start following the leads. It was winter in Amman, and when we walked into Saad's office he was sitting behind his desk at GID headquarters smoking Mu'assel out of a hookah, the picture of an Ottoman overlord. "You really look like a pasha," I said.

"Ali, come here, come here and give me a hug," he said, beaming.

The CIA became uncomfortable with the relationship we had built with the Jordanians. One day Saad took Pat D'Amuro to a family celebration. The next day, the CIA chief voiced his disapproval to Pat. He was furious that Saad had invited Pat without him. Another evening, two GID officers invited us to an *iftar*, a breaking of the fast during Ramadan; they did not invite the CIA officers. Apparently Fred complained to Alvin, who, without checking with us first on the circumstances, and believing whatever Fred had told him, passed a complaint to one of Saad's deputies: "Your guys"—he named the two GID officers—"are dealing with the FBI without authorization." The deputy reported the complaint to Saad.

Saad called the two officers in. "What are they referring to?" he asked them.

"We invited Ali and the other FBI agent to an *iftar* with us," the senior officer replied. "Apparently the CIA thought we should have asked their permission first."

Saad laughed. "Those guys," he said, waving his hand dismissively, "when will they grow up?"

On November 30, 1999, the GID intercepted a phone call between Abu Hoshar and Abu Zubaydah during which Abu Zubaydah said, "The time for training is over." There was no context. The Jordanians, understandably, didn't want to take chances. They rounded up all the individuals we had been monitoring; sixteen were taken in, including Abu Hoshar. Deek and Abu Zubaydah were in Pakistan, and Hijazi was in Syria, so they were not among those detained.

The Jordanians interrogated the operatives and quickly gained confessions and some additional details of the plot. Hijazi's younger brother and co-conspirator revealed the motto for the millennium attacks: "The season is coming, and bodies will pile up in sacks." The information the operatives gave included the location of hideouts. The GID raided several, recovering detonators (including the walkie-talkies Hijazi had purchased in London), weapons, forged passports, and the CD version of Deek's *Encyclopedia of Jihad*.

Initially we couldn't find any chemicals. The operatives were questioned further, and one explained where a trapdoor for the makeshift basement could be found. His directions led GID officers to the spot. When the hatch was opened, a terrible stench drifted up. A ladder was in place, and one of my GID friends was sent down it. He rushed back up a few seconds later and said that the basement was full of urns of chemicals. The acids were leaking and the floor was covered. The GID official started coughing and shouted, "I've been poisoned. I can't breathe."

He had indeed inhaled dangerous chemicals. Someone quickly brought him some milk and instructed him to drink it, telling him it would clear the poison from his system. After drinking the milk, and to the amusement of those present, he said he felt better.

After the arrest of the operatives in Jordan, and after the detainees had detailed Deek's role in the plot, the Pakistani authorities agreed to arrest him. They raided his center and took him into custody. There he was blindfolded—with blackout goggles put over his eyes and duct tape wrapped around the goggles—making it impossible for him to see. The Pakistanis did not tell him what they would do with him. They contacted the GID, which sent a military plane to Pakistan to pick him up. Once in Jordan, still with no one saying a word to him, and still blindfolded, he was taken to a GID jail and placed before a picture of King Abdullah II, who had assumed power ten months earlier, after the death of his father, King Hussein.

Only then were the goggles and duct tape removed. It took a few seconds for Deek's eyes to adjust to the light. He focused on the picture in front of him. His face dropped. He knew that the game was up and that the plot had failed.

Another graduate of Abu Zubaydah's Khaldan camp was Ahmed Ressam. A wily Algerian, he falsely claimed political asylum in Canada in 1994, using a fake passport and a story about persecution. He supported himself in Canada through crime and dealing in fake passports. While there he met a veteran of Khaldan who recommended that he head there for training.

Before he left for Khaldan in 1998, Ressam acquired a legitimate Canadian passport through a fixer who had stolen a blank baptism certificate from a church. Using the passport, he traveled easily to Pakistan and then to Afghanistan, where he went to Khaldan. There he received basic terrorism training and learned how to build explosives. He got to know Abu Zubaydah, who was impressed with Ressam's ability to procure passports and quickly put him to work. Eventually Ressam returned to Canada, with the intention of planning an attack in the United States with other Algerians he had met at Khaldan. They spent time discussing and planning attacks, with Abu Zubaydah offering advice on launching them. Ressam returned to Canada fully expecting his fellow Algerians to follow him. When they couldn't get the documents to enter the country, he decided to strike without them. He rented a Chrysler sedan, hid explosives in the spare tire, and drove to the car ferry at Victoria, Canada, which was to sail to Port Angeles, Washington. He intended his final destination to be Los Angeles International Airport, which he would bomb on the millennium.

On December 14, I was called into a secure room in the U.S. Embassy in Amman to receive a call from FBI headquarters. They told me that an Algerian named Ahmed Ressam had been arrested trying to bring explosives into the United States from Canada. They didn't yet know exactly what he intended to do, but they suspected a millennium attack.

While Ressam had cleared the Immigration and Naturalization Service (INS) preinspection station in Victoria—his passport was a legitimate Canadian one, so there were no red flags—it was his suspicious activity on the other end that prompted the attention of an astute customs official. Rather than getting off the ferry with his Chrysler when it was his turn, Ressam waited for every one of the other drivers to get their vehicles off first. Apparently he thought that the last car off would receive less attention. The customs officer noticed not only this but the fact that Ressam seemed nervous, and he referred him to an official for a secondary inspection.

When the agent at the secondary inspection began to pat Ressam down—a standard procedure—he panicked and tried to run away. He was quickly stopped, and his car was searched. At first, the customs staff thought that he was connected to drug smuggling, but once the timing devices were found they realized that there was a bigger issue, and the FBI was called in to take over.

I shared this information with the Jordanians. It seemed, from our inquiries, that Ressam might possibly be connected to the other millennium bombers—all or most had trained at Khaldan. Ressam's apprehension underscored the importance of Abu Zubaydah's camp and provided a warning that terrorists were plotting to strike not only Jordan but elsewhere.

Having learned that Deek and Abu Zubaydah worked closely with the UK-based operative Mozzam Begg to raise funds, we passed this information on to our friends in SO13 and MI5. The British authorities were already aware of Begg's activities and his connections to suspected terrorists in Pakistan and Afghanistan.

I worked in both Jordan and the UK during this period. One morning in 2000, while I was in England working with SO13 on a separate investigation, a clearly surprised Alan Fry and John Bunn told me that MI5 and SO12 (the intelligence counterpart to SO13) had raided al-Ansar, a bookstore operated by Begg, and Begg's home in Birmingham. They had arrested him. Because SO13 hadn't spent time building a case against him, however, after a preliminary interview he was released—and, like Liby in Manchester, escaped the country. We only caught Begg years later in Pakistan, after 9/11.

Bassam Kanj was born in Lebanon in 1965. In 1984 he moved to the United States and married an American woman, becoming a naturalized U.S. citizen. He then followed a path that was becoming familiar to us: fighting the Soviets in Afghanistan, he returned to the United

States when the war ended and in subsequent years regularly traveled back to Afghanistan to train at Khaldan.

It was under Abu Zubaydah that he picked up the alias Abu A'isha and met Raed Hijazi, Khalil Deek, and others with U.S. citizenship who frequented the master terrorist facilitator's camp. In 1995 Kanj moved to Boston and started driving a cab for the same company as Hijazi. The two were good friends. They had roomed together before Kanj was married and continued to share quarters when Kanj's wife was away. In 1998 Kanj left the United States and went to Lebanon, where he joined a radical group that called itself Takfir wal-Hijra.

On New Year's Eve 1999, Kanj led a group of around 150 Sunni terrorists to the Dinnieh mountain region in northern Lebanon. The group was predominantly Palestinians and Syrians; Kanj had met many of them in training camps in Afghanistan. Their stated aim was to impose Sharia law in Lebanon.

They first ambushed an army unit in the village of Assoun, killing a few soldiers and kidnapping a commanding officer. When the Lebanese army sent in troops, the terrorists went on a rampage and for four days battled the troops, killing anyone who got in their way. The slaughter did nothing to further the terrorists' singleminded devotion to their goal of imposing Sharia law. Another in the millennium series of plots was disrupted.

With Abu Hoshar, Deek, and the others in custody in Amman—and the group's explosive materials confiscated—we had successfully thwarted the plot in Jordan. Those who were jailed provided significant information about the terrorist network. The only loose ends we knew about were Hijazi, who was still on the run—when we rounded up the suspects, he had been traveling back from Pakistan, and was somewhere in Syria, and so he never returned to Jordan—and Abu Zubaydah, who was somewhere in Afghanistan or Pakistan.

Until the millennium dawned, however, we obviously wouldn't know for certain whether we had apprehended everyone. I stayed in Jordan, and on New Year's Eve I went with Stephen Gaudin (then rotating in the country) to Abdin Circle, the main square in Amman:

the Jordanian equivalent of Times Square. We told the New York FBI office we'd update them on what did or didn't occur.

As the clock struck midnight, we heard small explosions and saw people running in every direction. We ran behind a parked car to take cover. What had we missed?

I asked people in Arabic what was happening. It turned out that a stage holding fireworks had collapsed, sending them shooting into the crowd. Stephen and I looked at each other with relief and started laughing.

I called the New York FBI office from my phone and was put through to John O'Neill in the JTTF command center in New York. "Jordan's okay. Everything is good," I told him.

"Happy New Year," he said. "You guys did a great job."

I put my cell phone back in my jacket and turned around to speak to Stephen, who had been standing next to me, but he wasn't there. Then I saw him in the distance at an ATM. Like everyone, he had been reading stories of accounts getting messed up at the millennium— switching from 1999 to 2000 was said to be hard for bank computers— so he wanted to check that his money was safe.

He withdrew some cash, saw that his account was untouched, and walked back to me smiling and waving his Jordanian banknotes.

PART 3

USS *COLE*

8

A Naval Destroyer in Yemen?

The terrorists sitting in Bayt Habra, a safe house in Sanaa, nodded in agreement. They wouldn't ask bin Laden for his approval of their operation. It was a tough decision for them, but they felt that it was the right one. While they revered their emir, they knew that the al-Qaeda leader felt a close personal connection to Yemen: his father had been born there, and one of his wives was a Yemeni. The operatives doubted that he could bless an operation against the Yemeni government. But they had to act; their friend Abul al-Hasan al-Mihdhar would soon be executed. On May 5 he had been sentenced to death in a Yemeni court. What they had in mind was no less than Mihdhar's rescue from jail. To fund the operation, they planned a series of car thefts. It was May 1999.

On December 28, 1998, Mihdhar's group, the Islamic Army of Aden-Abyan, had kidnapped sixteen Western hostages (twelve Britons, two Americans, and two Australians) who were touring Yemen. The group had announced that they would release the hostages only if the Yemeni government released nine Islamists being held in jail and if international sanctions on Iraq were lifted. The Yemeni government had refused to accept their demands and had launched a rescue operation the next day.

When the kidnappers saw Yemeni soldiers approaching, they took cover behind the hostages and started firing at the soldiers. During an intense firefight, two kidnappers and four hostages—three Britons and one Australian—were killed. The Yemenis arrested the remaining kidnappers and rounded up any members of the group they could find. Mihdhar himself was captured and brought before a judge, who sentenced him to death. His friends and fellow terrorists in Yemen, among them many al-Qaeda members, resolved to rescue him—they just wouldn't tell bin Laden.

To fund the rescue operation, Mihdhar's supporters had come up with the car theft plan. They would steal and then sell cars from an American rental company in Yemen. With the proceeds, they would buy weapons and vehicles. Before they got very far, the Yemeni authorities learned of the plot and made numerous arrests. The Yemeni Criminal Investigative Division (CID) raided the al-Qaeda safe house in Sanaa after learning that al-Qaeda members were involved.

One of the al-Qaeda terrorists staying in the safe house at the time of the raid was Abu Jandal. He had recently returned to Yemen to get married—at least that's what he'd told bin Laden. He confided to friends that finding a bride wasn't the only reason he had left Afghanistan. He was unhappy with bin Laden's pledging *bayat* to Mullah Omar, the leader of the Taliban, and with bin Laden's endorsement of the honorific bestowed upon Mullah Omar in 1996 following the Cloak of the Prophet spectacle: Amir al-Mu'minin. Abu Jandal felt that al-Qaeda's aligning itself with the Taliban was a distraction from the organization's broader goals. It was not what he had signed up for.

Like many operatives, he also wasn't happy that Egyptians were running al-Qaeda. Traditionally, Arabs from the Persian Gulf are accustomed to having Egyptians work for them. In al-Qaeda Egyptians took many of the top positions: they headed most of the training camps and were in other positions of power as well, and they tended to order the Gulf Arabs around. Of the nine members of the *shura* council, seven were Egyptian. And of the heads of al-Qaeda's various committees, other than bin Laden himself and Abu Hafs al-Mauritani, all were Egyptians. The division extended to recreation: when al-Qaeda members played soccer on Fridays, the teams were usually Egyptians versus Saudis and Yemenis (and everyone else).

Bin Laden understood the resentment, but there was little he could do. Part of the problem was that Egyptians joined al-Qaeda permanently, while those from the Gulf states, especially Saudis, fought for a couple of months and then returned home. Bin Laden called it "vacation jihad," and jihadi strategist Abu Musab al-Suri often joked that the Gulf Arabs came for a few months to "cleanse themselves after a week of spending time with whores in Bangkok."

When Abu Jandal told bin Laden that he was returning to Yemen to find a wife, he also told him that he wanted to settle down and that this meant that he could no longer serve him. The al-Qaeda leader seemed unconcerned and gave Abu Jandal $2,500 in cash as a wedding present, telling him to "go and think about it after you are married." Bin Laden appeared confident that Abu Jandal's absence would not be permanent.

Sometime after Abu Jandal's departure for Yemen, bin Laden outlined a plan to his driver, Salim Hamdan: he and Abu Jandal should marry two sisters, as they were two of his most trusted followers and he wanted to bind them in this way. Hamdan did exactly as he was asked. Abu Jandal's growing misgivings with the direction al-Qaeda was taking were laid aside, and ultimately the two married sisters.

The Yemeni authorities who had raided Bayt Habra questioned Abu Jandal for an hour and a half, concluded that he was not part of the plot, and released him. Four hours later he bumped into another al-Qaeda operative, Ibrahim al-Thawer, alias Nibras (later to become one of the *Cole* suicide bombers), who warned him that the Yemeni police were searching for him again to ask more questions. Abu Jandal wasn't going to stay around and see what they wanted. Telling himself that "there is no one for you but the sheikh"—bin Laden—he fled to Afghanistan. Other al-Qaeda members who hadn't been picked up also left the country.

Bin Laden, pleased to have his trusted bodyguard back, gave Abu Jandal a warm welcome. When Abu Jandal told him about the raid, bin Laden asked worriedly: "Was it against us specifically or did someone do something wrong?" Abu Jandal outlined the full sequence of events, and told the al-Qaeda leader that the arrests seemed to have been made in response to the car thefts, not because the Yemenis were cracking down on al-Qaeda. "That is good to hear," bin Laden said, and a look of calm relief passed over his face as he invoked the president of Yemen: "The ship of Ali Abdullah Saleh is the only ship we have."

Mihdhar was executed in front of officials from the Yemeni prosecutor's office and the interior ministry on October 7, 1999. The al-Qaeda members who were arrested and found to be part of the plot were given jail sentences. As their weeks in jail progressed, their thinking about the Yemeni state changed. So, too, did the thinking of their fellow al-Qaeda comrades living in Yemen who regularly visited them. Until then al-Qaeda members had viewed the Yemeni state as a friend who sometimes erred. They therefore mostly avoided operations in the country. This episode ended that view, and now they saw the Yemeni state as an accomplice of the West. Other actions by the Yemenis around this time helped to poison the relationship, among them the arrest and incarceration of Khallad (Walid bin Attash), apparently in a case of mistaken identity.

One of the men most deeply affected by his time in jail was Hassan al-Khamiri, who spent nine months behind bars. Khamiri was older than most other al-Qaeda members and was "considered like a father by all the brothers," in the words of Abu Jandal. He returned to Afghanistan as soon as he was released, and his al-Qaeda brothers saw a changed man. He had become bitter and had developed a deep loathing for the Yemeni government. He already hated the United States: the emir of an al-Qaeda training camp in Afghanistan, he had lost a few of his men when the camp was bombed by the Americans in retaliation for the 1998 East African embassy attacks.

Khamiri and other al-Qaeda members tried to pressure bin Laden into launching a big operation in Yemen as punishment for their incarceration. "The brothers in Yemen are frustrated and need to do something. If you don't authorize it, they'll do it alone," Khamiri warned bin Laden.

"Have the brothers be patient," bin Laden replied. "An operation in Yemen is coming, and you will be involved. You need to be patient and discreet."

Khamiri returned to Yemen to help plan the operation and regularly visited the operatives who were still in jail. He spent a good deal of time speaking to Khallad, and to Khallad and Muhannad bin Attash's younger brother Abdul Aziz bin Attash (al-Bara). Although al-Bara's sentence was up, because of his family's close ties to bin Laden, the Yemenis continued to hold him, citing national security reasons. They thought that he could be a future bargaining chip with bin Laden. "Don't worry," Khamiri told al-Bara, "the sheikh understands our concerns. Some kind of action is coming."

In the summer of 2000 Khamiri sent al-Bara a letter saying that bin Laden and Saif al-Adel had asked him to no longer visit him and their other al-Qaeda brothers in prison; he had to remove himself from "suspicious activities." Khamiri concluded, "Soon you will hear the good news." It was a clear message that he would be involved in an operation.

Al-Bara smiled and burned the letter—while sitting in his Yemeni prison cell.

October 12, 2000. The darkness of the night was only beginning to retreat as I drove my car from my apartment in Brooklyn to the FBI offices in Manhattan. It was around 6:00 AM, and it wasn't unusual for me to be awake and on my way to the office at that early hour. The hours before daybreak were in many ways my favorite part of the day. New York was silent and peaceful, traffic and honking almost nonexistent. Not only did the quiet remind me, somehow, of my years in rural Pennsylvania, but it also gave me time to think clearly and without interruption before things started getting busy.

I was midway through my drive, deep in thought on a case I was working on—and almost exactly in the middle of the Brooklyn Bridge—when my cell phone rang. It startled me. A call at this hour meant that either something was wrong or a friend in the Middle East had forgotten the time difference. Having recently worked in Jordan to thwart the millennium attacks, I half-expected phone calls at early hours from the Middle East. But it wasn't someone from Jordan on the phone; it was Kevin Cruise, supervisor of the I-45 squad, dedicated to the investigation into the East African embassy bombings.

"Did you hear what happened?" Kevin asked, skipping a hello and other niceties.

"I heard on NPR earlier," I began cautiously. "Israel bombed Arafat's headquarters. We probably need to take precautions . . ." As the words came out, I knew something else must have happened. That alone wouldn't warrant a 6:00 AM call.

"Not that," he interrupted, not allowing me to finish my sentence. "A navy ship in Yemen was bombed. There are a lot of casualties, and some sailors are missing."

"Yemen?" I asked. "Why on earth do we have a navy ship in Yemen?"

Yemen was well known in the intelligence community to be full of radical Islamists, including al-Qaeda members. Radical Islamist fighters developed a close relationship with the Yemeni authorities during the country's civil war, when President Ali Abdullah Saleh reportedly used Arab mujahideen veterans of the Afghan-Soviet war to help him lead the North to defeat the socialist South. In return for the mujahideen's help, the government turned a blind eye to radical Islamist activities in the country as long as they weren't directed against the government or didn't harm the country's interests.

As a result al-Qaeda sympathizers could be found throughout Yemeni institutions, including in the intelligence services. Some would help terrorists obtain visas and fraudulent documents, or tip them off when foreign governments were looking for them. Many non-Yemenis involved in the 1998 East African embassy bombings, for example, used fraudulent Yemeni passports to hide their real identities.

Yemen is a convenient place for a terrorist base, as it has a weak central government and tribes that in many ways operate as autonomous minigovernments. Some tribes are sympathetic to extremists, and others are willing to aid terrorists for reasons ranging from monetary reward to help in battles with rival tribes. The weak central government also means that the country's borders are largely unsecured, allowing terrorists to enter and leave easily. To top it off, the country has a thriving arms market, giving terrorists access to the weapons and explosives they need.

"We're looking into that," Kevin replied to my question. "Just get in as fast as you can." In situations like this, Kevin was curt and to the point. A former military man, he was efficient in emergency situations. He was a devout Catholic, a family man, and someone committed to the truth. I remember him telling me after 9/11, when the bureau was being incorrectly blamed for not stopping the attacks (before the 9/11 Commission told the real story), that he felt that people in church were looking at him differently. It saddened him that the American people were being misled and that the FBI's reputation was being smeared.

"I'm on my way," I told Kevin. Why on earth do we have a navy ship in Yemen? I said out loud to myself after hanging up. The question kept repeating itself in my mind as I hurried toward the office.

Ten minutes later I pulled up outside the NYO. I parked my car across the street in what was a no-parking zone, not wanting to waste the time looking for a spot and for once not caring whether I'd get a ticket.

Details of the attack were filtering in: at 11:22 AM Yemen time, the USS *Cole*, a navy destroyer weighing 8,300 tons and carrying almost 300 sailors, was making a routine fueling stop in the Port of Aden. Suicide bombers pulled alongside the destroyer in a small boat and blew themselves up. At this point 12 sailors were confirmed dead and many more were reported injured. News of deaths and casualties was still coming in, and the numbers were expected to rise.

Details of the attack were first sent in by Col. Robert Newman, a military attaché based in Sanaa. He saw and felt the explosion firsthand and alerted the embassy. The explosion was so powerful, Newman later told me, that it was heard as far as two miles away. The first ship on the scene to provide aid to the *Cole* was the British Royal Navy's HMS

Marlborough, which was in the vicinity. Sailors with the gravest injuries were flown to a French military hospital in Djibouti before being transferred to a U.S. hospital in Germany. Rescuers and crew members focused on trying to stop the *Cole* from sinking, a very real danger.

Marines from the Interim Marine Corps Security Force, based in nearby Bahrain, arrived soon after to secure the area around the ship. They didn't know if a second attack was planned and were taking no chances. They were followed by a U.S Marine platoon, which helped secure the *Cole* itself. The marines also secured a nearby hotel, the Mövenpick, where U.S. troops, investigators, diplomats, and the press would be staying when they arrived.

At the office I found the answer to the question I had been asking myself on my way in: the *Cole* needed to refuel in Aden because it was making a 3,300-mile transit from the Mediterranean, where it had last refueled.

Djibouti, on the Horn of Africa, had been used for several years as the refueling port for U.S. vessels, but in January 1999 it was dropped in favor of Aden. The Eritrea-Ethiopia War (1998–2000) had made Djibouti less appealing to the United States, although in intelligence reports it was never ranked as being as dangerous as Aden. The real reason for the switch was that while Yemen had supported Saddam Hussein in the first Gulf War, the Clinton administration had launched a major diplomatic initiative aiming to bring Yemen into the U.S. orbit. Trusting Yemen with hosting U.S. ships, along with the economic benefits that hosting provides, was part of that effort. The State Department and its country team in Yemen concurred that the security situation in Aden was acceptable.

While the diplomatic corps supported the move, security agencies warned against it. An intelligence report by the Naval Criminal Investigative Service's Multiple Threat Alert Center (MTAC) warned that security in Aden was tenuous and that the central government had little or no control. Nor would this be the first time that radical jihadi terrorists were responsible for plotting an attack against a U.S. target. In December 1992, during the Yemeni Civil War, when Ali Abdullah Saleh was using Islamic militants to help the North defeat the South, terrorists bombed the Gold Mohur Hotel, aiming to hit U.S. Marines who were en route to Somalia to take part in Operation Restore Hope. The bombs missed their intended mark (the marines had already left) but killed a Yemeni citizen and an Austrian tourist.

All U.S. ships, before they visit a foreign port, are required to file a force-protection plan. The *Cole*'s plan—approved by higher U.S. military authorities—was that it would operate under threat or force condition "bravo," which is a heightened state of readiness against potential attack. (The lesser condition is alpha; beyond bravo is charlie; delta signifies the most critical state.) Under bravo, security teams on deck are armed with shotguns and other small arms and looking for threats.

My later review indicated that the sailors and the captain of the USS *Cole* did everything they could under the circumstances. The fact that the *Cole* was a sitting duck and identified as such by the terrorists was the fault of those responsible for designating Aden a safe port. At such close quarters, it would be next to impossible for sailors on a destroyer to ascertain in a minute or two whether a small boat pulling alongside was a friend or an enemy.

Bob McFadden, the NCIS special agent with whom I later partnered in the *Cole* investigation, told me when we first met: "I've been coming here since 1997 and have a good sense of the atmosphere of Aden and the harbor, and when a ship pulls in there's a lot of bustling activity. Small boats that service navy vessels routinely pull up to and away from the ship. It's inconceivable that a nineteen-year-old sailor with a twelve-gauge shotgun would be able to distinguish friend from foe under those circumstances."

JTTF supervisors gathered in Pat D'Amuro's office in New York to discuss the bombing, although Pat himself was out of the office at firearms training. (His was the most spacious office for a meeting of this kind.) Senior officials from FBI headquarters in Washington, DC, participated via speakerphone, and the JTTF supervisors asked me to join them in the room.

A week earlier I had written a memo suggesting that an al-Qaeda attack was imminent. It was based on a video bin Laden had just released, in which the al-Qaeda leader, wearing a *jambiya* (a traditional Yemeni dagger) and standing in front of a map of the Near and Middle East, issued threats against America. John O'Neill had distributed that memo across the law enforcement and intelligence community. Because of the memo, and because of the previous al-Qaeda and EIJ-related cases I had been involved in (such as the East African embassy bombings, Operation Challenge in the UK, the millennium plot in Jordan, and operations in Albania) that had direct links to Yemen, the JTTF supervisors asked me to brief everyone on the history of Yemen, terrorism in Yemen, and who was likely responsible. This last point was especially relevant because of the bureau's office of origin system: if al-Qaeda were behind the bombing of the *Cole*, the NYO would be charge of the investigation.

The Washington field office representatives on the call made the case that this wasn't an al-Qaeda plot. Their view was that the Islamic Army of Aden-Abyan, Mihdhar's group—still operational after his death—was behind the attack. I argued that it was more likely that al-Qaeda was behind the incident, as an attack of that magnitude required planning, funds, and greater operational capability than a local terrorist group would have. Bin Laden's video threat strengthened this view.

After hearing both arguments, FBI director Louis Freeh decided that agents from the two offices should go to Yemen until we found out who was behind the attack. Having to replace a WFO team with a NYO team, or the reverse, would waste the precious first weeks after an attack, when evidence is still on the ground and witnesses' memories are fresh.

The next decision to make was who would represent the NYO. Pat Fitzgerald and another assistant U.S. attorney from the Southern District of New York, David Kelley, were consulted. They would be handling any prosecutions for the bombing, and they said that they wanted me. I had worked closely with both men on the 1998 East African embassy bombings, the millennium attacks in Jordan, and other cases. I was happy to be working alongside them again.

In terrorism prosecutions it's necessary to have a case agent who is an expert in the organizations involved and who understands what is legally required to prosecute the culprits. Half the battle is determining who is responsible; the second half is capturing them and ensuring they're prosecuted. With Fitzy's much-vaunted memory came a dedication that put work before everything. He had a stove in his apartment in New York that wasn't hooked up for ten years. When Heather, my girlfriend, joked with him about it, he said: "I don't like to rush things." He is the son of a doorman and went to school on a scholarship.

Kelley is a Renaissance man: a great lawyer and prosecutor, a sharp-witted intellectual, a volunteer professor at a law school, an NFL referee, and an athlete who keeps himself in top shape. I remember once checking security with John O'Neill on the roof of our hotel in Aden. We spotted Kelley swimming solitary laps. Everyone else was too worried about personal safety to use the pool. David wasn't going to let the terrorists ruin his regimen. Instead of going to a gym, he ran up and down the hotel stairs. Whatever he does, he works hard to be the best at it. He's also a pretty funny guy. When he first met Heather, he asked her what she did and she told him, "Social work. I work with children with challenges." David said, "So that's how you met him," pointing at me.

Normally big teams of agents are sent to investigate an attack of the magnitude of the USS *Cole* bombing, but I was told that I could pick only three people from the New York office to go with me initially; the U.S. ambassador to Yemen, Barbara K. Bodine, was limiting the number of country clearances she was approving. (Unless the United States is at war, the State Department can limit the number of U.S. personnel allowed into a foreign country.) My superiors assured me that more would be allowed soon, but that in the meantime we should go ahead and start investigating.

I picked three colleagues from my I-49 squad: Steve Bongardt, George Crouch, and an NYPD detective stationed with the JTTF, Tom Ward. Steve was an obvious choice, as he was my partner on most of my cases at the time, and we worked well together. We were also close friends and spent a lot of our free time together, even double-dating. It is common for agents to spend their free time with other agents. You feel a kinship, having shared many of the same life-and-death experiences, but beyond that, because of the classified nature of the job, they're the only people you can discuss your work with outside the office.

Steve is a former navy pilot, and, as we'd be working with the navy on the investigation, this background would be useful. He has that Top Gun mentality of navy pilots, which allows him to think outside the box and take on issues that others might be too timid to touch. This attitude later placed Steve at the forefront of the FBI's pre-9/11 battle to break down the lack of intelligence sharing between the FBI and the CIA. He would not just go along with restrictions that damaged national security. It was in his nature to fight back. This showed itself on every level: despite having pulled a muscle in his back a week before the departure for Yemen, which made walking and sitting difficult, he refused to stay home.

George Crouch is a first-class investigator and has a great sense of humor. When working overseas on operations in hostile countries, you work, eat, and sleep in close proximity to your colleagues. You're with them twenty-four hours a day, for months on end. A big consideration when choosing a team is who you'll get along with. If the people don't get along, it can harm an investigation. George is a former marine captain (he was in the Judge Advocate General's Corps), and so he, too, would know how to work with the navy. The most important things in George's life are his wife, Laura, and his family, and I've always had a special respect for him. He and Laura became close friends of Heather's and mine.

Tom was assigned from the New York City Police Department to the JTTF; he is street-smart, with lots of investigative skills, and he pays close attention to detail. I never saw non-FBI members on the JTTF as outsiders—I include everyone from NYPD to CIA officials—so I didn't think twice about taking Tom.

We only had a few hours before we had to leave for Yemen, and that time would be spent at the office, planning and preparing for the investigation. There was no time to go back home and pack for the trip, so I'd have to travel in what I was wearing and get anything I needed from stores near the FBI's office or in Yemen. The command center was in full crisis mode: analysts were collecting data; agents were digging up old files on Yemen; allied intelligence services around the world were exchanging information; and senior officials were gathered on the main platform, discussing the case. As I finished preparing, I remembered that I had a date with Heather that evening. I tried calling her to tell her I'd have to rearrange, but I couldn't reach her; she was at school, teaching a class. I left it to the ASAC's secretary to tell her that not only did I have to cancel the date, but I didn't know when I'd return.

An NYPD detective stationed with the JTTF drove Steve, George, Tom, and me to Andrews Air Force Base, and we met the team from the WFO there. A hostage rescue team (HRT)—an elite FBI SWAT team—came as well to provide protection. We couldn't leave immediately, however, as we had to wait a couple of hours for our country clearances to be approved by Ambassador Bodine before we could take off. As we waited, news came through that there had been another terrorist attack in Yemen: a grenade had been thrown at the British embassy in Sanaa, blowing up one of its electric generators.

Once the clearances came we boarded a military cargo plane loaded with vehicles, weapons, and equipment. There were no seats, only netting on the side that we could rest on. The mood on the flight was anxious, as the FBI had no operational relationship with the Yemenis and we really didn't know if we'd be welcomed or attacked. It was also possible that al-Qaeda might be stronger in Yemen than we thought, and that the USS *Cole* attack was a ploy to trap more agents in Yemen and then kill the new arrivals—us. In our investigation into the East African embassy bombings, we learned from interrogating one al-Qaeda member that this was a not uncommon maneuver.

We were also aware of problems that Yemeni officials had with the United States. Not long before the attack, Yemeni president Ali Abdullah Saleh had said that if he shared a border with Israel, he would engage in jihad against the country because of the ongoing Arab-Israeli conflict. He went on to lambaste the United States for supporting Israel—so it didn't seem that we were heading into friendly territory. That's why we had the HRT with us: they would provide extra firepower if something went wrong. With Somalia in the back of our minds—the image, from

1993, of U.S. soldiers overwhelmed by hostile fighters in Mogadishu and dragged through the streets and killed—we were determined not to go down without a fight if something happened.

No one was in the mood to talk much on the plane. I tried sleeping, but there was too much going through my head, so I reviewed the information we had on Yemen.

More than twenty hours later, after a refueling stop in Germany, our plane descended in Yemen. Looking at the country for the first time out of the plane window, I saw that it was even more sparsely populated than I had imagined. As we taxied on the runway and slowed down to a stop, we saw that we were surrounded by what appeared to be Yemeni Special Forces. Soldiers wearing camouflage uniforms had trained their AK-47s on us. Alongside them were military vehicles and jeeps with their machine guns pointed at us.

At first no one moved. We had no idea what was happening and didn't want to trigger any reaction. Eventually, after what may have been a very long fifteen minutes, the U.S. defense attaché stationed in the country, Colonel Newman, came aboard. "What the hell is going on?" someone demanded. He said that he was unsure but that they were "working on it." In the meantime, he said, the Yemenis told him that we should put all our weapons in a big duffel bag and give it to them.

That didn't sound right. Walking unarmed into a country where U.S. sailors had just been killed was not something we were prepared to do, especially given the "welcome" we appeared to be receiving. The HRT bluntly refused. Meanwhile, I told George and Steve that I was going to try to find out what was going on. From the open door of the plane I picked out the Yemeni official who appeared to be in charge. Although armed, he was dressed in civilian clothes and was carrying a walkie-talkie, and he appeared to be issuing orders to the soldiers.

I stepped off the plane and walked toward him. I was still wearing my New York fall clothes, and it was like walking into a sauna. Sweat trickled down my forehead. "As-Salāmu `Alaykum," I said.

"Wa `Alaykum as-Salām," he replied.

"It's hot. Are you thirsty?" I asked, continuing in Arabic and pausing to wipe some of the sweat off my brow. His face registered surprise, and he looked me up and down.

"Yes," he said slowly, nodding at the same time.

"I have some bottles of water for you and your soldiers," I said, waving to George to bring them down to me from the plane. I handed him the bottles.

"Is this American water?" he asked.

"Yes." Apparently American bottled water is a luxury in Yemen. The official distributed the bottles. Some soldiers drank the water, while others instead put it in their bags, perhaps to take it home to show their families.

That broke the tension, and a few Yemeni soldiers smiled. Some even said "thank you" in English.

I asked the Yemeni: "What's going on? Why have you surrounded our plane?"

"Don't worry, it's only for your protection."

"We appreciate that," I told him, "but if someone is going to attack us, they will attack from outside, so your weapons need to face outward, not at us."

"No, no," he replied, "this is the best way."

"Well, at least lower the weapons," I said, "because otherwise an accident is going to happen and none of us wants that." He ordered the soldiers to lower their weapons.

The Aden airport was old and basic, with just a single runway, two halls (one for regular passengers and one with chairs and couches for "VIP" passengers), and a few offices for administrative staff and security officials. We had equipment, supplies, and vehicles that we wanted to unload from the plane; the Yemenis, at the same time, wanted to inspect and approve everything that came off. They wrote down every detail, right down to the serial numbers of our weapons. We were stiff and exhausted from the long and uncomfortable flight and had little patience for all this red tape.

The airport was also swarming with Yemeni officials: all of the different national and local law enforcement, intelligence, and military agencies were represented. There were airport security personnel; the military; the ministry of the interior's internal security force; the intelligence service, called the Political Security Organization (PSO); the regular police; and Aden security services. It appeared that none had ultimate jurisdiction and that all intended to monitor us.

Overlapping jurisdictions and blurred boundaries between security agencies are deliberate in some countries. Having one agency means that there's a potential power base that may dominate the country. The presence of many jurisdictions, however, comes with its own problems: agencies spend their time fighting turf wars with each other, with the president of the country serving as the arbitrator. While such a situation may prevent one group from launching a coup, it doesn't help outsiders trying to work with the different agencies. Every time we needed to do something in the airport we needed to coordinate it separately with each of them.

I found myself acting as the mediator between our side and the Yemenis and managed to establish rapport with them. I told them that we would give them any information they wanted and that we had nothing to hide. We were simply trying to investigate what had happened to our ship and wanted to work with them in the investigation. They appreciated this straightforwardness and the fact that we wanted to work with them. They also liked that I spoke their language.

I was told that my last name, Soufan, was a "Sada" name in Yemen. *Sada* is the plural of *sayyid*, which means "prestigious" and connotes social status. According to the Yemenis, Soufan is the family name of people descended from the Prophet. Some government ministers apparently also had the name, and the Yemenis at the airport eagerly inquired whether my family was from Yemen. "Perhaps a long time ago," I answered, wishing neither to lie nor surrender a useful advantage. In tight situations people often want to find someone they can relate to, and I was happy to be that person for the Yemenis.

I also showed the Yemenis that I understood their perspective and told them that I knew that they had to square the image of American officials "invading" their country with jeeps and weapons with their local population, many of whom were very anti-American. They told me that earlier in the day marines had set up a base camp and (as is their custom) planted an American flag on the ground, which had upset the locals.

I later found out from a Yemeni friend that the harsh treatment we received when we first landed was due partly to a humiliation the Yemenis had suffered the day before. According to the Yemenis, when the marines' Fleet Antiterrorism Security Team (FAST) landed hours after the attack, the Yemenis surrounded their plane, as had happened with us. The marines exited the plane in their Humvees and in a quick projection of force surrounded the Yemenis and took over the airport— without even firing a shot. It was an embarrassment for the Yemenis to have had their own airport seized so quickly.

Many of the Yemenis I dealt with sympathized with our loss. Especially among the law enforcement and intelligence community, there were those who shared our desire to seek justice for the murdered sailors. Many of the officials and officers I met at the airport—from the ministry of the interior, from state security—remained friends during my time in Aden. Whenever a U.S. plane landed in Aden, if I was free, I went with either the military attaché or a State Department representative to help smooth the entry. Many of the friends I made in Yemen then I still consider my friends today.

While I was dealing with the red tape, the HRT remained by the plane and monitored our gear to make sure that things weren't being tampered with or taken. Everyone else sat on the side in the main terminal waiting for our entry to be sorted out. It took a couple of hours of sometimes tense negotiation to determine what we could and couldn't take off the plane. The Yemenis insisted that we could not take certain vehicles and weapons. We didn't really have a choice but to comply: it was their country, and the State Department officials at the airport said that we had to accept the Yemenis' restrictions.

Our long guns had to be left on the plane, too, the State Department representatives at the airport told us. These M-4 machine guns and shotguns weren't the weapons we routinely carried—we used handguns for that purpose—but we'd planned to keep them in the car in case we needed them. We tried negotiating but were told that Ambassador Bodine had insisted we didn't need them. "The ambassador said that the Yemenis will protect you," one State Department representative offered unconvincingly. We were unhappy, but, again, we didn't have a choice. Because we needed to leave many things behind, some HRT squad members stayed behind as well to guard the plane and our equipment until it could return to the United States.

When we were finally ready to leave the airport, the State Department arranged pickup trucks for our luggage and equipment and a bus for us. We loaded up, and Yemeni soldiers climbed on top of the trucks to guard them. A convoy of Yemeni Special Forces in 4x4 jeeps with Dushkas—12.7 mm submachine guns—pulled up and said they would ride alongside us. The Yemenis told us to get into the bus and the convoy would head to the Mövenpick.

At this point I was exhausted. I was also hot, and the air-conditioned bus was appealing. But at the same time I didn't want to get in it because if any problems arose, I wanted to be available to work with the Yemenis. I assumed that they would appreciate my gesture of riding with them rather than in the bus. As everyone else was filing into the bus, I started climbing to the top of one of pickup trucks. The soldiers were in mid-conversation when my head came up over the side. "You're meant to be in the bus," one told me flatly.

"No, I'm not," I replied. "I'll be riding on top with you." I said it with certainty, and that apparently convinced them not to argue. They shrugged their shoulders and resumed talking to each other.

A few seconds later I heard someone else climbing up to the top of the truck. It was George. He had seen me and didn't want me to be alone. The Yemenis glanced at him, looked at me, and turned back to talk to each other.

With everyone else inside the buses and our equipment in the trucks, the convoy set off. I have always disliked traveling in official convoys in foreign countries. My reaction is the same whether I'm given a bullet-proof limousine with a police escort or a military convoy. While some may enjoy the luxury and sense of importance convoys provide, the attention always makes me feel unsafe, because it lets potential attackers know exactly where I am. Often when I traveled to foreign countries, I asked local authorities to provide a discreet pickup rather than lights and sirens.

As the convoy moved along, I focused on the other cars on the road. The road out of the airport passed a large construction site where a new airport was being built. George and I both did a doubletake when we saw the giant billboard that had been erected next to the site. It read: "Binladin."

The sign, we realized, referred to the company that was building the new airport—the Saudi Binladin Group, one of the biggest construction companies in the Middle East. But to George and me, it was as if we were being told who was behind the attack and who we were looking for.

As a safety precaution, we moved at the speed of the other traffic, and the Yemenis tried hard to ensure that we never had to stop. The jeeps traveling ahead of us cleared the road. For most of the journey the system worked, and we passed through intersections and roundabouts without slowing down. But as we got closer to the Mövenpick, we encountered heavy traffic at one roundabout and the jeeps were unable to clear the road in time. As we slowed, one of the soldiers on our pickup truck started furiously signaling with his fingers at cars. George's face registered shock. "I can't believe what he's doing," he said to me. At first I didn't understand George's complaint. A couple of seconds later it dawned on me. In the Middle East the signal to slow down involves putting the tips of your fingers together. I was familiar with it from my childhood in Lebanon. But in the United States that gesture could easily be mistaken for a rude one.

The Mövenpick was ringed with Yemeni security officials who checked the credentials of everyone entering. U.S. Marines were stationed on the roof and inside the hotel. While it was comforting to see that the hotel was protected, it also reminded us that we were entering hostile territory and that our lives were under threat.

9

The Hall of Death

A few hours after arriving in Yemen we went to visit the *Cole*, and as we approached the destroyer, our eyes couldn't miss the gaping hole in its port side. It reminded me of a wounded lion I'd seen on the National Geographic Channel: its majesty was still apparent, but the wound, and the pain, were clearly deep. It was impossible not to feel overcome by sadness. We were all silent as we pulled alongside.

The feeling got even worse once we climbed on board. The ship had the stench of death. Bodies draped in American flags were lying on the main deck. Sailors walked around with blank and sullen faces, and they all had bags under their eyes. They were working day and night to save the ship. Many had cuts and bruises on their bodies, and their eyes told of immeasurable sorrow. They still hadn't come to terms with what had happened. Some never would. It was heartbreaking.

We walked down to see the blast area. Blood was splattered across the floor. Bodies lay twisted and trapped in the metal. NCIS and FBI technicians were carefully trying to untangle them while keeping a lookout for pieces of evidence. We realized that this was an exceptionally tough job psychologically for crew members, and since the FBI and

NCIS had the apparatus, we did as much as we could. Agents collected body parts from the floor.

Forensic experts were examining the wreckage and evidence. I watched one trying to determine whether the blackened object he was holding was part of a person, the ship, or from the suicide bombers and their boat. Divers searched the surrounding harbor waters. The hall outside the blast area, where bodies were first placed, was unofficially known as the "hall of death." I felt sick.

With George taking the lead, we started interviewing crew members. We also had the team that was stuck in Germany, waiting for country clearances, interview injured survivors who had been flown to the Landstuhl Regional Medical Center—the largest American hospital in the world outside the United States. Between those survivors and others who were still on the *Cole*, we managed to piece together the last few minutes before the explosion.

After the *Cole* entered Tawahi Harbor at approximately 8:30 AM, the crew secured the starboard side to the "dolphin"—the fueling station. Refueling began. As is usual during refueling, small boats swarmed around the *Cole*, bringing supplies, taking trash, and doing maintenance jobs. A small boat approached, with two men aboard. The boat was approximately 35 feet long and 6 feet wide, powered by an outboard motor. It had a red carpet on its deck. It slowly pulled alongside the *Cole*, port side. The occupants waved. The crew waved back. The boat looked no different from others going to and from the *Cole*. There was no sign of explosives or of anything suspicious. The men cut the boat's engine. Seconds later, at 11:22, the boat exploded. A huge hole, 40 feet in diameter, was blown in the side of the ship. A fireball injured and killed sailors who were waiting to eat lunch in the galley. Black smoke rose up to the sky.

The first days of an investigation are among the most crucial, as the memories of witnesses are still fresh and crime scenes are less likely to have been touched, and so it was frustrating for us that John O'Neill, the special agent in charge and our on-scene commander, along with others from the NYO, were not yet allowed into Yemen. Ambassador Bodine wouldn't grant them country clearances and kept saying that we had enough officials on the ground. FBI headquarters tried explaining to her that to conduct an investigation, you need security and technical staff, divers, forensic experts, interrogators, detectives, and others, lots of them. The appeals had no effect; she felt she knew best.

We tried making the best of the situation and assigned everyone roles. The hostage rescue team, under Bob Hickey, was in charge of security at the hotel and in convoys. Steve Bongardt, though he continued to serve as co–case agent, remained in the command center because of his back problems, handling administrative issues and coordinating the exchange of information with the CIA. While our aim was to track those responsible and bring them to justice, it was likely that we would come across intelligence, so we'd give that to the CIA. And while the CIA's focus was intelligence efforts, it was likely they'd uncover information helpful to us. As one of my former FBI colleagues, Don Borelli, likes to put it: "We're the bird catchers and the CIA are the bird watchers."

George Crouch was in charge of all personnel at the crime scene itself, the USS *Cole*. We planned to send a big group to the ship to examine evidence and interview every sailor. While there were more than three hundred sailors on the *Cole*, we thought that it was important to talk to each one individually. It was possible that one might have seen something nobody else had noticed, and we also felt that speaking to all of them would provide psychological benefits: many had not slept since the explosion and had spent every waking minute trying to save colleagues and the ship, and we wanted them to feel as if they were part of the investigation.

Tom Ward was in charge of investigating different sites. And I, as the case agent, would lead the investigation and alternate between all the different groups to ensure that everything was working smoothly. I would also take the lead in coordinating our investigation with the Yemeni authorities. We agreed that each morning our entire team would have a meeting at 7:00 to report on progress.

. . .

The Mövenpick was full of military and intelligence personnel, many having flown in directly from other places in the Middle East where they were stationed. And over the next couple of days the hotel would fill up even more, as FBI, CIA, NCIS, military intelligence, United States Central Command (CENTCOM), marines, and State Department officials—everyone from the United States who was in Aden in any official capacity—were told to stay at the hotel. For security reasons the State Department wanted all Americans to stay in one place; even members of the press got rooms there.

Living together in the same quarters created close bonds among different U.S. government entities used to working independently. At the moment of crisis, no one cared which U.S. government agency you were from; we all represented the United States and were all focused on one thing: finding out who was behind the murder of the sailors and bringing them to justice. It was a welcome change from Washington's turf wars.

The ninth floor of the hotel was designated the command floor, and armed marines in full combat gear with loaded weapons guarded every entrance. All agencies and intelligence groups had offices and secure lines on that level, and no hotel staff or unauthorized personnel were permitted. The floor was headed by the NCIS assistant special agent in charge of the Middle East field office, Mike Dorsey. Mike was one of the first American law enforcement officers on the ground in Aden after the attack, having flown in straight from nearby Bahrain, where he was based. One of Mike's many qualities is that he is a team player, and for him it is always about the mission and never who is in charge, so he was perfect for coordinating the different arms of the government and ensuring that everyone worked together. The NCIS had assets on the ground in Yemen—they had helped the government remove mines left over from the civil war—and Mike put all his assets at our disposal and told us that however he could help, he would.

The Mövenpick was one of two supposedly five-star hotels in Aden, but it was cramped. Three to four people were put into rooms that only had two beds, so people took turns sleeping on the floor. I roomed with George and Steve. We were the lucky ones, however, as some people didn't even get rooms. The HRT slept on the floor of the hotel ballroom. When we asked whether there were other hotels, we were told that Barbara K. Bodine wouldn't allow anyone to stay anywhere else.

Bodine was a tough, thin woman in her forties who had previously served as an ambassador in charge of terrorism for the State Department. While she was a seasoned diplomat, she gave people strange looks when they spoke, as if she were trying to catch them out. When we interviewed USS *Cole* sailors, some told us that Bodine treated them as if they were responsible for the bombing and as if they had unnecessarily inconvenienced her. We couldn't believe that this was how a U.S. ambassador treated U.S. sailors who had just been victims of a terrorist attack.

As usual following an attack on U.S. citizens in a foreign country, the State Department prepared to put out a REWARD FOR JUSTICE poster, asking locals to help with the investigation. Such posters often produce useful leads, as they had with the East African embassy bombings. Without coordinating with us on the ground, Bodine's staff worked on translating a standard poster to be published in Yemeni newspapers. When I opened a paper the next day to look at the ad—written, of course, in Arabic—I saw that rather than asking for cooperation, it warned the local population not to cooperate with us. Apparently no one in the embassy had noticed the colossal mistake.

Bodine had a tendency to be overly sensitive to how she felt the Yemenis would react to actions we took. Her attitude reminded me of a story my colleague and coauthor Daniel Freedman likes to tell about George Shultz. When Shultz was secretary of state, before a new ambassador would head off to his or her country of destination, Shultz would call the person into his office and say: "Before you leave, you have one more test. Go over to that globe." He would point to a giant globe he had in the corner of his office. "Show me that you can identify your country," he would say. Without exception, the ambassador would spin the globe and point to the country to which he or she was heading.

Shultz would gently correct the ambassador by pointing to the United States and saying, "No, this is your country."

On October 18, almost a week after we had arrived in Yemen, we watched on a hotel television the memorial service being held for the victims of the *Cole* at the Naval Station Norfolk, in Virginia. President Clinton led the service. Many of the injured sailors, sitting in wheelchairs or resting on crutches, were present. The sky in Virginia was gray and overcast, a fitting backdrop for the ceremony. President Clinton said all the right things. He warned those responsible: "You will not find a safe harbor. We will find you, and justice will prevail." That cheered our spirits. With the president making a declaration like that, we believed strong support for our investigation would be forthcoming.

And initially it looked good. Ambassador Bodine was overruled by her superiors in the State Department, and the team in Germany with John O'Neill was finally allowed into the country. I went to the airport to prepare for John's arrival. We didn't want his group to have the same problems that we had encountered when we'd landed. The Yemeni official in charge of the airport had become my friend from our first day in Aden. I told him that John was "a very, very important man in the FBI." I knew that because of the class and rank consciousness of Yemeni society, this would make entry easier for John.

"How important?" the official asked. "Special agent in charge" doesn't translate well into Arabic, so I told him that John was the "boss of my boss, the equivalent of a general." The Yemeni official was impressed and told me that he would personally welcome John on the runway. It was only fitting that he, as the most important official at the airport, greet a general, he reasoned, and I nodded solemnly. I also suggested that he open the VIP lounge for the new guests, and he agreed that it would be appropriate.

The official set up a formation of soldiers on the tarmac to greet John. As soon as the plane landed, I went into it to find John. At first I couldn't see him. The plane was packed with people. Then I heard his voice shout "Ali." He had spotted me. I waved him to the door, and he pushed his way through the other passengers and we hugged. Kevin Donovan, who later became the assistant director of the New York office, was one of the officials with him. I explained what was waiting on the tarmac. They were relieved and even laughed, as it was the opposite of what they were expecting.

John was already familiar with most of the problems that we were having with the Yemenis and Ambassador Bodine, and as we walked through the airport he put his arm around me and said: "Don't worry, we'll deal with all these problems. There's a new sheriff in town." John always inspired confidence. He had such a reassuring presence, and those who worked for him knew he would do anything he could to support his agents. Still, I was skeptical despite John's reassurance; knowing as I did both Ambassador Bodine's personality and John's, I guessed that the two would clash.

Because of the rapport I had developed with the Yemenis at the airport, and because of John's status as a "general," we passed easily through airport security to the waiting escort. I pointed out to John the Binladin construction site with the big billboard as we passed it.

The first thing John did at the Mövenpick was speak to our team. He told them what he told me: that he'd deal with the problems we were having. John's presence lifted their spirits. Next I took him to see the *Cole*. The sight of the giant hole on the side, the blood on the floor, the sullen look on sailors' faces—it was all just as chilling every time I went to the destroyer.

We spoke to the captain of the *Cole*, Commander Kirk Lippold. John asked him, "How are you doing?" Lippold responded by speaking about his sailors. He told us who was killed, who was injured, and of the efforts being made to save the ship. He spoke slowly, clearly still coming to terms with the magnitude of what had happened. He was a brave and kind man, and it seemed as if each one of the sailors killed was one of his own children. John put his arm around the captain and asked him again, "How are you doing?"

Commander Lippold replied, "I'm not worried about myself." He then paused and added: "The navy eats its own."

It was sad to hear that the captain felt that his career was over. It shouldn't have been. Commander Kirk Lippold was a rising star in the U.S. Navy. He was an Annapolis graduate and had all the right talent and assignments to become a future senior leader in the Department of the Navy. He was not responsible for his ship's choosing to dock in the port, nor was there anything he could have done to prevent the bombing. And a commander who cared so deeply about his men was someone the navy should hold on to. We told him that. "It doesn't matter," he told us, and focused on what needed to be done: his only concern was saving the ship. His courage and resolve were inspiring. The same traits were displayed by everyone else on the ship.

After speaking to sailors and inspecting the blast site, John and I took a walk around the deck of the *Cole*. From one side we could see the hills of Aden lined up against the horizon. For a few minutes neither one of us spoke. We just leaned on the rails, thinking our own thoughts.

I broke the silence. "If we are right that al-Qaeda is responsible for this attack, as I believe we are, I am sure they had someone in those hills to record the operation to use it for propaganda purposes. That means there's at least one more person involved in this operation, and he's still out there."

John nodded. "So let's find him."

It was at the hotel that I first got to meet some members of the CIA's Counterterrorism Center, led by Hank Crumpton. One of the CTC officers—Ed—had been mentioned to me by fellow FBI agent and al-Qaeda expert Dan Coleman, who had worked with him in Pakistan, and Dan spoke highly of him. When Ed introduced himself, I mentioned Dan's high estimation of him. He was friendly and said that he had heard good things about me, too, from CIA colleagues. (I would later encounter Ed in Guantánamo Bay, after 9/11, and then during the interrogation of Abu Zubaydah.)

With John and the rest of the team on the ground we had the manpower to really start investigating. We established an early-morning meeting that everyone, from the case agent to the technical staff staying at the hotel, would attend. No matter his or her role in the investigation— whether guarding a door, searching a site, or interrogating suspects—

everyone is important. Without any one of them, our team wouldn't function properly. In addition, all of them were risking their lives every day by being in Yemen. That deserved to be recognized, and so everyone was included in the morning meeting.

There were obstacles we faced, however, starting with the Yemenis. As was the case at the airport, all the different Yemeni agencies were trying to monitor us and were demanding that we clear everything with them. This meant that a large part of our day was spent negotiating the same terms again and again. Even when we just wanted a convoy to get to the *Cole*, it wasn't enough to clear our visit with the PSO. We had to clear it with military intelligence, with the local police, and with other entities.

A second problem was that the highest levels of the Yemeni government were disputing whether the attack on the *Cole* was or was not a terrorist attack. After the bombing, President Saleh had first claimed that the bombing wasn't a terrorist attack but an accident. Echoing this line, some Yemeni government officials tried to convince the United States that the explosion was caused by a malfunction in the *Cole*'s operating systems, and Saleh asked the United States government for money to repair the damage the United States had "caused" in the port. When it had become indisputably clear that the bombing was an attack, Saleh tried blaming Mossad, Israel's national intelligence agency.

Hostility came from other quarters: clerics in mosques denounced our presence and warned people not to cooperate with us, and Yemeni parliamentarians claimed we were invading their country. We were also under the constant threat that extremists would try to attack us. Another concern we had was that a number of Yemeni officials we met were clearly sympathetic to al-Qaeda. The relationship made us question whether these officials had had anything to do with the attack. Many appeared to be playing a game with the extremists: they would let them operate as long as they didn't harm Yemeni interests. The good news was that for many Yemeni officials, that line was crossed with the bombing of the *Cole*.

Finally, we were given reason to frankly mistrust some Yemenis. One morning during our 7:00 briefing, an HRT member entered the room and whispered something into his commander's ear and then pointed up to the ceiling. We all looked up and saw that a wire with a small microphone was hanging down from the ceiling. Someone was trying to listen in. Because the hotel was made of cement, the wire was literally taped to the ceiling and was easy to spot. It must have been put in overnight. We followed the wire from the ballroom (where our meeting was taking place) through the hotel up to the mezzanine level, where it went behind a partition.

A U.S. Marine was standing nearby with a sniffer dog. Knowing that Yemenis in general are scared of dogs, I asked her to come with us. We went around the partition and saw a Yemeni man sitting at a desk monitoring cameras and listening to an earpiece. The Yemeni saw the dog, which snarled helpfully, and the man jumped onto the desk, shaking. When the dog started barking, he jumped off the desk and ran away from the listening post.

We looked at the cameras and examined the wires and saw that the Yemenis had set up monitoring devices in quite a few of our rooms. As we were looking at them, some other Yemeni officials ran into the area, but before they could speak, I angrily asked: "What is going on here? Why are you monitoring us? There are going to be problems."

"No, no," one officer responded, "this is for your own protection."

"These ones," I said, gesturing to the wires and cameras monitoring us inside the hotel, "aren't. Outside the hotel is fine. But inside our rooms is not. Get rid of them."

Convincing the Yemenis that the attack on the *Cole* was in fact a terrorist action and not a malfunction of the ship was a kind of game. We didn't think they believed their official story—no intelligent person could, we thought—but it was their country and their rules, so we had to play along.

We took senior Yemeni officials representing all their intelligence and security agencies to the *Cole*. The delegation included the head of the PSO in Aden, Hussein Ansi; the head of President Saleh's security team, Hamoud Naji; the chief of staff of the Yemeni military; and the governor of Aden. Navy engineers demonstrated that the damage done to the ship—the blast hole clearly went inward, not outward—meant that the explosion had to have been caused by an external attack. Sailors then recounted what they saw moments before the blast: the boat and the men on board. There was little to argue about, and when the Yemenis saw the blood, the bodies, and the pain on the faces of the sailors, they seemed genuinely touched, and expressed their sympathies.

We went directly from the ship to our hotel for a meeting with the Yemenis, and we were expecting a positive discussion as to how we could move forward with the investigation. We all gathered in a big conference room. We sat across from each other, Americans on one side, Yemenis on the other. John faced Naji, and I faced Ansi and translated for our side. Ansi was the first to speak. He was a short, mustached man with salt-and-pepper hair, and he liked to assume a pious air. What seemed to be an involuntary smirk often appeared on his face when he spoke. It gave the impression that he thought he was the most intelligent person in the room and that he was secretly laughing at everyone else.

"After reviewing the evidence," Ansi began, "we believe that the attack on the *Cole* was in fact a terrorist attack." I translated. Everyone nodded. "However—" He began again, and then he paused, and the smirk appeared for a few seconds. "The people responsible for the attack are dead, they blew themselves up, and so there is nothing to investigate. The case is closed." I was initially too stunned to translate. I couldn't believe my ears. Was he serious? I started arguing back without pausing to translate for the others. It was a struggle for me to mask the anger I felt.

"As you know, if a terrorist attack occurs, there are not only those who conducted the attack. There are also the people who facilitated the attack. Then there are the bomb makers, the providers of the safe houses, and the people who helped them buy the boat and the explosives. There is therefore still a lot to investigate. The case is far from closed."

John and the others didn't know what was happening. I was the only Arabic speaker among our team in the room. But my colleagues knew me well enough to realize from my tone of voice and facial expressions that whatever was being said, it wasn't good.

After I replied to Ansi, I translated the exchange for the others. There was anger on our side and John especially was agitated. "Now look here," John said, "We are here to work as a team with you. But you should know that this is something we are very serious about. We are not messing around. We want to get to the bottom of this. And we won't leave until we figure it out. We would, however, like to work with you." I translated. Ansi nodded but said nothing. The meeting was adjourned.

As I was leaving the room, Naji approached me. "Can I speak to you?" he said. I stepped to the side with him. "Don't worry," he said, touching my arm, as if trying to calm and reassure me. "Everything will get done, just have patience." I felt relieved. As the head of Saleh's security detail, he was the president's personal envoy to the meeting. If he said things would get done, they would.

Naji remained true to his word. That night General Ghalib al-Qamish, the head of the PSO and Ansi's superior, came to Aden from Sanaa. John and I went straight to meet him. Qamish is a small, skinny, bald man who looks like a Yemeni version of Gandhi.

"We can work together," were Qamish's first words to us. He then said: "I understand why you are in Yemen and the importance of your investigation. At the same time, you have to understand the sensitivities of Yemenis." He explained that some viewed our presence as an invasion, and that there was anger toward the United States for its support of Israel against the Palestinians. He made it clear that he didn't agree with this hostility to us but was just explaining the situation.

Qamish was knowledgeable about al-Qaeda. When the PSO was responsible for utilizing Islamists against the South during the civil war, he was one of the key players. Yemen was a country where things couldn't be viewed in black and white but shades of gray. Whatever Qamish's role in the past in dealing with Islamists, during the *Cole* investigation, with us, he was one of the good guys, and we were glad he was at the top. We agreed that we would primarily deal with him rather than Ansi.

With the Yemenis, when negotiating for access to evidence and witnesses, it was often a question of persistence. We had experienced similar problems when working elsewhere overseas, so we knew how to handle it: we needed to remain polite but be firm. And we needed to make it clear that we would not back down.

One of the first things we had done on arriving in Yemen was to ask the Yemenis for their harbor surveillance video from the time of the attack. As we watched the tape it was clear that the Yemenis had tampered with it—the time stamp and certain frames were cut out. I told Qamish that we'd been given a doctored tape and that we would like the original; he got it for us. The full tape didn't show us much more, so it didn't make sense that the Yemenis had edited it. We deduced that they were trying to waste our time or test us in some way.

FBI director Louis Freeh was aware of the problems we were having in Yemen and decided to fly to the country to help move the investigation forward. At the airport and again at the Mövenpick, we briefed him and the senior officials accompanying him. We then took the director to see President Saleh.

For security purposes, the presidential palace is up in the hills overlooking Aden, far from the general population. As we drove up the winding road to the palace, we saw down below us beautiful virgin beaches and bays. Great for scuba diving, I thought to myself.

President Saleh greeted us at the palace. He was shorter than I had expected and very reserved. The visit was mostly a matter of protocol: Director Freeh was coming to show President Saleh that the United States was serious about the investigation, and Saleh, in turn, was meeting him to show that Yemen would cooperate. The meeting started with a statement from President Saleh in which he said that it had yet to be determined who was responsible for the terrorist attack. He added that the weapons used in the attack were made in the United States or Israel. (The Yemenis were still keen at that point to blame Mossad.) And then, in a bizarre shift, Saleh added Libya's Muammar al-Gaddafi to the mix, claiming that he was getting involved in Yemen's affairs. Freeh politely sidestepped Saleh's comments, saying it was too early to determine where the weapons had come from and that the United States was eager to work alongside the Yemenis and investigate the attack. He added that the United States would be the "junior partner" and that the Yemenis would take the lead. This pleased President Saleh because Yemen's competence was acknowledged. President Saleh responded by saying that the Yemenis would fully cooperate with us, and he confirmed that John O'Neill should deal directly with Qamish.

Freeh went next to visit the *Cole*. He spoke to the sailors, listened to what they had to say, and promised to track down those responsible. We returned to the Mövenpick to discuss the investigation, gathering in John's room. Director Freeh sat on a chair, John and I on the bed, and a couple of FBI officials on the desk, while everyone else leaned against the walls. The first question the director had was whether he should hold a press conference. A few people worried that it would upset the Yemenis by suggesting that the United States was taking charge. After everyone gave their views, the director turned to me and said, "Ali, what do you think?"

I was surprised to be asked—there were far more senior FBI officials for him to consult. I told him that because he had already had a successful meeting with President Saleh, there could be no harm in holding a press conference to announce that progress had been made. If anything, it would make the Yemenis look good. He agreed.

Immediately after Director Freeh's visit, we met again with Qamish to discuss practical issues. We agreed that a joint committee with U.S. and Yemeni officials would be formed to run the investigation. We agreed to establish rules that both U.S. and Yemeni investigation teams would abide by. As always, this was crucial: we needed the rules of engagement to be binding by U.S. law if we ever wanted to prosecute anyone using evidence and statements collected in Yemen. The main negotiation for these rules took place between David Kelley and a Yemeni judge. Naji represented the Yemeni intelligence community and President Saleh; Ambassador Bodine represented the State Department; and John O'Neill, the FBI. Kelley had negotiated a similar agreement with the East African governments in 1998.

The judge was unfriendly from the start. He looked at things from a political perspective that was tainted by his negative views of the United States rather than from a legal perspective. We repeatedly had to explain to him that we had legal requirements to be met. The idea that people being questioned needed to be read the Miranda warning was a foreign concept to the Yemenis.

Kelley was clearly surprised by some of the things the judge said. He expected higher standards from someone representing the Yemeni judiciary. He shot me surprised looks as I translated what the judge was saying. Most of the pressure during the negotiation was on me. As a case agent who was also translating, I found myself required to mediate between the two sides.

The judge at times got annoyed with me, thinking that I was creating difficulties for him. He didn't seem to understand that Kelley's demands were U.S. legal requirements. At one point he angrily said to me, "You're working with them," as if I were not an American, and was inventing problems for Yemen. Other times, he tried to insult me, and I sensed that he was hoping I would get angry so that new problems—distractions from the main issues being discussed—would arise. I refused to engage him.

Our major success in the negotiation was securing an agreement that all suspects we questioned jointly would be read an Arabic version of the Miranda warning. This meant that any testimony gained would be admissible in U.S. court. We also established procedures for obtaining access to any leads the Yemenis found. A point that was problematic for us, and which the Yemenis refused to back down on, was their demand that no one be extradited from Yemen to the United States. Any trials or sentencing would take place in Yemen, they insisted, claiming that that was in the Yemeni constitution. Only suspects we caught outside Yemen could be taken back to the United States.

We didn't trust the Yemeni justice system or its government to keep al-Qaeda terrorists locked up, and we also strongly believed that those with American blood on their hands should be prosecuted in the United States, but politically we had to accept these rules. Our fears about doing so were realized years later when, after the terrorists had been caught and prosecuted, they "escaped" from Yemeni jails, and were eventually pardoned by President Saleh.

Another sticking point was how the interrogation of suspects would work. The Yemenis said that only their officials could talk to Yemeni suspects and that we wouldn't be allowed to question anyone directly. Given our early experience with Ansi, we didn't have much faith in the types of questions detainees would be asked if someone from their domestic intelligence service conducted an interrogation. Once again, because of political pressure from our State Department, we had to accept the Yemenis' terms. By the end of a single day, the initial terms of engagement were finalized. The rules for conducting joint interrogations would take many more weeks to establish.

We also decided that all our requests would go through Qamish—sweeping aside the problem of dealing with competing agencies. This didn't mean it was a smooth ride. Qamish was a tough negotiator, but, unlike Ansi, he was pragmatic—and friendly. It was clear that he understood our perspective, which helped. Night was when deals were done in Yemen, and almost every night when Qamish was in Aden, we would spend hours talking and joking with him—cajoling him and bargaining with him to give us access to sites, witnesses, and evidence.

I first heard the name Bob McFadden at 3:00 one morning, the day after John O'Neill had arrived in Aden. I was in a room at the command center, exhausted but unwilling to go to sleep until I had finished following up on some leads and writing reports. John entered the room, spotted me in a corner, beckoned to me, and said he wanted to speak to me privately. I followed him into another room.

"Ali," he began. In his voice was a tone he usually reserved for unpleasant tasks, and there was also a hint of stress. "Sometimes we have to work with others from outside the FBI. There is a guy here called Bob McFadden who is the case agent for the NCIS. He's said to be one of the best operational people in the region. He's an Arabic speaker, too." John then made a self-deprecating joke about the quality of Arabic an Irishman could speak. "You need to try to work with him," he added.

I was confused. "Boss, I don't understand," I said. "Why is Immigration working with us on this?" In my sleep-deprived state, NCIS had sounded like INS—the Immigration and Naturalization Service.

John smiled. "No, the NCIS. It's the navy."

"Sorry, it's late," I said, laughing. "That makes more sense. No problem. We'll do our thing, and if he wants to contribute we'd be grateful for any help we can get."

Many view it as an insult to be asked to work alongside officials from other agencies, and this antipathy is a recurring problem. I never shared the view. In fact, my first partner when I joined the JTTF was from the CIA. And when I was in charge of a squad, I made sure to partner every FBI agent with a non-FBI official. I believed it was a constructive process that helped improve relations and cooperation.

"Now, go to sleep—that's an order," John said. He had, I noticed, been studying my face. None of us were sleeping much. With the blood of sailors on the ground, we didn't feel we had a right to sleep. John, however, was rightly concerned about the health of his team. Still, I had work to do.

"Let me just finish this report and I'll go," I told him.

An hour later John returned to the command center and found me working. He didn't like being disobeyed, especially when he believed you were harming yourself. He pushed down the lid of my laptop. "That's it," he said. "Leave." He stood there, his hand resting on the laptop as I walked out.

The next day Robert McFadden introduced himself. He had been in U.S. Air Force intelligence before joining NCIS, where he had learned Arabic and served in offices throughout the Arab world. We would become partners in the investigation, doing most of our traveling, interrogations, and interviews together. Bob is polite and gentle, with an acerbic wit. He has a penetrating mind and is hard to fool. Working almost twenty-two-hour days together, we were in sync on everything, from how to prioritize leads and plan investigative strategies to how to interrogate suspects. We became quite close, and consider each other best friends to this day.

10

"We're Stubborn, but We're Not Crazy"

The initial leads we followed with the Yemenis came to nothing, and as days passed, frustration mounted on our side. One day Ambassador Bodine came from a meeting with President Saleh with some evidence for us. It turned out that a few days earlier the Yemenis had brought in a twelve-year-old boy named Hani for questioning. His older brothers reported to the police that Hani had seen men they believed to be the bombers come with a Nissan truck and a boat on a trailer. From under a bridge nearby, Hani saw them park close to the water and bring a crane to lower the boat into the water.

Out of curiosity Hani had moved closer to watch. As he watched them, the men spotted him. They motioned for him to come over and offered him 100 Yemeni rials to guard their truck. While the sum is worth less than a dollar, to Hani it was a significant amount, and he agreed. After the *Cole* exploded, he waited for their return. He got increasingly nervous as time passed and they didn't show up. After a while he left, too scared to remain. He then went to his older brothers and told them what had happened, and they thought it best to tell the police.

Hani led the police to the truck. It was a beige Nissan 4x4 with a wooden trailer. In the truck there were a few objects, including ownership papers for the boat in the name of Abdullah Ahmed Khalid Sa'id Musawa, with a black-and-white passport-sized photo attached, a pair of Ray-Ban sunglasses, and what seemed to be pills for hepatitis.

After the Yemenis finished examining the evidence, President Saleh offered it to Ambassador Bodine, and she accepted it and brought it to us at the hotel. We were surprised to see the ambassador turn up with evidence, as it was contrary to protocol for her to accept it. Most ambassadors would have said that the evidence should be given directly to the FBI or the regional security officer (RSO), the Department of State law enforcement officer of the embassy.

According to chain of custody protocol, since Ambassador Bodine had handled the evidence, she could be called as a witness in the trial and could be questioned about her handling of the evidence and whether she had tampered with it. It is considered unusual for an ambassador to handle evidence or appear in court. In my 302, I had to explain how we had come to get the evidence through this unusual channel.

After we had examined the evidence, we asked the Yemenis to take us to where the truck had been found. When we arrived at the site, the truck and the trailer were gone. The Yemenis told us that they were impounded at police headquarters. They saw no need to leave the evidence where it was found. They didn't understand the importance of leaving a crime scene untouched until investigators finished with it. Forensics appeared to be a foreign science to them.

In the United States the area would have been sealed. Nothing would have been moved until investigators had finished combing the area. Instead, the Yemenis stomped all over the place and removed the vehicle. We explained our protocol to the Yemenis and asked them to be more careful with future evidence. In the meantime, our forensic experts worked on analyzing what was left at the scene.

We asked the Yemenis if we could question Hani. Our gut instinct was that more information could be gained from him. We didn't know if the Yemenis had information they weren't passing on or if they just hadn't gotten anything else. Either way, we wanted to speak to the boy.

At first they refused. So we pushed up the chain of command and asked Qamish. Eventually he agreed, and Bob went to speak to Hani.

Hani was being held in jail, which was surprising. "If this is how they treat innocent children who are helpful witnesses, no wonder people don't cooperate," Bob later said to me. At first Hani wouldn't say anything: speaking had landed him in jail. It didn't help, either, that white-skinned Bob was clearly not a Yemeni or a native Arabic speaker. He was probably the first Westerner the boy ever met. But Bob wouldn't give up. He spoke gently to Hani and said he was a friend. He gave him some candy and chatted about football (soccer) and fishing—Hani's passion, according to his father.

Hani gave Bob more details about the men and what had happened. He told Bob that his family lived in Little Aden, a small, impoverished neighborhood. He spent his free time watching ships and playing around the bay. He had been fishing on the morning of October 12 when he saw the scene that he had already described to the Yemeni investigators. Bob extracted from him additional details about the boat, and Hani confirmed that the deck was covered in a red carpet. Much of what he told Bob about the crane and the offer of the 100 rials corroborated what we had been told by the Yemenis. Hani also said that one of the men had put on a life vest. It might seem strange that someone about to blow himself up would be concerned with not drowning. The reasoning behind this, however twisted, is similar to the reasoning that spared Owhali's life during the East African embassy bombing: suicide is explicitly forbidden in Islam.

The terrorists view martyrdom as the one exception to that rule. If their death is a product of martyrdom, it's permissible. Otherwise they have to stay alive. In the event of the failure of the operation, the terrorists would not be allowed to let themselves drown, just as Owhali couldn't blow himself up after he had carried out his role in the embassy bombing.

Bob, a seasoned interrogator, sensed that Hani knew more about the men than he was telling. Going with his instinct, Bob asked, "When did you see these men before?" Surprised that Bob knew to ask, Hani first nodded. He then told Bob that he had seen two of the men, with a third man, a couple of months earlier, in August. He couldn't remember the exact date. The men took their boat to the water, but rather than using a crane they simply pushed it in. They then invited Hani and his family to take a ride around the bay, saying that they had just bought a new boat and were testing it.

I guessed that the purpose to be served in taking the boy's family for a ride was to test how much weight the boat could take, so the terrorists could calculate how much explosive power they could use without sinking it. I assumed, too, that because the boat was empty the first time, they could just slide it into the water, whereas the second time—for the bombing—they needed a crane because it was heavy with explosives.

It was not just Hani who had problems remembering dates. We found this to be common among many Yemenis we encountered. Linear thinking is less important to them than it is to those in many other cultures. In particular, they are not used to paying attention to ages, dates (especially birthdays), and times. Many of our questions confused the Yemenis—and their answers frustrated us. When Bob asked Hani's father how old Hani was, he replied, "He is between ten and twelve, closer to ten." One witness I spoke to said of a suspect, "He was born about twenty years ago."

"How old is he?" I asked.

"Oh, twenty-five years old."

Many of the suspects we questioned said that they were born on January 1. We first thought that perhaps it was a joke they were playing on us, but we learned that in Yemen, January 1 is commonly given as a birthday so that people won't have trouble "remembering" their birthday if asked.

Other potential witnesses besides Hani who lived around the harbor had seen a third man, known to the locals as Abdu, participate in what we continued to assume was the test run. The neighborhood is small; people know each other, and outsiders are easily spotted. In addition, two of the three men, known as Abdullah and Khalid, had been seen by several people on the day of the *Cole* bombing. They were the suicide bombers, we guessed. The description of Abdullah that was provided by these witnesses matched the picture of the man, presumably named Abdullah Ahmed Khalid Sa'id Musawa, whose vehicle owner-ship papers we had found with the sunglasses and hepatitis pills in the abandoned truck. Khalid was referred to by locals as the "handsome one." Witnesses reported that Abdu appeared to be the leader of the two other men. We also located the crane operators. They confirmed that they had rented a crane to two men for 10,000 rials.

An FBI artist worked on creating sketches of the men. He was the same artist who had drawn the WANTED sketch of Timothy McVeigh, the Oklahoma City bomber. It was a tortuous process, as he didn't speak Arabic and had to work through a translator. Despite the difficulty, the witnesses said that the final sketches were realistic likenesses.

Days after we arrived in Yemen, one of my Yemeni friends told me confidentially that some pieces of the USS *Cole*, including parts of the protective fiberglass cover on the outer surface of the radar, had washed ashore. He said that Yemeni officials from the ministry of the interior had taken them. My friend was one of those Yemenis who sympathized with the United States and was firmly committed to getting justice. We had not heard anything about the boat parts from the Yemenis.

Under our agreement with them, they were to notify us of any new evidence that came in. Any and all parts of the *Cole* were U.S. property. I asked Ansi about the wreckage and he denied knowing that anything had washed ashore. Still other Yemeni friends, however, confirmed that parts had been found and told me how to find the lab in which the wreckage was being kept.

One afternoon, while our convoy was traveling from one location to another, I directed our drivers to take a detour and head to the lab. I hadn't wanted to give the Yemenis advance warning that we were coming. The lab was simply a fenced-in house with a courtyard and a gate; inside, there were a few rooms. We surprised the Yemenis at lunch, and they cautiously welcomed us in.

"What can we do for you?" the lab supervisor asked.

"As you know, we are working together on the *Cole* investigation." He nodded. "So we've come to see whether there is anything here that we can work on together."

"We don't have anything," he replied.

"There is nothing here from the *Cole*?"

"No."

"Okay, then." I walked past him to look into the next room.

"What are you doing?" he asked, his face showing confusion.

"We have approval to look here, and we're going to see what you have," I said, and signaled to my colleagues to start looking around. The official protested but seemed unsure what to do. I offered him my phone and said, "Do you want to call someone to confirm what you should already know?" He was hesitant. It was just after lunchtime; most senior officials would be taking their midday nap, and he didn't want to wake them unnecessarily. We went on with our search as he followed us nervously.

Within a couple of minutes of searching the rooms we found parts of the *Cole*'s radar cover along with other pieces of wreckage from the destroyer. I told my team to load them into our trucks. "What are you doing?" he asked, running up to me. "Stop! You can't take that!"

"Now you listen to me," I told him. "When we came you told us you didn't have anything from the USS *Cole* here. This is from the *Cole* and this belongs to the United States, and I'm taking it with me."

"Wait a second," he said, "let me speak to someone first." He started dialing a number on his phone.

"Let's go!" I told my team. I didn't want to hang around. We jumped into the cars and drove off.

"Keep your heads down," George shouted. We didn't know if they would start shooting. We made it safely out and back to our hotel. No Yemeni official ever mentioned the incident to me.

From Hani's family and local fishermen we learned that the men with the boat had been seen coming from Madinat al-Sha'ab, another impoverished area of Aden. We spoke to Aql al-Hara—a Yemeni term for the unofficial mayor of the neighborhood—and he said that a couple of Saudis had been spotted going into and out of a certain house with a boat. They were identifiable as Saudis because of their dialect. Ansi and a few other Yemenis took us to the house. As we approached, we saw that it was one story high, surrounded by a wall, with a courtyard in the back. One of the surrounding walls also served as a wall of the house, and another of the outside walls had a gate in it wide enough to let a truck in and out.

Ansi and the Yemenis told us that we had to wait outside, and they went in first. After a few minutes they came out and told us, "There is nothing in the house. We can move on."

"Can we look?"

"You'll be wasting your time," they told us, "but if you insist, sure, go ahead."

To the Yemenis, unskilled in forensics, a house with no obvious clues (IDs, papers, weapons) is useless. But to FBI forensic investigators, the house was a treasure chest: we found hairs, what later proved to be RDX and TNT residue, and other pieces of evidence. (RDX, or cyclotrimethylenetrinitramine, is a nitromine that forms the basis for a number of explosives.) We made no effort to hide the fact that what we found was important. Realizing that he and his team had made a mistake, Ansi tried telling us that we needed to leave the house and return later. We weren't going to risk losing all these clues, and we insisted on staying.

Ansi didn't have sufficient cause to make us leave, so he and the other Yemenis watched in surprise as we began collecting bits of what we hoped would prove to be evidence. Some of them chuckled as we collected dirt from the floor to check for DNA and other evidence; later, however, they came to appreciate our methods. When the terrorists were eventually prosecuted in Yemeni courts, our lab reports were used in the trial. I briefed the Yemeni prosecutor general on the lab reports beforehand so that he could explain their importance to the judge in court.

Next we tracked down the owner of the house. He said that he had rented it to a man he was introduced to as Abdu in 1999; the description he gave matched the description given at the harbor. Beyond that, the owner denied knowing anything about the men and said he was simply looking to rent the house and make some money. The name on the rental agreement was Abda Hussein Muhammad. We didn't think we had heard it before. The Yemenis said that it didn't mean anything to them, either, and the trail seemed to stop cold.

I kept mulling over the name Abda Hussein Muhammad. On second thought, it sounded somewhat familiar, but initially I couldn't remember why. I returned to our command center, went to the storage room, and took out the photo-book from the 1998 East African embassy bombings, which at the time was still the FBI's main al-Qaeda photo-book. The first two pages contained a list of names of everyone in the book, and as I looked through, it hit me: Abdul Rahim Hussein Muhammad Abda al-Nashiri could be Abda Hussein Muhammad. It was just the three middle names in a different order.

During the Nairobi bombing investigation, the failed suicide bomber, Owhali, had told us about overhearing another terrorist, Abdul Rahim Hussein Muhammad Abda al-Nashiri, discussing a plan to attack U.S. vessels in Aden using missiles. Nashiri's name had also come up because he was a cousin of one of the Nairobi bombers, Jihad Ali. As we knew, it was Nashiri who had helped prepare Jihad Ali for the operation; and the phone call to his aunt, Jihad Ali's mother, informing her that her son had been martyred, had actually been placed by Nashiri a day before the bombing: he had wanted to avoid his cousin's being linked directly to the East African incident, so he had announced his death in advance. We were also aware that Nashiri had played a role in attempting to smuggle Sagger antitank missiles into Saudi Arabia.

My instinct was that this was one and the same person, and I pointed out the inversion of the name to others. They were skeptical, however, as Nashiri wasn't known to be an important al-Qaeda figure, and only a few people had even heard of him. I was insistent; to me, it fit together. I explained my theory to John O'Neill. "It could be him," he said, "but your suspicion is not enough. You need more proof."

We went to General Qamish, and I shared my theory about Nashiri with him. "I guess you're on to something," he said. The Yemenis had found car registration papers for Abdul Rahim Hussein Muhammad Abda al-*Nashr* in the Nissan truck, along with the boat papers. In Yemen, car registration IDs contain a photo of the owner and resemble driver's licenses. "It's the same name, but spelled Nashr," Qamish said, producing the ID. The photo, however, did not match the picture of Nashiri in the photo-book. Either my theory was wrong or someone was trying to mislead us as to Nashiri's appearance. We theorized that perhaps Nashiri had deliberately left the fraudulent photo ID in the truck so that we would think he was dead. It was also strange that the Yemenis were only now mentioning that they had found the ID. Why hadn't they given it to us with everything else they had found in the truck, or at least mentioned it? There were no immediate answers.

We showed the 1998 picture of Nashiri to the fishermen and to Hani, all of whom confirmed that he was Abdu. The Abda Hussein Muhammad who had leased the house was in fact Nashiri. Returning to the landlord, we asked how he'd come to know Nashiri, and he explained that a man named Jamal al-Badawi had introduced them. Witnesses we questioned said that Badawi had been spotted in the neighborhood, as had Musawa. The Yemenis told us that Badawi was a known local al-Qaeda operative and that they would try to track him down. The landlord added that he had found the house deserted at the beginning of January. Nashiri hadn't notified him that he and the other tenants were leaving. They didn't even leave the keys, and he never heard from them again.

We thought that perhaps the person pictured in the Nashr ID was the second suicide bomber and that the other was Musawa. That would fit with our smokescreen theory. Hani and the fishermen didn't recognize the Nashr photo, however, so we sent it around to all the intelligence community and embassies to see if anyone knew anything about him.

A few weeks later, in January 2001, the man pictured on the Nashr ID walked into the U.S. Embassy in Sanaa. He waited in line and, when he got to the head of the line, told the clerk that he wanted a U.S. visa. The clerk looked at him, and his eyes widened: the man's face matched the WANTED picture that was circulating around the embassy. The clerk alerted security and the message was passed to us.

It sounded too good to be true; no suspect had ever been served up this easily. A decision was made by Ambassador Bodine not to arrest him. He had come in for a service, and an arrest could be viewed, she

felt, as kidnapping, leading to a diplomatic incident—an understand-
able concern. Instead we notified the Yemenis, and we instructed the
embassy staff to tell the man to return in the afternoon for an answer.
As he walked out, the Yemenis arrested him. The man was questioned
for hours and denied knowing anything about the *Cole*. He said that
he didn't know why his picture was on an ID for "Nashr." He seemed
confused and shocked by the accusations, and his reactions were so
obviously genuine that we eventually determined that he was telling
the truth. We guessed that he had probably gone to get his passport
picture taken in a store, and that someone had swiped a copy to use on
a fake ID. It was an unfortunate coincidence for him, but in any case he
was not given a U.S. visa. (He was the one person whom the Yemeni
authorities had no problem with us questioning as much as we wanted.)

At this point, given all the evidence we had discovered so far, including the role of Nashiri, it was clear that al-Qaeda was behind the bombing. The Washington field office began making preparations to leave
Aden and to hand over the case fully to the NYO. Everyone—the White
House, the military, the CIA, CENTCOM—were all briefed on the
fact that the bombing of the *Cole* had been an al-Qaeda operation. We
waited for an official U.S. response against al-Qaeda. And we waited.

Within a few days of Badawi's name being mentioned by witnesses,
the Yemenis found him in Sanaa and picked him up for questioning.
We weren't allowed to question him, however. The United States
and Yemen were in the final stages of working out an interrogation
agreement—it became known as the Joint Yemeni-American Investiga-
tive Committee—and Kelley and the judge were still negotiating terms.
In the meantime, we kept pushing Qamish for more information on
Nashiri. At one point, frustrated with all my queries, he said to me,
"Look, Nashiri doesn't matter. Badawi told us that a terrorist called
Khallad introduced him to Nashiri. Khallad is the main guy, anyway."
Qamish folded his hands.

"Khallad?" I recognized the name from the conversation I had had
months earlier with my source in Afghanistan, who had spoken of the
one-legged al-Qaeda terrorist, and from reports of his mistaken arrest

around the time of the Bayt Habra car thefts to finance Mihdhar's escape. Rumor had it that, following Khallad's arrest, bin Laden himself had written a letter to the Yemenis, addressed "To Whom It May Concern of the Brothers in Yemen," asking for the "bin Attash son to be freed." Khallad was not mentioned by name but the subject of the letter was clear. The letter reportedly went on to threaten the Yemenis with severe consequences if they didn't release bin Laden's errand boy.

This letter has never been found, and its existence was never confirmed by the Yemenis. However, it would not have been surprising for bin Laden to have written and sent such a letter: the al-Qaeda leader at that stage was viewed in Yemen not as an international terrorist but rather more as a respected mujahid from the first Afghan war, and he was known, feared, and respected. Al-Bara, however, was still in a Yemeni jail, ostensibly for his involvement in the Bayt Habra car theft plot. My source in Afghanistan had told me that al-Bara and Khallad looked like each other, a fact confirmed by other al-Qaeda operatives I questioned: when I showed them pictures of al-Bara, at least one identified the man in the photo as "Khallad when he was younger," and almost all were in agreement about the likeness.

All this information from my source was classified, and I wasn't permitted to tell Qamish that we knew about Khallad and al-Bara. I pulled John aside and told him what Qamish had said and asked for permission to reveal what I knew. John quickly got approval from Washington.

We went back to Qamish. "My friend," John said to him, "given that you said Nashiri doesn't matter and that Khallad is the key person, we'd like to ask you for pictures of both Khallad and al-Bara. Al-Bara is still in your custody, right?"

Qamish was surprised. "Yes, al-Bara is still in jail," he replied matter-of-factly.

"We understand you've had him in custody since the Bayt Habra incident. You also arrested Khallad around that time. I'd like their photos and files," John continued.

Qamish appeared unsure of how to respond. He had never mentioned al-Bara to us and was not expecting that we would know much, if anything, about him, let alone that the Yemenis had him in custody. John asked me to brief Qamish about Khallad and al-Bara, which I did. Qamish told us what they knew about the two men, giving us some new information.

It was, of course, difficult to get information from him in this way, but the slow back-and-forth wasn't unusual. No intelligence agency (even that of an ally) readily gives up information unless its officials know that the other party has much of it already, or knows something about it, or unless their officials believe that it is in their own interests to share it. In that case, they don't want to be seen as being noncooperative. If an agency thinks that we don't know much about a suspect or a subject, however, they're less likely to give up what information they themselves have.

The next time I met with Qamish, on November 22, he handed me an envelope. Inside, he told me, was a picture that Khallad had submitted when he had applied for a commercial license to open a shop in Sadah. (The business was a cover; Khallad planned to use the place to store explosives.) The name on the license was Tawfiq Muhammad Salih bin Rashid. "Over to you," Qamish said with a smile.

In the picture, Khallad looked to be in his early thirties, with a long face, a mustache, and black hair. He had a faraway look in his black eyes. When you are tracking someone, before you know what he looks like, you form an image of him in your mind. It's always surprising when you see an actual picture. Khallad was not how I had imagined him.

When I returned to the hotel that evening, I circulated Khallad's picture within the U.S. intelligence community. A colleague at the FBI office in Islamabad showed it to my source in Afghanistan when he saw him a few days later, and the source confirmed that it was the same Khallad. All U.S. intelligence agencies received this confirmation.

As for Khallad's false arrest, we later learned that he had been picked up in a car belonging to a well-known Yemeni weapons and explosives dealer named Hadi Muhammad Salih al-Wirsh (known as Hadi Dilkum), from whom he had been buying matériel. The pickup occurred around the time of the Bayt Habra incident. After taking the car late at night, Khallad had stopped at a phone booth to make a call, and when he returned to the car he found himself surrounded by Yemeni domestic intelligence officers.

When I asked about Hadi Dilkum, the Yemeni officials initially refused to acknowledge his existence and said that there was no one by that name for us to question. One of the few pieces of information we had been able to learn about Hadi Dilkum was that he had a close relationship with many influential Yemenis, and at the time I had to assume that this had spared him jail time. Later, we learned that the authorities had used him (and others like him) to supply the mujahideen with weapons for use against South Yemen during the civil war. After the North's victory in the war, Dilkum had been unofficially allowed to operate freely in the country as long as his actions didn't harm Yemeni interests.

The circumstances of Khallad's arrest and release were never made clear. The Yemenis were secretive about the episode, and I believe they were embarrassed as well. We learned from sources that when Khallad was brought in, the local Yemeni officials had accused him of being Hadi Dilkum. Based on this, some members of our team speculated that when the Yemenis arrested Khallad, they really intended to arrest Dilkum. It was Khallad's bad luck to have been borrowing Dilkum's car at that point. This explanation tallied with the account that Khallad, when released, took his explosives with him. They were in the trunk of his car, which the Yemeni intelligence officials apparently never searched.

An alternative explanation was that Hadi Dilkum had tipped them off that Khallad seemed to be up to no good. Hadi Dilkum may have been worried that an operation in Yemen using his explosives would get him in trouble with the authorities—hence the tip-off. This, we reasoned, would explain why the Yemenis didn't want us questioning Hadi Dilkum.

When we showed the picture of Nashiri from the East African embassy photo-book to the fishermen, besides confirming that he was Abdu, they told us about an incident that had occurred ten months earlier: on January 4, 2000, a group of local *shabab* (young men) went down, as usual, to the bay before daybreak. They described themselves as fishermen, and their daily routine was to hang out by the water in a fishing shack. There were five of them, aged between seventeen and the early twenties, and we nicknamed them the Beachboy Five.

When they came down that morning, they spotted a boat with a top-of-the-line Yahama engine near the water. They waited to see if the owner of the engine would return to claim it. When no one came, they cautiously went over to the boat, each encouraging the other. The boat had a red carpet, and when they lifted up the carpet and the plywood below, they saw lots of compartments. They were confused to find what seemed to be extra batteries with wires hanging out. Below that were what they termed "bricks," with Russian writing on them. The bricks had a hole through them, and a cord running through the hole. They thought, at first, that the bricks might be hashish, and that the boat belonged to smugglers, who often operated out of the area. They tried cutting into the bricks to see if they tasted like hashish. They didn't, but they assumed, still, that they had found something of value.

The first thing they wanted to take was the motor, which they knew was valuable. They estimated that it was worth five thousand dollars. The five young men weren't big or strong—Yemenis are often quite small, by Western standards—and when they removed the motor they ended up dropping in into the water. Eventually they managed to get it to their shack. They then formed a chain and started removing the "bricks" from the boat, throwing them to each other and piling them in the shack. The young men never realized that the bricks were explosives, that the cord was a detonation cord, and that the batteries were detonation devices that had been disconnected.

At daybreak, while the young men were still passing the bricks, a truck pulled up and three men ran out, one of whom they later identified as Abdu, the second as Musawa; the third went away and never reappeared, and they never learned his name. Abdu stepped forward; he was clearly the leader, and he had a look of horror on his face, presumably because the boys were happily tossing explosives. He asked them to put down the bricks, telling them that he owned the boat. They replied that they had found it abandoned and that it was theirs. He told them that it had gotten stuck in the water and that he was now collecting it, and he demanded that they give him the motor and the explosives back.

They refused. They began negotiating with Abdu, whom they described as a savvy businessman. At one point the five huddled together and decided to try to drive a harder bargain. Abdu replied with fury: "I'm Za'im"—a term denoting a well-connected or important person— "don't fool with me." Intimidated, the young men conferred with one another again and soon reached a deal with Abdu.

With the young men watching, Abdu and Musawa set about working to remove the boat from the water. First they brought in a front loader. They tried a few times to remove the boat with it but couldn't. Frustrated, they gave up for the day. Before they left, however, they removed the boat's steering wheel and throttle, along with wires that were to be used with the explosives. They carried off all of these items, as well as the motor and the explosives, and they returned the front loader. They told the young men that they'd be back to collect the boat.

They returned the next day, Musawa having obtained a crane. Once they started using it, however, it got stuck in the sand ten meters from the boat. Abdu flagged a passing Yemeni military truck and told the driver that he would pay him to help them drag the crane out. The driver agreed, but after examining the crane, he said that his truck couldn't take the weight. Still, he agreed to remain at the site to lend a hand. A decision was made to engage another front loader—to get the crane out of the sand. Eventually this was accomplished and the boat was lifted out of the water and put into the military truck. The convoy—the front loader, the crane, and the military truck holding the boat—then headed off.

The five young men told us that they initially saw the boat as a reward from heaven for their having fasted through Ramadan. Laylat al-Qadr, or the Night of Destiny—when the Prophet Mohammad is said to have received the first and the last of his divine revelations—had been widely celebrated on January 3 that year. The young men believed that their apparent good fortune was a reward from heaven for their piety. The Yemeni intelligence officers in the room during the questioning couldn't contain smirks and giggled under their breath.

This was nine months before the *Cole* attack. It was clear al-Qaeda had been planning something else. What had we stumbled on, we wondered.

As the Nashiri and Khallad leads were being followed, our team was following another lead after witnesses reported having seen a boat matching the description of the one used by the bombers being towed from the al-Burayqah neighborhood. We put out an alert, asking if any law enforcement personnel in the area had seen anything suspicious, and a policeman who directed traffic between al-Burayqah and another neighborhood, Kud al-Namer, came forward.

He had noticed, coming from the direction of al-Burayqah, a truck and trailer that matched the description. The boat being towed was bigger than the typical Yemeni craft—the equivalent of a limousine. Its size reduced the number of places the bombers could have purchased it within the country; it might have been purchased outside of Yemen. Based on information gained at the harbor, a team of FBI and Yemeni investigators headed to al-Burayqah. Known by locals as "little Kandahar," the neighborhood is an al-Qaeda recruitment hub (we were to learn that the organization even maintained a safe house there), sending ranks of youths to the Taliban capital to fight. We handed out pictures of the suspects, and over a period of a few days investigators knocked on doors, stopped in shops and restaurants, and asked pedestrians if they had seen the truck or the men.

Our involvement in the investigation occurred in fits and starts, with Ansi repeatedly coming up with reasons we couldn't proceed on any given day. More and more locals told us that they had seen the boat, each one remarking on its size. A few construction workers remembered having seen the truck go over a speed bump and then stop; one of the passengers had hopped out to check that the trailer hadn't become disconnected. They said that all the men were dressed in white. We were directed to a house that they had been seen entering and exiting. Its appearance gave me a chill across the back of my neck: it was eerily similar to the houses used by the bombers in the Kenyan and Tanzanian embassy bombings. A single-story detached white-brick villa, it was enclosed partly by wall and partly by fence; a gate controlled access. In the yard were engine parts, tools, and bomb-making materials.

In the master bedroom we found a prayer mat facing north, and the bathroom sink had some body hair in it, indicating that the bombers had performed the pre-suicide bombing rituals, "purifying" themselves. We collected hair samples and a razor they had left behind, giving the evidence to our forensic team for testing.

The Yemenis tracked down the landlord, who claimed not to know that the men were terrorists. According to the rental agreement, the lease had begun in the summer. It was made out to Abdullah Musawa. We showed the landlord the photo we had of Musawa, and he confirmed that it was the same man who had rented the house. He identified the two others seen at the harbor on the day of the bombing, Abdu and Khalid, as having been in the house.

After more questioning, we learned that the men had also visited a local mechanic, whom we tracked down. He admitted to having worked on their boat, although he claimed that he didn't know what they were planning on using it for. The men had come in with an engine problem, which he had fixed. Then they had asked him to build a fiberglass floor for the boat, creating a compartment between the actual bottom and the fiberglass. They explained that they needed it for storage—presumably of explosives.

The USS *Cole* was towed out of Aden on October 29, 2000, on a Norwegian salvage ship, the *Blue Marlin*—to the strains of the "The Star-Spangled Banner" and Kid Rock's "American Bad Ass" on a PA system. By that time we had what is known as the "intelligence case" that al-Qaeda was behind the attack. We had, in other words, enough evidence to remove any doubt among senior U.S. government officials, but it wouldn't be enough to convict those responsible in a U.S. court of law. Our next step was to widen the search and get more evidence. It was possible, we reasoned, that the terrorists had been spotted elsewhere in the city. We sent investigators to other neighborhoods with photos and sketches of the suspects.

The men had also been seen in the Tawahi neighborhood. Using regular police methods—knocking on doors, stopping pedestrians, and checking rental offices—we eventually located an apartment they had used, and the landlord from whom they had rented it. Abdullah Musawa had rented the apartment for four months, with the rent paid in advance. Neighbors said that there had been other men in the house, and that they had claimed to be fishermen and had kept to themselves.

The apartment overlooked the harbor, a perfect location for the terrorists to watch boats coming and going and from which to record any attack, which al-Qaeda would then try to use in propaganda videos. The known local al-Qaeda member Fahd al-Quso was identified by neighbors as having been in the apartment, and the Yemenis said that they would try to track him down.

Throughout this part of the investigation—in all three neighborhoods and at the harbor—Ansi watched us closely. At times he seemed to be encouraging witnesses not to talk to us; he would glower at them when they gave us information. Sometimes he would smirk when we didn't get the information we needed. He also invented excuses for getting annoyed with us. When we moved from site to site, we plugged each of the locations into our GPS devices so that other team members could locate them (by and large, the country does not use a system of formal addresses). Ansi protested, telling us in all sincerity that the devices could be used for marking targets we planned to bomb. He informed other Yemeni officials of his suspicions.

We explained to him how the GPS system worked and why it was useful. Curious, he asked if he could have a device. We ordered a box of top-quality GPS devices from Dubai for him and his team as a gift. Later he complained that they didn't work: he didn't understand that they needed to be programmed. When we left Aden, I noticed they that had been put back in their boxes. Similarly, when we dredged the sea floor below the *Cole* for evidence, Ansi didn't understand what dredging was and claimed that we were trying to mess up their harbor. Everything to him was a conspiracy.

Ansi's attitude and lack of cooperation were annoying and time-consuming, and sometimes our frustration boiled over. Once, John and I were in a conference room in PSO headquarters in Aden speaking to Naji and Ansi about some leads we wanted to follow, and Ansi was being his usual difficult self. John stared hard into his eyes and said, "With you it's like pulling teeth." Ansi took a step back, shocked. His English was very basic, and he thought that John was threatening to pull out his teeth. I quickly explained the saying. John often made references to teeth, although I never knew why. When we had problems with other Yemeni officials, he would sometimes ask, his face a study in seriousness, "Are you a dentist?" Surprised by the question, they'd reply, "No, why do you ask?"

"Because with you it's like pulling teeth," he'd tell them.

For all the problems we had with Ansi, our friendship with his boss, General Qamish, made up for it. Qamish knew that Ansi wasn't keen on helping us, so he tried to stay in Aden as much as possible to help us out himself. Almost every night we met with him. We grew fond of each other, and he would call John "Brother John" and me "Brother Ali." Often while I was translating Qamish's words for John, he would slap my thigh—a sign of friendship in Yemen.

Once when I noticed that Qamish's personal bodyguards were using the small AK-74s used by Soviet Spetsnaz, I joked with him that they were using bin Laden's jeffreys. (The guns were referred to in Yemen as jeffreys.) The al-Qaeda leader was known to carry a small AK-74 that he claimed to have taken from a Russian soldier he had killed in Afghanistan during the May 1987 Battle of Jaji. A few days later Qamish told me he had a gift for me in his office in Sanaa. It was a jeffrey. I was touched by the gesture and also found it ironic that while Ambassador Bodine wouldn't allow us to carry weapons, claiming that the Yemenis objected, the head of Yemeni intelligence wanted to give me one. I was never able to take it back with me to the United States; the paperwork was too complicated.

I was traveling from Aden to Sanaa one day to meet with PSO officials, and the embassy gave me a diplomatic pouch to carry. Under the 1961 Vienna Convention on Diplomatic Relations, diplomatic bags, which contain articles for official government use, have immunity from search or seizure, as does their courier. We'd had problems in the past with pouches being searched, and to try to minimize such problems, I had told the Yemenis in advance that I would have one. I was convinced, of course, that some agency would insist upon a search.

After I was dropped off by colleagues at the airport, a PSO official in civilian clothes—I had seen him in the airport on various occasions before—came running toward me shouting, "Ali Soufan, Ali Soufan, come with me." Oh, no, I thought, here we go. He told me to follow him, and I braced myself for drama as he led us to the VIP lounge. Sitting there to greet me was Qamish, with a big smile on his face. "You weren't expecting me?" he asked, half rhetorically, and I shook my head. "I'm going to travel with you to make sure you have no problems." The trip was the smoothest of all my time in Yemen. We spent the journey discussing our lives. He told me about his time in the military academy, and about his family.

Earning Qamish's friendship didn't result in his anticipating everything we might want. He only gave us what we asked for, and often we had to push hard for it. But unlike Ansi, when we were on to information, he didn't try to cripple our investigation. And he was always friendly, even when saying no.

One evening, John, Naji, and I were in a car, discussing the problems we were having and how hard it was to get information from some Yemenis. Naji spoke English well, so there was no need for me to translate from Arabic for John. Naji told us: "You have to remember we Arabs are stubborn people—that's why we're hitting a rock. You'll have to back down, because eventually things will work out."

"You're dealing with another Arab, and I'm also stubborn," I replied with a smile, reminding him of my childhood in Lebanon.

"The Irish are even more stubborn than the Arabs," John interjected, and told us a story about his clan in Ireland. The O'Neills were known for their strength and bravery. "Every year in their village there was a boat race to a giant stone in the middle of the local lake, and every year the O'Neill clan won. One year, another clan's boat took the lead, and it looked as if they would win. My great-grandfather took his sword, cut off his own hand, and threw it at the rock so that he would touch it first. You two got anything that can match that?"

"We're stubborn," I said with a smile, "but we're not crazy."

As the weeks passed, our morning meetings became increasingly upbeat. The focus shifted from problems with the Yemenis or Ambassador Bodine to progress that was being made on various fronts. There was a sense that we were getting closer and closer to nailing those responsible. And then a new problem arose.

Before we arrived in Yemen, there had been some confusion about what information could be shared between intelligence and criminal investigators. In 1995, Attorney General Janet Reno had instituted new rules concerning the division between criminal and intelligence investigations, partly because of alleged problems with the use of the Foreign Intelligence Surveillance Act (FISA) in past investigations. FISA governs the conduct and use of surveillance and physical searches of foreign powers and their agents inside the United States.

There are some differences between intelligence and criminal investigations: in a criminal investigation, in order to listen in on someone's conversation, you first need probable cause and a judge's approval. For intelligence gathering, you need reasonable suspicion, a much lower bar. Attorney General Reno's guidelines were meant to ensure that criminal investigators and prosecutors were not taking advantage of lax rules on the intelligence side to obtain information for their cases. But the rules never were designed to prevent FBI agents from cooperating when they were working on the criminal and intelligence sides—definitely not when the efforts were part of the same case. Yet that is how the guidelines came to be interpreted, despite objections from field agents.

When Steve Bongardt, the on-the-scene liaison with the CIA, initially asked the CIA for information, he was told, absurdly, that they would give it to him but that he couldn't share it with the rest of us. The CIA team said that they couldn't share intelligence with criminal agents. Steve refused to not pass on information. "What use is it," he asked, "to have information and not share it with the agents on the ground who need it to apprehend the terrorists?" The CIA said that if he was going to pass it on, they wouldn't share the intelligence.

For an investigation to proceed effectively, and for the United States to meet its national security goals and arrive at a successful outcome, the two sides need to work in tandem. After John O'Neill arrived on the ground, we briefed him on this "new issue" between criminal and intelligence that Steve and our team were facing. John made an agreement with a senior CIA official, Hank Crumpton, to let the CIA attend all our meetings, and vice versa. The agreement worked well initially. In the evenings we would meet with the CIA officers and analysts and update them on information we had gained during the day, and they, in turn, gave us the intelligence connected to our case.

While we were working with Hank and the CTC officials in Aden, Steve Bongardt moved to Sanaa to liaise with the embassy and the appropriate Yemeni agencies. Soon he began reporting problems with the CIA chief and his team, which was withholding intelligence-related material. Absurdly, this included material we had shared with them in Aden, expecting them, in turn, to share it with Steve in Sanaa. We began to suspect something was afoot.

Part of the problem was that Steve was dealing with a CIA official whose rank within the agency was lower than Hank's, and lower, too, than the members of the CTC team he had been dealing with in Aden. Because that officer was further down the CIA chain of command, the CTC team in Aden bypassed their own man, instead sending information straight to CIA headquarters. To complicate matters, that officer fell under the agency's Near East division rather than strictly under CTC jurisdiction. The state of affairs understandably left him upset, and he took it out on Steve and the FBI, claiming we wouldn't give him information. And when we later moved to Sanaa, we no longer dealt with Hank and the CTC—they had left the country—but only with that officer, from whom we got minimal information: apparently he was exacting his revenge. Information sharing began to be a one-way street.

We didn't retaliate; that would have been doubly absurd—punishing not the CIA but our country by making us less safe.

The idea of not sharing information with us because we were on the criminal side was nonsense. The FBI is also an intelligence agency. It deals with sensitive intelligence on a daily basis. The bureau respects and is fully aware of the differences between intelligence and law enforcement. We had been building cases against terrorist networks, foreign intelligence networks, and state sponsors of terrorism, and had never incurred any violations. The CIA had worked with us on many of these cases without dispute.

The claim that criminal agents could have no access to intelligence reports was a false reading of the FISA rules, especially as FISA rules don't necessarily apply to intelligence gained overseas. The 9/11 Commission found that the guidelines had been misinterpreted, and not only by the CIA; many in FBI headquarters had done so, too, much to our frustration. This error was identified by the 9/11 Commission as one factor in the failure to stop the attacks on New York and Washington. The commission found that the procedures governing information sharing between intelligence and criminal sides "were almost immediately misunderstood and misapplied." It also found that the Office of Intelligence Policy and Review (OIPR), the FBI leadership, and the United States Foreign Intelligence Surveillance Court (FICA) built barriers, discouraging information sharing. At the time, we tried explaining that the rules were being misread, but to no avail.

Even after he left Yemen, right up till 9/11, Steve Bongardt was furiously battling "the wall," as it came to be known. Often he would demand of people who were refusing him access to intelligence: "Show me where this is written that we can't have access to intelligence." They couldn't, but they would insist it was the law. It was a widespread misconception that no one at the top ever refuted. These problems—the problems identified by the 9/11 Commission—started in Yemen. Day by day it got worse. At one point I got the Pink Floyd CD *The Wall*. And whenever an issue came up and we were told we couldn't have information because we were on the criminal side, we would play it.

When I returned from Yemen I met with a delegation from the Department of Justice, led by Fran Townsend, to discuss intelligence-sharing problems. The meeting was convened in my supervisor Pat D'Amuro's conference room. "Imagine an instance where one agent on a squad is handling intelligence," I said to the delegates, "and another is handling the criminal investigation. It's likely that one agent would have half of the plot, and the other would have the other half. And yet they won't be allowed to piece it together. Imagine if someone wants to bomb the World Trade Center and our agents are unable to connect the dots since one half isn't allowed to tell the other half what it knows."

I said this not because I thought there was an attack coming, but because until 9/11, the previous major terrorist attack in the United States had been the 1993 bombing of the World Trade Center. The delegates were sympathetic and understood our problem, but in government it is very difficult to change anything, and nothing happened.

11

The Human Polygraph Machine

Witnesses who had seen Nashiri and the other al-Qaeda operatives around the Tawahi apartment told us that they had observed some of the suspects visiting a mechanic in the area. We tracked him down, and he confirmed the visits. He told us that the suspects had carried AK-47s and that they had brought in a white Dyna pickup truck and asked for a steel plate to be added to one of its sides.

Terrorists add steel plates to trucks that are to be used as conveyances for bombs; the plates help to direct the explosion toward the target. The trucks used in the East African embassy bombings, for example, were modified this way (they were Dyna trucks, too). We started investigating the truck in question in this case and found the dealership that had sold it. The truck had been purchased by Jamal al-Badawi—the second time that Badawi's name had appeared.

The Yemenis searched for the truck but were unable to find it. This meant, most likely, that it was still available, fitted for a possible suicide attack. Sources told us that Yemeni extremists were becoming increasingly agitated by the U.S. presence in the country, and the U.S. National Security Agency had picked up chatter traffic (the term used for intelligence collected using technical means to eavesdrop and intercept e-mail) about an immiment attack. With every American in Aden packed into a single hotel, it was clear where the most effective strike would be. We heightened all our security, strengthening the hotel perimeter protection; and the Yemenis blocked off one side of the street with cement blocks.

John, Kevin Donovan, and I were having a meeting one evening in October in the command post when we heard shooting outside. When we realized that we weren't being shot at, we edged toward the side of the windows to see if we could make out what was going on. A minute later Bob Hickey, the on-the-ground commander of the FBI hostage rescue team that was responsible for protecting us, rushed into our room and said that he was going to send some of his team outside to check what was going on.

"Hold on," I said. "If there is a problem outside, non–Arabic-speaking HRT guys are unlikely to help the situation but may find themselves new targets. Let me go out. I have a better chance of blending in with the Yemenis." Bob agreed that that made sense, handed me a bulletproof vest, and said he was coming with me.

Before we left, HRT snipers took positions on the roof to cover us. Bob carried a radio to keep in touch with them. As a security precaution, we decided to take the stairs down; if anything happened, we didn't want to be trapped in an elevator. As we started down, John called out to me, with a hint of nervousness in his voice, "Ali, be careful." It was unlike John to publicly show anxiety.

The lobby was empty, and we ran through it and opened the hotel's front door slowly. The street was eerily silent. There were no cars around and the roads appeared blocked off. The silence was only broken by an ambulance going by, although it didn't have its siren on.

We saw a group of Yemeni security agents standing at the end of the street. They were not wearing uniforms but traditional Yemeni dress, and they were carrying AK-47s. They noticed us seconds after we spotted them, and started walking toward us. Right behind them was a car, moving at their pace. Driving it was a Yemeni whom I recognized as the former chief of police in Aden.

They came to a stop right in front of us. "What's going on?" I asked the driver.

"Nothing," he replied.

"What was the shooting we heard?"

"Nothing. There was just a wedding, and people were shooting in celebration."

"Why did you close the streets?"

"Don't worry."

"The ambulance?"

"Don't worry," he said again, and drove off.

We reported the incident to headquarters. It was the tipping point for them, and they decided to evacuate everyone from the hotel. Everyone, "no exceptions," we were told, had to leave. We packed all our gear, equipment, and weapons into trucks, and we went to the pier, where a team of marines were stationed. They had a small base there to monitor who boarded and left the *Cole*. Loading our stuff in boats, we headed out to the USS *Duluth*, a navy ship not far from the harbor.

Her captain and officers were waiting on deck to greet us. They were very hospitable; officers bunked together so that we would have rooms to sleep in. The plan was to stay on the *Duluth* for a couple of days while we monitored what was happening on shore. The *Duluth* moved constantly: since the attack on the USS *Cole*, no U.S. ships were permitted to remain stationary in the vicinity of Aden. We had to keep moving our satellite to keep in contact with FBI headquarters and took turns, day and night, positioning it.

Ambassador Bodine was annoyed when she learned that we had evacuated the Mövenpick. She felt it was an unnecessary insult to the Yemenis. It implied, in her view, that we thought that the Yemenis were unable to protect us adequately. That was true, of course. The bombing of the *Cole*, along with the fact that there was a truck suited for a suicide bombing loose on the streets of Aden, was evidence of that. Not to her, however.

She registered a complaint through the State Department against John, whom she blamed for "unnecessarily" ordering the evacuation.

Because of her complaints, Kevin Donovan, myself, and some other officials were called to the bridge of the *Duluth* to speak to senior officials in headquarters about John's performance. Once the purpose of the call became clear to me, I got very frustrated. "Look," I told them, "we're working here nonstop day and night. Our lives are being threatened and yet we're making important progress. John is doing a great job. What we need here from you is support, not criticism."

One of the senior FBI officials responded apologetically: "We just needed to have this conversation because the State Department is complaining."

A couple of days went by, and we decided that a few of us would head back to shore to check the situation, as we didn't want the investigation to come to a complete halt. John, Kevin, and I, along with Bob Hickey and a few members of his hostage rescue team, were selected to return to the hotel. We climbed down a rope ladder to a waiting boat and began sailing back to Aden. As we approached the harbor, the HRT guys scanned the shoreline and hills for threats. They noticed a couple of men with binoculars on top of a rugged hill watching us as we pulled in. On shore, we asked the Yemenis if the men on the hill were security officials. They didn't know anything about them.

The hotel was empty and silent. Previously the corridors had been filled with U.S. officials moving to and from meetings, and a constant buzz of activity was heard; now very few people were around. We found one room with military officials from CENTCOM. We didn't know if they had stayed or come back.

We spoke to Yemeni officials and evaluated the security situation on the ground. While we planned to return to the *Duluth* that evening, we were worried about the men we had spotted watching us with binoculars, as they could be al-Qaeda operatives planning to strike. We consulted Department of Defense officials, who said that it would not be safe to head back to the *Duluth* in a boat. Instead they said that a helicopter would be sent from the USS *Tarawa*, the command ship of the three-vessel amphibious readiness group of which the *Duluth* was a part, and that it would take us to the *Duluth*.

We needed permission from Ambassador Bodine, but she vetoed the decision. She refused to give the helicopter from the *Tarawa* a country clearance to come pick us up. We had come in a boat, she maintained, and we could leave in one. The Yemenis had told her that they didn't like military helicopters flying into and out of Aden, and she decided that it was unnecessary. Her decision angered military officers, who felt she was risking U.S. lives.

On the DoD's recommendation, we decided to stay in the hotel until the situation was resolved. Stuck there for the night, we went in search of food. Most hotel staff had departed for security reasons, but the few left managed to make us something. Although the hotel was empty, we still bunked with roommates for security reasons.

Early the next morning we were told that Ambassador Bodine had been overruled by her superiors in the State Department. They had ordered her to give us permission to take a helicopter back to the boat, and she reluctantly signed the authorization. The plan was to fly us first to the *Tarawa*; from there we would get to the *Duluth* in a boat. We prepared to take off from the Aden airport, the pilot aiming out to sea. It should have been a simple ride. But as soon as we were airborne, the helicopter's alert siren went off. We were being "painted"—a missile system was locked in on us. The pilot swung into action and began emergency evasive maneuvers. He kept changing the direction we were flying in to try to lose the lock. There was silence in the cabin as we all held our breath and held on to the straps tightly (as if they would save us if a missile hit). After a series of maneuvers, the system stopped blinking red. The pilot had successfully evaded the lock. Seconds later we were out on the ocean heading toward the *Duluth*. We had no idea whether it was the Yemeni military or al-Qaeda locking on us. We didn't know if it was a test or a warning, or if someone was really trying to shoot at us. It was a terrifying experience, and I learned then firsthand what it means when people say they've seen their life flash before their eyes.

We arrived at the *Duluth* flustered and angry. On the boat, military personnel were tracking the incident. They told us that it was the Yemenis who had painted our helicopter—the first time it had happened, as the U.S. military had been flying helicopters into and out of Aden without problems till then. From then on, painting became standard Yemeni practice, and not only for helicopters. Whenever a U.S. plane landed in Yemen—and they were constantly coming in and out, bringing supplies, personnel, and equipment—it would be painted. And whenever a U.S. plane is painted, the pilot, not knowing whether it's a "friendly" procedure or an actual threat, has to go into standard emergency procedures to evade the missile lock.

Part of the emergency procedure for planes is to shoot flares. This helps to throw any incoming missiles off course, as the missile follows the flare rather than the plane. To all but the most experienced, flares look like small missiles, so when a U.S. plane came in and responded to the painting with flares, it seemed to the local Yemenis that the United States was shooting at them. The cycle of suspicion and mistrust worsened.

I was once at the airport with the local U.S. military attaché, Colonel Newman, when a C-130's flares came directly at the airport, creating confusion and panic. The general who headed the military at the airport demanded to see us and angrily asked: "What's going on? You're making us look bad."

"Let me ask the pilot what happened," I replied.

Colonel Newman went to the pilot and asked why he had fired flares over the airport. He told Newman: "We were painted. They locked a missile on us. So we went into standard evasive procedures." I returned to the Yemeni general and explained what the pilot had said.

"Well, don't shoot flares, you're scaring our population," he said.

"Well, don't paint them," I told him. "And you know," I continued, "when you paint a plane and we see that a missile is locked on it, to us that counts as an act of war. Are you declaring war on the United States? Because you're painting our planes left and right."

"No, no," he said, "this is just training for our missile defense system."

"Well, train on your own planes," I angrily told him.

Newman jumped in. "Are you declaring war on the United States? Are you?"

"No, no," said the general.

Back in the New York office there was mounting concern about the escalating threats we were facing. Eventually the decision was made to send everyone other than nonessential personnel back to the United States. Having fewer people on the ground would make us easier to protect and would offer a less appealing target to would-be attackers. John, myself, and other top officials organized the exodus. Military planes carried people to Germany, the United States, and Bahrain.

For those of us who remained, a decision was made to move to a different hotel, the Gold Mohur—site of the failed attack allegedly sponsored by al-Qaeda on U.S. Marines in December 1992. By moving there, we joked, we were either tempting fate or betting on the terrorists' not striking the same place twice. Gallows humor, they call it.

Despite the history of the hotel, it was judged to be the safest place for us in Aden, and I understood the logic. The hotel was set far away from other buildings, surrounded by water except on one side. It could be easily secured, as anyone approaching could be seen from a distance.

While the hotel was safer, we still needed to move around Aden and visit sites, follow leads, meet with the Yemenis, and interrogate suspects. This was when the risk was greatest, so we took all the precautions we could. We traveled in unmarked cars and varied our route and times of departure and return every day. Still, there were daily scares. One day, for example, while we were on our way to an interview, we heard a bomb explode. The sound came from the direction of a route we often took. At our destination we asked the Yemenis the source of the explosion. "We'll check it out," we were told. Later, in the interrogation room, we were given assurances: "We checked it out, don't worry, a tire exploded."

"Come on," I said. "We know the difference between a tire and a bomb." But they insisted.

A few hours later, on our way back to the hotel, we passed an area near the harbor where there was a facility built by the British and saw from our car windows that the place was scarred and damaged. It was clear that a bomb had exploded. The next day I said to the Yemenis: "We saw the damage from the explosion." They continued to insist that it was a tire. "Okay, you stick to your story," I told them, laughing uncomfortably at their ridiculousness.

Steve Corbett was the Naval Criminal Investigative Service commander on the ground and also served as assistant special agent in charge for the NCIS. Their commanders remained on-site a long time, a better policy than that allowed by our thirty-day rotations for commanders, which kept only the team of agents and me in place. We also parted ways with the HRT. In their place the NYO sent over a SWAT team to handle security. Among the agents was Carlos Fernandez, who is like a brother to me. It took pressure off me to have him on the ground: he was someone I could bounce ideas off and discuss problems with in complete confidence.

Another of the new FBI agents was Joe Ennis. A skinny redhead from Alabama, his nickname in the FBI was "Alabama Joe." Easygoing and good-natured, always smiling and willing to help, Joe quickly became loved by the FBI team.

It had taken Joe a while to adapt to New York, however. On his first day he drove into New York City in his pickup truck with Alabama plates, wearing a cowboy hat. That same day, a small Ku Klux Klan rally was taking place near our offices, and opposite it was a much larger anti-KKK rally. As Joe drove into the city, he passed through the anti-KKK rally and they mistook his car and hat as signs of his allegiance to the KKK. He barely escaped.

Those of us in Yemen had never met Joe before he arrived in Aden, as he had been transferred to New York after we'd left. We received a phone call from New York one day at the Gold Mohur Hotel that a new agent would be arriving the following day. Because of the time difference, we thought he was coming a day later than he actually was, so Joe arrived at the Aden airport (his first time in Yemen) with no one waiting for him. He called to let us know that he was in town, and we rushed to the airport to find him standing and laughing with a group of Yemenis. His southern demeanor enabled him to bond easily with people, despite the language barrier.

Joe's efforts to befriend the Yemenis were a constant source of entertainment. Many whom we worked with were from South Yemen—the half of the country that had lost the civil war. Joe would tell them, "I'm from the South, too. I know what it's like to lose a civil war." The Yemenis were by turns confused and amused to learn that an English-only-speaking white-skinned redhead from the United States thought he had something in common with them.

Once he had learned some Yemeni words, Joe told the Yemenis that they should call him Yusef al-Kabili al-Janubi. Yusef is Joseph in Arabic; Janubi means southerner; and Kabili means tribal. Joe thought that Kabili was the Yemeni equivalent of "redneck." The Yemenis couldn't stop laughing.

Alabama Joe was one of the most hardworking agents I have ever met, and he fit in well with our group, which worked around the clock. Joe was in charge of administrative issues. In a case of the magnitude of the *Cole*, you need a first-rate agent handling administration. If that gets messed up—registering evidence, tracking documents—the entire case collapses.

Joe shared a room with George Crouch, and one day George came to me looking agitated. "Ali," he said, squaring his hand on his jaw as he always did when he was focusing on a problem, "you have to speak with Joe."

"What's wrong?" I asked. It turned out that when Joe slid his slim frame into bed, he barely mussed the covers; when he slid out in the morning, the bed looked almost untouched. It left the impression that he hadn't been in his bed at all. When the Yemeni housekeepers came into the room, they would see what they thought to be one used bed and one unused bed, and two men in the room. They would wink at George, as if they "knew" what was going on. It didn't sit well with George.

John O'Neill and Ambassador Bodine continued to clash. As the top FBI official, it fell to John to represent our interests in meetings with her. Whoever represented the FBI in meetings would have had the same problems he did, but Bodine's persistent complaints through the

State Department to the FBI led to a second review, by headquarters, of John's performance.

A few days after we had moved into the Gold Mohur, the assistant director in charge of the New York office, Barry Mawn, came to visit. Barry was newly appointed and I had never met him, but it annoyed me (and the others) that my boss's boss was coming to ask me about my boss.

"We're trying to investigate a major attack on a U.S. ship, and rather than helping us deal with the Yemenis, people seem more concerned about them," I told John. He shrugged. He never openly let this type of thing bother him.

"We can only do our best, Ali," he said, "and hope that others come to recognize situations for what they are."

Our team in Yemen often felt that headquarters wasn't supporting us enough, with regard to our problems both with the State Department and with the CIA. Over time, I began to see that this stemmed in part from the fact that no one in headquarters really understood what we were up against in Yemen. They probably never guessed that the U.S. ambassador was more concerned about the feelings of Yemeni officials than with meeting the needs of the investigative team. Moreover, none of them understood the nature of the country itself. Their lack of knowledge was summed up in a single incident that took place one day when John was on the phone with headquarters and we were in the backyard of the al-Burayqah house. John told headquarters that he needed evidence sent to Washington, DC, for DNA analysis. Headquarters, weary of Ambassador Bodine's complaints of us not trusting the Yemenis, asked him: "Why don't you just have the Yemenis do the testing?"

To anyone who knew Yemen, this was a ridiculous question: the Yemenis didn't have any forensic labs or expertise in the area. But to some in headquarters who had never operated in third world countries, every country was presumed to have the same equipment as the United States. John replied in frustration, "Look, these guys don't have shoes on their feet, and you want them to do forensics?"

When Barry Mawn came to look into Ambassador Bodine's complaints against John, we vented our frustration, explaining that the problem was not with our boss, who was representing our needs ably, but with Ambassador Bodine and the Yemenis. We told him that we were disappointed that, rather than helping us find justice, he was here to investigate John. Barry appeared genuinely sympathetic to what we said. Once again, headquarters had simply been forced to respond to complaints from the State Department. Before very long he had taken our side and become a friend and a great supporter of our investigation.

The lack of support we were receiving from the White House and the State Department, and the pressure they were putting on FBI headquarters, never ceased to surprise us. While people in the United States were focused on the presidential election, we still thought that everyone would make it a priority to see that an investigation into a major terrorist attack was given full support. We didn't quite know how to explain the lack of support, but we tried to remain hopeful. "We'll soon have a new administration," I said to John, "and we'll get the support we need."

John disagreed. "It's not that the administration doesn't want to support us. The problem is the director," he said. John felt that because of the bad relationship Director Freeh had with the Clinton White House—stemming from the agency's investigation into the Clintons' personal lives—he had limited access to the president to make the FBI's case to him.

"We have to remember we are a government agency," John added. His position was that unless the director of the FBI was close to the president, the secretary of state was likely to get the final say in any disagreement between the FBI and an ambassador. So, in disagreements between Ambassador Bodine and John, she would usually win. I was uncomfortable with John's criticisms of Director Freeh, for whom I had, and still have, much admiration.

"Well, either way, there will be a new administration soon, and we'll find out," I replied.

President Clinton told the 9/11 Commission that before he could launch further attacks on al-Qaeda, he needed the CIA and the FBI to "be willing to stand up in public and say, we believe that he [Bin

Ladin] did this." One of Clinton's top aides, Sandy Berger, said that the intelligence agencies had reached "no conclusion by the time we left office that it was al-Qaeda." That just wasn't true, and I was surprised to read it. Not long after the attack, we had concluded that al-Qaeda was responsible—which was why the FBI's Washington field office was pulled out and the New York office placed in charge.

I had worked for a Republican senator in Pennsylvania after college and identified with the seemingly strong national security approach of the party, so later in November, when President George W. Bush won the election, I (and many in the bureau) felt happy, especially because as a candidate Bush took a hard line on the *Cole*, telling CNN: "I hope that we can gather enough intelligence to figure out who did the act and take the necessary action. There must be a consequence." After President Bush's election, I hoped that things would change. I expected more support for the *Cole* investigation and in our battle against al-Qaeda. We waited and waited. No change came.

Much later, in June 2001, when we had to move our investigation to Sanaa because of the threats from al-Qaeda against our lives, we had a meeting with a member of the Senate Intelligence Committee, along with his chief of staff. After our official meeting ended and the senator walked out, the chief of staff closed the door, trapping us in the room. "Just a moment," he said. Thinking we were about to get some deep insight, we waited. "I'm sympathetic to everything you're saying," he said, "but you have to be patient. Unfortunately, people in the White House can't have al-Qaeda linked to the *Cole* attack." His tone was apologetic and sympathetic, as if he were trying to help us understand what was coming.

We looked at him in shock. "What do you mean not linked?" I said. "Al-Qaeda is already linked. Everyone with access to intelligence briefings in the U.S. government knows that."

"Look," he said nervously, "you need to understand what's really going on." He paused. "To tell you the truth, we completely don't agree with the White House on this one, but from their perspective they don't want bin Laden involved in the USS *Cole*. The president is weak right now. The country is not united behind him and is still split over his election victory over Al Gore. He's not going to risk capital going after al-Qaeda in Afghanistan and splitting the country more. But if the *Cole* bombing is publicly declared to be an al-Qaeda attack, he's going to look weak on national security if he doesn't act. So the White House doesn't want al-Qaeda blamed for the *Cole*."

"That may be," I replied to the chief of staff, "but we report the facts. And the fact is that al-Qaeda is behind the attack on the USS *Cole*. What the White House does with that information is above our level."

Bob McFadden and I brushed past him and walked out, as did the others. We were getting daily death threats from al-Qaeda while investigating the death of seventeen U.S. sailors, and for political reasons it seemed that no one in Washington gave a damn.

According to the 9/11 Commission, some members of President Bush's team opposed responding to the USS *Cole* attack. The commission reported that defense secretary Donald Rumsfeld "thought that too much time had passed and his deputy, Paul Wolfowitz, thought the *Cole* attack was 'stale.'" Maybe to them, but not to us, not to the victims and their families, and certainly not to bin Laden and al-Qaeda.

Toward the end of November John left the country to go home for Thanksgiving. When he tried to return, Ambassador Bodine refused to issue him a country clearance. This shocked FBI headquarters, as it was the first time in memory that an ambassador had banned a senior U.S. government official from entering a country to investigate a terrorist act. I was also out of the country at the time, following leads first in Jordan and then in the United States.

At that stage we were finished investigating the crime scenes, and the leads we were following had been taken as far as they could. We were waiting to see what happened with two Yemeni interrogations then under way: of Badawi and Quso. Quso, whose alias was Abu Hathayfah al-Adani, had turned himself in after some of his family members were questioned. Aden PSO head Hussein Ansi, our old nemesis, initially told us that Badawi and Quso had sworn on the Quran that they were innocent. Ansi had told us that he planned to let them go. General Qamish had overruled him and ordered the men to be subjected to further questioning. The Yemenis were to question the two men alone; our agents would not be allowed to join the interrogations, as David Kelley's painstaking negotiation of the interrogation agreement, though by now nearing its final stages, was as yet—unbelievably—not finalized. That soon changed.

While I was in the United States, I received an urgent call from Kelley. "Ali, you need to get to Yemen right away," he said. "We've finally signed the agreement with the Yemenis allowing us to interrogate Badawi, but there's no one who can interrogate him."

"What about Bob and George?" I asked, "They're both first-class interrogators and are capable of handling the interrogation."

"They can't," Kelley replied. "The Yemenis gave their own interrogation reports to our team, and Bob, George, and everyone else read it." I understood the problem: a person reading the existing interrogation report would not know how the Yemenis had conducted their sessions—whether they had used reliable methods or had obtained information by torturing the detainee, for example. But the information would be in their minds, affecting their questions and their judgment, and thus any information gained would be potentially tainted and unreliable. It's a risk we were not prepared to take, as it could jeopardize the prosecutions. "You're the only team member who hasn't read the report," Kelley added.

"Okay," I said, "I'll leave as soon as possible."

"Whatever you do," he added, "don't read anything about Badawi from the Yemenis before you interrogate him."

I caught a flight the next day to Aden.

My main partner for the Badawi interrogation was an NCIS agent, Ken Reuwer. He and I prepared extensively for the interrogation, studying everything we knew about al-Qaeda, especially anyplace Badawi may have visited or information concerning any al-Qaeda operative he may have interacted with. All this was standard preparation—you can't pause during an interrogation and ask suspects to repeat names and places, or be unaware of basic information. If you do that, they'll realize they're giving you information you don't know. At best they'll simply slow down, but their train of thought will be ruined.

You have to convince the detainee that you know all about him, and that any lie will be easily uncovered. To do this you plan the interrogation around what you know. You prepare different hypothetical situations to predict what the suspect might say and where the evidence can lead, thereby lessening the chances of the suspect's taking you by surprise.

The interrogation room in Aden was oddly shaped. It was divided into two; a wall with a window-shaped gap was in the middle. Interrogators sat on one side of the wall and suspects on the other, and we spoke through the gap.

Badawi was plump, with a potbelly and a round face, dark eyes, black hair, and a full black beard. I read him the Arabic version of the Miranda warning, which he said he understood, and he waived his right to remain silent. He said that he had nothing to hide.

He was initially uncooperative, however. While he admitted to training with al-Qaeda in Afghanistan and purchasing a boat, he claimed that he thought it was for business and commerce and denied any knowledge of the attack. We could see that his "admission" followed the standard al-Qaeda counterinterrogation process, a method we were familiar with from the Manchester Manual. The manual advised al-Qaeda operatives to admit things they knew the interrogator knew, giving the impression that they were cooperating, while withholding the real truth and any new information.

I asked Badawi about Khallad and Nashiri. He admitted to knowing them, and as he was pretending to cooperate, he gave me more information on them—details that he thought were unimportant. But often these small, "unimportant" details that suspects give are very useful to us, as they were in this instance. Badawi told us that Nashiri and Khallad were intimate with bin Laden. "Is Osama bin Laden involved in the *Cole*?" I finally asked him.

"I'm not going to tell you that bin Laden was involved so you can write in the paper that Badawi said bin Laden was involved."

"Do you think we're waiting for you to tell us that?"

After that, Badawi tried downplaying Khallad's role, claiming that Khallad wasn't in Yemen and had just introduced him to Nashiri via a letter of introduction.

We pretended to "accept" whatever Badawi told us, trying to draw out some more details that might help us. Badawi at one point mentioned that Nashiri had him help purchase a truck to pick up a boat. Later we found the dealership at which the sale had been made and searched the records of the transaction. An ID had been submitted by the buyer: it featured a picture of Nashiri over the name Sa'eed al-Mansouri. Thus we learned another alias that Nashiri used.

When I was asking Badawi questions, Ken sat silently next to me, as he didn't speak Arabic. But whenever he thought of something I should ask Badawi, he would write a note on a sticky pad and pass it to me. Badawi did not know what the notes were for, and I saw him repeatedly glancing at them. He seemed unnerved by them. I guessed it confused him why Ken never opened his mouth and just passed notes.

"I see you looking at these notes," I said. "You're wondering what's written on this paper?" I held up one of the notes, with the blank side facing him.

"No, no," Badawi replied, his face turning red like a schoolboy caught cheating. "No, I wasn't." He paused and then continued, "It's your business, I don't care." He tried to look disinterested, but his eyes kept darting back to the notes.

"Well," I continued, "I'll tell you anyway. My friend here is like a human polygraph machine. He's an expert in human behavior. And every time you lie, he passes me a note telling me that you're lying." Ken had no idea what I was saying and just stared at Badawi, unsmiling, as before. This only seemed to unnerve Badawi even more.

From then on, whenever Badawi was going to lie, he would either move away from the window and attempt to maneuver himself into an angle that would prevent Ken from seeing him, or he would look to see whether Ken was reacting. Instantly we knew he was lying. Badawi himself became a human polygraph machine.

. . .

"What passport did you use to travel to Afghanistan?" I asked Badawi.

"My passport," he replied.

"In your name?"

"Yes, in my name."

"Which name?"

"Jamal."

"Jamal what?"

Puzzled, he asked, "What do you mean?"

"Is it Jamal al-Badawi, or is it one of the other names you use? Is it the name you used to travel to Bosnia?" Here I was guessing, but almost everyone we questioned had a second (fraudulent) Yemeni passport.

Badawi hesitated. I looked at Ken, and Badawi fidgeted. "Look, I've got a copy in our other office of the passport in the other name you use. Do you want me to get it?" I asked.

"No, no, it's Jamal al-Tali."

I had been bluffing, knowing that al-Qaeda terrorists like Badawi like to think they're outwitting you. They don't want to be caught lying. It's both a game to them—one they want to win—and a question of honor, as they don't like being called liars. As self-proclaimed religious Muslims, it's embarrassing for them to be caught lying.

The PSO interrogator present told me during a break that he was shocked that Badawi had admitted to using the name. Now we had an admission of one of his aliases, and we put out a search to see where the passport had been used. We found that a pager had been bought under the name, and we questioned Badawi about it. He admitted that it was for the attack: he would be paged when the attack was about to be under way so that he could record it, using a videotape provided by Nashiri for the purpose.

Bit by bit, we teased out details about the operation from Badawi. Throughout, he tried minimizing his own role. He consistently told us that it was Nashiri who had both provided the videotape and instructed him to buy the pager. He had passed both duties on to Quso, who became his deputy for the operation; he had trained Quso in how to use the video and the pager. Quso had not recorded the attack, however, Badawai claimed, because he had overslept.

Al-Qaeda members commonly had the same problems with time-lines that Yemenis did. Part of the reason is cultural: in the West we are trained to think in a linear manner, and we learn that the truth can be arrived at by following a series of logical steps. Al-Qaeda members, however, are greatly influenced by conspiracy theories, and they suspend their critical thinking. Rather than logic, they have a culture based on relationships and impressions, and there is considerable willingness, on their part, to accept conspiracy theories to explain certain events. Bin Laden capitalized on this by reiterating long-standing assertions that America, Israel, and the West were trying to subjugate the Arab and Muslim world and destroy the Islamic faith.

Concomitant with pledging *bayat* to their leader, and in preparation for the possibility of capture by Western intelligence, al-Qaeda operatives are trained to come up with a false narrative that follows linear thinking; but they find it hard to stick to lies when questioned in minute detail. A key part of successful interrogations is to ask detailed questions related to time and whereabouts. Such questions are easy for a detainee to answer if he is telling the truth, but if he is lying, it is hard for him to keep the story straight. Often Badawi would not lie completely but give a partial lie. By zeroing in on the details, we could see where he was lying. I would point it out, he would correct himself, and slowly we'd get the full picture.

Going through events in great detail eventually trips up most liars. At times it felt, as John put it more than once, like pulling teeth. We would ask a series of questions and trap Badawi in a lie. When he was caught or felt that he was about to be caught, he would change his story slightly, inserting more of the truth. He also got angry sometimes when he was caught in a lie, and then he would spill more information. The process required patience; interrogators can't show frustration. That would only encourage the detainee to hold out, thinking the interrogator would soon give up. Instead you have to show you're not in a rush, and are prepared to spend as long as it takes. Persistence is of paramount importance. A mistake some people make is giving an interrogation a fixed time slot. Doing so only alerts the suspect to the fact that all he needs to do is outlast you.

One day of interest was January 3, when the five young fishermen had reported finding the boat on the beach. It seemed to us that al-Qaeda had been planning a second attack, but that something had gone wrong. We checked with the U.S. Navy to determine what ships had been in the area at the time and found that on the night of January 3, the USS *The Sullivans*, a guided-missile destroyer, had been scheduled to be there. It was named after five brothers who had died when their ship, the USS *Juneau*, was sunk in November 1942 by the Japanese. This was the greatest military loss that any one family had suffered during World War II in any single action.

We guessed that Badawi must have known about a planned attack because he had been helping Nashiri. Eventually he admitted that there were two separate plots. Based on the January 3, 2000, timing, we concluded that the initial plan was to attack the USS *The Sullivans*. That plan had failed, and the plotters had turned their full attention to the USS *Cole*.

Badawi eventually pieced together for us his history with al-Qaeda, his friendship with Khallad, and his role in the *Cole* bombing. He also named operatives and training camps, and provided a lot of other detailed information on al-Qaeda. His confession was enough to warrant a full conviction for his role as a co-conspirator in the death of the seventeen U.S. sailors.

12

"What Is al-Qaeda Doing in Malaysia?"

Having gotten Badawi's confession, next came that of his deputy, Quso. Bob McFadden hadn't been able to interview Badawi, because he'd seen the Yemeni interrogators' report of their questioning of him; this was problematic, as they hadn't followed U.S. legal procedures. That hadn't happened with Quso, so Bob joined me in the interrogation room.

Quso laughed and joked with his guards as he walked into the interrogation room. He looked healthy and well rested. He was a small, lanky young man, with a long, narrow face and a scraggly beard he liked to tug on. As soon as he sat down, Ansi, the head of the PSO in Aden, walked into the interrogation room, glanced at us, and then kissed Quso on each cheek, whispering what seemed to be words of encouragement in his ear. Quso turned to us, smiled, and folded his hands.

"Hello," I said to Quso in Arabic, but before I could continue he interrupted me.

"I'm not going to speak to you," he said, waving his hand dismissively. "I'm waiting for the interrogator."

He apparently thought I was a translator and didn't realize that I was an FBI agent. "Well, you'll be waiting a long time, then," I told him.

"I'm the interrogator. I'm with the FBI." He had a look of disbelief on his face, so I showed him my FBI credentials.

"Now that we've got that sorted out, let me introduce myself," I said. Bob introduced himself and we read the Miranda warning. Quso wouldn't sign a declaration, but he nodded and verbally waived his rights. A reluctance to sign a document was common among al-Qaeda members, as some couldn't read so weren't sure what they were signing. Others feared that, once they signed a document, a confession would be added—something they apparently had been warned about.

I learned this later from questioning al-Bara, Khallad's younger brother, who had been locked up by the Yemenis since the Bayt Habra plot to free Mihdhar. He refused to sign the Miranda warning but was prepared to verbally waive his rights, so I asked him, "Why don't you guys sign this?"

"So you don't add anything," he replied.

He explained that in the Arabic version of the Miranda warning, there is a big space between the end of the words and the signature line. He (and other al-Qaeda members, evidently) worried that a "confession" would be added above their signature.

"How about if you cross out the white so that nothing can be added?" I asked. He was happy with that, and with a pen squiggled throughout the white space and then signed the paper.

We started off the interrogation by telling Quso that we knew all about his role in the attack on the *Cole* and that it would be best if he cooperated. He responded angrily, thumping the table and denying any knowledge of it. While our job with Quso should have been relatively easy because Badawi had confessed to both their roles, Quso made it clear that it would not be a smooth process. At times he accused me of being an Israeli intelligence agent. "I don't think you're really a Muslim. You're Mossad," he said.

We worked on connecting with Quso on a personal level, speaking about his desire to one day get married. I expressed sympathy regarding his single status, which seemed to bother him, and said I hoped that one day he would find a suitable bride. I told him that his life was still ahead of him, and that if he gave us information that we needed, there was more of a chance that he would have a future.

Quso had an inflated view of his own intelligence. From the outset he seemed convinced that he could outwit us, and at first he denied any knowledge of the attack. But like Badawi, Quso couldn't keep his timeline straight, as he, too, had a problem with linear thinking. Over the course of the interrogation he repeatedly switched his story when we caught him out.

His initial focus, after admitting a little, was to minimize the culpability of Badawi and himself. He said that he had supported the attack in theory but had not been a part of it, and asked sarcastically if expressing opinions was a crime under American law. Midway through the interrogation he switched to claiming that he and Badawi had attempted to alert the Yemeni authorities. Of course, no record of this attempt was ever found. Quso next tried claiming that he and Badawi had never intended to record the bombings, and that Badawi had told him "to go late." Then he said he had overslept. He also first claimed that he had never asked Badawi who was behind the attack, because "it was a big operation and my culpability was possible, so I did not ask." Later, he admitted he knew what he was meant to record.

We also played the two against each other. We told Quso that Badawi had told us all about his role, and Quso in turn told us that Badawi had told him that the operation would involve a boat laden with explosives ramming a U.S. warship. He had agreed to help after Badawi had told him that the attack would be against a ship that "zealously attacked Muslims" and that the warship was on its way to Iraq to kill innocent citizens. Badawi added that America was an enemy of Islam, which was why the attack was permitted.

Switching to religion, I asked him about the concept of Ahed al-Aman—which promises security and protection for non-Muslims by Muslims. As the Yemeni authorities welcomed the United States to Aden, Ahed al-Aman should apply. Quso countered that the "sheikh overruled that" because of the "evil America does."

"Who is the sheikh?" I asked.

"You know who," he replied. "It's bin Laden."

. . .

We used our knowledge of al-Qaeda to wear down Quso and impress upon him that we understood the inner workings of the organization and the extent of his involvement. After repeatedly getting caught in lies, he began to suspect that I had infiltrated the organization: nothing else could explain my intimacy with its practices. His conviction was so thoroughgoing that at one point he exclaimed, "I saw you in Afghanistan!" Later, he told me, "I saw you in Kandahar."

"Maybe," I said with a smile.

Gradually Quso became almost boastful about his relationship with bin Laden and al-Qaeda. He thought that we knew most of what he was telling us. We didn't.

After finishing high school in 1998, Quso traveled to Afghanistan with two friends from his neighborhood—Taha (who went by a single name) and Mamoun al-Musouwah. Musouwah went on to become a Yemeni policeman and arranged fraudulent documents for al-Qaeda. The young men's trip was sponsored by a radical network run through a school they attended in Taiz: Sheikh Aqeel University, a known al-Qaeda feeder institution. In Afghanistan, Quso traveled from guesthouse to guesthouse. Finally, Abu Khubaib al-Sudani (Ibrahim Ahmed Mahmoud al-Qosi) picked him up and took him to a guesthouse whose emir was bin Laden bodyguard Abu Jandal. Quso said that Abu Jandal had a Saudi accent but Yemeni features; he told us that he found him likable. He described watching Abu Jandal care for an al-Qaeda terrorist who was ill during Ramadan. The terrorist had fasted despite having just had his stomach stapled, a dangerous and foolish thing. Abu Jandal's ministrations brought him back to health. Quso became familiar with other high-ranking al-Qaeda members, including Saif al-Adel, Ayman al-Zawahiri, and Mohammed Atef. We showed Quso a photobook of top members and he was able to identify them.

Quso also met bin Laden at Abu Jandal's guesthouse. His feeling for the al-Qaeda leader bordered on infatuation: he told us that he felt serene and peaceful whenever bin Laden spoke. Bin Laden lectured about aggressions committed by Americans against Muslims and how Muslims had a duty to expel infidels from the Arabian Peninsula. Quso approached one of bin Laden's bodyguards about having an audience with the al-Qaeda leader and was granted one with Taha and Mamoun al-Musouwah. Quso described bin Laden as "very open." They discussed the justification for jihad. Bin Laden impressed upon the three that "if an inch of Muslim land is occupied, Muslims must undertake jihad."

Bin Laden's topic would vary depending upon who was present. When only close associates were in attendance, he spoke freely and at length. When he didn't know his listeners, he was more guarded and hesitant. That Quso knew the difference was an indication that bin Laden came to view him as a trusted associate.

Quso slowly filled in more details about the attack. He said he had learned about it a month and a half beforehand. Badawi had approached him and said that he himself had been charged with the task of recording it but that he would "be busy that day"; so he had asked Quso to step in. He took him to the Tawahi apartment and taught him how to use the camera, a small Sony model. From the window Badawi pointed to two different dolphins (fueling stations) in the harbor and said that the attack would occur at one of them. Quso and Badawi then practiced recording the attack. Quso said that they deleted each practice recording but kept the same tape in the camera. There was also, Quso told us, a new, unused tape in a camera bag.

After their instruction sessions, Badawi gave Quso a pager and told him that he would receive a "010101" page alerting him that the operation was imminent. As soon as he received the page, he should head to the apartment and begin recording the action at the harbor. Badawi gave Quso a key to the apartment.

Quso told us that on the morning of the *Cole* bombing, a Thursday, he woke up early and went to the mosque to read the Quran until sunrise, and then went for morning prayers. There he met his friend Mohammed al-Durrama, who invited him back to his father's house for breakfast. They ate and took a nap, sleeping till around 9:00 or 9:30, and proceeded to the mosque to study the Quran, as they had a test Monday.

Only then, around 9:45 or 10:00, Quso said, did he notice the page; the pager had been on vibrate. He assumed that the page had come while he was sleeping.

He immediately packed up his things at the mosque and went to Badawi's house, where the video camera was stored. Badawi wasn't there—he was at the Ibn al-Amir Institute, a radical religious school in Sanaa—so Quso entered the house using a spare key Badawi had given him. He moved on to his father's house, where the Tawahi apartment key was stored. While there, he also took a spare key for his sister's house. He then jumped in a taxi and headed toward the Tawahi apartment.

When he reached the main street of Ma'alla, a neighborhood near Aden's harbor, he heard a big explosion. He knew that it was the bombing of the ship, and that he had missed it. He told the driver to turn around, and he went to his sister's house. No one was home, and he let himself in using the spare key. He hid the video camera and called Badawi in Sanaa. Quso reported to Badawi that the operation had taken place but that he hadn't videotaped it.

Next Quso headed to al-Ridda Mosque for the noon prayer. On the way, he received a page from Badawi and stopped at a calling center near a taxi stand to get in touch with him. Badawi asked him to "report the news." Quso told him that he heard ambulances heading toward the harbor but didn't know anything else. Badawi asked Quso to go to his (Badawi's) house to collect three bags and drop them off at his in-laws'. He told Badawi that he was nervous about the situation in Aden and was planning to head to Sanaa. Badawi agreed that it was a good idea. Their conversation was "anxious," Quso said.

Later, in the Ba-Nafa' souk, Quso received a third page from Badawi, who again asked about "the news." Quso said that he had new information: his sister had told him that she had heard from neighbors that a boat had collided with a military ship. Badawi told Quso he had a new, "important" job for him. "The truck and trailer are still at the launch site," Badawi said. "I need you to get them. The keys are in the truck." Quso refused, telling Badawi that a police unit was stationed near the bridge and that it would be dangerous.

"Everyone in my neighborhood knows that I don't have a truck and a boat," Quso continued. "If I am seen after the explosion driving a truck with a boat trailer, it will attract suspicion. I'll be picked up."

"If you don't pick it up," Badawi replied, "then all of Burayqah will be under suspicion."

"It's too dangerous, I can't. I'm coming to Sanaa tonight." And Quso hung up.

Quso headed toward Badawi's house to get the three bags. En route, he bumped into his friend Yasser al-Shini, another al-Qaeda operative, who said he'd help him. The two picked up the bags: a green bag, a briefcase, and a leather purse. Quso asked Shini to close the safe house and warn all the other brothers to leave Aden. Next Quso went to pick up his friend Mohammed al-Durrama, who had told Quso he would leave for Sanaa with him.

The three headed toward Quso's house so that he could get some personal items. On their way, Quso received a fourth page from Badawi, checking on the status of the bags. Quso told him that he had the bags with him but that, rather than dropping them at Badawi's in-laws', it would be easier for him to drop them somewhere closer, so that he and Durrama could head to Sanaa sooner. Badawi was insistent that they drop the bags at the in-laws'.

Quso did so, and then he and Durrama headed toward Sanaa. As they passed over the al-Burayqah bridge, Quso saw that the truck and trailer were still parked under it. They arrived in Sanaa after midnight and called the al-Amir Institute, and Badawi instructed a guard to let them in.

A few days later, Quso said, security forces came and picked up Badawi. Quso remained in Sanaa until the following week, evading the authorities. He called his parents in Aden, only to find that his father had been taken into custody. Realizing that the noose was tightening around him and that his family was paying the consequences, he went back to Aden and surrendered himself to the PSO.

I was never convinced that Quso had in fact overslept. When the PSO went to Quso's sister's house, they found the camera where he said he had put it, but only one tape was found. There should have been two—the practice tape and the spare tape. Quso couldn't explain what had happened to the second tape.

Acting on a hunch, I asked him, "So who videotaped the operation, then, if you didn't?"

"Maybe the *jinn* did it," he replied, smiling. No sooner had he invoked the "genie" than Naji, the head of President Saleh's security team, terminated the interrogation, citing Quso's need for rest.

The moment was lost. In interrogations you often have one moment where a suspect makes a slip, and only if you seize on it immediately can you pursue it. If you don't, he has a chance to reorganize his story and cover up.

Throughout our interrogations of Quso, Ansi paid extra close attention to what we were asking and what he was answering. He seemed to have more of a personal interest in the Quso interrogation than in Badawi's or any others'. Often when Quso was in a tight spot and trapped by our questioning, Ansi would call for a break in the interrogation.

One day, after we had finished questioning Quso, Ansi asked me to take a ride with him in his car. I hesitated, as we had strict security procedures and were never to travel without the FBI SWAT agents responsible for our protection, but I didn't want to insult Ansi by saying I didn't trust him. Perhaps he had something important to tell me, I reasoned. I got into his car, and from the side mirror I saw a worried-looking Carlos Fernandez in the FBI convoy following us.

He drove very slowly, which made me nervous. After a few minutes of silence, he began talking about the interrogations and our investigation. We discussed the evidence we were building up and the progress that was being made. Eventually he said to me, "I believe Quso is a good, simple youth. I believe that Badawi is the man who needs to be prosecuted."

It was strange that he was trying to portray Quso as a good person and place the blame on Badawi. "Well, it seems that there are a lot of people who are bad and are involved," I replied, and he returned to the hotel without raising the topic again.

Ansi also got agitated when our investigation led us to al-Qaeda sympathizers among Yemeni officials. At one point we interrogated two Yemeni police officials, Yasser al-Surruri and Mohammed al-Murakab, who, under questioning, admitted to having helped terrorists obtain fraudulent passports. We had found these two officials through Quso's friend Mamoun al-Musouwah, the corrupt policeman. As I emerged from the session with Surruri and Murakab that had yielded that information, I saw Ansi—in the courtyard of the PSO prison where we were conducting the interrogation—and asked, "Can we have the pictures of the operatives Surruri and Murakab identified?"

"No."

"Why? They're possible suspects and we need to look into them."

"No," Ansi repeated. "Why are they important, anyway? You don't know if they're involved. Just because they have beards, it doesn't mean they're terrorists."

"You're missing the point," I replied. "These are known al-Qaeda members getting fraudulent documents. Surruri and Murakah already admitted it. And, yes, they are terrorists." The next time we spoke to Surruri and Murakab, Ansi yelled at them for speaking directly to us rather than to Yemeni interrogators and slapped Murakab.

Ansi later complained that, by talking directly to suspects, we were violating the rules agreed upon by David Kelley and the judge, as the rules spelled out that we were to ask the Yemeni officials our questions for them to repeat. But this system soon broke down: once we had established rapport with the Yemeni interrogators, they saw no reason for us not to ask questions directly. It was comical for me to ask a question in Arabic and then for the Yemenis to repeat it; it made no sense and just wasted time. Even the suspects got frustrated.

Our problems with Ansi continued to multiply. One day, when I arrived with FBI agent Andre Khoury to conduct interrogations, a PSO guard told us apologetically, "Sorry, there will be no interrogations today." I asked why. "Hussein Ansi told us so." Again I asked why. "We don't know. That's just what he ordered us to say."

Andre and I went looking for Ansi and found him at his desk, reading the Quran. "Good morning, Hussein," I said to him as pleasantly as

I could. "We were told there would be no interrogations today. What's going on?"

"I am busy today," he replied, a smirk briefly crossing his face.

"I can see," I said, pointing to the Quran. "It is heavenly work you are busy with." He smiled. "So we can't talk to suspects today?" I asked.

"No," he replied. We both smiled, continuing the pretense.

I started walking around his office. His desk was opposite the door; chairs and couches surrounded it. Behind were bookshelves filled with memorabilia, books, and binders. I paused in front of one of the book-shelves. Ansi tried to look at the Quran but kept nervously glancing up to see what I was doing. I pretended not to notice him looking and started removing memorabilia and books, as if I were interested in their content. After taking out something, I would deliberately put it back in the wrong place. Andre did the same.

"Don't touch my things," Ansi said after about a minute, his eyes flashing in anger. It apparently drove him crazy that we were ruining the organization of the shelves.

"He has nothing else to do," Andre said with a smile, "so he is going to mess up your office until you give him something to do."

"Okay, okay," Ansi replied. "You have access to the prisoners."

"Thank you, Hussein," I replied with a smile.

During our interrogation of Quso we also covered his activities during the week before the bombing. On the day before the *Cole* attack, he said that he was at Ibn al-Qayyim Mosque in al-Burayqah and that four brothers from Sanaa had walked in. One of them, Abdullah al-Rimi, he'd known since 1994, when they had studied at Sheikh Aqeel University; in subsequent years, Rimi had become an important al-Qaeda recruiter. Quso greeted them and invited them to his residence, Bayt al-Shabab—the House of Youths. The al-Qaeda guesthouse operated under the claim of *da'wa*, a calling for the faith. Fellow al-Qaeda members and potential recruits could linger and talk.

The men accepted his invitation and stayed for a half-hour, drinking tea. Another operative, Yasser Ahmad Qassem, came as well and spoke to Rimi privately. Rimi, Qassem, and a driver departed, while Quso left the house to arrange for lunch at the house of Yasser al-Azzani, a known al-Qaeda operative. After the noon prayer they all gathered at Azzani's. Other local al-Qaeda operatives joined them, including Ahmad al-Shini and Mohammed al-Durrama.

One discussion at lunch centered on funding jihad, and some of those present accused Rimi of "favoritism" with regard to expenditures and allocation of funds. Quso initially agreed, until Rimi said that, as he worked hard to raise the money from donors, he was free to decide how to spend the money. Quso agreed that it was a valid point. Rimi then told Quso that they wanted to go swimming in the sea, and everyone but Quso went off to find trunks. Following the afternoon prayer, Quso returned from the mosque and was told that the visitors had already gone back to Sanaa.

When Quso described this occasion, at first it sounded to us like a good-bye luncheon for the *Cole* bombers. He identified a photo of Musawa and said that he had been present; by now we identified him as Hassan al-Khamiri, using the alias Abu Ali. That wasn't the only connection between the luncheon and the attack: another of the guests had fought, in Afghanistan, under Taha al-Ahdal, who was meant to be the *Sullivans* suicide bomber. If the luncheon was a final send-off for the bombers, it would have meant that many in Yemen had had advance knowledge of the attack and of the fact that the *Cole* was coming. When we looked further, however, we found that Rimi was simply trying to get fraudulent passports for al-Qaeda terrorists for future operations. There was no apparent direct operational connection between the lunch and the *Cole* attack.

After covering Quso's path to al-Qaeda and his actions in the days before the *Cole*, we broadened the discussion to cover the months prior to the *Cole*. One episode stood out, although to Quso it wasn't a big deal, which is perhaps why he didn't see any problem in telling us about it. In late December 1999, Quso had received a phone call from Khallad, whom he knew well from Afghanistan. The two men had become so friendly there that at one point they had even discussed Khallad's marrying Quso's sister, although that didn't end up happening.

Quso described Khallad as having a slight build, thick hair, a Saudi accent, a full beard, and "pretty eyes," which matched my own observation, based on the ID Qamish had shown me—except for the beard: though the operatives tended to have beards while they were in Afghanistan, when they traveled for operations they cut their beards to try to blend in. Khallad claimed to be twenty-five, but Quso thought that he was older. The two had remained in contact even after Quso had left Afghanistan, and Khallad had told Quso that if he ever wished to return, Khallad's father, Mohammed bin Saleh bin Attash, would fund his trip.

Khallad had an important favor to ask Quso. Khallad's father had sent $36,000 from Saudi Arabia to an al-Qaeda operative named Ibrahim al-Thawer, alias Nibras, in Sanaa. We were still unaware, when we interrogated Quso, that Nibras was one of the *Cole* suicide bombers. Quso knew Nibras from Afghanistan; they had fought on the same front and at one point had stayed in the same guesthouse. (Nibras had also fought in Bosnia.) According to Quso, Khallad said that the money was for a new prosthesis. Khallad was in Asia at the time, and he had told Nibras to take the money to Singapore, where he'd meet him and collect it. But Khallad felt that, for customs reasons, $36,000 was too large an amount for Nibras to carry alone. Without hesitation Quso agreed to help.

As Quso told us about the phone call, his tone and demeanor livened up. It was clear that he was proud of his connection to Khallad, an important al-Qaeda member, and of the status conferred upon him by Khallad's having enlisted his help.

Quso went to Sanaa, and he and Nibras had dinner and discussed the trip. Nibras told Quso to shave and to wear trousers (instead of the traditional Yemeni garb) in order to blend in and not attract attention at the airport. They had to be careful, he warned, especially as they already had Pakistan entry and exit stamps on their passports from their time fighting in Afghanistan. Quso returned to Aden, waiting for Nibras to finalize their tickets.

On January 4, 2000, they set off for the airport. (Quso thought that the driver was a relative of Nibras's, possibly his uncle, Abu Saif—the leader of the al-Qaeda cell in Sanaa who, in October 2003, would be killed in a confrontation with the Yemeni authorities.) The two divided the $36,000 between them, Quso putting $9,000 in one trouser pocket and $7,000 in the other. They flew to Bangkok via Abu Dhabi, and from there they planned to head to Singapore, having been told by their travel agent in Sanaa that they could purchase visas for Singapore in the airport in Bangkok. That turned out to be untrue, and after several attempts to negotiate with Thai authorities in their limited English, they gave up. Stuck in Bangkok, they negotiated a thirty-day visa to stay and checked into the Washington Hotel.

From there they called Abu Saif in Sanaa and told him what had happened; they assumed that Khallad might have called him when they had failed to show up in Singapore. They told Abu Saif that they would wait in the hotel until they received further instructions. Quso also phoned his family and gave them the same message in case Khallad contacted them. Khallad, however, also didn't know that a visa was needed in advance to enter Singapore, and he, too, was turned back—at the Kuala Lumpur airport he was departing from. He called Nibras's uncle, who updated him on what had happened to Quso and Nibras. Khallad got in touch with Quso and Nibras at the Washington Hotel and told them to stay put; he would come to them. In passing, he mocked them for not getting visas, neglecting to mention that he had made the same mistake.

Khallad arrived in Bangkok the next day. He embraced Quso and Nibras warmly and, when they had handed over the $36,000, thanked them for their help, whereupon the two couriers purchased new tickets and returned to Yemen.

The story left Bob and me puzzled. Why, in the midst of planning an attack as big as the bombing of the USS *The Sullivans*, would al-Qaeda transfer $36,000 out of Yemen? Quso's explanation that the money was for a new prosthesis for Khallad seemed highly unlikely; they usually didn't cost more than $2,000. We sent a lead to the FBI agent based in Bangkok, suggesting that he go to the Washington Hotel to investigate. At the same time, we checked phone calls made between the hotel and Abu Saif (Nibras's uncle) and were able to determine which room in the hotel Quso and Nibras had used. Next we ran a reverse dump (checking incoming calls) on Quso's Aden number, Abu Saif's Sanaa number, and the phone number of the Washington Hotel room they had stayed in, and found that they were all in contact with a number in Kuala Lumpur. After further investigation we determined that the Kuala Lumpur number was a pay phone.

This, we deduced, must have been where Khallad was contacting them from. What was Khallad doing in Malaysia? And was this pay phone something al-Qaeda regularly used? We didn't know the answers, so we asked the CIA—the U.S. government entity responsible for gathering intelligence outside the country.

At each step of our investigating the Yemen–Bangkok–Malaysia connection, every time we gained an important lead or had new questions, we sent the CIA an official request (through the director of the FBI) asking if they had information. (It is standard procedure for any official request from the FBI to the CIA, or vice versa, to go through the office of the director. This doesn't mean that the director personally signs off on it or sees it, but it means, rather, that it is an official, high-level request.)

It was in November 2000 that we asked the CIA whether they knew anything about Khallad being in Malaysia or about an al-Qaeda meeting there. The CIA responded (also through the official channels) that they didn't know anything about al-Qaeda gatherings in Malaysia, and suggested we ask the National Security Agency. The NSA didn't have the answers for us, either.

In April 2001, after our Legat's investigations turned up the pay phone number in Kuala Lumpur that we had by then determined had probably been used by Khallad, we sent the CIA a second official request—called, in the FBI, a teletype—asking if they knew anything about the number. This request again went through the office of the director. No response came.

Our third official request was sent in July 2001, when we learned some new details. (Each new request was sent because we had new details or questions, not because we suspected the CIA hadn't responded

truthfully to our previous inquiries.) Again we asked if they knew anything about Khallad and al-Qaeda being in Malaysia or about the phone
number. No information was passed along to us.

Notwithstanding our successes in the interrogation room, the security situation in Aden deteriorated, as protests against our presence by
Yemeni clerics and parliamentarians multiplied, as did the death threats.
Sources told us with increasing frequency that al-Qaeda operatives in
the country were plotting to strike at us, including a cell that had traveled to Aden with that purpose. By June 2001 the situation was judged
by headquarters to be so dangerous that those of us remaining in the
country moved from Aden to Sanaa—viewed as a safer location. The
Yemenis agreed to transfer the suspects we needed to interrogate to
Sanaa.

We initially stayed at the Sheraton Hotel, but as the threats only
continued to increase in number—and as the cell that had moved to
Aden to attack us had reportedly followed us to Sanaa—we moved to
the U.S. Embassy. Another change we made was to hold our interrogations at night; and we traveled in unmarked cars. We also helped the
Yemenis track down the cell threatening us, and in June they arrested
eight men whom they accused of plotting to bomb the U.S. Embassy
and attack us and Ambassador Bodine.

Staying in the embassy was far from an ideal situation; space and
services were limited. We slept on the floor and showered in Marine
House, where the marines live within the embassy compound. The
cafeteria couldn't prepare enough food, so we had to order from outside, befriending a Lebanese restaurant owner, who delivered meals
every day.

Ambassador Bodine ordered that every member of the FBI and
NCIS investigation team pay five to ten dollars a day to the embassy
cleaning staff. This came out of our pockets; the FBI doesn't pick up
the tab when agents stay in an embassy or any government facility. FBI
and NCIS headquarters were furious that an ambassador would charge
agents for sleeping on the floor of an embassy. The cost didn't bother

us; what mattered was that it left us feeling that we weren't even welcome in our own embassy.

With our long guns locked in the embassy safe by order of Ambassador Bodine, we got around their absence in two different ways. The marines in charge of the safe deliberately left it unlocked in risky situations so we could access the guns if needed. They had again included us in their training, and so needed us to have easy access. Fellow FBI agents like Don Borelli took shifts on the roof of the embassy. Some embassy personnel also purchased long guns at the local market, joking about how easy it was for anyone to get a gun in Yemen, unless you were a U.S. official who needed it more than anyone else.

Meanwhile, on June 11, 2001, a CIA official, Clark S., went with Maggie Gillespie, an FBI analyst assigned to the CIA's bin Laden unit, and Dina Corsi, an FBI analyst stationed at bureau headquarters in Washington, DC, to meet with members of the USS *Cole* team in New York. They said that they had some questions about the case. I was in Yemen, but Steve Bongardt, my co–case agent, was in New York, and he led the team.

For the first few hours of the meeting, Steve and the team briefed the three visitors on progress made in the investigation. Once they had finished, at around 2:00 PM, Clark S. asked Dina to show photographs to the *Cole* team members. She put three crisp surveillance pictures on the table in front of them.

We learned months later that Dina had been given the three pictures by Tom Wilshire, a CIA official, and that she had been told only that they had been taken in Kuala Lumpur, and that one of the men in them was named Khalid al-Mihdhar. She had not been told who he was or why the CIA was monitoring him. Tom, we later learned, was fishing to see if the FBI knew anything about the men in the photos.

Clark S. asked Steve and the team whether Fahd al-Quso was in any of the pictures, and whether they recognized anyone else. Quso wasn't in any of the three pictures, Steve said after studying them, and they didn't recognize anyone else.

Steve then fired off a series of his own questions: "But who are these guys? Why are you showing these pictures to us? Where were they taken? Are there other pictures? What is their connection to the *Cole*?"

He was told that they couldn't tell him, and when he asked why, he was told that it involved "information that can't be shared with criminal agents." Dina later said that annotations on the reports indicated that they couldn't be shared with criminal investigators without permission from the Justice Department's Office of Intelligence Policy and Review. (The 9/11 Commission later reported that Dina had never sought OIPR approval. Either way, she could have shared the information with Steve, as he was a designated intelligence agent.)

Steve and the team started arguing back—it was the same wall that Steve had gone up against when he was in Yemen—and a shouting match ensued. Steve and the team tried to convince and cajole Clark S. to share the information. As far as they knew, the pictures were somehow relevant to our investigation in Yemen. Why else would the CIA be coming to the *Cole* team and asking about Quso? Who were the men, and what was the meeting that the CIA had monitored? Was there another plot we should be aware of? Clark S. wouldn't say.

Steve and the team argued harder, in part because of the threat those of us still in Yemen were under: we had moved to Sanaa from Aden because of the threat to our lives, and now it was reported that the threat had followed us to Sanaa. Perhaps the men in the photos were part of that threat. Or perhaps they could help with final pieces of the *Cole* puzzle, allowing us to come home sooner.

"One of these men is named Khalid al-Mihdhar," Dina eventually said.

"Who is Khalid al-Mihdhar?" Steve asked. "Why have you been monitoring him? Can you tell us anything about him?"

Silence.

"What's his passport number? Do you have his date of birth?"

Silence.

Steve and the team were desperate for any information. A name alone isn't much help when you are trying to search for someone about whom you know nothing—someone who could be anywhere in the world.

Clark S. refused to provide any information, and eventually he, Dina, and Maggie left.

For the next few weeks and months, Steve contacted Dina, asking for more information. Each time, she told him that, according to the "rules," she couldn't share information with him. He protested up the chain of command—to headquarters—but was told to "stand down." (After 9/11, Wilshire told investigators that he had asked if he could share the information with the FBI, but that his superiors in the agency had never responded.)

It wasn't only Dina who misunderstood the rules regarding information sharing. The problems were right across the U.S. government, and they were to the point of being absurd. In February, Steve had been at a meeting in Yemen with Yemeni officials and Howard Leadbetter, who was on a thirty-day rotation as the FBI commander. At some point Leadbetter asked Steve to step out of the meeting while he spoke to the Yemenis about some intelligence.

"Come on, if the Yemenis can know it, I can know it," Steve said.

"Sorry."

One day in Sanaa—we had been there for about a week—we were told that we were to be evacuated from Yemen. New, verified threats had surfaced that all those in residence would be assassinated—Bob McFadden and I, the ambassador, the CIA chief, and the defense attaché. We shredded all our documents, packed up all our gear, and boarded cars to head for the airport.

But the gates of the embassy wouldn't open. The head of the Marine Security Guard (MSG), responsible for guarding the embassy, apologetically told us that he had received a call from the State Department's regional security officer, who said that Ambassador Bodine had ordered that the gates not be opened until she had spoken further about it with the deputy secretary of state, Richard Armitage. "I'm sorry, it's nothing personal, but these are my orders," the MSG head told us. We had a good relationship with the marines. They had asked us to help them in their drills to secure the embassy, and so we often trained with them. We took turns on guard duty. With all nonessential personal gone from the embassy, they needed all the help they could get. We had readily pitched in, and a friendship developed between us. But here they had no choice: the ambassador was their boss.

Mary Galligan, who was doing the thirty-day rotation in charge of the FBI contingent, and Steve Corbett, NCIS on-ground commander, went to speak to Ambassador Bodine, who told them that the message sent by everyone's leaving the embassy would be damaging to our relationship with the Yemenis. However, she told Mary and Steve, if Bob and I stayed, she'd let everyone else leave. That way, she reasoned, the Yemenis would take comfort: she knew that they liked us.

Bob and I were prepared to accept this deal, and Mary conveyed that to FBI headquarters. "No, one team, one fight," the message came back. In addition, they reported that Bob and I were on the top of the target list for the terrorists, who knew that we were the ones spearheading the investigation and interrogating their operatives.

The director of the FBI called the secretary of state and explained the situation. The secretary intervened, and Ambassador Bodine was ordered to unlock the doors and let us leave. We flew to Fort Dix, where John O'Neill and Kenny Maxwell were waiting for us, and we drove with them back to New York City.

It was frustrating to be out of Yemen. Despite the threats, we had made important progress in the *Cole* investigation, and we had enough evidence to start prosecuting Badawi and Quso. Moreover, the real threats that prompted us to leave were a strong indication that al-Qaeda was still strong in Yemen. We needed to track those people down. There were other people that the Yemenis had in custody, ostensibly unconnected to the *Cole* bombing; we wanted to interrogate them because of their importance to al-Qaeda. High on this list were bodyguard Abu Jandal and al-Bara, Khallad's brother.

Then there was the lingering issue of Khallad and Malaysia. We kept asking the CIA about it, and they continued to insist that they didn't know anything about it. We wanted to try to investigate that further. Because of all these questions and issues, we kept pressing headquarters to grant us permission to go back.

In August we got the green light and returned to Yemen to meet with their officials to discuss terms for the FBI and NCIS team to return in safety to the country. I went with Kenny Maxwell and other officials to Sanaa to speak to the Yemenis. It was Kenny's first time in Yemen.

Ambassador Bodine was pleased to see the FBI reengaging in Yemen, and she offered the assistance of the mission to accomplish this goal. The long gun issue was still a point of contention, but by now no one could ignore the true nature of the threat. Bodine agreed that long guns could be carried, but only by agents from the Diplomatic Security Service (DSS), who would guard us.

The second item on the agenda was to find a secure location for the team to be based. Ambassador Bodine's deputy showed us an apartment in the Russian City area of Sanaa. Playing the tour guide, he pointed to a room where "you sit on the ground, talk about your day, and chew qat." We explained to Kenny that qat is an addictive drug, illegal in the United States but common in Yemen. About the fifth time the State Department official had mentioned, in utter seriousness, how convenient the apartment was for chewing qat, Kenny couldn't contain himself. He looked at the official, then at me, disbelievingly, and said without a trace of emotion, "Isn't that wonderful." Here we were, trying to restart the investigation into the murder of seventeen U.S. sailors, and the guy kept talking about the pleasures of chewing qat. "Welcome to Yemen," I said to Kenny with a sad smile as we walked out.

Kenny is a big Irish guy, a former state trooper, and he comes from a long line of law enforcement officials. He's straitlaced and absolutely focused on the job, and while he has a sense of humor, when the topic is national security he won't mess around. After meeting with the Yemenis, we returned to New York, and John O'Neill came over to JTTF and asked Kenny how he had enjoyed his first visit to Yemen. Kenny replied, "John, I don't know what you've been talking about with regard to problems with the ambassador. She strikes me as such a wonderful lady. She asked me to teach a class in Santa Barbara"— Ambassador Bodine's hometown. John gave him the finger, grinned, and walked out.

John's last act in the FBI was to sign an order for our return to Yemen. The last time I saw him was on August 22, 2001, his last day at work.

He had decided to leave the bureau because of mounting frustration with the way things were being run. He was upset that headquarters wasn't more forcefully supporting our efforts to investigate the *Cole*. He complained that the bureau had become a timid bureaucracy, too afraid to push when necessary and get things done, and he warned that lives would be lost.

John also had an investigation hanging over his head. In July, while attending an FBI conference, he received a page and removed himself to another room to take it. Thinking he'd be back in a few minutes, he had left his briefcase in the room full of FBI officials. His call took longer than expected, and when he returned, the other agents had left and his briefcase was missing. It contained some classified e-mails and a sensitive report on national security operations in New York. The director of the FBI and the attorney general were notified.

The briefcase was found a few hours later, and while some personal items had been stolen, none of the documents had been removed. A fingerprint analysis revealed that the documents had not been touched. Nonetheless, the Justice Department ordered a criminal inquiry.

The lack of support that the bureau gave him on this issue, coupled with everything else, made him feel that it was time for him to leave. He had been offered a well-paying job as the head of security for the World Trade Center. It was a sad decision for him, as he loved the bureau and the work we did.

John and I walked to Joe's Diner, across the street from our offices, and John ordered a ham and cheese sandwich. "You don't want to change your infidel ways?" I joked, pointing to the ham. "You'll go to hell."

I told John that I was planning to propose to Heather, my girlfriend. In the past, John had been critical of marriage. It probably didn't help that his own personal life was tangled and messy. But this time there were no anti-marriage barbs from him. Instead he simply said: "She has put up with you all this time. She must be a good woman."

John then showed me an e-mail he had written to Lou Gunn, whose son, Cherone, was killed on the USS *Cole*. It read, in part: "Today is my last day. In my thirty-one years of government service, my proudest moment was when I was selected to lead the investigation of the attack on the USS *Cole*. I have put my all into the investigation and truly believe that significant progress has been made. Unknown to you and the families is that I have cried with your loss. . . . I will keep you and all the families in my prayers and will continue to track the investigation as a civilian. God bless you, your loved ones, the families and God bless America."

"Don't be a stranger," John said as we said good-bye outside the diner. "Remember, I'm only down the road."

"I'm not sure they'll let me visit you," I said with a smile, referring to FBI officials in headquarters who didn't like John.

"Fuck them," he said with a half-grin, half-frown, and after giving me a hug he walked off down the street.

The next day, on August 23, 2001, Maggie Gillespie sent a message to the FBI, Customs, and the State Department asking that two individuals, Khalid al-Mihdhar and Nawaf al-Hazmi, be watchlisted, meaning that they'd be arrested if they attempted to enter or leave the United States.

Earlier in the summer, she had been asked by Tom Wilshire to look through materials the CIA had related to Khalid al-Mihdhar "in her free time." She had started looking at the end of July and continued through August. Maggie had found a CIA cable noting that Mihdhar had a U.S. visa, and a second cable noting that Nawaf al-Hazmi, labeled an associate of Mihdhar's, had flown to Los Angeles in January 2000. On August 22 Maggie went to the INS to investigate further and discovered that Mihdhar had entered the United States on January 15, 2000, and then again on July 4, 2001. She reported back to Wilshire and also passed on the information to Dina Corsi.

Dina sent an e-mail to Jack Cloonan, the acting supervisor of the I-49 squad. Labeled "IT: al Qaeda" (IT standing for International Terrorism), the e-mail asked that the squad investigate whether Khalid al-

Mihdhar was still in the United States. Her message stated that because of Mihdhar's possible connection to the *Cole*, he was a threat to national security. Beyond that, the e-mail gave no real details about Mihdhar or his connection to al-Qaeda. Dina also wrote that only intelligence agents could be involved in the search. However, she accidentally copied Steve Bongardt on the e-mail. He called her as soon as he had read it.

"Dina, you've got to be kidding me. Mihdhar is in the country?" He could hardly contain his anger.

Steve remembered the name from the June 11 meeting and the stonewalling he and the team had received. As far as he knew, based upon what had been implied by the June 11 meeting, Mihdhar was somehow connected to the *Cole*, which made him a threat to the United States. Now Steve was being told Mihdhar was in the United States. How had the FBI not been told?

"Steve, you've got to delete that," Dina replied nervously. "We'll have a conference call about it tomorrow."

Dina called the next day, with a senior CIA official also on the line. Steve was told by the senior official that he had to "stand down" regarding Mihdhar. He was furious to hear—again—that this was intelligence that couldn't be shared with criminal agents.

"If this guy is in the country, it's not because he's going to fucking Disneyland," Steve retorted.

"Stand down," the senior official replied.

The following day, Steve sent Dina an e-mail: "Whatever has happened to this—someday someone will die—and wall or not—the public will not understand why we were not more effective and throwing every resource we had at certain 'problems.' Let's hope the National Security Law Unit will stand behind their decisions then, especially since the biggest threat to us now, UBL [Osama bin Laden], is getting the most 'protection.'"

Only FBI personnel, and Steve Corbett and Bob McFadden of NCIS, returned to Yemen in late August 2001; the NYPD and City Hall decided that it was too dangerous to send their people. The head of our team was my old supervisor Tom Donlon, and we stayed at the Sanaa Sheraton.

Delegations from Washington occasionally visited us. Alabama senator Richard Shelby and his wife, Annette, stayed in the ambassador's house. I was invited to join them for dinner, and during the meal I briefed them on the *Cole* investigation and what we were doing in Yemen. As I was leaving the residence, Senator Shelby walked out with me, and, putting his arm around my shoulders, said, "You have to promise me something."

"What is that, Senator?"

"Don't leave the FBI before you finish investigating this case."

"I'm not planning on it, sir."

While FBI headquarters was barely on speaking terms with Ambassador Bodine, I always had a cordial relationship with her. Her anger was primarily directed at John and others. As the case agent, I tried to keep my eyes on the ball, and she was always kind and polite to me.

One evening in the embassy, during a conversation, she told me that she had been in Kuwait when Saddam invaded, launching the first Gulf War. She hadn't felt unsafe then, she told me; nor did she feel unsafe in Yemen. The only time she had felt unsafe in her life, she continued, was when she took part in a protest in Santa Barbara and a policeman held a gun to her face and told her to go home.

What surprised me most about Ambassador Bodine was that she attacked the FBI in the pages of the *Washington Post* years later, in May 2008, when the Yemeni government released some of the terrorists responsible for the *Cole* bombing—terrorists we had helped lock up. Instead of holding the Yemenis accountable, she was quoted as saying that the FBI had been slow to trust Yemeni authorities and had been "dealing with a bureaucracy and a culture they didn't understand. . . . We had one group working on a New York minute, and another on a 4,000-year-old history."

It was shocking to read those words, especially given the centrality of the *Cole* to the 9/11 attacks. I responded in an opinion piece: "In fact, our team included several Arab American agents who understood the culture and the region. Even so, such comments were irrelevant. The FBI left Yemen with the terrorists in jail. It is true that while tracking the terrorists we worked 'on a New York minute.' We owed that much to the sailors murdered on the *Cole* and to all innocent people who remained targets as long as the terrorists were free. It is also true that we did not trust some Yemeni officials. We had good reason not to." The Yemenis themselves later reluctantly admitted that our distrust of some officials was merited: after Quso and Badawi "escaped" from jail in April 2003, we pressured the authorities to look into the matter, and Hussein Ansi was arrested, questioned, and sacked (but they never prosecuted him).

The difficult relationship we had with Ambassador Bodine was no secret to the Yemenis, who knew that if they had any problems with us they could turn to her. This often undermined progress. Many Yemeni officials were even sympathetic to us in this situation. One day, while I was interrogating a suspect, the head of President Saleh's security team, Naji, came running into the room and said, "Can I talk to you outside?"

I stepped out, thinking it must be important. "Well," he said with a grave look on his face. "I don't know quite how to say this to you, but a plane has been hijacked."

"What plane?"

"Your ambassador is on the plane."

"What's the situation? Is she okay?"

"It's all okay," he replied. "It was some crazy guy. He didn't even know the ambassador was on board. And while he was in the cockpit, all the passengers escaped via one of the emergency doors. The hijacker was then hit over the head with a fire extinguisher by a crew member." Naji couldn't contain a big smile at this point. He found it highly ironic that Ambassador Bodine had been hijacked when she downplayed our concerns about safety. Naji was also fond of John and knew he hadn't returned because Bodine wouldn't give him clearance.

We had seventeen main reasons for returning to Yemen and pressing ahead despite the death threats and all other complications. They were:

Hull Maintenance Technician 2nd Class Kenneth Eugene
    Clodfelter
Electronics Technician Chief Petty Officer Richard Costelow

Mess Management Specialist Seaman Lakeina Monique
    Francis

Information Systems Technician Seaman Timothy Lee Gauna

Signalman Seaman Cherone Louis Gunn

Seaman James Rodrick McDaniels

Engineman 2nd Class Marc Ian Nieto

Electronics Warfare Technician 2nd Class Ronald Scott Owens

Seaman Lakiba Nicole Palmer

Engineman Fireman Joshua Langdon Parlett

Fireman Patrick Howard Roy

Electronic Warfare Technician 1st Class Kevin Shawn Rux

Mess Management Specialist 3rd Class Ronchester Manangan
    Santiago

Operations Specialist 2nd Class Timothy Lamont Saunders

Fireman Gary Graham Swenchonis Jr.

Ensign Andrew Triplett

Seaman Craig Bryan Wibberley

Those are the seventeen U.S. sailors who were murdered on the USS *Cole* by al-Qaeda. Each of their names alone was justification enough for our being in Yemen. And until their murderers were tracked down and justice was served, we did not feel that we could rest. We owed it to each one of these sailors and their families to find their killers. Those of us from the FBI, the NCIS, the CIA, and the military who investigated the *Cole* bombing believed that no American death should go unpunished. America sitting idly by would be a message to future terrorists to strike without fear of reprisal.

To this day what keeps me awake at night is the disgraceful way that so many in the U.S. government treated the memory of the sailors. I cannot understand the lack of support for our investigation. For reasons unknown, both Democrats and Republicans in the White House and in senior government positions tried to ignore what had happened to the USS *Cole*. Families of the murdered sailors told me with sadness that President George W. Bush refused to meet with them.

13

Bin Laden's Errand Boy

Walid bin Attash, or Khallad, was as close to being al-Qaeda royalty as possible. His father was friends with bin Laden, Abdullah Azzam, and Omar Abdul Rahman, the Blind Sheikh. His older brother, Muhannad, had been a trusted bin Laden lieutenant and pivotal in the recruitment of the Northern Group. Khallad himself had joined al-Qaeda in 1994, when he was only fifteen.

A defining moment in Khallad's life had come in 1997, when he and Muhannad, along with other al-Qaeda fighters, had fought with the Taliban against the Northern Alliance at Murad Beg, north of Kabul. Muhannad had been killed in the battle, and Khallad had lost his left leg when a howitzer misfired, releasing shrapnel into it. He had been rushed from the battlefield to a hospital, but the leg could not be saved and was amputated below the knee.

He had received a prosthesis from an NGO, but it hadn't fit properly and had left him in severe pain. Khallad had already been plunged into a state of depression over the death of Muhannad, and his leg pain had caused even more anguish. Al-Qaeda had sent him to Karachi for therapy, accompanied by his younger brother, al-Bara, who had fought with him at Murad Beg. They had spent the afternoons at the beach in Karachi, with al-Bara pushing Khallad in a wheelchair.

Khallad's misery had been relieved by the arrival of a personal letter from bin Laden, praising both his dedication to the cause and Muhannad's martyrdom. Khallad had resolved to take his brother's place as a central al-Qaeda figure. He was inordinately proud of having received a personal letter from the emir, and he treasured it.

On his return to Afghanistan, Khallad had dedicated himself to al-Qaeda, picking up another alias, Silver, after Long John Silver, the infamous one-legged pirate. He had first worked as a bodyguard and had carried out administrative duties for bin Laden, Saif al-Adel, and other senior al-Qaeda leaders. Over time, he had been given more responsibilities, including personal missions for bin Laden, sometimes requiring months of travel. Bin Laden had come to value him; he was Muhannad's brother in every way.

Khallad became known in al-Qaeda circles as a trusted bin Laden aide. When other members wanted to see the leader, they would often approach Khallad and ask him to arrange a meeting. Among those he helped secure a private audience was Nibras. Khallad was always pleasant to others and was well liked by the brothers, who appreciated his sense of humor. Their only criticism was that he didn't offer much guidance to his own younger siblings, al-Bara and Omayer.

The two younger siblings were very close. As boys, they had been put on a plane by their father and sent to Afghanistan. Their father had not told them where they were going. Al-Bara had been involved in gangs in Saudi Arabia and had been sent to reform school. His family had worried that he would get into drugs and make life even worse for himself, and this had been their justification for shipping him off to Afghanistan to join bin Laden. They had feared the same would happen to Omayer.

When the young men had arrived in Afghanistan and had discovered where they were, they had become very upset. Al-Bara, especially, preferred to be in Saudi Arabia with his friends rather than within the strict confines of an al-Qaeda camp. In the guesthouse to which they were first taken, al-Bara had run to the bathroom and cried. Khallad and Muhannad had soon joined them in Afghanistan, however, and had helped convert them to the al-Qaeda way of life. And, like Muhannad and Khallad, al-Bara and Omayer had been accepted into the inner circles.

At Murad Beg, al-Bara had gone missing behind enemy lines, and the Taliban had been forced to send a helicopter to the area to rescue him.

It was in early 1998 that bin Laden first seriously started thinking about launching a big operation targeting U.S. interests in the Arabia Peninsula. His first idea was to do four simultaneous bombings, targeting anything with a U.S. flag—oil tanker, cruise ship, military vessel—at four ports in Yemen. The ports of al-Hudaydah, Aden, Ash Shihr, and al-Mukalla would be suitable, bin Laden told al-Qaeda's *shura* council. He explained that the most important part was that the four actions take place simultaneously. That is what would grab the world's attention.

Yemen was chosen because its weak central government, loose borders, and easy access to weapons and explosives made it the easiest place in the region to target U.S. ships. Al-Qaeda had been using Yemen increasingly for operations. As a neighbor of Saudi Arabia, it provided a convenient place from which to smuggle Saudis out of Saudi Arabia to conduct operations elsewhere. Yemeni passports were also easily obtained and were used as cover, especially for Saudis, who would then go to Pakistan and Afghanistan. They didn't want those stamps on their real passports, as they would arouse Saudi authorities' suspicions. To get a passport in Yemen, all you had to do was show up at a local government office with two witnesses who confirmed your identity.

Bin Laden discussed his ideas with Khallad, repeatedly changing his mind about the nature of the operation as he read new information about the U.S. military. When he read that U.S. aircraft carriers carried four thousand soldiers and were nuclear-powered, he told Khallad that attacking one of them would be even more sensational than his first plan, and they started planning this operation.

They decided that al-Qaeda would need four boats to attack the four boats that bin Laden had read protected each carrier. Then they'd need a big boat to attack the carrier itself. Khallad started researching the best type of boats for the operation, and he learned what boats locals used in Yemeni ports so that al-Qaeda's attack boats would blend in and not attract attention.

By their next discussion, bin Laden had changed his mind again. He had read that U.S. destroyers on their way to Iraq refueled in Yemen. The symbolism of hitting one of those ships would be even greater, he had decided. Khallad liked the idea and told bin Laden that he wanted to be one of the suicide bombers for the operation. Bin Laden said that he would see. In the meantime, he sent Khallad to Yemen to study the ports in the south of the country—Aden, Ash Shihr, and al-Mukalla. He sent Nashiri to do the same type of research in the northern port of al-Hudaydah. Bin Laden didn't tell Khallad and Nashiri that they were casing for the same type of operation.

Khallad and Nashiri had become two of bin Laden's top operatives, and so it was natural that he tasked them with the casing. Both were born in Saudi Arabia and were of Yemeni descent. Khallad's father had been thrown out of Yemen because of trouble he had caused with the then-communist South. He had been born into the bin Yusifi, a prestigious tribe. Bin Laden calculated that if Khallad got into trouble with Yemen, he could rely on the family name to help him. The al-Qaeda leader was savvy in manipulating tribal advantages.

Independently of each other, Nashiri and Khallad busied themselves researching the ports that bin Laden had sent them to. They noted the types of local boats used, the security in the area, and whether any U.S vessels docked there. They also traveled around, looking into purchasing boats and explosives. When they passed through Sanaa, they stayed at Bayt Habra, the al-Qaeda guesthouse. Eventually their stops there overlapped.

They knew each other well. Both were part of the Northern Group, and both had become al-Qaeda special operations people. In any case, with fewer than four hundred members, al-Qaeda was a small organization—everyone knew everyone else. During their conversation they learned that they were working on the same operation. It didn't surprise them that bin Laden hadn't told each of them about the other. Al-Qaeda operated that way: if one cell was broken, the others wouldn't be compromised, and the mission could still be carried out.

They parted ways and completed their initial research, and then both returned to Afghanistan and reported to bin Laden. They had reached the same conclusion: no ports other than Aden hosted U.S. ships. Bin Laden told them to focus together on an operation in Aden.

Bayt Habra was also frequented by al-Qaeda operatives who were in Yemen to get fraudulent passports. Two of the operatives in residence with Nashiri and Khallad were Hassan al-Khamiri and failed Nairobi bomber Mohamed Rashed Daoud al-Owhali. When Owhali's father needed to contact him in Yemen, he reached him at the guesthouse. Khamiri's application for a Yemeni passport used the telephone number of the guesthouse as its contact number.

Nashiri helped Owhali get the fraudulent passport that he used for the 1998 East African embassy bombing operation. Owhali later said that while he was in the guesthouse, he overheard Nashiri discussing a plot to attack an American ship in Yemen with Katyusha missiles while it was in port.

In the summer of 1998, as the date of the East African embassy operation was nearing, bin Laden ordered Nashiri and Khallad to return to Afghanistan. He wasn't sure what America's response to the attacks would be, and he didn't know if the United States would pressure Yemen and other countries that al-Qaeda operated from to crack down on its operatives; and he didn't want to take any chances. Nashiri and Khallad did as they were told.

When they arrived in Afghanistan, bin Laden instructed them to help prepare Owhali and Jihad Ali (Nashiri's cousin) for the bombings. Khallad secured plane tickets and made travel arrangements and worked with the young men on their martyr videos. On bin Laden's instructions, he told them to say that they were members of "the Islamic army to liberate the holy places." They hadn't heard that before; it was something new, made up by bin Laden. Their first few practice recordings had to be discarded because each time they attempted to say the phrase, they started laughing. They had to redo the video a few times until they were able to get through the script with a straight face.

In January 1999, after U.S retaliation for the 1998 embassy bombings appeared to have ended, bin Laden told Khallad and Nashiri to return to Yemen. Now Khallad set up his base in Sadah, a rugged area near the Red Sea and the Saudi border. It is viewed as no-man's-land and, with weapons and explosives readily available, is a major Yemeni connection to the Saudi smuggling market. Nashiri, in the meantime, worked with Taha al-Ahdal.

Nashiri and Khallad occupied themselves with collecting explosives, a process Khallad had started on his first trip to Yemen. He had enlisted the help of the well-known dealer Hadi Dilkum, whose Yemeni government connections made him a valuable ally. As Khallad was making these arrangements, bin Laden instructed him to try to acquire a U.S. visa. Another operation—the "planes operation"—was being planned, and al-Qaeda needed to get operatives into the United States for it. In April Khallad applied for a visa using the alias Saleh Saeed Mohammed bin Yousaf.

His cover story for the visa application was that he needed to visit a medical clinic in the United States for a new prosthesis. A fellow al-Qaeda member had connected him with someone in the United States who had helped him find a "suitable" clinic. As he waited for confirmation of an appointment, he continued to run the boats operation, as it had come to be called, with Nashiri.

Khallad also decided to get fraudulent Yemeni identification papers to protect his identity. He applied for the fraudulent ID under the name Tawfiq Muhammad Salih bin Rashid. Dilkum was one of the witnesses who swore to the authorities that the name was valid. It was at this time that Khallad also bought, using the same fraudulent name, the ID that Qamish had handed over to us. Using that, and with Dilkum's assistance, he rented the space to store the explosives. Khallad also bought a boat in al-Mukalla.

. . .

In May, Khallad enlisted the assistance of an al-Qaeda operative based in Aden, Jamal al-Badawi. Khallad and Badawi had met and become close friends in Afghanistan. During their initial training at the Jihad Wal camp, Badawi had become very sick, and Khallad had taken care of him. From then on Badawi had felt a debt of gratitude to Khallad, and he had gone out of his way to help him whenever needed.

Khallad thought that Badawi would be of use in the boats operation. Not only was he an experienced fisherman, but he was a Yemeni and knew the Port of Aden. Khallad was sure that Badawi would readily agree to help him. The only problem was that they had lost touch with each other. Khallad knew to check the al-Jazeera Hotel in Sanaa, a favorite place for operatives to gather and socialize. On any given day, a couple of operatives would be there chatting and drinking coffee or tea. Khallad went to the hotel and greeted the operatives there. They told him that Badawi was working in the tractor business and could be found on the street where all tractor businesses were located; in Sanaa, companies are localized by type.

Khallad went to the street and found Badawi. The two men embraced. Badawi was pleased to see his old friend. Khallad told Badawi that he was working on an operation and needed his help, and Badawi of course agreed. Khallad told him that he needed a boat for the operation. It had to be approximately nine meters long, and it needed to look like the other boats in Aden so that it would blend in and go unnoticed. Badawi said he'd go to Jizan, Saudi Arabia, to get it. He explained to Khallad that among Yemenis Jizan was known to be an easier and cheaper place to find a boat of that size than Aden. It was a place where one could buy and sell repossessed and used boats. In addition, Badawi felt that from a security point of view, Jizan was safer. Aden was a relatively small community, and if Badawi turned up with a large sum of money to buy a boat, people would start talking, and the authorities might get suspicious.

Khallad also instructed Badawi—along with Badawi's brother, Hussein al-Badawi, and another operative, Mu'awiya al-Madani, who together formed his initial cell in Aden—to go to the port and watch

U.S. ships. They went out in a fishing boat and recorded how much time ships spent in the area. Nashiri and Ahdal did the same in al-Hudaydah. The two groups later compared information, calculating how long it took ships to travel from one part of Yemen to another.

At one point during these exercises, the Yemeni authorities picked up Nashiri, Mu'awiya al-Madani, and Hussein al-Badawi. The three were far out at sea and looked suspicious. They claimed that they were just fishermen who had gotten lost. The Yemeni authorities accepted their story and released them.

Khallad and Nashiri continued to work on accumulating explosives. When they had about five hundred to seven hundred pounds of maté-riel, they decided to move some of it from Sadah to al-Hudaydah. To effect the transfer, Khallad asked to borrow Dilkum's car one night. It was the action that would lead to his arrest. After packing the car, he pulled over at a bank of pay phones to make some calls. When he returned to the car he found himself surrounded by Yemeni PSO offi-cials, who brought him in for questioning.

When Nashiri learned that Khallad had been arrested, he panicked, thinking that the Yemenis had learned of the plot. He fled to Afghani-stan to inform bin Laden. "To Whom It May Concern of the Brothers in Yemen," the letter bin Laden sent the Yemeni authorities in response to Khallad's jailing, was said to have reached General Qamish, who passed it on to President Saleh. Released, Khallad reclaimed Hadi Dilkum's car, the explosives untouched.

The U.S. visa application that he had submitted before being jailed was rejected—not because of any terrorism connections but because of insufficient information on his form. Nashiri returned to Yemen with instructions from bin Laden. The al-Qaeda leader didn't want Khallad in Yemen anymore because the authorities were now focused on him. He was "too hot," and bin Laden didn't want to compromise the boats operation. Khallad was instructed to transfer full control to Nashiri. Having put a lot of work into the operation and grown excited about its potential, Khallad was keenly disappointed, but it was inconveivable that he would ever disobey an order from bin Laden. Using a refrigerated truck, he helped Nashiri move a portion of the explosives from Sadah to Aden. In addition, he provided Nashiri with the names of all of his contacts in Aden, including Jamal al-Badawi and another operative, Salman al-Adani. Word went out that Nashiri was now fully in charge.

After he left Yemen, Khallad remained involved in the boats operation, acting as the liaison between bin Laden and Nashiri. To avoid detection, bin Laden never used e-mail or the phone, instead relying on a network of operatives in the field. Khallad regularly traveled from Kandahar, where bin Laden was based, to Karachi, where he'd speak on the phone to Nashiri.

Beyond acting as a liaison to Nashiri, bin Laden told Khallad that he wanted the rest of his time devoted to helping with the planes operation. Bin Laden said that the mastermind of that operation was a jihadist who had joined al-Qaeda after the East African embassy bombings, Khalid Sheikh Mohammed.

Khallad spent a lot of time in Karachi planning with KSM and also traveled around the Middle East and Asia to help with the plot. In September 1999, he administered a forty-five-day special course in hand-to-hand combat at al-Qaeda's Loghar camp to select trainees, including Khalid al-Mihdhar, Nawaf al-Hazimi, and Ahmed Mohammed Haza al-Darbi—all viewed as promising recruits.

Al-Qaeda's decentralized system of management meant that once bin Laden decided who would be in charge, it was left to that person to work out the details. Bin Laden only instructed Nashiri that Salman al-Adani and Taha al-Ahdal would be the suicide bombers for the boats operation; Nashiri was in charge of making all the other decisions. He would relay them through Khallad to bin Laden for his sign-off.

Nashiri had felt, since the end of the summer, that they were ready to attack the next ship that entered Aden harbor. He and Khamiri had carefully surveyed the port for possible launch points. Finally, on January 3, 2000, they saw the USS *The Sullivans* enter the harbor. Nashiri sent the designated suicide bombers, Taha al-Ahdal and Salman al-Adani, to strike at the ship under cover of night while he waited in a hiding place, ready to view the explosion.

Ahdal and Adani placed the boat in the water, not realizing it was low tide. Because of the weight from the explosives, the boat got stuck in the sand. They tried a few times to move it, but it wouldn't budge, so they gave up and returned home, leaving the explosive-laden boat. Nashiri was waiting to videotape the operation from an apartment he had rented in Tawahi, and as daybreak approached, he realized that something had gone wrong. He went to the house where the bombers had been living before the operation to see if there were any clues to what had happened and was surprised to see them there, sleeping. He angrily woke them and they explained what had happened. After a firm rebuke he took Salman with him and, with Khamiri also in tow, rushed down to the harbor in a truck. When they saw the boat, they froze. The Beachboy Five were removing the explosives and throwing them casually to one another. Nashiri, Salman, and Khamiri approached cautiously, in case something exploded, and Nashiri negotiated to get the explosives back.

Nashiri, Taha, and Khamiri fled to Afghanistan, Nashiri reporting to bin Laden. The al-Qaeda leader said that they should keep out of sight and wait to see what happened in Yemen. No reports of the Yemenis or the United States investigating the incident reached them, however, and they became increasingly confident that, ultimately, their plans had not been compromised.

Nashiri returned to Yemen within a few months and reconnected with Badawi and the local cell. New suicide bombers were chosen, as Ahdal had been killed in Afghanistan fighting for the Taliban, and Adani had died after jumping into a sewer to try to save a boy who had fallen in. Although Khallad had regularly petitioned bin Laden to use him as a suicide bomber, the al-Qaeda leader wished to use Mu'awiya al-Madani. In fact, however, by September, when the boats operation was ready to be carried out, Nashiri substituted Nibras and Khamiri.

Newly married, Salim Hamdan was visiting Yemen when the attack on the USS *Cole* occurred. He knew nothing about it in advance but recognized the al-Qaeda hallmarks: suicide bombers and a U.S. target. One of his first responses to the attack was fear of arrest because of his well-known connections to bin Laden. But when he heard President Saleh saying on Yemeni television that the attack was an Israeli Mossad operation, he relaxed, as that, too, made sense to him: Israel was an enemy of Yemen and wanted to provoke the United States against Yemen. It would be illogical, on the other hand, for al-Qaeda to risk angering Yemen, which until then had been such a welcoming place for extremists, including al-Qaeda operatives. Hamdan traveled with his in-laws from Sanaa to Saudi Arabia for al-Umra, a minor pilgrimage. From Saudi Arabia he returned to Afghanistan to resume his duties for bin Laden.

When he arrived in Kandahar, bin Laden welcomed him back and asked him if there was "any news from Yemen regarding the attack on the American destroyer." Hamdan said that he had heard President Saleh blaming Mossad. Bin Laden smiled and walked away. Later that day, Hamdan bumped into Nashiri. Like bin Laden, Nashiri asked what the news was from Yemen. Hamdan repeated what he had told bin Laden. Nashiri started laughing. He then gestured in bin Laden's direction and said, "It's all from his head." Hamdan now understood why bin Laden had smiled earlier in the day—the *Cole* was an al-Qaeda operation.

It also now made sense to Hamdan why a few months earlier in Kandahar he had seen Nashiri experimenting with explosives in the company of Abu Abdul Rahman al-Muhajir, al-Qaeda's explosives expert and master bomb maker. He had watched the two men detonating and exploding bombs in the body of an old vehicle. Hamdan knew that Muhajir only instructed people when specifically instructed to do so by bin Laden. If he was involved, one could assume that it was an important operation. He also noticed that Nashiri was spending a lot of time with Khallad, Abu Hafs, and bin Laden, further indication of his involvement in an upcoming operation.

Not everyone in Kandahar agreed with the wisdom of hitting a U.S. target in Yemen. Many al-Qaeda members were either Yemenis or had family ties to Yemen, and they feared the effect an attack would have on their families and their ability to travel home. They also questioned the wisdom of upsetting a country that had been very useful in providing refuge to them.

Hamdan was one of the al-Qaeda members who questioned the wisdom of the attack. His wife was a Yemeni, and he feared that they would be prevented from returning to Yemen after the attack. When he spoke to his brother-in-law in Yemen, Hamdan was told that the PSO was looking for him. Yemen was a no-go country for him for now.

When they were alone, Hamdan asked bin Laden, "Sheikh, why in Yemen, when that was always a safe haven for the brothers?" Bin Laden did not respond directly and changed the subject.

Other al-Qaeda members would not dream of questioning bin Laden, and Nashiri fell into this camp. He believed that bin Laden always knew best. Abu Jandal described Nashiri as someone who would commit a terrorist act "in Mecca, inside the Kaaba itself" if he believed the cause demanded it.

Bin Laden was convinced that the United States would retaliate against al-Qaeda for the bombing of the USS *Cole*. At a minimum, he expected al-Qaeda's training camps to be bombed, as had happened after the East African embassy bombings. Before the *Cole* attack, bin Laden moved to protect himself and his followers.

Training camps were temporarily shut down, and operatives were ordered not to plan or carry out any terrorist acts. Bin Laden himself kept on the move, traveling from one safe house in Afghanistan to another. He first went to the hills around Kabul, then on to Khost and Jalalabad. After that he returned to Kandahar, moving between safe houses there. He also sent Abu Hafs and Ayman al-Zawahiri to separate locations in Kabul. That way, if one of them were killed, the others could continue running al-Qaeda.

Yet there was no retaliation from the United States, to bin Laden's surprise. They would have to hit harder to get America's attention, he told his aides. Hamdan later told me, "You [the United States] brought 9/11 on yourselves; you didn't respond to the *Cole*, so bin Laden had to hit harder."

As days and weeks went by, rumors that al-Qaeda was behind the

Cole attack reverberated around the Muslim world. The image of the attack on the *Cole*—a small boat bringing down a mighty destroyer—was a powerful one. Bin Laden would later say that "the destroyer represented the capital of the West and the small boat represented the Prophet Muhammad." In Kandahar, bin Laden, Abu Hafs, and Saif al-Adel met to discuss how best to further capitalize on the attack to boost al-Qaeda's fund-raising and recruitment. They decided to make a video about the bombing.

Bin Laden instructed Ali al-Bahlul to produce the video. He and other members of al-Qaeda's media office spent six months on the project, which included a reenactment of the *Cole* bombing, along with images of al-Qaeda camps and training sessions. It opened with the voice of Abu Hajer al-Iraqi, reading passages from the Quran—he was in jail in the United States for his role in the East African embassy bombings. The touch was significant: before the *Cole* bombing, bin Laden had issued a warning to the United States to release prisoners, among them Abu Hajer. Operatives later noted that the voiceover was bin Laden's creative flourish—one of many improvements and revisions insisted upon by the al-Qaeda leader.

Al-Qaeda distributed the video internationally, and it aired around the world. Money and recruits started pouring in, and in appreciation bin Laden promoted Bahlul; it was at this point that he attained the dual position of al-Qaeda's public relations secretary and bin Laden's personal propagandist.

At the al-Farouq camp, bin Laden addressed new recruits who came in following the *Cole* attack. He thanked God for the success of the *Cole* operation, promised future attacks, praised the martyrs Khamiri and Nibras for their heroic actions, and asked God to receive them as martyrs and "provide us with more like them." He also encouraged the trainees to prepare for jihad themselves. The Yemenis in the camps were proud that Yemeni al-Qaeda operatives were behind the *Cole*. They marched and chanted in unison during training: "We, the Yemenis, are the ones who blew up the *Cole*." Bin Laden also named two of al-Qaeda's main guesthouses after Hassan and Nibras—honoring them and hoping to encourage others to follow in their footsteps. Many new recruits volunteered for suicide missions.

In January 2001, in Kandahar, bin Laden celebrated al-Qaeda's successes at the wedding of Hamza, his seventeen-year-old son. The young man married the fourteen-year-old daughter of Abu Hafs al-Masri. To commemorate the occasion, bin Laden read a poem:

> *A destroyer: even the brave fear its might.*
> *It inspires horror in the harbor and in the open sea.*
> *She sails into the waves*
> *Flanked by arrogance, haughtiness and false power.*
> *To her doom she moves slowly*
> *A dinghy awaits her, riding the waves.*

In June 2001, Hamdan and Nashiri were sitting together in a guesthouse in Kandahar, and their conversation turned to the *Cole*. Nashiri, laughing, told Hamdan that while transporting the boat to be used for the operation, he had been stopped by a Yemeni policeman, who had asked to see the requisite papers for the craft. He didn't have any papers, so instead he had convinced the officer to turn a blind eye to the incident with "qat money." How easy it was to bribe a policeman in Yemen, Nashiri thought to himself, flushed with this success.

Hamdan was struck by how Nashiri gloried in his own role in the operation, failing to credit even Khamiri and Nibras, who were heavily involved in the planning and, of course, had lost their lives. This especially upset Hamdan, as the men had been friends of his. He and Khamiri had fought together in the front lines against the Northern Alliance. Nibras had been a witness at his wedding in Yemen. It was the last time Hamdan had seen him.

After the 2001 invasion of Afghanistan, an office used by al-Qaeda's military committee was raided. One of the documents found, in a plastic sleeve, was Hasan al-Khamiri's martyrdom letter. It was his farewell to his brothers. In the letter he spoke about jihad and al-Qaeda, and said his good-byes. On the side of the letter were doodles, with flowers on them.

September 9, 2001. After a long day working in Sanaa, George, Bob, and I were preparing to head to sleep in the room we were sharing in the Sheraton Hotel when the news came through that Ahmed Shah Massoud, the leader of the Northern Alliance, had been assassinated.

Two men claiming to be Belgian journalists of Moroccan origin had met with him for an interview and had blown up their camera's battery pack, which was filled with explosives, killing him. We later learned that their letter of introduction had been forged by Zawahiri and that they were Tunisian members of al-Qaeda.

Massoud was a committed Muslim and had been endorsed by many Islamic leaders, including Abdullah Azzam, who declared, after meeting him, "I have seen the true Islamic jihad, and it is Massoud." But he opposed the Taliban and al-Qaeda, seeking a moderate alternative.

Massoud was a national hero, and his death meant the splintering of the Northern Alliance. His reputation and charisma were instrumental in keeping his group united, and he was one of the few unifying figures who could command the respect of most of the country.

I confided to George and Bob my fear that the assassination was not strictly about Massoud and the Taliban; that it was an action with wider meaning and resonance. "This is bigger. Al-Qaeda is trying to do something huge, and needs the Taliban's support—so they killed Massoud, something the Taliban would be forever grateful for."

"Dude, you scare me when you say this stuff," George said. He brought up the memos I had written before the East African embassy bombings and before the *Cole* attack. "And look what happened. I hope you're wrong."

"I hope I'm wrong, too."

The next day, September 10, the Taliban began a major offensive against the shaken Northern Alliance—one that had been clearly prepared for months in advance.

PART 4

THE ATTACK THAT
CHANGED THE WORLD

14

The Binalshibh Riddle

August 29, 2001. Ramzi Binalshibh was awakened at 3:00 AM in his Hamburg apartment by the sound of the phone ringing. "Hello?" he answered groggily.

"Hello," a voice replied. He instantly recognized it as that of his friend and former roommate Mohammed Atta.

"What's going on?" Binalshibh asked.

"One of my friends related a riddle to me and I cannot solve it, and I called you so that you can solve it for me," Atta told him.

"Okay."

"Two sticks, a dash, and a cake with a stick down," Atta continued, and then he stopped speaking. Binalshibh was silent, waiting for Atta to say something else.

"Is this the riddle?" Binalshibh asked. He was confused, and half asleep. "You wake me from a deep sleep to tell me this riddle? Two sticks and I don't know what else?"

There was still silence from Atta on the other end. He was waiting for his friend to understand the code the two had regularly used in the past. Binalshibh finally comprehended. "Okay," he said to Atta. "Tell your friend that he has nothing to worry about. It's such a sweet riddle."

"Good-bye."

There was more Binalshibh wanted to say to his friend, as he knew he might never speak to him again, but it was too risky to do so on the open line. KSM had explicitly warned them to be careful, and there was too much at stake to take any risks. So Binalshibh kept his emotions to himself and put the receiver down.

He tied up loose ends in Hamburg, and on September 5, he went to Pakistan. From there he sent a trusted messenger to bin Laden and KSM, who were in Afghanistan, with the message: "The big attack on America will be on Tuesday, 11 September."

That was the meaning of Atta's riddle: the two sticks represented the number 11; the dash was a space; and the cake with a stick upside down was a nine. Together that made 11-9: 11 September. It meant that Atta had all his hijackers in place and had picked the date for al-Qaeda's planes operation.

Ramzi Binalshibh was born in 1972 in Ghayl Bawazir, Yemen, and first tried getting to the United States in 1995, but his visa application was rejected. The United States at the time was suspicious of Yemeni visa seekers, believing they'd attempt to become illegal immigrants. Binalshibh tried moving to Germany—pretending to be a Sudanese citizen and applying for asylum under the name Ramzi Omar. He lived in Hamburg while this request was being investigated, and he attended mosques there, but eventually the request was denied. After returning to Yemen he then went back to Germany, this time under his real name and as a student. He was permitted to stay.

He continued attending mosques in Hamburg, now more regularly, and soon met an Egyptian student named Mohammed Atta. Born in Kafr el-Sheikh in 1968, Atta had moved to Hamburg to further his education in architecture. While they had different personalities—Atta was serious, dogmatic, and a focused student, and Binalshibh was outgoing, carefree, and a poor student—they shared an extremist outlook and became fast friends.

They eventually got an apartment together, which they shared with a student from the United Arab Emirates, Marwan al-Shehhi. Younger than Mohammed Atta and Binalshibh (he was born in 1978), like them Shehhi had become more religious in Germany, and frequented the same mosques.

Binalshibh became close friends with a Lebanese student named Ziad Jarrah, whom he also met at a Hamburg mosque. In Beirut, Jarrah had been known to regularly attend parties and discos, and initially in Germany he kept up that lifestyle. At some point he began dating a young woman named Aysel Senguen, the daughter of Turkish immigrants, and regularly slept over at her apartment. While he gradually appeared to become increasingly dogmatic in his faith, he never gave up his relationship with Senguen.

The four men regularly got together in the apartment shared by Atta, Binalshibh, and Shehhi to discuss jihad and Islamic theology. They propelled each other to become ever more observant Muslims. Increasingly, they viewed themselves as devoted religious messengers. They took themselves very seriously. Atta even wrote on his rent checks that he resided at Dar el Ansar ("house of the followers").

The group was influenced by a preacher named Mohammed Haydar Zammar, who often spoke at Hamburg's al-Quds Mosque. Zammar had fought in Afghanistan in the first Soviet jihad, and he told his listeners that they, too, had a responsibility to wage jihad.

The four men initially resolved to travel to Chechnya to wage jihad but were advised to go to Afghanistan instead because of the difficulties of moving around Chechnya. To effect this plan, they met with Mohamedou Ould Slahi, a relative of Abu Hafs al-Mauritani's. Slahi, a member of the al-Qaeda *shura* council, headed the religious committee. He told the four men to get visas for Pakistan and how best to proceed to Karachi. From Pakistan they were taken by al-Qaeda operatives to Afghanistan, where they met bin Laden. After some indoctrination, they pledged *bayat* to him.

Their arrival was celebrated by bin Laden, KSM, and other al-Qaeda leaders working on developing the planes operation. Here were four men who were perfect for the plot. As they were based in Germany, they would have an easier time getting U.S. visas than operatives based in Afghanistan or Pakistan. And their education levels meant that they were probably intelligent enough to qualify for pilot training.

The mission was presented to them, and they accepted it. It was the perfect opportunity to wage the ultimate jihad and have their names heralded as the greatest of mujahideen. Al-Qaeda leaders encouraged this thinking, reinforcing the idea that the martyrs would receive seventy-two virgins in heaven and would be celebrated as heroes across the Muslim world. They were put into al-Qaeda's special operations branch, the organization's name for its terrorism branch. Led by the head of the military committee, Abu Hafs al-Masri (whose given name was Mohammed Atef), and the head of the security committee, Saif al-Adel, the branch itself has individual cells and operations, each functioning separately from the others for security reasons.

Mohammed Atef—the former Egyptian police officer whose services Zawahiri had offered bin Laden back in the late 1980s, and who had risen to prominence in al-Qaeda—briefed them on the details of what they were to do, and they were also trained in communicating with each other through code.

While they were in Afghanistan, bin Laden kept them segregated from most other al-Qaeda operatives, as the plot was kept highly confidential. Only trusted al-Qaeda members, among them bin Laden chauffeur Salim Hamdan and Ali al-Bahlul, bin Laden's propagandist, were allowed to interact with them. Bahlul roomed with Jarrah when he was in Afghanistan. The group filmed individual martyrdom videos, directed by Bahlul. As the four had only minimal knowledge of classical Arabic and the Quran, they had to go through several takes before their pronunciation seemed genuine. It was a source of amusement to the four and to Bahlul, and after each mispronunciation they would burst into laughter.

After their training was complete, the four returned to Germany, and, following instructions, they began to assume a less radical appearance. They shaved their beards, wore Western clothes, and stopping visiting extremist mosques. They also started looking into flight training. An al-Qaeda facilitator named Ammar al-Baluchi (Ali Abdul Aziz Ali), KSM's nephew, sent them flight simulator programs. Ultimately, the four decided that the German flight schools they had seen weren't good enough, and that it was best to learn to fly in the United States. They requested approval from bin Laden, and he gave this new plan his blessing.

Before applying for U.S. visas, the four applied for new passports, claiming that they had lost their originals. They worried that the Pakistani visas on their passports might harm their prospects of being given U.S. visas. When the new passports arrived, they applied for the visas. On January 18, 2000, Shehhi's came through. There was nothing for a few months, and then on May 18 Atta's came through, and on May 25 Jarrah's application was approved. Binalshibh's, however, was rejected. He attempted three more times to get a visa, but each time, his application was rejected—not because of suspicions about terrorism but for the same reason his visa application had been rejected a few years earlier: he was a Yemeni, and U.S. authorities at the time were nervous that Yemenis would try to stay in the country illegally.

As he couldn't get into the United States, bin Laden and KSM tasked Binalshibh with being KSM's main assistant for the plot and the liaison between the German cell and the al-Qaeda leadership. Nawaf al-Hazmi, one of the thirty operatives who had been singled out two years before by the leadership for special training from Khallad at Loghar, was selected by bin Laden as Atta's "deputy."

Once Atta, Shehhi, and Jarrah were in the United States, Binalshibh arranged for money to be wired to them and exchanged coded phone calls with Atta, who by that time had been appointed by al-Qaeda to lead the operation in the United States. In their phone calls, Atta and Binalshibh pretended to be students discussing their course work, but in reality a word such as "architecture" referred to the World Trade Center, and "arts" referred to the Pentagon. The two men also met a few times in Europe, for instance in Berlin in January 2001 and in Madrid in July 2001.

. . .

Binalshibh's inability to get a visa was problematic for al-Qaeda, as their plan was to hijack four planes and simultaneously crash them into four buildings: the twin towers of the World Trade Center, the Pentagon, and the U.S. Capitol. KSM would later claim to CIA interrogators that he originally planned to use ten planes for 9/11, the tenth to be flown himself. He said he had planned to land the plane at a U.S. airport, kill all male passengers on board, and then give a speech to the world attacking the United States for supporting Israel and repressive Arab governments.

It's clear, however, that this was never a real plan but rather an effort by KSM to boost his credentials—consistently, his motivation was always to make himself appear to be the ultimate terrorist mastermind, affording him greater notoriety than that enjoyed by his nephew Ramzi Yousef. His description of himself is also likely the product of his having watched too many of the terrorist movies that he screened for the 9/11 hijackers. The initial al-Qaeda plan was to launch attacks in the United States and Southeast Asia simultaneously, but the latter plan was abandoned as being overly complicated.

One person al-Qaeda was cultivating as another potential pilot was Zacarias Moussaoui, a Moroccan with French citizenship. His French passport would allow him to obtain a U.S. visa easily. The problem with Moussaoui, however, was that he was not very intelligent; the leadership wasn't confident that he was up to the role. Moussaoui thought of himself as a tough guy, and he liked showing off his strength by wrestling with other al-Qaeda members. Abu Jandal enjoyed angering Moussaoui by telling him that he could beat him in a wrestling match, and then refusing to wrestle with him. His position as bin Laden's bodyguard made him Moussaoui's superior, and there was nothing Moussaoui could do but fume and complain.

In 2000 KSM sent Moussaoui to Malaysia for flight training, but he couldn't find a school he liked, and instead he got involved in other terrorist operations there. KSM later instructed him to travel to London in October, and Binalshibh visited him in December. On February 23, 2001, Moussaoui went to the United States and attended flight school in Oklahoma and Minnesota, where he didn't perform well. He was arrested on August 16, 2001, and charged with an immigration violation after a flight instructor became suspicious and reported him.

Given Moussaoui's unimpressive track record, al-Qaeda's leaders were happy when a better candidate for fourth pilot presented himself in Afghanistan in 2000. Among the new recruits at al-Farouq was a man who was already a trained pilot: Hani Hanjour. Born in Saudi Arabia, in 1991 Hanjour had studied English in Arizona. He returned to Saudi Arabia and in 1996 moved back to the United States to learn how to fly, obtaining a private pilot's license in 1997 and then a commercial pilot's certificate. After that he went back to Saudi Arabia to find work.

When bin Laden and KSM discovered that they had a trained pilot in one of their camps—on joining al-Qaeda, new recruits were asked if they had any specific skills—they enlisted him. He accepted the mission readily; it was considered an honor for a new recruit to be handpicked by bin Laden.

After teaching Hanjour the code words he needed to know, al-Qaeda's leaders instructed him to procure a visa for travel to the United States. Khallad explained to him how to get in touch with Nawaf al-Hazmi once he was in the United States. On June 20, 2000, he returned to Saudi Arabia, and on September 25 he received a U.S. visa.

This group of would-be pilots joined the ranks of those already selected by bin Laden to be part of the operation—Khalid al-Mihdhar, Nawaf al-Hazmi, and Khallad. Born in Mecca, Hazmi and Mihdhar were Saudis, and they had no problem getting U.S. visas. Khallad's visa application, however, was rejected because he was a Yemeni.

Mihdhar and Hazmi were to be among the muscle hijackers—those whose task it would be to overwhelm the crew and any troublesome passengers. They were sent, with other hijackers, to al-Qaeda's Mes Aynak camp, in Afghanistan, where they underwent physical fitness training and received instruction in combat and weapons. They were also given the best available food in order to keep them healthy and boost their spirits. KSM personally helped train both the pilot and the nonpilot hijackers, teaching them how to hide knives in their bags and how to slit passengers' throats. He made them practice slitting the throats of goats, sheep, and camels.

KSM and others briefed them about the United States at a facility nicknamed by many involved "The House of Martyrs." (KSM nicknamed it "The House of Ghamdis" because a few of the hijackers were from the Ghamdi tribe.) KSM taught them English phrases, showed them how to read phone books and make reservations, and had them read aviation magazines and watch movies with hijacking scenes. Among the phrases taught were "get down," "don't move," "stay in your seat," and "if anyone moves I'll kill you."

After the training, Hazmi and Mihdhar traveled to Kuala Lumpur, where a 9/11 summit meeting took place. From there the two men departed for Bangkok with Khallad. Upon Nibras and Quso's delivery, to Khallad, of the $36,000 in cash, Mihdhar and Hazmi purchased first-class tickets to Los Angeles, leaving Bangkok on January 15, 2000.

Their fellow muscle hijackers arrived in the United States in the summer of 2001. Most were Saudis (twelve of the thirteen), and most were unemployed, unmarried, and uneducated. They had applied for visas in Saudi Arabia, and, once those applications were approved, they had traveled to Afghanistan for training. Atta and Shehhi coordinated their arrival in the United States, found them places to stay, and settled them in.

KSM's nephew Ammar al-Baluchi and Mustafa al-Hawsawi, an al-Qaeda financial operative, helped coordinate their travel and money both before departure and once they were in the United States. Upon arrival the hijackers were given Baluchi's or Hawsawi's number. Also promptly on arrival, they opened bank accounts and deposited the money they had brought with them. Each hijacker had been given six to eight thousand dollars by KSM or Hawsawi and had been told to keep a few thousand for himself and to give the rest to Atta.

On August 4, 2001, an al-Qaeda member named Mohammed al-Qahtani landed in Orlando, Florida, on Virgin Atlantic Airlines Flight 15 but was refused entry by a U.S. Immigration and Naturalization Service agent and shipped out of the United States on a later flight. As he was departing, he vowed, "I will be back." On August 28, 2001, Ammar al-Baluchi applied for a one-week travel visa to the United States, beginning September 4, 2001. The visa would expire on September 11. Baluchi's request was denied.

Atta's biggest challenge was finding four flights that would be in the air at the same time on one day—and on planes that Shehhi, Jarrah, Hanjour, and he himself knew how to fly. He ran a number of searches on Travelocity and found that everything matched up on September 11, 2001. Once that was established, he phoned Binalshibh to give him the message.

Once the date was set, the hijackers went out to enjoy their last days alive. Some attended strip joints; others went to bars and got drunk. Atta was spotted doing a series of shots. While it might seem surprising that these men who were later proclaimed by al-Qaeda to be religious martyrs were debasing themselves, the reality is that most weren't truly religious. At best, they had only a superficial knowledge of Islam, and most were either simple people swayed by convincing recruiters or macho individuals looking for a way to look tough and impress friends. But even while on missions, they never fully left their old lifestyles behind. Jarrah even traveled back to Germany a few times to hook up with his girlfriend. This activity was common across al-Qaeda. Nashiri, the mastermind of the USS *Cole* bombing, for example, at one point lived with a prostitute in Dubai.

In anticipation of the attack, and with the knowledge that the United States would likely strike back hard, bin Laden moved continuously from Kabul to Khost to Jalalabad with his most trusted aides. None of the bodyguards, and not even Salim Hamdan, the driver, ever knew the destination of the convoy. A minute or so before they were about to leave, bin Laden would tell them.

Sometimes bin Laden would order a change of direction mid-trip. At times he would just stop en route and order them to make camp. At times he himself had no idea where they would end up. He would camp in the middle of nowhere so he could not easily be found. They wouldn't even know their exact coordinates. These procedures made bin Laden feel safer.

In Kabul bin Laden spent a lot of time in the homes of Abu al-Khair al-Masri and Mohammed Saleh. Former EIJ *shura* council members and close associates of Ayman al-Zawahiri, they were the two Egyptian Islamic Jihad leaders who joined the al-Qaeda *shura* council following the March 2001 official merger of al-Qaeda and EIJ.

After the merger, bin Laden and Zawahiri went around visiting al-Qaeda training camps and facilities, accompanied by Abu Hafs al-Masri, who had become the number three in the group (Zawahiri had taken the number two spot), and a Kuwaiti named Salman Abu Ghaith, whose importance in the group had been steadily growing; he became the spokesman for the organization. Later, all four appeared in al-Qaeda's propaganda videos. The name al-Qaeda was officially changed to Qaeda al-Jihad, a combining of the names al-Qaeda and Egyptian Islamic Jihad. The name change was purely a formality, and the organization is still commonly known as al-Qaeda.

On September 11, 2001, bin Laden seemed especially excitable to those who knew him. Only a few members of his entourage knew why. Late in the afternoon, bin Laden told Ali al-Bahlul to switch on the satellite in his media van so they could watch the news. Bahlul tried but couldn't get any reception. Bin Laden told him instead to get the news on the radio. They alternated between channels, first the BBC, then Voice of America, till they got a consistent signal. For about forty-five minutes they listened to regular news reports. Finally a news flash came in: at 8:46 AM in the United States (EDT), a plane had hit the north tower of the World Trade Center in New York City. The report said that it seemed to have been an accident.

But bin Laden knew that American Airlines Flight 11, scheduled to fly from Logan International Airport in Boston to Los Angeles International Airport, had been successfully hijacked by Mohammed Atta, Abdulaziz al-Omari, Waleed al-Shehri, Wail al-Shehri, and Satam al-

Suqami. Before the plane crashed, a flight attendant had reported that a passenger had been stabbed and that it was hard for him to breath, leading investigators to later suspect that Mace had been used. But this report didn't get through till later.

Bin Laden smiled, and the al-Qaeda members with him started celebrating. "Allah Hu Akbar" (God is great), they shouted, firing their AK-47s into the air. Most were simply happy that the "Great Snake," the United States, had been hit. But based on bin Laden's smile and the lack of surprise on his face, they began to suspect that this had been an al-Qaeda plot.

"Calm down, calm down. Wait. There is more," bin Laden said, raising his hand to silence the celebrants. Here was confirmation of their suspicions. They were silent, wondering what was next. Only a few senior al-Qaeda members knew what to expect.

Another news flash came: at 9:03 AM, a second plane had hit the south tower of the World Trade Center. This was no longer looking like an accident, the newscaster said. The two most visible skyscrapers in New York City were going up in smoke. People were trapped inside and jumping out of windows.

Bin Laden's smile broadened. United Airlines Flight 175, scheduled to fly from Logan International Airport to Los Angeles International Airport, had been successfully hijacked by Marwan al-Shehhi, Fayez Banihammad, Hamza al-Ghamdi, Ahmed al-Ghamdi, and Mohand al-Shehri. Bin Laden knew all the hijackers personally. He had approved their selection and helped guide their training. He was elated. Once again the al-Qaeda members present started shouting and firing into the air. "Calm down, wait, there is more," bin Laden said again.

The next breaking news flash said that a plane had hit the western side of the Pentagon at 9:37 AM. It was beginning to look like a coordinated attack, the announcer said. "This can't be a coincidence."

"What's going on?" someone asked. Bin Laden grinned.

American Airlines Flight 77, flying from Washington Dulles International Airport to Los Angeles International Airport, manned by Hani Hanjour, Nawaf al-Hazmi, Khalid al-Mihdhar, Majed Moqed, and

Salem al-Hazmi, had succeeded in its mission. The celebrations started again, and once again bin Laden told them to hold off. "There is more," he said.

As al-Qaeda operatives listened intently to the news, more updates on what was going on in the United States came in: reports were that President Bush was in hiding, and that both towers of the World Trade Center had collapsed. Smoke was billowing from the ground. "It's horrific," the announcer said. Fires raged through the Pentagon. Casualties were unknown but estimated initially to be at tens of thousands. The Great Snake had been brought to its knees by al-Qaeda.

Then news of a fourth plane came: at 10:03 AM, United Airlines Flight 93, traveling from Newark International Airport, in New Jersey, to San Francisco International Airport, crashed in a field in Stonycreek Township, Pennsylvania. There had been a Mayday message at 9:28, and at 9:31 one of the hijackers had announced that he had a bomb. This later led investigators to suspect that the hijackers had used fake bombs. Some passengers who used their cell phones to make calls reported that the hijackers wore explosives on their belts.

Bin Laden was disappointed. He told his followers that the Americans must have shot the plane down. Ziad Jarrah, Ahmed al-Nami, Ahmed al-Haznawi, and Saeed al-Ghamdi did not reach their target. But given the success of the first three planes, bin Laden's disappointment didn't last long.

The al-Qaeda leader announced that they would head to Mohammed Saleh's house for a proper celebration. In one of the cars, a pickup truck that Hamdan was driving, bin Laden and Ayman al-Zawahiri sat together in the back and discussed the operation. "If the Americans hadn't shot that plane it could have hit that big dome," bin Laden told Zawahiri, referring to the Capitol.

At Saleh's house, the celebration began. Many of al-Qaeda's top leaders were present. KSM came to the house and briefed those present on the operation. He explained the background and training involved and announced the names of the martyrs. Many of those present who knew the hijackers well felt proud of their association with them.

"May God Bless Mokhtar for this great work," said bin Laden, using a nickname for Khalid Sheikh Mohammed. Bin Laden then asked KSM to travel to Kandahar to brief Abu Hafs. Because of back problems, he hadn't been able to leave Kandahar when everyone else had been evacuated; driving along the rugged roads would have been too painful.

Bin Laden then ended the celebration and told his convoy to head toward Khost.

15

"What Dots?"

September 11, 2001. "Hi, Heather, how are you?" I was speaking on the phone from an office in the U.S. Embassy in Sanaa; Heather was in New York. We had finally been allowed to return to Yemen a week earlier, and I was busy with my colleagues reestablishing our operation against al-Qaeda members responsible for the USS *Cole* bombing.

As I asked that question, Joe Ennis —Alabama Joe—rushed into the room. "Ali, a plane hit the World Trade Center," he said breathlessly. "We're watching the news in the ambassador's office. Come quickly!"

"You mean a helicopter?" I asked Joe.

"No, they said a plane," he replied.

"Ali," Heather said into my other ear, "the TV is showing smoke coming out of the World Trade Center." I repeated that to Joe and he let out an expletive.

"Switch on the TV," she replied. "One of the buildings is on fire."

My gut told me that it was something bigger, but I didn't want to alarm Heather. "I have to go and see what's going on, and I'll call you back. I love you."

"I love you."

• • •

I dialed John O'Neill's number in New York. He had just started his new job in the World Trade Center. His phone rang and rang and then went to voicemail. Joe Ennis rushed into the office again, screaming: "Another plane just hit the World Trade Center!"

"What?"

"It's a passenger plane. Oh my God, a big plane."

I tried calling John again. Once again the call went to voicemail, and again I hung up without leaving a message. I tried yet again and got his voicemail, but this time I left a message: "John, it's Ali, I just heard what happened. I'm in Yemen, give me a call."

I ran into the ambassador's office. Ambassador Bodine had left the country, and the new ambassador, Edmund Hull, had not yet arrived, so the office was empty, but the television was on, and all the agents, the entire team from the New York field office, had gathered to watch the breaking news from New York. For about a minute we stood silently, in shock, unable to look away from the screen, as images of what had just happened were shown again and again: The first plane flying in . . . the burst of flames . . . and then the second plane.

Forcing myself to look away from the screen, I picked up the phone on the ambassador's desk and tried calling the FBI's New York office. The call wouldn't go through. "Are you speaking to New York?" a colleague asked me, seeing the receiver in my hand.

"I'm trying," I said. "Lines are tied up." Being unable to reach headquarters only increased the tension and fear people felt. I kept trying to get through, but again and again I heard a busy signal. On the tenth attempt, my call went through to one of my colleagues in New York.

"We've just seen the images here," I said. "Do you know what's going on?"

"We're trying to find out. At the moment, we've got about thirty agents who were in the vicinity missing. We're treating this as a terrorist attack."

After checking the embassy's security and loading our own personal weapons, we all gathered in a secure conference room and waited for news from New York. More bad news reached us by television: bomb threats in DC, more planes allegedly hijacked, and finally the tragic news of United Airlines Flight 93 crashing over Shanksville, Pennsylvania.

Tom Donlon waited on the phone for fifteen minutes and at last was patched through to headquarters. The call lasted only a couple of minutes, and Tom didn't say much other than "yes, I understand."

"Okay," he said, putting the phone down, "the instructions are for everyone to evacuate Yemen immediately and get on the first plane back to New York. Yemen is deemed unsafe. We don't yet know who was behind the attacks in New York and Washington, or if more attacks are coming. But given the problems we've had in Yemen in the past, we're to get out. Pack up and be prepared to leave in a few hours."

For once none of us disagreed with an order to return home. As important as our mission in Yemen was, it could wait. Thousands of Americans were reported killed, and our colleagues were missing. We wanted to get home to help. We packed our bags, shredded documents that we weren't taking with us, and, the next day, September 12, we headed to the airport.

"Ali!" The CIA officer in Sanaa came up to me as I waited in the airport with the rest of the team to board the plane.

"What's up?" I asked.

"FBI headquarters is trying to reach you. You need to speak to them."

"Who at headquarters? What do they want?"

"I don't know, but they've sent a number." I asked Tom Donlon if he knew why I was wanted, but he was unaware that headquarters was trying to reach me.

Tom and I went to a quiet corner outside the airport terminal, where our team's communication technician mounted a portable dish and established a secure satellite line. The number belonged to Dina Corsi, the FBI analyst in headquarters who had clashed with Steve Bongardt during the June 11, 2001, meeting in New York. "Ali, there has been

 1. Osama bin Laden, emir. Deceased.

 2. Ayman al-Zawahiri, Egyptian. Succeeded bin Laden as head of al-Qaeda. Formerly second in command and head of the media committee.

 3. Abu Hafs, Egyptian. Head of the military committee; *shura* council member. Deceased.

 4. Saif al-Adel, Egyptian. Head of the security committee; *shura* council member. At large.

 5. Abu Hafs al-Mauritani, Mauritanian. Head of the religious committee; *shura* council member. Extradited to Mauritania.

 6. Sheikh Sa'eed al-Masri, Egyptian. Head of the administrative committee; *shura* council member. Deceased.

 7. Abdul Hadi al-Iraqi, military commander; *shura* council member. In custody.

 8. Mohammed Saleh, Egyptian. *Shura* council member. Deceased.

 9. Abu Mohammed al-Masri, Egyptian. Commander of training; *shura* council member. At large.

 10. Abu al-Khair al-Masri, Egyptian. *Shura* council member. Deceased.

11. Raising the black banners at an al-Qaeda training camp in Afghanistan.

12. Zawahiri, bin Laden, and Abu Hafs, at one time the top three commanders of the terrorist network.

13. Mohammed Atta and Ziad Jarrah. The photo was taken when they stayed with Ali al-Bahlul, al-Qaeda propagandist, at a facility in Kandahar.

14. Bin Laden with Abu Jandal, the only bodyguard showing his face.

15. During John Miller interview with bin Laden, 1998. Miller later became the FBI assistant director for public affairs. He is the only U.S. official to have met the terrorist leader.

16. Jamal al-Badawi and Fahd al-Quso in court during the USS *Cole* trial in Yemen.

17. Ibrahim al-Nibras and Hassan al-Khamiri, the two
suicide bombers in the attack of the USS *Cole*.

18. A photo of the
USS *Cole* at the Aden
harbor taken from the
apartment rented by al-
Qaeda as an observation
post to videotape the
operation. The damage
can be seen on the side
of the ship.

19. The hole of death.

20. The USS *Cole* being transported on the *Blue Marlin*, October 2000.

21. Abu Zubaydah upon his capture in Faisalabad, Pakistan, 2002.

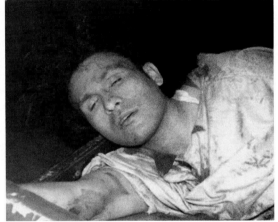

22. John O'Neill in one of the last photographs taken of him in his office, August 22, 2001, giving his signature hug to Ali Soufan's partner Bob McFadden.

23. Just prior to his delivery of the Eid sermon in Kandahar, bin Laden is seen with his trusted bodyguard Salim Hamdan (wearing black-and-white headdress). The man leaning forward is Abu Assim al-Maghrebi, then the head of bin Laden's security detachment.

24. Bin Laden's hideout was a million-dollar home in Abbottabad, Pakistan, close to the country's elite military academy.

25. Ali Soufan with Pat D'Amuro.

26. With NCIS and FBI team in Yemen after 9/11. (Standing, left to right) Ray Holcomb, Jeff Ringel, Ali Soufan, Tom Donlon, Dan Fethiere, Steve Corbett, Bob McFadden; (kneeling) Andre Khoury, Carlos Fernandez.

27. Ali Soufan with George Crouch in Afghanistan in bin Laden's hideout, 2002.

28. Ali Soufan with Andy Arena and Chuck Frahm.

29. Ali Soufan with his wife, Heather, and FBI director Robert Mueller.

a change of plans," she said. "You and Bob McFadden need to stay in Yemen."

"What do you mean?" I asked. "We have been attacked back home; we need to figure out who did this. Whatever is going on here can wait."

"We do need to figure out what just happened, which is why we need you to stay in Yemen. It's about what happened here. Quso is our best lead at the moment."

"Quso? What does he have to do with this?"

"The CIA has some intelligence for you to look over."

"Okay, I'll talk to Bob. We'll stay."

"One final thing, your instructions from the top are to identify those behind the attacks, and I quote, 'by any means necessary.'"

"We'll find them," I replied.

"One more thing, Ali," Dina said.

"Yes?"

"Be safe."

I ran to Bob, who was waiting for me to board the plane, and repeated the instructions I had just received. "'By any means necessary,'" I said, giving him the exact command I had been told. He nodded gravely. We assembled our FBI and NCIS colleagues who were also waiting to board and told them about our change of plan. Tom Donlon and Steve Corbett, the NCIS supervisor on the ground, decided to stay as well to help with the investigation, and two New York SWAT team agents also volunteered to stay and provide protection. Everyone else got on the plane, and we returned to the embassy.

"Let's go to my office," the officer said. He and I were alone, and he closed the door. He took out a file and silently handed it me.

Inside were three pictures of al-Qaeda operatives taken in Kuala Lumpur, along with a report of their activities there. The report and photos were all dated January 2000 and had been provided to the CIA by the Malaysians.

For about a minute I stared at the pictures and the report, not quite believing what I had in my hands. We had asked the CIA repeatedly during the USS *Cole* investigation if they knew anything about why Khallad had been in Malaysia and if they recognized the number of the pay phone in Kuala Lumpur that we suspected he had used. Each time we had asked—in November 2000, April 2001, and July 2001—they had said that they knew nothing.

But here in the file was a very different answer: they had in fact known since January 2000 that Khallad had met with other al-Qaeda operatives in Malaysia. They had pictures of them meeting and a detailed report of their comings and goings from the Malaysians.

As for the phone number, the report listed it as being assigned to a pay phone that the al-Qaeda operatives were using to communicate with colleagues everywhere. The phone booth was across from a condominium owned by an al-Qaeda sympathizer in Malaysia, which was where all the al-Qaeda members had stayed. Our deduction that Khallad had been using it was right.

The report also detailed Khallad's travels: it stated that he had attempted to fly to Singapore but had been rejected because he hadn't had a visa. He had returned to the Kuala Lumpur condominium and then had traveled to Bangkok. The report even stated that Khallad had been using a fraudulent Yemeni passport, under the name Sa'eed bin Saleh.

All this had been recorded and given to the CIA by the Malaysians in January 2000. None of it had been passed to us, despite our specifically having asked about Khallad and the phone number and its relevance to the *Cole* investigation and to national security. I later found out that the three photos in the report that the CIA gave me were the three photos shown, with no explanation, to Steve and my *Cole* colleagues at the June 11, 2001, meeting in New York. The *Cole* team had asked about the photos—who the people were, why they were taken, and so on—but Clark S., the CIA official present, said nothing.

Also in the file was a report that Khallad had flown first class to Bangkok with Khalid al-Mihdhar and Nawaf al-Hazmi. We soon would learn that they were listed as passengers on American Airlines Flight 77, which had hit the Pentagon. Based upon the chronology in the report, it was clear that the day after Quso and Nibras had met Khallad and given him the $36,000, Mihdhar and Hazmi had bought first-class tickets to the United States. Was that $36,000 used to buy their tickets? And had the rest of the money been intended for their use in the United States? My gut told me yes.

My hands started shaking. I didn't know what to think. "They just sent these reports," the CIA officer said, seeing my reaction. I walked out of the room, sprinted down the corridor to the bathroom, and fell to the floor next to a stall. There I threw up.

I sat on the floor for a few minutes, although it felt like hours. What I had just seen went through my mind again and again. The same thought kept looping back: "If they had all this information since January 2000, why the hell didn't they pass it on?" My whole body was shaking.

I heard one of the SWAT agents asking, "Ali, are you okay?" He had seen me run to the bathroom and had followed me in.

"I am fine."

I got myself to the sink, washed out my mouth, and splashed some water on my face. I covered my face with a paper towel for a few moments. I was still trying to process the fact that the information I had requested about major al-Qaeda operatives, information the CIA had claimed they knew nothing about, had been in the agency's hands since January 2000.

The SWAT agent asked, "What's wrong, bud? What the hell did he tell you?"

"They knew, they knew."

Another agent came in to check what was happening, and I told him what had just happened and why we had been ordered to stay in Yemen. We hugged and walked out.

I went back down the corridor to the CIA officer's office to get the file. "Ali?" he asked as I walked in. I looked him squarely in the face and saw that he was blushing and looked flustered. He clearly understood the significance of what the agency had not passed on.

I didn't have time to play the blame game. New York and Washington were still burning, colleagues of ours were missing, and we all had to focus on catching those responsible. "Is there anything else you haven't passed along?" I asked.

He didn't say anything, and I walked out, file in hand.

I went to the room where Tom Donlon, Bob McFadden, and Steve Corbett were working and dropped the file on the table. "The CIA just gave this to me," I said.

Bob looked up and saw the anger on my face. He didn't say anything, just took the file. Bob knew me well enough to know that something was very wrong. He looked through the contents and then turned to me in outrage. "I can't believe this." Those were his only words.

Tom and Steve's faces also dropped once they looked through the file; it was too much for any of us to take. "Now they want us to question Quso," Bob said, his voice rising in anger. "They should have given this to us eight months ago."

FBI special agent Andre Khoury had been stationed elsewhere in the Middle East when the planes hit the twin towers. He was reassigned to join us in Yemen, and after he arrived and saw the file, he wanted to confront the CIA officer. I held Andre back.

"They knew! Why didn't they tell us?!" Andre said.

"You're right," I said, "and I'm just as angry. Believe me. But now is not the time to ask these questions. One day someone will ask the questions and find out, but right now we have to focus on the task at hand."

In New York, a few hours after the attacks, Steve Bongardt and Kenny Maxwell joined a conference call with people in FBI headquarters in Washington, DC, including Dina Corsi and an FBI supervisor named Rod Middleton. Kenny asked if there were any names of suspected hijackers. Dina replied that they had some, and she began reading out names. The first few names didn't mean anything, but when Dina read the name "Khalid al-Mihdhar," Steve interrupted her.

"Khalid al-Mihdhar. Did you say Khalid al-Mihdhar?" he asked, his voice rising. "The same one you told us about? He's on the list?"

"Steve, we did everything by the book," Middleton interjected.

"I hope that makes you feel better," Steve replied. "Tens of thousands are dead." Kenny hit the mute button on the phone and said to Steve: "Now is not the time for this. There will be a time, but not now."

A few days later, once regular communication with New York was established, Steve called me in Yemen and repeated the conversation. "I hope they're fucking happy that they did everything by the book."

Over the next few days, weeks, and months, information about what else the CIA had known before 9/11 and hadn't told the FBI kept trickling out. In late 1999 the NSA had told the CIA that they had learned, from monitoring Ahmed al-Hada's number, that several al-Qaeda members had made plans to travel to Kuala Lumpur in early January 2000. They knew them by the names "Nawaf," "Khalid," and "Salem." Khalid had been identified by the CIA as Khalid al-Mihdhar, Hada's son-in-law, and they had tracked him arriving in Kuala Lumpur on January 5, 2000.

After we had uncovered Hada's switchboard during the 1998 investigation into the embassy bombings, we had made an operating agreement with the CIA under which they would monitor the number and share all intelligence with us. They hadn't done that.

We also learned that en route to Kuala Lumpur, Mihdhar had stopped off in Dubai. There his hotel room had been searched and his passport photographed and sent to CIA headquarters. In his passport he had a multi-entry U.S. visa. The CIA had passed this information on to foreign intelligence agencies but had not told the FBI, the Immigration and Naturalization Service, or the State Department.

Because no U.S. agency had been told, Mihdhar's name had not been put on a terrorist watchlist. As a consequence, he had not been stopped from entering the United States, or even questioned. In March 2000 the CIA had learned that Nawaf al-Hazmi had also flown to Los Angeles International Airport on January 15, but, again they hadn't told us, the State Department, or INS.

In June 2000 Mihdhar had left California and had gone back to Yemen to visit his family following the birth of a daughter. He had then traveled to Saudi Arabia and Afghanistan before traveling again to Mecca in June 2001. He had returned to the United States on July 4,

2001. But because the CIA had not informed us, no one stopped him from entering.

It was on June 13, two days after the June 11 meeting in which Clark S., the CIA supervisor, had refused to answer any questions from Steve and the *Cole* team about Mihdhar, that he was issued a new visa.

While they were in the United States, both Mihdhar and Hazmi had used their real names to get driver's licenses and to open bank accounts. Hazmi had even registered his car and was listed in the San Diego phone book. He had used his debit card to buy tickets for American Airlines Flight 77 for himself and his brother, Salem.

It was not until August 23, 2001, that the FBI, Customs, and the State Department were told that Mihdhar was in the United States.

Qamish, who was with his chief of staff, Nabil Sanabani, came straight up to me and gave me a hug. In his eyes there was a look of genuine concern and sadness. "It's terrible news," he said, after releasing me. "Is everyone okay?" He was referring to the many Americans he had met as part of the *Cole* investigation.

I shook my head. His question made me choke up, and it took me a few seconds to pull myself together. "John—" My throat swelled up. "Brother John is missing," I finished, "as are other colleagues." Qamish's face now registered unmistakable grief.

We updated him on the news from New York and Washington. At the time, reports were that more than fifty thousand people had been killed, and we thought that that number included many of our colleagues who were in the vicinity, and with whom we had lost contact. As we spoke, emotion overcame us each one by one. Nabil handed us tissues to wipe our tears.

"How can we help, Brother Ali?" Qamish asked me after we had finished briefing him.

"We need to speak to Quso," I said. "I believe that he has information on the attacks, and I need to interview him."

"I'll get him for you," Qamish replied immediately.

He picked up the phone and called the PSO office in Aden and was patched through to Ansi, whom we knew well from the *Cole* investigation.

"Put Quso on the next plane to Sanaa," Qamish told Ansi. "Ali needs to interview him."

An argument ensued, and Qamish's voice rose, his tone turning angry. "I don't care. The plane can't leave without him. You listen to me—"

When he had finished, Qamish turned to me and said, "Don't worry, I'll make sure Quso is brought here." It wasn't a surprise to us that Ansi was trying to stop us from interviewing Quso. He had made his sympathies clear during the *Cole* investigation.

Qamish next called the airport and issued an order to a PSO official based there. "Go find the pilot of the last plane from Aden to Sanaa and have him call me immediately." A few minutes later Qamish's phone rang. The PSO official at the airport had the pilot on the line.

"I have a prisoner that I want on your plane," Qamish told the pilot. "Don't leave without him. If he's late, the plane must wait."

It was clear Qamish thought that Ansi might deliberately bring Quso to the airport late so he would miss the plane. He was right—Ansi did bring Quso late. To Ansi's surprise, the plane was waiting.

During the late evening of September 12, Bob and I went to a PSO facility to meet Quso. He was brought straight from the airport, and as soon as he saw us waiting for him he started yelling. "What is this? So if anything happens in New York or Washington you blame me?"

"Hold on," I said. "How did you know we were going to ask you about that?" Quso was silent. My question caught him off-guard. "I was actually just going to ask you about the *Cole*, but since you bring it up, what do you know?" Quso slumped down in his chair.

We read Quso the Miranda warning; he waived his rights, and then we started questioning him. "So what do you know about what happened?"

"I don't know anything."

"Okay," I told him, "but you do know about al-Qaeda, right?"

"Yes, we've been through that."

"Okay, so we'll return to the *Cole*."

I asked Quso a series of questions about his having delivered the money to Khallad in Bangkok. I showed him the three pictures I had been given by the CIA, one of which was of Khalid al-Mihdhar, taken in Malaysia. Quso didn't identify him as Mihdhar but said he thought he looked like Khallad.

It took a lot of self-control for us to remain calm while questioning Quso. The $36,000 he had delivered to Khallad from Yemen had in all likelihood been used for the 9/11 attack, probably paying for tickets for two of the hijackers, Hazmi and Mihdhar. We had only just learned from the CIA that they knew that the two had been with Khallad in Bangkok, and from there had flown to Los Angeles. Next we showed Quso pictures of al-Qaeda operatives and asked him to identify those he knew. Some of the analysts in Washington were convinced that Quso was in the photos, though Bob and I, who had spent many hours with him, knew it wasn't the case. Nonetheless, the analysts requested that we get Quso to identify himself. After going over the photos, we dwelled on the individual they thought was Quso. He noticed and told us, "I know what you're thinking. It's not me. It looks like me, but it's not me." Included were pictures of the men we suspected of being the hijackers, although we didn't tell him the significance of those photos. Quso identified numerous al-Qaeda members but didn't recognize any of the suspected hijackers' photos except one. "That's Marwan al-Shehhi," he said. Shehhi had been on United Airlines Flight 175. We suspected that Shehhi was a hijacker, but at this stage we had no proof. Quso helped provide proof by identifying him as an al-Qaeda member.

"Okay," I said nonchalantly, "how do you know him?"

"I once stayed at the same guesthouse as him in Afghanistan."

"And?"

"It was during Ramadan, and Shehhi had apparently had some kind of stomach operation to help him lose weight, so really it was dangerous for him to fast, but he decided to fast anyway. As a result he got very sick, and the emir of the guesthouse had to look after him."

"Anything else happen with him?"

"I remember he had arrived in Afghanistan with a friend whose alias was Abas, but he was killed during a training exercise. Apparently he didn't realize the gun he was using had real bullets in it, and he shot himself." Quso laughed to himself.

"And in the guesthouse where you met Shehhi," I asked, "who was the emir?" Although I of course knew the answer, I wanted him to say the name for the benefit of the PSO officials present.

"Abu Jandal," he replied.

I asked Quso a couple more questions about other people, because I didn't want him to know the significance of what he had just told me, and then I suggested to the Yemenis that we all take a break.

From our anonymous source in Afghanistan we knew Abu Jandal's importance to bin Laden. We also knew that the Yemenis had him in custody. They had refused to give us access to him in the *Cole* investigation because they had said we had no evidence that he had anything to do with the attack on the destroyer. But now we had Quso linking him to one of the 9/11 hijackers.

"We need to talk to Abu Jandal," I told one of the Yemeni intelligence officers in the room. "Quickly!"

While we waited for Abu Jandal, we continued questioning Quso and in total spent about four days talking to him, going through all his interactions with other al-Qaeda members. We questioned him during the night and spent the days preparing for the next interview. At one point I collapsed from exhaustion and was taken to the emergency room, but as soon as I was revived I checked myself out and returned to work.

We took breaks from the interrogation to write up the information we had gained and file it with Washington. When we informed headquarters that we had shown Quso the three pictures and that he had misidentified the picture of Mihdhar as being Khallad, they told us that the CIA had just come up with a fourth picture.

"What fourth picture?" I asked in frustration. "Look, how many pictures are there?"

"As far as the CIA told us, that's it. There are only four pictures, but we are still pushing. We'll let you know."

Headquarters sent us the fourth picture—it was of Khallad, talking in a phone booth. The Malaysians had listed, in their report, the phone number assigned to the booth. It was the number that we had explicitly asked the CIA if they had recognized, to which they had replied no. Quso positively identified the man in the fourth photo as Khallad.

This fourth picture had been in the CIA's possession when Steve Bongardt and the *Cole* team had been shown the first three pictures on June 11, 2001. If it had been shown to the *Cole* team, Steve and the other agents at the meeting would have identified the man in the picture as Khallad. We knew exactly what Khallad looked like from the *Cole* investigation. And if we had learned that the CIA had had a picture of Khallad in June 2001, and had been monitoring him, we would have gone straight to headquarters saying that the CIA had lied about not knowing about Khallad, and we would have demanded that they hand over the information.

If that had happened, at a minimum, Khalid al-Mihdhar would not have been allowed to just walk into the United States on July 4, 2001, and Nawaf al-Hazmi, Atta's deputy, would have been arrested. At a minimum.

What really upset Bob and me now was that it was only Quso's misidentification of Mihdhar as possibly Khallad that had caused the CIA to share the fourth photo. Even now, after 9/11, they weren't properly sharing information with us. We wondered if there were other photographs from the Malaysia meeting that were still being kept from us.

August 2003. "Watch it, Ali, they seem to want your head," Kevin Cruise said, walking up to my desk. He'd just finished meeting investigators from the 9/11 Commission.

"What do you mean?" I asked.

"They're asking a lot of questions about you. It seems our friends at Langley have been talking about you. Just be careful when you see them tomorrow." It was clear that the CIA officials behind the withholding of information pre-9/11 were nervous about what I would say and were trying to discredit me. It was unfortunate that this was how they were spending their time: rather than addressing mistakes and working out how to ensure that errors weren't repeated, they wanted to cover it up and fight the FBI instead.

"Thanks, Kevin, will do."

The National Commission on Terrorist Attacks Upon the United States was set up in late 2002 by an act of Congress, with the mandate "to prepare a full and complete account of the circumstances surrounding the September 11, 2001, attacks." When the investigators arrived in New York, they spoke first to senior FBI officials like Kevin Cruise, who was one of two supervisors overseeing the 9/11 investigations. The next day they spoke to field agents.

The first agent they called was me. After introducing themselves and asking some basic background questions, one of the investigators asked me: "So, Agent Soufan, why does the CIA hate you?" I was taken aback by the question, and paused as I debated how to answer it.

"You must be talking to the wrong crowd down there. Hate is a big term," I replied. "But to answer your question, I think you'd have to ask them." The commission team started laughing.

"Let's move on and focus on al-Qaeda," said one of the investigators, Douglas J. MacEachin, a thirty-year CIA veteran. "Here's my question: if you want to look at al-Qaeda and understand what happened, where would you start?"

"Nineteen seventy-nine is where I'd start," I answered.

Doug's face lit up. "I must tell you," he said, "I'm very pleased you said that. Everyone else we've spoken to answers by starting just before 9/11, or with the East African embassy bombings or the USS *Cole*. But in my opinion, you are right. Tell me, why 1979?"

I explained to him what I had told John years earlier, explaining why 1979—with events like the Soviet invasion of Afghanistan and the Iranian revolution—was an important year.

"That's the best explanation we've heard, thank you," one of the staffers said. "Why don't you now take us through what has happened since 1979 and the cases you've been involved in investigating."

I talked them through a series of cases, including the East African embassy bombings, Operation Challenge, the thwarted millennium attacks in Jordan, and the USS *Cole* bombing. During this discussion, I sensed that the relationship between us was changing. While they had clearly been briefed negatively about me by some in the CIA, they saw I knew my material, and they were reevaluating me in their minds.

I finished off by mentioning that, as part of the *Cole* investigation, we had asked the CIA about Khallad and other al-Qaeda operatives being in Malaysia, and that they had denied any knowledge of it. I also mentioned that the CIA had known in January that hijacker Khalid al-Mihdhar had a U.S. visa, and that they had known in March that he was in the United States—but that they hadn't shared this information with the FBI until August 2001.

"The CIA told us," one investigator interjected, "that as they told the congressional Joint Inquiry, the FBI was told about Khallad being in Malaysia, and the FBI was told about Khalid al-Midhar and Hazmi being here." (The Joint Inquiry into Intelligence Community Activities before and after the Terrorist Attacks of September 11, 2001, or JIICA-TAS911, was conducted by the Senate Select Committee on Intelligence and the House Permanent Select Committee on Intelligence between February 2002 and December 2002, and it was widely seen as a failure. This is why the nonpartisan 9/11 Commission was set up.)

"That's not true," I replied, "and you can look through all the files we have to see that that information was never passed along. As you know, if information was passed along, it would be in these files. The government works electronically, and there's a record of everything. In the USS *Cole* files you'll see all the requests we made, and their responses saying they didn't have any information."

"We want to see all the USS *Cole* files."

"Sure. We have lots of files. It could take days."

"That's not a problem. We have lots of people to go through them."

I called in one of my FBI colleagues and asked that all the files for the USS *Cole* be brought to the investigators. We had files on every individual involved, every witness we had questioned, and every scene we had investigated. Included among the material were thick files with information we had sent to the CIA. A separate file contained information the CIA had passed to us, and that was very thin.

As the files were being brought in, we took a break and I went to speak to Pat D'Amuro. He was with Joe Valiquette, the FBI's spokesman. "How's it going, Ali?" Pat asked.

"The challenge I'm facing is that they are claiming the CIA gave us the information on Mihdhar and Khallad being in Malaysia."

"But they didn't," Pat replied.

"Exactly, boss, and in the USS *Cole* files we've got all the documents proving that. What I want to know is whether it's okay with the bureau that I point out to the investigators exactly where to look. Otherwise they're just searching through hundreds of files."

"Absolutely, give them everything they want and need," Pat replied.

This was a marked change from how the bureau approached the Joint Inquiry, where agents were told that the FBI leadership was just going to accept the "blame" for 9/11 in order not to upset anyone in the CIA and rock the boat. This decision outraged the agents who were on the front lines against al-Qaeda and who knew that the truth was very different. As I walked back into the room the commission investigators were using, I felt liberated.

At one point during my discussions with the 9/11 Commission investigators, I was called into the office of my assistant special agent in charge, Amy Jo Lyons. "Ali, we've been getting complaints from the CIA about things you're saying to the commission," she said. It seemed that the investigators were going back and asking the CIA new questions based on the information I had given them. And the CIA had complained to FBI headquarters.

"That's okay with me," I replied to Amy, "but if people in headquarters are unhappy with me telling the commission what really happened, they can tell me in writing not to cooperate, and I won't cooperate."

"No, no," Amy said, "I just want to know what's happening here."

"It's simple," I told her. "The commission started asking questions about the *Cole* and 9/11, and I quickly realized they had been told a series of lies. With Pat's approval I went through actual documents with them and showed them what really happened."

"If that's the case," Amy replied, "you didn't do anything wrong. You did exactly what needed to be done."

When the 9/11 Commission published their findings, everything I said was confirmed by their investigation. On page 355 of the report, they list "Operational Opportunities." Included in that summary list are:

1. January 2000: the CIA does not watchlist Khalid al-Mihdhar or notify the FBI when it learned Mihdhar possessed a valid U.S. visa.

2. January 2000: the CIA does not develop a transnational plan for tracking Mihdhar and his associates so that they could be followed to Bangkok and onward, including the United States.

3. March 2000: the CIA does not watchlist Nawaf al-Hazmi or notify the FBI when it learned that he possessed a U.S. visa and had flown to Los Angeles on January 15, 2000.

4. January 2001: the CIA does not inform the FBI that a source had identified Khallad, or Tawfiq bin Attash, a major figure in the October 2000 bombing of the USS *Cole*, as having attended the meeting in Kuala Lumpur with Khalid al-Mihdhar.

5. May 2001: a CIA official does not notify the FBI about Mihdhar's U.S. visa, Hazmi's U.S. travel, or Khallad's having attended the Kuala Lumpur meeting (identified when he reviewed all the relevant traffic because of the high level of threats).

6. June 2001: FBI and CIA officials do not ensure that all relevant information regarding the Kuala Lumpur meeting was shared with the *Cole* investigators at the June 11 meeting.

The CIA's own inspector general's report into 9/11 came to the same conclusions regarding CIA shortcomings and its failure to share intelligence. The report states: "Earlier watchlisting of Mihdhar could have prevented his reentry into the United States in July 2001. Informing the FBI and good operational follow-through by CIA and FBI might have resulted in surveillance of both al-Mihdhar and al-Hazmi. Surveillance, in turn, would have the potential to yield information on flight training, financing, and links to others who were complicit in the 9/11 attacks." The report goes on to say: "That so many individuals failed to act in this case reflects a systematic breakdown." The inspector general recommended that an "accountability board review the performance of the CTC chiefs." (This never happened.)

My discussions with the 9/11 Commission investigators resumed, and we started discussing the "source" in Afghanistan.

"He's an FBI source developed in Afghanistan before 9/11. We agreed to share him with the CIA. Our agreement with them on the source was that anything gained from the source—he was a criminal investigation source—had to be shared with us."

"And what happened?"

"After 9/11 we learned that the CIA went behind our backs and showed the pictures of the Malaysia summit meeting—the pictures they wouldn't share with us—to the source. They didn't tell us that they had shown him the pictures, nor did they share with us what he told them about the pictures. He didn't know that the CIA wasn't sharing information with the FBI; nor was he told why these pictures were important. When the source was shown the pictures from Malaysia in January 2001, he told them he didn't recognize who Mihdhar was, but he was 90 percent certain that the other person was Khallad.

"We were not told this. This shows that the CIA knew the significance of Malaysia, Khallad, and Mihdhar but actively went out of their way to withhold the information from us. It's not a case of just not passing on information. This is information the FBI representative working with the source should have been told about. It was a legal requirement. Instead we were deliberately kept out of the loop."

"We were told by the CIA's Counterterrorism Center that they shared all their information with the FBI from the source and that nothing was hidden," a commission member responded.

I paused and, thinking out loud, asked, "Did you check all the regular cables?"

"Yes."

"Did you check operational traffic?"

"That must be it," Doug said, smiling broadly. At first only he understood the point I was making, and he received puzzled looks from other staffers. But then he explained it to them.

Operational traffic refers to cables sent during an operation. The officer will list procedures, leaving a record in case something goes wrong or something needs to be referred to. Because these cables are strictly procedural and not related to intelligence, they would not be sent to the FBI. If someone wanted to hide something from the FBI, that's where he would put it. Because Doug had worked for the CIA, he knew what operational cables were, while other members of the team might not have.

After investigating the episode, the 9/11 Commission found that this intelligence was indeed hidden in operational traffic.

When an FBI colleague from New York, Frank Pellegrino, briefed the commission after me, a staffer commented about investigators being "unable to connect the dots."

"What dots?" Frank angrily replied. "There are no dots to connect! It was all there, written in front of them."

Later I was asked by the 9/11 Commission to travel to Washington with Dan Coleman, Debbie Doran, and a few senior FBI officials to deliver a briefing about al-Qaeda to the full commission. The CIA was represented by some analysts, and the meeting was chaired by the executive director of the commission, Philip Zelikow.

Doug MacEachin, the former CIA official who had become a supporter of mine after our meeting in New York, told me beforehand to give the same briefing I had given them, which I did. The CIA analysts then gave a presentation about the structure of al-Qaeda.

"Is that accurate?" a commission team member asked me.

"No, unfortunately, there is a series of errors in what they think is the structure of al-Qaeda."

"For example?"

"Well, they said that Khalid Sheikh Mohammed runs al-Qaeda's media committee. This is under the control of Ayman Zawahiri. KSM runs the media office, a cover for their operational planning unit."

"Can you support your claim?"

"Yes. We found some documents in Afghanistan explaining the structure."

"What else?"

"Then there's what they said about Khallad," I replied. "They said Khallad has never been to the United States. Debbie can tell you that's false."

"Yes," Debbie interjected, "we found that Salah bin Saeed bin Yousef—this is the alias Khallad traveled under—was listed as having traveled to LAX during the millennium."

"We have Khallad in our custody," a CIA analyst said, "and he told us he's never been to the United States."

"You may be right, but if he wasn't there, why is his alias on the flight manifest?"

These are a few of the points we raised, among many others. Some are classified; others I simply cannot recall after all these years. As we walked out of the room at the conclusion of the meeting, one commission staffer came up to us and said: "I have a feeling that between the three of you, you forget more things than they will ever know."

Years later, on April 23, 2009, Philip Zelikow commented, in a piece on foreignpolicy.com: "I met and interviewed Soufan in the course of my work at the 9/11 Commission, while he was still doing important work at the FBI. . . . My fellow staffers and I considered Soufan to be credible. Indeed, Soufan is fluent in Arabic, and he seemed to us to be one of the more impressive intelligence agents—from any agency—that we encountered in our work."

Until Debbie, Dan, myself, and other agents briefed the commission, senior FBI managers in Washington didn't understand the situation.

Part of the problem was that the FBI leadership had changed in August 2001. There was a new director, Robert Mueller, with a new senior team, and very few of them had been involved with the significant terrorist cases of the preceding years.

The leadership of the FBI didn't know that we had been requesting information and that the CIA hadn't shared it; and they just wanted to move on and start fresh. President George W. Bush had told the FBI and the CIA that he wanted everyone to get along. Again, the implication was that the FBI should just take the criticism and blame for 9/11.

But those of us who knew the truth stated exactly what had happened when we were asked about events under oath before the 9/11 Commission. And when senior FBI officials heard about our performance before the commission, they were surprised. At one point I was asked to brief John Pistole, one of Director Mueller's chief deputies, prior to his testifying publicly before the 9/11 Commission, but at the last minute the briefing was canceled, as the leadership didn't want to cause problems for the CIA.

Later, when John Miller, the former ABC journalist who had interviewed bin Laden in 1998, was appointed assistant director of the FBI's Office of Public Affairs, he understood the need to correct the narrative. When Lawrence Wright asked for access to people, John told the director: "We need to do this for history. It isn't about CIA or FBI. We need to tell the American people the truth about an important era." The director agreed, and the bureau gave Larry access. He then wrote the best-seller *The Looming Tower*, and he later profiled me in the *New Yorker*. Between his book and the 9/11 Commission, the truth began to come out.

Those in the CIA who were responsible for not passing on information did their best to ensure that the truth didn't come out. With approval from the bureau, around the same time we spoke to Wright, Joe Valiquette arranged for Dan Coleman and me to brief a senior journalist from one of the major newspapers. After he spoke to us in New York, he went to the CIA with a bunch of questions.

"What you were told by the FBI is completely false," a CIA official told him. The journalist asked to see evidence, whereupon the CIA official pointed to a stack of documents, describing the files as consisting of "information disproving everything the FBI said, but it's all classified, so I can't show it to you." The journalist decided to tone down the story. Wright was told the same thing, and veiled threats were made (with reference to his daughter). But he's a courageous reporter who could read through bluffs, and he had done enough research to be confident in what the truth was, and he wouldn't be pressured by threats. He wrote his book, and won the Pulitzer Prize for it.

After *The 9/11 Commission Report* was published and everything I had told the journalist was verified, the journalist contacted Joe Valiquette, told him what the CIA had said, and apologized for not running with the truth. "I was duped. I trusted them," the journalist told Joe.

What really upset a few people on the seventh floor of Langley—the executive floor—was that the 9/11 Commission flatly contradicted the CIA's claims about sharing intelligence. The commission showed the American people that if information had been shared, 9/11 might have been prevented.

The most damning passage in *The 9/11 Commission Report* is found on page 267: "DCI Tenet and Cofer Black testified before Congress's Joint Inquiry into 9/11 that the FBI had access to this identification [of Khallad in Kuala Lumpur] from the beginning. But drawing on an extensive record, including documents that were not available to the CIA personnel who drafted that testimony, we conclude this was not the case."

In a footnote to that line, one of the sources is "Al. S." Those in the CIA who had not shared the intelligence knew that this referred to "Ali Soufan," and they hated me for it.

16

The Father of Death

September 17, 2001. It was dark outside as Bob and I walked into the interrogation room at PSO headquarters in Sanaa. We had agreed with the Yemenis that it was safest to conduct our interrogations at night. Under cover of darkness there was less of a chance that we would be spotted traveling to and from the prison.

The security threat was greater than ever before, as the new suspect we were about to interrogate, Nasser Ahmad Nasser al-Bahri—widely known as Abu Jandal—was Osama bin Laden's former personal body-guard. Al-Qaeda and its supporters certainly didn't want him talking to us. He was a potential treasure trove of information on the enemy that had just six days earlier murdered so many Americans. The final tally was not yet known, as bodies were still being recovered, but among the dead were friends like my former boss John O'Neill. At the very least, Abu Jandal knew Marwan al-Shehhi, one of the suspected hijackers of United Airlines Flight 175.

Getting information on the hijackers and al-Qaeda in general was a top priority for the U.S. government. The U.S. military was prepar-ing to invade Afghanistan to go after al-Qaeda, and the government was trying to build an international coalition to support its efforts. All U.S. intelligence, military, and law enforcement personnel were under pressure to learn as much as they could about the enemy's capabilities, plans, locations, and numbers to help the military prepare for war. We were also asked to find evidence to show conclusively that al-Qaeda was behind the attack.

Several world leaders whom the United States wanted to include in its coalition, including Egypt's Hosni Mubarak and Pakistan's General Musharraf, were not convinced that al-Qaeda was responsible. Musharraf was particularly important given Pakistan's proximity to Afghanistan. Abu Jandal was the best lead the United States had so far; we hoped to obtain information from him that might remove these leaders' doubts and give our military information on the enemy we were about to attack.

We knew of Bahri—born in Saudi Arabia and of Yemeni descent—by his fearsome reputation. In a famous picture of bin Laden walking with his bodyguards, all of the bodyguards have their faces covered to protect their identities except Abu Jandal, who wanted to show he had no fear. Our anonymous source had spoken of Abu Jandal as someone fiercely dedicated to, and trusted by, bin Laden, and someone whom other al-Qaeda members both feared and respected.

He had been arrested by the Yemenis at Sanaa International Airport in February 2001 as he was trying to leave the country to return to Afghanistan. Initially the Yemenis wouldn't let us question him; they were only letting us interrogate those we could prove were connected to the *Cole* attack. Although Abu Jandal was a known al-Qaeda member, nothing linked him to the *Cole* bombing. The Yemenis were holding him because they knew his connection to bin Laden and were suspicious as to why he had been traveling into and out of the country. It was only because Quso had provisionally linked Abu Jandal to 9/11 that we now had access to him.

Bob and I settled into chairs on one side of the table and waited for Abu Jandal to be brought in. We were glad that our usual Yemeni interrogation partners, Colonel Yassir and Major Mahmoud, were with us. We had been working well with them in the *Cole* investigation. They were talented law enforcement operatives, and we knew that they shared our commitment to justice.

About ten minutes later guards knocked on the door. The door opened and Abu Jandal walked in, very much at ease. He had a thick black beard, closely cropped black hair, balding on top, and piercing brown eyes—which at that moment were glaring at us, as if he wanted to know how we dared to interrogate him.

He wasn't wearing shackles, handcuffs, or even a prison uniform. Instead he wore a blue thawb and slippers. He didn't act or dress like a prisoner. He looked healthy and well-rested, and it was clear that he had been treated well during his several months in prison.

Abu Jandal held his head high, and his body language displayed confidence and control. Our Yemeni partners had asked that their names not be said out loud—they didn't want Abu Jandal to know who they were. They were apparently afraid of him.

When he had taken his seat across the table from Bob and me, with Yassir and Mahmoud against the wall, we began the interrogation. "Hello, Nasser," I said in Arabic, using his first name to emphasize my familiarity with him. "My name is Ali Soufan, and I'm with the FBI." I took out my FBI credentials and placed them in front of him on the table.

I wanted to take him out of his comfort zone: he was used to being feared and having deferential Yemeni guards. I wanted him to know that things were different now: he was with Americans and we weren't scared. "And this is my colleague Bob McFadden, from the Naval Criminal Investigative Service," I continued, pointing to Bob, who nodded, "and we'd like to ask you some questions. But first I want to advise you of your rights, which I will now read to you."

Before I could continue, in one quick movement Abu Jandal stood up, swung his chair so that it faced away from us, and sat back down. Now he had his back to us. He turned his head to the side toward Yassir and Mahmoud, and told them, his brown eyes still glaring: "I will not talk directly to them. If there are any questions, you ask me, not these Americans. They can't talk to me. You know the rules." For the next few minutes he lectured them about how they should not allow Americans to question him.

Abu Jandal apparently had been told by sympathetic PSO officials that the Yemenis were meant to be intermediaries between us and any Yemenis we questioned. It was what we had agreed to during the *Cole* investigation. But the practice had been dropped: to Yassir and Mahmoud and most of the other Yemenis we worked with, it was seen as a waste of time. Why have them repeat, in Arabic, what I had just asked in Arabic? It made little sense and even made them look foolish, and so they had begun to let us speak directly in Arabic to the suspects.

When Abu Jandal finished his rant, I turned to Mahmoud and said dismissively in Arabic, "Go ahead, repeat what I said. If Nasser wants to waste his own time by hearing the same thing twice, that's fine with me." I wanted to show Abu Jandal that I wasn't intimidated; nor did it matter to me if Mahmoud or Yassir had to repeat things. If he was trying to score any psychological points, he had failed. Abu Jandal was silent.

"His name is Ali Soufan, and he's with the FBI. He wants to ask you some questions, but first he will read you your rights," Mahmoud said.

"Okay," Abu Jandal replied, looking at Mahmoud.

"Right," I said. "Nasser al-Bahri, you have the right to remain silent. Anything you say can and will be used against you in a court of law . . ." I continued reading from the form in Arabic. After I had finished, I said: "Do you understand these rights as they have been read to you?" Silence from Abu Jandal. I nodded to Mahmoud.

"Nasser al-Bahri, you have the right to remain silent. Anything you say . . . ," Mahmoud began, and he repeated verbatim in Arabic what I had just said in Arabic.

"I don't need a lawyer, I can answer any question. I'm not afraid. I've done nothing wrong. I'll answer your questions," Abu Jandal replied, full of confidence.

"Will you sign a declaration saying you understand yours rights?" I asked.

Abu Jandal was silent. He still had his back to Bob and me and he stared at Mahmoud. Again Mahmoud repeated what I had said: "Will you sign a declaration saying that you understand your rights?"

"I won't sign, but I verbally tell you it's okay," Abu Jandal replied.

"Okay," I said. "So, Abu Jandal, how are you today?"

Silence. I nodded to Mahmoud. "How are you today?" Mahmoud repeated.

"Good," Abu Jandal replied to him.

"Good," Mahmoud told me. I noticed Abu Jandal smirking to himself; the skit amused him. "So you are Abu Jandal, bin Laden's personal bodyguard?" I asked.

Silence. Mahmoud repeated the question.

"Yes," he said, "I can't deny that, because there is only one Abu Jandal, and I am Abu Jandal." He couldn't help grinning as he said this. Abu Jandal was clearly proud of his reputation and status in al-Qaeda.

"And you were bin Laden's personal bodyguard?" I asked. Mahmoud repeated my question.

"Yes," Abu Jandal replied, "I was, but I left al-Qaeda and am now being held for no reason."

"How did you join al-Qaeda?" I asked. Mahmoud repeated the question.

"I first went to Bosnia to protect Muslims from Serb brutality, then I went to Afghanistan, where I met bin Laden," he told Mahmoud, who repeated it to me. We went through a series of basic questions—covering his identity and his role in al-Qaeda—and he answered all our questions, through Mahmoud and Yassir.

While it appeared that Abu Jandal was cooperating, he was in fact practicing a classic counterinterrogation technique. He knew that we were fully aware of who he was, his position in al-Qaeda, and other basic information about him. He knew there was no point denying it, so he readily admitted it in order to appear to be cooperating. But in reality he wasn't giving us any new information, only basic stuff that he assumed we knew. This made it difficult for us to accuse him of not cooperating.

To get Abu Jandal to cooperate properly and gain new intelligence, we first had to get him to talk directly to us, rather than through the Yemenis. A key to a successful interrogation is to establish rapport with the detainee—a nearly impossible task if he won't even talk to you. Bob and I began to ask Abu Jandal a series of seemingly irrelevant questions. While they wouldn't necessarily give us any actual intelligence, they would, importantly, encourage him to open up and talk.

"Why would someone join al-Qaeda?" I asked. Mahmoud repeated the question. It was an open-ended question designed to give Abu Jandal a chance to lecture. Abu Jandal responded by talking about the Islamic tradition of fighting injustice and tyranny, and linked that to the American "occupation" of Muslims lands and Israel's actions against the Palestinians. I guessed he had spoken about the subject countless times, probably to motivate new al-Qaeda recruits.

We followed up with a series of similar soft questions, ones that Abu Jandal wouldn't see as problematic to address—ones he would want to respond to. At the same time, the questions made him more emotional, as these were matters close to his heart, and as a result he lost some of his control and deliberation. I asked him about the "injustices" he referred to, and about what he had seen in Bosnia and Afghanistan.

As he got increasingly involved in replying—thinking perhaps that he was convincing me, given the earnestness and respectful tone of my questioning—at times he forgot to wait for Mahmoud to repeat the question and responded directly to me.

We broke in the early hours of the morning, happy to have succeeded in getting Abu Jandal to speak and look directly at us. Our first objective had been achieved.

Bob and I returned to the U.S. Embassy in Sanaa (then our home and office) and started reviewing our conversation with Abu Jandal and preparing for the next evening's interview. After a few hours we took a break and went to a nearby local supermarket for some food. As we passed the bakery section, Bob pointed to some sugarless cookies and said to me, with a twinkle in his eye: "Let's get them for him. We'll give him the message that Americans are good. Habibi, we are good." "Habibi" is an Arabic word that literally means "my beloved" but is used as a term of friendship and endearment. Bob was being sarcastic.

During the interrogation we had put some cookies on the table for Abu Jandal, but he hadn't touched them. We'd asked Yassir why, and he had told us it was because Abu Jandal was diabetic. While I asked more of the questions, Bob focused on manipulating the atmosphere of the interview. Even while taking a break from preparation, he was thinking about how to establish rapport with Abu Jandal.

The next evening, we returned to PSO headquarters and went back into the interrogation room with Mahmoud and Yassir. As Abu Jandal was escorted into the room by his guards, before he had a chance to sit down I greeted him: "As-Salāmu `Alaykum."

He shook his head and then slowly replied, "Wa `Alaykum as-Salām." In Islamic culture, if someone says "peace be upon you," you need to respond in kind. Knowing the culture, we used it to our advantage and got him to start off that evening as he had finished the previous one: speaking directly to us.

I then read Abu Jandal the Miranda warning (we did this every day): "You have the right . . ." Abu Jandal was silent, and he turned his head and glared at Mahmoud, clearly trying to reestablish the boundaries he had had the previous night before he had engaged with us. I nodded to Mahmoud, who repeated the Miranda warning. Abu Jandal again verbally waived his rights, saying he had nothing to hide.

"How are you today?" I asked him. He was silent and looked at Mahmoud.

I nodded to Mahmoud and he repeated my question.

"Good," Abu Jandal replied.

"Good," Mahmoud told me.

"We know you didn't eat the cookies we put out for you yesterday because you have a sugar problem. So today we brought you some sugarless cookies that you can eat."

Abu Jandal's face registered surprise. He had been taught to expect cruelty from Americans, not kindness. He seemed at a loss for how to respond.

"Shukran," he said slowly, looking at me and again shaking his head. Under Islamic traditions, you need to thank someone for a kindness, and Abu Jandal was well versed in Islamic etiquette. Now he looked at me, rather than Mahmoud, waiting for the next question.

We started off by asking him light personal questions, ones he'd have no problem answering. The aim was to warm him up. Every detainee is different. Abu Jandal was by nature talkative. He liked to lecture and liked being listened to. He was intelligent and well read, unlike many other al-Qaeda terrorists I had interrogated, so we used leverage on his personality and engaged him intellectually.

"So you left al-Qaeda in 2000?" I asked, accepting his claim from the previous evening that when he returned to Yemen in 2000 it was because he was leaving al-Qaeda.

"Yes," he replied directly to me. "Although the fact that I'm here talking to you shows that you can't really leave," he said in a sarcastic tone.

"In fact," he continued, "Abu Mohammed al-Masri told me, 'If you think by leaving Afghanistan they [the Americans] will leave you alone, you are wrong. This is a war. Either we will win or die. There is no place for turning back.'" He had used an alias for Abdullah Ahmed Abdullah, the al-Qaeda *shura* council member and mastermind of the East African embassy bombings. He paused, as if for effect, and then continued with a shrug and a half-smile, "And he's right, here I am with you, even though I left."

"Why did you leave al-Qaeda?" I asked, ignoring Abu Jandal's comment and sticking to our plan of having him talk about comfortable topics.

"For many reasons," he replied. "First of all, because of my wife and children . . ." He explained that his son Habib had a bone condition and that they couldn't get adequate treatment in Afghanistan. Another reason for leaving, he told us, was because his wife was unhappy in Afghanistan.

"Why was she unhappy?" I asked.

"Because Bin Laden had given me money to bring to someone in Yemen, which turned out to be for a new bride for bin Laden himself. She was very young, and the other wives resented me for bringing her, and in turn were mean to my wife." Abu Jandal told us that he thought he was being sent with the funds for what he termed a "martyrdom operation" and was upset to learn that he was simply being used as a courier for wedding arrangements.

"So it was only for those personal reasons that you left al-Qaeda?" I asked. "There were no ideological reasons?" If there were ideological differences, it would be a good basis upon which to tease information out of Abu Jandal, Bob and I had calculated.

"No, there were," he replied. "I also didn't agree with some things bin Laden did."

"Like what?" I asked.

"Like when he pledged *bayat* to Mullah Omar."

"Why did you object to that?" I asked. Our conversation was a steady back-and-forth at this point.

"It meant that all al-Qaeda members who had pledged *bayat* to bin Laden were obligated to follow Mullah Omar. To me that's not what al-Qaeda is meant to be, and not what I signed up for. I didn't sign up to join the Taliban."

"What is al-Qaeda meant to be?" I asked. Abu Jandal gave his views, which were based on bin Laden's 1996 declaration of war and liberating the holy lands and the Arabian Peninsula from the presence of crusaders and Jews. From this topic, Bob and I steered the conversation toward his religious justifications for joining al-Qaeda. I gently challenged those religious justifications, citing passages from the Quran that appeared not to square with his view. I wanted to test Abu Jandal's knowledge and see how firmly committed he was to his religious views, and to impress on him that I, too, was well versed in Islamic theology.

Abu Jandal countered by citing Islamic scholars who supported his position, and I replied by citing scholars who disagreed with his scholars. We had a spirited yet friendly debate, quoting authorities and passages from the Quran between us. Abu Jandal seemed to be enjoying himself, and enjoying the challenge. He voiced his wonder at one point, saying: "It's fascinating to me how you can be a Muslim, know so much about Islam, and yet have such a radically different view from mine about America, al-Qaeda, and jihad."

"I hope this leads you to rethink some of your stands," I told him with a smile.

Our conversation veered into revolutions, which we had learned, the night before, was a favorite topic of Abu Jandal's. After telling us about the Islamic tradition of revolutions for the sake of justice, he told us, "Revolutions don't only happen in the Islamic world because of injustice. Non-Muslims also have revolutions."

"Oh?" I asked.

"It's true. In fact a revolution in Scotland started because the British general ruling the country insisted on sleeping with every woman before she got married, and one man refused. As a punishment they killed his wife, and in response he declared war on the British and . . ."

"Hold on," I said, interrupting him, "are you talking about a movie? It's *Braveheart*, right?" I recognized his description of the Mel Gibson movie.

"Yes, yes," he said excitedly, grinning broadly. When he smiles, Abu Jandal's face lights up, and the gaps in his front teeth become visible. "I saw it with my wife. I loved that film." We agreed that it was a great movie, and for a few minutes we discussed it and compared our favorite scenes.

"You know, Abu Jandal," I told him, ending the *Braveheart* conversation, "I know about the revolutionary tradition in Islam, and you're clearly very well read in it. But did you know that America also has a revolutionary past?" He shook his head and leaned in. He was curious. He liked learning new things, especially on his favorite topics.

"It's true," I continued. "We Americans understand revolutions. We had our own revolution. America used to be ruled by the British. But in 1776 Americans had enough of British cruelty and taxes, and under George Washington, who was then a general but later became the first American president, we revolted against the British and defeated them. Only then did America become a country." Abu Jandal was fascinated and asked me questions about the American Revolution.

He was now speaking directly to us, and Bob and I moved to the second stage of the interrogation: asking him more detailed questions about himself and al-Qaeda. While he continued answering our questions directly, he was still practicing the classic counterinterrogation technique of admitting to what he knew we knew and to things that were of no value, so as to appear cooperative.

We needed to snap him out of this counterinterrogation technique.

"We're going to do something different now." I reached into my brief-case and took out one of our al-Qaeda photo-books, placing it on the table and sliding it toward him. "This is filled with people you know," I said. "I'd like you to confirm who you know."

"Sure," Abu Jandal said. "I'll take a look." He picked up the book and began looking through it.

While he appeared to earnestly study each photo—his eyebrows furrowed and his forehead wrinkled, a few seconds allotted to each— he kept shaking his head and said he knew almost none of the people. There were about sixty photos. By the end, he had only identified Osama bin Laden, Abu Hafs al-Masri, Ayman Zawahiri, and few other known operatives. Those were people he couldn't deny knowing, given his admission that he had been Osama bin Laden's bodyguard. Abu Hafs was, at the time of Abu Jandal's service, bin Laden's anointed successor.

"That's all you recognize?" I asked, deliberately adding surprise to my voice.

"Yes, I don't recognize anyone else, sorry," he responded.

"Are you sure?"

"Yes," he replied.

"Please look again, my friend. Do you think I ask without knowing that you know many of these people? I'm confident you know more people. Look again."

"Okay, I'll look again," he said, again trying to show that he was cooperating, and maintaining the friendly relationship we had built.

He looked slowly through the book, spending a few more seconds than before on each photo. "Sorry, there's no one else I know."

"Are you sure?" I asked, eyebrows raised.

"Yes."

"Well, for friendship's sake, would you look one more time?"

"Okay, for you I will," he said with a smile.

He looked at picture after picture, shaking his head after examin-ing each one. As he got about halfway through, I laughed and turned to Bob. "See?"

"What?" Abu Jandal asked somewhat nervously, trying to work out what was going on. He didn't like being on the outside of a joke.

"I knew you wouldn't be straight with us," I told him. "I told Bob you wouldn't admit to knowing people."

"What do you mean?" Abu Jandal asked, his voice sounding a bit less confident than usual.

"Come on," I said, "take this picture." I pointed to a photo on the page he had been looking at. "Are you claiming you don't know al-Sharqi?" Sharqi was an al-Qaeda alias for Shehhi, the hijacker who Quso had told us had stayed in Abu Jandal's guesthouse.

Abu Jandal was silent, with a poker face. "Do you think I don't know about your relationship with him?" I continued. "Remember Ramadan 1999, when he was sick in your guesthouse? And as his emir you cared for him and gave him soup and nursed him back to health?" Abu Jandal began to blush. "So do you really not know him?" I asked.

"Yes, I do know him," he admitted sheepishly. After a pause, as if calculating the situation, he added, "Sorry." We didn't mention anything about Shehhi being one of the 9/11 hijackers; and Shehhi's name had not yet been released to the press as a suspected hijacker.

"When I ask you a question, I most probably know the answer," I told him. "I am just testing you to see if you are cooperating and being honest, as you claim you are. Now, if you don't want to cooperate, just say so, but please don't lie to me and waste my time by pretending that you don't know these people." Abu Jandal looked down, embarrassed. He had been caught lying, undermining not only his claims of cooperating but, more importantly in his book, of being a religious person—in Islam, as in other religions, lying is a sin. "Look," I continued, "I thought you were an honest guy. Feeding someone soup is very personal. How do you think I know about it? I know about your relationships with many in this book. I didn't fly all the way from America to interview you knowing nothing. You don't know how many of your friends I have in my custody, or who worked for me, and how many have spoken about you. So please let's not play games, and let's go through this honestly."

"Okay, okay," Abu Jandal said.

"Let's start at the beginning of the book," I replied. He went through and identified one al-Qaeda operative after another. We never let on that the only person we knew he knew for certain was Shehhi. He identified, as al-Qaeda members, seven of those who were later identified as 9/11 hijackers, including hijacker leader Mohammed Atta, whom he had met in the bin Laden compound in Kandahar, and whom he identified as Abu Abdul Rahman al-Masri. Abu Jandal said he thought he had met Nawaf al-Hazmi in bin Laden's main Kabul guesthouse. He also recognized Salem al-Hazmi, whom he had seen on the front lines in Kabul. He went on to recount where he had seen Ahmed al-Ghamdi and Mohand al-Shehri. He gave us all the nationalities and al-Qaeda aliases of the hijackers, something we hadn't known at the time.

When shown a picture of Khalid al-Mihdhar, Abu Jandal recognized him by the alias Sinan al-Maki. "Now, Sinan," Abu Jandal told us, "is married to the sister of Abu Jaffar al-Yemeni, who died in 1997. Abu Jaffar was the son of Ahmed al-Hada. Abu Jaffar was a good friend of mine, and he wanted me to marry one of his sisters, but she changed her mind."

Ahmed al-Hada was the Yemeni whose phone number was used as an al-Qaeda switchboard. "Is Hada a member of al-Qaeda?"

"Yes, and he even fought on the front lines."

"What did you think of him?"

"Sinan told me that Hada was known to be very cheap, and that his family in Saudi Arabia didn't approve of him marrying into a lowly Yemeni family."

We continued the discussion along these lines, still not saying anything to Abu Jandal about the men being 9/11 hijackers. To him they were just people he had met in safe houses and training camps in Afghanistan and Pakistan, no different from the other al-Qaeda operatives he had identified. Abu Jandal was unaware that al-Qaeda was behind 9/11. The terrorists whose pictures we had shown him were also those involved in the USS *Cole* and East African embassy attacks, and he assumed that our questions were related to those incidents.

But for us, this was the first time we had definite confirmation that seven of the suspected hijackers were in fact al-Qaeda members. We now knew for certain that al-Qaeda was behind 9/11.

After he had finished identifying people, I closed the book and said, "Thank you for looking at this. Let's switch to other topics." We started talking about the operatives he had identified who were part of the 1998 East African embassy bombings.

I asked Abu Jandal, "Where does Islam allow suicide bombers? Suicide is forbidden in the Quran."

"Generally that's true," he conceded, "but it's different in war, which is what we're in. These are our weapons against the missiles of the other side. And so it's allowed."

"What about the women and the children that your suicide bombers kill?" I countered. "Where does the Quran justify killing innocents?"

"Like who?" he asked.

"In the East Africa bombings," I replied, "women and children were killed, and many of them were Muslims."

"In war there are casualties," he countered. "If they were good Muslims then God will accept them as martyrs."

"Hold on," I said. "I worked the East African bombing. I remember, for example, that we found the remains of a woman and her baby in a bus in front of the Nairobi embassy. Both were incinerated. The mother's arms were wrapped around the baby, as if trying to protect it. Tell me, what crime did the baby commit? What's the justification for killing that baby?"

Abu Jandal had a ready reply: "The baby's reward will come in heaven. Those deaths were a small sacrifice for the wound the bombing inflicted on our enemy and for the inspiration it gave to hundreds of others to become martyrs. Any innocent Muslims killed will be rewarded for their sacrifice in heaven." A classic attempt to explain away the murder of innocent bystanders, often given by al-Qaeda's alleged theologians.

Abu Jandal then quoted bin Laden's 1998 declaration of jihad and told us, "God chooses a contractor [referring to bin Laden] and high school students to defend his religion and launch jihad against his enemies." This was the first time Abu Jandal had mentioned bin Laden launching attacks. "High school students" referred to the young age of al-Qaeda fighters.

"So this is why there are attacks like what happened recently in New York and Washington?" I asked, seizing on his comment.

"The reason for such attacks and the reason for your [pointing to us] presence here [pointing to the ground] is America's foreign policies—your occupation of the Arabian Peninsula, the continuous blockade and attacks on Iraq, and the support of Israel in killing and occupying the land of the Palestinians." He added, "For every action there is a reaction."

"So were you guys behind the attacks last week?" I asked.

"I am not aware who did it," he replied.

"I think you guys did it," I said. Our voices were rising.

"No, this is just a plan for you to attack Afghanistan. And if you do, the mujahideen will rebel, and operations will happen in America itself." He paused and then said: "The war has not started yet, but if we can hit more, we will."

Coincidentally, Bob pointed out a Yemeni newspaper from that day, which had been lying on Mahmoud's desk, with a headline reporting that two hundred Yemenis had been killed in the World Trade Center. (This figure later turned out to be a mistake.) I read the headline out loud—"Two Hundred Yemenis Die in New York Attack"—and showed Abu Jandal the newspaper.

"God help us," Abu Jandal said, clearly shocked by the number of Yemenis killed.

"Is this justifiable?" I asked.

"No, it's a horrible crime," he replied.

"So what do you say to the families of these Yemenis killed in the World Trade Center on behalf of al-Qaeda?" I asked. "What type of Muslim would do this?"

"Bin Laden didn't do this," he countered. He waved his hand as if to dismiss my comment. "The sheikh is not crazy," he added.

"I know al-Qaeda did this attack." I was staring hard at him.

"How do you know?" he asked.

"Someone told me."

"Who told you?"

"You did. You identified the hijackers of the planes as being al-Qaeda members." As I completed the sentence, I placed on the table the photos of the seven hijackers he had identified, including Mohammed Atta, Khalid al-Mihdhar, and Marwan al-Shehhi. "These are the hijackers," I said, pointing to them. "They killed the two hundred Yemenis."

Abu Jandal slouched back in his chair as if he had been punched in the stomach. His face registered complete shock. After looking blankly ahead in disbelief, his head dropped and he rested it between his hands, with his elbows propped on his knees. He was silent.

About a minute later I repeated: "These are the hijackers. These are the men who murdered thousands of innocent people."

"I don't know," he said, shaking his head. "Can I have five minutes, please?"

"Okay," I said, and signaled to Bob that we should walk out. Yassir walked out with us.

"What just happened? Why did you walk out?" Yassir asked. "You had him." He didn't understand why we'd let the moment pass. "Why did you agree to give him five minutes?"

"Let him compose himself," I said. "He knows he has just identified al-Qaeda as being behind the attacks. It's a big admission. We need it to sink in to his mind, too. The moment isn't lost. We've got him now."

We walked back in two minutes later. Abu Jandal still had his head between his hands. "What do you think now?" I asked. He was quiet for a few moments, then looked up and stared directly at me.

"I think the sheikh went crazy. I know these guys. They are all bin Laden's followers. We used to hang out together." He shook his head and paused. "I don't know what to say," he continued. "This is not what I believe in. I will cooperate fully. What do you need?"

We started off by asking Abu Jandal to tell us everything he knew about the hijackers he had identified. True to his word, he cooperated fully. This was a different person from the Abu Jandal we had first met. He gave us details and valuable information. Among the terrorists he spoke about was Zacarias Moussaoui, who had been arrested on August 16,

2001, by the FBI for suspicious activities related to airplanes. In Abu Jandal's estimation, Moussaoui was a simpleton.

After discussing the hijackers we turned to members of al-Qaeda's leadership. Many of the names he supplied were new to us, as was a lot of the organizational structure. The U.S. government's knowledge of al-Qaeda's day-to-day operations was dated to when the group was in Sudan.

The 1998 East African embassy bombings had put al-Qaeda on the international terrorism map and had increased the group's size and funding. This, and the move to Afghanistan, had changed the way it operated. (Neither Junior nor Kherchtou had moved back to Afghanistan with bin Laden.) Abu Jandal filled in the gaps and gave us a more complete picture of the enemy we were now facing.

He outlined the al-Qaeda *shura* council, and described the personal habits of Abu Mohammed al-Masri, Saif al-Adel, Abu Hafs al-Masri, Abu Hafs al-Mauritani, Sheikh Sa'eed al-Masri, Ayman al-Zawahiri, and Abu Assim al-Maghrebi, whose real name was Abdullah Tabarak. We knew that Abu Hafs al-Mauritani (a Mauritanian, as his alias indicated) was the only person in al-Qaeda with religious training; he headed the theology, or fatwa, committee. Sheikh Sa'eed al-Masri, an Egyptian, had taken over the finances and administration of al-Qaeda from Madani al-Tayyib. Abu Assim al-Maghrebi was an old colleague of bin Laden's who had fought with him against the Soviets and who had gone with him to Sudan; it was after the East African embassy bombings that bin Laden had asked him to head the bodyguard detachment.

Abu Jandal explained how and when the operatives and the leadership held meetings. "Abu Hafs and some of the others would regularly meet with bin Laden. But when they all met, the brothers would joke, 'Al-Shiba [the old men] are meeting, may God help us.' Because they knew it meant a big operation was coming." Abu Jandal grinned at the memory.

"Then there's the military committee, headed by Abu Hafs al-Masri," Abu Jandal continued. "He also heads the special operations committee, in which Saif al-Adel is involved, and Saif, too, is a senior member of al-Qaeda. He heads the security committee."

"Is this Abu Hafs?" I asked, showing a picture.

"Yes." After Abu Jandal had identified Abu Hafs, he laughed.

"What's funny?"

"I'm just remembering the story of when, during the battle of Jaji, Abu Hafs killed a Russian soldier, and then called up bin Laden while standing on the soldier and told him, 'I've got a Russian officer under my shoe.'"

When we showed him a picture of Saif al-Adel, Abu Jandal said, "It's out of date."

"Why?"

"Well, Saif has a scar under his right eye from when a bullet ricocheted and hit him."

"Do you like him?"

"Members from the Arabian Peninsula don't usually like his rough manner," Abu Jandal replied with a grin.

We showed him a series of pictures and he identified everyone he knew in the movement, though often he knew them only by their aliases. "This is Yaqoub al-Dusari, who assists Abu Hafs in the military committee," he told us, studying one picture. We knew the person in the photograph as Fazul Abdullah Mohammed, alias Harun Fazul, from the East African embassy bombings.

"What are the other committees?" Bob asked.

"The public relations committee is headed by Abu Hussein al-Masri and Abu Annas al-Yemeni," he said. (Ayman Zawahiri had taken over the committee sometime after Abu Jandal was put in jail.) "And the finance committee is headed by Sheikh Sa'eed al-Masri, who is director of funds, and al-Fateh al-Masri, emir of salaries. Finally, there is the theology committee, headed by Abu Hafs al-Mauritani. That is the senior leadership." Abu Hussein al-Masri was a son-in-law of Zawahiri's; Abu Annas al-Yemeni was Ali al-Bahlul, the operative who had created the al-Qaeda propaganda video following the *Cole* attack.

Below those people, Abu Jandal explained that there were key operatives like Khallad, whose job was to help and motivate the operatives carrying out the attacks. Khallad didn't plan, but he was assigned tasks outside Afghanistan, such as distributing money, providing fake passports, giving instructions to operatives from bin Laden, and relaying their replies. Abu Jandal seemed to admire him.

"Although Khallad is young, his influence is very notable," Abu Jandal told us. Khallad was in his twenties. Abu Jandal's only criticism of him—and this was echoed by other al-Qaeda members we interrogated—was his neglect of his younger brothers, Omayer and al-Bara, after the death of their elder brother, Muhannad. Abu Jandal told us that at one point he had confronted Khallad because Omayer was living with *takfiris*. *Takfiris'* enemies are the near enemy, the governments of their own countries; they don't believe in the global enemy that al-Qaeda believes in. While al-Qaeda adopts some *takfir* ideology, it isn't overwhelmingly *takfiri*; and *takfiris* disliked bin Laden because he took their operatives and distracted them from the near enemy to his global jihad. "You're not acting like Muhannad would have," Abu Jandal had lectured Khallad, which had prompted Khallad to set his brother straight.

These stories about al-Qaeda members were useful both in helping us to understand the personalities of the people we were up against and in terms of future interrogations. We could show suspects that we were intimately familiar with their lives and that denial would be pointless. So we encouraged Abu Jandal to tell us as much about operatives as he could. And he did. Saif al-Adel, for example, according to Abu Jandal, had a "notorious temper and quick tongue and is known to make threats against al-Qaeda members who anger him."

Our conversation moved on to bin Laden's personal security detail, something with which Abu Jandal was intimately familiar. "The sheikh's bodyguards are personally selected by him. They are then trained by Saif al-Adel and Abu Hafs al-Masri, who teach security procedures."

Abu Jandal explained that bin Laden's bodyguards were trusted and important members of al-Qaeda, even sleeping in the same room as the al-Qaeda leader. Abu Jandal had his own room, however, because he was a noisy sleeper, a source of some embarrassment to him: he made "noises" with his "teeth" and didn't want to awaken bin Laden. He detailed the weapons the bodyguards carried. Their arsenal included SAM-7 and Stinger missiles, AK-47s, RPGs, and PK machine guns (similar to an M60).

Of particular importance, Abu Jandal said, was Abu Assim al-Maghrebi (Abdullah Tabarak), appointed head of the bodyguard detachment after the East African embassy bombings. According to Abu Jandal, Tabarak was on the al-Qaeda *shura* council. (Documents we found later indicated that he wasn't, but often sat in on meetings because he was close to bin Laden.) Tabarak was at one point in U.S. custody in Guantánamo Bay, but was handed over to the Moroccans, who later freed him. As of this writing, he is a free man in Morocco.

To Abu Jandal, al-Qaeda was an extended family. He told us that the way bin Laden structured the organization was as one big tribe, with himself as sheikh. It was a way to create loyalty and bonds among members, and bin Laden encouraged not only Abu Jandal and Saqr but other members to intermarry. When speaking about Hamdan, Abu Jandal told us that when his own son, Habib, was born, minutes after he came out of the womb, Saqr quickly took the newborn and ran to bin Laden before Abu Jandal could stop him. "Sheikh, Sheikh, here's Abu Jandal's son, Habib," Saqr cried. The al-Qaeda leader took the baby, chewed some dates in his mouth, and removed a piece or two and put them on Habib's lips, reciting *adhan*, the Islamic call to prayer, in both of his ears. Both Abu Jandal and Saqr were proud that the first taste Habib experienced was from bin Laden's lips.

Despite learning that bin Laden was behind 9/11, from our conversation it was clear that Abu Jandal still cherished his connection to the al-Qaeda leader and was somewhat enthralled by him. Bin Laden's daily routine was to rise before dawn, pray at the mosque, and then return home. He spent time with his family (he had four wives and many children) and went back to the mosque for more prayers. Afterward, he met with his followers and dealt with al-Qaeda affairs. Abu Jandal described bin Laden's house as "very simple, with not even a carpet on the floor." He smiled, as this had triggered a memory. At one point when Abu

Jandal was sick, bin Laden came to visit him. When the al-Qaeda leader saw furniture, a bookshelf, and a carpet in Abu Jandal's home, he told him with a smile: "Look at all this, and you call yourself a mujahid." Abu Jandal relished the visit.

Even when recalling bin Laden's nonreligious or non–al-Qaeda-related actions, Abu Jandal was in awe. He told us that often they would play soccer, and that bin Laden was a good player. "Everybody wants Abu Abdullah on their team because he scores goals," Abu Jandal said.

We spent time talking about al-Qaeda's different training camps and compounds—all important information for our military. The emir of each camp and each housing complex filed reports on activities and members, and bin Laden himself met with the various emirs. The security reports and personnel data were retained by Saif al-Adel.

We turned to the equipment the group used, starting with their communication system. "To communicate with each other," Abu Jandal said, "al-Qaeda uses the Yaesu brand radio system, which is solar-powered. Messages are encrypted through a small Casio computer, and an operator reads numbers through the radio. An operator on the other end takes numbers and puts them into the computer to decipher them. Abu Ata'a al-Tunisi implemented the system. The sheikh doesn't use it himself, but Sa'eed al-Masri does it for him."

For transportation, al-Qaeda used Toyota pickup trucks (the Hilux model), along with fourteen passenger buses. Bin Laden got the Toyotas from the United Arab Emirates and liked them because of their "maneuverability." When bin Laden traveled, his security team followed certain procedures to secure the areas, including looking for buried land mines.

Abu Jandal outlined for us the weapons al-Qaeda used, from the air defense weapons and radars (and how they were stored and transported) to the handguns bodyguards carried. He also told us everything he knew about the weapons and capabilities of al-Qaeda's Taliban hosts. When we asked Abu Jandal if he thought the Taliban would remain supportive of al-Qaeda if the United States attacked, he told us that the Taliban leader, Mullah Omar, once said, "Only if the whole country of

Afghanistan was burned and every Afghani killed would we be permitted to surrender a Muslim to the infidels."

Abu Jandal outlined the al-Qaeda training process and the facilities they had available for use. "When trainees arrive they first go through an orientation at the guesthouse, usually given by the public relations emir. He emphasizes the heavenly rewards bestowed on those who are patient and disciplined during training, and he also stresses the importance of morals and Islamic behavior."

Next they would go to a training camp, where they studied military discipline, administrative issues, and military formations. The trainees were taught to use light weapons, and they took courses in artillery, topography, first aid, and basic explosives, finally advancing to guerrilla warfare. Training concluded with military exercises in which targets were attacked.

"That's regular training," Abu Jandal continued. "But some trainees, because of their dedication, morals, and discipline, are selected to attend advanced and specialized training. Saif al-Adel gives an advanced security session. It teaches trainees how to select a target for an operation, gather information on the target, take photographs, and anything else that's necessary." Advanced training in explosives and electronics was provided by Abu Abdul Rahman al-Muhajir and Tariq al-Tunisi, but only if authorized by bin Laden himself, and usually for operatives tasked with a mission.

Saif al-Adel also put out regular security announcements, warning brothers not to speak about official business, and instructed them in what to do before traveling outside Afghanistan, such as having a barber cut their hair and beard so they would blend in. Abu Jandal then listed some more of the advice operatives received before traveling.

"Is bin Laden involved in the training?" I asked.

"Yes," Abu Jandal replied, "the sheikh often helps with training. I remember once we went into the desert and he gave us a training session he called Desert Fox, on how to maneuver at night in the desert. At another point, he took us to the desert on a very hot day and told us to run to the top of one hill in the sand and back. When we returned, he told us, 'Your path is as difficult and hard as running, but at the end, as on the peak of the hill after conquering it, it is God's paradise.' The men were all inspired."

There were exercises where trainees learned how to hijack planes and were taught assassination techniques. In one exercise they built a skeleton base behind the Khaldan camp and raised an American flag on one of the buildings. Trainees were told to imagine that the base was an American base and to attack it.

Another topic we covered was how al-Qaeda planned an attack, including who would be involved and what the different stages would be. Usually bin Laden met with his military committee—its head, Mohammed Atef, and others, including Abu Mohammed al-Masri and Saif al-Adel. He also met with the consultative committee, which included Sa'eed al-Masri, Abu Hafs al-Mauritani, and Ayman al-Zawahiri.

Abu Jandal added that if there was to be a major operation, senior members had to be informed of the justification. Before the East African embassy bombings, they were told, as justification for bombing the embassies, that U.S. Operation Restore Hope had killed thirty thousand Muslims and that the embassies were centers of U.S. intelligence in East Africa.

While on the subject of the embassy bombings, we asked Abu Jandal what he knew about them. He confessed that he had asked bin Laden if he could be a suicide bomber for the attack—a contradiction of his earlier claim of opposing suicide attacks. Bin Laden told him, "This isn't your time," and counseled patience.

He told us what he knew about those involved, including Owhali. Abu Jandal remembered seeing Owhali's picture in the paper under a fake name after the bombing. "I think the alias was Khalid Salem," he said.

"What do you think we should do with him?" I asked.

"The best thing you can do is execute him," Abu Jandal said.

"Why?"

"He wants to be a martyr and doesn't want to live," Abu Jandal said sincerely, in consideration of Owhali's interests.

After discussing East Africa, Abu Jandal also told us what he knew about al-Qaeda's London cell, headed by Fawwaz, former head of the Kenyan cell. When the news came that Fawwaz had been arrested, bin Laden was upset. "He told us that he had told Fawwaz to leave London and come to Afghanistan, but he didn't listen," Abu Jandal said, recounting what bin Laden had told him. Bin Laden went on to praise Fawwaz, according to Abu Jandal, and told him that Fawwaz was "a good example and had a capacity that we hope God will compensate us for in return."

We moved on to other al-Qaeda operations, including the USS *Cole* bombing. The conversation started after we showed Abu Jandal a picture of Hassan al-Khamiri, one of the suicide bombers. He said he knew him: "This is Hassan, may God bless his soul."

"How do you know he is dead?" I asked.

Abu Jandal replied, "A feeling inside me tells me he is." He then admitted that he had seen Khamiri's photo in a newspaper, identifying him as one of the *Cole* suicide bombers. Abu Jandal told us that Khamiri had been the emir of the al-Farouq training camp, hit by U.S. missiles in response to the East African embassy bombings. The experience had a devastating effect on Khamiri. Abu Jandal took us through the other operatives he knew who were involved in the *Cole*, such as Nashiri.

We discussed Americans he had met who had converted to Islam and had gone to Afghanistan. The conversation segued into a discussion of attempts by outside intelligence agencies to try to infiltrate al-Qaeda. Abu Jandal told us that one operative had been recruited by a foreign intelligence agency after being taken to a hotel room, shown pornographic movies, sodomized, and then blackmailed. He folded after Saif al-Adel accused him of being a spy, confessing that in fact that was the case. There were similar stories involving the intelligence of other countries.

The interview with Abu Jandal lasted the entire night. We wanted to get everything we could in that session, in case he changed his mind later about cooperating. When we eventually finished, he seemed relieved and said to me, "Can I ask you a favor?"

"Sure."

"Please," he said, "please send my condolences to the American people from a terrorist who used to be part of al-Qaeda."

At the start of the next evening's session, I greeted Abu Jandal and said, "Remember what I told you about America's revolutionary history?"

"Yes," he replied eagerly.

"Well, here's a book on that topic. I think you'll enjoy it." I handed him a book (in Arabic) about George Washington and the history of the American Revolution that I had found in the U.S. Embassy.

"Thank you," he said, taking the book gratefully.

We spent that session and every evening for the next week and a half speaking to Abu Jandal and following up on matters raised in the second night's session that we wanted more information on. Abu Jandal came to enjoy our conversations, and would give us all the information we wanted as we joked and drank tea together. Much later, when we bade him farewell and left Yemen, he hugged Bob and me and invited us to visit his house in Yemen "when I am free and out of jail."

Abu Jandal talked to us about his path to al-Qaeda. Though he was born in Jeddah, his family later moved to Yemen. His strong religious devotion surfaced around 1988. He started attending a mosque in Sanaa and began studying theology and the Quran. As the war in Bosnia raged, inspired by his teachers and provoked by images and stories of massacres and the rape of Muslim women and children by marauding Serbs, he traveled to Bosnia to help the Muslims fight back.

Back then you couldn't travel to Bosnia from Yemen directly, so he took a roundabout route. From Sanaa he flew to Damascus, Syria; from there, he drove to Istanbul, Turkey; and from the Turkish capital he flew to Zagreb, Croatia. From Zagreb he drove to Zenitsa, Bosnia, where he was received by the Mujahideen Brigade, the name given to the Arab mujahideen, mostly veterans from Afghanistan, who fought in

Bosnia. He gave them his passport and valuables to look after, so that if he was killed in battle no one could identify him as a foreign fighter, and he trained in a camp for forty-five days.

He learned how to use Kalashnikov machine guns, PK machine guns, and RPGs, and also learned topography and combat tactics. After completing the training course, Abu Jandal went to the front lines and engaged in combat against Serb forces. He didn't fight for long, however, because soon after he went to the front, the Dayton Peace Accords were signed, and Abu Jandal, along with other foreign fighters, was deported. Abu Jandal said that leaders of the foreign fighters, including Abu al-Hareth al-Liby, Abu Hamza al-Jaza'eri, Abu Ziad al-Najdi, and Abu Hammam al-Najaji, were assassinated during this period, after which Abu Jandal and his group were told that they had to leave the country and were no longer needed.

To conceal their identities from spies of their home governments and other intelligence entities, all fighters were given aliases. Abu Jandal had originally picked "Abu Hamza" but was told that it was too common. An Egyptian acquaintance suggested that "Abu Jandal," with its implication that the bearer of the name could be an agent of death, would be fitting.

In 1996 Abu Jandal traveled to Somalia to help Muslim fighters who were trying to take over the country. They were battling invading Ethiopian forces who opposed their taking control. However, the Somalis, he discovered, were selective with regard to who could fight. From among the group that Abu Jandal had arrived with, only he was accepted—because his dark complexion allowed him to blend in easily. To "avoid complications," the Somalis declined to use anyone who was patently foreign-born: they wished to maintain the appearance of a native force. Abu Jandal's description of his route to Somalia matched the route that L'Houssaine Kherchtou had told us al-Qaeda used to transport fighters.

After being accepted, Abu Jandal was approached by ministers from the Islamic Union Movement, or Itihad Islami (his hosts), and asked if he had money to give them "for our cause." This put Abu Jandal over the edge. "We are not here for the jihad of money, nor the jihad of color," he angrily told them. He didn't like their attitude toward fighting and toward fellow Muslims. Without having fought a battle in Somalia, he returned to Yemen.

Later that year he met Muhannad bin Attash, Khallad's elder brother, at the al-Qaeda guesthouse on October Street in Sanaa. Muhannad, an inspiring figure, convinced Abu Jandal to go to Tajikistan with him to wage jihad. They traveled to Karachi first and met up with other foreign fighters, and this group became known, unofficially, as the Northern Group. Abu Jandal was among the members of the group who in 1996 pledged *bayat* to bin Laden. He identified the members of the group for us.

Abu Jandal went to the front lines to fight alongside the Taliban against the Northern Alliance. During a battle he injured the bottom of his foot and was evacuated to Khost. He spent three months recovering, and then went to Kandahar to join bin Laden. He served as one of the guards—along with Khallad, Hamdan, and others—during the May 1998 press conference of bin Laden's following the ABC interview.

After the East African bombings, bin Laden enlisted Abu Jandal, Saqr al-Jadawi, Fayadh al-Madani, and Mu'awiya al-Madani as his bodyguards. Bin Laden gave Abu Jandal a gun with two bullets and told him, "If I am ever about to be captured, kill me first." The gun and those bullets became Abu Jandal's most prized possessions.

After a trip to Yemen, Abu Mohammed al-Masri recommended that Abu Jandal be made emir of the Kabul guesthouse. There had been a dispute between al-Qaeda operatives from Egypt and al-Qaeda members from the Arabian Peninsula as to who should be in charge of it. Bin Laden realized that he needed someone who was respected by both groups—and he felt that Abu Jandal fit that bill. Abu Jandal was honored to be appointed.

As emir, his job was to interview people who came to stay, find out why they had come to Afghanistan, and test them to see if they were suitable candidates for membership in al-Qaeda. For this duty he was paid $64 a month by bin Laden. Abu Jandal also traveled around to different training camps, meeting recruits and advocating jihad against America and the importance of al-Qaeda.

Later he moved from Kabul to Kandahar, where he stayed in the bin Laden compound and was paid $94 a month by bin Laden to help protect him. At this point he was recognized as a central figure in the entourage.

Abu Jandal treasured the book on George Washington. (Attorneys who years later interviewed him for the Hamdan trial told me that he still had it and showed it to them.) He read it immediately, devoting an entire day to it, and discussed it with us that evening. He excitedly told me: "Bin Laden is like George Washington. They're both revolutionaries."

"No, they're not," I replied with a smile.

The intelligence Abu Jandal gave was disseminated across the intelligence and military communities. It was celebrated as a major success. Edmund Hull, Barbara Bodine's replacement as ambassador to Yemen, called Bob and me into his office and told us: "Congratulations. The Abu Jandal interrogation has caused General Musharraf to accept that al-Qaeda is behind 9/11, and to join the coalition. Well done. That's a huge success."

The Abu Jandal 302 to this day is viewed as the most successful interrogation of any al-Qaeda operative. It was immensely valuable in the war in Afghanistan; it was crucial to successful interrogations of many future al-Qaeda operatives that we apprehended; and it provided much of the basis for our knowledge of al-Qaeda. It is still used in interrogating and prosecuting al-Qaeda operatives. (I can talk about Abu Jandal in greater detail than I can about other detainees because his 302 was declassified by the Senate Judiciary Committee.)

The information gained about al-Qaeda's capabilities, communication systems, and training was eagerly digested by the military community. The war against Afghanistan was delayed so that the information could be best used. Our team was brought to Bahrain to brief military officials, most prominent among them Vice Adm. Charles "Willy" Moore, commander of U.S. Naval Forces Central Command. We briefed the admiral on everything Abu Jandal had revealed to us. Our briefing ended late in the day, and we had to spend the night in Bahrain. We intended to fly back to Yemen the next morning. It was the first free evening we'd had in weeks, so we went to a restaurant for dinner.

As we walked out of the restaurant, a group of young men who had congregated in a parking lot nearby started to yell at Bob and another FBI colleague who were walking ahead of the rest of us. The young men grew more and more belligerent, finally grabbing Bob and trying to push him into one of their cars. He resisted, and my friend and FBI colleague Carlos Fernandez and I tried fighting back. But they outnumbered us, and we weren't carrying any weapons.

From what they were shouting to each other in Arabic, I realized that they were disgruntled Shiite youths who were wannabe Bahraini Hezbollah operatives. They apparently did not like Bob; with his fair skin and blue eyes, he was the most Western-looking of all of us. Bahrain had experienced significant problems with the Shiite segment of their population.

"What are you doing, you fools?" I shouted at them.

"We are terrorists. We are Hezbollah."

I knew then for sure that they were just bored kids with nothing to do. A real member of Hezbollah won't call himself a terrorist.

I approached the one who appeared to be the gang leader. "I am Lebanese. I am the real Hezbollah from Lebanon. You're interfering in my business. Go away."

He froze, then tried to give me a hug. "Brother, you are one of us, we want to help you," he said excitedly.

"No, you're not. I appreciate your sentiment, but get out of here and take your buddies with you before you get into trouble."

They let go of Bob, apologized, and started embracing me: "We are your Bahraini Hezbollah allies. Long live Hezbollah!" They were drunk.

"Okay, okay, go home now," I shouted, pushing them off me. They ran to their cars, saluted, and drove off.

We flew back to Yemen the next morning.

• • •

"Now can we speak to Ahmed al-Hada?" I asked Qamish.

"Why? He's just an old man. He's got no direct connection to terrorism," Qamish replied. "We've been through this before."

"We have been through this before, but now is different."

The Yemenis had been giving us the "he's just an old man" line since the East African embassy bombings. The surviving Nairobi bomber, Owhali, had confessed to FBI interrogators that he had called Hada's number in Yemen after the attack to let al-Qaeda know what had happened to him and to request a fake passport and money. Still, the Yemenis maintained that Hada was just an old man whose home was used.

"He's not just an old man, my friend," I said to Qamish. "Abu Jandal just told us that not only is Hada a member of al-Qaeda, but he is the father-in-law of Khalid al-Mihdhar, one of the hijackers of American Airlines Flight 77, which crashed into the Pentagon."

Hada was brought into the interrogation room in Sanaa and seated before us. Andre Khoury, Bob, and I introduced ourselves and read him the Miranda warning, explaining it to him. He waived his right to a lawyer and signed the Miranda document using a thumbprint, as he was illiterate and didn't know how to write his name.

"As-Salāmu ʿAlaykum," I began, and told him that we were investigating the terrorist attack on America.

"I don't know anything about terrorism," he replied, "I'm just an old man."

"You don't know anything about al-Qaeda?" I asked.

"No."

"Okay, then, tell us about your son-in-law Khalid al-Mihdhar."

"I don't know anything about my son-in-law. I didn't even know that that's his name."

"You don't know your own son-in-law's name? So how did your daughter get married?"

"One day men came to the mosque and asked about my daughter and said they wanted their friend to marry her."

"And you agreed?"

"Yes."

"And you never met or spoke to your daughter's husband?"

"No."

"You're a disgrace," one of the Yemeni officers present shouted at Hada, unable to contain himself. "How can you be a son of a tribe, how can you be an Arab? How do you claim to be Yemeni and say something like this? This is your daughter you are talking about. Your own flesh and blood. This is your honor." Hada went red.

Andre chimed in: "No self-respecting Arab would do such a thing. What's wrong with you?" Hada shrugged and didn't say anything. It was very telling that protecting al-Qaeda was more important to him than his own reputation.

For several hours Hada maintained that he knew nothing. In order to catch him out, Andre and I began testing him about what we knew about him. We would ask him about a specific fact, acting as if we didn't know the answer. He would reply, denying that he knew the answer. We would demonstrate that he did know the fact. Because Hada was extremely embarrassed to be caught lying, he would then concede that he did indeed know the information, and admit more details. For example, when he claimed not to know the identity and names of his sons-in-law, we showed him photographs of them. Only then did he acknowledge that he knew them and give us information about them. Sometimes we'd ask a question, not knowing the answer, but he'd think we were trying to embarrass and test him again, and so he would tell us what we wanted to know. We slowly built up information this way.

Ahmed al-Hada was originally from Thamar, Yemen. His brothers were well respected in the community, but he was considered the black sheep of the family, which was not financially well off. Hada's son Abu Jaffar went to Afghanistan and joined al-Qaeda soon after bin Laden returned there from Sudan in 1996; he was a member of the Northern Group.

Around 1997, Abu Jaffar arranged the marriage of two of his sisters to two al-Qaeda operatives he had befriended in Afghanistan: Khalid al-Mihdhar and Ahmed Mohammed Haza al-Darbi. Both Darbi and

Mihdhar traveled to Yemen to meet their future brides and got married in a double wedding ceremony attended by other al-Qaeda operatives. A few months later they returned to Afghanistan with their wives.

Hada's other daughters also married al-Qaeda fighters. One of these sons-in-law was Mustafah al-Ansari, who used the alias Abed al-Kareem al-Maki. Mihdhar had introduced the family to Ansari. Like Darbi and Mihdhar himself, Ansari was a Saudi of Yemeni descent. We knew of him because he had been imprisoned in the Bayt Habra car theft incident, but we were not aware that he was related to Hada. Ansari was later killed while conducting an attack in Yanbu, Saudi Arabia, against Western workers at an oil installation. The other of Hada's al-Qaeda sons-in-law was Abed al-Wahab al-Maki, who was killed in 1999 in Juzor al-Molluk, Indonesia.

Hada was a cog in al-Qaeda's operations in Yemen. Bashir al-Shadadi was the organization's main travel facilitator in the country; he had also participated in the jihad in Bosnia, Tajikistan, and Afghanistan. His role was to move recruits from Yemen to camps in Afghanistan. The person who helped him organize this movement of mujahideen was Abdul Razaq Saleh al-Nijjar, who was married to Shadadi's sister. Yemeni recruits were received at the Kandahar guesthouse by Abu al-Kholoud, who was married to Shadadi's other sister. The operative tasked with training recruits in the al-Farouq training camp was another brother-in law of Shadadi's named Husam al-Deen al-Himyari. It was felt that blood loyalty would extend beyond ideology, making infiltration of the group less likely. Bin Laden's son Mohammed, considered by al-Qaeda members to be most like his father, married the daughter of al-Qaeda's then military commander, Abu Hafs al-Masri.

With his children all being al-Qaeda members, or married to them, Hada's house in Sanaa naturally became a place where al-Qaeda operatives would meet. On most days someone was there having meetings or just stopping by for a chat. This is what led to his number's becoming the al-Qaeda switchboard in Yemen. At one point Hada became upset at how high his telephone bill was, prompting Mihdhar to joke that Hada was a "penny-pincher."

Tragedy struck Hada's family when Abu Jaffar was electrocuted in 1999 while fishing in Duranta Lake in Afghanistan. He was in a boat with another al-Qaeda member while a third was on shore operating an electric transformer. They communicated by reflecting sun rays, using a mirror. The person on shore misinterpreted the movement of the mirror on the boat as a signal and flipped the switch while Abu Jaffar was still in the water collecting fish. He died instantly. Hada traveled to Afghanistan to visit his son's grave and stayed with his then-pregnant daughter and her husband, Ahmed Mohammed Haza al-Darbi, who at the time was a trainer at al-Farouq.

Hada decided to join al-Qaeda. He underwent military training at Loghar. Bin Laden met him there and honored him because of his age and known loyalty. Other operatives took to calling him Am Ahmed (Uncle Ahmed). At the end of the training, a thirty-kilometer march was required, and the instructors at first excused Hada because of his age. He became upset, and they responded by appointing him leader of the march. He was proud of leading the formation and carrying its flag. The fighters referred to him as "Umda," an Egyptian term that translates to "Mayor."

After training, he wanted to participate in jihad. He was dispatched to the front lines to fight against the Northern Alliance troops of Ahmed Shah Massoud. Due to his age, he was kept in the rear, next to the artillery. Another of his sons, Samir (alias Abed Al-Rahman), joined him in Afghanistan and attended an al-Qaeda training camp. Samir was later killed when he blew himself up with a hand grenade after being cornered by Yemeni security during an al-Qaeda operation in Yemen.

Hada stayed in Afghanistan for about five months. On his way back to Yemen, he stopped in Kandahar, where bin Laden was hosting a dinner. Hada was honored by being seated next to bin Laden. After his return to Yemen, Hada encouraged his third son, Abu Khalil, to travel to Afghanistan to join al-Qaeda.

By the time we had finished, the Yemenis realized that Hada wasn't just an ignorant old man.

. . .

One of the operatives Abu Jandal and Hada had mentioned was Abdul Aziz al-Janoubi, an alias of Ahmed Mohammed Haza al-Darbi. We didn't know his real name at the time, so we referred to him as Abdul Aziz. Because of the information we already had about him, including the fact that he had been in the same close combat class from which Mihdhar had been selected as a hijacker, we initially thought that Darbi might be among the 9/11 hijackers, but no one fitting his description was registered on any of the flights.

After ruling out that possibility, I had asked Abu Jandal: "Do you think Abdul Aziz is operational?"

"He is in the special operations division," Abu Jandal had replied, "but to know for sure if he is operational right now, you should check where his family is. If he sent his wife back to her family, that means he's probably on a mission." We now asked Hada, the wife's father, and confirmed that Darbi's family was back in Yemen staying with him at his house.

From the descriptions Abu Jandal and Hada had given us of Darbi, we were able to further identify him, and we got a picture of him from the Yemenis—he had applied for a Yemeni passport under a different name. We sent out a worldwide alert to police forces and intelligence agencies; a few months later, when I was back in the United States, I stopped at a grocery store in Manhattan and did a double-take when I saw an NYPD WANTED poster for him behind the cash register. Eventually Darbi was captured while attempting to visit his mistress in Azerbaijan.

PART 5

A NEW WORLD ORDER

17

Bin Laden's Escape

"What's this?" a Northern Alliance commander asked me, in early 2002, as we walked through the rubble of what had been bin Laden's hideout in Kabul. A U.S. fighter plane had flown overhead and dropped thousands of leaflets, a few of which settled on the ground near us.

I picked one up. "It's a note offering twenty-five million dollars for information leading to the capture of Osama bin Laden," I said. The sum was written out as a numeral, with its impressive string of zeros.

"That won't work," he said, shaking his head. "You won't get any information."

"Why not?"

"Well, for a start, most people in this area can't read. But beyond that, they don't believe that amount of money exists in the world. They are simple folks. If you would write, say, a hundred rupees, that would be more believable, and you'd probably get more responses."

After the Taliban refused an ultimatum from the U.S. government to stop harboring al-Qaeda, on October 7, 2001, the U.S. military launched Operation Enduring Freedom and attacked Afghanistan. Primary strikes were launched at the capital, Kabul, at the country's main airport, at Kandahar, where Mullah Omar was based, and at Jalalabab—all cities considered central to the Taliban and al-Qaeda. Supported by U.S. air cover and Special Operations Forces, the Northern Alliance pressed forward against Taliban positions.

Once the U.S. attack began, the leaders of different terrorist groups came together for a meeting. Among those present were representatives of al-Qaeda, Jemaah Islamiah, and the Libyan Islamic Fighting Group. Independent operatives like Abu Zubaydah and Ibn al-Shaykh al-Liby, of Khaldan, also participated. They all agreed to put their personal and ideological differences behind them and unite to fight the invading U.S. forces.

Abdul Hadi al-Iraqi, one of al-Qaeda's military commanders, was appointed commander of all the Arabs. He was assisted by Abdel al-Wakeel al-Masri, one of the 1998 East African embassy bombing co-conspirators. Abdel Wakeel toured al-Qaeda bases and instructed fighters to dig trenches around their bases. He told several al-Qaeda operatives, "The United States will only attack by air and drop bombs. They won't put troops on the ground." Al-Qaeda's military preparations were premised on this assumption.

When U.S. forces appeared in Afghanistan, it was a surprise to most al-Qaeda members, including Salim Hamdan. For years he had sat through speeches by bin Laden in which the al-Qaeda leader had told those gathered that the United States was a weak country that retreated when attacked. It was a shock, therefore, to see the United States responding to the attacks in New York and Washington by invading Afghanistan, and to see al-Qaeda and Taliban leaders on the run.

Once the invasion began, bin Laden and his entourage kept constantly on the move, traveling between Kabul and Jalalabad, areas bin Laden was very familiar with, having lived and traveled in the region since the beginning of the Soviet jihad. At one stop, in a small village, Hamdan timidly approached the al-Qaeda leader and asked for a brief leave. His wife was pregnant and ill. He promised to return.

Bin Laden granted permission. With his personal driver and confidant gone, he decided to change his entourage. He realized that his life would now be that of a fugitive. While before he had been a guest of the ruling Taliban, he now needed operatives with different skills around him. The new group he picked included three of his most trusted advisers and operatives: his son Uthman; Hamza al-Ghamdi, the leader of the Northern Group; and Khallad. Among the others were Khalid al-Habib, an Egyptian; Yousef al-Qanas ("the sniper"), a Kuwaiti; Abdulrahman al-Taezi, a Yemeni; and Abu Saeed, a Saudi.

Where the Taliban could no longer hold their lines, the foreign fighters took over security for the cities. Saif al-Adel, one of al Qaeda's chief military operatives, was sent by bin Laden to Khandahar to help organize the defense of the city. Realizing the situation was getting increasingly dangerous, bin Laden gave the order for al-Qaeda fighters to take their families out of Afghanistan. The one leader who hadn't fled from al-Qaeda's main camp was Abu Hafs, al-Qaeda's main military commander, who was unable to travel because of his back problems. In mid-November a U.S. airstrike leveled the house he was staying in, killing him and seven other al-Qaeda members. One of the seven was Zachariah al-Tunisi, who (one of his friends confided in Abu Zubaydah) was involved in the 1993 battle against U.S. forces in Somalia. He had in fact fired the RPG that took down the U.S. helicopter in the episode that became known as Black Hawk Down. Also killed was Moaz bin Attash, the youngest member of the bin Attash family, at the time assigned to take care of al-Qaeda's main guesthouse in Kandahar. After the strike killing Abu Hafs, surviving al-Qaeda members ran to the site, removed the rubble by hand, and buried the bodies nearby. The death of Abu Hafs was a great loss for al-Qaeda, and bin Laden personally delivered a taped eulogy from his hiding place.

In late 2001, as Taliban-controlled cities began falling to the Northern Alliance and U.S. Special Operations Forces started hunting al-Qaeda and Taliban leaders, bin Laden gave the order for fighters to head to Tora Bora, a mountainous region in eastern Afghanistan. Located in the White Mountains, near the border with Pakistan, Tora Bora's interconnected caves were well known to bin Laden and other operatives from the Soviet jihad days. The treacherous terrain and well-hidden bunkers all but prevented easy penetration by invading forces, and the mountain range offered escape routes into Pakistan.

Bin Laden knew, however, that it was just a matter of time before U.S. Special Operations Forces, guided by Afghani allies, successfully breached the cave network, so after al-Qaeda regrouped, he ordered operatives to head into Pakistan and the lawless tribal regions. These were places into which it would be difficult for U.S. Special Operations Forces and Northern Alliance fighters to follow them. To avoid attracting attention, bin Laden traveled with only Hamza al-Ghamdi and Qanas. Other operatives watched as bin Laden and the two walked off and disappeared into the mountains. Bin Laden's circle had just gotten smaller. (When we learned about bin Laden's new entourage a few months later in Gitmo from detainees, it was clear that the key to finding the al-Qaeda leader lay with those two men. These details were shared across the U.S. government.)

The head of bin Laden's bodyguard staff, Tabarak, went off with a group of thirty operatives, taking bin Laden's satellite phone with him. Among this group was the entire bin Laden security detachment, including Bahlul, bin Laden's secretary, who had disbursed to each operative leaving Tora Bora one hundred dollars for expenses. Every so often Tabarak would switch on the satellite phone to put U.S. intelligence teams monitoring it on his tail rather than bin Laden's. The thirty were picked up by the Northern Alliance as they tried to cross the border.

By mid-December the mountain range had been overrun by U.S. Special Operations Forces and their Afghani allies, but the al-Qaeda leadership was long gone.

Bermel, a town in Paktika province, on the Afghan-Pakistan border, became a main transit point for the escaping Arabs. Al-Qaeda operated a safe house in town, where many al-Qaeda members stayed, including Abdul Hadi al-Iraqi, the commander of all Arab fighters in Afghanistan; his deputy, Abdul Wakeel; and senior commander Abu Mohammed al-Masri, alias al-Zayat. Some operatives camped in the local school.

Within the group, there were debates about whether to stay in the area or head into Pakistan proper. Abu Mohammed al-Masri was against leaving and decided to stay on the Afghani side of the border. Others, like Saif al-Adel, crossed into the tribal areas on the Pakistani side.

Those who chose to leave were evacuated by Afghani sympathizers to Bannu, Pakistan. From there, operatives from the Pakistani terrorist group Lashkar-e-Taiba (LeT) smuggled them to Lahore, Karachi, and Faisalabad. In guesthouses in Pakistan, operatives waited for instructions. Some were told to leave Pakistan to plan operations abroad, and others were told to wait for a plan to be developed for them to return to Afghanistan. While waiting, they met with Riyadh al-Jaza'eri, al-Qaeda's travel facilitator, who made the smuggling arrangements.

In the guesthouse where Abu Zubaydah was staying were two operatives, with American and British passports, who told him that they wanted to launch a major operation against the United States—and with their passports they had the ability to travel. He referred them to KSM, who, following the death of Abu Hafs, had been appointed by bin Laden as head of the group's global military operations.

Al-Qaeda's nature was rapidly changing. Before 9/11, the network had acted like a state in many ways: it had a highly centralized command and control structure and a defined territorial sanctuary. After the United States responded to 9/11 decisively, and effectively dismantled what was then considered al-Qaeda's "center of gravity," the terrorist network adapted. Instead of the centralized command and control that had been its trademark, it became less "Chief Operator" than "Chief Motivator," a move that helped spur Internet recruitment and domestic terrorism— a great problem faced today by the governments of the United States and other countries fighting terrorism.

The terror network's focus turned to manipulating regional, local, tribal, and sectarian conflicts in order to promote its interests. It also "franchised" the al-Qaeda name and encouraged other terrorist groups in places such as North Africa, Southeast Asia, and parts of the Middle East (later, notably, Iraq) to operate under the al-Qaeda banner.

Bin Laden ordered top operatives like KSM, Khallad, and Nashiri to spread their fighters around the world and launch plots—with the aim of ensuring that America would never have peace: "I pledge to he who raised the skies [God] that America will not live in peace before peace reigns in Palestine, and before all the army of infidels depart the land of Muhammad, peace be upon him." Many al-Qaeda operatives later referred to this October 2001 statement by bin Laden as an oath from their leader: it was his pledge to continue the fight.

When Hamdan was arrested crossing back into Afghanistan, in his car was a note from KSM directed to Abu Obadiah, the alias of Ramzi Binalshibh, the 9/11 plotter who had worked as the liaison between KSM and head hijacker Mohammad Atta. The note instructed Abu Obadiah to send to the United States and England all available operatives with the ability to travel there.

KSM was planning operations in the United Kingdom and elsewhere in Europe, and he also was reactivating the network in Southeast Asia that he had worked with during the foiled 1995 Bojinka plot. Among the operatives instructed to launch attacks in the United States was Richard Reid, a British-born al-Qaeda operative, who, on December 22, 2001, attempted to use a shoe bomb to blow up a plane traveling from Paris to Miami.

Another place KSM targeted was Tunisia, where he instructed a twenty-four-year-old named Nizar Nawar (Saif al-Islam al-Tunisi) to plan an attack. On April 11, 2002, Nawar detonated a natural gas truck rigged with explosives at the ancient El-Ghriba Synagogue, killing twenty-one people—fourteen German tourists, two French citizens, and five Tunisians—and injuring more than thirty others.

As KSM focused on these areas, Nashiri was organizing attacks in the Arabian Gulf. Following the success of the bombing of the USS *Cole*, he had been appointed commander of al-Qaeda's naval operations. With Ahmed al-Darbi, he had set up base in Dubai and was organizing the smuggling of al-Qaeda operatives into the Gulf region using a small ship they had purchased. From there they planned to launch operations in Yemen, Saudi Arabia, and Qatar. Nashiri was also interested in attacking ships in the Strait of Gibraltar, and he sent to Morocco two

Saudis who had married Moroccan women—unions arranged by Abu Assim al-Maghrebi.

In January 2002 Nashiri was on a boat off the coast of Dubai with four other Yemenis, all of whom had at one point been members of bin Laden's bodyguard detachment. Now they were under Nashiri's command in his dual position as head of operations in the Arabian Peninsula and head of naval operations. The four were Omar Hasan Saeed Jarralla, alias Ibn Hafeez; Fawzi Yahya Qasim al-Hababi, alias Abu al-Shahid al-Sannani; Fawzi Muhammad Abed al-Qawi al-Wajih, alias Abu Mu'ab al-Taezi; and Bashir al-Safari, alias Salman al-Taezi.

Nashiri outlined to them his plans to conduct a series of attacks in Yemen, one of which would be a naval attack, similar to the bombing of the USS *Cole*. This time, however, Nashiri wanted to target an oil tanker off the coast of al-Mukalla in South Yemen. Before the *Cole* attack Nashiri had considered an attack on an oil tanker, and had done casing for the operation, so he knew exactly what was needed.

After 9/11 Abu Ali al-Harithi had been chosen by bin Laden to be al-Qaeda's main representative in Yemen. He was a veteran mujahid with a strong Yemeni tribal background, which enabled him to operate with tribal protection. His cell would assist Nashiri's men in whatever way was required.

Nashiri told his operatives to get explosives for the oil tanker operation from Abu Ali, and told them what else he wanted: a small boat, a villa to prepare the boat, a Dyna pickup truck to move the boat, fraudulent documents to purchase the boat and truck, and a place to store the explosives.

18

DocEx

In December 2001 I returned to the United States, where the FBI's al-Qaeda team had gone through a reorganization: headquarters didn't want the investigation into 9/11 and al-Qaeda to be run out of the New York field office anymore, despite the institutional knowledge base there, and created a new squad based in Washington, DC, known as the 9/11 Team.

My boss, Pat D'Amuro, was reassigned from New York to Washington to oversee it, and many agents from New York were temporarily moved with him. Later, all veteran terrorist investigators returned to New York. Many New York agents felt that their expertise was unwelcome in Washington, where a new leadership, mostly from the West Coast and appointed by Director Robert Mueller, was running the show. Excluding Pat, none of them had experience in dealing with al-Qaeda. The division was compared, within the FBI, to the East Coast/West Coast rap wars going on at the time. Pat's deputy running the team, which was now responsible for operations against al-Qaeda around the world, was an assistant special agent in charge from Detroit named Andy Arena.

Prior to the Iraq war, when there was a lot of pressure on the FBI from the White House to produce a "link" between Saddam Hussein and al-Qaeda, the 9/11 Team's assessment, again and again, was that there was no link. The White House didn't like that answer, and told the bureau to look into it more and "come up with one." Andy refused, and in an exchange (now famous among bureau agents), he told Robert Mueller: "Sir, in the FBI, we present facts. We don't manufacture reasons for White House wars." The director agreed, and the message went back that the assessment wouldn't be changed.

I was temporarily reassigned to Washington, as were George Crouch, who had worked with me on the USS *Cole*; veteran FBI al-Qaeda expert Dan Coleman; and Debbie Doran, who was assigned to DocEx, a program that involved sorting through the thousands of documents that had been recovered from battlefields, guesthouses, and various facilities in Afghanistan and Pakistan. Coordinating the organization and translation of all the documents was a complicated task, but Debbie had played a similar role in the East African embassy investigation. Boxes and boxes of evidence were shipped to Washington, and translation teams, made up of contractors with no background in al-Qaeda or terrorism, were set up to deal with them.

"Ali," Pat said, calling me into his office. I had been assigned to help Pat. "DocEx is naturally going to be slow. The translation teams write up documents without knowing what is and isn't important. You know al-Qaeda and you've got the language skills. Can you please look through the boxes of evidence that come in before they go to DocEx and flag anything you think is important? There might be some items we'll need to follow up on immediately."

I started searching. In one box, which consisted of evidence found in the rubble of the house where Abu Hafs had died, I found martyr videos and a video of what appeared to be a casing operation. From the license plates of the cars visible in the background, the latter seemed to have been in Singapore.

I recognized three of the people in the martyr videos: Ramzi Binalshibh; Muawiyah al-Medani, who was involved in the casing of the USS *Cole* and who Abu Jandal had told me was once a bodyguard for bin Laden; and Gharib al-Taezi, also identified by Abu Jandal as a one-time bodyguard for the al-Qaeda leader. None of them were known to have killed themselves in operations, which indicated that something they were involved in was likely to be under way.

In one of the tapes was a man I didn't recognize. He was unsmiling and had a glassy look in his eyes, as if he were somewhere else. His long face was partially covered by a medium-sized beard.

Another tape had no sound, but the man in it didn't look, or act, like the others: instead of exuding confidence and pride, he appeared to be in distress. The handwritten label on the tape said "Abdul Rahman." We later learned that he had been accused by al-Qaeda of being a foreign intelligence agent sent to spy on the group. After al-Qaeda arrested him, they forced him to tape a confession.

In another box I found a letter, which seemed directed at the al-Qaeda leadership, in which the writer explained his reasons for getting involved in the organization and his desire to be part of a martyrdom operation. Attached to the letter was a passport-sized photo: it was of the operative I didn't recognize. In the letter, he stated that he was a Tunisian who had immigrated to Canada, where he had gone to college. The letter was signed using a name and an alias: Abderraouf bin Habib bin Yousef Jdey and Farouk al-Tunisi.

I took the letter to Pat and told him about the video featuring the same unknown operative. "We might have a big problem on our hands," I said. "If this guy is a Canadian, it will be very easy for him to enter the United States." Pat contacted the liaison to our Canadian counterpart, the Canadian Security Intelligence Service (CSIS), who was based in the Canadian Embassy in Washington, DC. A few hours later he came to our headquarters with a fellow CSIS officer. They told us that they were aware of Jdey's terrorist connections and knew he was somewhere in Canada but that they had lost track of him. He had disappeared with another Tunisian Canadian they had been monitoring named Faker Boussora.

We put this information together, and Robert Mueller and Attorney General John Ashcroft held a press conference announcing the first Most Wanted Terrorists Seeking Information list.

On November 12, 2001, shortly after American Airlines Flight 587 took off from New York's John F. Kennedy International Airport, it crashed into the Belle Harbor neighborhood of Queens. A total of 265 people were killed, 260 on board and 5 on the ground.

In May 2002 Mohammed Mansour Jabarah, a Canadian active in both al-Qaeda and Jemaah Islamiah, was arrested by Omani authorities and sent to Canada, whereupon authorities delivered him to the United States. He said that one of KSM's lieutenants, Abu Abdelraham, had told him that both Richard Reid and Jdey had been designated shoe bombers, and that Jdey had succeeded on Flight 587.

In 2004, al-Qaeda released a list of eighteen attacks they claimed to have successfully perpetrated against the United States. Of those listed, seventeen were known to the U.S. government, and the other was Flight 587. To date, Jdey has not been found. The U.S. government has denied that Flight 587 was a terrorist attack, and it is possible that Jdey was killed somewhere else and that al-Qaeda, to boost morale and recruitment, instead claimed that he bombed Flight 587.

We recovered al-Qaeda propaganda material praising Jdey for the attack, but there was no indication that he or any other suspects were on the plane; and all passengers were accounted for. In addition, after a lengthy and thorough investigation, the National Transportation Safety Board ruled that the crash was caused by the first officer's overuse of rudder controls.

In one of the boxes directed to DocEx, I found a handwritten note. The writing was later identified as Khallad's; the note was addressed to someone called Mokhtar (who we later learned was KSM). Khallad described some surveillance he had done for the 9/11 plot. When he was later interrogated, he told his interlocutors that he had never written anything down. "How about this?" they asked, showing him the note. Shocked, he remained silent briefly and then said, "That was the only time."

Also in the boxes were hundreds of applications and contact sheets filled out by recruits who had just arrived in Afghanistan. On the forms, the new recruits listed their sponsors (those who had recommended them to al-Qaeda), expertise, specialties, and personal data and aliases. Listed with the personal data was the name of the person who should be notified if anything happened to them.

One of the applications was Abu Abdullah al-Muhajir's. He listed his expertise as carpentry. His alias didn't mean anything to us until I interrogated Abu Zubaydah, who informed me that Abu Abdullah al-Muhajir was actually an American named Jose Padilla.

I also came across a short letter from an operative indicating that he was going on a mission in Yemen. It was signed Furqan al-Tajiki. The alias al-Tajiki usually would indicate that the operative was from Tajikistan. However, I recognized this alias as belonging to one of the al-Qaeda operatives who had been arrested in the Bayt Habra car theft incident. Furqan's real name was Fawaz al-Rabeiee, and he was a Yemeni national born in Saudi Arabia. "If Furqan did head to Yemen from Afghanistan," I told Pat, "he most probably reconnected with his old friends from Bayt Habra, and my guess is that they'll all be planning an operation together."

On February 11, 2002, the FBI added Furqan's name, along with those of sixteen others connected to the car thefts, to the Seeking Information list. Those of us involved in the *Cole* investigation pointed out that several of those terrorists were still locked up in Yemen, so on February 14, six of the names were removed.

The others were considered dangerous threats, and there were indications that a major operation was planned for Yemen, the site of al-Qaeda's big attack prior to 9/11, the October 12, 2000, bombing of the USS *Cole*. A fusion team comprised of U.S. officials from many different agencies (except the CIA, which didn't want to take part) was put together and sent to Yemen, under the leadership of Marine colonel Scott Duke. Stephen Gaudin was the FBI's permanent representative on the fusion team and he was joined by a Washington field office agent, who was working on other, related investigations. Bob McFadden and I reconnected with General Qamish, the head of Yemeni intelligence, with whom I had developed a good relationship during the *Cole* investigation. Colonel Yassir and Major Mahmoud, the two Yemeni intelligence officers who had sat in on our interrogation of Abu Jandal, were to work alongside us.

19

Black Magic

December 14, 2001. Singapore's famed domestic intelligence service, the Internal Security Department, better known by its initials, ISD, briefed an American security liaison officer on a plot by the pan-Asian terrorist group Jemaah Islamiah to attack the U.S., Israeli, British, and Australian embassies in Singapore. The ISD was just then thwarting the operation, and the liaison officer told the ISD about the casing and martyrdom videos found in the rubble of Abu Hafs's home and sifted through during the DocEx investigation. It had been determined that the Singapore sites being cased in the video were locations usually frequented by U.S. military personnel. The ISD asked for a copy of the videotape, which it received on December 28.

On December 15 the ISD arrested a Singaporean JI member, Khalim Jaffar, and subsequently found, in a search of his home, the master copy of the same tape. He had made and produced it with the help of another Singaporean JI member, Hashim Abas. Khalim Jaffar told ISD investigators that he had screened a videotape of sites around Singapore's Yishun Mass Rapid Transit station in Abu Hafs's home. He said that he had made notes and had drawn diagrams of the station to explain his plan. While al-Qaeda had given the attack its support, operational defects had prevented its being carried out.

The tape provided concrete proof of the connection between JI and al-Qaeda.

September 2001. The phone rang twice in the ISD duty office in Phoenix Park, Singapore, before an inspector, Charlie, answered it. The muted television in the office showed search and rescue efforts at ground zero, where the World Trade Center towers had once stood. The caller, whose distinctive accent Charlie's trained ear recognized as being that of a Singaporean Malay, told him about a man named Mohammad Aslam bin Yar Ali Khan who said he knew Osama bin Laden, had fought against the Soviets in Afghanistan, and intended to return there soon to rejoin the mujahideen.

Pranksters knew better than to call an ISD office, but Charlie still had to verify the information. An investigation showed that Mohammad Aslam bin Yar Ali Khan was serious, and uncovered associates of his who had been part of Darul Islam (DI), an Indonesian group that had fought for independence against the Dutch and then, after independence, had fought to turn the country into an Islamic state. DI emir Abdullah Sungkar would go on to form Jemaah Islamiah, a DI splinter group.

Jemaah Islamiah was very security conscious and used a system of codes to arrange meetings. When they gathered for what were supposed to be prayer sessions in private homes, they all brought their shoes into the house instead of leaving them outside, as Singaporeans usually do. The members also stayed away from mainstream religious activities, and dressed in modern fashions, abandoning the usual Middle Eastern–style robes that DI members wore for T-shirts, jeans, and the like. They also shared with each other a subscription to *Playboy* magazine (banned in Singapore). The deliberate attempts to blend in seemed reminiscent of the pre-9/11 preparations of Mohammed Atta and Ramzi Binalshibh's Hamburg cell.

On October 4, Mohammad Aslam bin Yar Ali Khan made a move to leave Singapore on a flight to Pakistan, and, after weighing the situation, the ISD decided to let him go. There was little to hold him on, but, more importantly, his arrest would alert the rest of the group that they were being watched. Two weeks after Aslam left, an Asian who called himself Mike arrived in Singapore and met with group members. Many knew him from a bomb-making class he had given in Malaysia in 2000. Mike told the group that an al-Qaeda operative with the alias Sammy would be arriving shortly to plan a terrorist attack, and that they should help him.

When Sammy arrived from Kuala Lumpur on October 13, members of the group met him in a hotel just outside Singapore's Orchard Road shopping district and drove him to a car park in Marina South, a quiet area on the outskirts of the business quarter. There Sammy briefed the Singaporeans on his plan to use truck bombs to attack the U.S. Embassy, the Israeli Embassy, and U.S. naval bases in Singapore.

He asked the group members if they had other suggestions, and they proposed the Australian and British diplomatic missions as possible targets—because they were located close to the U.S. Embassy. The group also explored attacking "soft targets" such as commercial buildings housing U.S. companies.

Using a video camera, Sammy and group members cased the selected targets, creating a tape that they labeled "Visiting Singapore Sightseeing" to disguise its contents: the soundtrack to the video was the theme music from the Hollywood hit movie *Armageddon*. Mike had other operatives purchase seventeen tons of ammonium nitrate, case the U.S. naval bases, and find suitable warehouses where they could prepare the truck bombs. They were given five thousand dollars to cover expenses.

Through data mining and investigative footwork, the ISD later identified Mike as an Indonesian named Fathur Rohman al-Ghozi, who was based in southern Mindanao and traveled on a Philippines passport under the name Alih Randy. Sammy was identified as the Canadian who had been arrested in Oman, Mohammed Mansour Jabarah. When I interrogated Jabarah with fellow FBI agent George Crouch, he told us that he had tried to get a Yemeni al-Qaeda member to be a suicide bomber in Singapore, as none of the Singaporeans wanted to martyr themselves.

Jabarah's path to al-Qaeda began with his training in camps in Afghanistan in 2000 and 2001, after which he pledged *bayat* to bin Laden, who assigned him to an operation in Southeast Asia under KSM. In mid-August 2001, Jabarah stayed with KSM for three weeks in Karachi and was trained by the 9/11 mastermind in surveillance and stealth travel techniques. He was also taken to meet Riduan Isamuddin, a JI commander more commonly known as Hambali, who had responsibility for Singapore and Malaysia, and who was a close associate of KSM's: through him, Hambali had joined al-Qaeda and had pledged *bayat* to bin Laden.

Jabarah was first sent to Malaysia to aid JI members seeking to attack the U.S. and Israeli embassies in the Philippines, and KSM gave him explicit instructions to leave Pakistan before Tuesday, September 11, 2001. He met with JI operatives about a week after his arrival in Malaysia—in mid-September—and surveyed the U.S. Embassy in Manila before traveling to Singapore to plan an operation there.

In December 2001, after the Singaporean JI members were arrested, Hambali told Jabarah to flee to Southeast Asia. He went instead to the United Arab Emirates. KSM told him to travel to Oman to set up a safe house for al-Qaeda members fleeing Afghanistan and heading to Yemen. In Oman Jabarah was arrested.

The ISD commander overseeing the operation against the group in Singapore, Brian, had his team of investigators watching almost a hundred people, and he would have liked to watch the plot mature further, as there were still many unanswered questions: Who else was involved in the plot? How extensive was this terrorist network in Singapore and the region? How were these groups linked to al-Qaeda? And what other acts of violence were they planning?

Brian, a seasoned investigator and commander who had honed his interrogation skills on espionage cases and had a nonconfrontational style that encouraged suspects to talk, had his hand forced after the press reported that Aslam had been arrested by the Northern Alliance in Afghanistan. His teams moved in, and in a series of raids (the last of which was December 24, 2001), a total of twenty-three men were arrested. Those who were not positively identified as group members were allowed to flee with their families to Malaysia, as the ISD was confident that they could track them if they returned.

At Singapore's Whitley Road Detention Centre, the head of ISD, Andrew, reviewed the case in Brian's office. Standing before a flip chart, Andrew began reworking the organization's structure in his cursive script as investigators pointed out subordinate cells they had uncovered, spelled out names, and debated the role of peripheral characters.

When they had first mentioned the name Jemaah Islamiah, liaison security services didn't have any information, and one had even laughed dismissively: "It means 'Islamic community.' Why should it concern us?" But what the ISD had discovered was a pan–Southeast Asian terrorist network with multiple cells in Singapore, Malaysia, Indonesia, and the Philippines and with direct links to al-Qaeda in Afghanistan.

Just as 1979 had been a pivotal year for al-Qaeda, it was also a very important year for Islamist terrorist groups in Southeast Asia. Members of many organizations traveled to Afghanistan to help fight the Soviets and also to experience the "thrill" of jihad and victory over a superpower.

Not without reason did a January 2003 Singapore government white paper on JI label the Soviet jihad as "perhaps the most significant factor in the radicalization of the militant Islamic groups in the region." Abdullah Sungkar, who went on to found Jemaah Islamiah with the cleric Abu Bakar Bashir and other senior Darul Islam members, had traveled to Afghanistan in the 1980s to arrange for his members to participate in the jihad. They maintained a connection with operatives who went on to form al-Qaeda. By the mid-1990s select JI members were being sent to train in al-Qaeda camps in Afghanistan, learning "sophisticated terrorist tradecraft and expertise," as the white paper reports, and "they transferred the skills to other members of their organizations."

They forged links with other terrorist groups based in Southeast Asia whose members had fought in Afghanistan, including the Moro Islamic Liberation Front.

The Afghanistan connection gave al-Qaeda members easy access to Southeast Asia. A number of JI members I later spoke with told me that they had met KSM and other al-Qaeda members when they went through the region. Khallad and 9/11 hijackers Khalid al-Mihdhar and Nawaf al-Hazmi passed through Southeast Asia between December 1999 and January 2000, and Hambali helped with their lodging and travel. Hambali was central to cementing the relationship between al-Qaeda and JI. A disciple of Sungkar, he had been sent by him to train in Afghanistan in 1986, where he also fought the Soviets. He remained in the country for eighteen months, building a relationship with KSM in the process.

As with other regional terrorist groups it tried to co-opt, al-Qaeda funded JI, thereby tying the two groups to each other. While Hambali embraced al-Qaeda and swore allegiance to bin Laden, other JI members resisted the connection, preferring to focus on their near enemy rather than al-Qaeda's far enemy, the United States.

Other JI commanders I later spoke to, including Nasir Abbas, told me that they had opposed Hambali and had refused to endorse his operations. He had control over Singapore and Malaysia, which is where al-Qaeda's initial focus in the region was because that was where its members were. At times he managed to bypass local commanders and run operations in their fiefdoms, including in Indonesia itself. Hambali's efforts were helped after Sungkar died, in 1999, and Abu Bakar Bashir took over. Bashir supported Hambali's relationship with al-Qaeda and gave Hambali freedom to do almost whatever he liked.

December 13, 2001. Hambali was furious when he learned of the arrests in Singapore. This was yet another failure for him: he had orchestrated a series of bombings of Christian churches across the Indonesian archipelago on Christmas Eve 2000, but several of the bombs had been badly placed and had failed to kill anyone. Still, 19 people died that night, and 120 were injured, in what came to be known as the Christmas Eve bombings. With the Singapore plan in ruins and key operatives in custody, Hambali decided to improvise and met several of the Singapore JI fugitives in Johor on December 13. He ordered them to bomb targets in Singapore to retaliate against the arrests. He found an eager terrorist conspirator in Mas Selamat Kastari, who had taken over as operational commander of the Singapore JI network from Ibrahim Maidin in 1999, and gave him approval to hijack a Singapore-bound airplane and crash it into Changi Airport, Singapore's international airport, in what an accomplice would later describe, referring to the World Trade Center, as "a WTC on Changi."

The group had previously identified the airport as a potential target and had taken reconnaissance photos, so with the legwork already done, Mas Selamat handpicked four of his most trusted cell members and accompanied them to Thailand. Hiding out in the seaside resort of Pattaya, they bought five business-class tickets on Aeroflot to Singapore and planned the details of their attack. (The choice of a Russian airline was deliberate; Kastari wanted to avenge the killing of Chechen Muslims by Russian soldiers.)

ISD broke up the plot. On December 29 it alerted all its security partners, and Mas Selamat's photo appeared on the front pages of Thai newspapers. Their cover blown, Mas Selamat and his cell were forced to flee Thailand. ISD tracked Mas Selamat down in Riau a year later and informed the Indonesian police, who arrested and jailed him for immigration violations. He was eventually deported to Singapore in 2006, as were two of his accomplices.

In 2001, the Indonesian government of Megawati Soekarnoputri was ambivalent about the threat posed by Jemaah Islamiah. The government's complacency was reinforced when Singaporean authorities named the Indonesian cleric Abu Bakar Bashir as the spiritual leader of JI. But while Bashir appeared to be harmless and well respected, in reality he was firmly committed to violence and had let Hambali effectively run the group. Megawati's own vice president led the chorus of skeptics who muttered darkly about Western conspiracies, insisting that Jemaah Islamiah simply meant Islamic community. All that changed on October 12, 2002, when two massive bombs ripped through the heart of Bali. This was the second anniversary of the USS *Cole* attack, a thought that immediately went through my mind when I heard the news.

Hambali's first successful operation in Indonesia was the bombing of the Filipino ambassador in Jakarta in August 2000. While the ambassador's Mercedes-Benz withstood the blast of the parcel bomb left outside his front gate (it was detonated as his car drove in), he was badly injured, and an Indonesian guard at the gate and a street vendor were killed.

The bomb maker was the Indonesian Moro Islamic Liberation Front–trained JI operative Rohman al-Ghozi. Cooperation between Singapore and Philippines intelligence led to Ghozi's arrest in Manila on January 15, 2002, as he tried to board a flight to Bangkok. He was on his way to pick up funds from JI leaders for the purchase of explosives meant for an attack in Singapore.

JI had other bomb makers, including a Malaysian called Azahari Husin, and Hambali called for a meeting in Bangkok in early February 2002. Also present were Indonesian JI leaders Mukhlas (Huda bin Abdul Haq) and Zulkifli Marzuki, and Malaysian JI leaders Wan Min bin Wan Mat and Noordin M. Top.

They discussed small-scale bombings in bars, cafés, and nightclubs frequented by Westerners in Thailand, Malaysia, Singapore, the Philippines, and Indonesia. After debating the locations, the group decided to target the Indonesian tourist resort island of Bali for maximum impact.

After the Bangkok meeting, Hambali sent Mukhlas $35,500 through Wan Min, and Mukhlas roped in his brothers Amrozi and Ali Imron for the operation. Ali Imron, a bomb maker who had taught weapons handling in an al-Qaeda camp in Afghanistan in the mid-1990s, later told me that while he didn't know Hambali well, and he wasn't his usual commander, he had agreed to join the operation because his brother Mukhlas trusted him.

On the evening of October 12, 2002, Ali Imron placed a box-shaped bomb on the sidewalk outside the U.S. Consulate in Denpasar, the provincial capital of Bali, and then drove a Mitsubishi L-300 van packed with a ton of potassium chlorate and 20 kilograms of TNT to the junction of Legian Street in the tourist hub of Kuta, where another man took the vehicle. Just after 11:00 PM, a cell phone call activated the bomb outside the U.S. Consulate, injuring a passerby, but no one in Kuta heard anything beyond the pop music pulsating out of pubs. The party was in full swing in Paddy's Pub when a young Indonesian man walked in, looked around, and detonated his vest bomb.

As survivors stumbled outside to escape the fireball, the man who had taken the car from Ali Imron drove his mobile bomb to the front of the Sari Club and pressed the detonator.

A total of 202 people died in Bali that night: 88 Australians, 38 Indonesians, 24 Brits, 7 Americans, 6 Germans, 5 Swedes, and 32 nationals from 17 other countries. Two bodies were never identified.

Ali Imron, along with the cell's operation commander, Imam Samudra, and the rest of the attackers, left Bali the next day. Indonesian police, now focused on the threat and aided by the countries whose citizens had lost their lives, discovered the chassis of the Mitsubishi L-300 at the blast site, leading to the first break: the van had been sold to Mukhlas's brother Amrozi. His name was familiar to Indonesian investigator Benny Mamoto, as he had heard about him from the ISD when he had come to interview the Singapore JI detainees months earlier. Amrozi's arrest, in the East Java village of Lamongan, gave Indonesian police key documents and a list of cell phone numbers that were traced to other members of the network, and by July 2003, more than eighty-three suspects were under arrest, and Hambali was on the run.

August 11, 2003. Police major general Tritot Ronnaritivichai, of the Thai Special Branch, knew he was on the verge of capturing Asia's most wanted terrorist, Hambali, in an operation he called Black Magic. He had begun his manhunt for Hambali by interviewing JI operatives in custody in Singapore, Malaysia, and Indonesia who knew him.

Mukhlas, then in Indonesian custody, identified Hambali from an array of photos, apparently out of resentment: he was angry that KSM had made Hambali the leader of al-Qaeda in Southeast Asia when he himself was two years older.

After the arrest, in March 2003 in Pakistan, of an al-Qaeda operative named Majid Khan, Tritot was informed by a foreign intelligence service that Majid had been in Bangkok in December 2002. A search of immigration manifests showed that he had entered under his own name and had stayed at a hotel in the center of the city. The Thai Special Branch checked the hotel computer and found that Majid had made more than fifty calls from his room. Five phone numbers popped up, one of which eventually led to one of Hambali's key aides, a Malaysian named Bashir bin Lap, alias Lillie.

By June 2003, General Tritot had pinpointed Lillie's likely location, even though he did not know his identity or what he looked like, and one day the Thai Special Branch put the Bangkok apartment building Lillie was thought to be in under surveillance and jammed all cell phone communication to lure him out. As Tritot watched, a man who was clearly a foreigner came out to use his cell phone. Tritot sent his team in to grab him, sensing he was an operative. He later told a Singaporean friend, Susan Sim (a multitalented woman who has been an ISD officer, a high-level diplomat, and a reporter, and is now a colleague of mine): "I'm trained in police intelligence. I can tell you when something looks wrong. He just looked out of place."

It was not Lillie but another close Hambali associate, Mohamad Farik Amin, alias Zubair. Zubair, however, initially refused to cooperate, and Tritot—who videotapes all his operations—in the meantime reviewed the footage of the takedown and spotted a man hiding behind a building column when Zubair was arrested. The man appeared to be trying to observe the operation without being seen.

Tritot showed the photo to Zubair, who, once he started cooperating, identified the man as Lillie and told Tritot where he was likely to be.

Hambali was in Thailand when he learned of Zubair's arrest, and he assigned to Lillie, who had escaped arrest and returned to him, the task of obtaining new fake passports. He worried that Zubair had confessed their false identities. Hambali didn't think Zubair would confess too quickly, so he thought he had some time to maneuver.

Tritot's team, however, was already watching the fake passport syndicates in Thailand, and when Lillie turned up to collect new Spanish passports for Hambali and himself, he was arrested. By nightfall, Lillie had told Tritot where Hambali was hiding: a rental in an apartment block of fifty flats in an area of Ayutthaya popular with Indian, Chinese, Korean, and Japanese businessmen and workers. Lillie also told Tritot that Hambali was heavily armed, having purchased from the black market along the Cambodian border an M16 and two Norinco-made pistols, with a total of 380 rounds.

Tritot was determined to capture Hambali alive. To lure him downstairs, he told the owner of the apartment block to go up to Hambali's flat and say to him in pidgin English (which he had taught him): "Come downstairs. Your friend telephone you."

Tritot knew that Hambali was expecting a call from Lillie, and that there were no telephones in the flats, so he hid behind the stairway with two Special Branch officers, and another two officers hid in the bathroom along the passageway to the public telephone. Hambali followed the landlord down the stairs, but as soon as the landlord reached the bottom he ran out of the building, alerting Hambali that something was wrong. He swiveled around, spotted Tritot, and reached for a gun he had on him. Tritot ran to him and grabbed the gun, and as the two struggled for the weapon the other Special Branch officials ran out of their hiding places and subdued Hambali. They put him in a van and drove straight to Bangkok. Hambali appeared surprised by his capture, but he said nothing. It was 10:00 PM on August 11, 2003.

Upstairs in the rental flat, Tritot found Hambali's wife, Noralwizah Lee Abdullah, sitting calmly on the bed, Hambali's second pistol next to her. She said nothing, but later confessed that she had thought of committing suicide when she'd heard the noise downstairs and knew Hambali had been taken. Then she apparently realized that instead of dying she could be free of the austere lifestyle Hambali had imposed on her. He never gave her money; she even had to ask the Thai Special Branch officers for money to buy sanitary pads. She never asked to see Hambali.

Back in Bangkok, Tritot began Hambali's interrogation by asking, "Are you Hambali?" To his surprise, Hambali replied, "Yes. I surrender to you." Hambali told Tritot that he knew he would be caught if he stayed in Thailand too long, even though he believed Zubair would not talk, but he had not counted on Tritot's getting Lillie to confess straightaway.

Hambali told Tritot that he had invested half a million Thai baht in two companies run by Muslims: one a computer service shop in Narathiwat and the other a wholesale rice supplier in Yala. Both companies had promised to pay him interest, but he had not insisted upon a contract to that effect, and they never paid it. He asked if Tritot could get him his money, but Tritot said that without proper documentation he could not help him. It was a strange query from Hambali, who must have realized, given his role in the Bali bombing and other terrorist acts, that he'd never see the outside of a prison cell again.

Tritot interrogated Hambali for five days.

Hambali told the Thai Special Branch about his brother, Rusman Gunawan, also known as Gun Gun, who was with a cell in Pakistan called al-Ghuraba: "the foreigners" in Arabic (they weren't from Pakistan). On September 18, members of that cell—thirteen Malaysians and five Indonesians—were arrested. The thirteen Malaysians, aged between seventeen and twenty-five, were enrolled at Abu Bakr Islamic University and Madrasah Jamiat Dirasat, the latter a religious school controlled by Lashkar-e-Taiba. Investigations showed that many of them were products of Luqmanul Hakiem, a JI-run religious school in Ulu Tiram, closed down by the Malaysian authorities in early 2002.

Many of the students were trained in both religious studies and military and terrorist skills, and were being groomed to be the next generation of JI leaders. A few had traveled to Afghanistan for guerrilla training some months before 9/11 and had met bin Laden in Kandahar. As it turned out, the cell had not yet committed any acts and weren't plotting anything; they were training and studying. In November the eighteen students were repatriated to their home countries.

On February 9, 2006, Fran Townsend, assistant to President George W. Bush for Homeland Security and Counterterrorism, previously in the Department of Justice, told reporters in a press briefing that after

9/11, KSM planned to launch a West Coast plot, aiming to hit the tallest building on that side of the United States. During a hearing at Guantánamo Bay in March 2007, KSM revealed that the intended target was the Library Tower in central Los Angeles. He had worked with Hambali and recruited four members for the cell, and he trained the leader in shoe-bombing techniques. Townsend stated: "The cell leader was arrested in February of 2002 . . . at that point, the other members of the cell believed that the West Coast plot [had] been canceled, was not going forward."

A May 23, 2007, White House "Fact Sheet" echoed that the plot was foiled in 2002: "In 2002, we broke up a plot by KSM to hijack an airplane and fly it into the tallest building on the West Coast."

Advocates of the coercive interrogation methods authorized by the Bush administration later claimed that it was their use on KSM that prevented the West Coast attack. The problem with this argument is that KSM was arrested in March 2003, long after the plot had been derailed. KSM, practicing classic counterinterrogation techniques, told interrogators about that plot, leaving them to think he was cooperating, but in reality he was giving information that was outdated. The plot was over: the then cell leader had been captured, as Townsend noted.

In a declassified memo entitled "Detainee Reporting Pivotal for the War Against Al-Qai'da," the CIA claimed that in March 2003 KSM gave information on Majid Khan, who in turn gave up information. "Based on that information, Zubair was captured in June 2003." The memo then claims, "We used the information Zubair provided to track down and arrest Hambali." To put it charitably, this is a loose interpretation of what happened.

The memo also tries to boost the importance of Gun Gun and the al-Ghuraba cell, stating: "Hambali admitted that some members of the [Pakistani] cell were eventually to be groomed for U.S. operations— at the behest of KSM—possibly as part of KSM's plot to fly hijacked planes into the tallest building on the U.S. west coast." This "eventually" and "possibly" was the best that analysts could conclude, despite 183 sessions of waterboarding, the coercive interrogation technique that simulates drowning. The reality is that the al-Ghuraba cell wasn't involved, which is why the United States didn't request the arrest of its members and they were sent to their home countries.

And while KSM was "confessing" to plots already thwarted, and those running the EIT program thought that this was important news, he didn't tell them about plots that hadn't yet happened but which he definitely knew about because of his position as al-Qaeda's military commander, such as the cells working in Madrid, London, and Jakarta. Pleased with the success of the first Bali attack, in October 2002, KSM gave Hambali $100,000 as "a sign of congratulations" and another $30,000 for further operations. Hambali gave the money to Noordin Top and the bomb maker Azahari Husin to fund the bombing of the JW Marriott Hotel in Jakarta on August 5, 2003, approximately five months after KSM was arrested.

While Hambali's capture cut off the remnants of the JI network from al-Qaeda central, operatives like Noordin Top now had acquired a taste for violence. With Azahari, Top went on to carry out three more terrorist attacks in Indonesia, including a second attack in Bali. Azahari was killed when Indonesian police raided his hideout in East Java in November 2005, and Noordin Top was tracked down to a safe house near the Indonesian royal city of Solo in Central Java, where he died in a hail of bullets on September 17, 2009. After that, the Indonesian police discovered a terrorist training camp in Aceh and rounded up several dozen more JI operatives and their new recruits.

PART 6

THE FIRST
HIGH-VALUE DETAINEE

20

Abu Zubaydah

March 29, 2002. I was in the middle of packing my suitcase in my New York City apartment, preparing to take a long-awaited vacation and spend Easter with family in Pennsylvania, when my cell phone, house phone, and pager all rang consecutively. It was my assistant special agent in charge, Kenny Maxwell, calling from the Joint Terrorism Task Force in New York, ordering me to travel to a private airstrip at Dulles Airport, outside Washington, DC, for a special mission. Abu Zubaydah, America's first high-value detainee since 9/11, had been captured the night before. I was to help interrogate him.

The FBI had been looking for Abu Zubaydah for a while. He was originally wanted for his connection both to Ahmed Ressam's attempt to bomb Los Angeles International Airport on New Year's Eve 1999 and to the millennium plot in Jordan. Abu Zubaydah's name had come up with increasing frequency in intelligence reports after the millennium plot. While he was not a member of al-Qaeda, his role as external emir of Khaldan was of considerable importance. Senior al-Qaeda members, such as Khallad, regularly turned to Abu Zubaydah for help with passports and travel. In turn, al-Qaeda guaranteed Abu Zubaydah's protection elsewhere in Afghanistan, and he often stayed in their guesthouses. He was one of the most important cogs in the shadowy network that we were struggling to disrupt.

I emptied my suitcase and packed a duffel bag. Ten minutes later I was in a cab heading to LaGuardia Airport. In Washington, acting FBI deputy assistant director Charles Frahm met me to drive me to Dulles. With him was Stephen Gaudin, my former colleague from the New York office, who had just been assigned to headquarters.

On the way to Dulles, Frahm, who at the time was seconded, or assigned, to the CIA, told me that Abu Zubaydah had been captured the night before in a gunfight in Faisalabad, Pakistan. He had been tracked down after the FBI helped trace one of his calls to an apartment building after monitoring his communications. The FBI worked with the CIA and Pakistani security services to raid the building.

After the gun battle, the occupants of the apartment surrendered or were overwhelmed and subdued. All were taken in for questioning. Abu Zubaydah was not recognizable at first. He had been shot in the thigh, groin, and stomach while trying to escape by jumping from the roof of one apartment building to another, and his wounds were serious. In addition, he had altered his appearance in an effort to conceal his identity. Before, he had looked like a businessman, with a carefully trimmed beard, glasses, and relatively short hair. Now his beard had been shaved off and his hair had grown long and straggly; he was taken for a low-level terrorist. Soon, however, the FBI and CIA teams on the ground saw through his disguise, and he was separated from the other prisoners. A decision was made by the CIA to fly him to another country—its name is classified—where he would be interrogated at a secure location.

The FBI case agent responsible for the monitoring of Abu Zubaydah was Craig Donnachie. I knew Craig well. He was assigned to the JTTF in New York and was knowledgeable about Abu Zubaydah. We had worked together on previous I-49 cases, and initially FBI headquarters had decided that Craig and I would be partners on this mission. In the car, however, Frahm told me that Craig wouldn't be joining me, as they couldn't get in contact with him. (It turned out that he was on a train back to New York to spend Easter with his family.) Instead, Stephen Gaudin would come.

Frahm told us that our orders were to assist the CIA team, and that we were being brought in to help because of our knowledge of Abu Zubaydah. He told us, more than once, that it was to be a CIA-led intelligence-gathering operation and that we were there to support them as needed. We were not to read the Miranda warning or worry about the admissibility of evidence in court. We were to stay as long as the CIA needed us.

At Dulles we were joined by two medical personnel contracted by the agency, a doctor and an anesthesiologist, who were to help care for Abu Zubaydah. As the anesthesiologist had never worked with the CIA before, an agency officer took him into a telephone booth at the terminal to explain, and have him sign, a confidentiality agreement. Also with them was a cadet who had been pulled out of the new CIA officers' class and assigned to the mission because he had training as a medic. He was to assist the doctor and the anesthesiologist in that capacity. We boarded a plane chartered by the CIA and took off. After a lengthy journey we arrived at our destination.

We were met by officers from the local CIA station who took us to a small plane. We flew to the safe house where Abu Zubaydah would be held. Local CIA officers warmly welcomed us. As Abu Zubaydah was to be arriving shortly, we set about cleaning and preparing the facility for his arrival, setting up a makeshift hospital room for him. We also tried to make the place hygienic for the rest of us to use. It was a very primitive location. One day I walked into the bathroom and saw a cobra curled up in the corner, head raised and hissing at me. I ran out and called a guard who was assigned to provide perimeter security. He found a V-shaped branch on the ground and caught the snake, then took it out of the bathroom. This was not an uncommon problem.

We had been told that the CIA's Counterterrorism Center, tasked with conducting interrogations on behalf of the agency, had decided not to send a team to join us. They didn't believe it was actually Abu

Zubaydah who had been captured. Others in the CIA did, which is why he was flown to a CIA safe house, and why we were flown to meet him. (We later discovered that the CTC team was supposed to have been on the plane with us.) The CTC was now being run by Alvin, the chief of operations who had made mistakes in Amman during the millennium investigation.

I later found out that the CTC's confusion stemmed from our anonymous source in Afghanistan, who had told them that the man captured was not Abu Zubaydah. They had shown the source a picture of the captured man. While usually reliable, the source was not skilled at identifying people in photos. Photographs were foreign to him, as he had grown up under the Taliban, of whose members there were no pictures. And he certainly couldn't recognize a beardless Abu Zubaydah. Confident in the source, the CTC didn't want to waste their time by coming. We, and others at the CIA, trusted the positive identification of Abu Zubaydah by the arresting team on the ground in Faisalabad.

Given the CTC's absence, I assumed we would be supporting the local CIA team in interrogating Abu Zubaydah, as Frahm had made it clear that it was a CIA operation. We were there to support them and not to take control. As soon as Abu Zubaydah arrived and was set up, I went to the CIA chief of base and asked when they were planning to start interviewing him. He was surprised at my question. "Who? Us?" he asked. "I don't know anything about this guy, and neither do my guys. But I understand you FBI guys know something about him, so why don't you do the interviews? We're all working for Uncle Sam."

Stephen and I walked into the makeshift hospital room we had helped set up a few hours earlier. Abu Zubaydah was lying in the center on a gurney. His face was covered by a bag, a normal procedure when transporting terrorists. He was barely moving. Parts of his body were bandaged up, and elsewhere he had cuts and bruises. He was in critical condition. His wrists were handcuffed to the gurney.

I removed the bag from his head. His eyes flickered as they adjusted to the light. They darted around the room and at us, taking everything in. I studied his face. One of his eyes was a cloudy green from an infection. He had cuts and dried blood on his face. His hair was long, curly, and messy. I understood why the source hadn't recognized him. I judged that he was around my age, thirty-two.

"What's your name?" I asked him in Arabic.

"Daood," he replied. David, in Arabic. I smiled. His given name was Zayn—he was born Zayn al-Abidin Muhammad Husayn Abu Zubaydah—but I knew that Daood was one of his aliases.

"Okay," I said, smiling, "how about I call you Hani?"

This was his mother's nickname for him when he was a child. His face registered shock, and he also wore a guilty "oh, shit, my game is up" look. He sighed, paused, and then slowly nodded his head in agreement.

"Okay," he said. In a few seconds both his identity and cooperation had been confirmed.

He stared at me with curiosity. I guessed he was trying to calculate how I could know such an intimate detail about him. He now wanted to know more about me. "Who are you?" he asked.

"I'm with the FBI," I told him.

"I don't believe you," he replied.

We were speaking in Arabic, and he apparently assumed that we were either Arab or Israeli intelligence agents. His image of FBI officials was of white-skinned tough guys, not native Arabic speakers. Stephen and I took out our FBI credentials and showed them to him. Again his face registered surprise.

"Okay," he said, accepting that we were who we claimed to be.

"Now, look," I told him, "you have been caught. The battle is up. If you are smart enough, and I think you are, you will realize that you are caught. We know everything about you. So don't play games with me, Zayn."

He nodded. "What do you want to know?" he asked.

"Let's start with what you were working on before you were captured."

He began telling us about an operation he was involved in just before his capture: a plan to raise funds and conduct terrorist activities in a country closely allied with the United States. There had been an attack in that country not long before, and Abu Zubaydah wanted to do something similar. The plot was far along, and he told us all about the sources he had received money from, where the money was going, the individuals involved, and logistical and operational details, along with other valuable intelligence. This was all in our first hour with him.

As the information related to an attack in the works was naturally time sensitive, we took a quick break from Abu Zubaydah and put everything he told us into a cable while the medical team attended to his wounds and evaluated his condition. All cable traffic from the safe house went through CIA channels to headquarters in Langley. There the information was quickly verified, and the director of the CIA, George Tenet, was briefed. The attack was thwarted based on the information we gained.

People seated around the table at the meeting in which Tenet was briefed later told me that he registered obvious surprise at how quickly Abu Zubaydah was cooperating. The CIA had commissioned a report in December 2001 from two psychologists who argued that an approach that used cruelty and humiliation to subdue terrorists would be needed to make high-value detainees talk, and that the process took time.

Tenet instructed his aides to send his congratulations to the two CIA officers doing the interrogation. There was an uncomfortable silence in the room. The briefers told him that it was actually two FBI agents who had gained the information. He was furious and angrily slammed his hand on the table. "Why isn't the CTC running the interrogation?" he demanded. He was told that they hadn't believed that it was Abu Zubaydah who'd been captured. "Get them there now and have them take over," he ordered.

After filing our report, we returned to Abu Zubaydah. We took his fingerprints and a DNA sample—standard procedure—and recorded his voice, because of the CTC's initial conclusion that the suspect really wasn't Abu Zubaydah. The voice sample would be sent to other sources for verification.

We knew a great deal about Abu Zubaydah before his capture, and during our interrogation he filled in the gaps. A Palestinian, Abu Zubaydah was born in 1971 in Saudi Arabia, where his father held a teaching position. He grew up as a typical middle-class Palestinian expat there, and he even went on a high school trip to the United States. He also studied in India and married an Indian woman. He said that she was obsessed with "sex, sex, too much sex," and he ended the marriage when he left India. Later he was swayed, like so many other top mujahideen, by the fiery speeches on jihad of another Palestinian, Abdullah Azzam, and resolved to wage war on the Russians. He traveled to Afghanistan to fight against the Soviet-backed Najibullah regime (1989–1992).

During a battle, he was hit in the head by shrapnel. The shrapnel wiped out his memory. He didn't even know who he was. He was rushed to a hospital for treatment, and it was judged too dangerous to remove the shrapnel. To this day, he has a hole in his head.

After treatment, he was taken for therapy to a guesthouse in Peshawar. He was shown his passport. As was standard for mujahideen, it had been stored with an emir at a safe house while Abu Zubaydah had been fighting on the front. To help him with his therapy, everyone in the guesthouse would tell him, "Your name is Abu Zubaydah." This is why he was one of the few terrorists who operated under his actual name rather than an alias.

In the guesthouse, as part of his therapy to try and piece together his past, Abu Zubaydah began keeping a diary that detailed his life, emotions, and what people were telling him. He split information into categories, such as what he knew about himself and what people told him about himself, and listed them under different names (Hani 1, Hani 2, Hani 3) to distinguish one set from the other. When the diary was found, some analysts incorrectly interpreted the use of the different names as the symptom of multiple-personality disorder.

Even after Abu Zubaydah's therapy was completed and he had left the guesthouse, he kept writing in his diary. We later evaluated it, and it both provided us with new information and confirmed information he had given us. The diary, for example, contained details of how, days before 9/11, he began preparing for counterattacks by the United States, working with al-Qaeda to buy weapons and prepare defensive lines in Afghanistan. Another entry, from 2002, details how he personally planned to wage jihad against the United States by instigating racial wars, and by attacking gas stations and fuel trucks and starting timed fires. He went into greater detail later in our interrogation.

When he felt well enough, Abu Zubaydah decided to leave the guesthouse. He again wanted to wage jihad and decided to try to join al-Qaeda. He went to the al-Qaeda training camp in Jalalabad headed by Abu Ata'a al-Tunisi. A Tunisian, Abu Ata'a was the commander of al-Qaeda troops in Afghanistan prior to Abdul Hadi al-Iraqi, who, as of this writing, is in Guantánamo Bay.

After interviewing Abu Zubaydah, Abu Ata'a was reluctant to accept him, given his memory loss and poor mental state. He told Abu Zubaydah that he would speak to bin Laden and the al-Qaeda leadership in Sudan. The leadership backed up Abu Ata'a's assessment, and Abu Zubaydah was denied membership. The rejection came as a colossal insult, and Abu Zubaydah never fully forgave al-Qaeda. Still committed to waging jihad, he resolved to do his part independently and prove al-Qaeda wrong.

And he did. Over time he became a successful independent facilitator, well known for smuggling people and raising money. He worked closely with the majority of the Arabs in Afghanistan, many of whom were al-Qaeda members. Over the years, a relationship with al-Qaeda developed, and he often sent them top graduates from Khaldan, such as Ahmed Ressam. Another al-Qaeda operative who went through Khaldan was Owhali, the failed East African embassy suicide bomber. Abu Zubaydah was so effective a facilitator that al-Qaeda invited him to join the organization. He refused. Having been turned down initially, he would never join. He had his pride.

Even before he told us this, we knew from previous investigations that Abu Zubaydah was not a member of al-Qaeda; nor had he ever been. But especially given that he reiterated this to us—and we dutifully wrote it up and sent it in cables to Langley—it was very surprising to see him publicly described by Bush administration officials as being a senior al-Qaeda member, and even the terrorist group's number three or four in command.

Bush administration officials kept insisting that Abu Zubaydah was a member of al-Qaeda, and they inflated his importance, not only publicly but in classified memos. A now declassified May 30, 2005, memo from the principal deputy assistant attorney general of the Justice Department, Steven G. Bradbury, to John A. Rizzo, then the senior deputy general counsel of the CIA, states that, according to what the Justice Department had been told by the CIA, prior to his capture Abu Zubaydah was "one of Usama Bin Laden's key lieutenants," al-Qaeda's third or fourth highest-ranking member, and that he had been involved "in every major terrorist operation carried out by al-Qaeda." (This memo and other, related memos, issued from the Justice Department's Office of Legal Counsel, have since come to be known as the "OLC Memos.") None of this was true; nor should it have ever been believed. It was not until the Obama administration was in office that U.S. officials stopped calling him a senior al-Qaeda member.

When Abu Zubaydah was much later interviewed by the Criminal Investigation Task Force (CITF) in Guantánamo Bay, Cuba, he was shown a picture of Abu Hafs al-Masri. He put his hand on the photo, slid it back to the interrogator, and said: "Now this is the number three in al-Qaeda." When asked why he had in the past "admitted" to CIA interrogators that he was the number three in al-Qaeda, he said that he had realized that they would keep torturing him until he said what they wanted to hear.

As we interrogated Abu Zubaydah, we were simultaneously fighting to keep him alive. He was in terrible shape. The bullet that had hit him in his left thigh had shattered coins in his pocket. Some of this freak shrapnel entered his abdomen. We had to take breaks during the interrogation as the medics opened his wounds and cleaned them to prevent infection. He couldn't eat, drink, or even clean up after himself. As we interrogated him, I placed blocks of ice on his lips to give him some liquid, and Stephen cleaned him up after he soiled himself.

Abu Zubaydah knew that his situation was dire. His eyes showed fear. "I don't want to die," he would say in moments of immense pain. We told him that it was all in the hands of God, and that the doctors were doing their best. "I hope so. I don't want to die." Tears rolled down from the eye that was not infected. We were in a strange situation: we were fighting to keep alive a terrorist dedicated to killing Americans.

But we needed to get information from him, and he was of no use to us dead.

That first evening, after Abu Zubaydah fell asleep and we filed our cables to Langley, everyone went to a nearby hotel to sleep. I decided to stay at the safe house with Abu Zubaydah in case he woke up and had something to say. I set up in a cot in the room next door to him. I spent much of the night reviewing what we knew about Abu Zubaydah and other terrorists who were in his network, along with the information he had given us that day, in preparation for the next day's interrogation.

As I was drawing up an interrogation plan, at around 3:00 AM, the CIA medic tending to Abu Zubaydah came to my room. "Hey, Ali, how important is this guy?" he casually asked. He knew nothing about Abu Zubaydah and was only at the location because of his medical skills.

"He's pretty important," I replied.

"Does he know a lot of stuff?"

"Yes, I believe so."

"Well, if you want anything from him you'd better go and interview him now."

"Why? What are you talking about?"

"In the morning I don't think he'll be alive. He's septic." All this the medic said in a matter-of-fact tone.

I called the hotel where Stephen, the medical team, and some local CIA officials were staying and woke them up. When they arrived twenty minutes later I repeated what the medic had told me. The doctor evaluated Abu Zubaydah and concurred: "If we don't do something, he will be dead by morning."

Our first problem was that we didn't have the necessary medical equipment at the safe house to treat Abu Zubaydah. A proper hospital was our only chance of keeping him alive. The second problem was that we were FBI agents and CIA officers; our presence in this country was supposed to be a secret. If that information slipped out, it would alert other terrorists to where Abu Zubaydah was being held, and it would probably cause problems for our host country, too.

The CIA chief of base cabled Langley, explaining our situation and asking for guidance. A cable came straight back: "Death is not an option." That was clearance to do whatever it took to keep Abu Zubaydah alive. His early cooperation and clear intelligence value saved his life. Our challenge was how to get him to a local hospital without attracting notice.

The chief of security at the local station, Allen, came up with a plan: we would pretend to be soldiers training nearby. Our cover story was that Abu Zubaydah was a fellow soldier who had gone crazy during an exercise and had needed to be shot to be contained. That's how we would explain, to hospital staff, his injuries and why he was handcuffed. We all put on military uniforms and dressed Abu Zubaydah in one, too.

On the way to the hospital Abu Zubaydah's condition deteriorated even further. Stephen, Allen, and I sat in the back of the ambulance with him and watched the doctors fight to keep him breathing. The anesthesiologist performed a tracheotomy by cutting a hole in his neck and putting a tube through it. We took turns physically pumping air through the tube into his lungs. He was still alive as we pulled up outside the hospital. We were nervous as we pushed him through the hospital entrance on a stretcher. We didn't know if our cover story would be accepted, and there was a good chance that Abu Zubaydah would die at any moment. People stared, no doubt trying to understand why all these soldiers were wheeling an injured and handcuffed fellow soldier through. We spoke to the hospital staff, and Abu Zubaydah was rushed into the operating room. Minutes later, the doctors began surgery.

We sat in the waiting room, watching television to pass the time. What if he dies? I thought. If he's alive, what should we discuss next? These thoughts were only interrupted when a doctor came out and told us that the operation had been a success.

A doctor from Johns Hopkins had been flown in by the CIA to evaluate Abu Zubaydah's condition. He consulted with the surgeons, wrote a report, and left. Stephen and I stayed in Abu Zubaydah's hospital room, waiting for him to regain consciousness. We repeatedly asked the doctors and nurses tending to him and changing his bandages how long they thought it would be before he came to. Eventually he opened his eyes.

Abu Zubaydah later told me that when he first opened his eyes, he saw that he was surrounded by women who were all covered up—nurses wearing uniforms and surgical masks—and thought perhaps that he was in heaven. The vision evaporated when he saw Stephen and me in our military uniforms looking over him. He smiled as he said this.

As soon as he opened his eyes and it was clear he was lucid, I gave him a stern lecture. "Don't you try to make a scene," I warned him. "You just play along. We're doing this to save your life. If you play any games, you're only endangering yourself." Without delay, Stephen and I started asking him questions. When he found it difficult to speak, we held out an alphabet chart for him to point to letters to communicate his answers.

At the safe house we had focused primarily on plots he was involved in just before he was captured. Our first priority was to stop any plots in the works. In the hospital our goal in the first session was to get more details on pending threats and to see what information he could give us on bin Laden and al-Qaeda's senior leadership. That's where we steered the conversation.

Abu Zubaydah told us he had first met bin Laden in 2000, at a time when the Taliban was under pressure from bin Laden to close down non–al-Qaeda terrorist training camps so that he could control all Arab fighters in Afghanistan. The Taliban agreed to shut down a few, and one of those was Khaldan. With his camp closed, Abu Zubaydah traveled to Kandahar, where bin Laden and much of the al-Qaeda leadership had gathered. On learning that Abu Zubaydah was in town, as a sign of respect to someone who had been of such help to al-Qaeda over the years, bin Laden invited Abu Zubaydah to visit him. Abu Zubaydah told us, proudly, that when he walked into the room to meet bin Laden, al-Qaeda's then military chief, Mohammed Atef (Abu Hafs), who was killed by a U.S. airstrike in November 2001, greeted him by saying: "So this is the Abu Zubaydah we hear all about."

After Abu Zubaydah described that interaction, I asked him about the most recent time he had seen bin Laden. That, he told me, came after 9/11, when Musharraf switched his allegiance from being a supporter of the Taliban to joining America's side in the war against al-

Qaeda and the Taliban. When the news broke that Musharraf had changed sides, Abu Zubaydah and his partner Ibn al-Shaykh al-Liby, Khaldan's internal emir, met with bin Laden and other al-Qaeda leaders. Bin Laden was furious with Pakistan for having sided with the United States against the Taliban. He said that Musharraf's switch was a "clear betrayal."

"Is bin Laden planning any attacks?" I asked Abu Zubaydah.

"Yes. Bin Laden has people working on plots," he replied.

"Like who?"

"Azayet."

Azayet was an alias for Abdullah Ahmed Abdullah. He had been indicted for his role in the East African embassy bombings, and as Stephen and I had both worked on that case, we were very familiar with him. I asked Stephen to get me a picture of him, to double-check that Abu Zubaydah was talking about the same person.

We didn't have any of our FBI photo-books with us, because we were only meant to be supporting the CIA and hadn't brought our own interrogation materials. So Stephen downloaded on his Sony device, similar to a Palm Pilot, the FBI's Most Wanted Terrorists list. The list, published for the first time after the attacks of September 11, 2001, contained the names of twenty-two terrorists indicted by grand juries for terrorist crimes. Azayet's picture was on it because of his role in the embassy bombings.

Stephen repeatedly tapped on his device to zoom in and handed it to me as it was still loading. Without pausing to look at the picture, I put the device in front of Abu Zubaydah's face and asked, "Is this Azayet?"

"No." He shook his head. "It isn't."

"No? It isn't?" I repeated. "What do you mean, no, it isn't?" Raising my voice slightly, I told him: "I can't believe we just saved your life, cleaned up your shit, and have been really good to you, and you are playing games."

Abu Zubaydah seemed surprised by my reaction. "I'm not playing games. Please, brother, don't play games with me."

"I'm showing you the picture of Azayet, and you say it isn't him. So indulge me, who the fuck is this?"

"You know who it is." He was clearly shaken by my anger. "It's Mokhtar."

When I heard Mokhtar, my stomach churned. Trying to maintain my calm, I quickly looked at the picture. "Oh, sorry, you're right, wrong photo, our mistake." Stephen had zoomed in accidentally on the wrong picture, bringing up a picture of Khalid Sheikh Mohammed. "But since Mokhtar's picture is up, tell me about him."

"You know who he is. Please don't play games with me, my brother. You know." Abu Zubaydah's voice showed fatigue now. I was silent. "You know Mokhtar is the guy who did the planes operation," he said.

When he first said the name, I recalled a video we had found after 9/11 of bin Laden describing the plot and bragging about his expertise in putting it together. A couple of times in the clip, he looks at an individual who is either videotaping or next to the person videotaping, and gestures toward him, saying, "Mokhtar." He even gives him some credit for the attacks.

Later in the same video clip, talking about a dream someone had had about 9/11, bin Laden says: "And in the same dream he saw Mokhtar teaching them karate." At the end of the tape, al-Qaeda members surround a U.S. helicopter that had been shot down in the Ghazni province of Afghanistan. The terrorists are taking pictures of the wreckage, and some can be heard saying, "Hey, Mokhtar, come see this." From this we knew that Mokhtar was important; but we didn't know who he was. It was tremendously frustrating for the U.S. intelligence community. Mokhtar can mean "mayor," and it can also mean "the chosen." Either way, it is a name that denotes respect.

At the same time, the intelligence community had been hearing chatter traffic about "the man whose brain flew away"—*Le moch tar* in Arabic. Some analysts thought that the phrase stood for bin Laden, but my suspicion, based on the chatter traffic, was that it was another way for operatives to refer to Mokhtar, deepening his cover. Now, from Abu Zubaydah, we finally had an answer to the riddle. KSM was Mokhtar! We had no idea.

KSM was on the FBI's Most Wanted list for his role in the Bojinka plot with his nephew Ramzi Yousef. The U.S. intelligence community until now had had no idea that KSM was even a member of al-Qaeda (he was believed to be an independent terrorist), let alone the mastermind of the 9/11 attacks. I had to be careful, as I didn't want Abu Zubaydah to know that this was a big breakthrough for us. A key to a successful interrogation is to never let the suspect know that he is giving you information you didn't know. That only lessens the chances of his giving you more information, as he realizes he's said too much. But I also had to let Stephen know what had happened.

Stephen realized from the tone of the conversation that something was going on, but as he didn't speak fluent Arabic—he only knew a few words—he didn't know the details. I turned to him and said: "Stephen, what's up? You showed me the wrong picture." As I handed him his electronic device, I pointed at the picture of KSM on his screen. As Stephen took the device, I simultaneously asked Zubaydah about KSM in an effort to maintain the pace of the interrogation.

"I know Mokhtar did 9/11. But speaking of Mokhtar, why the heck do you guys call him 'Le moch tar'? Did he really lose his brain?" I said this with a smile, wanting to conceal from Abu Zubaydah that we knew nothing about KSM's role in al-Qaeda and instead make him think that I was familiar with Mokhtar. It worked.

Without pausing, Abu Zubaydah responded, "No, it's a code. It sounds similar."

"A code that can't be cracked?" I replied in jest. He smiled.

During this exchange Stephen walked out of the room with Allen, who had been observing the interrogation. We had grown close to Allen since we had arrived, and we liked him. His expertise was not in Middle Eastern terrorists, so the photo of KSM meant nothing to him. Stephen took him outside to explain what had just happened.

I pressed on with Abu Zubaydah. "Since your buddy Mokhtar came up, let's talk about him now." Again I was going with my instinct. I didn't know that they were friends, but I guessed that, given Abu Zubaydah's knowledge of KSM's role in 9/11, they must be—and again I wanted to make Abu Zubaydah think that I knew all about their relationship.

"What do you want to know about him?" Abu Zubaydah asked.

"Let's see if your knowledge of how the plot started matches mine," I told him.

Piece by piece, Abu Zubaydah outlined what he knew of how KSM had come up with the idea of 9/11 and how it was carried out. During his years as a terrorist facilitator, Abu Zubaydah had come to know KSM well. KSM, originally as a freelance terrorist operative, often approached Abu Zubaydah for help with plots he was hatching. Abu Zubaydah's reputation as a facilitator was well established, and KSM knew that if Abu Zubaydah couldn't help him, at least he might put him in touch with people who could.

One day KSM went to see Abu Zubaydah. He excitedly outlined a new idea he was working on: flying Cessna planes into the World Trade Center. But KSM lacked the resources for such a plan. He thought Abu Zubaydah might be able to provide funds and recruits or point him in the right direction.

"I like the idea," Abu Zubaydah told KSM, "but flying Cessna planes into the World Trade Center will only break windows. Why only break windows? At least fill the planes with explosives."

"That's a good improvement," KSM replied, "so will you help me?"

Abu Zubaydah said he lacked the resources for a plan of that scale, but told him, "Bin Laden could help you."

KSM was wary of approaching bin Laden. He prized his independence, and a condition for working with bin Laden was pledging *bayat* to him and joining al-Qaeda. Moreover, KSM wanted to be recognized as the architect of the attack, and he didn't want the credit to go to bin Laden. But KSM understood that he had no other option. He couldn't undertake the plan alone, and only al-Qaeda had the resources.

He asked to meet with bin Laden and Abu Hafs, who consented to see him because of his connection to his nephew Ramzi Yousef, a hero in the eyes of al-Qaeda. KSM outlined his plan to them. Bin Laden nodded. "It's a good idea, but why go to war with an ax when you can use a bulldozer?" he asked. KSM had found his backer and agreed to join al-Qaeda. The planes operation was formed.

Bin Laden later outlined a vision of hijacking airplanes going from the East Coast to the West Coast and using them to strike at the World

Trade Center and other major targets in the United States. KSM liked bin Laden's improvements.

When we finished talking with Abu Zubaydah about KSM, I said, "Now let's go back to Azayet." This time, Stephen zoomed in on the correct picture, and Abu Zubaydah positively identified him. He gave us more details on plots Azayet was involved in, including an attack in the works on a U.S. military base. The information led to the thwarting of the attack.

Abu Zubaydah's identification of KSM's role in 9/11 was celebrated as a major breakthrough in Washington.

We did not have a secure line at the hospital, so I waited few days until I was back at the safe house to call Kenny Maxwell, head of the Joint Terrorism Task Force, under whose remit KSM fell. The JTTF was also spearheading major parts of the 9/11 investigation, so this information was an important part of the puzzle they were piecing together. I was eager to find out what they thought of the news, and wanted any ideas they could send my way.

"Kenny, what do you think of the news?"

"What news?" He sounded puzzled.

"Kenny," I said slowly, "do you know who did 9/11?"

"Who?"

"The guy Frank Pellegrino is working on," I told him. Frank was the FBI case agent for KSM.

"Who?" Kenny asked again.

"The guy from Manila Air," I told him, using another name for the Bojinka plot.

"You're shitting me." Kenny was stunned. "He isn't even a member of al-Qaeda," he added.

"Think again," I said. I couldn't believe that the JTTF hadn't been given the news. I told Kenny to get the information we had sent to Langley so that JTTF agents like Frank could act on it and send us any questions they had.

When I eventually returned to New York, I found out that little of the information we had cabled daily had ever reached the JTTF.

· · ·

Over the next few days in the hospital we interrogated Abu Zubaydah every moment we could, utilizing the alphabet chart when he was unable to speak, and gained many more pieces of actionable intelligence. We paused only when he had to sleep or when doctors treated him. At times he underwent tests. When he needed an MRI and his body was found to be too big for the machine, Stephen and I had to squeeze him into the hole.

One conversation we had with Abu Zubaydah centered around the assassination, days before 9/11, of Ahmed Shah Massoud. Abu Zubaydah was fascinated with the logistics of the assassination by operatives posing as journalists. He told us that the Taliban had been exceptionally grateful to al-Qaeda for killing their arch-rival, and had told the leadership: "You Arab mujahideen have embarrassed us with your kindness."

After 9/11, with the news that America was preparing to invade Afghanistan, and as the Northern Alliance pushed forward against Taliban positions, there was a move among the Taliban and their Arab allies to evacuate people from Kandahar. Abu Zubaydah made the trip in a plane. Another passenger was Hamza al-Rab'ei, an Egyptian al-Qaeda operative who rose to a high operational position. He was later killed.

The two started talking, and, prompted by Abu Zubaydah's questions, Hamza explained how the Massoud assassination had been planned. I suspected that Abu Zubaydah was somewhat involved, too, as two Tunisians played a part in the assassination, and the majority of Tunisians in Afghanistan went through Khaldan. I intended to ask him about it later, but we had more important things to focus on first.

During the times in the hospital when Abu Zubaydah slept, we went through his phone book, diary, and other personal effects, removed from the apartment building upon his capture in Faisalabad. The items had been found in his briefcase. It all helped give us a fuller understanding of his links to the terrorist network across the world, and helped us prepare for our interrogation sessions. Also found was a videotape in which he urged everyone to rally behind bin Laden as the leader of the mujahideen in Afghanistan. In the video, Abu Zubaydah says: "We and the sheikh are one. We have been working together for almost ten years, but we were hoping to keep this work secret . . . hidden." I questioned Abu Zubaydah about this statement, asking, "So you're saying bin Laden became your emir?"

"No," he said, "we were at war in Afghanistan and I wanted to rally all different groups together. I thought that if I signaled that I was behind bin Laden it would rally recruits and money for our case." Abu Zubaydah said all of this with the utmost seriousness. He really believed in his own importance and the effect his announcement would have on other independent terrorists in Afghanistan. In fact, his impact wasn't as significant as he believed it to be. While he was an important facilitator, he did not attract recruits or have his own following.

Abu Zubaydah went on to explain that while there were divisions among various mujahideen groups in Afghanistan after 9/11, he thought that everyone should unite against the invaders. He went off on a tangent about how he disagreed with the al-Qaeda propaganda committee's policy of sending out tapes. He thought that media outlets would pay for the exclusive use of the tapes, and didn't understand why they just handed them out for free. He planned to sell his tape urging people to unite behind bin Laden for a large sum of money.

Although Abu Zubaydah believed that everyone should unite together behind bin Laden, and he met with al-Qaeda's leaders to make such plans, he wouldn't take an oath of loyalty to bin Laden. Once spurned, never fully forgiven was his mind-set. It also surprised him how much al-Qaeda members revered bin Laden. They spoke about him "as if he was someone not from this world," Abu Zubaydah said. He was uncomfortable with the hero worship.

Even his old friend KSM, who had once prized his independence, became overly reverent after joining al-Qaeda. During a meal that KSM and Abu Zubaydah shared at the main al-Qaeda guesthouse in Kandahar, it was announced that bin Laden was coming to join them. KSM got nervous and started looking around for a head covering. He told Abu Zubaydah that he wanted to put something on to honor bin Laden. Abu Zubaydah, surprised, asked KSM rhetorically, "What happened to you?"

Abu Zubaydah spent most of his time until 2000 in Pakistan. From there he facilitated travel for operatives to and from Afghanistan and accessed his network of recruits and funds. But in 2000 he started spending more time in Afghanistan. In Kabul, he visited old colleagues and friends. While his circle consisted mostly of single men, there were a few married men, too, and the single men would go to their houses for meals.

One person he fondly remembered was Mozzam Begg, the Pakistani from the UK. Begg had trained in camps in Afghanistan. Abu Zubaydah told us about his bookstore in Birmingham, al-Ansar, and how he had used it as a front to send money and recruits to Abu Zubaydah. I was familiar with Begg from counterterrorism operations in the UK: how he had been picked up in Britain in the summer of 2001 by MI5 and SO12, his store raided, his belongings searched. I mentally reviewed the case: SO13 had not been briefed on the raid and was not prepared to build a terrorism case against him. Upon his release, Begg had fled to Kabul.

Abu Zubaydah liked to visit Begg. His wife, Zaynab, was a good cook, and there was always food in the house. Abu Zubaydah laughed, remembering that Zaynab used to get upset with him because he used too much olive oil on his food, an extravagance that depleted their larder. Begg today is a free man in Britain.

21

The Contractors Take Over

This period of cooperation with Abu Zubaydah lasted for about ten days in the hospital and ended when the CTC finally arrived in the country from Washington, DC. The CIA group included their chief operational psychologist, whom I will call Wilson; an interrogator, Ed; and a polygrapher, Frank. There were other CIA personnel: analysts, support staff, security personnel. With them was a psychologist, Boris—a contractor hired by the CIA.

At first I was pleased when the CTC group arrived. Although I was meeting Frank for the first time, I knew Wilson and Ed well. I held Wilson in high regard and had worked with him before. He had always impressed me with his professional expertise and integrity, and we found that we had similar views on issues back then. Ed and I had worked together a few times. We had first met in Yemen investigating the USS *Cole* bombing, and we partnered a few times in interrogations of terror suspects. I respected Ed and had enjoyed working with him in the past. I was glad to see someone of his caliber on the team. With the two of them present, I assumed that we would all work together as we had done in counterterrorism operations and interrogations elsewhere, and that this too would be a smooth operation.

While Abu Zubaydah was in the hospital, Stephen and I, along with local CIA officers, stayed in a nearby hotel. When Wilson and the CTC team arrived at the hotel, Wilson asked Stephen and me to join them for a meeting. After greeting us and exchanging pleasantries, Wilson said to us, "Washington wants to do something new with the interrogation." He introduced us to Boris, who he said had developed the new method of interrogation.

"Why is a change needed?" Stephen asked Wilson. "I know we haven't gotten everything from him yet, but so far it's been a series of successful interrogations."

Stephen was visibly annoyed. "I've interviewed terrorists before. It's a process. This guy is cooperating, and we're on the right track, so why stop?"

"I know," Wilson said, "but Washington feels that Abu Zubaydah knows much more than he's telling you, and Boris here has a method that will get that information quickly."

"What's your method?" I asked Boris, turning to him. He said that he would force Abu Zubaydah into submission. His idea was to make Abu Zubaydah see his interrogator as a god who controls his suffering. Everything would be taken away from Abu Zubaydah: his bed, his sheets, and even his clothes. If he cooperated he would be given these things back, and if he failed to cooperate, harsher and harsher techniques would be used. "Pretty quickly you'll see Abu Zubaydah buckle and become compliant," Boris declared.

"For my technique to work," he said, "we need to send the message to Abu Zubaydah that until now he had the chance to cooperate, but he blew it. He has to understand that we know he was playing games, and that the game is now over." He finished by telling us: "You two will only see Abu Zubaydah one final time. You will tell him that your 'boss' will take over. He alone will speak to Abu Zubaydah. He will determine when Abu Zubaydah eats and sleeps, and whether he lives or dies. After that you will never see him again." Boris added that the boss would be the CTC interrogator, Ed.

As Boris explained his plan, Stephen and I looked at each other in surprise. "Why is this necessary," I asked, turning to Wilson and Frank, "given that Abu Zubaydah is cooperating and has been giving us very important intelligence?"

Boris interrupted. "You may have gotten results, but it relies on you spending time talking to Abu Zubaydah and outwitting him, while my method is more effective. He'll become fully compliant without us having to do any work."

I had heard enough. Boris clearly didn't understand the nature of ideologically motivated Islamic terrorists like Abu Zubaydah. "These things won't work on people committed to dying for their cause," I warned him. "People like Abu Zubaydah are prepared to blow themselves up and die. People like him are prepared to be tortured and severely beaten. They expect to be sodomized and to have family members raped in front of them! Do you really think stripping him naked and taking away his chair will make him cooperate? Do you know who you're dealing with?"

"This is science," was Boris's response. He seemed shocked to have someone challenging him. Former colleagues of his later told me that he always viewed himself as the smartest person in any room and disliked anyone who questioned him. But I wasn't finished.

"So why are you going down a path that can jeopardize the endgame?"

"We don't need to go down the path," Boris replied. "It's easy. He'll fold quickly."

"Don't you realize that if you try to humiliate him, you're just reinforcing what he expects us to do and what he's trained to resist?" I had no idea at that point that Boris's plans would warp into what later became known as EITs.

"You'll see," said Boris. "It's human nature to react to these things. You'll soon see how quickly he folds. Human beings always want to make life better for themselves. You'll see."

"He's not a prostitute or a common criminal," I replied. "His life getting better involves us all being killed or converting to his brand of Islam. This won't work."

"You'll see," Boris responded. He had a condescending look on his face, as if he couldn't be bothered with speaking to such simpletons.

"Have you ever questioned an Islamic terrorist before?" I asked him.
"No."

"Have you ever conducted any interrogations?"

"No," he said again, "but I know human nature." I was taken aback by his response. I couldn't believe that someone with no interrogation or terrorism experience had been sent by the CIA on this mission.

I spoke to Wilson and Frank privately and asked, "Is this a joke? What's going on? The guy has no experience. This is ridiculous."

"Give him a chance," Wilson said. "His ideas might work." Frank told us that Boris was very well known in his field: psychology. He added that we had no choice but to go along with his methods.

"He is in charge," Frank added.

Wilson then said, "You know what, Ali, he's meant to be an expert. Let's just give this guy a chance." Wilson seemed to hope that Boris's technique would work. Stephen and I had no choice. The CIA was in charge and our orders were to assist the CIA officers.

Stephen and I went into Abu Zubaydah's hospital room. We repeated what Boris had told us to say: that we wouldn't see him anymore and that Ed, who had walked in with us, was our boss and that now he alone would be in charge.

Abu Zubaydah looked shocked. "What's going on?" he asked me. "I am cooperating. What's with these games?" He looked searchingly at Stephen and me, as if we should back him up. But we couldn't say anything. He then took a hard look at the CTC interrogator, Ed, who is of Middle Eastern descent. Correctly guessing what country he was from, he asked us to confirm it. "No," I told him, "he is an American, and he is my boss." And we walked out. I had a sinking feeling in my stomach that a big mistake was being made.

Abu Zubaydah was taken out of the hospital and brought back to our original location. It had been transformed in our absence. An actual cell had been built for him, monitored by hidden cameras and microphones. It took me a long time to fall asleep that night. I stared at the ceiling, struggling to understand why a contractor with no interrogation or Islamic terrorism experience was running our nation's high-value detainee interrogation program. It didn't make sense.

Boris's first action was to order Abu Zubaydah to be stripped naked. Nudity would humiliate him, Boris said, and he'd quickly become compliant in order to get his clothes back. The guards and the medical team were all instructed by Boris to put on masks, so that Ed's face was the only face Abu Zubaydah would see.

Ed went into the cell, as instructed by Boris, and said, "Tell us what you know." Abu Zubaydah seemed confused.

"What do you want to know?"

"You know," Ed responded, and walked out. Ed had replied as he had been told to by Boris.

Boris announced that loud music would be blasted into Abu Zubaydah's cell. The nudity would continue as well. The music, Boris said, would become so unbearable that Abu Zubaydah would start speaking to end the noise. The same track of rock music was blasted into the cell, over and over, for a whole day. Those of us listening in the monitoring room soon got sick of the music, and we could only imagine what Abu Zubaydah was going through. Boris sent Ed into the cell. "Tell us what you know," Ed told Abu Zubaydah.

"What do you want to know?" Abu Zubaydah responded. Ed walked out.

A white noise machine that Boris had requested arrived. Boris told us that the reason the loud music had failed was because it was the wrong type of noise. He had intended to use the white noise machine all along—he was just using the loud music as a stopgap measure until the machine arrived. It was about three feet tall, and I thought that perhaps it must be something special. But when it was switched on, it made the same sound as a commercial white noise machine that people use when sleeping. "This will make him talk?" I asked Wilson. "You've got to be kidding me."

Stephen said, "They could have just turned on the air-conditioning, which makes a similar noise." This went on for three or four days, with the same question and response between Ed and Abu Zubaydah ("Tell us what you know." "What do you want to know?"). No intelligence was gained from Abu Zuabydah.

Boris then said that what was needed to make Abu Zubaydah talk was sleep deprivation. Stephen and I questioned whether sleep deprivation would actually harm Abu Zubaydah and render him less useful to us. The CIA officers on the ground were in agreement with us about the risk of such an approach, and they requested guidance from Langley.

The message came back that Boris could deprive Abu Zubaydah of sleep, but for no more than twenty-four hours. Boris was jubilant, and said that after the sleep deprivation, Abu Zubaydah's will would be broken and he would automatically give up all the information he knew.

The sleep deprivation lasted for twenty-four hours. But like the nudity, the loud noise, and the white noise, it didn't work. Abu Zubaydah kept asking, "What do you want to know?" And Ed would walk out. Abu Zubaydah didn't give up a shred of information.

Every moment that Stephen and I had previously spent with Abu Zubaydah, from our first hour with him, we had gained intelligence from him. Slowly but surely he had cooperated, giving information that saved lives. Now we had to sit and watch for days as nothing was gained through techniques that no reputable interrogator would even think of using.

I tried reasoning with the CIA officers present in the hope that they would appeal to their headquarters. Terrorists are trained to resist torture. As shocking as Boris's methods might be to us, the training terrorists receive in training camps prepares them for much worse—the sort of torture they would expect if caught by dictatorships, for example. Being attacked by dogs, being sodomized, and having family members raped in front of them are some of the things they are physically and mentally prepared to endure. And Abu Zubaydah was not an ordinary terrorist trainee. He was the external emir of Khaldan; he had *supervised* the training process there. Sleep deprivation and nudity would be unlikely to work on a regular terrorist, let alone someone of Abu Zubaydah's stature and experience.

. . .

After the failure of sleep deprivation, Wilson began having doubts about Boris. He contrasted our previous successes with the dearth of information under Boris's regime. He began to realize that our evaluation of Abu Zubaydah—as a major terrorist facilitator, but not the number three in al-Qaeda—was correct, as was our warning that Boris's experiments wouldn't work on a terrorist like this one.

Other CTC officials and local CIA officers also began to develop doubts, and their original openness to trying Boris's techniques was replaced by growing skepticism. They had limited or no interrogation experience and didn't know anything about Abu Zubaydah, so at first didn't know better. Boris had seemed to know what he was talking about.

But then they saw that Boris's experiments were evolving into a risky situation with possible legal ramifications. They also began to realize that while Boris came across as being full of confidence, in reality he was just experimenting. His experience was limited to the classroom. He'd never been involved in an actual interrogation of a terrorist before. Wilson led the effort to put Stephen and me back in control of the interrogation.

Boris dismissed any questions about what he was doing. He tried to rally his supporters and explain away his failure by saying that in fact a twenty-four-hour period of sleep deprivation wasn't enough. "A minimum of forty-eight hours is really needed for sleep deprivation to be successful," he announced.

Shortly after the initial CTC contingent had arrived with Boris, a team of CIA analysts, mostly young, had followed. They were unfortunately very receptive to the arguments Boris made, as they believed that Abu Zubaydah was the number three or four in al-Qaeda and therefore wasn't cooperating. Almost all of them admired Boris and seemed convinced that we were failing with Abu Zubaydah. Some of the young analysts believed that talk was boring and that we needed to be tough. Boris sent a request to CIA headquarters asking for permission to try a longer period of sleep deprivation.

CIA headquarters wasn't being challenged only by our vocal minority at the location. After a few days of getting no information, there were inquiries from other parts of the U.S. intelligence community asking why, all of sudden, no information was being transmitted. The result of all this push-back and questioning was that CIA headquarters authorized Stephen and me to reengage with Abu Zubaydah. Although Boris was not called off the case, this was an admission that his experiments weren't working; it was also breaking Boris's cardinal rule that only one person would deal with Abu Zubaydah—his "god." Boris was unhappy, but he had no choice—for once CIA headquarters was taking our side.

Before speaking to Abu Zubayah, I had a condition that I made clear to Wilson. "We won't go in while he's naked, or while Boris is playing any of his games." He told us to do whatever we wanted. I took a towel to Abu Zubaydah. He was sitting naked on the floor and looked surprised to see us. I gave him the towel, and he nodded. I knew that given his cultural and religious taboos regarding nudity, my action was appreciated. He covered himself. Then he looked at us.

"Why are you doing this?" he asked, referring to Boris's experiments. His facial expression was one of genuine bewilderment. While we understood and agreed with his sentiments, we couldn't tell him. Abu Zubaydah would then know that our side was dysfunctional, and he would clam up altogether, even with us.

"You need to cooperate, Zayn," I told him. He had a puzzled look on his face. "We told you, our boss is not happy. He knows that you are not cooperating and are still playing games." I shifted the focus of the conversation and started chatting. Slowly, over a period of a few hours, we reengaged him.

Frank, the CTC polygrapher, worked with Stephen and me when we went back in. He was a trained interrogator and shared our views. We took turns with Abu Zubaydah.

Frank's technique in working with Abu Zubaydah was to focus on convincing him that it was in his interest to cooperate. He would tell him, "Don't lie; it's better to tell the truth. We know all about you, so lying just drags out the process." He focused on behavioral psychology.

Stephen and I had a different approach. We worked on establishing rapport, and on showing Abu Zubaydah—with our knowledge of his background, his friends, and of the international terrorist network—that we knew all about him and that it was just silly to lie to us. It would just embarrass him. And as we had formed a relationship with him, his lying would be an insult to us, his "friends."

When one of the three of us was in the interrogation room, the others were in an adjacent room watching on a closed circuit television (CCTV) screen. Boris and CIA analysts monitoring and supporting the interrogations were in the room, too, and I quickly learned that Boris hated Frank. This was presumably because Frank was an actual interrogator, and by word and action made it clear that he disagreed with Boris and supported our approach to interrogation.

When Frank was in with Abu Zubaydah, Boris often made sarcastic remarks about Frank to the others in the room: "He's boring the hell out of him," he might say, or "You know what Abu Zubaydah is saying right now? He's saying, 'Just shoot me.'" Some of the young analysts would laugh at anything Boris said. Stephen and I had no idea what he said about us when we were out of the room, but we could guess.

Ignoring Boris, we picked up with Abu Zubaydah where we had left off in the hospital. We began discussing plots and other important subjects, and pretty soon he began giving us a steady stream of intelligence. This was around April 20, 2002, and we led Abu Zubaydah to a discussion of his movements after 9/11.

He told us that he and other terrorists had been evacuated from Kandahar, and then Afghanistan in general, because of the Northern Alliance's advance on Taliban positions. He had traveled primarily with people connected to Khaldan. He had picked a group to travel with him from Bermel, on the border between Pakistan and Afghanistan, to guesthouses in Pakistan.

As a rule, for security reasons, Abu Zubaydah usually only traveled with people he knew. But on this occasion he had agreed to travel with two individuals he didn't know, because of the passports they carried. One was a man of Eritrean or Ethiopian origin who had a fraudulent British passport, and the second was someone who seemed to be from Latin America, with an American passport. Abu Zubaydah said he was "Hispanic" and looked "like he's from Peru."

Foreign passports, especially British and American ones, were a prized commodity. Having one meant that there was no need for visas or false documents; the holder of such a passport could get into countries easily. While the British passport was fraudulent, Abu Zubaydah told us that he had examined it, it was a very good fake, and he believed it would work. He viewed himself as an expert in fraudulent documents.

Abu Zubaydah's group was smuggled by Lashkar-e-Taiba. The group stayed for about ten days in the Federally Administered Tribal Areas (FATA) region, then traveled to Lahore, where they remained in one guesthouse for about another ten days and a second for about twenty days. From there they moved to the apartment building in Faisalabad. Abu Zubaydah had been in Faisalabad for about four weeks when he was captured during the U.S.-Pakistani raid and brought to the secret location.

In the guesthouse in Faisalabad, the situation was tense; Abu Zubaydah's group kept to themselves. They were out of their comfort zone and worried about being betrayed. Abu Zubaydah had his own room and avoided most of the others. Often he would go to other locations to meet other top operatives and find out what was going on in Afghanistan.

There were two Saudis in the guesthouse, Abdullah al-Muslim (alias al-Sharbi) and Jobran. They stayed up all night and slept during the day, interacting little with those in the guesthouse who had more traditional sleeping habits. Abdullah had studied in the United States and spoke English well. When the other operatives discovered this, they asked him to teach them English. One such operative was Mohammed Samir (alias Akrama al-Sudani), a member of the Khaldan *shura* committee.

Abu Zubaydah kept an eye on the two individuals with the British and American passports. They were constantly with each other, using the computer and talking behind closed doors. They sought out Abu Zubaydah and told him they had a plan to follow up on 9/11 and deal a devastating blow to America.

"What's your plan?" he asked, curious.

"We'll create a dirty bomb and strike at an American city," one of the men said.

With their passports, they told Abu Zubaydah, they could easily get into the United States. "That's true," Abu Zubaydah said, "but how do you plan on getting uranium for your bomb?"

"We'll hijack a truck that carries it to a hospital or a research facility in a university," one of the men told him. "We've worked it all out."

Abu Zubaydah was surprised at their ignorance. "It's not that easy. Anyway, after you get the uranium, how do you plan on enriching it?"

"That's the easy part. We've looked it up on the Internet. All we need to do is swirl it around quickly in a bucket." They showed him white extremist websites that explained how to do it.

Abu Zubaydah thought they were fools, but because of their passports they could be of use for another mission, so he didn't dismiss them. He packed the two off via train to KSM in Karachi, informing him that he "might be able to use them for something else because of their passports. If not, give them some money and I'll use them."

"What were their names?" I asked Abu Zubaydah. He didn't recall their real names, but gave me their aliases and a description of each man. The one with the British passport was known as Talha and the American as Abdullah al-Muhajir. We cabled this information straight to Langley, recommending that an international alert be put out for the two. This was done.

A message came back from the CIA station in another country that they had passport pictures of two individuals fitting those descriptions. A sharp CIA officer there had made the connection. The Pakistanis had detained the two as they tried to leave Pakistan, suspicious that their passports were fraudulent. The passports were sent to the British and American embassies, respectively, to check whether they were legitimate.

The U.S. Embassy responded that the American passport, belonging to Jose Padilla, was legitimate, as indeed it was. The British said their passport, under the name Binyam Mohamed, was fraudulent—so much for Abu Zubaydah's estimate. As a result the Pakistanis had released Padilla and held Mohamed for further questioning.

The two passport photos were scanned and sent to us, and the next morning I showed the two pictures to Abu Zubaydah. "Recognize these men?" I asked.

"Yes," he replied, eyes wide open, shocked that we had their pictures. "Didn't I tell you from day one that you do not know what I know?" I asked. An international search for Padilla began.

In the meantime, I asked Abu Zubaydah about his comment to KSM that if he didn't have a use for the two men, he, Abu Zubaydah, would use them. "What would you have used them for?"

"I planned to fill lots of apartment buildings across America with explosives. I would then tell [President] Bush to release all brothers who are prisoners in U.S. jails, including Sheikh Omar Abdul Rahman [the Blind Sheikh], or I would blow up the buildings. Because no one would know how many buildings across the country had explosives in them, it would create chaos and confusion," he said.

"How did you plan to speak to President Bush?" I asked.

"I'd call the White House and say put me through to Bush. If they didn't, I would blow up buildings until they did."

"Just like that you'd call?"

"Yes," he replied, shrugging his shoulders, as if he didn't think it was a big deal.

Abu Zubaydah also said he planned to attack gas stations across the country and a major bridge in New York. "Which bridge in New York?" I asked.

"I don't remember the name," he said.

I started listing them: "Brooklyn, Manhattan, George Washington . . ."

"I've got it," he interrupted, snapping his fingers. "It's the one in the second Godzilla movie." We checked on the Internet and saw it was the Brooklyn Bridge.

"Why the Brooklyn Bridge?" I asked.

"We were watching *Godzilla* one day, and we saw what happened when Godzilla stepped onto the bridge, and we imagined the devastation we could cause by blowing it up."

While talking about Padilla, I asked Abu Zubaydah, "How do you refer to yourself? Are you a terrorist, a mujahid, a brother?"

"What's the difference?" he replied. "They're all the same."

"So you'd refer to yourself as a terrorist?"

"Sure, why not?"

"Really?"

"Yes, sure. You're acting as if terrorism is a bad word," he said.

"Isn't it?"

"No," he replied, "terrorism was first mentioned by God." And he quoted a passage from the Quran: "Make ready for them whatever force and strings of horses you can, to terrorize thereby the enemy of God and your enemy . . ." (8:60). The passage really is saying to put fear into the enemy so that they don't attack you—it's about deterrence—but Abu Zubaydah took it literally.

Continuing with the combination of interpersonal, cognitive, and emotional interrogation strategies that had already yielded so much, we requested, and were granted, permission from Langley to use three classified wiretapped conversations involving Abu Zubaydah. I put the three tapes in the interrogation room. To give the impression that we had a full library of such tapes, we bought a few dozen blank tapes and labeled them. We set them up and brought in Abu Zubaydah.

I started by asking questions that I knew the answers to, based on the recorded tapes. "Do you know about ———?" I asked, naming a subject.

"No," he replied.

"Are you sure?"

"Yes."

"Why are you lying?"

"I'm not."

"Okay," I said, and played a tape with his voice speaking about the subject. He went red.

I asked another question, this time about certain funds being used by a terrorist organization. "I don't know anything about it," he said.

"Are you sure?"

"Yes."

"Again you're lying."

I then played a tape of him talking about it. He went red again. We repeated this one more time.

Finally, I asked him about a large amount of money coming from

Saudi Arabia for a terrorist operation—something I knew had happened but that I didn't have any details on. "Are you going to tell me about this and stop pretending you don't know, or shall I just play the tape?" I asked him.

"Okay, okay," he responded, "there is no need." He gave us the information. Jackpot.

My fluency in Arabic was a definite plus in carrying out this ploy, as the recordings were all in Arabic and I did not need a translator; nor could Abu Zubaydah deny or lie about the context. But there were many tricks we used to outwit Abu Zubaydah that didn't require Arabic.

Professional interrogators know that one of the central points of influence on a detainee is the impression he has of the evidence against him. The interrogator has to do his or her homework and become an expert in every detail known to the intelligence community about the detainee. The interrogator then uses that knowledge to impress upon the detainee that everything about him is known and that any lie will be easily detected.

In contrast, attempting to "break" detainees into compliance without knowing anything about them or the level of their involvement can have disastrous consequences. Interrogators will not know whether information they are given is accurate, pointless, or false.

The interrogator also uses the fear that the detainee feels as a result of his capture and isolation from his support base. People crave human contact, and this is especially true in some cultures. The interrogator turns this knowledge to advantage by becoming the one person the detainee can talk to and who listens to what he has to say. He uses this to encourage the detainee to open up.

Acting in a nonthreatening way isn't what the terrorist expects from a U.S. interrogator. This adds to the detainee's confusion and makes him more likely to cooperate. Our approach also utilizes the need the detainee feels to maintain a position of respect and value to the interrogator. Because the interrogator is the one person speaking to and listening to the detainee, a relationship is built—and the detainee doesn't want to jeopardize it. This was very much the case with us and Abu Zubaydah, and we were able to capitalize on it.

• • •

As Stephen and I were in the middle of writing our report on Padilla, Abu Zubaydah's plan to fill American apartment buildings with bombs, and the other intelligence he had given us, Boris walked into our room with a big smile. He came up to me, shook my hand, and said, "I had you all wrong. It was great."

Stephen and I looked at each other in surprise. Our success had undermined his entire approach and had shown that our technique was the effective one. All I could say in response was: "There is a lot of work to do here." I suspected that Wilson had told Boris to come to us to try to repair the relationship. At that point Wilson was still higher up than Boris, as he was a CTC employee and Boris was just a contractor.

Based on the intelligence we got, on May 17, 2002, FBI headquarters sent out threat warnings to American apartment building owners generally, and extra security was added to the Brooklyn Bridge. At the same time, the international manhunt launched for Padilla was closing in on him. The Pakistanis knew that he had headed to Egypt. From there we discovered that he had gone to Switzerland. He was tracked to Zurich, where he boarded a plane for Chicago. A contingent of Swiss officials followed him onto the plane. FBI agents based in New York headed to Chicago to pick him up.

The New York office was given the Padilla case because of his al-Qaeda connection. Kenny Maxwell and the JTTF were in charge, and on a secure line I spoke to Kenny about Padilla. Kenny told me that they planned to arrest him as soon as he landed. He sounded annoyed with this decision. His preference, he said, was to instead monitor Padilla and see who met up with him in Chicago.

I fully agreed with Kenny. I found it strange that Padilla was heading to Chicago. He was raised in Florida and lived in New York. "What is the Chicago connection?" I asked.

"That's what I'd like to find out," Kenny agreed. He said that headquarters had decided to pick up Padilla on arrival out of fear of losing the tail. They didn't want to take any risks and thought it was safest to just arrest him. I understood their concerns.

As Padilla stepped off the plane at Chicago's O'Hare International

Airport, FBI agents pulled him aside, executing a material witness warrant issued by the Southern District of New York. He was searched and was found to have ten thousand dollars with him, along with a cell phone and a personal telephone book. (Padilla is in a U.S. jail today, while Binyam Mohamed is a free man in Britain.)

The material witness warrant was issued based on an affidavit sworn to by Joe Ennis—Alabama Joe. While the "Ennis affidavit" remains classified, parts of it have been quoted in unclassified court documents: "on or about April 23rd CS-1 (Abu Zubaydah) was shown two photographs." The affidavit states that Abu Zubaydah identified the men in the pictures as being Padilla and Binyam Mohamed. Both the Ennis affidavit and the material witness warrant were signed by the then chief judge of the Southern District, Michael Mukasey, who went on to become President George W. Bush's third attorney general.

After Padilla was apprehended, John Ashcroft, Bush's first attorney general, held a press conference on the arrest in Moscow, where he was traveling at the time. He described Padilla as a "known terrorist" who was pursuing an "unfolding terrorist plot" to launch a dirty bomb in an American city. This wasn't true; the former attorney general was misinformed. While Padilla was a committed terrorist set on trying to harm America, he was a brain transplant away from making a dirty bomb, and there was no unfolding plot. Padilla was the plot. Later, when I returned to New York, I was shocked to see Padilla on the cover of magazines labeled as "the dirty bomber."

What Ashcroft said just didn't fit with the information we had cabled to Langley. The exaggeration of Padilla's expertise and ability unnecessarily instilled fear in the American people. Ashcroft's statement was not only inaccurate, it also made us look foolish in the eyes of al-Qaeda and others who knew their real intentions. The message was that it was easy to fool the United States.

While we continued to question Abu Zubaydah, CIA officials at the location whom we had grown close to told me that Boris and his backers in Washington were agitating for him to retake control. They were still pushing for a longer period of sleep deprivation, having settled on the argument that the only reason his experiments on Abu Zubaydah had failed was because sleep deprivation hadn't gone on for long enough. In the meantime Boris tried interfering with our interrogation a few times.

One morning Stephen and I walked into Abu Zubaydah's cell for a session, and we shivered. The room was very cold. We saw that Abu Zubaydah's skin was a bit bluish. It was clear that the room temperature had been deliberately lowered. Boris was trying temperature manipulation, even though we were in control of the interrogation and had been assured that his experiments would be stopped.

I walked out and told Boris that Abu Zubaydah was cold. "Are you playing with the temperature?" I asked directly.

"No, I'm not."

"Go check." I told him, "The room is very cold." Boris put on a mask—he was still trying to play his game of not having Abu Zubaydah see anyone's face other than Ed's, despite the fact that Stephen, Frank, and I didn't wear masks—and went through the motions of checking the temperature and Abu Zubaydah's pulse. Boris then walked out, past Stephen and me, and announced to the team of CIA analysts, "Everything's fine." There was a hint of sarcasm in his tone, as though he thought Stephen and I had been making things up.

I wasn't going to play games with Boris. "Just turn it up right now," I said. I checked with the local CIA officers; none of them were aware of Boris's having received permission for temperature manipulation. I told Boris as much, and he walked off, muttering, and said he'd turn the temperature up.

I made some tea and brought it in to Abu Zubaydah. "Here. This will warm you up." He was silent. I studied him. He looked shaken. He had always been friendly and would engage us as soon as we entered the room. Now he was silent and unsmiling.

"Who are you?" he suddenly asked me. I knew he was playing a game. He couldn't have forgotten us already; nor could the chill in the room have done that kind of damage.

"Who are you?" I responded, rather than answering.

"I'm Mahmoud el-Meligi," he said. Stephen looked blankly at Abu Zubaydah. The name meant nothing to him. Nor did the CIA support staff watching through the cameras have any idea.

I smiled, because I knew. "Okay, Mahmoud el-Meligi," I told Abu Zubaydah, "if that's who you are, I'm Adel Imam. And when Hani comes back, I'll come back," and I walked out. I didn't stop to see Abu Zubaydah's reaction. I wanted him to see me walk straight out.

Mahmoud el-Meligi was a famous Egyptian actor. Not many people know Egyptian actors, so the name meant nothing to Stephen or the others. But I recognized the name and knew that Abu Zubaydah was playing a game and was not really delusional. I had told him I was Adel Imam because that's the name of another famous Egyptian actor—one who specializes in comedy—signaling to him that I knew he was playing a game. I also called him Hani to remind him that I knew all about him.

I poured myself a cup of tea and walked back into Abu Zubaydah's cell. He smiled at me. He was amused that I had caught him out. "Can I ask you a question?" I asked.

"Sure," he said.

"Where the hell did Mahmoud el-Meligi come from?" He laughed.

"I thought I'd try it," he said. "Once, I was picked up in Pakistan by local police. They asked me who I was. They were searching for terrorists, so I couldn't tell them who I really was. So I said I was Mahmoud el-Meligi. For some reason that was the first name that came to my head. They had no idea who that was and they accepted it. They just made me sign a paper saying I was Mahmoud el-Meligi, which I did, and then they set me free. I thought I'd try it again now to confuse you." We all laughed.

22

"We Don't Do That"

Boris wasn't the only person at the location giving us difficulties. He was in many ways just the front man for powerful backers in Washington. By this time, the Department of Justice was giving verbal permission to Langley to use the coercive interrogation techniques on Abu Zubaydah. The powers behind Boris in Washington had lots of other minions at the location as well. Every day, the contingent of wisecracking CIA analysts who sided with Boris challenged what we were doing and lectured us about how we were failing to get Abu Zubaydah to cooperate fully. In their minds, Abu Zubaydah was a senior member of al-Qaeda. Based on this assumption, they believed that he should be able to give detailed information on the leadership, down to bin Laden's hiding places. Therefore, to them, the information we were getting from Abu Zubaydah wasn't significant enough, and Boris and his techniques were necessary.

To people who knew what they were talking about, the insistence that Abu Zubaydah was the number three or four in al-Qaeda was flatly ridiculous, as were the claims that he wasn't cooperating. But the analysts kept writing reports that Abu Zubaydah was the number three or four in al-Qaeda, and they managed to get that announced to the American people.

One young CIA analyst, to "prove" to Stephen and me that Abu Zubaydah was the number three in al-Qaeda, took to lecturing us about Abu Zubaydah's role in the millennium plot in Jordan. I listened to what he had to say. He had all his facts wrong. As politely as I could, I told him: "Listen, you've got the millennium plot all wrong, and maybe that's why you've got the wrong idea about Abu Zubaydah." I began to list his mistakes.

As I corrected him, he got increasingly annoyed, his face registering a who-the-hell-are-you look. "How do you know you're right?" he demanded. "I've read all the briefing notes."

"I was in Jordan during the millennium," I told him. "I was the case agent for the plot that you're trying to quote to me. Stephen was with me in Jordan. We experienced firsthand what you're trying to tell me from a briefing paper you read."

Even on the smallest of things, the CIA analysts would challenge us, to demonstrate their expertise and point out our "failings." During one interrogation session, I got intelligence from Abu Zubaydah about two terrorists whom he identified as brothers. The CIA analysts told me afterward that Abu Zubaydah was tricking me, and that the two terrorists were not in fact brothers. Evidence, they said, that Abu Zubaydah wasn't cooperating.

I had personally gone through Abu Zubaydah's personal effects upon his capture. Among the documents was a letter from the two terrorists to their parents, which clearly indicated that they were brothers. Since the document was in Arabic and the CIA analysts couldn't read it, I patiently explained to them what the document said.

"You're wrong," one of the analysts responded. "Our translators in CTC did not say what you're saying."

"Go back and ask them to review it again," I told them. For the next few days, even more tension than usual existed between us and the CIA analysts.

A few days later, their supervisor, Jen, came up to me and gave me a hug. I was shocked. What was this about? "They were brothers. I'm sorry, you were right. The linguists back at Langley had it wrong," she said.

That apology was a rare one, and for the most part the analysts were skeptical of anything Stephen and I said. There were one or two exceptions, but their voices were drowned out. The analysts felt they knew it all and had no need for us. They'd read the briefs. That was enough. But because they had no experience with terrorists beyond reading some memos about them, they really didn't understand the broader terrorist network. Stephen put it this way: "These guys read a lot of Tom Clancy novels, but they have no idea about how things work in the real world."

At the time, this was only my personal conclusion regarding our problems with the people running the CIA interrogation program; later, it was confirmed by John L. Helgerson, the inspector general of the CIA. Helgerson investigated the program at the urging of CIA professionals who spoke out against the mistakes being made. His report, published in 2004 and declassified a few years later, details the lack of experience among the CIA people running the program. The report states: "According to a number of those interviewed for this Review, the Agency's intelligence on Al-Qa'ida was limited prior to the initiation of the CTC Interrogation Program. The Agency lacked adequate linguists or subject matter experts and had very little knowledge of what particular Al-Qa'ida leaders—who later became detainees—knew. This lack of knowledge led analysts to speculate about what a detainee 'should know,' [which] information the analyst could objectively demonstrate the detainee did know."

The report goes on to state: "When a detainee did not respond to a question posed to him, the assumption at Headquarters was that the detainee was holding back and knew more; consequently, Headquarters recommended resumption of EITs." It was a case of the blind leading the blind. It was because of this lack of knowledge in the CIA that Boris was introduced, because they didn't understand that Abu Zubaydah was cooperating, and that he wasn't "twelve feet tall"—a term my friends in the FBI used to refer to the insistence, on the part of Boris's backers in Washington, that Abu Zubaydah was a senior al-Qaeda member. It was another reference to *Braveheart*; in one scene, William Wallace, the Scottish revolutionary leader played by Mel Gibson, appears before the Scottish army and announces: "Sons of Scotland, I am William Wallace." A young soldier, having never met William Wallace before and having only heard stories about him, tells him that he can't be Wallace, because "William Wallace is seven feet tall." Wallace replies: "Yes, I've heard. Kills men by the hundreds. And if HE were here, he'd consume the English with fireballs from his eyes, and bolts of lightning from his arse."

The CIA analysts at the location, however, were representative of the views of their masters back at Langley, and soon an order came through that Boris was to be put back in charge. The line taken by experts was the same as before: Abu Zubaydah was not cooperating; he hadn't given up the information that the number three in al-Qaeda would know, and so Boris was allowed to experiment further.

While Boris in our first meeting had confidently said that Abu Zubaydah would open up easily and quickly with one or two of his techniques, telling us, "It's science," by now his tone and explanations had changed. It was as if he had come to realize that working with terrorists in person was different from classroom theory. He began speaking about how his methods would be "part of a systematic approach to diminish his ability to resist." He announced that Abu Zubaydah would be deprived of sleep for forty-eight hours now, and that they would reintroduce nudity and loud music at the same time. He had the approval from Langley. We were out. Abu Zubaydah was stripped naked, loud rock music was blasted into the cell, and he was forcibly kept awake.

Wilson had assumed that the madness of Boris's experiments was over. He protested vigorously to his superiors in Langley but got no satisfactory response. Finally, he announced that he was leaving. He packed up his things. As he waited for a car to pick him up, I sat with him. He told me, "We are almost crossing the line. There are the Geneva Conventions on torture. It's not worth losing myself for this." Wilson was referring to his morals and his license to practice. He returned to the United States.

The CTC polygrapher, Frank, repeatedly voiced his disapproval. Ed, the CTC interrogator who was playing Abu Zubaydah's "god," was also worried. Over the weeks that we were together, Ed and I had many conversations. I asked him, "Is this all approved? You do know we could get into trouble for even witnessing it if there is no approval."

"It has been approved," Ed replied, "by Gonzales." Alberto Gonzales, George W. Bush's White House counsel, was the author of a controversial January 2002 memo questioning Geneva Convention protection for al-Qaeda detainees and other terrorists. He went on to serve as Bush's second attorney general, resigning in 2007 amid allegations of perjury before Congress on a separate matter.

"Who the hell is Gonzales?" I asked, as I had never heard of him before.

"They say he's Bush's lawyer," Ed told me.

"So he's not from the Department of Justice?"

"No, he's from the White House."

"That's not enough. We need DOJ clearance for these types of things."

"You're right."

A few days later Ed came to me and said, "Our guys met with the DOJ lawyers and briefed them, and they said there's no problem with what's happening." Ed had apparently demanded a written DOJ clearance from his CIA superiors. He showed me the cable he had received. The identities of the DOJ lawyers were not mentioned in the cable, which just noted that the techniques had been verbally approved by the DOJ.

"I'd like to see something in writing from the DOJ," I told Ed. "I wouldn't rely on their word." There is a saying in government that if it's not on paper it doesn't exist: "One day the pendulum will swing the other way and someone will be blamed for this."

Ed agreed. He told me: "I'm keeping a record of every order they give me, because one day this is going to be a bad thing."

As to why Boris himself insisted on reintroducing experiments that he had seen fail firsthand, perhaps the high fees the government was paying him had something to do with it. Reports later indicated that he was paid a thousand dollars a day.

During the period of forty-eight hours of sleep deprivation, Ed would go in and tell Abu Zubaydah, "Tell us what you know." Abu Zubaydah would either ignore him or say, "What do you want to know?" Ed would walk out.

Once, Ed went through Boris's routine and told Abu Zubaydah, "Tell me what you know." Abu Zubaydah just responded by tilting his head to his left side. Boris leaped up. "Aha," he declared triumphantly, "from how he tilts his head it is clear the technique is working."

About three seconds later, we watched through the CCTV system as Abu Zubaydah tilted farther and then fell asleep. He was simply exhausted from the sleep deprivation. I would have laughed if there hadn't been lives at stake.

At another point during the forty-eight hours, at Boris's instruction, a piece of paper and a crayon were put in front of Abu Zubaydah in the hope that he would write down "intelligence." He didn't. I couldn't believe that those responsible for running the program believed that this would work, and would be so careless with an important intelligence asset.

During this whole time, we were detailing the situation on the ground and registering our protests at what was happening in classified memos to our FBI headquarters through Langley, though we didn't know whether the memos were actually reaching FBI headquarters. The information we had obtained through the use of our techniques, and the lack of information when the newly imposed techniques were used, was clear in the daily stream of cables—ours and the CTC's—to Langley. Everything, down to the crayon attempt, was reported. But it didn't make a difference. Boris had authorization from the top, and there was nothing any of us could do or say. He was allowed his forty-eight hours.

When the second round of Boris's experiments failed, once again CIA headquarters reluctantly told us that we could go back in to interrogate Abu Zubaydah. Our terms were again that Boris's experiments were stopped; otherwise, we refused to go in.

We gave Abu Zubaydah back his clothes, we switched off the music, and we let him sleep. We also gave him time to clean himself (during sleep deprivation this was refused).We gave him a Quran and let him pray.

We found it harder to reengage him this time. Boris's techniques had affected him. He was very sullen and seemed scared, but eventually we succeeded, and he reengaged. We went through photos with him, along with his diary, phone book, and the rest of his personal effects. He identified many terrorists from their pictures—people we had previously known nothing about—and what various events recorded in his diary referred to.

He told us who the numbers in his phone book belonged to and explained the roles of those people in the terrorist network. Abu Zubaydah also told us about operations that he was familiar with through his connections with Algerians and North Africans who had gone through Khaldan. He told us about operatives who passed through his camp and had been referred, by him, to al-Qaeda.

We followed up on Padilla's dirty bomb idea by asking Abu Zubaydah if he was aware of a WMD or nuclear program that al-Qaeda was working on. He said that al-Qaeda had heard about anthrax from U.S. news sources, and that he had spoken to an Egyptian chemist called Abu Khabab al-Masri who worked on poisons for al-Qaeda. He had a camp called Duranta that developed these. Abu Zubaydah said that they wanted to use anthrax but that Abu Khabab lacked the expertise to make it. At that, Abu Zubaydah passed wind—because of his stomach injuries he was only eating dietary supplements, which gave him gas. He joked, "Sorry, I apologize, but you wanted WMD, now you got it."

At times he seemed to enjoy interacting with us. During one session Stephen wrote up on a white board the information from the training manual used at Khaldan on how to survive interrogations. Next to it Stephen wrote up the behavior Abu Zubaydah was exhibiting at certain times when he wasn't fully cooperating. The idea was to show him that we knew exactly what he was doing when he was playing games.

Abu Zubaydah and I sat in chairs next to each other facing the board, and Stephen said, "Today we are going to have a class, and you and Ali are students." Abu Zubaydah raised his hand and asked, "Will there be any tests on this?"

"Yes," Stephen replied, smiling.

"But that's not fair. You're working together, so I'm sure Ali knows the answers," he said with a big grin. "Play fair, Steve Austin." He'd heard me call Stephen "Steve," and somehow he'd also seen the television show *The Six Million Dollar Man*. He would hum the theme tune when he saw Steve—the only person with this first name he had ever met. He asked him his ethnicity, and Stephen told him that he was Italian. Abu Zuabydah started singing a children's song in Italian that he had learned as a child, though he didn't know what the words meant. Stephen was familiar with the song, and, laughing, he joined in.

That was one side of Abu Zubaydah. The other showed itself when he spouted the violent rhetoric you'd expect to hear from a committed terrorist. At one point he ranted about his hatred of the West and capitalism, and the evils of big companies, globalism, and America's control of the world economy. He accused America of destroying grain and other food supplies to control prices. He also mocked Americans for spending millions of dollars on their pets when so many people were dying of hunger elsewhere in the world.

We would let him talk about these subjects, not to debate him, but to gain insight into his mind-set and learn how to outwit him in a later interrogation. We noticed that, unlike other Islamic terrorists, who would complain about the American "occupation" of Islamic lands, for example, his arguments more closely resembled those of Che Guevara. They were about social issues rather than religion; he sounded like a Communist radical. At one point I wanted to change the subject and told him, "You're giving me a headache. I'm going to get a soda. What would you like?"

"A Pepsi," he replied.

"What?" I said, feigning shock at his choosing an American brand after everything he had just said.

"Yes, I am embarrassed," he laughed. "You got me with that one."

Every terrorist I've questioned is different. Sometimes humor is needed to establish rapport. As our job is to get intelligence from them, we use whatever legal tools we can to put them at ease and gain their cooperation. It was odious to sit and laugh with a committed terrorist.

I would think of John O'Neill, my former boss and mentor, who was murdered in the World Trade Center. I would think of Lenny

Hatton. Lenny was on his way to work on the morning of 9/11 when he saw the first tower on fire. Instead of continuing to the FBI office, he went to the scene to help. And when the second tower was struck, Lenny ran into the collapsing building to help firemen and other rescuers lead people to safety. He led people out and returned for more. He was killed in the tower. I also thought of the seventeen U.S. sailors killed on the USS *Cole*. It wasn't easy talking to Abu Zubaydah. But we had to do it. To save lives and get intelligence, we'd smile as much as needed.

While there were jokes, and even though we were caring for Abu Zubaydah and saving his life, he remained committed to his cause and never stopped seeing us as the enemy. One day he was telling us about an idea he had to behead people on camera (this was before al-Qaeda actually started doing it). "That's disgusting. How can you think about beheading a human being?" I said.

"It worked when the Chechens did it to the Russians. It put fear in their hearts," he replied.

"Now that you've met us, and we've looked after you, if you captured me, would you behead me?" I asked, intending it as a joke.

He replied, "Absolutely, you're the enemy, not a question." His face was serious.

Stephen, laughing, said, "But you wouldn't kill me. We're friends?"

Abu Zubaydah looked at him and said, "No, I'd kill you first."

"Why?" Stephen asked.

"Because you used to be in the U.S. military."

"Now you've hurt my feelings," Stephen told him. I looked at Abu Zubaydah and felt so relieved that this guy was in our custody.

Abu Zubaydah told us what he thought of many of the terrorist operatives he had interacted with. One he disliked was Sawad al-Madani, a known extremist from England who had fought in Bosnia and Afghanistan, where the United States later captured him. Abu Zubaydah picked up Madani in Pakistan to smuggle him to Afghanistan. He said that Sawad annoyed others in the guesthouse because—like Zacarias Moussaoui—he wanted to wrestle people the whole time. When they first met, and Abu Zubaydah was going through customary security precautions, Sawad said to him: "Don't tell me you're Mister Intelligence. You're dealing with me now"—as if Abu Zubaydah were putting on airs or wasting both their time. At one point Abu Zubaydah went to see someone about a visa and left Sawad in his car. When he returned he found Sawad blasting music from the car and dancing—trying to pretend he wasn't a radical and blend in. "These are guys I had to deal with," Abu Zubaydah told us, shaking his head disdainfully at the memory.

As we continued to succeed with Abu Zuabydah, Boris and the CIA analysts were also now pushing an explanation as to why the forty-eight hours had failed. As one of them said, "Forty-eight hours isn't enough sleep deprivation," and "the body only breaks after forty-eight hours." One day at the safe house I saw a big coffin leaning against a wall. One of the CIA officers told me that Boris was requesting authorization to place Abu Zubaydah in it. It was clear that Boris wanted to conduct a mock burial as the next stage in his force continuum once he took over.

The CIA officers told me that Boris expected the approval to come. The coffin had been built for the purpose, a clear indication that people at CIA headquarters supported the plan. "You've got to be kidding me," I told the CIA official. He shrugged his shoulders, as if to say, We have no choice.

I opened the coffin and looked inside; some kind of padding or carpeting lined it. I told the CIA official I wanted to try it. I lay down inside, and he closed it. It was pitch black in there. It was just possible to move my head and arms a little. After a few seconds I told him to open the cover. It was chilling, despite knowing that I could get out at any time. The CIA official opened the cover and I quickly climbed out. "This is insane," I told him, and walked off. He nodded in agreement, with a discouraged look on his face.

I realized that CIA headquarters was not going to stop Boris's experiments. Our protests were being ignored. Boris was being given a blank check by the White House and CIA headquarters, and was being urged on by CIA analysts on the ground. Their lack of expertise and fear of the unknown would just lead them to authorize crazier and more abusive things that wouldn't work. The experiments would become more and more cruel, thus reducing the chances of getting reliable intelligence from Abu Zubaydah in the future. For the first time, I began to wonder whether the real intent of the people back in Washington was to collect intelligence.

What I had seen Boris try until now struck me as borderline torture. I had stayed on because I had hoped in my heart that someone in Washington would put a stop to the madness and allow us to continue to interrogate Abu Zubaydah. Until now I hadn't wanted to give up the chance of getting useful intelligence from him again. But each time Boris tried crazier things, I got more upset, and began to worry about the people running the program.

On seeing the coffin, I realized that my hopes of Boris's being removed were in vain. The person or persons running the program were not sane. With this coffin the interrogation was stepping over the line from borderline torture. Way over the line.

That's it, I said to myself. I picked up the secure phone and phoned FBI headquarters. This was the first time I had called headquarters directly. All our previous messages had gone through the standard channels, which was via e-mails sent through the CIA that were meant to be delivered to the FBI liaison, Chuck Frahm, at CIA headquarters. The situation demanded communication outside the regular channels, and I worried that our previous complaints hadn't made it to the director.

I asked the operator at FBI headquarters in Washington to put me through to the assistant director, Pat D'Amuro. I considered him a friend, and I respected him as a principled public servant and had no doubt he would be outraged by what was happening. I was right.

I explained to Pat what had happened over the past weeks, and what it looked like they were going to do next with the coffin. I finished by telling him: "I can no longer remain here. Either I leave or I'll arrest him." Beyond the immorality and un-American nature of these techniques, I couldn't stand by as we abused someone instead of gaining intelligence that would save American lives.

Pat told me that Stephen and I should immediately leave the location and go to a nearby city to wait for instructions. He was going to consult with the director of the FBI, Robert Mueller, on how best to proceed. Frank, the CTC polygrapher, joined us. As we walked around the city, Frank told me, "Hiring that guy was the worst thing I have done." There was regret and shame in his voice.

We visited the local CIA station. We had built a great relationship with all the officers. For the most part, they were on the same page as us. The CIA chief made it clear to Stephen and me that he was apprehensive about what was happening.

A day later the message came back from Mueller: "We don't do that." Pat ordered us to leave the location immediately and return to the United States. I packed up and flew back to New York.

Stephen didn't. When he reported through his chain of command and said he was going to leave, he was told to hold off leaving until further instruction. Stephen reported through his usual channel—to headquarters. Stephen and I had different chains of command. I was a field agent and reported through the New York chain of command. Stephen wasn't an operational agent at the time. He was an assigned supervisory agent in headquarters in Washington, and reported through those channels. Other people in headquarters didn't agree with Pat's order and saw a need for our continuing involvement at the site. They allowed Stephen to stay. Stephen said: "Look, Ali, things might change, and they might realize we should be in charge. And if I leave, do you trust these fucking idiots to run the program? Every time they go in, Abu Zubaydah stops talking. We need someone to do the job. What do you think?"

"Stephen, I can't stay here any longer," I told him. "This is out of control, un-American, and downright dangerous. The director agreed that we don't do this, and Pat ordered us to leave. I'm leaving. But you do what you want."

"I'm going to stay."

"Be careful," I told him, and said good-bye.

A few weeks later Stephen returned to Washington for a meeting on Abu Zubaydah. It was only then that Pat found out that Stephen had stayed. (Pat was based in Washington, and I returned to New York and so didn't see him, and no one else briefed him on Stephen's decision.)

Pat was furious that Stephen had not followed his orders, and to this day he hasn't forgiven him. He ordered Stephen not to return to the location. The FBI would not be party to the harsh techniques.

While others in headquarters disagreed with Pat and felt we needed to be part of the CTC program, Robert Mueller sided with Pat and me. He understood that things had already gone too far, and that those pushing these techniques were not prepared to turn back. And he had the final say. Stephen stayed in Washington. That was the end of the FBI's involvement in Abu Zubaydah's interrogation.

After we left, Boris had to keep introducing harsher and harsher methods, because Abu Zubaydah and other terrorists were trained to resist them. In a democracy such as ours, there is a glass ceiling on harsh techniques that the interrogator cannot breach, so a detainee can eventually call the interrogator's bluff. And that's what Abu Zubaydah did.

This is why the EIT proponents later had to order Abu Zubaydah to be waterboarded again, and again, and again—at least eighty-three times, reportedly. The techniques were in many ways a self-fulfilling prophecy, ensuring that harsher and harsher ones were introduced.

Cruel interrogation techniques not only serve to reinforce what a terrorist has been prepared to expect if captured; they give him a greater sense of control and predictability about his experience, and strengthen his resistance. By contrast, the interrogation strategy that Stephen and I employed—engaging and outwitting the terrorist—confuses him and leads him to cooperate. The art of interview and interrogation is a science, a behavioral science, and we were successful precisely because we had it down to a science.

Evidence gained from torture is unreliable. There is no way to know whether the detainee is being truthful, or just speaking to either mitigate his discomfort or to deliberately provide false information. Indeed, as KSM, who was subjected to the enhanced techniques, later told the Red Cross: "During the harshest period of my interrogation I gave a lot of false information in order to satisfy what I believed the interrogators wished to hear in order to make the ill-treatment stop."

Boris's methods were aiming at compliance rather than cooperation. In compliance you get someone to say what he thinks you'll be happy hearing, not necessarily the truth. A good example of this is the case of Ibn al-Shaykh al-Liby, Abu Zubaydah's partner at Khaldan. Liby later confessed that he "decided he would fabricate any information the interrogators wanted in order to gain better treatment and avoid being handed over to [a foreign government]." For the same reason, after undergoing waterboarding, Abu Zubaydah "confessed" to being the number three in al-Qaeda, which was a lie and a dead end for the investigators. A 2006 investigation by the Senate Select Committee on Intelligence (SSCI) found that the CIA relied heavily on information from Liby to assess connections between Iraq and al-Qaeda. This information played a crucial role in making the Bush administration's case for the 2003 U.S. invasion of Iraq, outlined in Secretary of State Colin Powell's presentation to the UN weeks before the invasion.

In contrast, the Informed Interrogation Approach yields information that is accurate, actionable, and useful in our legal process. A major problem with Boris's techniques is that they ignore the endgame. After getting intelligence from terrorists, at some point we have to prosecute them. We can't hold people indefinitely. Whether it is one year later or ten years later, eventually a trial becomes necessary; otherwise they'll have to be released. But information gained from torture is inadmissible in court. Even in military commissions—courts run and staffed by military officers, with rules and requirements different from those of regular courts—it is problematic.

I had a conversation with Ed about this, and I asked him, "What's the endgame with Abu Zubaydah after using these techniques?"

"I guess they intend that he'll go to a military commission."

"Military commissions may have a lower standard of evidence than regular courts," I replied, "but we both know that they're not kangaroo courts."

Ed and I were familiar with the operation in Guantánamo Bay, and the preparation used in other cases for military commissions. Already, in early 2002, military lawyers were telling investigators to be careful with evidence, and to keep notes. There was also the discovery process;

and anything we had we were required to share with the defense. It was clear to me that even in a military commission, evidence gained from harsh techniques wouldn't be admissible. Ed agreed.

Coercive interrogations are also slow. Days were spent on each unsuccessful technique, with nothing to show for it. We were, in effect, playing right into the hands of the enemy. The Manchester Manual instructs captured terrorists to hold off answering questions for forty-eight hours, so that their comrades can change safe houses and phone numbers, even flee the country. There is always the possibility of a "ticking time bomb" scenario hanging over any interrogation of a terrorist, which is why wasting minutes or hours, let alone whole days, is completely unacceptable.

A July 29, 2009, report by the Justice Department's Office of Professional Responsibility (OPR) stated that Boris's techniques "were not expected or intended to produce immediate results. Rather, the goal of the CIA interrogation program was to condition the detainee gradually in order to break down his resistance to interrogation." I wonder if the person who wrote the word "gradually" had any idea of the urgency of counterterrorist operations.

I later learned that Boris's path from being an independent contractor with no interrogation or Islamic extremism experience to running one of the most crucial fronts in our battle against al-Qaeda—our interrogation program of high-value detainees—had its origins on September 17, 2001. On that day, President Bush gave the CIA the authority, in an authorization known as a memorandum of notification, to capture, detain, and interrogate terrorism suspects.

In previous decades, the CIA had primarily operated as an intelligence collection agency. It was the FBI, along with military outfits such as the NCIS, the U.S. Army Criminal Investigation Command, and the U.S. Air Force Office of Special Investigations, that had interrogated suspects. John Helgerson's 2004 report on detention and interrogation activities explains in detail that the post-9/11 CIA detention program "began with almost no foundation, as the Agency had discontinued virtually all involvement in interrogations after encountering difficult issues with early interrogation programs in Central America and the Near East."

In their July 29, 2009 report, OPR investigators wrote that CIA acting general counsel John Rizzo had told them that throughout most of its history the CIA had not detained subjects or conducted interrogations. Before 9/11, CIA personnel debriefed sources (these portions were censored and do not appear in the report), but the agency was not authorized to detain or interrogate individuals. Consequently, the CIA had no institutional experience or expertise in that area. (Rizzo was incorrect. Before 9/11, the CIA's polygraph division, formerly known as the interrogation branch, was responsible for interrogations abroad. After 9/11, this responsibility was taken out of their hands and given to the CTC.)

Because of this lack of institutional experience, when President Bush ordered the CIA to institute the detention program, they needed to find someone to run it. Brought to their attention—it's not yet publicly known by whom—were two contractors, Boris and another psychologist. Helgerson writes: "In late 2001, CIA had tasked an independent contractor psychologist [Boris] . . . to research and write a paper on Al-Qaida's resistance to interrogation techniques." Boris collaborated with a Department of Defense psychologist, and "subsequently, the two psychologists developed a list of new and more aggressive EITs that they recommended for use in interrogations." (Military personnel who knew the two contractors described Boris as extremely arrogant, and his partner—whom I never met—as someone with a terrible temper. Arrogance and anger—a dangerous combination.)

I later found out from a Senate investigation that in December 2001, CIA officials had asked Boris and his partner to analyze al-Qaeda's Manchester Manual. It was on the basis of the information in this manual that the two reportedly concluded that harsh techniques would be needed to break al-Qaeda detainees. This constituted a misreading of the Manchester Manual, and in fact Boris's techniques played into what the manual instructed captured terrorists to do.

A few weeks after I left the location, I saw Pat D'Amuro. He told me that Robert Mueller had had a conversation with George Tenet, during which Mueller had asked about the lack of intelligence coming from Abu Zubaydah. (This was after Stephen and I had left the location.) Tenet had replied, "Your guys really messed him up. We have to fix him all over again." It was clear that after we left, Boris's experiments continued to fail. His backers were struggling to find a new excuse to explain away the failure.

In 2006, when President Bush gave a speech acknowledging the existence of the harsh interrogation program and listed its "successes," I received a phone call from an assistant director of the FBI. "Did you see the president's speech?" he asked.

"No," I replied. I was overseas at the time, working on a project.

"Just remember, this is still classified. Just because the president is talking about it doesn't mean that we can."

I later read through the speech and understood the phone call. The president was just repeating false information put into classified CIA memos. (I believe that President Bush was misled and briefed incorrectly regarding the efficacy of the techniques.) From that speech, and from memos on the program that were later declassified, I learned that backers of the EITs in Washington went on to claim credit for having obtained the information about Padilla's attempted operation and other intelligence from Abu Zubaydah. They also claimed credit for the news that KSM was Mokhtar, despite the fact that the CTC team wasn't even at the location when we learned that information.

The May 30 Bradbury memo states: "Interrogations of Zubaydah— again, once enhanced interrogation techniques were employed . . . identified KSM as the mastermind of the September 11 attacks." Zubaydah, according to the memo, also "provided significant information on two operatives, [including] Jose Padilla [,] who planned to build and detonate a 'dirty bomb' in the Washington DC area." And the apartment buildings and Brooklyn Bridge plots that we got from Abu Zubaydah, the CIA claimed to have gotten from KSM a year later. Apparently they had no success of their own at any time, and so they had to use ours.

There are many other errors. The May 30 Bradbury memo states that Padilla was arrested "on his arrival in Chicago in May 2003." He was arrested in May 2002. Another declassified memo states that Ramzi Binalshibh was arrested in December 2002. He was arrested in September 2002. These incorrect dates led officials to erroneously state that Padilla was captured because of waterboarding that began in August 1, 2002. In reality, this would have been factually impossible.

With the declassification of several memos, I had a chance to see the CIA's "psychological assessment" of Abu Zubaydah. The assessment was used by Jay S. Bybee (then assistant attorney general in the Department of Justice's Office of Legal Counsel) to write a memo for Rizzo on August 1, 2002, giving the CIA permission to use the enhanced interrogation techniques.

The Bybee memo states, referencing the psychological assessment: "According to this assessment, Zubaydah, though only 31, rose quickly from very low level mujahedin to third or fourth man in al Qaeda. He has served as Usama Bin Laden's senior lieutenant. In that capacity, he has managed a network of training camps. . . . He also acted as al Qaeda's coordinator of external contacts and foreign communications. Additionally, he has acted as al Qaeda's counter-intelligence officer and has been trusted to find spies within the organization. . . . Zubaydah has been involved in every major terrorist operation carried out by al Qaeda. . . . Moreover he was one of the planners of the September 11 attacks."

To this day, I don't understand how anyone could write such a profile. Not only did we know this to be false before we captured Abu Zubaydah, but it was patently false from information obtained after we captured him. Yet this psychological assessment was cited for the next couple of years in internal government memos.

The psychological assessment also says that Abu Zubaydah wrote al-Qaeda's manual on resistance techniques and that he is "a highly self directed individual who prizes his independence." Apparently they didn't even pay attention to their own rhetoric. Why would someone who "prizes his independence" (which is true) join an organization that requires blind obedience to a leader? And if he wrote al-Qaeda's manual on resistance techniques, why would they think harsh techniques (which pale in comparison to what they expect) would work? It seems they just put down on paper whatever they could to show that Abu Zubadyah was "twelve feet tall."

According to the CIA inspector general's 2004 report by Helgerson, official CIA memos about Abu Zubaydah not only hid the successes we had with him before we left but even made it look as though we had never been there: "To treat the severe wounds that Abu Zubaydah suffered upon his capture, the Agency provided him intensive medical care from the outset and deferred his questioning for several weeks pending his recovery. The Agency then assembled a team that interrogated Abu Zubaydah." In fact, questioning wasn't deferred at all, and it was successful.

What's especially notable about the memos authorizing the techniques is their unquestioning acceptance of information from CIA officials. Bradbury acknowledged that "he relied entirely on the CIA's representations as to the effectiveness of the EITs, and did not attempt to verify or question the information he was given." He told the OPR: "It's not my role, really, to do a factual investigation of that." With such an attitude, the watchdog was little better than a lapdog.

It wasn't only the Justice Department that really slipped up. A footnote to Bradbury's comments to the OPR that his role was not to check the facts states that one official "urged AG Gonzales and White House Counsel Fred Fielding to have a new CIA team review the program, but that the effectiveness reviews consistently relied on the originators of the program." Is it fitting for the backers of EITs to be tasked with evaluating their own effectiveness? That would be a sure, and easy, way to guarantee the conclusion they wanted.

The Bybee memo, which authorized the techniques, states: "Our advice is based upon the following facts, which you have provided to us. We also understand that you do not have any facts in your possession contrary to the facts outlined here, and this opinion is limited to these facts. If these facts were to change, this advice would not necessarily apply."

The "facts" granting authorization to use the harsh techniques were that Abu Zubaydah was not cooperating (he was) and that he was a senior al-Qaeda member (he wasn't). While the authors of the memo may not have been aware of the truth, those providing the content for the memos, and those requesting the authorization to initiate Boris's experiments, certainly were. Because the advocates of the harsh techniques were allowed to state these lies and claim our successes as their own, Boris and his partner (under the guidance of their sponsors in Washington) were then granted control over all future high-value detainees captured. Abu Zubaydah was the first person on whom the techniques were used. It was in many ways a trial or test run for the techniques. And because people in Washington rewrote the results to show that they passed the "test case," they could successfully argue that the techniques be used in the future. Boris and his partner were given control of other high-value detainees.

Back in FBI headquarters, the situation was clear. We gained information using a tried and tested and scientific approach, while what Boris was doing was un-American and ineffective. We were confident that the contractors and their crazy ideas would soon be abandoned. Little did we know that there was a wider effort to disseminate misinformation even to Justice Department officials.

I later learned—from the July 29, 2009, OPR report—that the CIA had initially requested that twelve EITs be used in the interrogation of Abu Zubaydah. They were as follows (the descriptions are from the report):

1. Attention grasp: The interrogator grasps the subject with both hands, with one hand on each side of the collar opening, in a controlled and quick motion, and draws the subject toward the interrogator.

2. Walling: The subject is pulled forward and then quickly and firmly pushed into a flexible false wall so that his shoulder blades hit the wall. His head and neck are supported with a rolled towel to prevent whiplash.

3. Facial hold: The interrogator holds the subject's head immobile by placing an open palm on either side of the subject's face, keeping fingertips well away from the eyes.

4. Facial or insult slap: With fingers slightly spread apart, the interrogator's hand makes contact with the area between the tip of the subject's chin and the bottom of the corresponding earlobe.

5. Cramped confinement: The subject is placed in a confined space, typically a small or large box, which is usually dark. Confinement in the smaller space lasts no more than two hours and in the larger space up to eighteen hours.

6. Insects: A harmless insect is placed in the confinement box with detainees.

7. Wall standing: The subject may stand about four to five feet from a wall with his feet spread approximately to his shoulder width. His arms are stretched out in front of him and his fingers rest on the wall to support all of his body weight. The subject is not allowed to reposition his hands or feet.

8. Stress positions: These positions may include having the detainee sit on the floor with his legs extended straight out in front of him with his arms raised above his head or kneeling on the floor while leaning back at a forty-five-degree angle.

9. Sleep deprivation: The subject is prevented from sleeping, not to exceed eleven days at a time. [Note: as initially proposed,

sleep deprivation was to be induced by shackling the subject in a standing position, with his feet chained to a ring in the floor and his arms attached to a bar at head level, with very little room for movement.]

10. Use of diapers: The subject is forced to wear adult diapers and is denied access to toilet facilities for an extended period, in order to humiliate him.

11. Waterboard: The subject is restrained on a bench with his feet elevated above his head. His head is immobilized and an interrogator places a cloth over his mouth and nose while pouring water onto the cloth. Airflow is restricted for twenty to forty seconds; the technique produces the sensation of drowning and suffocation.

12. [When the document was released, this paragraph was redacted by the government.]

According to the OPR report, on July 24, a Justice Department lawyer, John Yoo, "telephoned Rizzo and told him that the attorney general had authorized him to say that the first six EITs (attention grasp, walling, facial hold, facial slap, cramped confinement, and wall standing [which is actually number seven]) were lawful and that they could proceed to use them on Abu Zubaydah."

Only on August 1, 2002, at around 10:00 PM, did the Department of Justice give the agency its written legal approval that ten specific enhanced interrogation techniques would not violate the Geneva Convention torture prohibition and could be used on detainees. The memo was primarily the work of Jay Bybee and John Yoo. (There are actually two versions of the memo, classified and unclassified, and together they are referred to as the Bybee memos.) According to CIA records, the classified Bybee memo was faxed to the CIA at 10:30 PM on August 1, 2002.

After the Abu Zubaydah interrogation, Boris and his partner and supporters in Washington were fully in control of the program. Only after that did the CIA even start "training" its interrogators. According to the 2004 OIG report, only in "November 2002" did the CIA initiate "a pilot running of a two-week Interrogator Training Course designed to train, qualify, and certify individuals as Agency interrogators." Of course, two weeks isn't enough to make someone a qualified interrogator. What makes someone a qualified interrogator is not only months of training but knowledge of the detainee and of terrorism.

Enhanced interrogation techniques is a term I first heard long after I had left the secret location. While I was at the location, there was no system to what Boris and his backers were doing. They appeared to be experimenting with techniques, with no clear plan. Not only was Abu Zubaydah the first terrorist they had ever interrogated, but he was the first Islamist radical they had ever met.

The techniques that I witnessed (and described as "borderline torture") were later declared by George Tenet, in guidelines issued on January 28, 2003, to be "Standard CIA Interrogation Techniques." According to Tenet, "these guidelines complement internal Directorate of Operations guidance relating to the conduct of interrogations." His guidelines state that the standard techniques "include, but are not limited to, all lawful forms of questioning employed by US Law Enforcement and military interrogation personnel. Among Standard Techniques are the use of isolation, sleep deprivation not to exceed 72 hours, reduced caloric intake (so long as the amount is calculated to maintain the general health of the detainee), deprivation of reading material, use of loud music or white noise (at a decibel level calculated to avoid damage to the detainee's hearing), and the use of diapers for a limited period (generally not to exceed 72 hours) . . ."—the rest is redacted.

What failed with Abu Zubaydah was later declared "standard" by George Tenet. It seems that the lesson was not learned.

For the next six years, until documents regarding this period were declassified, I had to remain silent as lie after lie was told about Abu Zubaydah and the success of the techniques. One public defender of the techniques was a CIA official named John Kiriakou, who stated on national television that Abu Zubaydah was uncooperative until he was waterboarded for thirty-five seconds. Kiriakou said he witnessed this himself. "It was like flipping a switch," Kiriakou said; after that, Abu Zubaydah spilled everything. Later Kiriakou admitted that he had given false information, and we learned that Abu Zubaydah had been waterboarded eighty-three times—and that no new valuable information was gained from him. (Today Kiriakou works as a staff member on the Senate Foreign Relations Committee.)

In FBI headquarters, Boris, his partner, and their high-level backers in Washington were referred to as the "poster boys," a reference to the FBI's Most Wanted list, where we believed their methods would one day land them.

What happened at the secret location with Abu Zubaydah was originally taped by the CIA. The tapes were destroyed by the CIA before investigators could see them. Declassified internal CIA e-mails show senior CIA officials stating the urgency and importance of destroying the tapes. According to one e-mail, which records a discussion between senior officials, "the heat from destroying is nothing compared to what it would be if the tapes ever got into the public domain . . . they would make us look terrible, it would be 'devastating' to us."

One of the most damning condemnations of the CIA program came with the declassification of the CIA inspector general's 2004 report. John Helgerson examined all the claims about the effectiveness of the techniques, and he had access to the CIA classified memos. He states that while regular interrogation (our approach) achieved many successes, "measuring the effectiveness of the EITs . . . is a more subjective process and not without some concern." Moreover, he said he couldn't verify that a single threat listed by the CIA as having been thwarted was imminent. Unfortunately, the report came two years too late.

In early 2008, in a conference room that is referred to as a sensitive compartmented information facility (SCIF), I gave a classified briefing on Abu Zubaydah to staffers of the Senate Select Committee on Intelligence. The staffers present were shocked. What I told them contradicted everything they had been told by Bush administration and CIA officials.

When the discussion turned to whether I could prove everything I was saying, I told them, "Remember, an FBI agent always keeps his notes." Locked in a secure safe in the FBI New York office are my hand-written notes of everything that happened with Abu Zubaydah while I was there.

PART 7

SUCCESSES AND FAILURES

23

Guantánamo Bay

February 2002. "So tell me," I asked the elderly Afghani man sitting across from me in a detention cell in Guantánamo Bay, Cuba, "what do you know about New York and Washington?"

"I don't know what they've done," he replied, "but I'm sure they are good people."

The Afghani knew nothing about al-Qaeda or 9/11, and even thought "New York" and "Washington" were the names of people. Our first challenge at Guantánamo was to distinguish al-Qaeda and Taliban members from those wrongfully rounded up.

I arrived at Gitmo in early February 2002. The United States had just begun bringing detainees captured in Afghanistan to the U.S. detention facility. Little was known about our new prisoners, and U.S. government agencies had sent their top investigators and interrogators to help the military question and sort them. Among those gathered at the base were Bob McFadden; Ed, the CIA officer with whom I later worked on Abu Zubaydah; and Andre Khoury and John Anticev.

We had all heard stories of how Northern Alliance fighters would drive in their trucks though Pashtun tribal areas in Afghanistan and offer villagers a ride. Many had never been in a car before and eagerly took the ride. The Northern Alliance fighters, who were mostly Tajiks and hated Pashtuns, would then drive to a nearby U.S. base and tell officials that their passengers were "Taliban/al-Qaeda," and receive a reward of fifty dollars a head for their efforts.

Other detainees, however, were important figures in the al-Qaeda and Taliban networks. Early on, Andre, Ed, and I interrogated Abdul Aziz al-Matrafi, head of the Afghan offices of al-Wafa, an NGO listed as a terrorist-affiliated entity by the United States. We knew that he was viewed in the Islamic world (and that he viewed himself) as an important person, so we treated him with a great deal of respect in order to make him feel comfortable. We steadily established rapport with him, first discussing non–al-Qaeda-related matters, like his family. When we asked about his children, he started crying and told us that he missed his daughters. We then started prodding him to see if he had had any disagreements with bin Laden.

He soon told us that bin Laden had upset him, and many Saudi clerics, when he had declared that traveling to Afghanistan with one's family was the Hijra of today, implying that anyone who didn't make the pilgrimage wasn't a proper Muslim. It was a clear insult to Matrafi's backers in Saudi Arabia and to many sympathetic clerics who weren't taking their families to Afghanistan.

Once Matrafi began listing his disagreements with bin Laden, we convinced him to cooperate with us, which he did, even telling us how his own supposedly humanitarian organization would purchase weapons for jihad. Matrafi was present at several key al-Qaeda meetings, including a lunch with bin Laden, Zawahiri, KSM, and the paraplegic Saudi mullah Khalid al-Harbi, who appeared with bin Laden in the infamous video praising the 9/11 attacks. (Found on November 9, 2001, the video was released by the Department of Defense on December 13.)

Many al-Qaeda sympathizers had traveled to Afghanistan shortly after 9/11, thinking that divine prophecies were being fulfilled and that it was the end of America. They quoted to each other apocalyptic hadith similar to the ones citing the black banners from Khurasan. Harbi is heard on bin Laden's 9/11 video speaking about mujahideen everywhere flying to Afghanistan as part of a heavenly plan.

Al-Wafa sponsored Harbi's trip, and he flew to Iran and from there was smuggled across the border into Afghanistan. Bin Laden, who considered Harbi a friend, held a lunch honoring him—the lunch attended by Matrafi. It was then, with KSM apparently videotaping, that bin Laden read his poem celebrating 9/11 and gave credit to Mokhtar, or KSM.

When fighters were picked up in Afghanistan after 9/11, they often had their real passports with them, as they were trying to flee the country; but their names meant little to us, as we primarily knew al-Qaeda members by their aliases. Our first challenge at Gitmo, therefore, was to match real names to aliases.

I looked through photos of detainees. One man of interest appeared to be Moroccan and in his forties, and fit Abu Jandal's description of Abu Assim al-Maghrebi, who supervised bin Laden's bodyguards. His name, according to the file, was Abdullah Tabarak, and the notes in the file said that he had been captured, with others, crossing the Afghani border into Pakistan. The whole group claimed that they were in Afghanistan to teach the Quran. Their cover story seemed suspicious. I began looking through the photos of the other group members to see if I recognized any of them as well. Ibrahim al-Qosi, a Sudanese, seemed to match a description I had been given by several al-Qaeda members, including L'Houssaine Kherchtou, Fahd al-Quso, and Abu Jandal, of Abu Khubaib al-Sudani, who had been with bin Laden from the start and served at one point as an accountant for al-Qaeda. He was also Abu Assim al-Maghrebi's son-in-law.

I asked for copies of the photos of Tabarak and Qosi to be sent to Mike Anticev, John's brother and a squad mate at I-49 in New York. They would be shown to Junior and L'Houssaine Kherchtou, the former al-Qaeda members who had become U.S. government cooperating witnesses. The message came back a day later from Mike that the witnesses had separately identified the men in the photos as Abu Assim and Abu Khubaib.

. . .

When the first detainees were brought to Gitmo, the base was split between two commanders: Maj. Gen. Michael E. Dunlavey, the commander of Joint Task Force 170, responsible for military interrogations; and Brig. Gen. Rick Baccus, the commander of Joint Task Force 160, responsible for running the base and guarding prisoners.

FBI agents at Gitmo operated under the auspices of the Defense Department's Criminal Investigation Task Force (CITF), headed by Col. Brittain P. Mallow, from the army's Criminal Investigation Command. (The latter is referred to as CID, an acronym formed from the original name of the unit, the Criminal Investigation Division.) Colonel Mallow's deputy was Mark Fallon, from NCIS. CITF was charged with investigating the detainees and deciding who should be prosecuted, a separate function from the military interrogators, whose mandate was just to get intelligence.

I took the pictures of Tabarak and Qosi to General Dunlavey. He told me that while other groups of prisoners were violent and regularly fought with guards and caused trouble, Tabarak, Qosi, and the other detainees in their bloc were "model prisoners." General Dunlavey asked, "What do you recommend doing?"

"First we need to take them out of their comfort zone," I said, "and show them that we know who they are and that the game is up. We also need to isolate them from their support base. Tabarak is the most senior al-Qaeda guy we have caught since 9/11. He's higher up than Abu Jandal. He's important and should be an amazing source of intelligence, if we handle him correctly."

General Dunlavey escorted Tabarak to the brig, at the time the only facility at Gitmo available to separate valuable detainees from the general population. One problem, however, was that the brig is located on the top of a hill in the middle of the island, and the cells had windows, enabling inmates to see where they were and who was coming and going. We were not allowed to tell detainees that they were being held in Cuba, though eventually they guessed (and later on they knew for certain, from Red Cross visits). We also didn't want them to see who was coming and going, so the guards covered the windows.

Once Abu Assim was installed in the brig, I went to see him. "Abu Assim, As-Salāmu `Alaykum."

"Wa `Alaykum as-Salām."

Speaking in Arabic, I got straight to the point. "I know who you are and I know your importance. The game is up."

"You've got the wrong person," he replied. "I don't know what you're talking about."

"Denial is pointless," I told him. "I have witnesses who have identified you, fellow al-Qaeda members. We are aware of your long journey with Sheikh Abu Abdullah. My sources told me a lot about you and your family." I invoked the bin Laden alias to convey the point that we understood the group's dynamics.

"My family, what about them?"

"There is a lot, after Abu Ata'a was killed."

"Who is Abu Ata'a?" he interrupted.

"Abu Ata'a al-Tunisi, your son-in-law, who was killed fighting against Ahmed Shah Massoud. Al-Qaeda even named a mountain after him on the front lines in Afghanistan. Do you remember him?"

Abu Assim did not respond. He was assessing me.

"Now, to go back to your family. Your widowed daughter got remarried to another brother, Abu Khubaib, the one who was apprehended with you." I wanted him to know that we had successfully identified all those who were picked up with him. The message to him was that we had sources and possibly other detainees already cooperating with us. It would make it easier for him to cooperate if he knew others were talking to us.

"I have to go, but when we next speak I hope you find it in your best interest to cooperate with me. In the meantime, rest up, because we've got a lot of talking to do." I wanted him to reflect on his new circumstances and realize that his cover was blown. Inexplicably, soon after, we were informed that Abu Assim was off-limits and that no one had access to him. I appealed to Blaine Thomas, the CITF commander on the ground. "This is a prisoner we identified. He's our subject."

"We've been told he is probably already off the island."

CITF protested up the chain of command, to no avail. When I asked others at the base if they knew what was going on with Abu Assim, no one seemed to have any information. There were plenty of other detainees to deal with, so I put his file to the side.

Months later, I was reading an Arabic newspaper and spotted an article saying that Abu Assim had been freed by a Moroccan judge. I made some inquiries and found out that soon after we identified him, the Bush administration had authorized his transfer to Morocco. After questioning him, the Moroccans eventually freed him.

"Is this a joke?" I vented my frustration to my partner Bob McFadden. "Tabarak was the most senior al-Qaeda guy we had in our custody. He was with bin Laden from the start and was his confidant."

"Man, the amount of intelligence he had surpasses anyone else in our custody," Bob said. "Not to mention that he deserved to spend his life behind bars."

Qosi, on the other hand, remained in Gitmo and was interrogated by Bob and me. We took time establishing rapport with him, and he offered valuable information about bin Laden and his security team. As the first bodyguard assigned to protect bin Laden after he was attacked in Sudan, he was well placed to do so. He also provided details on how he delivered money given to him by Abu Hafs al-Masri to an Egyptian operative in Ethiopia. Days after the delivery, the operative led a failed assassination attempt on Egyptian president Hosni Mubarak in Addis Ababa.

At one point Qosi asked me: "Has the U.S. invaded Iraq yet?" The U.S. invasion of Iraq didn't come until much later, in 2003, so it seemed a very strange question.

"No, we haven't, but why do you ask?" He told me that there was a hadith saying that the end of days would come after the land that is today Iraq is invaded by armies fighting over its black gold, a reference to oil. Later, other al-Qaeda detainees also quoted the black gold hadith. They all firmly believed al-Qaeda's rhetoric and use of questionable hadith and saw themselves as part of a divine prophecy.

Qosi also told me that bin Laden often said that his strategy to defeat America was through the death by a thousand cuts. Bin Laden knew that he could never defeat America straight up or with one blow, or even a series of blows, so his aim was to keeping pricking the United States, in a variety of ways, until life was made unbearable. This was not only through carrying out operations in the United States but by creating a constant source of worry. Qosi said that at times bin Laden had operatives talk about nonexistent operations on lines they thought the United States would be listening in on, so that the United States would waste time and resources chasing those "plots."

Years later, when Qosi's case went to trial, he pleaded guilty on the advice of his defense team.

There were many initial successes and frustrations at Gitmo. The problem was that there was no plan, and there were no rules of engagement aiming toward an endgame. The seasoned investigators started out doing everything by the book, but soon we were being given contrary orders from above.

The first new directive forbade the reading of the Miranda warning to detainees. Henceforth any confessions we got couldn't be used as evidence in any court, military or civilian. (The Uniform Code of Military Justice also requires that subjects be advised of their rights.) After many protested, especially the detectives assigned to various JTTFs who were reassigned to Gitmo, the bureau sent down a senior official, Spike Bowman, to tell us that Washington viewed Guantánamo at this stage as just an intelligence collection operation, and that we shouldn't worry about eventual prosecutions.

General Dunlavey often asked me for help when he was having problems with detainees, and at one point he told me that the detainees were on a hunger strike and the guards didn't know why. I interviewed some of them and was told that they were protesting because the guards had supposedly replaced the morning call to prayer with Bruce Springsteen's "Born in the U.S.A."

There was also a series of disagreements between experienced and novice interrogators about how interrogations should be carried out. The problem was that after 9/11, the U.S. military and other government entities rapidly expanded their teams that dealt with terrorism and put people in positions they didn't have the training or experience for. People were put on the job at Gitmo after just a six-week training course, without having ever conducted a real interrogation, let alone interrogated al-Qaeda terrorists. Their knowledge of al-Qaeda was thin and largely based on media accounts and press conferences.

When these inexperienced interrogators started doing their own interviews, they didn't have much success, and began trying different methods to get information. They were under pressure from officials in Washington to "produce results." One interrogator dressed up as a cowboy and blared country music into the interrogation room, thinking that somehow it would shock the detainee into cooperating. Later, I heard of reports of cruelty beginning to seep in, and harsher tactics were employed at Gitmo, such as the use of cinderblocks to hold detainees in stress positions.

The experienced investigators refused to be party to such interrogations and protested up our chain of command. CITF also organized training sessions for these fresh interrogators, and we tried explaining how to sort detainees, how to flip people (get them to cooperate), and how to utilize knowledge of al-Qaeda to gain information. The problem was that interrogation skills and knowledge cannot be picked up from a few sessions; they come from studying the group and the subject, and lots of interrogation experience working alongside experts.

Some of the military interrogators began to dress like FBI and CITF personnel, thinking that our successes stemmed from our appearance. At one point, Mark Fallon, the deputy CITF commander, even received a request from the military for two hundred CITF-logo polo shirts.

It wasn't only experienced interrogators who objected to what they saw, but also behavioral experts sent to the base to support the interrogations. Experienced experts like Tom Neer from the FBI Behavioral Analysis Unit; the CTC's Wilson; and Mike Gelles, NCIS's chief psychologist, all traveled to the base and voiced their objections.

Shortly after we arrived at Gitmo we had a series of discussions organized by CITF on how to sort and process the detainees. Years later Bob McFadden reminded me of what I told the group: "From here, within

Gitmo, we will either win or lose the war. After we interrogate people we need to sort them: who is guilty of crimes and who is innocent. If they're innocent, or if we're not going to be able to prosecute them, then we need to think of their detention here as a rehabilitation period. Otherwise we're creating new enemies. In the process we need to show them what the 'real America' is, and leave them with good impressions. And if we fail to process detainees, we'll lower the incentive for other detainees to cooperate, as they'll see cooperation doesn't change their situation. As for the guilty ones, we need to process them and put them on trial. Otherwise we're creating living martyrs."

This view was shared by the other experienced investigators, and after we'd finish our interrogations, we'd file any intelligence that could be used for operations and assess whether the people should be prosecuted or freed. We had an important advantage against many of the al-Qaeda members we interrogated at the start, as they were in deep shock to be in U.S. custody. For years they had been told by bin Laden that the United States was a cowardly country whose soldiers would flee when attacked. The al-Qaeda leader would cite the U.S. withdrawals from Lebanon and Somalia following attacks as examples of American "cowardice." But after 9/11, when we invaded Afghanistan, al-Qaeda's rhetoric was exposed as hollow. The image of al-Qaeda's leaders (rather than U.S. soldiers) scurrying into hiding places, and even fleeing Afghanistan, turned perceptions upside down. This made al-Qaeda members fear the United States for the first time, and made them more likely to cooperate than when they thought al-Qaeda had the upper hand.

The image of a confident and strong America was compromised when the Guantánamo guards were ordered to chain the detainees' hands and feet so they could barely move. When a detainee needed to be moved from his cell to an interrogation room, two guards would almost carry him, sometimes even putting him on a wheeled stretcher. "This actually plays into al-Qaeda's rhetoric and shows them that we are indeed terrified of them," I told the CITF. "We need to do it securely and safely, but this is overkill. It's a mistake."

In each interrogation I conducted, I had the guards take off the detainee's chains. I wanted to show that I wasn't afraid of the person I was interrogating. Taking off the chains also furthered the process, as detainees reacted well when treated with dignity.

"Why are you being nice to them?" one guard asked me in a sneering tone.

"I'm playing mind games with them," I told him, "playing on their notions of respect and dignity. When I treat them well, they feel they have to be polite and responsive, and in return I get the intelligence I need. For that, I'll be nice."

One day General Dunlavey called me, along with the CIA chief, whom I will call Matt, to his office. He told us that FBI director Robert Mueller would be arriving shortly and that he would like us to accompany him and the director on a tour. I had never met Mueller before; he was appointed just before 9/11, and I had been largely outside the United States on missions since his appointment.

When the director arrived, I had just come out of an interrogation and was wearing cargo pants and a polo shirt and had a beard, so I didn't look like an FBI agent. As we took him around the base, Dunlavey periodically asked me to explain things to Mueller, and I noticed the director looking at me strangely, as if he was trying to work out who I was. At the end of the tour, Dunlavey turned to the director and said: "Now that you've seen the operation, let me introduce you to the people who are making it happen." Rather than have a general introduce Mueller to one of his own agents, I quickly said: "Ali Soufan, FBI, nice to meet you sir," before Dunlavey could finish.

"You're Ali?" the director asked, and his eyebrows shot up. He looked me up and down again.

"Yes, sir."

"I should tell you that I just came from a trip overseas, and in many countries, when we landed, the foreign services would ask me, 'How is Ali doing?' I've heard a lot of great things about you, so I'm very happy to meet you."

"That's a great honor, sir. Thank you."

We continued on to the FBI house at Gitmo, where all our agents worked and lived, and gathered in the living room, where several rows of folding chairs had been set up. Matt, the CIA chief of base, was also invited to come, and he and I stood at the back of the room. No one sat in the front two rows, and as the director was about to begin his talk, he asked, "No one wants to sit in the front?" There was silence. "Where's Ali?" he asked, looking around, and when he spotted me at the back he beckoned me to the front: "Come sit here." I guessed that my name was one of the few he knew.

One evening in late June 2002, while I was working in FBI headquarters in DC—I was splitting my time between helping at Gitmo and other operations—Dan Coleman approached my desk. "Ali, do you know that there is a Salim Hamdan in Gitmo? Isn't he Abu Jandal's brother-in-law?"

"Seriously? Gitmo?"

"Yes, I've just been sorting through detainee files. Here's his arrest photo," Dan said, handing it to me.

"So this is the famous Saqr," I said, studying the photo.

Abu Jandal had once told us that he only knew Saqr by his alias. "Come on," I had told him, "are you really going to claim you don't know your own brother-in-law's real name?" Abu Jandal had blushed, caught in a lie. He had no idea how we knew of their relationship.

"It's Salim Hamdan," he'd said.

I went to see Pat D'Amuro and explained what I'd just learned, and we agreed that I would go interview Hamdan. At the time, there was no "fly team" (a specialized rapid response team) set up to interrogate new detainees, so Pat let me take whoever I wanted. I chose George Crouch, who had worked with me on the *Cole* investigation and was at the time temporarily assigned with me to headquarters. We sent word in advance to the FBI base at Gitmo that we were coming to interview Hamdan.

Bill Corbett, the Gitmo case agent at the time, met us when we landed. "I know it's late," I told him, "but we want to go straight to interview Hamdan."

"There's a problem," he said. "The CIA have suddenly decided to interrogate him right now."

"What suddenly pricked their interest?"

"I know," Bill replied, "there's something strange going on. Hamdan has been in custody for months, and the CIA has had plenty of time to interrogate him, but only now, when they heard that the FBI specifically asked to interview him and that HQ was sending you to the island, did they say they wanted to speak to him."

"Let's go to Hamdan anyway," I said. "I want to see what's going on."

We went straight to the interrogation room and asked the CIA interrogators inside to come out. One was a good friend whom I had worked alongside in the past, and we exchanged pleasantries. "Listen," I told him, "we've flown all the way from Washington to speak to Hamdan. We can do it together if you want, but this guy is important to us."

He readily agreed, but his colleague, a retired CIA officer working for the agency as a contractor, objected. When he wouldn't listen to reasoning, we took the matter to Matt, the CIA chief. We explained the situation and why we wanted to speak to Hamdan, and he sided with us and offered to help however he could. The CIA contractor argued back, but Matt had seniority.

"This is becoming a bad pattern with the CIA," George said to me, as we walked from Matt's office to the interrogation room. He had recently interviewed Abu Zubaydah's partner Ibn al-Shaykh al-Liby. Liby had been captured by Pakistani officials toward the end of November 2001 while trying to flee Afghanistan. He was handed over to the U.S. military and taken to Bagram Airfield, in Afghanistan's Parvan province. George and another of our team members, Russell Fincher, interrogated him in multiple sessions, and Liby cooperated, giving intelligence that included details of a threat against the U.S. Embassy in Yemen. Liby even showed them, on a map, how the plot could be disrupted.

During one session, Fred, the CIA officer who had caused problems in Jordan during the millennium investigation and had sent the faulty cables that had to be withdrawn, stormed into the room and began shouting at Liby: "I don't care what you've said about plots in Yemen. I want to know about plots in Israel."

George and Russell couldn't believe it. Did Fred really think that thwarting attacks against the U.S. Embassy wasn't important? Why was he disrupting the interrogation? Liby's face also registered confusion. "What's going on?" he asked, looking to George for guidance.

"If you don't tell me about what you are planning in Israel," Fred told Liby, "I'm going to bring your mother here and fuck her in front of you."

This was too much for Liby, and he turned away and refused to say another word to anyone. He was the internal emir of Khaldan and, in his mind, an important person; he wasn't going to take such abuse. The interrogation stopped for the day.

The general in charge of Bagram was furious when he heard what had happened and banned Fred from the airfield. Fred, however, filed his own report, and shortly afterwards, the CIA secretly came and rendered Liby to a third country (the name is still classified). There, after being tortured, he described the "links" between al-Qaeda and Saddam, which was a complete fabrication.

According to the Senate Select Committee on Intelligence's report on prewar intelligence on Iraq: "Postwar findings support the . . . February 2002 assessment that Ibn al-Shaykh al-Liby was likely intentionally misleading his debriefers when he said that Iraq provided two al-Qa'ida associates with chemical and biological weapons . . . training in 2000. . . . Al-Liby told debriefers that he fabricated information while in U.S. custody to receive better treatment and in response to threats of being transferred to a foreign intelligence service which he believed would torture him. . . . He said that later, while he was being debriefed . . . he fabricated more information in response to physical abuse and threats of torture."

Later, Liby was sent to Libya, where he died under suspicious circumstances. According to reports, he hanged himself. In some countries, it's not uncommon for prisoners to "commit suicide" in suspicious circumstances. One prisoner I heard about allegedly did so by shooting himself in the back of the head . . . three times. We have already seen

Bush administration, unsatisfied with an initial FBI report ₂ no links between Iraq and al-Qaeda, asked for a rewrite, a ₂t that senior FBI official Andy Arena refused.

George wasn't the only FBI agent who had bad experiences with Fred. I'd had my own with him in Jordan, of course, and saw him during the interrogations of al-Qaeda operatives Ramzi Binalshibh and another high-level al-Qaeda operative whom I will call Karim. The 2004 CIA inspector general's report by Helgerson also mentions mistakes Fred made.

"You cannot make that stuff up," I told George. "Thank God we have someone like Matt here."

Hamdan had a scowl on his face when we walked in; he glared at us as I began introducing myself. "This is my colleague George Crouch," I continued. "We're both from the FBI, and we've come to talk to you. You've been on our radar for a long time. I know your family. I know your position. I know the truth about who you are."

"Good for you," he sneered. "I have nothing to say to you. Everything I have said and will say is in my file. Go read it."

"I have no interest in your file. I'm here for something different."

"I don't care. I don't trust any of you. All of you are liars."

"You haven't dealt with me before, and I don't know who said what to you, but tell me, what are the lies?"

"I was repeatedly promised that I could call my wife to check that she was okay, but the promise was never kept."

"We're different," I told him, "but I won't speak to you tonight because you're clearly angry. So rest and we'll speak tomorrow. In the meantime, pray and do *istikhara*"—a term referring to asking God for guidance—"because what I know about you, your family, and your role in al-Qaeda will really shock you."

"How do you know things?" he asked, clearly curious.

"Let's just say Abu Jandal and I became good friends." He looked puzzled. "Maybe you don't believe me?" He shook his head. "Well, maybe all of us are liars, but do you remember when Habib was born?" I went on to remind him of the story of Abu Jandal's son's birth, and of how proud he was that Habib had tasted dates from bin Laden's mouth even before the infant tasted his own mother's milk. Hamdan didn't say anything but looked at me with his eyes wide open.

"Who else but a good friend would know this story?" I asked him. "We'll meet tomorrow, my friend. Good night."

"So, how did it go with Hamdan?" Matt asked as we walked into his office. We recounted the exchange.

"So he claims he's been lied to, and that appears to be hindering his cooperation. Is that true?"

"Let me check," Matt replied, and he pulled out the file. "Seems he's telling the truth. He was promised a few times that he'd be given a phone call, but that didn't happen."

"How about we let him have the phone call?"

"What good will that do?"

"He'll be less agitated and more likely to cooperate, for a start, and we can use that as leverage against him."

"Sounds like a good idea, worth a try. Go do it. Here's a satellite phone to use," Matt said, handing us one of the agency's phones.

Early the next morning George and I met Hamdan in an interrogation room. I instructed the guard to remove the shackles from Hamdan's arms and legs.

"Before we start, I want to tell you something: I checked whether you were promised a phone call, and I found that it's true. I am embarrassed that my colleagues didn't keep their promise. George and I always keep our promises. Even though you may not believe me, and even though you know from our conversation last night that we know everything about you and what you've done for al-Qaeda, a promise is still a promise, so let's go."

"What?" Hamdan asked, looking unsure if he understood me.

"Don't you want to make a phone call?" I asked. He nodded and started shaking.

We took him outside the cell to an area where phone service was available and gave him the phone to dial his wife. When she answered and he heard her voice, he started weeping. He told her briefly that he was okay, and asked how she and their children were doing. They spoke for a few minutes. We then ended the phone call and Hamdan fell on his knees and performed the *sejud*, kneeling in prayer, thanking God for the phone call. He was still crying.

We took him back to the interrogation room. For about fifteen minutes no one said anything. He just stared to the side, visibly shaking. I didn't say anything, not wanting him to think that we were taking advantage of his emotions. I poured him some water, which he drank.

"Thank you for the call," he finally said, with tears in his eyes.

"A promise is a promise."

"How is Abu Jandal doing?" Hamdan asked.

"He's good," I told him, "and he definitely helped himself by cooperating, as I'm sure you're now fully aware."

"Okay, I'll give you everything you need."

True to his word, Hamdan began to cooperate fully. We started off by talking about his childhood in Al-Therba, Yemen, where his father kept a grocery store. When Hamdan was about nineteen, his father died. An unsuccessful effort to take over the store was followed by the death of his mother. Hamdan moved to Sanaa, where he met Muhannad bin Attash at a mosque. Muhannad convinced him to go to Afghanistan and join what later became known as the Northern Group. When the members of the Northern Group met bin Laden, the al-Qaeda leader said to Hamdan, "You are from the Hadramout region of Yemen." Suitably impressed, Hamdan accepted an offer from bin Laden to serve as a driver.

For about six months he drove a truck hauling building materials for al-Qaeda's new compound. "This was a test for me," Hamdan told us. "They wanted to see whether I was committed and trustworthy. I was a hard worker, and after six months they appointed me as a driver for bin Laden's convoy."

"Who was the main driver?" I asked.

"At this point Saif al-Adel would drive bin Laden, and if he wasn't driving, it would be Muhannad bin Attash or someone else who had been with bin Laden for a long time. I drove one of the other cars in the convoy." Bin Laden paid him between two hundred and three hundred dollars a month and also covered his rent.

"When did you first drive bin Laden?"

"I was on the front, fighting the Northern Alliance, but they had the upper hand and were overrunning our lines. Saif al-Adel ran up to me and said that he didn't want bin Laden at the front anymore—it was too dangerous. Saif said that he had to stay and fight, so I should drive bin Laden to safety. Which I did."

"What was that battle?"

"I'm not sure, but Muhannad bin Attash was killed, and Khallad lost one of his legs."

Over the next days and weeks, Hamdan told us everything he knew. We'd bring him fish sandwiches from McDonald's, which he loved, and car and truck magazines, and he'd give us information about al-Qaeda. It became clear to us that Hamdan would be a great witness in trials prosecuting other al-Qaeda members. He had been present at many key moments in al-Qaeda's history, and while driving bin Laden he had overheard many details of plots. He had been with bin Laden, for example, when the al-Qaeda leader had released his 1998 fatwa, and he was present when bin Laden gave his press conference following the ABC interview. "And that's when I first met Zawahiri," Hamdan told us.

"Did you like him?"

"My first impression was very positive. He was very friendly. Later I saw the problems with the Egyptians running al-Qaeda."

Hamdan told us that he was present at al-Farouq when it was announced that al-Qaeda and Zawahiri's Egyptian Islamic Jihad would formally merge. He was present when various al-Qaeda plots were discussed, and he detailed what he knew about those involved—as, for example, when Abu Abdul Rahman al-Muhajir, al-Qaeda's chief explosives expert, explained to him exactly how the 1998 East African truck bombs worked.

He was also present when Abu Hafs al-Masri, al-Qaeda's military commander, and bin Laden discussed making a video about the USS Cole attack. Nashiri himself had told Hamdan during a private conversation that he was the mastermind of the attack. We talked about al-Qaeda's structure and the process by which the leadership selected people for different missions. Abu Mohammed al-Masri, emir of al-Farouq, was "most likely to identify potential suicide bombers," Hamdan concluded.

Hamdan talked about how bin Laden motivated his followers and convinced them to participate in al-Qaeda operations. "After the 1998 embassy attacks and the 2000 *Cole* attack, there was uncontrolled passion. We were all so proud of what we had done."

"You didn't think about the innocent people being killed?"

"You need to understand that while you are in al-Qaeda's midst, it's difficult to think clearly or objectively. Bin Laden was always encouraging us, so we felt there was no one who could stand up to us. It was difficult to isolate yourself from the surroundings. There was no media, no newspapers, only what bin Laden and al-Qaeda spread around. When one is part of that home, from the inside it is very difficult to think of what is happening on the outside. If you think Pelé is the best football player of all time, it is difficult for anyone to convince you there are any better players. Even though, for sure, there are players better than him, for you, he is the best. You see only his best plays. If he has a bad one, you ignore it. That was the way bin Laden was for me. All these things are going on around you, and you just go with it."

I've seen this with many operatives from different terrorist organizations: it's difficult to get through to them while they're operational. They're too busy planning attacks and hiding from the authorities. The time when terrorists can be turned is either during the recruitment stage or when they've been caught and are in jail.

"So what's changed now? Why do you not feel the same toward bin Laden?" I asked.

"My time in detention has opened my eyes to many things. I saw the technology of the Americans and was shocked to even see the military vehicles they moved in. I did not even think such vehicles and cars existed. Now I look back at my life and have regrets. At the time, it was difficult to see clearly."

• • •

I started working with David Kelley, from the Southern District of New York, with whom I had worked during the *Cole* investigation and in other cases, to come up with a plea agreement for Hamdan in exchange for pleading guilty and being a prosecution witness against other al-Qaeda members, especially all those involved with the *Cole* plot. One morning, I was watching CNN while getting dressed to go to the office and heard that Hamdan had been declared an "enemy combatant" by President Bush. I called Kelley immediately and asked if he'd seen the news.

"Yes," he replied gloomily.

"What does it mean?"

"I don't know. We'll soon find out. But I don't think it's good."

What it meant was that we could no longer have access to Hamdan to ask questions about other detainees, and could no longer use him as a witness in other trials. Instead he was given lawyers who helped him mount a lengthy (and successful) legal challenge against the military legal system that the Bush administration had set up at Gitmo, eventually forcing the administration to set up a new system.

What was most surprising to people in the FBI and Southern District about the "enemy combatant" label was that the Bush administration applied it without even consulting the primary agencies that had been putting together the Hamdan case, or the prosecutors preparing to try him. It was a move that undermined our efforts against al-Qaeda, especially at Gitmo.

When I testified against Hamdan in the trial as a prosecution witness, it was the first time I had seen him since he had been declared an enemy combatant. When he had me in his line of vision across the courtroom, he placed his hand on his heart and nodded to me—a sign of respect. Hamdan was ultimately sentenced to five and a half years in prison, a term that was largely wiped out based on time he had already served in Gitmo. After a few months he was released, and on January 8, 2009, he was back in Yemen.

During the trial, the defense criticized the government for throwing out a plea agreement whereby Hamdan would have served as a cooperating witness (and would have been sentenced to a longer prison term, as it turned out). "We hope one day the American people find out about this squandered opportunity." It was a rare instance where the prosecution's witness agreed with what the defense said.

In July 2002 a routine FBI fingerprint check on a group of detainees in Gitmo found that detainee No. 63, who until then had insisted that he knew nothing about al-Qaeda and that he had been in Afghanistan pursuing his interest in falconry, had given a false name. In fact, he was Mohammed al-Qahtani, who had vowed, "I will be back" after being refused entry to the United States on August 4, 2001, in Orlando. He had landed in Florida with almost nonexistent English, a one-way ticket, and $2,800 in cash. Asked who he was meeting, he said that there was someone "upstairs"; asked for the name, Qahtani changed his story and said that no one was waiting for him.

Now he was back, although not in the manner he probably expected. His file showed that he had been captured near the Tora Bora region of Afghanistan by Pakistani forces around December 15, 2001, and transferred to Guantánamo Bay on February 13, 2002. He was picked up with the other twenty-nine members of the group that included Abu Assim and Qosi, promptly nicknamed "the dirty thirty" by investigators for their false stories and close links to al-Qaeda leadership.

Given this background information and the proximity to 9/11 of Qahtani's entry attempt, we started looking for links between him and the hijackers. We found that on his landing card, he had listed a number belonging to Mustafa al-Hawsawi, KSM's administrative assistant for the 9/11 attack. Some of the hijackers also had Hawsawi's number on their landing forms. Next we discovered that on the day Qahtani had tried to enter the United States, between 4:30 and 8:30 PM a series of five calls were made from a pay phone in the airport to Hawsawi's number. The calls were made using a calling card bought with lead hijacker Mohammed Atta's credit card. Surveillance footage from the airport also revealed that at 4:18 PM a rental car used by Atta had entered the airport's garage, leaving at 9:04.

It seemed too big a coincidence that Atta, or someone using his card, would have been independently at the same airport making a call a few hours before Qahtani had arrived. I told a colleague to check whether the Virgin Atlantic flight that Qahtani was on had been delayed, and it turned out that it had been; it had been scheduled to land at 4:40 PM but hadn't gotten in till a few hours later. Atta (or one of his fellow plotters) had probably called to find out where Qahtani was and what had happened to the flight.

The evidence indicated that Qahtani was the missing fifth hijacker on United Airlines Flight 93. The other three planes each had five hijackers, while Flight 93 had four. He, and not Zacarias Moussaoui, as then attorney general John Ashcroft had been claiming, was the missing twentieth hijacker.

We took this information to General Dunlavey and explained Qahtani's connection to 9/11. Our team, assisted by behavioral experts, recommended that we remove him from the general Gitmo population and put him in the brig, as we had done with Abu Assim. The purpose of doing so would be to send him the message that his cover was blown and to isolate him from his support base. We also worried that if other detainees found out that we knew he was the twentieth hijacker, they might try to kill him to prevent him from giving us information about the plot. He was transferred and I was given clearance to see him.

"Why have I been moved?" Qahtani asked, clearly nervous as to why he had been put in the brig.

"We know who you are," I told him. "Your cover has been blown. We know how you tried to enter the United States in August. It's time for you to start telling us the truth."

"I don't know what you're talking about," he replied angrily.

I studied him for a few moments while letting my words sink in. He was short and skinny, and his eyes were glassy, as if there was not much there. He also was shaking and seemed afraid. It was just the two of us in the interrogation room, although other agents were watching through a video camera in another room.

"Okay," I said, "let's go through your story, then. Why were you in Afghanistan?"

"I was there because I like falcons and Afghanistan is great for falconry."

"How many times have you been to America?"

"Never."

"We have the details of your attempted entry in August."

"Oh," Qahtani stuttered, "that was my only time."

"And why were you trying to enter?"

"I wanted to buy cars."

"Where from?"

"I don't know."

It was soon clear that Qahtani didn't have a well-thought-out cover story. All he'd say was that he was in Afghanistan for falconry and had gone to the United States to buy "cars." To any additional questions about the U.S. episode, he answered, "I don't know." When we discussed nonterrorism-related matters, I saw that he wasn't very intelligent. I concluded that at best his intended role in 9/11 must have been as a muscle hijacker.

"We'll stop for now," I told him, "but you should realize we know who you are. You can play all the games you want to, but eventually you'll realize it's in your interest to talk to me."

Before my interview with him the next day, I put pictures on the wall of al-Qaeda members I knew he'd recognize, including KSM, Mohammed Atta, Ramzi Binalshibh, and Mustafa al-Hawsawi. They were all central planners of 9/11. We doctored the pictures, except the one of Atta, so that all the men appeared to be wearing orange jumpsuits, indicating that they were in our custody.

"Do you know these people?" I asked, gesturing to the pictures as he walked in. "We've got all your friends in custody. That's how we know all about you." He froze for a moment, and his face went red, but then he shook his head and said, "I don't know anything."

"I need to step out," I told him, "but I'll be back soon."

I left and went into the room where others were watching the interrogation through a video link. As we watched, Qahtani got out of his bed and slowly approached the wall where we had taped the photographs. He stared at them for a few minutes and then touched them gently, as if trying to communicate with the subjects.

I returned to the room and found Qahtani shaking. "Are you okay?" I asked him.

"I'm going on a hunger strike," he replied. When he was among the general population, some detainees had gone on hunger strikes to protest prison conditions. He thought that it might absolve him from cooperating.

"You are being silly," I told him. "You can play this game if you want to, and we'll wait for you to stop, but I'd prefer it if you just started being honest and stopped wasting both our time." He folded his hands and wouldn't say anything else, and he was taken to his cell.

I went and got hummus, tabouli, and kebab and brought it to him with some pita. "Here's food for you," I told him. "If you want, you can eat." I placed it in front of him and left the cell. From the room where the video cameras were, I watched him jump up and start eating the food. That was the end of his hunger strike.

Showing a detainee that I knew all about him and that further denial was a waste of time often worked if he had initially denied his role or refused to cooperate. It took time to wear down al-Qaeda members' resistance, because when silence didn't deter us, they would make small talk and deny wrongdoing, hoping to prove their "innocence" that way. That's when we would start questioning them on small details: Why did they go to Afghanistan? How had they traveled there? Who had arranged their trip? Who had convinced them to go? How was the trip funded? How did they get the money? Who vouched for them? Who picked them up at the airport? How did they enter Afghanistan? Where did they stay in Afghanistan? Whom did they meet?

In their minds, these were questions that weren't directly relevant to terrorism and could fit with their cover story, but their answers would eventually trap them in a lie, and they would have to revise their story, usually so that it was closer to the truth. Even so, we wouldn't just ask a question like "Did you meet bin Laden?" Instead, we'd tease out details. We'd ask: Who did you first meet in Afghanistan? Where did you first stay? How did you get there? Who was the driver? What route did you take? Who was in that guesthouse? Whom did you submit your passport to? Who was the emir of the guesthouse? What did you talk about? Where did you go next? When asked about specific details, it's very hard for anyone to maintain a false cover story.

Once the detainee named the emir, or the person who'd trained him, we'd begin to hear names we knew from past interrogations and investigations, which gave us an indication of how the detainee fit into the al-Qaeda chart. If, for example, the detainee said that his emir was Abu Musab al-Yemeni, one of the many regular instructors in al-Qaeda's camps, it was likely that he had done only basic training. If Saif al-Adel was involved, however, he might have been used for a special operation.

The process could take one hour or a week; each detainee was different. Eventually they'd start telling us what really happened. But to get to that point, the interrogator needs to be an expert in the subject, and you have to show you are familiar with what the detainees are talking about. You can't stop to ask them to start spelling names of people or places, as that would make it clear that lies aren't being picked up.

I got to the small talk stage with Qahtani and started developing a relationship with him. We even prayed together. I then had to leave Gitmo on another mission that was viewed as a higher priority, so I handed his case back to the agents who had originally handled him.

In my experience, people like Qahtani would only be able to tell us their specific role in a plot: how they were recruited and trained, the people they interacted with. All of which would be useful information to convict Qahtani and give us information on the plot itself, but it was unlikely to give us much information about other plots.

When KSM was later arrested, he told interrogators that Qahtani was "an unsophisticated Bedouin," and derided him for being unable to learn English phrases or even use e-mail. Al-Qaeda had also tried to put Qahtani through a special training course in the al-Banshiri camp, named after the al-Qaeda military leader and *shura* council member who had drowned in the ferry accident in Lake Victoria, but he had failed the course.

After I had left, other FBI agents worked on Qahtani and continued to make progress. But military interrogators, backed by political appointees in Washington, wanted to get "juicy" intelligence from Qahtani. They didn't understand that someone like Qahtani didn't have it. They argued that the FBI had been unsuccessful and that harsher interrogation techniques were needed. If you don't know what a detainee should know—and political appointees in Washington certainly didn't—there is no way to know what is success and what is failure.

While CITF and FBI members were having problems with the military command over interrogations, there was also friction within the two strands of the military—JTF 170, under General Dunlavey, and JTF 160, under General Baccus. The separation of responsibility into interrogations and base organization frustrated nonmilitary personnel at Gitmo, too, with the lack of a coherent command structure making it difficult to produce decisions. General Dunlavey felt that General Baccus was too soft on the detainees, and at one point he even asked the NCIS to investigate him for "consorting with the enemy." General Baccus was in fact just treating the detainees as required by military rules and regulations. While I was frustrated with both the lack of organization at the base and the way detainees were being handled, I never had any problems with General Dunlavey and always found him to be receptive to suggestions.

The complaints about the difficulty of the two command structures reached senior U.S. military leaders, and on October 9, 2002, General Baccus was relieved of his command, and JTF 160 and 170 merged. The military felt that someone else was needed to run both commands, and on November 8, 2002, Maj. Gen. Geoffrey Miller was placed in charge of the base. A few days later, General Dunlavey left.

General Miller was a strange choice for command of an operation whose focus was interrogating and sorting detainees. His background was in artillery, and he had no interrogation or intelligence experience. He had never even sat in on an interrogation, as he openly admitted. This inexperience showed when he ordered that interrogations be run like military operations: there had to be a fixed start time and end time, and he wanted a fixed number of interrogations to be conducted each day.

CITF tried explaining to him that interrogations don't work like that. Each detainee is different, knows different things, and has different triggers that will get him to cooperate. Giving fixed end times to interrogations is better for the detainee, as he knows he only needs to hold out for a certain period of time, after which the interrogation will be over.

I learned years later that the move to employ aggressive interrogation techniques at Gitmo started long before Qahtani was alleged to be not cooperating. The November 2008 *Senate Armed Services Committee Inquiry into the Treatment of Detainees in U.S. Custody*, declassified in April 2009, reported that back in December 2001, seven months before we even identified Qahtani and removed him from the general Gitmo population, the Department of Defense's general counsel's office, headed by William James Haynes II, requested help with detainee "exploitation" from the Joint Personnel Recovery Agency's military Survival Evasion Resistance and Escape (SERE) trainers. Haynes was a close friend of Vice President Dick Cheney's counsel, David Addington, and had been the best man at his wedding.

SERE was established to teach U.S. military personnel how to withstand interrogation techniques considered illegal under the Geneva Conventions. The strategies are partly based on tactics used by Chinese Communists during the Korean War to gain false confessions. The Senate report cites the deputy commander of the Joint Forces Command (JFCOM), the Joint Personnel Recovery Agency (JPRA)'s higher headquarters, saying that "the expertise of JPRA lies in training personnel how to respond and resist interrogations—not in how to conduct interrogations."

The wisdom of the Senate report was not available on September 16, 2002, when, following up on the earlier assistance, a group of military interrogators and behavioral scientists from Gitmo went to JPRA, in Ft. Belvoir, Virginia, for SERE training. On September 25, 2002, a delegation of senior Bush administration lawyers, including Jim Haynes and David Addington, along with John Rizzo and Michael Chertoff, then with the criminal division of the Justice Department (later director of Homeland Security), traveled to Gitmo for discussions on how interrogations should be run.

On October 2, 2002, the chief counsel to the CIA's Counterterrorism Center met with Gitmo staff. The Senate Armed Services Committee report notes: "Minutes of that meeting indicate that it was dominated by a discussion of aggressive interrogation techniques including sleep deprivation, death threats, and waterboarding, which was discussed in relation to its use in SERE training."

By the time the CTC chief counsel was giving this briefing, CIA contractors interrogating Abu Zubaydah had already been employing the aggressive techniques that I had seen used on him and had objected to, and which FBI director Robert Mueller had ordered his agents not to use. But when Mark Fallon and other members of CITF, and the FBI, tried to gain access to the September 25 and October 2 meetings, to argue against the use of aggressive interrogation techniques, they were turned away. It appeared to CITF members that a decision had been made to employ harsh techniques, and the Bush delegation didn't want to hear any contrary opinions. It was a strange situation, with lawyers giving orders on how interrogations should be run, and experienced practitioners not allowed to offer their views.

Following these meetings, on October 11, General Dunlavey sent a memo to his military superior, Gen. James Hill, requesting authorization for aggressive interrogation techniques. There were three progressively harsh categories. Category I included yelling at the detainee and allowing the interrogator to claim he was the citizen of a foreign country known for the harsh treatment of detainees. Among Category II techniques were the use of stress positions, isolation, twenty-hour interrogations, the removal of clothing, and the use of phobias (such as fear of dogs) to induce stress in the detainee. Category III techniques included scenarios designed to make the detainee believe that imminent harm was about to befall either him or his family, and the use of water to induce the "misperception" of suffocation. The techniques were defended in a legal memo by then Lt. Col. Diane Beaver, the senior-most lawyer at Guantánamo. The request passed through General Hill's office up through the chain of command and landed on Jim Haynes's desk for his recommendation to Donald Rumsfeld, then secretary of defense.

The way the legal system in the military worked was that lawyers from all services could offer opinions, but ultimate legal authority rested with the defense secretary's general counsel. The Senate report details various objections that different services had to the techniques. The Marine Corps, for example, stated that several techniques "arguably violate federal law, and would expose our service members to possible prosecution," and called for "a more thorough legal and policy review."

Ignoring the warnings, Haynes sent a one-page memo to Secretary Rumsfeld on November 27, as the Senate report notes, "recommending that he approve all but three of the eighteen techniques in the GTMO request. . . . Mr. Haynes's memo indicated that he had discussed the issue with Deputy Secretary of Defense Paul Wolfowitz, Undersecretary of Defense for Policy Doug Feith, and General Myers and that he believed they concurred in his recommendation."

On December 2, 2002, Secretary Rumsfeld signed the recommendation, adding a handwritten note at the bottom of the page regarding limits on the use of stress positions: "I stand for 8–10 hours a day. Why is standing limited to 4 hours?"

While Secretary Rumsfeld only officially approved the techniques on December 2, some were already being introduced in early October, after the Bush administration lawyers and the CIA's CTC general counsel left the base. Dogs were used to intimidate Qahtani and he was put into stress positions. Later a host of much more aggressive techniques were used on him over a period of three months. These included, according to the Senate Committee, being stripped naked and "made to wear a leash and perform dog tricks."

When Mark Fallon was shown the proposed interrogation plan for Qahtani by members of the military command at Gitmo, he said that it was "illegal" and that he would recommend that CITF members be barred from taking part in the interrogations.

"It can't be illegal, the secretary of defense authorized it," was the reply.

"The secretary of defense doesn't have the ability to change the law. He can't determine what is legal and illegal."

Fallon's boss, Brittain Mallow, initially disagreed with him: while he was completely opposed to the techniques, he thought that CITF agents could go in as observers and temper what the military interrogators did. Fallon's response was unequivocal: "It will put agents in a bad position. Either they'll watch the law being broken, or, as sworn law enforcement officers, seeing laws being broken, they may try to arrest the military interrogators. Nothing good can come of this."

Mark Fallon, a New Jersey native from a family of law enforcement officials, found himself in a position he had warned his staff members about during their orientation. "Even if I give you an illegal order," he told them, "you can't follow it. You are bound by the Constitution. Remember that at Nuremberg we prosecuted Nazis who claimed just to be following orders. And remember in the United States there are no secrets, only delayed disclosures. One day, whether one year away or ten years away, people will be looking at what we did, so make sure you act with the utmost integrity." He told Mallow that he would resign from CITF and from the government, if necessary, if Mallow authorized CITF agents to sit in on harsh interrogations. Mallow saw the wisdom in Fallon's logic and ordered CITF personnel not to take part in any interrogation in which harsh techniques were being used. This angered General Miller, who lambasted the CITF commanders: "You either are with us or you are against us, and your guys are out."

Like Fallon, NCIS chief psychologist Mike Gelles objected to what the military interrogators were doing, and together they went to see NCIS director David Brant. He agreed with them and they spoke to Alberto J. Mora, the navy's general counsel. Mora told them: "I don't understand how they can be doing these things. You guys are the ones with the interrogation experience. I suggest you go back to Gitmo and try talking to General Miller."

Fallon and Gelles flew to Gitmo to see General Miller and again explained their objections. Based on their experience dealing with terrorists, they told him, these techniques didn't get results. Furthermore, they were illegal under U.S. law. Miller dismissed them: "You have got to put on the same jersey if you want to be on the team."

"Listen, General," Fallon replied, "we don't work for you. We've got a separate chain of command. We're not going to participate and will continue to oppose these techniques."

When Mora learned of the conversation, he contacted Jim Haynes a few times to object to the use of the techniques. At one point, the Senate report states, he told Haynes that he thought the techniques authorized by Rumsfeld "could rise to the level of torture." Haynes ignored Mora's warnings.

Having failed to get Haynes or his superiors in the Pentagon to listen, on January 15, 2003, Mora drafted a memo saying that the techniques were clearly illegal and sent it to Haynes, warning him that he'd sign the memo by the end of the day unless the use of the techniques ended. A senior administration lawyer calling what the administration was doing "illegal" would cause serious problems; Rumsfeld, later that day, signed an order rescinding his approval of the techniques.

Mora's victory was short-lived, however. In March 2003, Rumsfeld secretly reauthorized twenty-four techniques, at which point Mora had left the navy for private practice.

The Pentagon, at the time of this back-and-forth, declared that Qahtani's questioning was "worthwhile," and a spokesman from the Defense Department said that he was "a valuable source of information." Unnamed Bush administration officials told reporters that his interrogation provided information about planned attacks and the financial networks used by terrorists.

Later, when the techniques were no longer being used, I was asked to go back to interrogate Qahtani because basic information was still missing. Despite claims of success, not only did those employing the harsh techniques not get any valuable information, they hadn't even managed to get the basic stuff.

I spoke to Qahtani and he gave me details we wanted about his training and his interactions with KSM and other plotters, among other information. He told me about his difficulties in learning English phrases and using e-mail, and KSM's frustrations, and told me that when Mustafa al-Hawsawi was training him, he would go to the beach at sunset to pray.

"What did you pray about?" I asked.

"I asked God to give me a sign showing whether he agreed with my mission. I told him if he agreed with my mission then he should facilitate my trip. If he didn't, then he should stop it."

Contrary to Bush administration claims about Qahtani's importance, nothing gained from Qahtani while he was subjected to the coercive techniques could have saved a single life. The 9/11 Commission concluded that he was a "muscle hijacker," as we had predicted from the start. To date, Qahtani has not been charged for his role in 9/11. All previous charges against him have been dropped. That he was subjected to the use of harsh techniques makes any trial legally difficult. As we warned when the techniques were being introduced, not only are they unreliable, ineffective, and un-American, they also ignore our long-term goals and make prosecution unlikely.

When the Department of Justice's inspector general investigated detainee abuse and asked Qahtani about me, he complained that I had put him in the brig and let no one else see him, but he said I had "some sense of humanity." The IG noted that the logs showed that I wasn't the only person who saw Qahtani; other agents saw him, including members of the FBI's Behavioral Analysis Unit.

Agents reading the report told me that it seemed as if the IG were almost trying to get Qahtani to say something negative about me. And Qahtani had reason to hate me: I was the face that he associated with his having been identified and taken from the general population— but I had "some sense of humanity." What was strange, however, was that the IG only asked Qahtani, the would-be twentieth hijacker, about me, and never asked for my version of what had happened. Per-

haps because Qahtani didn't say anything negative, the IG didn't feel
he needed to.

While Secretary Rumsfeld and members of his team such as Haynes,
Wolfowitz, and Feith were busy approving the use of these techniques,
they were also getting in the way of successful interrogations. FBI and
CITF investigators identified detainee No. 37 as a Yemeni al-Qaeda
operative called al-Batar, based on information and a description I had
gotten from Abu Jandal. Batar was the person to whom Abu Jandal had
delivered money—the sum turned out to be five thousand dollars—to
procure a Yemeni wife for bin Laden. As Abu Jandal had told me, he
went into the errand thinking that the money was for a mission. At the
airport in Sanaa, he was met by Nibras, one of the *Cole* suicide bombers, and Batar, and together the three men went to the al-Jazeera Hotel.
There Abu Jandal gave the five thousand dollars to Batar, who thanked
him and told him that the money was for a dowry. Disillusioned and
chagrined, Abu Jandal returned to Afghanistan shortly after.

Given his connection to bin Laden's Yemeni wife, I thought that
Batar would be especially valuable in tracking down the al-Qaeda
leader. After I had introduced myself to Batar, he said to me, "So you're
the FBI agent Ali?"

"Yes."

"Saqr told me about you," he said, referring to Hamdan by his alias.

"What did he say?"

"He told me that originally he wouldn't cooperate, but he met you,
and said you are trustworthy and said he cooperated with you."

"That's true."

"Saqr told me he releases me from my oath so that I can speak
to you."

"What was the oath?"

"When we were captured, we both swore to each other that whatever happened in interrogations, we would never admit to knowing
each other." (Hamdan had kept that oath, as he had never mentioned
Batar's name to me.)

"And?"

"Hamdan told me that you treated him well, and were honest, and let him check on his family to see that they were okay."

"I did."

"Hamdan told me he thought it was in our interest to cooperate. And so we canceled the oath."

"Great," I said. "Let's start with your background."

"I'll tell you everything, but I would also like to check that my family is okay."

"We can arrange that."

"What I'll do is that I'll tell you half my story. From what Hamdan told me, you know al-Qaeda well and will know whether I'm telling the truth. And then I will tell you the other half after I make a phone call."

I spoke to the FBI and the CITF commanders. They agreed that it made sense to let Batar make a call and said they'd get permission from General Miller. (Miller had instructed that any calls had to have prior approval from him.) I returned to Batar and told him he had a deal.

He admitted, for the first time, his true identity, and detailed his background, his path to al-Qaeda, and his connection to bin Laden. The investigators had recovered a document that appeared to be a handwritten martyrdom letter, signed by "Al-Battar," which he admitted was his. As promised, he was cooperating.

In the meantime, the CITF and FBI commanders had put through a request for permission from General Miller to make the call. He responded: "No prisoner can make a phone call without approval from Paul Wolfowitz," Rumsfeld's deputy secretary of defense. The commanders argued that there was a precedent in Hamdan; in that case, approval had come from General Dunlavey.

The approval never came, and we never heard the second half of Batar's confession. We could have learned important information about bin Laden's Yemeni wife, which would have helped us track bin Laden and others. When bin Laden was finally tracked down and killed, in May 2011, his Yemeni wife was among those with him. Who knows how much more quickly we could have gotten to bin Laden and what lives could have been saved?

While General Miller wouldn't approve a phone call, he had no qualms about employing harsh interrogation techniques on Qahtani without proper formal approval from the secretary of defense. The same is true of his bosses: they wouldn't let a detainee use a phone for a minute, which would have led to bin Laden, but they didn't mind disregarding the U.S. Constitution.

"Ali, you're heading to Gitmo, right?" asked a member of the 9/11 Team. It was August 2002, and I was leaving headquarters, preparing to head back to interrogate Hamdan further.

"Yes, I'm leaving shortly."

"While you're there, will you take a look at prisoner No. 39?"

"Sure, who is that?"

"His name is Ali Hamza Ahmed Suleiman al-Bahlul."

"What has he done?"

"We don't know. In fact, we don't know anything about him. He's been in Gitmo for several months, and, according to the military, he's fully cooperative. They do not believe he is a member of Al-Qaeda."

"But?"

"But we recovered, in Afghanistan, a phone book with the names and numbers of al-Qaeda operatives. Its contents range from the contact details of the terrorists involved in the USS *Cole* bombing, such as Quso and Nibras, to the address and phone number in Malaysia where the 9/11 planning summit was held. It's probable that whoever had access to the phone book knew about 9/11 and was a central figure in al-Qaeda. After it was tested for fingerprints, one got a positive hit: Bahlul.

"There's one more thing about Bahlul," the agent continued, "that makes us suspicious about him. He was picked up with the dirty thirty."

"Can I see the phone book?" I asked.

"Sure," the agent said, and handed me a copy. It was filled with the numbers of high-level operatives, including Khallad, identified by his alias Silver.

"Where did this book come from?"

"It was found in the car Hamdan was driving when he was arrested."

"And Bahlul's fingerprints?"

"They appear on pages eight and nine, so he had access to it. My gut feeling is that this person is important in al-Qaeda."

"I think you're right. I'll speak to him at Gitmo and see what I make of him."

Also found in Hamdan's car were two SAM-7 missile launchers, along with cards detailing numerical codes used internally to refer to al-Qaeda members, entities, locations, and specific tactical words: bin Laden was 4; Zawahiri, 22; Saif al-Adel, 11; and KSM, 10. The military command was 33; the al-Banshiri camp, 31; bin Laden's bodyguards, 47. Number 77 referred to families; 115, to chemicals; 129, to an ambush; 100, to a tank; 67, to food. Different locations at which fighters were based also had numbers: 108, for example, meant "in town."

When I arrived back at Guantánamo I requested access to Bahlul from the military, but the interrogators who had been handling him refused. He had been put in a restricted-access location, as he was deemed to be cooperating. The military interrogators explained that he had told them everything he knew, and that any questioning "by you guys from the FBI" was "unnecessary."

I talked to General Dunlavey about the phone book and the fingerprints. "I believe he's been lying to the interrogators." He agreed to grant me access, and I was given Bahlul's file. I saw that he had been in Gitmo for almost eight months and had been telling the same story consistently: he had been in Afghanistan teaching the Quran and knew nothing about al-Qaeda. It was the cover story that the rest of the dirty thirty had given. Otherwise, the file revealed little about Bahlul.

I was sure that during the previous eight months Bahlul had learned how standard military interrogations worked. I wanted to deliver the message that this interrogation was different, and I wanted him to arrive at different conclusions concerning who I was, why I was there, and what I knew.

The first thing I did was change the interrogation setting. Bahlul had been questioned in a standard room and kept cuffed. We took him to a room designed to look like a small living room, which we furnished with couches, a carpet, a coffee table, and pictures. Matt, the CIA chief, helped us obtain the location and set it up.

When Bahlul was brought into the room, I was sitting on a chair next to the coffee table, waiting for him. He was wearing an inmate's orange jumpsuit, and both his arms and legs were shackled, but he had a confident, bored look, as if to say, Here's yet another interrogator who I'm going to have to run through the same issues with. Once he was unshackled, he sat down on the couch, across the coffee table.

I asked him how he was being treated. "Acceptable." He went on to say that, while there were some instances where the Quran was desecrated "at the beginning," he felt that they had been dealt with. "Overall, the treatment has been good, and as Muslims, we have to acknowledge justice."

We started talking to Bahlul about his family and the place he was from in Yemen. I had spent a good deal of time in Yemen investigating the USS *Cole* bombing, and I surprised Bahlul with my knowledge of the land, people, and culture. "You know more about Yemen than the others did," he told me.

Next I asked him what had made him go to Afghanistan. He gave what appeared to be his stock answer, that he had gone to help people learn the Quran. He said that he had no interest in al-Qaeda or jihad, and that he had gone solely for religious reasons. He also insisted that he hadn't met any Arabs fighters there, and that he had spent all his time with poor Afghanis who needed religious instruction. We discussed his impressions of the country.

"What do you think of Osama bin Laden's fatwa to expel the infidel Americans from Muslim lands?" I asked.

"I don't believe in that fatwa, and there are religious scholars in Saudi Arabia who ruled that America's presence was not an occupation but legitimate assistance, as it had been requested by the king of Saudi Arabia."

I played devil's advocate and gave al-Qaeda's justifications for jihad in response. He countered them and we had a debate. That Bahlul was so familiar with arguments that countered al-Qaeda's arguments was a sign that he was familiar with al-Qaeda's arguments as well. When I kept responding with more of al-Qaeda's arguments, he continued to respond with religious ideas that contradicted them, but slowly his arguments got weaker and he seemed less sure of himself. It was clear to me that he was repeating things that he had been practicing to say if captured, not saying things he passionately believed in.

"Where is your family now?" I asked, switching topics. "Have you heard from them recently?"

"I don't know, but I hope that they made it home safely." I asked this to see whether he had taken his family with him to Afghanistan, following bin Laden's declaration that it was a religious duty for devout Muslims. The indication that they had been in Afghanistan was a sign that he was likely a member of al-Qaeda. Why else would people take their families to a war zone?

After a while I stopped taking notes, even though I was still asking questions and he continued to answer them. I also began to look disinterested, and at one point I even closed my notebook, put my hand on my head, and yawned. Bahlul looked puzzled—he was used to military interrogators writing down everything he said.

"Tell me again, why did you go to Afghanistan?" I asked.

"I came to teach the Quran, as I told you," he said. I gave him a big smile. "Why are you smiling?"

"The problem with you guys is that you didn't come up with better stories. If you and the friends you were captured with were smart, you would have divided yourselves up, saying numbers one to fifteen were studying the Quran, while numbers sixteen to thirty were teaching it. Saying you all are teaching the Quran is just stupid." Bahlul said nothing, but a smirk crossed his face.

I returned to talking about Islam, but I still wasn't taking any notes. At a certain point Bahlul could no longer contain himself and asked me sharply: "What?"

"What?" I asked back.

"Why aren't you taking notes anymore?"

"Did I do anything but respect you here?" I asked him.

He shook his head. "You did respect me."

"I did. I came here and dealt with you respectfully as one human being to another. But when you are not honest with me, I take that as sign of disrespect."

"But I'm telling you the truth," he protested.

"Please, please don't go down that route. You don't know what I know. I know who you are. I came here especially to speak to you."

"I'm telling you the truth."

"Look, you may consider yourself an important soldier in the war against the infidels, but as you sit here and give arguments that contradict what you swore you'd give your life for, you make me wonder how much you really believe in your cause. My question to you is: Do you really believe in these things?" Bahlul was silent. "If you do truly believe these things," I continued, "then your jihad is not over yet. It is your duty to continue advocating what you were fighting for.

"I have a deal for you," I continued. "It is time for noon prayers. We should stop and you should go and pray. And when you pray I need you to do an *istikhara*—I need you to ask God for guidance. Ask God if you should continue to hide behind your shadow, or whether you should be a real mujahid and admit to what you believe in." Bahlul gave a slight, somewhat uncomfortable-sounding laugh, as if trying to show he was still confident, and then left for prayers.

When he returned, he sat back down in his place on the couch, but this time I sat down next to him. He clasped his hands together between his knees and stared down at the table. "Taqabal Allah," I said—May God receive your prayers: a common saying among Muslims after prayer.

"Minna wa minkum," he replied: May God accept them from us and you. Then neither of us said anything for a minute.

"Would you like a cookie?" I said, breaking the silence. On the coffee table in front of us I had put some tea and a plate of cookies.

"Thank you," he said, removing a cookie from the plate. He took a bite and then said slowly, "I am Anas al-Mekki. I am *mas'oul*"—someone with responsibilities. "I am one of the officers of al-Qaeda. I am bin Laden's personal assistant. What do you want to know?"

I had heard the name Anas al-Mekki many times, in different investigations, and knew he was indeed important. "Would you like some tea?" I replied.

Bahlul coughed up some of the cookie that was still in his mouth. "I told you my position in al-Qaeda and you ask whether I'd like some tea?" He looked at me in disbelief.

"Well, I already knew that," I told him. "It didn't surprise me. As I told you, you don't know what I know. But now I know you're at least being honest and respecting me, which is why I'm offering you some tea."

I spent the next day and a half interviewing Bahlul. His story is very similar to many other Yemeni al-Qaeda members. Their families had lived and worked in Saudi Arabia until they were expelled in the aftermath of the first Gulf War due to Yemen's support of Saddam Hussein's invasion of Kuwait. We covered everything from his path to al-Qaeda—he, too, was inspired first by Abdullah Azzam—to specific roles he'd had. At one stage Bahlul had roomed with Mohammed Atta and Ziad Jarrah, two of the 9/11 hijackers. We spent time discussing the video he had produced celebrating the USS *Cole* bombing, which had led to his appointment as bin Laden's personal propagandist. We went through the tape, looking at the different scenes, and he outlined where he had taken them from: bin Laden's speeches, military training exercises at al-Farouq, scenes from Saudi Arabia, and the press conference at which bin Laden and others had expressed solidarity with the Blind Sheikh.

Bahlul's roles were wide-ranging. He had researched and written speeches for bin Laden, set up the satellite that had allowed bin Laden to listen to the details being reported about the 9/11 attacks, and kept minutes of meetings held by al-Qaeda's leaders.

When al-Qaeda members confessed their roles and gave us information, often it was because they were repentant, or wanted to pretend they were, in order to lessen their punishment. Bahlul was different in that he was not embarrassed about anything he had done for al-Qaeda, and he confessed with pride. He appeared convinced of my argument that if he truly believed in al-Qaeda's aims, he shouldn't lie and deny his involvement.

In a stomach-turning and appallingly cold manner, Bahlul detailed why al-Qaeda considered the World Trade Center a legitimate target. "The World Trade Center was the center of those who control the world economy and the World Bank, those who destroy other countries' economies and even deny small farmers their lands, and those who prevent Islamic banks and financial institutions from flourishing because they want to control all capital.

"The World Trade Center was the center of globalism, and exemplified the American domination of the world and its people." Bahlul went on to claim that anyone "who worked in it participated in crimes against politically and economically oppressed people all over the world."

"But the world economy and market prices are not controlled by the innocent people who worked at the World Trade Center," I countered.

He wouldn't even acknowledge the death of innocent people on 9/11: "They were legitimate targets because they paid taxes and so are funding America's wars against Muslims. We should kill Americans exactly as they kill us, an eye for an eye and a tooth for a tooth. We should keep killing them until every liter of blood they wasted from us is equaled by the liters of blood we waste from them." It was his hope, he said, that America would kill him, as his death would anger bin Laden. And if he was killed by Christians and Jews, his reward would be even greater than that of a regular martyr.

Bin Laden was very interested in the effects of the 9/11 attacks. He had instructed Bahlul to conduct research pertaining to what experts were predicting would be the economic results of the attack.

At one point, Bahlul asked me to send the message to President Bush that America should invade Iraq and "finish his father's unfinished job." To convince me, he told me that Saddam Hussein was a bloodthirsty individual who killed his own people, and that the Arab world would support an American attack. Like other al-Qaeda members, Bahlul was a firm believer in the hadith that said that the eventual victory of Islam would come after the final battle of Armageddon. According to his belief, the invasion of Iraq would be an important stepping-stone to fulfillment of the prophecy.

We showed Bahlul many photographs of al-Qaeda members, and he identified them. When he saw a picture of Abu Zubaydah, he said that he remembered seeing him in Afghanistan and had heard a lot about him as early as 1990. When he had asked Abu Hafs if Abu Zubaydah was a member of al-Qaeda, Abu Hafs had said no.

Bahlul also provided times and dates for information we had recovered in Afghanistan. When I showed him a video that our analysts believed was filmed after 9/11, he corrected them: "That's from before the attacks on New York."

"Why do you say that?"

"Because Abu Hafs is in the film. After the attacks on New York and Washington, everyone else left Kandahar, but Abu Hafs stayed because he had a herniated disc and couldn't move."

I worked with the prosecution to prepare for the Bahlul trial, as I was to be the main witness. The only difficulty came from certain people within the CIA, who objected to the prosecution's use of the phone book that had Bahlul's fingerprints on it and contained the reference to the 9/11 summit meeting in Malaysia.

"You can't use that in the trial. The fact that there was a Malaysian meeting is classified," a CIA representative told one of the prosecutors.

"What do you mean?" the prosecutor asked. "The Malaysian meeting isn't a secret. It's in *The 9/11 Commission Report*."

"Just because the commission revealed the information doesn't mean it isn't still classified."

"But your former director, George Tenet, also references it in his book."

"He's not the director anymore."

"But it had to be declassified for him to write about it."

"You can't use it."

The prosecutors were shocked by how far the CIA would go to

limit any public mention of the Malaysia meeting. There was no mention of it in the trial.

When I testified in Bahlul's trial, he would nod as I spoke, as if confirming what I had said. At one point, when I told the court that Bahlul had told me that he had produced the video celebrating the *Cole* bombing, he nodded, as if saying: Yes, I said that to him.

Bahlul was sentenced to life imprisonment in November 2008.

In 2004, I was in a military jail in North Carolina, helping with the interrogation of an uncooperative detainee, when I received an urgent phone call from the director of the FBI: a team of specialized military interrogators in Gitmo reported a confession, from an al-Qaeda member named Tarek Mahmoud el-Sawah, exposing al-Qaeda as the group behind the series of anthrax attacks that had occurred over several weeks shortly after 9/11.

The Pentagon had already briefed Congress on el-Sawah's confession. Congress asked the director to brief them on the anthrax investigation. A task force of very capable FBI agents, with high-level expertise in science, terrorism, and specialized investigations, was already working diligently on the case. No al-Qaeda links had been found. But due to the briefing to Congress, the director wanted to make sure that the intelligence was reliable, and he asked me to question el-Sawah. Not only had the military interrogators reported that he was the mastermind of al-Qaeda's anthrax program, they also said he had designed al-Qaeda's shoe bomb program.

I questioned el-Sawah, who was overweight and happiest when we'd bring him ice cream, and he was open about his al-Qaeda connections. He had fought in the original Afghan jihad and in Bosnia, where he had served as an explosives expert, and he knew senior al-Qaeda leaders from the period. He had decided to visit Afghanistan to see if, under the Taliban, it was a true Islamic state, as he had heard, because if it was, he would bring his family there to live. While there, he had visited old friends, among them Abu Hafs and Saif al-Adel. Abu Hafs had asked him to help train al-Qaeda operatives in explosives. "But you've got trainers," el-Sawah had said.

"At Banshiri," Abu Hafs replied, "we're graduating more people to heaven than out of the class." He explained that they had Yemeni trainers who really didn't know what they were doing. One blew up an entire class of Chinese Uighurs who had joined al-Qaeda. El-Sawah agreed to help, and he received specialized explosives training, including instruction in building improvised explosive devices (IEDs) and remote detonation devices, from Abu Abdul Rahman al-Muhajir. He went on to receive advanced explosives/electronics training from Abu Tariq al-Tunisi, learning how to make timers for IEDs using Casio watches as remote detonators.

Then, from June 2001, he gave instruction in explosives and wrote a four-hundred-page bomb-making manual. After the United States invaded Afghanistan, el-Sawah fought with al-Qaeda against the United States in the Tora Bora region before being wounded and caught.

When I asked him about al-Qaeda's anthrax program, he didn't even understand the question. We were speaking in Arabic, and he didn't know what the word *anthrax* was in Arabic. When I questioned him further, trying to work out where the military interrogators had got their information from, I learned that he had told them that once, when he was having lunch in Kandahar with Abu Hafs and Saif al-Adel, the two had asked him if he remembered a mutual friend who had a degree in chemistry and whom they had known in Egypt. El-Sawah said that he remembered the expert, and Saif al-Adel asked if he was still in contact with him; el-Sawah said he wasn't.

On that basis the interrogators wrote a report about "the anthrax program." As for el-Sawah's being the mastermind of any shoe bombing operation, I found out that the military interrogators had said to him: "You're an explosives expert. If you were to build a shoe bomb, how would you do it?" He had drawn them a diagram. That diagram constituted their "proof." It turned out that it was a bad drawing, unrepresentative of the shoe bomb Richard Reid used.

I went with FBI colleagues to the interrogators who had extracted the "confession" and told them that, based upon my interrogation, their claims didn't add up. They were novice interrogators and didn't understand that you can't just jump to those kinds of conclusions. They admitted that they had messed up.

Around the time I was interrogating el-Sawah, Matrafi—the head of al-Wafa, whom I had interrogated in the early days at Gitmo with Ed and Andre—was taken by the same specialized military team to a black site (a secret location) and interrogated. Apparently they didn't get much intelligence from him, so they asked me to come and talk to him again. A member of the team told me, "We know he knows about a threat, but he's not cooperating. Can you get through to him and tell him to talk to us?" I didn't have much faith in that specialized military interrogation team after the el-Sawah incident, but I felt that if there really was a threat that Matrafi knew about, I should help.

When I went in he was very angry, and before I could say anything, he said: "I told you everything I knew right at the start. I confessed everything. Why am I here? Why should I talk to you again?"

"I can't explain Guantánamo. I don't understand how it's being run," I told him. By this time the detainees knew exactly where they were. "But I can tell you that cooperation is always the best tactic, so I recommend you tell them everything."

"But I already told you everything. Why should I repeat it again? Didn't you write everything down?"

"What do you mean?" I asked him.

"The other interrogators just told me to repeat to them everything I told you when you interrogated me, so they can put it in their file."

"I'm sorry that I wasted your time," I told him, and walked out. It wasn't the only time that these inexperienced interrogators tried to "reinterrogate" detainees, telling them simply to repeat what they had told the seasoned interrogators. The point was that they could then claim that their techniques were successful and that they had gotten "intelligence."

On August 31, 2003, General Miller flew to Iraq to advise those running a prison in Baghdad called Abu Ghraib. Mark Fallon sent a CITF agent along with him, with instructions to warn the officials meeting

Miller that use of the techniques he would advocate were not the only way to run interrogations. The general wouldn't allow the agent into any of his meetings. In April 2004, General Miller became head of all prisons in Iraq that were under U.S. control.

In 2004, pictures of U.S. army personnel abusing detainees in Abu Ghraib were shown around the world. One of the photographs that went around the world was an image of one soldier, Lynndie England, holding a leash attached to the neck of a naked prisoner. Qahtani had endured the same treatment at Gitmo, also under General Miller's command.

Instructors from the JPRA SERE school also went to Iraq and participated in interrogations using SERE techniques. Col. Steven Kleinman, an air force reservist who is a highly decorated veteran of three major military campaigns (Operations Just Cause, Desert Storm, and Iraqi Freedom) and who is recognized as having been one of the most prolific interrogators during the first Gulf War, told the Senate Armed Services Committee in September 2008 that in Iraq he had witnessed abusive interrogations and had intervened to stop them. In one instance the JPRA team "took a hooded detainee to a bunker at the Task Force facility, forcibly stripped him naked and left him, shackled by the wrist and ankles, to stand for 12 hours."

In November 2005 Secretary Rumsfeld and the new chairman of the Joint Chiefs of Staff, Gen. Peter Pace, gave a press conference during which a UPI reporter asked them about allegations of torture by Iraqi authorities in prisons under Iraqi control. General Pace told the reporter: "It is the absolute responsibility of every U.S. service member, if they see inhumane treatment being conducted, to intervene, to stop it."

Secretary Rumsfeld interrupted him and said: "I don't think you mean they have an obligation to physically stop it; it's to report it."

"If they are physically present when inhumane treatment is taking place, sir, they have an obligation to try to stop it," General Pace responded.

24

45 Minutes

Mid-September 2002. "How did you get this information?" Samantha, the head of the CIA's high-value target (HVT) unit, was standing in the doorway of the office I was using at a CIA safe house in Kabul. She was waving a cable I had asked the chief of station to send to FBI headquarters. Before the 9/11 attacks, Samantha had been assigned to the CIA's station at a location where I had also worked, so we kind of knew each other.

"From the six al-Qaeda guys you let us interrogate," I replied, referring to a group of terrorists captured in a September 11, 2002, raid on apartments in Karachi that had also, and more importantly, netted Ramzi Binalshibh and Karim. The CIA had let me and my FBI colleagues Aaron Zebley and Mike Butsch question the six, but had barred us—on orders from Langley—from interrogating Binalshibh and Karim.

The Pakistani authorities had found the group based mainly on intelligence an FBI colleague got from the Saudi al-Qaeda operative Ahmed al-Darbi, whom he had interrogated at Bagram Airfield. We had learned about Darbi from his father-in-law, Ahmed al-Hada, and from Abu Jandal. Following the raid, the FBI had identified the terrorists, photographed them, and searched the apartments for evidence. One of the raids had resulted in a bloody gun battle, in which a number of al-Qaeda operatives were killed. In the apartment where Binalshibh and Karim were found there was a standoff, Binalshibh holding a knife to his own throat.

"If any of you step any closer," Binalshibh had declared, "I'm going to slit my own throat." He apparently didn't realize that in a hostage situation you need a hostage other than yourself, and that the Pakistanis were happy to take him dead or alive. There was no way they'd let him escape. He was soon subdued, and after the detainees were processed by an FBI team in Karachi, they were handed over to the CIA, by order of the Bush administration.

"Very impressive," Samantha said, referring to the memo we had written based on intelligence the six terrorists had given us. "This is some of the best intelligence I've read in a while. That's amazing that they gave it to you."

With that she was gone. Aaron, who was in the office with me, whispered, "Think they'll now realize they are being stupid not letting us have access to the other two?"

"Let's hope so," I replied.

A few hours later Samantha again appeared in the doorway. "Can we talk?" she asked.

"Sure." I followed her into the hallway. "What's going on?"

"As you know, we're not allowed to give you access to Binalshibh and Karim," she said, "because they want them to be interrogated by ————." She named two foreign countries—the names of which are classified—and then her voice trailed off. From her facial expression I could tell that she disagreed with the policy of barring us from interrogating them, and that she wanted my opinion.

"That's pathetic," I told her. "Why have other countries do the interrogating, when we have people who can do the job better?"

"And they have American blood on their hands. I don't want them to do our job. I know we can do it here, and we can do it right."

"I agree completely. So do you have a plan to give us access?"

"I do. I'm going to go against the instructions I've been given from

Washington, and I'm going to give you access to them for forty-five minutes each, and we'll see what happens. If they cooperate, then maybe the whole idea of rendition will be scrapped and we can continue interrogating them here."

"Sounds good, but did you say I can only have forty-five minutes with them?"

"Yes, forty-five minutes."

"Okay, I'll take what I can get."

September 11, 2002. "Hi, Ali, welcome back." Kevin Donovan, now the assistant director in charge of the New York office, had spotted me on the street outside the JTTF's New York office.

"Thank you, it's good to be home," I replied. I had just returned to New York from working with the fusion cell in Yemen.

"We're going down to ground zero," Kevin said, "and I'd like you and Steve Bongardt to carry the FBI wreath to the memorial."

"But there are others better suited than us."

"No, it would be an honor for the FBI to have you and Steve do this." Steve and I had been trying to get the CIA to share information with us before 9/11 that could have stopped the attacks, so I understood why Kevin wanted us to carry the wreath—the act would be symbolic.

As Steve and I walked, holding the wreath, I couldn't hold back my tears. The history of what had happened kept swirling around in my mind.

I felt almost physically unable to look at the site where thousands of Americans had died, in an attack that in my heart I knew we could have stopped. At one point I passed a picture of John O'Neill, and as I looked at John's face I felt a sharp pain in my chest. We laid the wreath at the memorial for law enforcement personnel who had died in the attacks.

After the walk, I returned to my office. Others were going to a nearby bar, but I was too emotional to deal with other people. As I sat at my desk, reliving what had happened a year earlier and trying to work, my phone rang. It was FBI headquarters in Washington telling me that Ramzi Binalshibh and Karim had been captured, and that the CIA had requested that I travel to Karachi to help with the interrogations.

I flew to Washington, DC, where I met Aaron and Mike and another FBI agent, Ray Holcomb, who would help with our security, and we got on a private plane chartered by the CIA and flew to Islamabad. CIA officers met us on the tarmac, and one, an older man, came up to me and asked, "Are you Ali Soufan?"

"Yes," I replied, "I am."

He stuck out his hand. "I've heard a lot about you. I look forward to seeing you in action."

"Thank you. We'll see how it goes."

A few hours later we took a small cargo plane from Islamabad to Karachi, and a new group of CIA officials flew with us. While the officials on the plane from DC and at the airport in Karachi were friendly, on this plane we were ignored. We recognized some of them, including Fred, the CIA official who had caused problems in Jordan during the millennium investigation and who had threatened Ibn al-Shaykh al-Liby, ruining that interrogation. It was a bad sign that he was involved.

In Karachi we were met by CIA officers and Pakistani special forces who were holding the detainees. The eight terrorists, who were all blindfolded and handcuffed, were one by one taken from a building on the side of the runway onto our cargo plane.

One of the CIA officers pointed at a detainee, identifying him as Karim; he didn't really look like his brother, whom I had interrogated in Yemen. The officer said to me: "That one is a troublemaker. He's very arrogant. He's even telling the others that they'll open an Islamic school in Guantánamo."

Once the prisoners were loaded onto the plane, we flew to Kabul, and there we met other CIA officials, including Samantha, from the HVT unit. The sun had set and Kabul was dark, and we boarded 4x4 jeeps and headed into the darkness. I was in the same vehicle as Samantha, and at first sat silently as we drove out of the city, watching as we passed remnants of destroyed Russian tanks and other military equipment, which the Afghanis had deliberately left as symbols of their victory against a superpower.

"Where are we going?" I asked Samantha after a few minutes.

"There's a detention facility outside the city that we use to question terrorists," she replied.

We were waved through the detention facility's gate by Northern Alliance fighters, who appeared to be in control of the place. The detainees were taken to cells, and we were instructed to sit in a waiting area.

We were eager to start interrogating the suspects. Aaron and Mike had both been assigned to 9/11 investigations and had been trailing Binalshibh for a year, and I was very familiar with Karim and his entire family. "If we are lucky," I said, "these guys might lead us to Khallad and even to bin Laden."

We had waited for about an hour when a CIA official came up to us and said: "You guys can interview the six, but not Binalshibh or Karim."

"Excuse me?" I asked. "Why not?"

"We received specific instructions from Washington that the FBI agents are not authorized to speak to the two main subjects. I'm sorry." Later, I learned that a cable from the CIA's Counterterrorism Center had ordered: "FBI Agent Ali Soufan is not, repeat NOT, to have access." The CTC was angry with me for my stark disagreement with them over the Abu Zubaydah interrogation.

"You guys flew us on a plane all the way from the United States just to tell us we can't actually interrogate the two main suspects?" I asked.

"That's the rule. You can have those six or nothing, your choice."

"We'll take the six, but please reconsider."

Aaron and Mike called FBI headquarters to see if they knew about any of this. They didn't, and were just as annoyed and confused as we were.

This wasn't the first time we had had conflicting messages from the CIA. It's a big agency, and within it there were some officials who had opposed the use of enhanced interrogation techniques, siding with me on the issue of the Abu Zubaydah interrogation. They were the individuals who wanted me to interrogate these detainees. Others, notably the CTC, which had brought in the contractors and the enhanced interrogation techniques, didn't want me involved.

Divisions in the CIA were also seen before we got to the Abu Zubaydah interrogation; the CTC, after all, hadn't bothered to show up originally, because according to their intelligence reporting, he wasn't actually Abu Zubaydah. Unfortunately for the CIA, those supporting the EITs seemed to have the final word—and the others were forced to go to the CIA's inspector general to register their complaints.

We began interrogating the six and soon gained valuable intelligence: on the movement of al-Qaeda operatives in Pakistan, their escape routes, and the smugglers who transport them into Pakistan and Iran. The six were surprised by what we already knew about the al-Qaeda network, the various operatives, the structure, and about their native country, Yemen—and this helped convince them to cooperate with us.

They told us about safe houses al-Qaeda used on both sides of Afghanistan's borders with Pakistan and Iran, and they detailed how operatives were smuggled from Bandar Abbas and elsewhere in Iran to Oman, Yemen, and other countries in the Arabian Peninsula.

We were naturally interested in ongoing operations, and they told us what they had been involved in before they were picked up. One detainee mentioned an al-Qaeda operative named Zubayr al-Riymi, who was putting together a cell to conduct "attacks in the Peninsula." Based on his name, we thought he was a Yemeni, but according to the detainee he was Saudi.

"Where in the Gulf is he planning to do an operation?" I asked.

"I don't know," the detainee replied, his eyes showing fear, as if he had told me too much.

"What if I told you that I know you know?"

"No, I am telling you the truth."

"And I am telling you the truth, too," I replied, looking him straight in the eye. "Brother, I have you here. How did I know where you were hiding with your buddies so I could capture you? You're smart. You see what I know about your group, about Yemen, about things that you thought were valued secrets. I am not going to tell you what I know, or how I know it, but I will let you figure it out by yourself. Much of what I know will allow me to assess your truthfulness." As I finished speaking, I put my hand gently on his shoulder.

He looked down for a few seconds, and then looked up at me. His face was a mixture of sorrow, guilt, and fear. "Look," he said, "I do not know any of the details, but I heard he was planning to do an operation in ———," and he named a country in the Arabian Gulf. "I swear, that is everything I know."

Later that night, CIA officials told Aaron, Mike, Ray, and me that they would come back and pick us up in a few hours. They never came, so we ended up falling asleep in a room that had red carpet all over the floor and walls. At night guards patrolled the base, and we were given to understand that unless we gave them the right password, we would be shot.

An Afghani fighter told us the password—it was in Tajik, the language the Northern Alliance fighters spoke—and we wrote it on our hands and went to sleep. In the middle of the night I woke up and had just stepped out to the toilet when I heard a guard shouting at me.

He was speaking Tajik, which made no sense to me, and because I was half asleep, it took me a few seconds to realize that he wanted the password. I tried to read my hand and shouted out the word, trying a few different pronunciations, and on the fourth or fifth attempt he signaled to me to pass.

Early the next morning, a few minutes after daybreak, I was awakened by Ray whispering a single sentence in my ear, over and over: "Ali, wake up, but don't move; Ali, wake up, but don't move." I opened one eye and looked at Ray, who was lying next to me. He appeared to be asleep—he wasn't moving, and his eyes were half closed—and I saw that his fingers were wrapped around his handgun.

"Look," he said, gesturing with his eyes toward the entrance to the room, "look at those guys watching us." Out of the corner of my eye I saw two Afghanis crouched by the door, staring at us. We woke up Aaron and Mike in the same manner that Ray had woken me, whispering and instructing them not to move. None of us spoke Tajik, and we weren't sure what to do.

After a few minutes I decided to break the deadlock, and I pretended to wake up. I stretched and slowly stood up, and then turned to the two Afghanis and said, "As-Salāmu `Alaykum." Though Arabic, it was a phrase that all Muslims would be familiar with, and one of the Afghanis gave me a big smile and gestured for us to follow him.

We picked up our gear and weapons and followed him cautiously out of our room into another, where a man, who we guessed was the commander, was sitting with breakfast laid out in front of him. He gestured to us to sit down and, pointing to the food, said, "Eat." That appeared to be the extent of his English, and he didn't make any more of an effort to talk to us after that.

There was tea, bread, and cheese, which we would have enjoyed if it wasn't already more than an hour after sunrise and the CIA still hadn't showed up—despite having assured us that they would pick us up last night.

We knew that the situation in Afghanistan was complicated, with tribes regularly switching alliances, so we began to fear that we might now really be captives and used as bargaining chips.

After returning to our room, we took a walk around the base, and spotted an old Russian jeep with a big picture of Ahmed Shah Massoud, the Northern Alliance commander assassinated days before 9/11, on the windscreen. As we stood around the jeep, I told the others: "Something is wrong, and for whatever reason the CIA are not showing up to pick us up. Either we stay here and wait and see what happens, or we borrow this jeep and head to Kabul."

The others agreed that we should take the jeep. We had no GPS and little idea how to get to Kabul, but staying seemed too risky. We signaled to the Afghanis, who had been watching us, that we just wanted to take the jeep for a ride around the area, which I explained by making a driving motion with my arms, and then a circle motion with my fingers. They smiled and nodded.

"Do you know how to drive on the other side of the road, Ali?" Aaron asked. The steering wheel was on the right-hand side.

"Do you see any roads around here to drive on?" I asked, and everyone laughed. There were just dirt paths and barren terrain all around.

Using our memory of how we had arrived at the base, we tried to navigate our way back. We passed lots of burned-out Russian jeeps and tanks and had to drive around a huge crater clearly made by a big bomb. By what we could only attribute to the grace of God we found our way back to Kabul and made our way to the local CIA base was. When the officials saw us, their faces turned white.

"What are you doing here? How did you get here?" one of them stammered.

"We borrowed a jeep," I replied.

"We were planning to get you—we just got busy with other things," another one said lamely.

From then on we used that jeep whenever we needed to travel, not wishing to rely on local CIA officials and get stranded again. When we returned to the United States, I left the truck near the CIA safe house, and when I returned a few months later it was still there—and I used it again.

From the CIA safe house we wrote up the intelligence we had gained from the six detainees and sent it through the CIA to FBI headquarters, as the CIA had insisted we only use their system to file any reports. That's when Samantha came to see me.

The arrangement she proposed was that I interview Binalshibh and Karim without Aaron or Mike present. A CTC officer would be in the room. I argued that my colleagues were in a better position to interview Binalshibh than I was, since they had been following him.

"Why does that matter?" Samantha asked. "You know al-Qaeda."

"Mike and Aaron have the small details, and that's what you use to show the detainees you know all about them, and how you catch them on any lies. Mike and Aaron know what questions to ask Binalshibh and what he should know. So either let them come in with me, or send them in instead, and I'll do the Karim interview."

"I'm sorry but only you can go in. They can stay outside and watch on CCTV. If you need to run anything by them, they will be there."

Since we had been using CCTV at Gitmo, we thought it might work, and as we had no choice anyway, we accepted.

"Okay," I told Samantha, "let's try that."

We went back to the detention facility, on the outskirts of the city, and while we waited for the Afghani guards to bring Binalshibh into the interrogation room, we discovered that the CCTV system had no audio. It meant that Aaron and Mike could watch what was going on but not hear anything.

The Afghanis brought Binalshibh into the room, pushed him onto the floor, and handcuffed him to the wall. He looked exactly like the picture we had of him on the FBI's Most Wanted Terrorists list, which was unusual, as terrorists rarely look exactly like the pictures we have of them. Usually they've changed their appearance to disguise their identities, or they try to appear serious in pictures. The pictures of Abu Jandal, for example, show an unsmiling, tough-looking character, but in person he's full of smiles, once engaged.

I shuddered inwardly as he walked in, because here was someone directly culpable for 9/11. While I had interrogated more important al-Qaeda members, Binalshibh was the first directly involved in coordinating the death of so many Americans. But to succeed with him, I needed to remain collected and in control of the situation, so I calmly asked the Afghanis to undo his handcuffs.

After the guards stepped out, I briefly introduced myself and told him: "Ramzi, I am not here to ask you for a confession or to elicit your cooperation. That is done. You already did it for me. You've given me everything that I need to know about 'the planes operation,' as you call it."

Binalshibh didn't say anything, but just stared at me with a confused look. This obviously wasn't how his interrogation had gone the day before with the CIA interrogators.

"What?" I asked. "You don't know what I'm talking about?"

Binalshibh had done an interview with al-Jazeera a few days earlier in which he proudly admitted his role in 9/11, providing a detailed account of the planning and execution phases of the plot. "Your interview with al-Jazeera is more then enough to fry you! Wow, Ramzi, we knew a lot about you before, but the details you provided were extremely helpful. Thank you. You told us everything about the plot and your involvement that we needed to know.

"This is a unique way to do an interrogation," I continued. "I am calling it 'interrogation in reverse,' because you already confessed. I bet you wished you had not bragged about your role on camera now. But you definitely made my life easier. You're screwed, and you should know you're screwed. Your only hope, as I'm sure you realize, is if you fully cooperate."

He nodded. "I know."

Binalshibh gave me lots of information about the planning for 9/11. He told me all about Atta and the Hamburg cell and how he had been the liaison between KSM and Atta. He explained how the hijackers were divided into two groups, the pilots and the muscle, and he outlined KSM's role as the coordinator. He told me about his last meeting with Atta, in Spain, and about Zacarias Moussaoui, whom KSM didn't want to interact with Atta.

After he gave me this information, I took a break to brief Aaron and Mike and verify what Binalshibh had told me. For the most part he was providing good information, but Aaron and Mike noticed minor discrepancies between what he was saying and evidence recovered by our investigation. This meant that he was testing our knowledge and practicing a classic counterinterrogation tactic.

On returning to the cell, I asked Binalshibh: "Did I tell you that I lost dear friends in the World Trade Center? I thought that maybe you had reflected on what you did and would at least try to make amends now, but it seems that you are still playing games."

"What do you mean? I am cooperating."

"No, you are not. You are like the one who puts poison in honey," I said, referring to a well-known Arabic proverb. "That is not cooperation. Do not think you can fool me. I have people outside who know everything about you, more than you probably realize yourself, and when you lie they will tell me.

"Look," I continued, "let me be honest with you. I am trying to control my feelings. I wish right now that I wasn't an FBI agent and I was not a U.S. government official, and that I wasn't wearing a badge. That's how I feel right now."

"I'm telling you the truth!"

"Oh, really?" I confronted him with the details that Aaron and Mike had provided, and he conceded that he had lied. "I hope we understand each other," I told him. "Every lie will be caught." He nodded.

We continued our interrogation, and I stepped out regularly and checked with Aaron and Mike to be sure that what Binalshibh was telling me squared with what we already knew. Not only were they able to tell me whether or not he was telling the truth, but they were able to cite, without notes, evidence supporting their points, from faxes, time-lines, and other information we had. Aaron is a lawyer by training—he left law to follow his dream of being an FBI agent—and his training was evident. He paid close attention to detail. Mike had similar skills, and I was impressed with how the two of them could instantly catch Binalshibh in lies.

After forty-five minutes, the CIA officials told us that our time was up, and they took Binalshibh away. Aaron and Mike called headquarters and reported the breakthrough we'd had, and headquarters requested that we write up the interview. As Aaron and Mike worked on that, I prepared for the interrogation with the second HVT, Karim.

Karim was naked when he was brought into the interrogation room, but he swaggered, with his chin held high; you might have thought he was dressed like a king and ruled the place. As an Afghani guard chained him to the wall, he sneered at me, spat on the floor to show his disgust, and uttered a series of insults.

I ignored him, took off his chains, handed him a towel to cover himself, and sat down on the floor next to him. He looked away. "This is not going to work, Karim," I told him. "You are in a tough situation. I'm going to ask you some questions. You cannot imagine how much I already know about you." He looked at me with a puzzled expression.

"Well, you are a [I gave his family's name], after all," I said with a smile, by way of explanation, and he couldn't help smiling back—he liked the compliment and the recognition of his family's importance.

"I know your family," I told Karim, "and I know you are a smart man and you realize what's happening to you. I promise to be honest with you, but I also want you to be honest with me." He listened.

"Let me tell you a story," I said, "a real story about a person in a situation similar to yours. He cooperated with me fully, and I would like to believe we became friends, mainly because of his honesty. You know in our Arab culture that the true man is judged by his traits. This is what strengthens his reputation and the stature of his family."

While Karim was looking at the floor and avoiding eye contact with me, I could tell that he was listening, because he held his head still.

"I know that he was honest with me," I continued, "and he proved to me that he was worthy of being called a man. I asked him questions that I already knew the answers to, and he replied truthfully. And when I asked about someone he did not want to talk about, instead of lying, he just told me, 'I do not want to discuss this guy with you.'

"Eventually the trust between us grew, and we discussed everything. After we finished the interrogation sessions, which lasted a few days, I asked him if I could help him in any way. He was a prisoner in the hands of a country that wasn't my own, and I had no influence over their officials, but I wanted to try to help him.

"Do you know what he said to me?" I asked. Karim didn't say anything but remained still.

"I remember very clearly the exact words he said to me. He said, 'The only thing I want is to kiss my mother's feet before I die.'"

As I said those words, I saw Karim shiver, and he then turned to look directly at me, as if trying to ensure he would hear every word I said as clearly as possible.

"While I could not help him kiss his mother's feet," I continued, "as that was out of my control, I understood his emotions and feelings, and I promised to work on arranging a phone call with his mother, so that she could hear his voice and know that he was okay. He was so happy and grateful when I told him this."

Karim began shaking, and, as if to steady himself, he placed the palm of his right hand on his forehead. I knew that he had figured out who the person in the story was.

"So I did my best to get him that phone call," I said.

He began crying like a baby. The confident and pompous individual whom the CIA had labeled as a troublemaker was now acting like a child, his shoulders slouched. It was as if all the suppressed feelings of his youth, which had been robbed from him when he was sent as a teenager to join al-Qaeda, suddenly came out.

I put my hand on his shoulder to try to calm him down, and told him: "I'm sorry. I'm not trying to play with your emotions. I know how close the two of you are to each other. But I wanted you to know the truth about my exchange with your brother."

His brother had been in jail in Yemen since the Bayt Habra incident. Even after the other al-Qaeda members arrested for the car thefts were freed, he had been held as a bargaining chip because of the family's importance to bin Laden. Karim hadn't seen his brother in many years.

Karim placed his head on my shoulder and began crying out loud: "My beloved ———, my beloved ——— [here he gave his brother's al-Qaeda alias]." It was a strange moment, having an al-Qaeda terrorist cry on my shoulder, but what instantly struck me was that he was calling his brother by his al-Qaeda alias rather than his real name. It showed how fully absorbed in the group Karim was: even during an emotional breakdown, he called his brother by his al-Qaeda alias.

"I know, I know you're telling me the truth," he said a few minutes later, with his head still on my shoulder and with tears running down his face. "My mother told me that there was an American who allowed my brother to make a phone call. She prays for you. I cannot believe it's you."

I gently patted his back and told him: "It's a small world. I'm glad that I was able to help your brother. He was very cooperative."

I waited a couple of minutes for Karim to regain his composure and stop crying. Once the tears had stopped, he looked at me differently, as if I were a link to his dear brother, someone who had done his brother a great kindness. All his original arrogance and animosity were gone.

He completely opened up and gave me specific information about al-Qaeda's operations in Afghanistan, including who was in charge of which region and where they were based. He told me everything he had done since 9/11, right through what had happened just before he got arrested. KSM and Khallad had been visiting him a few hours earlier.

Karim said he often helped KSM, who would give him detonators and explosives to transport to locations and use him as a liaison with different tribal groups. Fluent in Urdu, Karim could move around and interact with locals without attracting attention. Another role he had was as an assistant to Nashiri, the head of al-Qaeda in the Arabian Peninsula. Nashiri used him as a messenger to send instructions to different al-Qaeda operatives, and he would go to Internet cafés and send instructions on behalf of Nashiri to cells throughout the Arabian Peninsula. He gave me the methods he used on behalf of Nashiri, all of which we later verified.

"What's Nashiri working on right now?" I asked Karim. He had only been captured a few days before, so his intelligence would be extremely relevant.

"He's working on a few plots in the Arabian Peninsula," he told me, and he gave me the names of the individuals who were working with Nashiri.

Among those names, two stood out: Hussein al-Badawi, the brother of Jamal al-Badawi, who had been involved in the USS *Cole* plot; and Mu'awiya al-Madani, whose martyrdom video I had uncovered in the DocEx program and who Abu Jandal had told me was a former bin Laden bodyguard.

"What are they working on specifically?" I asked.

"I believe they are planning to do an operation against an oil tanker either in al-Mukalla, off the coast of Yemen, or in Bab al-Mandeb, a strategic strait connecting the Arabia Gulf with the Red Sea."

"How far along are they?"

"Nashiri has already purchased a boat for the attack, and the attack itself will be similar to the *Cole*. Beyond that I don't know the details. That is left to the people in the country to organize." He also gave me a list of local operatives in Yemen who he thought would be working on the plot.

My time with Karim was up, and the Afghani guards took him away.

I told Aaron and Mike what Karim had told me, and we wrote up the information and disseminated it through CIA channels. We also called FBI headquarters on a secure phone and let them know what had happened.

"That's the exact definition of actionable intelligence," said Pat D'Amuro, my boss. "If we act on it now, we should be able to stop the plot. And given your clear, undeniable success, they should give you more access to him and change their minds about rendition. I'm going to make sure everyone here is told the good news. Great work."

We were in a jubilant mood: we had gained actionable intelligence with each of the high-value targets, demonstrating that there was no need to fly them to foreign countries to be tortured. We waited in the office for instructions on how to proceed, with little doubt in our mind we'd be given access to the two of them again shortly.

About an hour after he spoke to headquarters, the CIA deputy chief of station stormed into our office. "Who the hell told the FBI HQ that these guys are cooperating?" he yelled at us.

"We did," I told him, "or, rather, we reported the facts of what happened in the interrogations. And there is clear, actionable intelligence. They cooperated, there's plenty of evidence of that."

"Don't you understand that nobody can stop these guys from being sent to ———?" He mentioned the names of the still-classified countries.

"That doesn't make sense. We got clear, actionable intelligence. There is no need to send them elsewhere. You're making a big mistake by doing that."

"This is bigger than you," he yelled. "This is an order coming from the White House. There is nothing you or the FBI can do. You can't stop this rendition." He almost spat out those words, acting as if he viewed us with complete disgust, and stormed back out.

We reported the conversation to FBI headquarters, including the "this is bigger than you" line, which indicated that decisions had been made at the very top of the U.S. government.

First we were told to stay put, as senior FBI officials tried to negotiate with the CIA and the White House to see if they'd at least agree to delay the rendition so we could talk to both detainees a bit longer. We were told about ongoing plots—ticking time bombs—and they were prepared to tell us more. Information from them could lead us to bin Laden. We had established rapport with the detainees; it made no sense not to give us access, at least for another couple of hours. Headquarters warned the White House that how they dealt with Binalshibh, especially now, would affect whether we'd be able to prosecute him down the line.

The message came back: the decision had been made to fly them to the designated countries. They could have told us bin Laden's whereabouts and still been deemed uncooperative.

A few hours later we received a phone call from headquarters. A frustrated Pat said that we had lost the battle, and that the decision had been made exactly as the CIA deputy chief of base had told us: they were denying that Binalshubh and Karim had cooperated with us, and said we were told lies.

Binalshibh and Karim were put on planes that evening and sent to ———, where they would be dealt with using interrogations tactics that were illegal in the United States.

"The rendition decision was made before you got to them," a colleague later told me. "The only reason they let you in for forty-five minutes was to cover their ass down the road. They didn't expect you to have any success in so little time, so they thought they'd give you access, and then, when asked, they'd say they had tried everything, even giving one of the FBI's top interrogators access, but the terrorists were not cooperating. But you messed up their plans, so they had to deny that you got intelligence."

I don't believe this theory, and I believe that Samantha, who had enabled us to conduct the interrogations, was a good CIA officer. When I worked at different locations, I came across some top CIA officials who were professional and talented and did the right thing. I believe Samantha fit into this category, and that she tried to do the right thing but ultimately failed because the steamroller was more powerful than anyone in the field.

Headquarters instructed Mike and Aaron to follow Binalshibh to ———— to see if they could get access to him again. Ray and I were told to return to Yemen to work with the fusion cell on disrupting the plot that Karim had told us about. The problem for us was that, after 9/11, the CIA had control of operations the FBI conducted overseas. According to Langley, the threat of an oil tanker explosion didn't exist: in their eyes, Karim had told lies.

25

The Crystal Ball Memo

October 6, 2002. "Hello?" I said, answering the phone in my hotel room in Sanaa.

"Switch on your TV." Col. Scott Duke, the marine in charge of the fusion cell in Yemen, was on the other end of the line. His voice was raised, and I could hear anger and emotion in his tone.

"What's wrong?"

"They did it," he replied. "An oil tanker is on fire off the coast of al-Mukalla. We could have stopped it if only they'd listened to us. If only they had listened to us . . ." I switched on the television and watched smoke billowing from an oil tanker at sea. Below the shot was a caption: "Breaking News: Explosion on Oil Tanker off the Coast of Yemen."

We ended the call and I switched off the television and stared out the window for a few minutes. There is no way to describe the feeling of knowing you could have stopped a terrorist attack if only your government had supported you. It was that terrible feeling again.

Hours later my phone rang. This time it was Andy Arena, the senior FBI official who had refused to link Saddam Hussein and al-Qaeda. "Ali," he said with panic in his voice, "I need to confirm something.

How widely did you distribute your memo warning of an attack off the coast of Yemen?"

"It was distributed across all U.S. government agencies through the DoD channels," I replied.

"I just got off the phone with Pat D'Amuro," Andy said. "He's sickened that the attack went ahead exactly as you had predicted in the memo, right down to an oil tanker off the coast of al-Mukalla—sickened that the warning wasn't listened to. He wanted to confirm that the memo had been widely distributed."

The memo had been put together with the help of the joint military and fusion cell. In a meeting with representatives from all U.S. agencies in Yemen, as well as the U.S. ambassador, Edmund Hull, Colonel Duke had asked for permission to intervene to stop the plot. The CIA had opposed our analysis.

One crew member was killed in the October 6 attack on the *Limburg*, a 332 x 58-meter oil tanker flying under a French flag off the coast of al-Mukalla. Twelve others were injured, and some 90,000 barrels of oil leaked into the Gulf of Aden.

After the phone calls with Duke and Andy, I went with Bob to the U.S. Embassy for a meeting in Ambassador Hull's office. Members of the fusion cell, State Department officials, and the CIA chief were gathered. I noticed that the chief looked agitated as I walked into the meeting with Stephen Gaudin, who at the time served as a permanent detailee to the fusion cell.

"I just returned from a meeting with Yemeni officials," the ambassador said, "and they told us that they believe the attack was an accident and not a terrorist attack." We were told that at the moment we had to go along with the Yemenis' verdict on the issue, and we were not to write reports saying it was a terrorist attack.

"On what basis are they saying that it's an accident?" Stephen asked.

"They looked into it. That's their position."

Stephen and I left the meeting with Colonel Duke, who muttered, "Accident my ass" on the way out.

"Like they said the USS *Cole* was an accident?" I replied.

"This cover-up won't work," Duke said.

"The truth will come out soon. The direction of the explosions, residue, witnesses—exactly like the *Cole*. You can't hide for long the fact that it was a terrorist attack," I said.

For three days the official position was that it was not a terrorist attack. We could not call it one, nor could we refer to the memo I had written before the attack, predicting it.

But on the third day a team from the Naval Criminal Investigative Service began testing the boat and found residue of TNT and other explosives. After an examination of the blast area, it was clear that the tanker had been attacked, and NCIS reported it up their chain of command. The director of the FBI assigned an FBI bomb team to investigate as well.

We investigated the attack with the Yemenis and found that what had happened conformed precisely to the information Karim had given me: two al-Qaeda suicide bombers, one of them Hussein al-Badawi, whom Karim had mentioned to me by name, pulled up alongside the *Limburg* and detonated the explosives in their dinghy.

The memo I had written became known in government circles as the "crystal ball memo," because it was so utterly and unanswerably accurate.

The joint military-FBI fusion cell had worked out that there were two separate cells operating in Yemen: one sent by Nashiri specifically to attack the *Limburg*; and a local group, run by Abu Ali al-Harithi, the post-9/11 bin Laden appointee to Yemen. Harithi's cell included Furqan al-Tajiki. Prevented from breaking up the *Limburg* cell, we had begun to focus on tracking the other operatives.

We learned that the local al-Qaeda cell had come up with a plan to target foreign embassies in Sanaa and planned to hit the U.S., British, German, French, and Cuban embassies. The Cuban Embassy was a target because of the detention of operatives at Guantánamo Bay. Apparently the al-Qaeda leadership wasn't aware that the facility is owned and operated by the United States and has nothing to do with the Cuban government.

The local cell's attack was to take place on August 13, 2002. Having cased the embassies, operatives had decided to hit the British and German with car bombs; the French and Cubans with explosives left nearby; and the U.S. with a missile, as it was deemed too well protected to be attacked with car bombs or bags of explosives. Three days before the operation, explosives expert Salman al-Taezi was adding to the missile's capacity and asked Walid Ashibi, the chief operative for the Yemen cells, to hold it while he did some rewiring. Ashibi trudged across the carpeted room. As soon as he touched the missile, the static energy that had accumulated from his traverse of the carpet caused the missile to light, and it shot right through Taezi, killing him instantly. The ignition also sent a huge shock though Ashibi, and he ran out of the apartment screaming and collapsed in the hallway. He died moments later.

Furqan and his brother, another operative, had both been resting next door. When they heard the explosion, they ran barefoot out of the building and down the street, screaming hysterically. That was the end of the planned al-Qaeda attack on the embassies.

But Furqan and the other members of the cell were still operational in Yemen.

We worked closely with our friends Colonel Yassir and Major Mahmoud, the two Yemeni PSO officials, to track down the local cell. Furqan often hid in the home of Abu Saif, Nibras's uncle. The Yemenis raided the home of Abu Saif, who was killed in a gun battle resisting arrest. In his house was evidence related to al-Qaeda and the local cell. We also found the suicide will that Nibras had left.

After the static energy fiasco, Furqan and his brother Abu Bakr (another local operative) had visited Abu al-Shahid al-Sanani, one of the *Limburg* operatives, and had told him that Harithi wanted to hit a helicopter belonging to an oil company. This was not an operation approved by Nashiri, but since the request had come from Harithi, Sanani gave Furqan help, in the form of cash, an operative for casing, and someone to train the group in weapons. Furqan rented a house in Sanaa and stocked up on weapons and ammunition, including a missile launcher. The plan was that Furqan would fire a missile at the helicopter, and another operative would shoot at it with an AK-47. Other operatives were assigned to drive the two getaway cars and videotape the operation.

When they spotted the helicopter, Furqan fired the missile but missed. The operative with the machine gun fired his entire magazine of 250 bullets but only managed to hit the helicopter twice, not doing any serious damage. Realizing that the plot had failed, the group jumped into the two cars and drove off. Abu al-Layth threw his gun under the front passenger seat and climbed in, and his brother, Huzam, got into the driver's seat. The AK-47 was not locked, and as they sped along a bumpy road, the gun went off and fired a round, hitting Abu al-Layth in the foot.

He cried out in pain and started screaming, "I'm shot, I'm shot." Not knowing where the shots were coming from, Huzam pulled the car over to the side of the road and ducked, thinking that they were being attacked. Abu al-Layth jumped out of the car, screaming in agony. The other group of operatives, among them Furqan, had no idea what had happened. Eventually, the unlocked AK-47 was found under the passenger seat, and the operatives took Abu al-Layth to the hospital.

His slipper, which had fallen off in the confusion, was left at the side of the road.

We investigated the attack on the helicopter. A big breakthrough came on November 3, when the bloodied slipper was found after witnesses reported a shooting in the area. The Yemenis checked local hospital records to see if anyone had come in with a gun wound to the foot, and indeed someone had: a known al-Qaeda operative named Abu al-Layth, in Furqan's cell. The Yemenis interrogated him and together we started tracking down the other members of the cell.

Entirely by coincidence, on November 5, analysts at the U.S. National Security Agency listening in on phone conversations got a location on Harithi, and a drone-launched missile was fired at his car. It killed him and the other five other al-Qaeda operatives riding with him. Among those in the car was his main assistant, a Yemeni-born U.S. citizen, Kamal Derwish, who had close ties to an al-Qaeda group in the United

States nicknamed the Lackawanna Six. (The group had often gathered in Derwish's apartment, near Buffalo, New York.)

Nashiri ordered the *Limburg* cell to assassinate the U.S. ambassador, Edmund Hull, in retaliation. After the *Limburg* attack the cell had gone into hiding, but once Nashiri ordered them to start planning a new attack, they reemerged and we were able to find and arrest them. They had mapped out the routes the ambassador took and were planning to fire missiles at his armored vehicle. We found the safe house they had rented and the weapons they had intended to use.

With operatives from both cells in custody, we worked with the Yemeni authorities to prosecute them. Yemeni prosecutor Saeed al-Aql was committed to justice and faced defense lawyers who tried promoting conspiracy theories, including the idea that al-Qaeda doesn't exist and that the plots were American fabrications. The detainees, meanwhile, sang songs in the courtroom praising bin Laden and al-Qaeda.

On the first day in court, the suspects spat on the floor in front of us as they walked in. I told a colleague to go up to them, collect their spit on pieces of paper, and say to them: "Thanks, now we have your DNA." He did, and they never spat in court again while we were there.

Qassim al-Rimi, one of Furqan's junior operatives, shouted at Aql as he read the charges, "I am going to break your legs."

"What did you say?" Aql replied. "You think someone like you can threaten me?" That same evening, a hand grenade was thrown at Aql's house when he was out. Thankfully, his wife and children were unharmed.

There were two trials, one for the *Cole* suspects and the second for all the other plots. Each of the trials was a success; the detainees were given a mixture of death sentences, life imprisonment, and long-term prison sentences. They remained in jail until February 3, 2006, when a group of twenty-three prisoners escaped by digging a tunnel to the women's bathroom of a mosque some 140 meters away. Among the escapees were Furqan and Qassim al-Rimi, once a low-level member of the Nashiri cell (at the time of this writing, he is one of the main leaders of al-Qaeda in the Arabian Peninsula), and operatives convicted years earlier for their roles in the USS *Cole* bombing.

A few months after the members of the Yemeni cells were prosecuted, I received a phone call from a friend at the CTC. "Ali, this is important," he said. "What's your STU number?" STU stands for secure telephone unit. I gave it to him and he told me, "I'm going to fax you something."

It was a memo from the CIA chief in Sanaa to CTC headquarters, reporting that Ambassador Hull had suggested that I go to Yemen to help with the investigation of USS *Cole* subjects who had escaped from prison in April 2003. (Ten al-Qaeda members, including Jamal al-Badawi, had escaped. They were caught the following year.) Hull had made the recommendation based upon my close relationship with General Qamish and other senior Yemeni officials. The CIA chief registered his disagreement, asking the ambassador to change his request. The Yemenis didn't like me, the CIA chief claimed, because I had "demanded access to people in al-Mukalla." I had never been to al-Mukalla and knew that the CIA chief, the same person who had blocked us from breaking up the *Limburg* plot, was making up lies about me.

I gave the memo to my FBI superiors, who demanded an apology from the CIA and a retraction. No official apology came, and instead a CIA official went to the FBI representative at the CTC and said, "We made a mistake."

PART 8

FINAL MISSIONS

26

Leaving the FBI

April 29, 2003. Undercover Pakistani domestic intelligence officers saw the truck they were waiting for pull into the arranged meeting spot. As it came to a standstill, one officer casually strolled over to the driver's window and peered inside. The officers were posing as arms dealers for a domestic terrorism case they were investigating—Shiite mosques were being blown up in Karachi—and a source had arranged the introduction between them and the men seeking to buy explosives.

One of the undercover officers studied the truck's occupants and shouted at the driver, "Why were you looking at my sister?"

"What are you talking about?" the driver asked. He laughed and replied, "We're not looking at your sister."

In a swift movement, the officer snatched the keys from the ignition. The driver, now agitated, continued to insist that he did not know what the officer was talking about. The man in the passenger seat smiled silently at his friend's dilemma and then stepped out of the truck, whereupon the undercover officers watching noticed that he had only one leg.

The driver had also stepped out of the truck, and a fistfight ensued between him and the officer. A crowd gathered, and within seconds the driver and the undercover officer were separated and the driver and the passenger subdued. The crowd was made up entirely of undercover officers; the "why are you looking at my sister" routine was a ploy to get the two men out of the truck. It was a good move, as the driver had a perfume spray bottle with cyanide in it, which probably would have been used if he had realized that the encounter was a sting.

The driver and the one-legged passenger were taken to the police station, where they denied any connection to terrorism. They weren't known to local officers as domestic terrorists or dealers. The driver, however, had in his possession a compact disc with a letter to Osama bin Laden and two images of the World Trade Center, with United Airlines Flight 175 crashing into the south tower. The police suspected an international link, and the case officer went to the FBI's Most Wanted Terrorists website to see if a picture of either man appeared on it. As only indicted terrorists appeared on the site, the men were not found.

One officer, bluffing, said to the one-legged passenger, "So I see that you're a very important guy?"

Without blinking, the one-legged Arab replied: "Whatever the Americans are paying you, bin Laden will double."

The passenger identified himself as Khallad bin Attash, bin Laden's key operative, and the driver was later identified as Ammar al-Baluchi, alias Ali Abdul Aziz Ali, KSM's nephew who had assisted the 9/11 hijackers and had himself tried to get a U.S. visa a week before the attack, perhaps to assist as a hijacker.

In one of the men's pockets was a letter from Saudi Arabian scholars to bin Laden, discussing al-Qaeda's strategy against the United States. Khallad and Baluchi wanted to buy explosives to attack the U.S. Consulate in Karachi. The two terrorists were handed over to the CIA. Later, defenders of enhanced interrogation techniques claimed that it was through their use on KSM that Baluchi and Khallad were arrested, but this was yet another falsehood propagated: the arrests were by chance, and entirely due to a quick-witted police officer, who told me the story himself when I later visited Pakistan to investigate the case.

Khallad was never given to the FBI for questioning, despite the fact that we knew more about him than anyone else in the U.S. government—from our anonymous source in Afghanistan, from the USS *Cole* investigation, from his brothers, from the East African embassy bombings case, and from Abu Jandal, Hamdan, Bahlul, and other al-Qaeda operatives we had successfully interrogated. Instead he was handed over to the very CIA contractors who had messed up the Abu Zubaydah interrogation. They had no knowledge of Khallad, and subjected him to harsh interrogation techniques.

The same happened with Nashiri, the mastermind of the USS *Cole* investigation. He had been captured in November 2002, and those of us involved in the USS *Cole* case, who knew all about him from the years we had spent in Yemen investigating the case and speaking to his operatives, weren't given access to him. Likewise KSM, who was arrested in March 2003 and put into the enhanced interrogation program: an FBI colleague who knew more about KSM than anyone else wasn't given access to him.

When I publicly commented on this years later, Philip Zelikow, executive director of the 9/11 Commission and a Bush administration official, publicly concurred with my assessment. The wrong people were questioning these top al-Qaeda operatives, with disastrous effects.

After Nashiri was arrested and bin Laden placed Khallad in charge of operations in the Arabian Peninsula, and before his arrest, Khallad was in contact with the al-Qaeda cell in Saudi Arabia. He gave them the order, from bin Laden, that operations in Saudi Arabia were approved. Previously, bin Laden had been reluctant to hit his homeland. Two weeks after Khallad's arrest, on May 12, 2003, residential compounds in Riyadh were attacked, resulting in the death of thirty-five people, including nine Americans. More than 160 people were injured. The bombing was led by Mu'awiya al-Madani and Zubayr al-Rimi. One of the six al-Qaeda operatives arrested with Binalshibh and Karim had told me that Rimi was involved in planning an attack in the area. Those interrogating Khallad had two weeks to get that information from him—a real ticking time bomb scenario. A few months later, on November 8, a suicide truck bomb exploded at another compound in Saudi Arabia, resulting in the death of eighteen people. One hundred and twenty-two people were injured. Khallad most probably knew of the operatives in Saudi Arabia and may even have given them their orders.

The same was true of KSM, who after 9/11 headed al-Qaeda cells around the world. It's highly unlikely that he didn't know about cells in London, Madrid, and Bali. But he was put into the EIT program, and on March 11, 2004, al-Qaeda bombs exploded in Madrid's train system, killing 191 people and injuring around 1,800; on July 7, 2005, al-Qaeda bombed London, killing 52 people and injuring more than 700; and on October 1, 2005, bombs in Bali killed 20 people and injured more than 100. All of these acts were perpetrated by cells that it's virtually impossible for KSM not to have known about. For example, Mohammad Sidique Khan, the oldest of the four suicide bombers who blew himself up in London, reportedly trained in camps in Pakistan and Afghanistan while KSM was running operations, and with Jemaah Islamiah in Southeast Asia, another part of KSM's fiefdom.

Approximately five months after KSM was arrested, the JW Marriott in Jakarta was hit, the operation funded by $100,000 KSM had given Hambali after the first Bali bombing as "a sign of congratulations." Another $30,000 had been given to Hambali for further operations; he gave the money to Azahari Husin and Noordin Top for the bombing. But KSM's interrogators never got this information.

Those of us in the FBI who had seen what had happened with Abu Zubaydah, Ibn al-Shaykh al-Liby, Qahtani, Ramzi Binalshibh, Karim, and others now had to sit on the sidelines as even more important al-Qaeda terrorists were put into a program that didn't work and created faulty intelligence.

On May 14, 2004, I arrived in Yemen at 11:30 PM with Carlos Fernandez. We had come to help the Yemenis prosecute the *Cole* suspects. Stephen Gaudin and his wife, Casssandra, met us at the airport; they had married earlier that year and I had been unable to attend the wedding, so I was excited to finally meet Cassandra and give my congratulations in person. Steve wasn't in the mood for well wishes, however. I saw that he was fuming.

"What's wrong?" I asked.

"Did you see yesterday's *New York Times* article?" There was anger in his voice. I hadn't seen the article; I had been on a plane, I told him. He said that the CIA had publicly taken credit for our successes in getting information from Abu Zubaydah. "They actually connected the success with KSM and Padilla to the special treatment," he said, making quotation marks in the air with his hands as he said *special treatment*.

The next day we met the ambassador, Edmund Hull, who said that he was happy we had come and that he hoped my special relationship with General Qamish would influence the Yemenis' cooperation with the *Cole* detainees.

On March 19, 2005, the Doha Players theater in Qatar was blown up by a suicide bomber. A British citizen was killed, and fifteen people were injured. The operation was possibly conducted by the same cell we were warned about by one of the Yemenis arrested with Binalshibh and Karim. A few hours after the attack, al-Jazeera's website posted a picture of the bomber: someone we had been searching for since the East African embassy bombings. Two days before the bombing, al-Qaeda in Saudi Arabia had released a recording hinting at an attack. One of the leaders of the Saudi al-Qaeda cell at the time was Zubayr al-Rimi, the operative we had been told was planning an attack.

I walked into Pat D'Amuro's office and showed him the picture of the bomber and asked, "What the hell are we doing here?" It was a rhetorical question. Pat was aware of all these issues, and he was as angry as I was. He had already announced that he was leaving the FBI and heading to a private consulting firm, headed by the former mayor of New York, Rudy Giuliani. I added, "Aren't you glad you're leaving? I wish I could leave, too, but I've got too many years left." To retire from the FBI, you need at least twenty years of service and to be age fifty or over. I had been in the FBI less than ten years.

"Why don't you come with me?" Pat asked. I thought he was joking, but then he kept asking, and after a series of discussions over several weeks, I accepted. It was one of the hardest decisions I've had to make in my life, but I realized that either I'd have a heart attack by the time I was forty or I'd have to leave.

It wasn't only that we weren't involved in investigations abroad; it was also clear that some high-level people at the CIA at the time were specifically targeting me—I was told that by more than a few FBI executives and CIA colleagues. Ever since I had been interviewed by the 9/11 Commission, I was a marked man. It didn't help that I had objected to what later became known as enhanced interrogation techniques.

In a number of instances, the FBI wanted to send me abroad for an investigation, and the CIA tried to bar me from traveling. Pat responded to FBI headquarters, which had delivered the CIA request: "Since when does the FBI let others decide who we send on missions?" The director of the FBI agreed, and I went on the missions.

In June 2003 I assisted in the investigation of a case in the United States where a suspect was in contact with al-Qaeda in Saudi Arabia. I questioned the suspect with another FBI agent, Bob Herrmann. The suspect had a lawyer with him, and when we asked a question, he'd reply: "Don't speak to me. Speak to my lawyer."

I ignored him and told him why he was important to our investigation, why he should talk, and that his answers could save lives. He responded to that speech by repeating, "Talk to my lawyer." To my surprise, the lawyer turned to his client and said: "Now, listen to me. Agent Soufan is saying very important things, and you had better listen to him, because cooperating is in your interest." We got the information we needed.

Bob and I were nominated for the internal "intelligence award" after that operation ended successfully. When you're nominated for the award by the FBI director, it's usually a formality for the director of Central Intelligence to sign it, but apparently it never left the DCI's desk.

"Before I leave," I told Pat, as I accepted his offer, "I first have to finish the undercover operation that I'm running." Some Americans were trying to join al-Qaeda, and, posing as Osama bin Laden's personal representative in North America, I had infiltrated their group.

On the day I announced my resignation, David Johnston, a reporter from the *New York Times*, told me that a few days earlier he had talked to the director of the FBI during a gala in New York and asked him: "Where do you see the future of the FBI?" The director had pointed at me and said, "That is the future of the FBI."

I was touched by his kind words, more valuable to me than any award. I told Johnston with a smile: "Then you only have yourself to blame. If you had told me that two days ago, maybe I would have stayed."

27

Undercover

March 4, 2004. "Do you have any questions?" I asked Tarik Shah, a martial arts expert and musician from the Bronx. Shah was under the impression that I was a personal representative of Osama bin Laden. He had been telling me of his desire to join al-Qaeda and kill infidels, and while outlining his credentials he had boasted that he was a master of hand-to-hand combat and knew how to rip someone's throat out.

"I'm talking about damage to the inside, so they would drown on their own blood."

"I can't make a decision on whether to accept you and your friend into al-Qaeda now," I told him. "I need to confer with my al-Qaeda superiors first. In the meantime, you should continue your training, and I will be in touch."

"Shukran," he said: thank you. I guessed he felt that speaking Arabic would demonstrate his commitment to the cause.

The fact that I was doing the undercover mission was strange: Shah's case belonged to a different squad, and I was a supervisory special agent—which meant that I was running my own squad and had my own agents to oversee. But the squad handling Shah had asked me to help. They didn't have anyone else available who knew enough about al-Qaeda or had sufficient training to fool Shah.

I spent weeks preparing for the mission, reviewing the case information, refreshing my knowledge of al-Qaeda and its recruitment process, and practicing what I would say in different scenarios. I started by researching everything known about Shah: his thoughts, ideas, and motivations. Next I determined where he fit into the operation, and then I worked on developing my cover story, down to the smallest details: I would need to answer with confidence and show no hesitation.

Undercover operations don't allow room for mistakes. If the wannabe terrorists find out who you really are, odds are they'll kill you. Not only are you a representative of the Western oppressor that they've been professing a desire to kill, but you're now the obstacle between them and their jihad. If you're lucky, you'll escape alive, but the operation will have failed, and the chance to catch them incriminating themselves will be lost.

In December 2003 Shah had been arrested by the City of Yonkers police for petty larceny, and during a search of his vehicle the police found phone numbers belonging to Seifullah Chapman—a member of an extremist group in northern Virginia, the Virginia Jihad Network, who was convicted in March 2004 of providing material support to a Pakistani terrorist group—and a second individual, who was known to have trained in foreign terrorist camps. Shah had also made inquiries in mosques and religious stores in New York about joining al-Qaeda—and those questions eventually reached us as well.

On December 16, 2003, we sent an informant whom I will call Saeed (a former convict and Black Panther) to befriend Shah under the guise of seeking bass lessons. Saeed succeeded, and as their friendship grew, Shah enlisted Saeed's help in finding a location for a martial arts studio where he could "teach the brothers . . . knives and stars and stuff like that" so that they could carry out terrorist activities. Shah also told Saeed of a network he had of others who also wanted to help al-Qaeda.

In January 2004 Saeed told Shah that he had "important news": he was in contact with an al-Qaeda recruiter from the Middle East who was interested in someone who could train a small group of fighters in hand-to-hand combat and martial arts. The brother's name was Ali, he was originally from Canada, and he was in fact bin Laden's personal representative in North America.

Shah said that he was interested and added that he had a close associate, Rafiq Sabir (also known as "the Doctor"), a Columbia University–trained emergency room doctor, living in Boca Raton, Florida, who would be interested in participating as well. He told Saeed to present himself and Sabir to Ali as a "package"—between the two of them, they could provide al-Qaeda with both martial arts services and medical services.

Saeed said he'd pass on the message and later told Shah that the recruiter was willing to meet Shah alone, and that the meeting would take place in Plattsburgh, in upstate New York, near the Canadian border. He warned Shah that Ali was part of a cell involved in jihad and was very security conscious.

On March 3, 2004, Shah and Saeed took a train from New York's Penn Station to Plattsburgh, and I met them the following day. Shah tried to impress me by telling me about his training in jujitsu and knife and stick fighting, and he said that he was "blessed" to have studied with a mujahid who had fought in Malaysia in 1969. He also showed me his prayer beads, which he said could be used as a weapon to strangle someone.

I told Shah that his application was promising, as many brothers had been arrested in Afghanistan and were in Guantánamo, and we needed new trainers. Shah then made the case for accepting Sabir as well, who he said was a "very, very, very close friend"; they had known each other for more than twenty years. He said Sabir used to be a student in one of his martial arts classes, and that he had "got the spirit." I told him I'd check with the brothers in light of his recommendation.

An undercover mission requires emotional and psychological preparation, as you are pretending to be someone you aren't. You experience competing emotions as you develop a relationship with the targets—

they trust you, and you become their "friend." You see their good side as well as the evil side. At the same time, you are using what they say to lock them in jail. You do it, of course, to protect the public from the death and destruction such people want to inflict.

With Shah, as my cover story was that I was a recruiter for bin Laden, I was reversing the usual scenario and playing this situation as if he had to work to gain my trust. It would have been unusual for bin Laden's personal representative to need to impress a wannabe al-Qaeda member, and the plan worked. He tried hard to establish his credentials with me, and it was clear that my presence made him nervous, as he felt he was mixing with an important terrorist.

On March 11, Saeed met Shah in his apartment in New York to deliver the message that I wished to meet "Doctor Rafiq" in Florida. On April 1, I met Shah in Orlando, Florida. Shah apologized and said that Sabir had had to leave the country for a family emergency. (He would be back, Shah said, on April 12.) I told Shah that I had spoken to the brothers about him, and that I had vouched for him. In light of his recommending Sabir, it was an acceptable risk for me to meet his friend. As Shah and I drove to a hotel where he was staying, because I wasn't familiar with the area, I accidentally missed the exit, so I took the next one and backtracked. Shah smiled at me and said, "I know what you're doing: You're trying to ensure we aren't followed."

"I have to do what's necessary," I replied. (The surveillance team later told me that they were worried about what was happening, and were debating whether to intervene but decided to hold off.) We arrived at his hotel and took a walk, and as we passed a little girl who was on her father's shoulders—she must have been less than two years old—she smiled at Shah and he smiled back. "She likes you," I said.

"Yes," he replied with a smile, and then he paused, and his expression turned serious, and he added, "but if needed, I could slit her throat."

I asked Shah to make a martial arts demonstration video for al-Qaeda and to prepare a syllabus. He said he wanted to train in camps in Afghanistan to learn about "chemical stuff" and how to use "explosives and firearms." He also said that he had trained many brothers who had gone to Afghanistan, including the individual whose number was found in his car and was known by authorities to have gone there.

Shah said he had wanted to start a martial arts school in New York just for Muslims, but that it wouldn't be permitted, as it would be viewed as discriminatory. What he planned to do instead was to create a "social club," because then "I can use the highest level of discrimination."

Before we parted, we discussed using a code to communicate in the future.

I had series of phone calls and e-mail exchanges with Shah. The members of the squad running the operation wrote the e-mails, as I was busy running my own squad, but they showed me each one before it was sent. The e-mails contained questions about Sabir, and Shah wrote that he was concerned about how "open" the e-mails were and worried about the security risk. I told him not to worry.

Over the period of my undercover work, Shah continued working toward helping al-Qaeda and found possible training centers for al-Qaeda terrorists in the United States, including a warehouse in Long Island, New York. He also traveled to Phoenix, Arizona, to scout for possible recruits there, and came up with a list of people he had met across the country who were sympathetic to the cause.

On March 20, 2005, I called Shah on a cell phone using a Yemeni country code. He answered thinking it was Sabir—now in the Middle East—and was surprised to hear my voice. He didn't know that I, too, was in the Middle East. I told him I was traveling, and in our agreed-upon code we spoke about the syllabus and the video. The handbook was almost complete, he said, and he was still working on the video. He assured me that he was still interested in our "business" proposal—code for his joining al-Qaeda.

On May 1, 2005, Sabir returned to the United States and stayed at a new apartment Shah had in the Bronx. I told Shah that I would return to the United States and would meet them both, which I did, on May 20, at Shah's mother's apartment, also in the Bronx.

With both of them present, Shah again attested to Sabir's value, and told me that the two of them had been kicked out of a mosque in the Bronx, where Sabir was an assistant imam, after Sabir brought in Shah to teach urban warfare. I said I was "impressed" with what he had told me about Sabir and trusted his recommendation. "Sheikh Osama considers doctors our number-one resource," I told Sabir. I said that we were ready for him and Shah to join the terrorist group.

I instructed them to continue their preparations. Shah still had not finished making his martial arts video for al-Qaeda to use. I warned him to wear a ski mask while on camera, in case the video "God forbid, falls into somebody's hands." I told them that before they were accepted as al-Qaeda members, they needed to pledge *bayat* to bin Laden. They readily agreed, Shah telling me, "We have been waiting for this for a long time."

They fell to their knees, took my hands, and repeated after me: "God's pledge is upon me and so is his covenant to commit myself to the orders of the guardians of the agreement, for the misfortune and for the prosperity. And to be a loyalist to the path of jihad, and to my brothers, until God's word is exalted. And to be protective of the secrecy of the oath and to the directives of Al-Qaeda." They embraced me, completing the al-Qaeda initiation process. They had taken the same oath as Mohammed Atta and the other 9/11 hijackers. I was now looking at two members of al-Qaeda.

Leaving the Bronx, I returned to the office, took off the wire I was wearing, and handed in my badge. That was my last day at work. I was leaving the FBI and heading into the private sector. At a farewell party that night, friends and colleagues wished me good luck.

"It's a big loss for us that you're leaving," my close friend and confidant Carlos Fernandez said.

"Well, the oath I took to defend the United States from enemies foreign and domestic doesn't end with a paycheck," I told him. "I'll still be doing my part, just from a different angle."

That was a Friday. The next day, Shah was arrested. In the interrogation booth, the agent questioning him asked, "Do you know someone called Ali?"

"No, I don't."

"You haven't met someone called Ali a number of times?"

"No."

"He looks like—" The agent went on to describe me.

"No, I don't know him," Shah said.

The agent realized that Shah truly believed I was a member of al-Qaeda and was trying to protect my identity. "Maybe you'll recognize him if I show you a picture," the agent said, and showed Shah an official FBI photo of me.

"Oh," Shah replied, and, realizing the game was up, he confessed to everything.

Shah and most of his group pled guilty, but Sabir didn't, so two years later, in 2007, I testified in court. That was the first time I had appeared before reporters—there had been many stories in the media full of speculation about who the undercover agent had been, and all of them had gotten it wrong.

We had done everything for the mission by the book, and the defense did little other than ask me to read the transcripts of my exchanges with Shah and Sabir.

Sabir was convicted.

Postscript

On April 16, 2009, the U.S. Justice Department declassified a series of memos on the CIA's enhanced interrogation techniques program. This followed an announcement earlier in the month by Leon Panetta, the new CIA director, that the agency's black sites had been shut down. "The CIA no longer operates detention facilities or black sites," he had written to his staff. On October 29, 2009, David Iglesias, a navy prosecutor (and the actual person on whom Tom Cruise's character in the film *A Few Good Men* is based), told me that in lectures to young Special Forces JAG officers, the military was teaching the "Ali Soufan Rule"—that intelligent interrogations are always more productive than coercive ones, and that interrogators need to remember the endgame.

The declassified Department of Justice memos dispassionately detailed the coercive interrogation methods approved by the Bush administration, including waterboarding, and also listed "successes" of the program as a justification for their continuation. Featured prominently in the memos was Abu Zubaydah, the first to go through the program.

Within hours of the memos' release, I received calls from outraged friends in the intelligence and law enforcement communities. As one friend put it, "This is why the United States ripped up the Constitution in dealing with these terrorists? The memos are full of lies. I can't believe they've got the cheek to claim these successes as theirs! Didn't any of the lawyers even bother to check the dates?"

I felt the same disbelief and anger. It was apparent from the memos that the introduction of EITs was based on lies. The proof resides in my notes—locked, as noted earlier, in FBI vaults. It's no surprise that those behind the EITs fought so hard to keep these memos classified. From the interrogation of Abu Zubaydah to the information leading to the capture of Ramzi Binalshibh to the arrest of Khallad, the memos are full of misrepresentations of facts.

I received nonstop inquiries from journalists and television shows asking me about the memos, as it was no secret that I had opposed the techniques—a previously declassified Department of Justice inspector general's report had made that clear. From 2002 to 2009 I was limited to closed-door briefings in classified settings.

I didn't, however, speak out immediately, as I didn't want to reopen a period of my life that I had been happy to put behind me. I also thought it would be pretty clear that the claims in the memos were false. Unfortunately, that wasn't the case, as the defenders of the EITs launched a media blitz campaign not only to defend the techniques but to argue for their reintroduction.

"As you always say, the oath you took to defend the American people against enemies foreign and domestic didn't end when you left the FBI. Indeed, that's why you agreed to be the government's main witness in the trials at Guantánamo," a former colleague reminded me, "and once again you have a duty to tell the truth. Otherwise there is a danger that the American people will become convinced the EITs were a success, and they'll be reintroduced, and that will be disastrous."

Some colleagues suggested specific journalists I might speak with, but my colleague and coauthor Daniel Freedman recommended that my first public comments be in my own words, on my terms, with no possibility of their being misconstrued. As I was weighing what to do, the *New York Times* contacted me and asked if I'd write an opinion piece, and I accepted.

The next day, Wednesday, April 22, 2009, the *New York Times* ran the piece, entitled "My Tortured Decision." It attracted attacks from both the left and the right, with the right upset that I was attacking the techniques and the left upset that I had argued against the prosecution of CIA officials involved in the program. I told people who questioned why I opposed prosecutions that many of the CIA officers I had worked with had themselves objected to the techniques. Some had left the location, and even the agency, in protest. Those who had used the EITs had done so on the orders of higher-ups, and with the support of administration lawyers writing legal opinions authorizing the techniques. Any prosecutions, I said, needed to start at the very top, where the orders originated, and not with some sacrificial lambs at the bottom of the chain. It's also important to remember that CIA officers complained about the program to their inspector general, which is why he launched his investigation in the first place.

Because of the op-ed, I was called to testify before the Senate Judiciary Committee, under oath, about what had happened. None of the people who had authorized the EITs would consent to appear before the committee against me. They probably didn't want to commit perjury. One of the other witnesses was Philip Zelikow, who also opposed the techniques during his time in the State Department.

I outlined for the committee what had happened with Abu Zubaydah and explained how interrogations should work, and why EITs wouldn't work. I concluded: "For the last seven years, it was not easy objecting to these methods when they had powerful backers. I stood up then for the same reason I'm willing to take on critics now, because I took an oath swearing to protect this great nation. I could not stand by quietly while our country's safety was endangered and our moral standing damaged."

The defenders of the program had propagated so many falsehoods about the alleged successes of the EITS that many people in Washington were deceived, including Senator Lindsey Graham, a respected committee member. This came out during one exchange:

> SENATOR GRAHAM: Now, about the interrogation of this
>   suspect, do you know a gentleman named John K-I-R-I-A-
>   K-O-U?
> MR. SOUFAN: Me?
> SENATOR GRAHAM: Yes.
> MR. SOUFAN: No, I do not know him.
> SENATOR GRAHAM: Okay. He gave an interview—he is a retired
>   CIA officer, and he said Abu Zubaydah—is that the guy's
>   name?
> MR. SOUFAN: Yes.
> SENATOR GRAHAM: Did I say it right? He said that they
>   waterboarded the guy and he broke within 35 seconds.
> MR. SOUFAN: Is this question for me, sir?
> SENATOR GRAHAM: Yes.
> MR. SOUFAN: Well, last week, he retracted that and he said
>   he was misinformed, and actually he was not at the Abu
>   Zubaydah location.
> SENATOR GRAHAM: Okay. So he just—
> MR. SOUFAN: He retracted that, yes, sir. That is one of the
>   things that was mentioned before.

President Barack Obama publicly denounced the EIT program and said that never again would those coercive techniques be used. He also set up a presidential commission to make recommendations on how to move forward and improve our interrogation program, and I was asked to brief the commission.

"You catch more flies with honey than vinegar," I began. I went on to explain that knowledge of the detainee and of the group, and of both the detainee's and the group's background, is crucial to any interrogation. I explained that torture doesn't work. "It produces at best compliance, but not cooperation, which is what you need for a successful and reliable interrogation."

"But," one commission member asked, "if al-Qaeda learns your interrogation method, won't they be able to train their operatives to prepare for it?"

"That's impossible," I replied with a smile, "because no two interrogations are ever the same."

"Why not?"

"Just as no two detainees are exactly the same. Whether it's a different childhood, a different experience in al-Qaeda, or a different intellect, no two interrogations are ever exactly the same. The Informed Interrogation Approach isn't about following a series of steps, it's about playing what you know about the detainee against him and outwitting him."

"So every time you got a detainee to cooperate, it was with a different approach?"

"Yes. With Abu Jandal, for example, we trapped him in his lies and his ego. With Ali al-Bahlul, bin Laden's secretary and propagandist, we played on his commitment to al-Qaeda and his religious knowledge. With L'Houssaine Kherchtou the important point was al-Qaeda's refusal to pay for a Cesarean section for his wife. And with Karim, it was his childhood feelings toward his brother that flipped him.

"To put it in different terms, think of dating. If you think there's a magic formula and five words that will win you success, you've never been on a date. The same remark that somehow led one person to throw a drink in your face might have an entirely different effect on someone else. Everyone is different. And naturally you'll have more success if you know all about your date's likes and dislikes.

"Every detainee is different, and for each interview you need to have a unique strategy—based on knowledge." That hit home.

Conclusion

"I'm back with the people I was with before," Abu Ahmed al-Kuwaiti told an old friend on the phone, according to the *Washington Post*. It was the spring of 2010, and Abu Ahmed, a Kuwaiti of Pakistani origin, was being deliberately vague in response to his friend's queries about what he was up to, with good reason: he was one of Osama bin Laden's key links to the outside world, serving as a courier. Any slipup from him could lead intelligence officials to the world's most wanted terrorist.

"May God facilitate," was the reply from the friend, as if he understood what Abu Ahmed wasn't saying. It also made sense to U.S. investigators listening in on the conversation: they had been monitoring the friend in the hope of snagging the Kuwaiti. Now they finally had his cell phone number.

In early 2002 detainees at Guantánamo told us about the last time they had seen bin Laden: escaping from the Tora Bora mountain range as Northern Alliance troops (backed by U.S. forces) advanced, accompanied only by Hamza al-Ghamdi, a Saudi, and Yousef al-Qanas, a Kuwaiti. Prior to arriving at Tora Bora, bin Laden had reshuffled his bodyguards and picked a group of nine trusted aides to accompany him, among them his son Uthman and the Saudi and Kuwaiti nationals.

At the same time, we also learned that a Kuwaiti operative (who would turn out to be Abu Ahmed al-Kuwaiti) was playing a central role in bin Laden's new, post–Tora Bora al-Qaeda. The CIA and others in the U.S. intelligence community put possible acquaintances and probable hangouts under surveillance, hoping to find Abu Ahmed. This paid dividends in the spring of 2010, and that recorded conversation gave investigators his cell phone number.

The number was monitored, and an investigation—using assets, sources, data mining, detective work, and both old-fashioned tailing by CIA operatives and sleek surveillance using the latest high-level technology—eventually led to a one-acre compound in the Pakistani city of Abbottabad.

The city, less than forty miles from the Pakistani capital, Islamabad, houses the Kakul Military Academy—a training academy often described as the Pakistani version of West Point or Sandhurst, the premier U.S. and UK military academies. Senior Pakistani officials, as well as important foreign visitors, often visit the academy. In February 2010, for example, U.S. general David Petraeus was a visitor.

Abbottabad was therefore, at first glance, one of the last places an al-Qaeda leader might be expected to hide, which, on reflection, is perhaps what made it attractive. While many intelligence analysts expected al-Qaeda's leaders to be hiding in rural areas, several senior al-Qaeda members had already been captured in major cities: Ramzi Binalshibh, for example, was caught in Karachi, and his boss, KSM, in Rawalpindi.

The compound was surrounded by twelve-foot walls topped by barbed wire. It had no telephone or Internet connections, making it impossible for the National Security Agency to listen in on conversations going on inside. CIA officials, who had set up a monitoring base nearby, watched the Kuwaiti travel ninety minutes outside the compound before even putting a battery into his phone to make a call.

It was clear that someone important was in the compound, but was it bin Laden? Estimates given to President Obama ranged from 40 percent to 80 percent likelihood, and different options for how to proceed were presented to him. One was to use missiles to destroy the compound and kill the inhabitants—as had been done in November 2001 with the hideout of Abu Hafs al-Masri, al-Qaeda's then military commander. One downside of such a plan was that it would be hard to confirm whether bin Laden was indeed in the compound and had been killed.

A second option would be to send U.S. Special Operations Forces into the compound to either capture or kill its inhabitants. That brought up memories of Black Hawk Down.

Plans for both options were drawn up: B-2 bombers, with their two-thousand-pound bombs, were put on standby, and Navy vice admiral William H. McRaven—the head of the Joint Special Operations Command (JSOC)—assigned a team of elite Navy SEALs, Team 6, to train for a possible mission. At 8:20 AM on Friday, April 29, 2011, President Obama approved the ground force option. "It's a go," he ordered. The next evening he donned his tuxedo and headed to the annual White House Correspondents' Dinner, delivering his lines without giving away what was really on his mind.

On Monday, May 2, conditions were determined suitable for the mission, and two Black Hawk helicopters carrying the SEALs took off from Jalalabad, in eastern Afghanistan. En route, one of the helicopters stalled over the compound's walls, forcing a hard landing. Those inside got out safely, but the helicopter was rendered unusable—so the SEALs destroyed it.

The entire raid lasted less than forty minutes. Bin Laden, one of his sons, and some aides were killed. Among the dead was Abu Ahmed, the courier. Upon exiting, the SEALs took with them computer drives and other hard evidence, and bin Laden's dead body, and flew away in the one still-functioning helicopter.

After it was confirmed that the body was indeed bin Laden's, the White House alerted media outlets that President Obama would be making a big announcement that evening. Rumors soon began circulating that bin Laden had been killed, and impromptu crowds gathered outside the White House, at ground zero, and at other significant locations to celebrate the news. Euphoria, as well as a sense of relief, filled the air.

I was at home with my wife, Heather, putting our newborn twins to sleep, when old colleagues—both from U.S. government agencies and services across the world—called, texted, and e-mailed to celebrate the historic moment. Some recalled my 1998 memo, and others the pivotal interrogations of 2002.

"Tonight, I can report to the American people and to the world that the United States has conducted an operation that killed Osama bin Laden, the leader of al-Qaeda, and a terrorist who's responsible for the murder of thousands of innocent men, women, and children," President Obama told an estimated 57 million Americans who watched him speak from a podium in the East Room of the White House.

The investigation into bin Laden that had begun in 1996—when FBI special agent Dan Coleman opened a case on him—was closed. An era of my life was over, too: following bin Laden had been a hobby in the early 1990s, and then turned into a mission when I joined the FBI in the mid-1990s. It had been almost twenty years of my life.

It was fitting that the man who motivated so many to commit violent acts by preaching that America was weak and would flee when attacked was killed in his home in Pakistan by American forces. It wasn't America that had been in retreat and hiding. The al-Qaeda leader had essentially been a prisoner in his compound for the final years of his life, able to communicate with the outside world only through couriers who brought him information on thumb drives. Videos meant for dissemination found in the compound showed him practicing, and often messing up, his lines.

Bin Laden's body was wrapped in a *kafan* (a white burial sheet), placed in a bag with heavy stones, and dropped into the North Arabian Sea on the day of the raid.

The same day, backers of coercive interrogation techniques began claiming that their use had led investigators to bin Laden. Similar false claims had been made following the capture of other al-Qaeda members, such as KSM, Khallad, and Jose Padilla. The great British prime minister Winston Churchill once remarked that "a lie gets halfway around the world before the truth has a chance to get its pants on," and that was true in this instance, too.

The American people soon learned that when KSM was waterboarded in 2003, and when al-Qaeda's operational chief, Abu Faraj al-Liby, was subjected to coercive techniques (but not waterboarding) in 2005, they were asked about Abu Ahmed. They denied knowing his true identity and downplayed his significance in al-Qaeda. This denial, which was patently false, was "proof" for defenders of EITs that the Kuwaiti was important to al-Qaeda, and their "proof" that EITs work.

We already knew in 2002—through the use of traditional interrogation methods with detainees—that the Kuwaiti was important. And the fact that KSM and Abu Faraj lied about knowing him showed yet again that the EITs *didn't* work. A successful interrogation is one in which detainees cooperate and confess, not lie. That may seem obvious, but apparently not to EIT supporters.

Not only did KSM know Abu Ahmed, the Kuwaiti was the 9/11 mastermind's protégé. They had similar backgrounds, and KSM entrusted him with management of the al-Qaeda guesthouse in Karachi, Pakistan: it was through that guesthouse that key al-Qaeda operatives and many of those involved in 9/11 passed, including Hambali, Khallad, Mustafa al-Hawsawi, and Ammar al-Baluchi. They also went through the EIT program and didn't reveal valuable information about the Kuwaiti either. Abu Ahmed was the perfect operative for KSM and bin Laden to use: he was an Arab and spoke the local language, understood the culture, and blended in easily.

More details about the Kuwaiti came from the Pakistani al-Qaeda operative Hassan Ghul, who was questioned by the CIA in July 2004. Senator Diane Feinstein, the chair of the Senate Intelligence Committee, said that Ghul gave up the information *before* he was subjected to harsh techniques.

A question I was asked after bin Laden's death was: why did it take so long to get him? We had the first important clue in 2002; why did we only get to him in 2011?

The reason is that professional interrogators, intelligence operatives, and investigators were marginalized, and instead of tried and tested methods being used, faith was placed in EITs. The highest-ranking al-Qaeda detainees in U.S. custody—the likes of KSM, Nashiri, and Khallad—all of whom would most likely have known Abu Ahmed and other couriers, or would themselves be in communication with bin Laden, were given to the EIT users to question.

Things only really changed when CIA director Leon Panetta completely ended the coercive interrogation program and closed down the black sites. It's not without coincidence that the eventual death of bin Laden came after the traditional methods of intelligence and investigation were resumed. The professionals were put back in control. We just lost important years, and knowledge and skills, in the years in between.

With bin Laden at the compound, and in the room with him during his final moments of life, was his Yemeni wife. It was the same wife whom Guantánamo detainee No. 37, the Yemeni al-Qaeda operative named al-Batar, knew well. He had helped facilitate her five-thousand-dollar dowry from bin Laden. Salim Hamdan had advised al-Batar to cooperate with me, and he had agreed—on condition that, like Hamdan, he be allowed to phone his family to let them know he was okay.

CITF and FBI commanders at Gitmo requested permission from General Miller, the head of the base, but he refused, saying he wouldn't allow it without permission from Paul Wolfowitz, Rumsfeld's deputy secretary of defense. When that approval never came, we pleaded again for permission, telling him that bin Laden's Yemeni wife could probably lead us to bin Laden. Our pleas were ignored.

Bin Laden's death followed the so-called Arab Spring of 2011, during which citizens of countries like Egypt, Tunisia, Yemen, Libya, Jordan, Algeria, and Syria challenged their rulers. I was in the Middle East during that period, and one of the most striking things about the protests was the absence of al-Qaeda rhetoric among the demonstrators.

Al-Qaeda differs from many other Islamic extremist groups in that its leaders urge people to focus on the United States (the far enemy) rather than the rulers of their own countries (the near enemy). Bin Laden had been very successful in convincing other groups to ally with al-Qaeda and focus on the United States—claiming that was the best way to topple the regimes they opposed. But the Arab Spring showed that, contrary to al-Qaeda's narrative, hated rulers can be toppled peacefully without engaging the United States. In fact, people saw the United States even supporting their efforts, further ruining al-Qaeda's claims. It also became apparent that those rulers used the threat of al-Qaeda to justify to other nations their oppressive reigns and to settle scores with other countries and opponents.

This solidified a drift away from al-Qaeda that had been occurring during the previous few years among former supporters in the Muslim world. Those people had grown increasingly sick of al-Qaeda's merciless killings and terrorist attacks—the majority of al-Qaeda's victims are Muslims—and had come to realize that the group doesn't have any political program or long-term ideas; it only kills.

Bin Laden's death was another blow to al-Qaeda. Not only was he the leader, but he embodied its members' belief that their version of Islam was correct, that terrorism was the right weapon, and that they would ultimately be victorious—as they believed the black banners hadith predicted. It was his personal appeal that was central to al-Qaeda's recruitment and fund-raising. With a bullet from a SEAL's gun, al-Qaeda suffered a mortal blow, losing its greatest asset.

On June 16, 2011, al-Qaeda–General Command announced that bin Laden's deputy, Ayman al-Zawahiri, would take charge of the group. (Saif al-Adel had been the interim leader after bin Laden's death.) Zawahiri, however, brings with him a host of problems for the group: he is seen as a divisive figure who lacks bin Laden's appeal and charisma, so he won't be able to pull in recruits and funds or keep everyone in line, as bin Laden did. The fact that he's an Egyptian will also count against him, given the rivalry between al-Qaeda's Egyptian and Gulf Arab members.

While bin Laden's death and Zawahiri's promotion weakened al-Qaeda, neither event killed the group. Some of al-Qaeda's leadership council members are still at large. They command their own follow-ers and are trying to launch operations to prove al-Qaeda's continu-ing relevance. And with al-Qaeda on the decline, regional groups that had aligned themselves with it may return to operating independently. This in many ways makes them deadlier—as they're harder to monitor and have a wider scope of operations. That the Zawahiri announce-ment came from al Qaeda–General Command rather than just from al-Qaeda hints that such divisions may already be emerging.

To ever fully defeat al-Qaeda, or the subsequent new groups that emerge, we need to realize that military operations, interrogations, and intelligence successes are only half the battle. The other half is in the arena of ideas—countering the narratives and recruitment methods that extremists use. We can keep killing and arresting terrorists, but if new ones keep joining, our war will never end.

As the Saudi king demonstrated with the "devil's box," and as Sun Tzu taught in *The Art of War*, understanding your opponents, and using that knowledge to undermine them, is the key to ultimate victory. Since I've left the government, countering the propaganda and rhetoric that al-Qaeda and other groups use to entice people to join them has become my new hobby.

Acknowledgments

There are hundreds of men and women I have encountered through-out my life and whom I have worked alongside—in the FBI and in other government agencies, both in the United States and abroad—who deserve my thanks, but space constraints, security rules, people's desire to stay out of the spotlight, and the limits of my own memory prevent me from directly naming everybody.

My wife, Heather, is the perfect partner in every sense of the word. Few people would put up with a spouse departing for weeks on end, and with not being told where he was going or even when he'd return, but Heather is a unique person. We have three young boys, Connor, Dean, and Dylan, who, with their laughs, smiles, and clear inner good-ness, inspire me anew every day.

My father, for installing in me the same passion, work ethic, and commitment to doing the right thing that he had. To my mother, brother, and sister, for a lifetime of love.

Daniel Freedman, my friend and coauthor, was instrumental in helping to write this book. His work ethic, keen intellect, and ener-getic nature are the bedrock of this project. I am immensely appreciative of his incredible hard work and dedication. Special thanks also go to his wife, Becky—for putting up with the long and late hours we spent on the book—and to the two of them for being friends and family to Heather and me.

I have been fortunate to serve alongside, and learn from, many exceptional people from the U.S. law enforcement, military, and intelligence worlds, and from allied countries. Among them are, from the FBI: Carlos Fernandez, who is a great friend, trusted confidant, and superb colleague; Pat D'Amuro, for his exceptional character and support; Kenny Maxwell, who was always a great boss and trusted friend; and, from the Naval Criminal Investigative Service, Bob McFadden, the best partner anyone can have.

There are many others who deserve mention, among them Mark Fallon, Steve Corbett, Ken Reuwer, and Mike Gelles, from NCIS; Col. Scott Duke and his fusion team; and Tom Donlon, Don Borelli, Steve Bongardt, Debbie Doran, Stephen Gaudin, Bob Herrmann, Ryan Plunkett, Tom Neer, Bill Corbett, George Crouch, Joe Ennis, Russell Fincher, Aaron Zebley, Mike Butsch, Brian Getson, Jeff "Gunny" Ringel, Kevin Cruise, Dan Coleman, Kevin Donovan, Andy Arena, Mary Galligan, Barry Mawn, Jack Cloonan, Andre Khoury, John Anticev, Mike Anticev, Chris Reimann, Chuck Frahm, Amy Lyons, Mark Whitworth, Jerry Cocuzzo, Jim Margolin, Joe Valiquette, Ray Holcomb, Dan Fethiere, April Phillips, Abby Perkins, Hank Shaw, Scott Jessee, Frank Pellegrino, Jen Keenan, Joe Landers, Chris Nicholas, and John Liguori, from the FBI. Kathy MacGowan, Rosie Lepore, Barbara Calandra (my former secretary), Anita Waddell (who retired and is my office manager), Dennis Baker, and the many others in the FBI and in other agencies who support the agents in the field—without them, we would have no success.

I also worked alongside many fine men and women from the CIA, but by definition their jobs require that they remain anonymous. Then there are the officials from the State Department and the diplomatic service. Thank you all.

A special thank you also goes to all the people whom I worked with on the Joint Terrorism Task Force in New York, within my squad and beyond. Roger Koury for his unwavering friendship. Tom Corrigan (who sadly passed away in July 2011), Kevin Yorke, Kevin Butler, Louis Napoli, Brian Dennigan, Wayne Parola, Tom Ward (who died of a 9/11-related illness), Terry McGhee, and Bobby Losada, from the NYPD. My team included men and women from the NYPD, the FBI, the Port Authority, and Homeland Security—it was an honor to work alongside you. In Yemen and across the world I served with members of the U.S. military—soldiers, sailors, and marines. You inspire me.

I'd also like to thank Mike Kortan, from the FBI's public affairs office, for his help and guidance, and his predecessor, John Miller, who helped me with the process. John in many ways is responsible for this book—because he consistently encouraged me to write one. Thanks are also due to the FBI's Prepublication Review Office, especially Zach Wright and Dennis Argall.

Every organization is only as good as its leaders. In the FBI I was fortunate to work under two directors, Louis Freeh and Robert Mueller. Our nation would greatly benefit if other leaders took lessons from your playbook.

Outside the FBI, the CIA, the military, and other agencies one commonly associates with fighting terrorism are the prosecutors—both in civilian and military courts—who work with us on the front lines to ensure that those we catch will stay locked up. I was fortunate to work alongside many of our nation's best, including David Kelly, Pat Fitzgerald, and Ken Karas, who is now a judge. The staff of the Office of Military Commissions, both from the prosecution and the defense, who every day remind the world of who we are and what our country is about—we all owe you our gratitude.

During my career with the FBI I was fortunate to serve alongside outstanding officials from other countries, from whom I learned a great deal and with whom I formed great friendships. To John Bunn, Alan Fry, Peter Clarke, in the UK; and to Giuseppe Petronzi and Massimo De Benedittis, in Italy, to name just a few. My good friend Saad al-Khair, from Jordan, is no longer alive, but he taught me a great deal.

My friends in Singapore deserve special mention: Susan Sim, a col-

542 ■ Acknowledgments

league and a friend, was a great help with this book, as she is in other areas; and my friends from the different government agencies have my deep appreciation. Most, unfortunately, cannot be mentioned, other than Interpol president Khoo Boon Hui, but we indeed owe thanks to those involved in security in Singapore.

I'd now like to turn to those friendships I've developed since I left government. A special mention goes to those I work alongside who are today still on the front lines, especially Mohammed al-Missned, who is more than a friend, more like a brother, and who is always a few steps ahead of everyone else. The gifted diplomat Umej Singh Bhatia is both a good friend and someone I've learned a great deal from.

Another person who deserves mention is Lawrence Wright—his dedication to pursuing the truth, put together brilliantly in his book *The Looming Tower*, is a lesson to every aspiring journalist. Barry McManus, Steve Kleinman, Stephen White, Philip Zelikow, Mark Pritchard, Karen Greenberg, Dan Benjamin, Tim Andrews, Mike Jacobson, and other friends also teach me a great deal. My thanks also go to Mayor Rudy Giuliani, who gave me my first job after I left the bureau, and to Dan Connolly at Giuliani Partners, a high-minded true friend.

I also owe a debt of gratitude to my colleagues at The Soufan Group: Mark Smith, Ahmad Khalil, Heidi Fink, Sandy Choi, Angie Hutcheson, John Waddell, Bud Aldridge, Jim McGee, Ray Mey, my friend Mohammed Hanzab, and all our instructors, language teachers, interpreters, and the whole team at the Qatar International Academy for Security Studies (QIASS)—I treasure your friendship. Michael Lomonaco and Tim Brown from the excellent Porter House are two caring friends, as well as excellent hosts. To Sayeed Rahman, Liora Danan, Jared Wigdor, and Samm Tyroler-Cooper, our research interns who helped with this book.

While most of those whom I'd like to thank I'm able to, some are sadly no longer with us. The seventeen sailors who died on the USS *Cole* are heroes, in every sense of the word, whom I will never forget; and neither should America. Lenny Hatton was a heroic FBI agent who died on 9/11, running into the burning twin towers to try to save lives. Finally, there's John O'Neill, my boss, friend, and mentor—who understood the threat more than anyone else. He died in the twin towers, too. John, more than anyone else, this is for you.

A special thank you goes to my agent, Andrew Wylie, who has guided me through the writing process, and to the team at his agency. Starling Lawrence, my very capable editor at Norton, and his team— Louise Brockett, Rachel Salzman, Melody Conroy, Bill Rusin, Nancy Palmquist, Don Rifkin, Anna Oler, and everyone else—did a wonderful job, and I owe my deep thanks to them for believing in this project and guiding it to fruition. Janet Byrne, who worked alongside Star as a second editor: her stunning skills and amazing tenacity transformed the original material into this book.

My final thanks go to the heroes of the country who are today still on the front lines—across the military, FBI, CIA, NCIS, and other agencies—and who every day put their lives on the line for us. Thank you.

Principal Characters

Nasir Abbas: A commander of the Southeast Asian terrorist group Jemaah Islamiah who opposed the efforts of Hambali to tie the group to al-Qaeda. He later left the group, and I spoke to him in 2010 in Indonesia.

Abdullah Ahmed Abdullah (aliases: Saleh, Azayet, and Abu Mohammed al-Masri): Headed al-Qaeda's East African cells following the death of Abu Ubaidah on May 21, 1996, and was indicted for his role in planning the 1998 East African embassy bombings. He is on the FBI's Most Wanted Terrorists list and is believed to be in Iran.

Abu Abdul Rahman al-Muhajir (alias of Muhsin Musa Matwakku Atwah): Al-Qaeda's explosives expert and master bomb maker; indicted for the 1998 East African embassy bombings. He was reported by Pakistani officials to have been killed in 2006 by an airstrike in North Waziristan, a claim confirmed by U.S. officials through DNA testing.

Abu Bakar Bashir: Cofounded the Southeast Asian terrorist group Jemaah Islamiah with Abdullah Sungkar, and after Sungkar's death in 1999 he took over the group. He supported Hambali's relationship with al-Qaeda.

Abu Hafs al-Mauritani (alias of Mahfouz Ould al-Walid): *Shura* council member and the only person in al-Qaeda with religious training; headed the fatwa committee following the arrest of Abu Hajer al-Iraqi. He resides in Mauritania, having spent a decade in an Iranian jail.

Abu Hafs al-Masri: (alias of Mohammed Atef): Al-Qaeda's military commander after the death of Abu Ubaidah in 1996. He was eventually killed in November 2001 by a U.S. airstrike on his hiding place; in the rubble of the house we found important evidence that became part of the DocEx program.

Abu Hajer al-Iraqi (alias of Mamdouh Mahmoud Salem): Kurd who fought in Saddam's army and then alongside bin Laden in Afghanistan, where the two became close friends. Although he wasn't a cleric, he memorized the Quran, and bin Laden appointed him head of al-Qaeda's fatwa committee. From that perch he wrote justifications for al-Qaeda's actions, including the killing of innocent civilians. He was arrested in Germany in September 1998 and extradited to the United States, where he was sentenced for participating in the 1998 East African embassy bombings.

Abu Jandal (literally, "father of death"; alias of Nasser Ahmad Nasser al-Bahri): Member of the Northern Group who was recruited to al-Qaeda in 1996 with the help of Muhannad bin Attash; rose within the organization to become bin Laden's personal bodyguard. He is the brother-in-law of Salim Hamdan, who served as bin Laden's driver and confidant; it was the al-Qaeda leader who encouraged the two to marry sisters. Abu Jandal had been arrested by the Yemeni authorities after the October 12, 2000, bombing of the USS

Cole, but they only let us question him after 9/11, when another al-Qaeda operative, Fahd al-Quso, linked him to one of the 9/11 hijackers, Marwan al-Shehhi. NCIS Special Agent Robert McFadden and I interrogated him, and he identified many of the 9/11 hijackers and provided invaluable intelligence on al-Qaeda's structure, operatives, and operations. To date that interrogation is viewed as the most successful in the war against al-Qaeda. Abu Jandal died of natural causes on December 26, 2015, in Yemen.

Abu Ubaidah al-Banshiri (alias of Amin Ali al-Rashidi): A member of Ayman al-Zawahiri's Egyptian Islamic Jihad before joining al-Qaeda, he was bin Laden's first deputy and then became the group's first military commander. He drowned in 1996 in a ferry accident on Lake Victoria.

Abu Zubaydah (full name: Zayn al-Abidin Muhammad Husayn Abu Zubaydah; alias Daood): Independent terrorist facilitator who served as the external emir of the Khaldan training camp and was the partner of Ibn al-Shaykh al-Liby. We first came across Abu Zubaydah during the Millennium Operation in Jordan. He was captured in a shootout in March 2002 and flown to a secret location, where Stephen Gaudin and I interrogated him. We gained important actionable intelligence from him, including his identification of Khalid Sheikh Mohammed as the mastermind of 9/11. He also told us about Jose Padilla and Binyam Mohamed's so-called dirty bomb plot. We left Abu Zubaydah when final control of his interrogation was given over to CIA contractors employing coercive interrogation techniques. Their techniques failed, and in secret memos they tried to claim our earlier successes as their own. He is being held in Guantánamo Bay, Cuba.

Salman al-Adani: Al-Qaeda operative tasked with being one of the suicide bombers for the January 2000 attack on the USS *The Sullivans*—which failed because Adani and his fellow suicide bomber, Taha al-Ahdal, miscalculated the tide and their boat got stuck in the sand.

He later died after jumping into a sewer to try to save a boy who had fallen in.

Saif al-Adel: Senior al-Qaeda operative who is a member of the *shura* council and heads the organization's security committee. After bin Laden's death, he was appointed the interim leader of al-Qaeda. He held that position until June 16, 2011, when Ayman al-Zawahiri officially became its new leader. He remains on the FBI's Most Wanted Terrorists list and reportedly lives in Iran.

Taha al-Ahdal: An al-Qaeda operative who, with Salman al-Adani, was one of the intended suicide bombers for the aborted January 2000 attack on the USS *The Sullivans*. He was killed while fighting for the Taliban in Afghanistan.

Alvin (not his real name): CIA chief of operations in Jordan during the Millennium Operation. He went on to become the CIA's Counterterrorism Center Sunni extremists chief.

Hussein Ansi: Head of Yemen's Political Security Organization in Aden while we were investigating the bombing of the USS *Cole*. He appeared to be sympathetic to al-Qaeda and often tried to frustrate our investigation. After two of the al-Qaeda members involved in the attack, Fahd al-Quso and Jamal al-Badawi, "escaped" from jail in April 2003, we pressured the Yemenis to look into Ansi's complicity, and he was eventually arrested, questioned, and sacked (but never prosecuted).

John Anticev: FBI Special Agent and I-49 squad member (and brother of Mike Anticev) who was the case agent for Operation Terrorstop, among other high-profile investigations. He also successfully interrogated both Mohamed Sadeek Odeh and Mohamed al-Owhali during the 1998 East African embassy bombings investigation, extracting from Owhali the phone number belonging to Ahmed al-Hada—which served as a virtual switchboard for al-Qaeda.

Mike Anticev: FBI special agent and I-49 squad member (and brother of John Anticev) who helped manage Jamal al-Fadl ("Junior").

Andy Arena: Assistant agent in charge at the Detroit office who was appointed Pat D'Amuro's deputy in investigating 9/11. He refused a request from the Bush administration to report links between Iraq and al-Qaeda.

Mohammed Atta: The leader of the 9/11 hijackers, he piloted American Airlines Flight 11 into the north tower of the World Trade Center. A member of the Hamburg cell, he roomed there with 9/11 coordinator Ramzi Binalshibh and hijacker Marwan al-Shehhi.

Abdullah Azzam: A Palestinian cleric who inspired many Muslims, including bin Laden, to join the mujahideen and fight the Soviet Union in Afghanistan. With bin Laden he founded Makhtab al-Khidmat (Bureau of Services), which channeled money and recruits into Afghanistan. He was a potential rival to bin Laden to head al-Qaeda and was assassinated on November 24, 1989. Many suspected that Ayman al-Zawahiri was behind his murder, but this has never been proven.

Jamal al-Badawi: Yemeni al-Qaeda member who was involved in the USS *Cole* bombing. He was a close friend of Khallad's; Khallad brought him into the operation. I interrogated him in Yemen with NCIS agent Ken Reuwer, gained his confession, and helped prosecute him in a Yemeni court. He was given a death sentence, "escaped," and was later pardoned by President Ali Abdullah Saleh. Badawi was reportedly killed on January 1, 2019, in a U.S. airstrike after being on the FBI's Most Wanted Terrorists list.

Ali al-Bahlul (alias of Anas al-Mekki): Served as bin Laden's propagandist and secretary, a position he was appointed to after putting together the propaganda video celebrating the bombing of the USS *Cole*. He was captured in 2002 along with a group of thirty other al-Qaeda operatives nicknamed the "dirty thirty." I gained his cooperation and confession in Guantánamo Bay, Cuba, and served as the key witness in his trial. He was sentenced to life in prison.

Ammar al-Baluchi (alias of Abdul Aziz Ali): Al-Qaeda operative who was the nephew of 9/11 mastermind Khalid Sheikh Mohammed and who helped the hijackers with money and logistics. He was arrested with Khallad in Pakistan on April 29, 2003, and identified by a quick-witted police officer. He is being held in Guantánamo Bay, Cuba.

Al-Bara (alias of Abdul Aziz bin Attash): Al-Qaeda operative who is one of the younger brothers of Khallad and Muhannad bin Attash. He was convicted and jailed in Yemen in connection with the Bayt Habra plot, and I interrogated him and gained his cooperation.

Mozzam Begg: British Pakistani extremist who operated al-Ansar, a bookstore in Birmingham, and helped raise funds for the Khaldan training camp. He escaped from England to Afghanistan when British authorities first tried to arrest him. He was taken to Guantánamo after being captured in Pakistan in 2002. In 2005 he was freed, and today he is a free man in the UK.

Muhannad bin Attash: Older brother of Khallad, al-Bara, Omayer, and Moaz bin Attash; a key aide to bin Laden and instrumental in recruiting members of the Northern Group in 1996. He was killed in 1997 fighting alongside the Taliban at Murad Beg, in the same battle in which his brother Khallad lost a leg.

Ramzi Binalshibh: Yemeni al-Qaeda operative who was the roommate of Mohammed Atta, the head 9/11 hijacker, and of another hijacker, Marwan al-Shehhi, in Hamburg. He was to be one of the 9/11 hijackers but was unable to get a U.S. visa. Instead he served as the liaison between the hijackers and mastermind Khalid Sheikh Mohammed. He was arrested on September 11, 2002, after information gained by an FBI colleague from Ahmed al-Darbi helped lead us to him. I was allowed to interrogate him for forty-five minutes shortly after his capture—but despite the fact that he cooperated, he was rendered to a foreign country by the CIA so that coercive interrogation techniques could be employed on him. He is being held in Guantánamo Bay, Cuba.

Osama bin Laden: A Saudi of Yemeni origins, he founded al-Qaeda in 1988 after raising funds during the first Afghani jihad, during which he worked alongside Abdullah Azzam in operating Makhtab al-Khidmat, which channeled money and recruits into Afghanistan. After founding al-Qaeda, bin Laden went back to his homeland, Saudi Arabia, in 1990 before moving the organization to Sudan (1991) and then back to Afghanistan (1996). In Afghanistan he pledged allegiance to Mullah Omar, the leader of the Taliban. From Afghanistan bin Laden planned many attacks, including the bombing of the USS *Cole* and 9/11. He was killed by U.S. Navy SEALs during a May 2, 2011, raid on the compound in which he lived in Abbottabad, Pakistan.

Barbara K. Bodine: U.S. ambassador to Yemen from November 1997 to August 30, 2002. Many in the FBI and the U.S. military investigating the USS *Cole* bombing felt she obstructed the investigation.

Steve Bongardt: FBI special agent and member of the I-49 squad who was my co–case agent during the USS *Cole* bombing investigation. He tried to challenge the CIA's refusal to share information with the FBI pre-9/11—information that may have stopped the attacks—but he was repeatedly told to "stand down."

Mike Butsch: FBI special agent assigned to the 9/11 investigation and tasked with tracking down Ramzi Binalshibh. With Aaron Zebley, we worked on interrogating Binalshibh, Karim, and six other operatives caught together on September 11, 2002.

Jack Cloonan: FBI special agent and member of the I-49 squad whom I worked alongside in many cases, including the recruitment of L'Houssaine Kherchtou.

Daniel Coleman: Senior FBI agent and I-49 squad member. He opened the FBI's case on bin Laden in 1996 and was an FBI expert on the al-Qaeda leader. He played a key role in many high-profile investigations.

Dina Corsi: FBI analyst who worked with the CIA. On June 11, 2001, together with a CIA official and another analyst assigned to the CIA, she met Steve Bongardt and other members of the FBI's USS *Cole* team and showed them three photos. She told them that one of the men in the pictures was named Khalid al-Mihdhar. Only the CIA official knew more than that, but he wouldn't say anything. After 9/11 we learned that those pictures were from al-Qaeda's 9/11 planning summit in Malaysia. If the CIA official had told us what he knew then, we might have stopped 9/11.

George Crouch: FBI special agent from the I-49 squad who was a member of the USS *Cole* investigation team. We conducted several interrogations together after the *Cole* investigation, including that of Salim Hamdan, bin Laden's driver and confidant, at Guantánamo in 2002.

Pat D'Amuro: The assistant special agent in charge of counterterrorism when I joined the bureau, he was my boss through my most important cases—the Millennium Operation in Jordan, Operation Challenge in the UK, the USS *Cole* bombing, the 9/11 investigation—and during key interrogations in Guantánamo and elsewhere. He fully supported my decision to object to the introduction of coercive interrogation techniques.

Ahmed al-Darbi (alias Abdul Aziz al-Janoubi): Al-Qaeda operative who was the son-in-law of Ahmed al-Hada and a close friend and brother-in-law of 9/11 hijacker Khalid al-Mihdhar. He and Mihdhar were in same combat class in Afghanistan, and it was from this class that Mihdhar was selected for the 9/11 operation. Darbi rose through al-Qaeda's ranks to become a deputy of Abdul Rahim al-Nashiri.

He was eventually captured in 2002 while visiting his mistress in Azerbaijan, and information gained from him by an FBI colleague led to the arrest of Ramzi Binalshibh, Karim, and six other al-Qaeda operatives on September 11, 2002. He is being held in Guantánamo Bay, Cuba.

Tom Donlon: Senior FBI official and the case agent in the 1993 World Trade Center bombing. He was the supervisor of the I-40 squad, which focused on Sunni extremists, when I joined the FBI, and he encouraged me to write and circulate memos on bin Laden and al-Qaeda. It was one of these memos that attracted the attention of John O'Neill. Donlon was on a thirty-day rotation in Yemen, as a supervisor of the USS *Cole* investigation, when we received the news about 9/11.

Kevin Donovan: Senior FBI official who did a thirty-day rotation in Yemen as part of the USS *Cole* investigation. Later he was promoted to assistant director in charge of the FBI's New York office.

Debbie Doran: FBI special agent on the I-49 squad; from a family of FBI agents. She played an important role in many operations. These included the 1998 East Africa embassy bombing investigation, the recruitment of L'Houssaine Kherchtou, and the DocEx program.

Maj. Gen. Michael E. Dunlavey: Commander of Joint Task Force 170 at Guantánamo; responsible for military interrogations from the opening of the base until November 8, 2002, when he was replaced in command by Maj. Gen. Geoffrey Miller. Many FBI and military personnel were critical of his leadership and attitude toward detainees, although my interactions with him on the whole were positive.

Ed (not his real name): CIA interrogator whom I first met in Yemen while investigating the USS *Cole* bombing. We worked together during the interrogation of Abu Zubaydah, and later we partnered a few times at Guantánamo. He was unhappy with the coercive interrogation techniques the CIA contractors were using on Abu Zubaydah, and demanded that his superiors provide in writing orders that he go along with the contractors.

Joe Ennis: FBI special agent nicknamed "Alabama Joe" because of his pride in his roots; he joined us in Yemen during the USS *Cole* investigation. The material witness warrant for Jose Padilla was issued based on an affidavit sworn to by him.

Jamal al-Fadl (alias Abu Bakr Sudani): Nicknamed "Junior" within U.S. government circles, he was an early al-Qaeda member who served as bin Laden's secretary before turning himself over to the United States in 1996 after getting caught stealing $110,000 from al-Qaeda. The information he gave us was central to our understanding of how the organization operated and evolved up till 1996, and he also became a key witness in subsequent trials against al-Qaeda members. He is in the U.S. Witness Protection Program.

Khalid al-Fawwaz: A trusted bin Laden lieutenant who first led al-Qaeda's cell in Nairobi; once it was operational he went to London to run al-Qaeda's operations there, focusing on logistics and public relations. In 1999 I helped the British build a case against Fawwaz and other members of the al-Qaeda–Egyptian Islamic Jihad cell in London. We won the case. Fawwaz was extradited to the United States from the UK in 2012 and was convicted of conspiracy by a New York court in late February 2015. He is serving a life sentence.

Harun Fazul (alias of Fazul Abdullah Mohammed; known mainly as Harun; another alias is Yaqoub al-Dusari): Al-Qaeda operative who served as Wadih el-Hage's secretary in Nairobi and helped investigate the drowning of Abu Ubaidah. He also helped plan and execute the 1998 East African embassy bombings, and often wrote reports for al-Qaeda leaders. He ran al-Qaeda operations in the Horn of Africa until his death, on June 10, 2011.

Carlos Fernandez: FBI special agent whom I served alongside in many operations.

Patrick Fitzgerald: Worked closely with the FBI when he was an assistant U.S. attorney from the Southern District of New York. He played a central role in gaining the cooperation of several al-Qaeda members, including Mohamed al-Owhali and L'Houssaine Kherchtou, and I worked closely with him on operations in London, Italy, and Yemen. He also successfully prosecuted many terrorists, including Omar Abdul Rahman, and al-Qaeda members involved in the 1998 East African embassy bombings.

Fred (not his real name): CIA official who wrote faulty cables during the Millennium Operation in Jordan that had to be withdrawn, and who tried disrupting George Crouch's successful interrogation of Ibn al-Shaykh al-Liby. Some of his other errors are discussed in the CIA inspector general's report on the CIA's coercive interrogation program.

Louis Freeh: Director of the FBI from September 1993 to June 2001. Aware of problems we were having during the *Cole* investigation, he flew to Yemen to speak to President Ali Abdullah Saleh, an effort that greatly helped us.

Stephen Gaudin: FBI special agent who was my partner in interrogating Abu Zubaydah. His mistake with the Palm Pilot–like device helped us identify Khalid Sheikh Mohammed as the mastermind of 9/11. During the 1998 East African embassy bombing investigation, he helped gain the confession of Mohamed al-Owhali, and after 9/11 he served as the FBI Legat in Yemen.

Ahmed al-Hada: Yemeni al-Qaeda member whose son Jaffar and sons-in-law Ahmed al-Darbi and Khalid al-Mihdhar (one of the 9/11 hijackers) also belonged to the organization. During the 1998 East African embassy bombing investigation, we discovered that his phone number in Yemen served as a virtual switchboard for al-Qaeda. The Yemenis only let us question him after 9/11; the interrogation was conducted by Bob McFadden, Andre Khoury, and me.

Wadih el-Hage: Lebanese al-Qaeda member who moved to the United States (and became a citizen) and was inspired by Abdullah Azzam to join the mujahideen. After the Soviet jihad he worked for bin Laden as his secretary, and in Nairobi he replaced Khalid al-Fawwaz (who had been sent by bin Laden to London). El-Hage was later arrested and sentenced to life in prison in the United States for his role in the 1998 East African embassy bombings.

Hambali: Commonly used name of Riduan Isamuddin, a commander of the Southeast Asian terrorist group Jemaah Islamiah with responsibility for Singapore and Malaysia. A disciple of Abdullah Sungkar, he was sent by him in 1996 to train in Afghanistan, where he built a relationship with Khalid Sheikh Mohammed. Through KSM he pledged allegiance to bin Laden and was central to cementing the relationship between al-Qaeda and JI. On August 11, 2003, he was arrested by Thailand's Special Branch. He is being held in Guantánamo Bay, Cuba.

Salim Hamdan (alias Saqr al-Jadawi): Al-Qaeda member who joined the organization as part of the Northern Group in 1996. He is the brother-in-law of Abu Jandal, and served as bin Laden's driver and confidant. I interrogated him at Guantánamo Bay, Cuba, with George Crouch, and gained his confession and cooperation. Without our knowledge, or that of assistant U.S. attorney David Kelley, who was prosecuting the case, Hamdan was labeled an enemy combatant by the Bush administration and barred from cooperating with us anymore. I served as the main witness in his eventual trial. He was convicted, but because of the mishandling of the case by the Bush administration (the enemy combatant label), he was sentenced to only five and a half years in prison. Based on time served, he was released after only a few months in prison. Today he is free in Yemen.

Mustafa al-Hawsawi: Al-Qaeda financial operative who worked with Khalid Sheikh Mohammed's nephew Ammar al-Baluchi in helping to coordinate the 9/11 hijackers' travel and money. He is being held in Guantánamo Bay, Cuba.

John Helgerson: Inspector general of the CIA who investigated the agency's coercive interrogation program after receiving complaints from CIA professionals unhappy with what was being done, and whose report was very critical of the program.

Edmund Hull: Barbara Bodine's replacement as ambassador to Yemen; served there from 2001 to 2004.

Ibn al-Shaykh al-Liby: An independent terrorist who worked closely with al-Qaeda, he was the internal emir of the Khaldan training camp—Abu Zubaydah's partner. After his capture he was interrogated by George Crouch and another FBI colleague, and provided actionable intelligence. He was taken away from the FBI and rendered by the CIA to another country, where he was tortured and forced to admit to false connections between al-Qaeda and Saddam. His "confession" was used by Bush administration officials to build its case for war with Iraq. He was later transferred to Libya, where he was put in prison and died under suspicious circumstances.

Abdul Hadi al-Iraqi: One of al-Qaeda's military commanders. A member of the *shura* council, after 9/11 he was appointed commander of all the Arabs in Afghanistan. In April 2007 it was reported that he had been arrested. The exact date of the arrest is unclear. He is being held in Guantánamo Bay, Cuba.

Kenneth Karas: We worked together when he was an assistant U.S. attorney from the Southern District of New York, gaining the conviction in the UK of members of the al-Qaeda–Egyptian Islamic Jihad cell in London. He is a federal judge.

Karim: A high-level al-Qaeda operative who was captured in a September 11, 2002, raid that also netted Ramzi Binalshibh and six other operatives—based on information given by Ahmed al-Darbi to an FBI colleague. I interrogated him for forty-five minutes after his capture. He cooperated and provided important intelligence but was taken from me and rendered to a foreign country by the CIA to be subjected to coercive interrogation techniques.

David Kelley: We worked closely together on many operations while he was an assistant U.S. attorney from the Southern District of New York, including during the USS *Cole* investigation and while building a case against Salim Hamdan. He later became the U.S. attorney for the Southern District of New York but still continued to personally oversee the USS *Cole* case.

Khallad (alias of Walid bin Attash; other aliases: "Silver," Saleh Saeed Mohammed, Sa'eed bin Saleh bin Yousaf, Tawfiq Muhammad Salih bin Rashid, and Saleh bin Saeed bin Yousef): Senior al-Qaeda operative from a family of al-Qaeda members, including older brother Muhannad and younger brothers al-Bara, Omayer, and Moaz. He joined al-Qaeda with the Northern Group, lost a leg in 1997—at Murad Beg, where his brother Muhannad was killed— and rose up through the organization to become a key bin Laden aide. He helped plan major attacks, including the bombing of the USS *Cole* and 9/11. The failure of the CIA to share information that the FBI requested during the *Cole* investigation prevented us from following his trail and possibly stopping the 9/11 attacks. He headed al-Qaeda operations in the Arabian Gulf after the November 2002 arrest of Nashiri, and he himself was arrested, by chance, in April 29, 2003, alongside Ammar al-Baluchi, by Pakistani police. He was put into the CIA's coercive interrogation program and the FBI was not given access to him. He is being held in Guantánamo Bay, Cuba.

Hassan al-Khamiri (alias Abu Yousef al-Ta'efi): Yemeni al-Qaeda member who was the emir of the al-Farouq training camp in Afghanistan until it was hit by U.S. missiles in response to the East African embassy bombings. That experience, along with his arrest in Yemen during the Bayt Habra car theft incident, pushed him to request a martyrdom operation from bin Laden. He was a suicide bomber, alongside Ibrahim al-Nibras, in the October 12, 2000, bombing of the USS *Cole*.

L'Houssaine Kherchtou (alias Mzungu): Early al-Qaeda member who served as bin Laden's personal pilot and ran errands for the group. In Morocco Pat Fitzgerald, Jack Cloonan, Debbie Doran, and I convinced him to become a U.S. government asset and witness, and on September 21, 1999, he flew with us to the United States. Nicknamed "Joe the Moroccan," he helped us understand al-Qaeda—picking up where Jamal al-Fadl left off (his knowledge stopped in 1996, when he defected)—and became a key prosecution witness in the trials of al-Qaeda members. He is in the U.S. Witness Protection Program.

Andre Khoury: FBI special agent whom I worked alongside in Yemen during the USS *Cole* investigation and in operations after 9/11. We interrogated several al-Qaeda members together, including Ahmed al-Hada.

Anas al-Liby (alias of Nazih Abdul Hamed al-Ruqai'i): Senior al-Qaeda operative and computer expert whose involvement in terrorist plots included casing the U.S. Embassy in Nairobi in preparation for the 1998 bombing. We tracked him down to Manchester, England, but because of a lack of immediate evidence and British rules on holding suspects, he was released and escaped. Later, among his possessions, I found what became known as the Manchester Manual—an al-Qaeda handbook full of lessons for terrorist operatives. This manual was later translated into English and misunderstood by CIA contractors and used to justify their use of coercive interrogation techniques. In reality these techniques played into al-Qaeda's tactics as outlined in the manual. In a daring raid in Tripoli, Liby was arrested by the FBI and the U.S. military and brought to the United States, where he died of liver cancer on January 2, 2015, while awaiting trial.

Mu'awiya al-Madani: Al-Qaeda operative who was a bodyguard for bin Laden and whom the al-Qaeda leader wanted to use as a suicide bomber for the USS *Cole* (in the end, he wasn't used). I uncovered his martyrdom video in the DocEx program. He died in the May 12, 2003, al-Qaeda attack on the residential compounds in Riyadh.

Major Mahmoud (not his real name): Yemeni investigator whom we worked closely with during the USS *Cole* investigation and on investigations after 9/11.

Abu al-Khair al-Masri: Egyptian Islamic Jihad *shura* council member and a close associate of Ayman al-Zawahiri; joined al-Qaeda's *shura* council following the March 2001 official merger of the two groups. He was killed in late February 2017 in a U.S. drone strike near Idlib, Syria.

Sheikh Sa'eed al-Masri: Al-Qaeda *shura* council member who ranked just below Madani al-Tayyib on the financial committee, and who took over from him after he left the group. He refused to give L'Houssaine Kherchtou the $500 he needed to pay for his wife's Cesarean section. He was killed by a U.S. drone attack in Pakistan in May 2010.

Ahmed Shah Massoud: Leader of the Northern Alliance who played a major role in defeating the Soviets and who was seen as the best hope for defeating the Taliban. He was assassinated by al-Qaeda on September 9, 2001, as a gift to the Taliban—helping to cement the relationship between the two groups.

Barry Mawn: Assistant director in charge of the New York office of the FBI during the USS *Cole* investigation.

Robert (Bob) McFadden: A Naval Criminal Investigative Service special agent who served as my partner during the investigation into the USS *Cole* bombing and in several subsequent investigations. Among the very successful interrogations we partnered in was that of Abu Jandal.

Khalid al-Mihdhar (alias Sinan al-Maki): One of the 9/11 hijackers, he was on American Airlines Flight 77, which hit the Pentagon. The son-in-law of Ahmed al-Hada and the brother-in-law of Ahmed al-Darbi, he was identified by the 9/11 Commission and the CIA's inspector general as the weakest link in the 9/11 plot. Both concluded that if the CIA had shared information about him with the FBI, as legally required and as the FBI had asked, 9/11 might have been averted.

Maj. Gen. Geoffrey Miller: On November 8, 2002, he replaced Maj. Gen. Michael E. Dunlavey and took control of Guantánamo. He refused to listen to the professional interrogators at the base and instead allowed coercive interrogation techniques to be used. On August 31, 2003, he flew to Iraq to advise those running the Baghdad prison Abu Ghraib.

Ali Mohamed: An al-Qaeda–EIJ double agent who served in the U.S. Army in the 1980s while also training terrorist operatives and helping plan attacks. Before joining Zawahiri's EIJ, he had a seventeen-year career in the Egyptian military. He was part of the cell that cased the Nairobi embassy in preparation for the August 7, 1998, bombing. He was arrested by the United States in September in connection with the bombing and pleaded guilty in May 1999. He is awaiting sentencing.

Binyam Mohamed (alias Talha): Al-Qaeda operative who plotted with Jose Padilla to attack the United States with a dirty bomb. Traveling on a fake British passport, he was arrested in Pakistan and was handed over to the CIA and taken to Guantánamo. He was never tried and is today a free man in the UK.

Khalid Sheikh Mohammed (nickname: KSM; alias Mokhtar): 9/11 mastermind; uncle of the 1993 World Trade Center bomber Ramzi Yousef and co-planner, with him, of the thwarted Manila Air (or Bojinka) plot. Originally an independent terrorist, he joined al-Qaeda to make use of its organization, operatives, and funds in plotting the 9/11 attacks. The United States only learned that KSM was behind 9/11, and a member of al-Qaeda, from the interrogation of Abu Zubaydah that Stephen Gaudin and I conducted. He was captured in Pakistan in 2003 and put into the CIA's coercive interrogation program, and the FBI was not given access to him. He is being held in Guantánamo Bay, Cuba.

Zacarias Moussaoui: Al-Qaeda operative who entered the United States on February 23, 2001, and attended flight schools in Oklahoma and Minnesota. He was arrested on August 16, 2001, and charged with an immigration violation after a flight instructor became suspicious and reported him. He was convicted for his role in 9/11 and sentenced to life in prison.

Robert Mueller: Became director of the FBI on September 4, 2001. Supported the decision of FBI agents not to get involved in the CIA's coercive interrogation program despite strong pressure from the Bush administration.

Hamoud Naji: Head of Yemeni president Ali Abdullah Saleh's security team during our investigation into the USS *Cole* bombing.

Abdul Rahim al-Nashiri (full name: Abdul Rahim Hussein Muhammad Abda al-Nashiri; aliases: Abda Hussein Muhammad, Abdu, Sa'eed al-Mansouri, and Mullah Bilal): Senior al-Qaeda special operations member who masterminded the October 12, 2000, bombing of the *USS* Cole. After joining the organization as part of the Northern Group in 1996, he rose through its ranks to eventually become head of operations in the Arabian Gulf. He was captured in November 2002 and put into the CIA's coercive interrogation program, and the FBI was not given access to him at the time. He is being held in Guantánamo Bay, Cuba.

Ibrahim al-Nibras (alias of Ibrahim al-Thawer): Yemeni al-Qaeda operative who, with Fahd al-Quso, transported $36,000 from Yemen to Khallad in Bangkok—money that was probably used by 9/11 hijackers Khalid al-Mihdhar and Nawaf al-Hazmi for their plane tickets to the United States and for spending money there. After delivering the money to Khallad he became a suicide bomber, alongside Hassan al-Khamiri, in the bombing of the USS *Cole*.

Mullah Omar: Reclusive founder and leader of the Taliban whose followers named him Amir al-Mu'minin, or "commander of the faithful"—emir of the country. Bin Laden pledged allegiance to him, and he in turn offered al-Qaeda refuge and protection. He died of health complications in 2013.

John O'Neill: Veteran FBI official who, on January 1, 1997, became the special agent in charge of the National Security Division in the FBI's New York office. He picked me to be the case agent of several important investigations, and became a friend and mentor. He left the FBI on August 22, 2001, to work in the World Trade Center, where he died on 9/11.

Mohamed Rashed Daoud al-Owhali (aliases: Moath al-Balucci and Khaled Saleem bin Rasheed): Al-Qaeda operative who joined the group in 1996 as part of the Northern Group; recruited with the help of Muhannad bin Attash. Tasked with being a suicide bomber for the 1998 bombing of the U.S. Embassy in Nairobi, he didn't end up killing himself, and was later interrogated (separately) by John Anticev and Stephen Gaudin. He confessed his role and was later convicted, and is serving life in prison.

Jose Padilla (alias Abu Abdullah al-Muhajir): American al-Qaeda member who, with Binyam Mohamed, intended to attack the United States with a dirty bomb. Stephen Gaudin and I learned about his intentions during our interrogation of Abu Zubaydah, and then our squad tracked him across the world before arresting him as he landed in Chicago's O'Hare International Airport. The Bush administration publicly exaggerated Padilla's capabilities. He was convicted and sentenced to seventeen years and four months in prison.

Frank Pellegrino: FBI special agent from the I-49 squad who was the case agent for Khalid Sheikh Mohammed but who was prevented by the CIA from interrogating him.

Mohammed al-Qahtani: Al-Qaeda member who attempted to enter the United States on August 4, 2001, but was refused entry by a U.S. Immigration and Naturalization Service agent. After 9/11 he was arrested in Afghanistan and taken to Guantánamo, where a fingerprint check identified him. He was taken from the FBI and subjected to coercive interrogation techniques, which didn't yield any new information. He is being held in Guantánamo Bay, Cuba.

Ghalib al-Qamish: Head of the Political Security Organization in Yemen whom we worked with during the USS *Cole* investigation and in investigations into, and after, 9/11.

Ibrahim al-Qosi (full name: Ibrahim Ahmed Mahmoud al-Qosi; alias Abu Khubaib al-Sudani): Al-Qaeda operative who was with bin Laden from the start and who served as an accountant for the organization. He is married to the daughter of Abdullah Tabarak. I identified him at Guantánamo and gained his cooperation and confession. Before his trial, he entered a guilty plea. He was released from Guantánamo to Sudan on July 10, 2012.

Fahd al-Quso (alias Abu Hathayfah al-Adani): Member of al-Qaeda in Yemen who was tasked with videotaping the *Cole* operation. He confessed his role to Robert McFadden and me, and also told us how he and Ibrahim al-Nibras delivered $36,000 to Khallad in Malaysia. We passed this information to the CIA and asked if they knew anything about Khallad's movements in the region; they replied that they didn't. After 9/11 we discovered that the CIA had known about Khallad's movements, and that he met with Quso and Nibras after coming from al-Qaeda's 9/11 planning summit in Malaysia. The $36,000 was probably used by 9/11 hijackers Khalid al-Mihdhar and Nawaf al-Hazmi to buy their tickets to the United

States and for spending money there. He was added to the FBI's Most Wanted Terrorists list in November 2009. On May 6, 2012, he was killed in a U.S. drone strike in Yemen.

Omar Abdul Rahman: Known as the Blind Sheikh (childhood diabetes left him sightless), he led al-Gamma'a al-Islamiyya (the Islamic Group), a rival of Ayman al-Zawahiri's Egyptian Islamic Jihad. After being imprisoned in, and then expelled from, Egypt in connection with the 1981 assassination of Sadat, he made his way to the United States to take control of Abdullah Azzam's U.S. operations. He was able to enter the United States after being given a visa by a CIA official, despite being on the U.S. State Department terrorist watchlist. He was arrested in the FBI's Operation Terrorstop and sentenced to life in prison. Rahman died on February 18, 2017, in a federal prison in Butner, North Carolina.

Ali Abdullah Saleh: President of Yemen who, during the Yemeni civil war, built a relationship with mujahideen fighters; they helped him lead the North to defeat the socialist South. That began a complex relationship with extremists and al-Qaeda that continues to this day. Saleh died in Sanaa on December 4, 2017, a casualty of the civil war.

Mohammed Saleh: Egyptian Islamic Jihad *shura* council member and close associate of Ayman al-Zawahiri who joined the al-Qaeda *shura* council following the March 2001 official merger of the two groups. On 9/11 al-Qaeda held a celebration of the attacks in his house. He was killed by a U.S. missile.

Marwan al-Shehhi: A member of the Hamburg cell and roommate of 9/11 lead hijacker Mohammed Atta and facilitator Ramzi Binalshibh, he was one of the hijackers on United Airlines Flight 175, which crashed into the south tower of the World Trade Center. Fahd al-Quso's confession to NCIS special agent Robert McFadden and me that Shehhi had stayed at one point in Abu Jandal's guesthouse enabled us to convince the Yemenis to let us question Abu Jandal.

Abdullah Sungkar: Leader of Darul Islam who founded the Southeast Asian terrorist group Jemaah Islamiah with the cleric Abu Bakar Bashir. He arranged for members to travel to Afghanistan in the 1980s to train and fight the Soviets. One of his key followers was Hambali. He died in 1999.

Adbullah Tabarak (alias Abu Assim al-Maghrebi): Close personal friend of bin Laden's dating back to their days fighting the Soviets together, he followed him to Sudan and was asked by the al-Qaeda leader to head his bodyguard detachment after the 1998 East African embassy bombings. He is the father-in-law of Ibrahim al-Qosi. Arrested with Ali al-Bahlul as part of the "dirty thirty" group after 9/11 and taken to Guantánamo Bay, Cuba. I identified him based on a description Abu Jandal had given me, and I took him out of the general population. Under suspicious circumstances, the FBI was barred from questioning him and he was released. Today he is free in Morocco.

Furqan al-Tajiki (alias of Fawaz al-Rabeiee): Yemeni al-Qaeda operative who was arrested in connection with the Bayt Habra car theft plot and was later involved in other al-Qaeda operations in Yemen. In February 2006 he escaped with other al-Qaeda members from a jail in Saana, and he was killed in October 2006.

Madani al-Tayyib (also known as Abu Fadhl al-Makkee): Al-Qaeda's first financial chief, he lost a leg during the Soviet jihad and was very close to bin Laden. He ordered Jamal al-Fadl to try to procure uranium for the organization. In the 1990s he traveled to Europe with the help of Khalid al-Fawwaz to get treatment for his leg, and in 1997 it was reported that he had defected from al-Qaeda—causing many operatives, including Harun Fazul, to panic. He cooperated with the Saudi authorities, who said that they shared the information he gave them with the CIA, but this information was never passed along to the FBI. At one point, the U.S. military mistakenly thought that they had him in custody in Guantánamo. Today he is in Saudi Arabia.

George Tenet: Director of the CIA from July 1997 to July 2004. Under his leadership the professional interrogators from the CIA were sidelined, contractors were put in charge of interrogations, and coercive interrogations were introduced.

Tom Ward: An NYPD detective assigned to the Joint Terrorism Task Force in New York whom I picked to be a member of our team for the USS *Cole* bombing investigation. He died on July 8, 2016, of cancer caused by his participation in search and recovery efforts at the World Trade Center site following the 9/11 attacks.

Wilson: CIA's chief operational psychologist with whom I worked during the interrogation of Abu Zubaydah and in Guantánamo. He left the interrogation of Abu Zubaydah after CIA contractors made it clear that they intended to use coercive interrogation techniques.

Colonel Yassir (not his real name): Yemeni interrogator whom we worked closely with during the USS *Cole* investigation and in investigations after 9/11.

Ramzi Yousef: Mastermind of the 1993 World Trade Center bombing, and nephew of Khalid Sheikh Mohammed, with whom he plotted the failed Manila Air (Bojinka) attack. He is serving a life sentence in a U.S. prison.

Ayman al-Zawahiri: Originally one of the leaders of Egyptian Islamic Jihad, he supported the group's merger with al-Qaeda and became bin Laden's deputy. He helped surround bin Laden with fellow Egyptians, ensuring that they dominated and shaped al-Qaeda. He is suspected of being behind the 1989 assassination of Abdullah Azzam. On June 16, 2011, al-Qaeda announced that he had been appointed the new leader of the group following bin Laden's death.

Aaron Zebley: FBI special agent with a legal background who was instrumental in apprehending and gaining a confession from Khalfan Khamis Mohamed, an operative involved in the 1998 East African embassy bombings. He was assigned to the 9/11 investigation after the attacks, and with Mike Butsch trailed Ramzi Binalshibh. Together the three of us worked on interrogating Ramzi Binalshibh, Karim, and the six other operatives caught together on September 11, 2002.

Key Documents and Articles Cited

Note: Spellings are as in original.

United States v. Usama Bin Laden, Indictment (unsealed November 4, 1998), http://jya.com/usa-v-laden.htm.

United States v. Usama Bin Laden, Muhammad Atef, Wadih El Hage, Fazul Adbullah Mohammed, Mohamed Saeek Odeh, Mohamed Rasheed Daoud Al-Owhali, Indictment, November 4, 1998, http://jya.com/usa-v-laden+5.htm.

USA v. Usama bin Laden et al. trial in the Southern District of New York (Days 1–76, Pre-Sentencing Hearing, Sentencing Hearing), February 5, 2001–October 18, 2001, http://cryptome.org/usa-v-ubl-dt.htm.

The 9/11 Commission Report: Final Report of the National Commission on Terrorist Attacks Upon the United States (New York: W. W. Norton, 2004), http://www.9-11commission.gov/report/911Report.pdf.

John L. Helgerson, *CIA Office of Inspector General Report on CIA Account-ability with Respect to the 9/11 Attacks*, June 2005, http://www.fas.org/irp/cia/product/oig-911.pdf.

U.S. Department of Justice, *Office of the Inspector General Report: A Review of the FBI's Involvement in and Observations of Detainee Interrogations in Guantánamo Bay, Afghanistan, and Iraq*, http://www.justice.gov/oig/special/s0805/final.pdf.

Department of Justice, *Office of Professional Responsibility Report—Investigation into the Office of Legal Counsel's Memoranda Concerning Issues Relating to the Central Intelligence Agency's Use of "Enhanced Interrogation Techniques" on Suspected Terrorists*, http://judiciary.house.gov/hearings/pdf/OPRFinalReport090729.pdf.

CIA Office of Inspector General, Counterterrorism Detention and Interrogation Activities (September 1–October 2003), May 7, 2004, http://luxmedia.com.edgesuite.net/aclu/IG_Report.pdf.

U.S. Senate, *Report of the Select Committee on Intelligence on Postwar Findings About Iraq's WMD Programs and Links to Terrorism and How They Compare with Prewar Assessments*, September 8, 2006, http://intelligence.senate.gov/phaseiiaccuracy.pdf.

Penttbom Timeline Briefing, FBI Headquarters, December 10–11, 2003, http://www.scribd.com/doc/20830948/Mfr-Nara-t1a-FBI-Penttbom-Timeline-Briefing-12-10-03-00265.

U.S. Senate, *Report of the Committee on Armed Services: Inquiry into the Treatment of Detainees in U.S. Custody*, http://armed-services.senate.gov/Publications/Detainee%20Report%20Final_April%2022%202009.pdf.

CIA Report, *Detainee Reporting Pivotal for the War Against Al-Qa'ida*, June 3,

2005, http://ccrjustice.org/files/CIA%20Doc%20Detainee%20Report ing%20Pivotal.pdf.

U.S Department of Justice, Office of Legal Counsel: Memorandum for John Rizzo, Acting General Counsel of the Central Intelligence Agency (Bybee Memo), August 1, 2002, http://media.mcclatchydc .com/smedia/2009/04/16/16/Taylor-OLC-CIAtorturememo-1 .source.prod_affiliate.91.pdf.

U.S. Department of Justice, Office of Legal Counsel, Memorandum for John A. Rizzo Senior Deputy General Counsel, Central Intelligence Agency (Bradbury Memo), May 30, 2005, http://media.mcclatchydc .com/smedia/2009/04/16/16/Taylor-OLC-CIAmemo3-1.source .prod_affiliate.91.pdf.

The CIA Interrogation of Abu Zubaydah (March 2001–Jan. 2003),* http://www.aclu.org/files/assets/CIA_Interrogation_of_AZ_ released_04-15-10.pdf.

Department of Defense Joint Task-Force 170 Guantánamo Bay, Cuba, Memorandum for Commander, United States Southern Command. Subject: Counter-Resistance Strategies, http://www.defense.gov/ news/Jun2004/d20040622doc3.pdf.

CIA Psychological Assessment of Zain al-'Abideen Muhammad Hassan, a.k.a. Abu Zubaydah, http://www.aclu.org/files/torturefoia/released/ 082409/cia_ig/oig39.pdf.

Government of Singapore White Paper, *The Jemaah Islamiyah Arrests and the Threat of Terrorism*, January 2003, http://www.mha.gov.sg/publica tion_details.aspx?pageid=35&cid=354.

---

*March 2001 is a typographical error; it should be March 2002.

Press Briefing on the West Coast Terrorist Plot by Frances Fragos Townsend, Assistant to the President for Homeland Security and Counterterrorism, February 9, 2006, http://georgewbush-whitehouse .archives.gov/news/releases/2006/02/20060209-4.html.

Fact Sheet, "Keeping America Safe from Attack—President Bush Discusses Intelligence Showing the Importance of Defeating Al Qaeda in Iraq," May 23, 2007, http://georgewbush-whitehouse.archives .gov/news/releases/2007/05/print/20070523.html.

Testimony of Ali Soufan before the United States Senate Judiciary, May 13, 2009, http://judiciary.senate.gov/hearings/testimony.cfm?id=3842& wit_id=7906.

"My Tortured Decision," by Ali Soufan, *New York Times*, April 23, 2009, http://www.nytimes.com/2009/04/23/opinion/23soufan.html.

Photograph Credits

1. FBI
2. Image from al-Qaeda propoganda tape
3. FBI
4. FBI
5. U.S. Government
6. U.S. Government
7. U.S. Government
8. U.S. Government
9. FBI
11. Image from al-Qaeda propaganda tape
12. Image from al-Qaeda propaganda tape
13. Image from al-Qaeda propaganda tape
14. Image from al-Qaeda propaganda tape
15. ABC News photo
16. Courtesy of Khaled Fazaa / Getty Images
17. FBI
18. Courtesy of the author
19. Courtesy of the author

20. U.S. Government
21. U.S. Government
22. Courtesy of the author
23. Image from al-Qaeda propaganda tape
24. Courtesy of Farooq Naeem / Getty Images
25. Courtesy of the author
26. Courtesy of the author
27. Courtesy of the author
28. Courtesy of the author
29. Courtesy of the author

Index

Abas, 295

Abas, Hashim, 356, 551

Abbas, Nasir, 361, 545

Abbottabad, 532

ABC, 14, 79, 84, 100, 304, 332, 455

Abdin Circle, 144–45

Abdu, *see* Nashiri, Abdul Rahim Hussein Muhammad Abda al-

Abdullah, Abdullah Ahmed, 54, 65, 77–78, 89, 90, 93, 119, 313, 322, 328, 332, 346–47, 385, 389, 456, 545

Abdullah, Noralwizah Lee, 366

Abdullah II, King, 141

Abouhalima, Mahmud, 47, 48, 49

Abraham, 22

Abu Abdelraham, 353

Abu Abdullah al-Muhajir, *see* Padilla, Jose

Abu Abdul Rahman al-Muhajir, 78, 112, 264, 327, 455, 481, 545

Abu Ahmed al-Kuwaiti, 531, 532, 533, 535, 536

Abu A'isha, *see* Abu Zubaydah, Zayn al-Abidin Muhammad Husayn

Abu al-Hareth al-Liby, 331

Abu Ali al-Harithi, 349, 504, 505, 506

Abu al-Khair al-Masri, 280, 560

Abu al-Kholoud, 337

Abu al-Layth, 506

Abu al-Shahid al-Sanani, 505

Abu Assim al-Maghrebi, *see* Tabarak, Abdullah

Abu Ata'a al-Tunisi, 79–80, 326, 380, 443

Abu Ayed al-Phalastini, *see* Deek, Khalil Said al-

Abu Bakar Bashir, 360, 361, 362, 546, 566

Abu Bakr, 505

Abu Bakr Islamic University, 367

Abu Bakr Sadeek camp, 129

Abu Bakr Sudani, *see* Fadl, Jamal al-

Abu Dhabi, 240

Abu Dijana, 42

Abu Fadhl al-Makkee, *see* Tayyib, Madani al-

Abu Faraj al-Liby, 535

Abu Ghaith, Salman, 280

Abu Ghraib, 482–83, 561

Abu Hafs al-Masri, 31, 41, 52, 54, 65, 79, 101, 129, 231, 264, 265, 266, 267, 274, 280, 283, 316, 322, 323, 324, 328, 337, 345, 347, 351, 356, 361, 381, 384, 388, 444, 455, 479, 480–81, 533

Abu Hafs al-Mauritani, 151, 273, 322, 323, 328, 546

Abu Hajer al-Iraqi, 31–32, 33–34, 44, 266, 546

Abu Hammam al-Najaji, 331

Abu Hamza al-Jaza'eri, 331

Abu Hanifa, Imam, 57

Abu Hoshar, Khadr, 133, 134, 135–36, 137, 140, 144

Abu Hurairah, xxi

Abu Hussein al-Masri, 323

Abu Jaffar, 36

Abu Jaffar al-Hada, 66, 318, 336, 338, 555

Abu Jandal, xix–xxi, xxii–xiii, xxv, 62, 65–66, 79, 80, 118, 150, 151–52, 231, 246, 265, 276, 295, 306, 307–34, 339, 352, 355, 441, 442, 449, 452, 454, 470, 484, 493, 498, 513, 529, 546–47, 556, 560, 565, 566

Abu Khabab al-Masri, 417

Abu Khadija al-Iraqi, *see* Abu Jaffar

Abu Khalil al-Hada, 338

Abu Khubaib al-Sudani, *see* Qosi, Ibrahim Ahmed Mahmoud al-

Abu Mohamed al-Amriki, *see* Mohamed, Ali

Abu Mohammed al-Maqdisi, 133

Abu Mohammed al-Masri, *see* Abdullah, Abdullah Ahmed

Abu Musab al-Suri, *see* Setmariam, Mustafa

Abu Musab al-Yemeni, 462

Abu Obeydah al-Maki, *see* Jihad Ali

Abu Qutadah, 135

Abu Rida al-Suri, 43–44, 45

Abu Saeed, 345

Abu Saif, 239, 240, 241, 505

Abu Sayyaf Group, 40

Abu Tareq, *see* Ridi, Essam al-

Abu Ubaidah al-Banshiri, 31, 49, 53–54, 61, 545, 546, 547, 554

Abu Ziad al-Najdi, 331

Abu Zubaydah, Zayn al-Abidin Muhammad Husayn, 119, 132, 133, 134, 135–36, 140, 141, 142, 143, 144, 175, 344, 345, 347, 373–92, 393–410, 411–12, 413, 414, 415–18, 419–21, 422–24, 427, 428–29, 430, 432–34, 435, 439, 465, 479, 488, 489, 513, 514, 515, 525–27, 547, 553–54, 555, 557, 562, 563, 567

Aceh, 369

Adani, Salman al-, 262–63, 547–48

Addington, David, 464

Addis Ababa, 444

Adel, Saif al-, 65, 78, 79, 99, 153, 231, 266, 274, 322, 326, 327, 328, 329, 345, 347, 454, 455, 462, 480, 481, 537, 548

Aden, 155, 159, 163–64, 165, 171, 173, 175, 177, 179, 180, 183, 201–4, 206, 210–14, 215, 221, 222–23, 228, 230, 233–34, 239, 242, 244, 256–58, 260, 262, 292–93

Advice and Reformation Committee, 42

Afghanistan, xix, 10, 11, 12–13, 17, 22, 23, 25, 27, 28, 30, 31, 32, 33, 37, 42, 47–48, 49, 52, 54, 56–58, 59–60, 61–64, 66, 68, 69, 71, 76, 80, 90, 91, 99, 100, 114, 117, 122–23, 131, 132–33, 142, 143–44, 150, 152, 194, 195, 196, 221, 223, 225, 231, 238–39, 255–56, 258, 260, 263, 264, 267, 274, 277, 278, 294–95, 297, 301, 306–7, 310, 311, 313, 318, 320, 327, 329, 332, 333, 336, 337, 338, 343, 344, 345, 351, 354, 357, 359, 360–61, 376, 379–80, 384, 386, 390–92, 401, 419, 439–41, 443, 450, 454, 459–60, 470, 472, 474–75, 479, 480, 481, 489, 491, 498, 513, 520, 521–22, 549, 551, 552, 556, 557, 558–59, 564

Ahdal, Taha al-, 238, 259, 261, 262–63, 322, 323, 363, 367, 374, 547, 548

Ahmed the German, *see* Alal, Hamdan Khalif

Air Force Office of Special Investigations, U.S., 425

Airman Flight School, 28

Alal, Hamdan Khalif, 78, 79, 89

al-Amir Institute, 234

al-Ansar, 143, 392, 550

al-Aqsa Mosque, 13

al-Azhar University, 47

Albania, 69, 100, 102, 107–11

al-Banshiri camp, 462, 481

al-Bara, *see* bin Attash, Abdul Aziz

al-Batar, 470, 536

al-Burayqah, 200, 218, 234, 237

al-Farouq camp, 89, 129, 266, 277, 329, 337, 338, 455, 456, 477, 558

al-Farouq Mosque, 11, 47, 71

Algeria, 12, 30, 131

al-Ghuraba, 367, 368–69

al-Hudaydah, 256, 257, 261

Ali, Ihab, 25, 28, 38–40, 49

Ali, Imam, 19–20

al-Iman Media Center, 134

al-Islamiyya, 32, 565

al-Jazeera, 493–94, 515

al-Jazeera Hotel, 260, 470

al-Kifah Center, 47

Allen, 383, 387

al-Masjid al-Haram, 11, 21–22

al-Mukalla, 256, 257, 259, 349, 502, 508

al-Mukhabarat al-Aamah, 70

al-Qaeda, xix, xx, xxi–xxiv, xxvii, 19, 25, 30, 31, 32, 33–34, 36, 38–39, 41–45, 49–52, 54, 56–62, 65, 66–67, 69, 70–72, 76, 77–79, 81, 82, 84, 86, 88, 89, 91–94, 97–98, 99, 101–2, 103–8, 110, 113–15, 117–19, 121–27, 128–29, 130, 131–35, 136, 138, 149–51, 152–54, 157–58, 161, 175, 176, 179, 182, 192, 194–95, 200–203, 209, 212, 215, 219–21, 223, 225, 226, 227, 229, 231–32, 234, 236–42, 246, 250, 253, 254–68, 272–83, 284, 287–89, 291, 293–95, 297, 298, 299, 302, 306–39, 343–49, 350–54, 357–61, 363–65, 369, 373, 379–80, 384–87, 388, 390, 399, 407, 411–15, 417, 424, 426, 428, 430, 439–40, 442–43, 444–47, 452, 454–58, 460–62, 469–81, 484–85, 489, 492, 493, 497–98, 502, 504–7, 512–17, 519–23, 529, 532–38, 545–48, 550–60, 562

al-Quds Mosque, 273

al-Ridda Mosque, 233

Al-Therba, 454

Alvin (CIA chief), 139, 140, 376, 548

al-Wafa, 440, 441, 482

Amin, Mohamad Farik, see Zubair
Amman, 134, 135, 136, 137, 139–40,
    142, 144–45, 376
Andrew (head of ISD), 360
Andrews Air Force Base, 161
Ansari, Mustafah al-, 337
Ansi, Hussein, 177, 178–79, 183, 189,
    190–91, 200, 202–3, 221, 228,
    235–37, 252, 293, 548
Anticev, John, 49, 71, 86, 88–89, 90,
    92, 439, 441, 548, 563
Anticev, Mike, 71, 441, 548
Aql, Saeed al-, 507
Arabian Peninsula, xxii, xxiv, xxv, 13,
    51, 63, 65, 70, 85, 100, 131, 231,
    256, 314, 320, 323, 349, 489,
    498, 507, 513
Arab League, 21
Arena, Andy, 350–51, 502–3, 549
Arizona, 26, 277
Armitage, Richard, 245
Army Criminal Investigation
    Command, U.S., 425
Army of Mohammad, 133
Army Special Operations Forces,
    U.S., 86
Arnett, Peter, 69, 99
Ashcroft, John, 353, 408, 459
Ashibi, Walid, 505
Ashraf, 107–8
Ash Shihr, 256, 257
Assoun, 144
Atef, Mohammed, see Abu Hafs al-
    Masri
Atlantic City, N.J., 30
Atta, Mohammed, xxiv, 271–72, 275,
    278, 279, 280, 296, 318, 321,
    348, 357, 458–59, 460, 477, 494,
    523, 549, 550, 565
Attas, Hamida al-, 11
Atwah, Muhsin Musa Matwakku, see
    Abu Abdul Rahman al-Muhajir

Austria, 45
Ayutthaya, 366
Ayyad, Nidal, 48
Azayet, see Abdullah, Abdullah
    Ahmed
Azerbaijan, 98, 102, 105, 339, 553
Aziz, King Abdul, xx
Azzam, see Jihad Ali
Azzam, Abdullah, 11, 23, 25–26, 28, 31,
    32, 47, 48, 61, 85, 87, 89, 254, 268,
    379, 477, 549, 551, 556, 565, 567
Azzani, Yasser al-, 238

Baccus, Rick, 442, 463
Badakhshan, 63
Badawi, Hussein al-, 260, 261, 498,
    504
Badawi, Jamal al-, 193, 194, 209, 221,
    222, 223–26, 228, 230, 232–34,
    235, 246, 252, 260, 262, 263,
    498, 508, 548, 549
Baghdad, 482, 561
Bagram Airfield, 450, 451
Bahlul, Ali Hamza Ahmed Suleiman
    al-, xxiii, 266, 274, 280, 323, 346,
    472–74, 476–80, 513, 529, 549
Bahrain, 156, 171, 215, 333–34
Bahri, Habib al-, 313, 325, 452
Bahri, Nasser Ahmad Nasser al-, see
    Abu Jandal
Baizid, Mohammed Loay, see Abu
    Rida al-Suri
Baku, 98
Bali, 363–64
Balucci, Moath al-, see Owhali,
    Mohamed Rashed Daoud al-
Baluchi, Ammar al-, 275, 278, 279,
    512, 535, 550, 557, 558
Ba-Nafa' souk, 233
Bandar Abbas, 489
Bangkok, 54, 240, 278, 288, 294, 363,
    365, 366

Banihammad, Fayez, 281
Banna, Hassan al-, 18
Bannu, 347
Bary, Adel Abdel, 96, 97–98, 100,
    101–3
Basheer, 43, 44–45
Bayt Habra, 149, 151, 195, 196, 229,
    257, 258, 337, 354, 497, 550, 559,
    566
BBC, 65, 280
Beaver, Diane, 465–66
Begg, Mozzam, 133, 143, 392, 550
Begg, Zaynab, 392
Beirut, 4, 7, 9, 273
Bekaa Valley, 41, 138
Bergen, Peter, 99
Berger, Sandy, 220
Berlin, 275
Bermel, 346, 401
bin Abdul Haq, Huda, see Mukhlas
Binalshibh, Ramzi, 52, 271–72, 275–
    76, 279, 287, 348, 351, 357, 428,
    452, 460, 484–85, 488, 492, 493,
    494, 495, 500, 501, 513–15, 532,
    549, 550–51, 553, 558, 565, 568
bin Attash, Abdul Aziz, 118, 153,
    195–96, 229, 246, 254–56, 324,
    550, 558
bin Attash, Moaz, 345, 550, 558
bin Attash, Mohammed bin Saleh,
    239
bin Attash, Muhannad, 60–61, 62–63,
    64, 65, 118, 153, 254, 255–56,
    324, 332, 454, 455, 546, 550,
    558, 563
bin Attash, Omayer, 255–56, 324, 550,
    558
bin Attash, Walid, see Khallad
bin Baz, Abd al-Aziz, 23, 100
bin Habib bin Yousef Jdey,
    Abderraouf, 352, 353
bin Laden, Abdullah, 35

bin Laden, Hamza, 267
bin Laden, Mohammed bin Awad,
    10–11, 337
bin Laden, Osama, xix, xxi, xxiii,
    xxiv, xxvii, 10, 11, 13–14, 17, 21,
    23, 25–28, 30–32, 33–34, 35,
    36–38, 39–42, 48, 50, 51–52,
    54, 56– 57, 61, 62, 63, 64–68,
    69–71, 72, 75–79, 80, 81–82,
    83, 84, 88, 90, 91, 93, 95, 96,
    98–100, 101, 117–18, 121–22,
    128, 129, 131–32, 134, 149, 150,
    151–53, 157–58, 195, 219–20,
    221, 223, 226, 230, 231–32, 250,
    254, 255, 256–59, 263–67, 272–
    75, 276, 277, 279–83, 304, 306,
    307, 310, 313, 316, 318, 319–26,
    328, 332, 333, 336, 337, 343–46,
    347–48, 349, 352, 357, 359, 361,
    367, 380, 384–85, 386, 388–89,
    390–91, 428, 440–41, 444–45,
    447, 453, 454–55, 456, 458, 470,
    471–72, 474, 475, 477, 478, 488,
    497, 498, 500, 507, 512, 513, 517,
    518, 521, 523, 531–32, 533–37,
    546, 547, 549, 550, 551, 552,
    554, 556, 558, 559, 560, 564, 566
bin Laden, Uthman, 345, 532
bin Lap, Bashir, see Lillie
bin Rasheed, Khaled Saleem, see
    Owhali, Mohamed Rashed
    Daoud al-
bin Rashid, Tawfiq Muhammad Salih,
    196
bin Wan Mat, Wan Min, 363
bin Yar Ali Khan, Mohammad Aslam,
    357–58, 360
Birmingham, UK, 143, 392, 550
Black Hawk Down, 41, 345, 533
Black Magic, 364
Blaine, Thomas, 443
Blind Sheik, see Rahman, Omar Abdul

Boca Raton, Fla., 520

Bodine, Barbara K., 159, 161, 166, 170, 172, 173, 174, 181, 185, 186, 193, 203, 205, 211–12, 213, 217–19, 221, 242–43, 245, 246, 247, 251, 252, 285, 333, 551, 557

Bongardt, Steve, 119, 120, 139, 159–60, 161, 162, 170, 172, 205–6, 207, 243–45, 250, 286, 288, 290–92, 296, 486, 551, 552

Borelli, Don, 170, 243

Boris (CIA psychologist), 393, 394–98, 399, 400, 401, 407, 408–9, 411, 413, 414, 415–17, 420–21, 423, 424, 425, 426, 432–33, 434

Bosnia, 30, 61, 62, 65, 310, 311, 330–31, 337, 480

Boston, Mass., 134, 144

Boussora, Faker, 352

Bowman, Spike, 445

Bradbury, Steven G., 381, 427–28, 429

Bragg, Fort, 76

Brant, David, 467

Brian (ISD commander), 359–60

British Royal Navy, 155–56

Bronx, N.Y., 518, 522–23

Brooklyn Bridge, 404, 407, 427

Bruno's, 24

Bukoba, 53

Bulbul, see Jihad Ali

Bunn, John, 104, 143

Bush, George W., 116, 220–21, 253, 282, 304, 367, 380, 404, 408, 415, 425, 426, 427, 435, 457, 478

Butsch, Mike, 484, 487, 488, 490, 492–95, 499, 501, 551, 568

Bybee, Jay S., 428, 429–30, 432

Caine, Michael, 104

Cairo, 40, 47

Camp David Accords, 21

Canada, 141–42, 352–53

Canadian Security Intelligence Service (CSIS), 352

Cape Town, 95

Capitol, U.S., 276, 282

Carter, Jimmy, 21

Casey, William, 28

Cedars of Lebanon, 25

Central Intelligence Agency (CIA), xxvii, 14, 28, 29, 47, 50, 52, 75, 76, 83, 91, 107, 108, 109–10, 116, 119–20, 138–40, 160, 170, 171, 184, 205–7, 218, 219, 241, 243, 246, 249, 253, 276, 286, 287–89, 291–92, 294, 296, 298–302, 304, 305, 365, 367–68, 374, 378, 380, 381–82, 389, 393–98, 399–401, 403, 405, 408–9, 411–13, 414, 416, 420–21, 424, 425, 427–33, 448–50, 479, 484, 485, 486, 487, 488, 490, 491–92, 497, 500, 501, 512, 515, 516, 525, 527, 532, 535, 550, 557, 559, 566, 567
see also Counterterrorism Center

Chapman, Seifullah, 519

Charlie (ISD inspector), 357

Chechnya, 30, 61, 62, 65, 273

Cheney, Dick, 464

Chertoff, Michael, 464

Chicago, Ill., 30, 407

Christmas Eve bombings, 361–62

Churchill, Winston, 535

Cité, 24, 30, 105

Clancy, Tom, 413

Clinton, Bill, 41, 90, 91, 156, 219–20

Cloonan, Jack, 99, 102, 107, 114–15, 116, 125, 249, 551, 559

CNN, 69–70, 84, 99, 220, 457

Cohen, David, 91

Coleman, Daniel, 14, 49, 68, 71, 72, 99, 102, 136, 175, 302, 303, 304, 351, 449, 534, 552

Congress, U.S., 415, 480

Corbett, Bill, 449–50
Corbett, Steve, 216, 246, 250, 287, 290
Corrigan, Tom, 83
Corsi, Dina, 243, 244, 245, 249–50, 286–87, 290, 552
Counterterrorism Center (CTC), 14, 29, 71, 119, 139, 175, 206, 302, 367, 375–76, 378, 393–96, 399, 407, 412, 413, 414–15, 416, 423, 427, 446, 465, 466, 488, 489, 492, 508
Criminal Investigation Command (CID), 442
Criminal Investigation Task Force (CITF), 381, 442, 443, 446, 447, 463–64, 466–67, 470, 471, 482, 536
Crouch, George, 159, 160, 161, 162, 166–67, 169, 170, 172, 190, 217, 222, 268, 351, 358, 449, 450, 451, 452, 453, 552, 555, 556, 557
Crouch, Laura, 160
Cruise, Kevin, 13–14, 83, 154–55, 296–97
Cruise, Tom, 525
Crumpton, Hank, 175, 206
Cuba, 442

Dairat al-Mukhabarat al-Ammah, *see* General Intelligence Directorate (GID)
D'Amuro, Pat, 10, 15, 29, 30, 83, 88, 91, 101, 103, 136, 138, 139, 140, 157, 208, 299, 300, 350, 421–23, 427, 449, 499, 500, 503, 515–16, 549, 552
Darbi, Ahmed Mohammed Haza al-, 79, 262, 336–37, 338, 339, 348, 484, 550, 552–53, 555, 558, 561
Dar es Salaam, 14, 42, 77, 78, 80–81, 83, 85, 89, 90, 91, 95, 96

Darul Islam (DI), 357, 360, 566
Dayton Peace Accords, 331
De Benedittis, Massimo, 112
Deek, Khalil Said al-, 132–33, 134, 135, 137, 140–41, 143, 144
Defense Department, U.S., 76, 212, 426, 440, 442, 464, 468
Denpasar, 363
Derwish, Kamal, 506–7
Desert Fox, 327
Dhahran, 51
Dilkum, Hadi, 196–97, 259, 261
Diplomatic Security Service (DSS), 247
Direction de la Surveillance du Territoire (DST), 124, 126
Dix, Fort, 246
Djibouti, 156
DocEx, 351, 353, 356, 498, 546, 553, 560
Donlon, Tom, 15, 16, 80–83, 97, 250, 286, 287, 290, 553
Donnachie, Craig, 374
Donovan, Kevin, 174, 210, 212, 486, 553
Doran, Debbie, 85–86, 123–24, 127, 302, 303, 351, 559
Dorris, Mike, 117
Dorsey, Mike, 171
Driscoll, Mike, 71
Drug Enforcement Administration (DEA), 116–17
Dubai, 93, 202, 279, 291, 348–49
Duke, Scott, 354, 502, 503–4
Dulles International Airport, 281, 373, 374, 375
Dunlavey, Michael E., 50–51, 442, 445, 448, 459, 463, 465, 471, 473, 553, 561
Duranta camp, 417
Duranta Lake, 338
Durrama, Mohammed al-, 232, 234, 238

Ed (CTC interrogator), 175, 393, 396,
    397, 409, 414–16, 424–25, 439,
    440, 483, 553–54
Ed Boardman Aviation School, 26
Egypt, 12, 17, 21, 22, 26, 31, 38, 40,
    45, 47, 65, 100, 102, 307
EgyptAir, 75
Egyptian Islamic Jihad (EIJ), 13, 25, 31,
    40, 48, 52, 75, 76, 82, 84, 97–98,
    100, 102–11, 114, 158, 280, 455,
    547, 554, 557, 560, 561, 565, 567
Eidarous, Ibrahim, 96, 97–98, 100,
    101–3, 108
Elaine's, 24
El-Ghriba Synagogue, 348
England, 8, 25, 27, 49
England, Lynndie, 483
Ennis, Joe, 216–17, 284–85, 408, 554
Ethiopia, 52

Fadhil, Mustafa Mohamed, 89
Fadl, Jamal al-, 34, 36, 42–45, 50,
    66–72, 107, 118, 129, 130, 322,
    441, 548, 554, 559, 566
Faisalabad, 347, 374, 376, 390, 402
Fallon, Mark, 442, 446, 465, 466–68, 482
Farouk, King, 18–19
Fawwaz, Khalid al-, 42, 45, 50, 75–76,
    77, 95, 97, 98, 99, 100, 101, 103,
    129, 133, 329, 554, 556, 566
Fayzabad, 63, 64
Fazhil, 66
Fazul, Harun, 42, 49–50, 54, 89, 90,
    93, 95, 323, 554, 566
Federal Bureau of Investigation (FBI),
    xx, xxvii, 3–4, 5–6, 7–10, 13, 14,
    15, 16, 17, 28, 29, 48–51, 55, 71,
    76, 83–88, 89, 91, 97, 98, 101,
    104, 107, 108, 112, 113, 117, 119,
    123, 125, 126, 129, 136, 137,
    142, 143, 145, 153, 154, 157, 158,
    159, 160, 161, 165, 166, 168–71,

172, 175, 176, 180–81, 196, 200,
    206–7, 210, 212, 216, 217–19,
    221, 228–53, 285–87, 289,
    290–91, 297, 300, 302–4, 322,
    335, 350, 353, 354, 358, 373–74,
    376–77, 385, 386, 407–8, 413,
    416, 421–22, 425, 434–35, 441,
    442, 446, 448–49, 452, 457, 458,
    462–63, 465, 469–71, 473, 480,
    484–87, 492, 493, 495, 499–500,
    504, 508, 512, 513, 515, 525–26,
    534, 536, 545, 548, 549, 551,
    552, 553, 555, 562, 563, 564, 565
Federally Administered Tribal Areas
    (FATA), 402
Feinstein, Diane, 535
Feith, Doug, 466, 470
Fernandez, Carlos, 216, 235, 334, 514,
    523, 555
Fielding, Fred, 429
Fincher, Russell, 450, 451
Fitzgerald, Patrick, 68, 92, 94–95, 99,
    102, 103, 112, 125, 127–28, 139,
    158–59, 354, 555, 559
Fleet Antiterrorism Security Team
    (FAST), 165
Foreign Intelligence Surveillance Act
    (FISA), 205, 207, 374
Frahm, Charles, 274–75, 376, 421
France, 128
Frank (CTC polygrapher), 393, 394–
    95, 396, 400, 401, 409, 414, 422
Fred (CIA liaison), 138–39, 140, 450–
    51, 452, 487, 555
Freedman, Daniel, 172, 526
Freeh, Louis, xxvii, 158, 180–81, 219,
    555
Fry, Alan, 104, 143
Ft. Belvoir, Va., 464

Gadahn, Adam Yahiye, 134
Gaddafi, Muammar al-, 52, 180

Galligan, Mary, 246
Gaudin, Cassandra, 514–15
Gaudin, Stephen, 86, 92, 94, 118,
    144–45, 354–55, 374, 375, 376,
    377, 381, 382, 383, 384, 385,
    387, 389, 390, 394, 396, 397,
    398, 399, 400, 407, 409, 412,
    413, 417–18, 419, 421–23, 503,
    514–15, 547, 555, 562, 563
Gelles, Mike, 446, 467–68
General Intelligence Directorate
    (GID), 136, 139, 140–41
Geneva Conventions, 414, 432, 464
Germany, 215, 272–75, 279
Ghailani, Ahmed Khalfan, 89, 90
Ghamdi, Ahmed al-, 281, 318
Ghamdi, Hamza al-, 63–64, 281, 345,
    346, 531
Ghamdi, Saeed al-, 282
Ghayl Bawazir, 272
Ghazni province, 386
Ghozi, Fathur Rohman al-, 358, 363
Ghul, Hassan, 535
Gibran, Kahlil, 130
Gibson, Mel, 315, 413
Gillespie, Maggie, 243, 245, 249
Giuliani, Rudy, 515
Gold Mohur Hotel, 157, 215, 218
Gonzales, Alberto, 415, 429
Gore, Al, 221
Graham, Lindsey, 528
Grand Mosque, 11, 13, 17, 22, 51
Guantánamo Bay, xxiii, 50, 175, 325,
    346, 368, 380, 381, 424, 439–83,
    487, 493, 504, 520, 526, 531,
    536, 547, 549, 550, 551, 552,
    553, 556, 557, 558, 561, 562,
    564, 566
Guevara, Che, 418
Gunawan, Rusman "Gun Gun," 367,
    368
Gunn, Cherone, 249

Gunn, Lou, 249

Hababi, Fawzi Yahya Qasim al-, 349
Habib, Khalid al-, 345
Hada, Ahmed al-, 88, 93, 94, 95, 291,
    318, 335–39, 484, 548, 552,
    555–56, 559, 561
Hada, Samir al-, 338
Hage, April El-, 26
Hage, Wadih El-, 25–26, 27, 34–36,
    38, 42, 46, 47, 48, 49–50, 54, 72,
    75, 94, 554, 556
Hamas, 10, 15
Hambali, 359, 361, 362–63, 364,
    365–67, 368, 369, 514, 535, 545,
    546, 556, 566
Hamburg, 271, 272–73, 357, 494, 549,
    550, 565
Hamdan, Salim, 63–64, 66, 78, 80,
    118, 151, 263–65, 267, 274, 279,
    282, 325, 332, 333, 344, 348,
    449–50, 452–56, 470–73, 513,
    536, 546, 552, 556, 558
Hani (Yemeni witness), 185–86, 187–
    88, 190, 193
Hanjour, Hani, 277, 279, 281
Haq, Ali Imron, 363–64
Haq, Amrozi, 363, 364
Harazi, Jihad Mohammed Ali al-, see
    Jihad Ali
Harbi, Khalid al-, 440–41
Hatton, Lenny, xx, 418–19
Hawsawi, Mustafa al-, 278, 458, 460,
    469, 535, 557
Haynes, William James, II, 464, 468,
    470
Hazmi, Nawaf al-, 96, 249, 262, 275,
    277, 278, 281, 288–89, 291, 292,
    294, 296, 298, 300, 301, 318,
    361, 563, 564
Hazmi, Salem al-, 282, 292, 318
Haznawi, Ahmed al-, 282

Helgerson, John L., 413, 425, 426, 429, 434, 452, 557
Help Africa People, 38, 75, 95
Herrmann, Bob, 516
Hezbollah, 10, 29, 41, 51, 138, 334
Hickey, Bob, 170, 210, 212
Hijazi, Raed, 133–36, 137, 140–41, 144
Hill, James, 465, 466
Hilltop Hotel, 89, 90
Himyari, Husam al-Deen al-, 337
Hizb Wahdat Islami, 63
Holcomb, Ray, 487, 490, 501
Homeland Security, U.S., 367, 465
Hoover, J. Edgar, 8
Horn of Africa, 41, 68, 71, 156, 554
hostage rescue team (HRT), 161, 162, 165, 166, 170, 172, 176, 210, 212, 216
House of Lords, 104
House Permanent Select Committee on Intelligence, 298
Hull, Edmund, 285, 333, 503, 507, 508, 515, 557
Hummel, Joe, 104, 106
Husin, Azahari, 363, 369, 514
Hussein, King, 141
Hussein, Saddam, xxii, 15, 31, 32, 156, 251, 351, 451, 477, 478, 502, 546, 557

Ibn al-Amir Institute, 233
Ibn al-Qayyim Mosque, 237
Ibn al-Shaykh al-Liby, 34, 119, 132, 424, 450–51, 487, 514, 547, 555, 557
Ibn Taymiyyah, Taqi ad-Din, xviii, 20, 32
Iglesias, David, 525
Ignatius, David, 137
Ilala, 95
Imam, Adel, 410

Immigration and Naturalization Service (INS), 142, 249, 278–79, 291, 564
India, 379
Indonesia, 40–41, 337, 360, 361, 363, 364, 369
Indonesian Moro Islamic Liberation Front, 363
Informed Interrogation Approach, 424
Interim Marine Corps Security Force, 156
Internal Security Department (ISD), 356–60, 362, 364, 365
International Islamic University, 23
Iran, xxi, xxii, 17, 21, 297, 489
Iranian Revolutionary Guards, 135
Iraq, 15, 149, 230, 257, 320, 424, 451–52, 478–79, 482–83
Iraqi, Abdul Hadi al-, 344, 346, 380, 557
Irish Republican Army, 10
Isamuddin, Riduan, see Hambali
Islamabad, 22, 55, 100, 117, 196, 487, 532
Islamic Army for the Liberation of the Holy Places, 85
Islamic Army of Aden-Abyan, 149, 158
Islamic Army shura, 40
Islamic Center, 46
Islamic Union Movement, 331
Israel, 17, 21, 31, 139, 179, 180, 264, 311, 320
Italian Division of General Investigations and Special Operations (DIGOS), 112
Italy, 105, 112, 128

Jabarah, Mohammed Mansour, 353, 358–59
Jadawi, Saqr al-, see Hamdan, Salim
Jaffar, Khalim, 356

Jaji, battle of, 63, 323
Jakarta, 363, 369, 514
Jalalabad, 63, 64, 265, 279, 344, 380, 533
Jalalabad camp, 61
Janoubi, Abdul Aziz al-, *see* Darbi, Ahmed Mohammed Haza al-
Japan, 27
Jarrah, Ziad, xxiv, 273, 274, 275, 279, 282, 477
Jarralla, Omar Hasan Saeed, 349
Jaza'eri, Riyadh al-, 347
Jeddah, 23, 330
Jemaah Islamiah (JI), 13, 40–41, 344, 353, 356–57, 359, 360–63, 364, 367, 369, 514, 545, 546, 556, 566
Jen (CTC supervisor), 412
Jenin, 132
Jerusalem, xxi, 13
Jessee, Scott, 136
Jihad Ali, 78, 80, 93–94, 118, 192, 258
Jihad Wal camp, 65, 260
Jizan, 260
Jobran, 402
Joe's Diner, 248
John Paul II, Pope, 54
Johnston, David, 517
Johor, 362
Joint Forces Command (JFCOM), 464
Joint Inquiry into Intelligence Community Activities (JIICA-TAS911), 298, 299
Joint Personnel Recovery Agency (JPRA), 464, 483
Joint Special Operations Command (JSOC), 533
Joint Task Force 160, 442, 463
Joint Task Force 170, 50, 442, 463, 553
Joint Terrorism Task Force (JTTF), 15, 30, 82–83, 86, 136, 145, 157, 159, 160, 161, 184, 247, 373, 374, 389, 407, 445, 486, 567

Joint Yemeni-American Investigative Committee, 194
Jordan, 12, 25, 133, 134, 136–40, 141, 143, 144–45, 154, 221, 298, 412, 450, 452, 487, 552
Juma, Ashif Mohamed, 53–54
Junior, *see* Fadl, Jamal al-
Justice Department, U.S., 84, 89, 92, 208, 244, 248, 367, 381, 411, 415, 425, 426, 428, 429, 430, 432, 465, 469, 525
Juzor al-Molluk, 337
JW Marriott Hotel, 369, 514

Kaaba, 22, 265
Kabul, 22, 60, 64, 79, 80, 254, 265, 279, 280, 332–33, 343–44, 392, 484, 487, 491–92
Kafr el-Sheikh, 272
Kahane, Meir, 46–47
Kakul Military Academy, 532
Kandahar, 59–60, 69, 79, 96, 262, 264, 265, 266, 267, 283, 318, 332, 333, 337, 338, 344, 345, 367, 384, 390, 391, 401, 479, 481
Kanj, Bassam, 143–44
Karachi, 26, 88, 90, 254–55, 262, 273, 332, 347, 359, 485, 487, 511, 512, 532, 535
Karas, Kenneth, 68, 99, 102, 103–4, 106, 557
Karim (al-Qaeda operative), 452, 484–85, 487, 488, 492, 495–99, 500, 501, 504, 513–15, 529, 551, 553, 558, 568
Kashmir, 41
Kastari, Mas Selamat, 362
Katibat al-Shimal, *see* Northern Group
Keenan, Jennifer, 117
Kelley, David, 158–59, 181–82, 194, 222, 236, 457, 556, 558
Kennedy's, 3, 18–19

Kenya, 14, 53, 88, 89, 101, 129
Khair, Saad al-, 24, 136–37, 139–40
Khaldan camp, 49, 92–93, 119, 131–
    32, 133, 135, 141–42, 143, 144,
    328, 344, 373, 380, 384, 390,
    398, 402, 417, 424, 451, 547, 557
Khalifa, Rashad, 45–46
Khalifa, Sam, 45
Khallad (Walid bin Attash), 66, 80, 96,
    118, 152, 153, 194–97, 200, 201,
    223, 224, 227, 229, 238–39, 240,
    241–42, 246, 254–62, 264, 275,
    277, 278, 288–89, 294–96, 298,
    299, 300, 301, 303, 323–24, 332,
    345, 347–48, 353, 373, 455, 472,
    488, 498, 512–14, 526, 534, 535,
    536, 549, 550, 558, 562, 564
Khamiri, Hassan al-, 91–92, 152–53,
    238, 258, 262, 263, 266, 267,
    329, 558–59, 563
Khan, Majid, 365, 368
Khan, Mohammad Sidique, 514
Kharijites, 20
Khartoum, 33–38, 40, 44, 51, 66, 77,
    91, 121, 123, 129
Kherchtou, L'Houssaine, 76–77, 121–
    30, 322, 331, 441, 529, 551, 553,
    555, 559, 560
Khomeini, Ayatollah Ruhollah, 17–18,
    21
Khost, 49, 79, 91, 129, 265, 279, 283,
    332
Khoury, Andre, 126, 236–37, 290,
    335, 336, 439, 440, 482, 556, 559
Khurasan, xxi, xxii, 440
King Abdul Aziz University, 23
Kiriakou, John, 433–34
Kleinman, Steven, 483
Kuala Lumpur, 240, 241, 243, 278,
    287, 288, 291, 358
Kunduz, 64
Kuta, 364

Kuwait, xxii, 25, 26, 27, 29, 32, 251
Lackawanna Six, 507
Lahore, 347, 402
Lamongan, 364
Landstuhl Regional Medical Center,
    169
Lang, Tom, 97–99, 102, 107, 108
Lashkar-e-Taiba (LeT), 347, 367, 402
Latif, Mohammed Abdel, 19
Layth, Huzam al-, 506
Leadbetter, Howard, 245
Lebanon, 5, 6–7, 15, 25, 29, 41, 143,
    144, 167
Lewinsky, Monica, 91
Library Tower, 368
Liby, Anas al-, 52, 76, 113–14, 559
Libya, 12, 22, 52, 131, 180, 451
Libyan Islamic Fighting Group
    (LIFG), 40, 52, 113, 344
Liguori, John, 119–20
Lillie, 365–67
Lippold, Kirk, 174–75
Little Aden, 187
Loghar camp, 96, 262, 275, 338
London, 42, 45, 50, 52, 69, 84, 90, 95,
    97–99, 100, 101–8, 113, 134–35,
    276, 329, 369
Los Angeles, Calif., 278, 294, 368
Los Angeles International Airport,
    142
Lubnani, Abed al-Sabour al-, see Hage,
    Wadih El-
Luqmanul Hakiem, 367
Lyons, Amy Jo, 299

Ma'alla, 233
Maboir, John Garang de, 96
MacEachin, Douglas J., 297, 302
Madani, Fayadh al-, 332
Madani, Mu'awiya al-, 260, 261, 263,
    332, 498, 513, 560
Madani, Sa'ad al-, 61, 62

Madani, Sawad al-, 419–20
Madinat al-Sha'ab, 190
Madrasah Jamiat Dirasat, 367
Madrid, 275, 369
Maghrebi, Yousef al-, *see* Kherchtou, L'Houssaine
Mahmoud, Major, 307, 308, 309–10, 312, 320, 355, 505, 560
Maidin, Ibrahim, 362
Makhtab al-Khidmat (MAK), 11, 31, 47, 549, 551
Maki, Abed al-Wahab al-, 337
Maki, Sinan al-, *see* Mihdhar, Khalid al-
Malaysia, 241–42, 246, 276, 288, 294, 298, 299, 301, 358, 359, 360, 361, 363, 364, 367, 479–80, 520, 552, 564
Mallow, Brittain P., 442, 467
Mamoto, Benny, 364
Manchester, 113–14, 559
Manchester Manual, 114–16, 223, 425, 426, 428–29, 559
Mand, Khirad, 63, 64
Manila, 54, 55, 359, 363
Mansfield University, 5, 8
Mansouri, Sa'eed al-, *see* Nashiri, Abdul Rahim Hussein Muhammad Abda al-
Maresco, Joe, 5–6, 7
Marina South, 358
Marine Corps, U.S., 466
Marine Security Guard (MSG), 245
Marka, 135
Marwan, *see* Odeh, Mohamed Sadeek
Marzuki, Zulkifli, 363
Masjid Tucson, 45–46
Masri, Abdel al-Wakeel al-, 344
Masri, Abdul Rahman al-, 112
Masri, al-Fateh al-, 323
Masri, Sa'eed al-, 79, 121–22, 322, 323, 326, 560

Massoud, Ahmed Shah, 60, 268, 338, 390, 443, 491, 560
Matrafi, Abdul Aziz al-, 440, 441, 482
Matt (CIA chief), 448, 449, 450, 452, 453, 474
Maududi, Sayed Abul A'ala, 20
Maurice (bartender), 15–16
Mawn, Barry, 218–19, 560
Maxwell, Kenny, 30, 246, 247, 290–91, 373, 389, 407
McFadden, Robert, xix–xx, xxii, 157, 183, 184, 187, 221, 222, 228–29, 240, 245, 246, 250, 268, 287, 290, 293, 294, 296, 306, 307–8, 310–12, 314, 315, 316–17, 320, 321, 330, 333, 334, 335, 355, 439, 444, 446–47, 503, 547, 556, 560, 564, 565
McRaven, William H., 533
McVeigh, Timothy, 189
Mecca, xxv, 11, 13, 17, 22, 56, 277
Medani, Muawiyah al-, 351–52
Medina, xxv, 56
Megawati Soekarnoputri, 362
Meligi, Mahmoud el-, 410
Mes Aynak camp, 277
MI5, 106–7, 143, 392
Middleton, Rod, 290
Mihdhar, Abul al-Hasan al-, 149, 152, 158, 195, 229
Mihdhar, Khalid al-, 79, 96, 243, 244, 249–50, 262, 277, 278, 281, 288–89, 290–92, 294–96, 298, 299, 300, 301, 318, 321, 335–37, 339, 361, 552, 555, 561, 563, 564
Mike, *see* Ghozi, Fathur Rohman al-
Miller, Geoffrey, 463, 467–68, 471–72, 482–83, 536, 553, 561
Miller, John, 14, 79, 100, 304
Mindanao, 358

Minnesota, 277
Mobruk, Moqadem Salah Abdel al-, 42–43
Mogadishu, 41, 42, 162
Mohamed, Ali, 32, 48, 49, 75–77, 94–95, 113, 129, 561
Mohamed, Binyam, 403, 408, 547, 561, 563
Mohamed, Khalfan Khamis, 89, 94, 95, 96, 567
Mohammed, Fazul Abdullah, *see* Fazul, Harun
Mohammed, Khalid Sheikh (KSM), xxiv, 32, 54, 55, 262, 272, 273, 275–78, 282–83, 303, 347–48, 353, 359, 364, 368–69, 386–89, 391, 403, 404, 423, 427–28, 440, 441, 458, 460, 462, 469, 494, 498, 512, 514, 515, 532, 534–36, 547, 550, 555, 556, 557, 561–62, 564, 567
Mokhtar, *see* Mohammed, Khalid Sheikh (KSM)
Moore, Charles "Willy," 333
Moqed, Majed, 281
Mora, Alberto J., 467, 468
Morocco, 12, 122, 124–25, 127, 131, 325, 348, 444
Moro Islamic Liberation Front (MILF), 40, 361, 363
Mossad, 176, 180, 229, 264
Mount Nebo, 134
Moussaoui, Zacarias, 276–77, 321–22, 419, 459, 494, 562
Mövenpick, 156, 166, 167, 171–72, 174, 180, 181, 211
Msalam, Fahid Mohammed Ally, 89–90
Mubarak, Hosni, 52, 307
Mueller, Robert, xxvii, 304, 350, 351, 353, 422, 423, 427, 448, 465, 562

mujahideen, 17, 22, 23, 25–32, 57, 59, 60–64, 84, 133, 154, 197, 320, 337, 357, 379, 390, 391, 441, 549, 556
Mujahideen Brigade, 330
Mukasey, Michael, 408
Mukhlas, 363, 364
Murad Beg, 254–55, 256, 550, 558
Murakab, Mohammed al-, 236
Musawa, Abdullah Ahmed Khalid Sa'id, 186, 193, 198–99, 201, 202, 238
Musharraf, 307, 333, 384–85
Muslim, Abdullah al-, 402
Muslim American Youth Association, 26
Muslim Brotherhood, 18–19
Musouwah, Mamoun al-, 231, 232, 236
Mwanza, 53, 54
Myers, General, 466
Mzungu, *see* Kherchtou, L'Houssaine

Nairobi, 14, 29, 38, 41–42, 49–50, 54, 75, 76–78, 80–88, 91, 93–94, 95, 96, 113, 121, 122–23, 124, 129, 192, 258, 319, 335, 559, 563
Naji, Hamoud, 177, 178, 179, 181, 203, 204, 235, 252, 562
Najibullah, Muhammad, 59, 60
Namer, Kud al-, 200
Nami, Ahmed al-, 282
Napoli, Louis, 49
Narathiwat, 367
Nashiri, Abdul Rahim Hussein Muhammad Abda al-, xxiv, 66, 80, 118, 188, 191–92, 193, 194, 197–99, 200, 201, 209, 223, 224, 225, 227, 257–59, 261–63, 264, 265, 267, 279, 329, 347–49, 455–56, 498, 504, 507, 513, 536, 552, 558, 562
Nasser, Gamal Abdel, 18–19, 21

National Commission on Terrorist Attacks Upon the United States, 297

National Geographic Channel, 168

National Islamic Front (NIF), 33, 34

National Security Agency (NSA), U.S., 83, 209, 241, 506, 532

National Security Council, 29

National Security Decision Directive (NSDD), 29

National Security Law Unit, 250

National Transportation Safety Board, 353

Naval Criminal Investigative Service (NCIS), xix, xxvii, 156, 157, 168–69, 171, 183–84, 216, 222, 242, 246, 247, 250, 253, 287, 308, 425, 442, 446, 463, 467, 504, 549, 560, 565

Naval Forces Central Command, U.S., 333

Naval Station Norfolk, 173

Navy Department, U.S., 175

Navy SEALS, U.S., 533, 551

Nawar, Nizar, 348

Nawawi, see Ali, Ihab

Nazis, 467

Neer, Tom, 446

Newburgh, N.Y., 55

New Jersey, 48

Newman, Robert, 155, 162, 214

New York, N.Y., 3, 9, 11, 15, 17, 24, 25, 30, 45, 46–48, 68, 82, 84, 86, 99, 101, 102, 103, 136, 139, 145, 153, 155, 157, 158, 159, 243, 246, 247, 280–82, 284–86, 289–90, 292, 297, 302, 320, 344, 350, 373, 404, 407, 408, 435, 441, 457, 479, 486, 519, 522, 555, 557, 558

New York Police Department (NYPD), 49, 83, 86, 159, 160, 161, 567

Nibras, Ibrahim al-, 151, 239, 240–41,

255, 263, 266, 278, 289, 470, 472, 505, 559, 562–63, 564

Nijjar, Razaq Saleh al-, 337

9/11 Commission, 155, 207, 219, 221, 244, 296, 298–305, 469, 513, 516, 561

9/11 Team, 350, 351, 472

Noori, Abdullah, 63

Norman, Okla., 28

North Carolina, 480

Northern Alliance, 60, 64, 79, 254, 267, 268, 332, 338, 343, 344, 345, 346, 360, 390, 401, 439–40, 455, 488, 490, 531, 560

Northern Group, 63, 64, 65–66, 80, 254, 257, 332, 336, 345, 454, 546, 550, 556, 558, 562, 563

Nosair, El Sayyid, 47, 48, 49

Nuremberg, 467

Oadah, Sheikh Salman al-, xxii

Obama, Barack, 532–33, 534

Obama administration, 381

Odeh, Mohamed Sadeek, 88–90, 94, 129, 548

Office of Intelligence Policy and Review (OIPR), 207

Okinawa, 54

Oklahoma, 277

Oman, 358, 489

Omar, Mullah, 57, 59–60, 69, 70, 72, 150, 314, 326–27, 344, 551

Omari, Abdulaziz al-, 280

O'Neill, John, xx, 3–5, 10, 15, 16, 23–25, 29–30, 82, 83–84, 90, 101, 105–7, 113, 116–17, 125, 126–27, 139, 145, 158, 159, 169, 173–74, 178–79, 181, 183, 192, 195–96, 203, 204–5, 206, 210, 211–12, 215, 216–19, 226, 246, 247, 248–49, 252, 285, 292, 297, 306, 418, 486, 553, 563

Orlando, Fla., 28, 278, 521
Owhali, Mohamed Rashed Daoud al-, 66, 78, 79, 86–88, 92–94, 95, 118, 187, 192, 258, 328–29, 335, 380, 548, 555, 563

Pace, Peter, 483
Paddy's Pub, 364
Padilla, Jose, 354, 403–4, 407, 427, 428, 515, 534, 547, 554, 561, 563
Pakistan, 11, 22, 23, 26, 27, 28, 30, 31, 32, 47, 48, 49, 55, 57, 59, 60, 63, 102, 117, 120, 131, 134, 140, 141, 142, 143, 144, 175, 272, 273–74, 307, 318, 345–47, 351, 357, 359, 365, 367, 374, 391, 403, 489
Paktika province, 346
Palestine Liberation Organization, 10
Palestinian Islamic Jihad (PIJ), 135
Panetta, Leon, 525, 536
Panjshir Valley, 31, 60, 64
Parola, Wayne, 86, 92
Pattaya, 362
Pelé, 456
Pellegrino, Frank, 302, 389, 564
Pennsylvania, 5, 9, 373
Pentagon, xiv, 28, 50, 275, 276, 281, 282, 288, 335, 468, 480, 561
Perkins, Abby, 96
Peshawar, 11, 26, 30, 32, 35, 37, 116, 134, 379
Petraeus, David, 532
Petronzi, Giuseppe, 112
Philippines, xxiv, 22, 30, 40, 54, 89, 359, 360, 363
Phoenix, Ariz., 522
Phoenix Park, 357
Pink Floyd, 207
Pistole, John, 304
Pittsburgh Pirates, 45
Plattsburgh, N.Y., 520

Political Security Organization (PSO), xix, 164, 176, 177, 179, 203, 204, 221, 225, 228, 234, 261, 265, 292–93, 295, 306, 309, 312, 548
Port Angeles, Wash., 142
Powell, Colin, 424

Qahtani, Mohammed al-, 278–79, 458–64, 466, 468–72, 483, 514, 564
Qamish, Ghalib al-, 179, 180, 181, 183, 187, 192–93, 194, 195–96, 203, 204, 221–22, 239, 259, 261, 292–93, 335, 355, 508, 515
Qanas, Yousef al-, 345, 346, 531
Qassem, Yasser Ahmad, 237
Qatar, 55, 348, 515
Qosi, Ibrahim Ahmed Mahmoud al-, 52, 231, 441, 442, 444–45, 458, 564, 566
Quantico, Va., 9
Quso, Fahd al-, xix, xx, 202, 221, 225–26, 228–36, 237–41, 243, 246, 252, 278, 287, 289, 290, 292–96, 307, 317, 441, 443, 472, 547, 548, 562, 564–65
Qutaybah, 64
Qutb, Sayyid, 18–19, 20–21, 23, 32, 47, 58

Rabat, 124, 125, 126, 127
Rab'ei, Hamza al-, 390
Rabeiee, Fawaz al-, see Tajiki, Furqan al-
Rahman, Abdul, 352, 477
Rahman, Omar Abdul, 32, 47, 48, 49, 103, 132, 254, 404, 555, 565
Rashidi, Amin Ali al-, see Abu Ubaidah al-Banshiri
Rawalpindi, 532
Reagan, Ronald, 29
Red Cross, 423, 442
Red Sea, 259

Reid, Richard, 348, 353, 481
Reimann, Chris, 117
Reno, Janet, 205
Ressam, Ahmed, 141–43, 373, 380
Returnees from Albania, 100
Reuwer, Ken, 222, 224, 225, 549
Riau, 362
Ridi, Essam al-, 25, 26–28, 34–40, 49
Rikers Island prison, 48
Rimi, Abdullah al-, 237
Rimi, Qassim al-, 507
Rimi, Zubayr al-, 513, 515
Riyadh, 85, 513, 560
Riymi, Zubayr al-, 489
Rizzo, John A., 381, 426, 428, 432, 464
Ronnaritivichai, Tritot, 364–67
Rossini, Mark, 139
Royal Court of Justice, 104
Ruffa, 71
Rumsfeld, Donald, 221, 466, 468, 470, 471, 483, 536
Ruqai'i, Nazih Abdul Hamed al-, *see* Liby, Anas al-

S., Clark, 243, 245, 288, 292
Sabir, Rafiq, 520, 522, 523, 524
Sadah, 196, 259, 261, 262
Sadat, Anwar al-, 21, 47, 75, 565
Saeed, Khalid al-, 51, 85
Saeed (FBI informant), 519–21
Safari, Bashir al-, 349
Salameh, Mohammed, 48, 49
Saleh, *see* Abdullah, Abdullah Ahmed
Saleh, Ali Abdullah, 152, 154, 156, 161, 176, 177, 179, 180–81, 182, 186, 235, 252, 261, 264, 549, 555, 562, 565
Saleh, Mohammed, 280, 282, 565
Salem, Mamdouh Mahmoud, *see* Abu Hajer al-Iraqi
Samantha (head of HVT unit), 484, 485–86, 487–88, 492–93, 501

Samir, Mohammed, 402
Sammy, *see* Jabarah, Mohammed Mansour
Samudra, Imam, 364
Sanaa, xix, 60, 62, 149, 150, 155, 161, 179, 193, 194, 203, 204, 206, 220, 233, 234, 237–40, 241, 242, 244, 245, 247, 257, 260, 264, 268, 284, 286, 293, 306, 311, 330, 332, 335, 337, 454, 470, 502, 504, 505, 566
Sanaa International Airport, 307
Sanabani, Nabil, 292
Sanchez, Linda, 75
Sari Club, 364
Saud, Turki bin Faisal al-, 70, 72
Saudi Arabia, xxii, xxv, xxvi, 10, 11–12, 17, 22, 23, 32, 33, 42, 51, 56, 58, 59, 63, 65, 69, 70, 72, 85, 121, 133, 192, 239, 254, 255, 256, 257, 260, 264, 277, 278, 307, 318, 337, 348, 378, 405–6, 440, 474, 476, 551, 566
Saudi Binladin Group, 11, 52, 167
Sawah, Tarek Mahmoud, el-, 282, 480–81
Sayyaf, Abdul Rasul, 26–27
Scotland Yard, 25, 95, 98, 101, 103–4, 106
Seidel, Charlie, 91
Senate, U.S., 426, 464, 466, 468
Senate Armed Services Committee, 465, 483
Senate Foreign Relations Committee, 434
Senate Intelligence Committee, 220, 535
Senate Judiciary Committee, 333, 527
Senate Select Committee on Intelligence (SSCI), 298, 424, 434–35, 451
Senguen, Aysel, 273

Setmariam, Mustafa, 99, 151
Shadadi, Bashir al-, 337
Shah, Tarik, 518–24
Shalabi, Mustafa, 47–48, 71
Shanksville, Pa., 286
Shehhi, Marwan al-, xix, 273, 275, 278, 279, 281, 294–95, 306, 317, 321, 547, 549, 550, 565
Shehri, Mohand al-, 281, 318
Shehri, Wail al-, 280
Shehri, Waleed al-, 280
Sheikh Aqeel University, 231, 237
Shelby, Annette, 251
Shelby, Richard, 251
Shepherd's, 104
Sheraton Hotel, 242, 250, 268
Shini, Ahmad al-, 238
Shini, Yasser al-, 234
Shultz, George, 172–73
Sibai, Hani al-, 105, 111, 112
Sim, Susan, 365
Singapore, 239, 240, 288, 351, 356–63, 364
Slahi, Mohamedou Ould, 273
SO12, 143, 392
SO13, 98, 104, 106–7, 113, 143, 392
Solo, 369
Somalia, 34, 38, 41, 42, 65, 96, 129, 157, 161–62, 331–32
Sorbonne, 34
Southwestern Louisiana, University of, 26
Soviet Spetsnaz, 63, 203
Soviet Union, 10, 17, 22, 29, 47, 57, 59, 62, 63, 133, 549
Special Operations Forces, U.S., 344, 345, 346, 533
Springsteen, Bruce, 445
State Department, U.S., 47, 84, 156, 159, 165–66, 171, 172, 173, 181, 183, 211–12, 213, 218, 219, 245, 247, 291, 527, 565

Stewart Air National Guard Base, 55, 90
Stonycreek Township, Pa., 282
Strait of Gibraltar, 348
Sudan, 32, 33–34, 37, 38, 40, 41, 43, 47, 48, 51, 52, 56, 57, 68, 76, 91, 95, 102, 121, 124, 131, 322, 336, 380, 444, 551
Sungkar, Abdullah, 357, 360, 361, 546, 556, 566
Sun Tzu, xix, xxvi, 538
Suqami, Satam al-, 280–81
Surruri, Yasser al-, 236
Survival Evasion Resistance and Escape (SERE), 464, 483
Swedan, Ahmed Salem, 89
Syria, 133, 134, 136, 140, 144

Tabarak, Abdullah, 80, 322, 325, 346, 349, 441, 442–44, 458, 459, 564, 566
Taezi, Abdul-rahman al-, 345
Taezi, Gharib al-, 352
Taezi, Salman al, 505
Taha, 231, 232
Taiz, 231
Tajiki, Furqan al-, 354, 504, 505–6, 507
Tajikistan, 29, 41, 61, 63, 332, 337
Takfir wal-Hijra, 144
Talha, see Mohamed, Binyam
Tali, Jamal al-, see Badawi, Jamal al-
Taliban, 12, 57–60, 69, 70, 72, 79, 118, 150, 200, 254, 256, 263, 268, 314, 326–27, 332, 343–45, 376, 384–85, 390, 401, 439–40, 480, 548, 550, 551, 560
Taloqan, 62, 64
Tanzania, 14, 53, 80
Tawahi, 202, 209, 232, 233, 263
Tawahi Harbor, 169
Tayyib, Madani al-, 42, 50–51, 66–67, 79, 322, 560, 566

Tehran, 21
Tel Aviv, 136
Tenet, George, 378, 427, 433, 479, 567
Texas, 26, 27, 28, 34
Thailand, 362, 363, 365
Thai Special Branch, 364–66, 367, 556
Thamar, 336
Thawer, Ibrahim al-, *see* Nibras,
    Ibrahim al-
Tirana, 108, 109
Tokyo, 54
Top, Noordin M., 363, 369, 514
Tora Bora, 345–46, 458, 481, 531
Townsend, Fran, 208, 367–68
Tripoli, 22, 76
Tucson, Ariz., 36, 45–46
Tunis, Zachariah al-, 345
Tunisi, Tariq al-, 327, 481
Tunisia, 348
Turabi, Hassan al-, 34
Turin, 112
Turkey, 134

Ulema Union of Afghanistan, 101
Ulu Tiram, 367
Uniform Code of Military Justice, 445
United Arab Emirates, 22, 59, 69, 273,
    326, 359
United Nations, 41, 60
United States, xxiii, 8, 10, 11, 21, 22,
    25–26, 27, 28, 31, 37, 44, 45–49,
    59, 62, 68, 70, 71, 75–76, 77, 87,
    91–92, 98, 100, 101, 103, 118,
    125, 127–28, 129–30, 132, 134,
    142, 143–44, 152, 161, 171, 179,
    180–82, 215, 219, 221, 222, 230,
    249, 250, 256, 258, 259, 263–64,
    265, 272, 275–82, 291–92, 298,
    301, 303, 307, 344, 347, 348,
    350, 353, 368–69, 377, 388–89,
    402, 408, 422, 439, 444–47, 467,
    481, 522–23, 536–37, 554

United States Agency for
    International Development
    (USAID), 77
United States Central Command
    (CENTCOM), 171, 212
United States Foreign Intelligence
    Surveillance Court (FICA),
    207
Uzbekistan, 28, 29

Valiquette, Joe, 299, 304, 305
Victoria, 142
Vienna, 108
Villanova University, 8
Virginia, 173
Virginia Jihad Network, 519
Voice of America, 280

Wajih, Fawzi Muhammad Abed al-
    Qawi al-, 349
Wakeel, Abdul, 346
Wallace, William, 413–14
Ward, Tom, 159, 160, 161, 170, 567
Washington, D.C., 29, 30, 82, 83, 157,
    218, 243, 250–51, 286, 289–90,
    292, 295, 302, 303, 320, 344,
    355, 373–74, 393, 408, 411, 413,
    421, 422–23, 427, 433, 434, 445,
    446, 449, 463, 486–87, 488,
    527–28
Washington, George, 315, 330, 333
Washington Hotel, 240, 241
White Mountains, 345–46
Whitley Road Detention Centre, 360
Wilshire, Tom, 243, 249
Wilson, 393–95, 396, 399, 407, 414,
    446, 567
Wilson, Charlie, 28
Wirsh, Hadi Muhammad Salih al-, *see*
    Dilkum, Hadi
Witness Protection Program, U.S., 71,
    127, 128, 130, 554, 559

Wolfowitz, Paul, 221, 466, 470, 471, 536
World Islamic Front, 13
World Trade Center, xix, xx, xxiv, 13, 15, 30, 48, 49, 54, 55, 208, 248, 275, 276, 280–82, 284, 285, 320, 357, 362, 388–89, 418, 478, 494, 512, 549, 553, 561, 563, 565, 567
Wright, Lawrence, 304–5

Yala, 367
Yanbu, 337
Yarmouk Palestinian refugee camp, 133
Yassir, Colonel, 307, 308, 309, 310, 311–12, 321, 355, 505, 567
Yemen, xix, xx, 10, 32, 41, 61, 63, 69, 88, 95, 105, 112, 130, 133, 149–53, 154–55, 158–67, 168, 170, 173–84, 185–208, 209–18, 221–27, 228–47, 251–53, 256–65, 272, 284, 286–96, 313, 330, 332, 333, 336, 337, 338, 348, 354–55, 359, 393, 450, 454, 474, 486,

489, 497, 498–99, 501, 502, 505, 514, 551, 554, 555–56, 557, 566
Yemeni Criminal Investigative Division (CID), 150
Yemeni Special Forces, 162, 166
Yishun Mass Rapid Transit station, 356
Yoo, John, 432
Yousef, Ramzi, xviii, 23, 32, 49, 54–55, 135, 276, 387, 388, 561, 567

Zammar, Mohammed Haydar, 273
Zawahiri, Ayman al-, 31, 32, 40, 62, 75, 79, 82, 95, 96, 98, 100, 101–2, 105, 107, 129, 231, 265, 268, 274, 280, 282, 303, 316, 322, 323, 328, 440, 455, 537, 547, 548, 549, 560, 561, 565, 567
Zebley, Aaron, 96, 484, 485, 487, 488, 490–95, 499, 501, 551, 567–68
Zelikow, Philip, 302, 303, 513, 527
Zia-ul-Haq, Muhammad, 28
Zubair, 365, 368

Ali Soufan, a former FBI special agent and the lead investigator on some of the world's most complex international terrorism cases, gained an international reputation as a top counterterrorism operative. He is the chairman and CEO of The Soufan Group, founder of The Soufan Center, and has been featured in books, films, television series, newspaper articles, and documentaries across the globe.